A TEXTBOOK OF
APPLIED ENTOMOLOGY

A TEXTBOOK OF
APPLIED ENTOMOLOGY

Volume–II
INSECTS OF ECONOMIC IMPORTANCE

Gursharan Singh
Former Professor of Entomology
and Dean of Postgraduate Studies
Punjab Agricultural University, Ludhiana, India

(Late) K.P. Srivastava
Former Professor and Head
Department of Zoology
Banaras Hindu University, Varanasi, India

(Late) G.S. Dhaliwal
Former Professor of Ecology
Department of Entomology
Punjab Agricultural University, Ludhiana, India

KALYANI PUBLISHERS
LUDHIANA - NEW DELHI - NOIDA (U.P.) - HYDERABAD
CHENNAI - KOLKATA - CUTTACK - GUWAHATI - KOCHI - BENGALURU

KALYANI PUBLISHERS

Head Office

B-1/1292, Rajinder Nagar, **Ludhiana**-141 008 • Ph : 0161-2760031, 2745756
E-mail : kalyanibooks@yahoo.co.in **Website :** www.kalyanipublishers.co.in

Administration Office

4779/23, Ansari Road, Daryaganj, **New Delhi**-110 002 • Ph : 011-23271469, 23274393
E-mail : kalyani_delhi@yahoo.co.in, kalyani_delhi@kalyanipublishers.in

Works

B-16, Sector-8, **NOIDA** (U.P.)

Branches

1, Mahalakshmi Street, T. Nagar, **Chennai**-600 017 • Ph : 044-24344684
Gopabandhu Lane, Behind Govt. Bus Stand, Badambadi, **Cuttack**-753 012 (Odisha) • Ph : 0671-2311391
4-3-65/2/A, Behind HVS Public School, Raghunath Bagh
Sultan Bazar, **Hyderabad**-500 095 • Ph : 040-24750368
10/2B, Ramanath Mazumdar Street, **Kolkata**-700 009 • Ph : 033-22416024
Arunalaya, 1st Floor, Saraswati Road, Pan Bazar, **Guwahati**-781 001 • Ph : 0361-2731274
Koratti Parambil House, Convent Road, **Kochi**-682 035 • Ph : 0484-2367189
No. 24 & 25, 1st Floor, Hameed Shah Complex, Cubbonpet Main Road, **Bengaluru**-560 002

12 + 360 = 372 Pages 20" x 30" 46.5 Formes

KPP Q 32216 1

Fourth Enlarged Edition, 2021

Datalink Computer
(PEST2-19)

ISBN 978-81-272-6752-0

PRINTED IN INDIA
at Diamond Agencies Pvt. Ltd., B-125, Sec. 63, NOIDA

PREFACE

Prof. K.P. Srivastava's *A Textbook of Applied Entomology* was published in two volumes; the first volume appeared in 1988 and the second one in 1993. Both the volumes were revised in 2020 to update the information on various emerging areas. These volumes found a great favour among students and teachers in view of the thorough coverage of the subject matter in concise manner, use of easy-to-understand language and well-meaning illustrations. The book had dominated the scene of Entomology in India for over a decade. However, the book needed another revision in view of the change in pest, pesticide and pest management scenario at the national and global level. Prof. Srivastava was very keen to revise the book, but he expired on October 10, 2002 after a brief illness and hence, the task could not be undertaken. When Prof. Srivastava's family and the publisher contacted me to do this job. I could not think of a better opportunity to pay my humble tribute to this great teacher, scientist and above all, a human being.

While maintaining the basic format of the book as per Prof. Srivastava's vision, all the chapters in both the volumes have been thoroughly revised, and recent information included wherever available. In volume I, the chapter on Applied Control : General Methods has been expanded and developed into three independent chapters, viz. Physical, Mechanical and Legal Control; Cultural Control and Host Plant Resistance. In adition, two new chapters, viz. Biotechnological Approaches, and Integrated Pest Management : Progress and Perspectives, have been included. In volume II also, three new chapters, viz. Pests of Mushrooms, Pests of Spices, and Insect Vectors of Plant Diseases, have been added. In addition, all the scientific names of the insects and their placement have been checked and the changes incorporated wherever required.

Some of the topics which do not form a part of the approved syllabus have been excluded. The descriptions of several new pests have been included, the banned and withdrawn pesticides have been taken out and the latest recommendations for management of pests have been added. Many of the illustrations have been redrawn, a few excluded and some new ones have been added. The information on current status of apiculture, sericulture and lac culture in India, has also been incorporated. The bibliography has been given a new outlook by including leading publications that had appeared in the last decade.

I express my gratitude to Prof. Srivastava's and Dr. G.S. Dhaliwal family, for imposing confidence in me to undertake the revision of the book. I am also grateful to Mr Raj Kumar, Kalyani Publishers, for his keen interest and enthusiasm to bring out the revised version of the book. I hope the book would meet the requirements of the students and teachers in applied entomology, and their valuable suggestions would be most appreciated.

2021 **Gursharan Singh**

CONTENTS

Ch.No.	Chapter	Pages

PART–I : INTRODUCTION

PART–II : AGRICULTURAL ENTOMOLOGY

PART–III : FOREST ENTOMOLOGY

INTRODUCTION

PART-I

- ECONOMIC IMPORTANCE OF INSECTS

1 CHAPTER

ECONOMIC IMPORTANCE OF INSECTS

INTRODUCTION

Insects have lived on Earth for about 350 million years, compared with less than 2 million for humans. Of an estimated 5-10 million species of insects, probably not more than a fraction of 1 per cent interact, directly or indirectly, with humans. The fact that insects do more good than harm would probably come as a surprise to lay persons whose familiarity with insects is generally limited to mosquitoes, house flies, cockroaches, etc. and to farmers who protect their crops and livestock against a variety of pests. Humans have long recognized the importance of insects in their well-being. Production of silk from silkworm pupae has been carried out for almost 5000 years. Similarly, the usefulness of honey bees has been known to man from prehistoric times. The services rendered by insects in pollination of crops, biological control of pests, soil builders and scavengers have been well recognized. Insects and/or their products have been eaten by humans for thousands of years. Locust swarms, which originally may have been an important seasonal food for humans, took on new significance as humans turned to a farming rather than a hunting existence.

Several features of recent human evolution like increase in population, a trend towards urbanization, increased geographic movement of people and agricultural products, and intensification of agriculture to feed more people, have led to increase in the severity of harmful insects. The relatively crowded conditions of urban areas enable insects parasitic on humans, both to locate a host and to transfer between host individuals. Thus, urbanization has facilitated the spread of insect-borne human diseases such as typhus, plague, and malaria. An increasing need to produce more and cheaper food led to the practice of monoculture. By simplifying the ecosystem, humans encourage the buildup of populations of the insects that compete with them for food being grown. A massive increase in human geographic movements and a concomitant increase in trade led to the transportation of a number of species, both plant and animal, into areas previously unoccupied by them. Some of these were able to establish themselves and, in the absence of normal regulators of population (especially parasitoids and predators), increased rapidly in numbers and became important pests.

A. BENEFICIAL INSECTS

Insects may be beneficial to humans in various ways, directly or indirectly. The most important beneficial species are those whose products are of immense commercial value. The insects which bring about pollination of crops are also of considerable importance. There are other beneficial insects which are used as food, for biological control of insect pests and plants, soil scavengers, in medicine and research, and for aesthetic value.

COMMERCIALLY VALUABLE INSECTS

The best known insects which provide commercially valuable products are the honey bee, silkworm, lac insect and wax scale.

Honey Bees

There are four species of the honey bee, viz. *Apis cerana, Apis florea, Apis dorsata* and *Apis mellifera*; the first three are indigenous, and the last one has been introduced and acclimatized in India for the last about 50 years. The honey bee originally occupied the African continent, most of Europe (except the northern part), and western Asia. Bee management was probably first carried out by the ancient Egyptians. Honey bees were brought to North America by colonists in the early 1600s, and today honey and beeswax production is a billion dollar industry.

The honey yield of *A. mellifera* averages 50-100 kg per colony per year as compared to very low yield (3.6-4.5 kg in hills and 1.3-2.2 kg in plains) of *A. cerana*. The world honey production is estimated at about 1.31 million tonnes, China is the world's largest honey producer (0.27 million tonnes), accounting for almost 20 per cent of the total. According to recent estimates there are more than 3,50,500 beekeepers in India maintaining 1.5 million colonies. The total production of honey in India is about 92000 tonnes (including wild honey), out of which more than 23,600 tonnes is exported to Germany, USA, Middle East countries and South Africa. In Punjab alone, there are about 30,000 beekeepers maintaining more than 2,50,000 A. mellifera colonies producing 18000 tonnes of honey annually, out of which more than 90 per cent is being exported.

In addition, beeswax is produced at the rate of about 1 kg for every 50-100 kg of honey; its value varies between one and three times that of honey. There is also a significant world trade in pollen which is used not only by beekeepers to supplement the reserves in the hive but also in the health-food industry. Other products that are collected include propolis (bee glue), venom (used to desensitize patients with severe allergies to bee stings), and royal jelly which is added to certain food supplements.

Silkworm

There are four species of silkworm in India, which can be exploited for commercial silk production. These are mulberry silkworm, *Bombyx mori*; tassar silkworm, *Antheraea paphia*, muga silkworm, *Antheraea assama;* and eri silkworm, *Philosamia ricini*, among which the first one is the most important. Silk production has been commercially important for about 4700 years. The industry originated in East Asia and spread into Europe (France, Italy and Spain) after eggs were smuggled from China to Italy in the sixth century A.D. The production of silk remains a labour intensive industry, making production costs high. In 1988, world silk production was about 67,000 tonnes. By the end of 1998, production had increased slightly to 72,000 tonnes. At present, China is the leading producer of silk with about 70 per cent of the world total, followed by India and Japan. India is producing over 30,000 tonnes of raw silk every year, accounting for about 18% of the world's total raw silk production. The annual export of silk and silk products from India is around US$400 million. The US has been the largest importer of Indian silk and silk products over the recent years, followed by China — the world's largest silk consumer, and the UAE — one of the fastest growing silk importers in the world.

Lac Insect

The lac insect, *Kerria lacca*, is a scale endemic to India and Southeast Asia that secretes about itself a coating of lac, which may be more than 1 cm thick. The twigs on which the insects rest are collected and either used to spread the insects to new areas or ground up and heated in order to separate the lac. The lac is a component of shellac, though its importance has declined. The important lac producing countries are India and Thailand. India produced 23,230 tonnes of lac in 2006-07, which declined to 20,640 tonnes in 2007-08 and to 16978 in 2014-15 showing a gradual decline.

Pela Wax Scale

The pela wax scale, *Ericerus pela*, has been used in China for commercial production of China wax, mainly in Sichuan province, for more than 100 years. It is the second instar males that produce economically valuable wax. Wax production peaked in the early 1900s and in a good year the production reached 6000 tonnes. Most of this wax was used in the manufacture of candles. However, with the coming of electricity and discovery of other waxes (particulary paraffin wax), interest in China wax declined and currently about 500 tonnes is harvested every year. It is used for a variety of horticultural, industrial and pharmaceutical purposes, viz. grafting agent for fruit trees, insulation of electrical cables and equipment, manufacture of molds for precision instruments, production of high-gloss, tracing, and wax paper, as an ingredient of furniture and automobile polishes, and coating candles and pills.

INSECT POLLINATORS

The human beings would have remain devoid of many fruits and vegetables , had there been no insects acting as pollinators. It has been estimated that roughly one-third of the world's agricultural production relies either directly or indirectly on insect pollinators. Many species of insects and plants have evolved a mutualistic relationship, in which plants produce nectar and pollen for use by insects, while the latter provide a transport system for effective cross-pollination. In the self-pollinated plants, pollen grains from the anthers automatically fall on to their stigmas. However, even these plants may produce more and better fruits or seeds by cross-pollination than by self-pollination. In the case of cross-pollinated plants, the chief agents which carry the pollen from plant to plant for pollination are the wind and the insects. More than two-thirds of all the flowering plants depend upon insects for pollination.

Cereals and grasses are wind-pollinated crops and flowers of such crops are generally small, inconspicuous with dull coloured and poorly developed petals and brush-like stigmas; their pollen are dry and light, and are produced in large number. Horticultural crops like fruits, vegetables and ornamental plants and field crops like cotton and tobacco are pollinated by insects. These crops have coloured and scented flowers with well-developed showy petals of conspicuous size with nectaries and their stigmas are sticky, and their pollen grains are sticky and are produced in large numbers. Insect pollination results in a uniform crop and in some cases in the improvement in the quality of the fruit.

Nectar is secreted by insect pollinated flowers to attract the insects. As they visit flowers for nectar, the pollen grains get dusted all over the body and transferred to the stigma of the flower they visit, thus bringing about pollination. The important pollinators are the honey bees, solitary bees like *Xylocopa, Andrena* and *Halictus,* and bumble bees, *Bombus* spp. Other insects which are useful as pollinators are the stingless bee (*Trigona* spp.), wasps, many kinds of flies (*Syrphus, Bombylius* and *Sacrophaga*), beetles, black ants, thrips, butterflies and moths like *Acherontia* spp. and *Deilephila* spp., leaf cutting bees or the mason bees.

Bumble bees are generally too few in number to serve as effective pollinators in nature. However, they are valuable in the case of crops whose flowers are large enough, as cotton and lady's finger, to facilitate pollen transfer and where the corollas are long and tubular with deep-seated nectaries in which case short tongued bees may not be of any value.

By far, the honey bees remain the most important pollinators of crops. The potentiality of honey bees can be imagined from the fact that members of a colony visit about 100 flowers during a field trip and make about four million field trips. Fruits like apple, pears, plum, blackberry, raspberry, strawberry, citrus, mango, fig, grapes, papaya and cherry; vegetables like asparagus, brinjal, melons, lady's finger, cucumbers, pumpkins, squash, cabbage, cauliflower, onion and tomato; and oilseeds like rape, mustard, toria, and sunflower; seed crops such as clovers, fennel, pepper, and sunflower; and many ornamentals, depend upon honey bees for pollination.

Some plants like many fruits particularly figs, peas, beans, tomatoes, many vegetables, sunflower, seasonal flowers, chrysanthemum and many ornamental plants would produce no fruits unless pollinated by insects. It has been estimated that 50-70 per cent of the grain crops are pollinated by insects, bulk of it by bees alone. Every time the bees collect honey worth Rs 100, they make Rs 2000 worth of seeds and fruits by pollinating the flowers. In India, it has been found that visit by honey bees resulted in magnificient increase in yield of agricultural and horticultural crops (Table 1.1).

Table 1.1 Increase in yield of agricultural and horticultural crops due to pollination by honey bees

Agricultural crop	Increase in yield (%)	Horticultural crop	Increase in yield (%)
Mustard	128.1 – 157.8	Apple	180 – 6950
Rapeseed	12.8 – 139.3	Pear	240 – 6014
Sunflower	21 – 3400	Cherries	56 – 1000
Niger	60.7 – 173	Strawberry	17.4 – 91.9
Berseem (seed)	24.3 – 33150	Litchi	4538 – 10246
Buckwheat	62.5	Orange	47 – 900
Egyptian cotton	16 – 24	Citrus	7 – 33.3
Coffee beans	16.7 – 39.8	Guava	70 – 140

Source : National Bee Board, New Delhi

Realising the importance of honey bees in pollination of crops, bee colonies are being hired out to orchard growers in many parts of the world. The practice of renting bee colonies for pollination service started in USA by about 1910. In California, about 1.4 million hives are rented annually to augment natural pollination of almonds (about 50% of the hives), alfalfa, melons, and other fruits and vegetables. In USA alone, USD 15 billion worth of crops (fruits, vegetables, flowers) are pollinated by domesticated honey bees each year. Under such conditions, the value of bees as pollinators may be up to 140 times their value as honey producers. However, the mortality among honey bees in transit has to be guarded against. For pollination services, honey bee colonies have to be transported from a distance, have to be packed properly, loaded on a truck, then unloaded at the destination and taken to the site of placement. In USA, providing honey bee colonies for pollination is a professional job with some beekeepers, but in India this degree of sophistication has not been achieved so far. The movement of honey bee colonies from lower altitudes or the plains to the apple orchards is being practiced at a reasonable scale with very promising results.

The number and strength of colonies for pollination work are different than those required for honey production. Although much of the efficiency of pollination depends on the vigour and foraging habits of the colony, and the climatic conditions, but a colony should be sufficiently strong. A pollination colony may preferably be on two chambers having a strength of 50,000 bees or one chamber having a strength of 25,000 bees. The number of colonies to be kept in an orchard or field crops should be given due consideration. The number of colonies per unit area depends upon the concentration of flowers, their attractiveness, presence and abundance of other pollinating insects, and presence of competing crops in the vicinity. However, it is usually recommended that five colonies are maintained for two hectares of crop and it should be more in case of profusely flowering field crops like alfalfa and red clover. A colony should be kept for pollination as near the orchard as possible to avoid waste of time and energy on the part of bees in making to and fro trips. The colonies should be moved into the field or orchard for pollination, just when sufficient number of plants have flowers for the bees to work.

ENTOMOPHAGOUS INSECTS

Entomophagous insects are those which feed upon other insects destroying our crops and stored grains. They constitute the greatest single factor to check the phytophagous species from gaining overwhelming predominance over other animals in the world or at least from causing much more damage to cultivated crops. This check by entomophagous species on phytophagous insects is much more effective than all other efforts of man through multifarious means. It is only relatively recently that humans have gained an appreciation of the importance of insects in the regulation of populations of potentially harmful species of insects. Entomophagous insects can be divided into two groups, viz. predators and parasitoids.

Predators

A predator is usually larger than its prey, kills its prey and requires more than one prey to complete its development. Predators are usually active in habits and have structural adaptations for catching the prey with well developed sense organs and capacity for swift movements. Many predators remain stationary and suddenly seize the prey when it comes within its reach, whereas others capture the prey while on its wings. Some of them have cryptic colourations and deceptive markings as in praying mantids and robber flies. The insect predators are spread over a wide range of orders including Coleoptera, Neuroptera, Diptera, Hemiptera, Hymenoptera, Dictyoptera, etc.

Coleoptera. Adults and larvae of ladybird beetles (Coccinellidae), *Brumus* and *Scymnus* feed upon aphids, coccids and other soft-bodied insects. *Rodolia cardinalis* feeds upon cottony cushion scale, *Icerya purchasi; Cryptolaemus montrouzieri* is predaceous upon scales and mealy bugs ; *Menochilus sexmaculatus* feeds on aphids and mealy bugs ; and *Chilocorus nigritus* feeds on coconut scale insect, *Aspidiotus destructor.* Ground beetle (Carabidae), *Callida splendidula* feeds upon caterpillars of *Opisina arenosella* and *Orthaga exvinacea. Pheropsophus sorrinus* predates on the larvae of *Oryctes rhinoceros.* Tiger beetles (Cicindelidae), *Cicindela* spp. are large, active and prominently coloured beetles feeding upon a variety of insects. Larvae of tiger beetles are also predaceous, remain at the mouth of deep burrows and seize any insect that passes by.

Diptera. The adults of robber flies (Asilidae) catch insects on flight. The adult hover flies (Syrphidae) are good pollinators, but the larvae are predaceous. The green apodous maggots feed upon aphids by sucking their body fluids. The maggots of the fly *Acletoxenus indicus* (Drosophilidae) are predaceous on castor and pomegranate aleyrodids.

Hymenoptera. The wasps (Vespidae) collect various insects and feed them to their larvae. Mud wasps (Vespidae) and digger wasps (Sphecidae) construct nests made of mud and provide various caterpillars to the young ones in the nest. About half of the members of the ant family (Formicidae) are predaceous upon various kinds of insects.

Neuroptera. The adults of aphid lions or green lacewings (Chrysopidae) are not predatory, but the larvae with their long sharp mandibles grasp and puncture the bodies of aphids and other soft-bodied insects such as psyllids, coccids and jassids, and mites and suck their body fluids.

Dictyoptera. The nymphs and adults of praying mantids (Mantidae) are cryptically coloured with long prehensile fore legs. Nymphs feed on aphids and leafhoppers while adults feed on caterpillars, grasshoppers, wasps and even spiders, *e.g. Mantis religiosa.*

Odonata. The naiads of dragonflies (Coenagrionidae) feed on aquatic insects and the adults on insects like mosquitoes, flies and moths while on the wings. The naiads possess prehensile labium and the adults are swift fliers at a speed of 100 kmph and have basket-like legs. *Sympetrum frequens* preyed upon the larvae of *Anopheles sinensis* in rice fields in Japan. Similarly, dragonflies have proved useful in reducing the population of *Nilaparvata lugens* in rice fields in Indonesia.

Hemiptera. The stink bug, *Eocanthena furcellata* (Pentatomidae) feeds upon *Amsacta albistriga* larvae, whereas *Andrallus spinidens* is predaceous on *Spodoptera litura, Helicoverpa armigera, Semiothisa pervolgata* and *Anticarsia irrorata.* The assassin bug, *Harpactor costalis* (Reduviidae) preys upon *Dysdercus cingulatus, Platymerous laevicollis* on *Oryctes rhinoceros,* and *Rhinocoris fuscipes* on the larvae of *Helicoverpa armigera* and *Spodoptera litura.*

Parasitoids

A parasite is an organism which is usually much smaller than its host and a single individual usually does not kill the host. A parasitoid is a special kind of parasite which is often about the same size as its host, kills its host and requires only one host (prey) for development into a free-living adult. The majority of the parasitoids utilized in biological control of insect pests belong to two orders, namely Hymenoptera (especially wasps of the families Ichneumonidae, Braconidae, Eulophidae and Trichogrammatidae) and Diptera (flies, particularly of the family Tachinidae). About 66 per cent of all successful biocontrol programmes have involved parasitoids that belong to the insect order Hymenoptera. One of the reasons for the success of these species is their having a modified ovipositor that can be used to lay eggs, to secrete venom to paralyse prey and to locate prey via sensitive neural receptors. In general, the dipteran parasitoids in the family Tachinidae appear to be less host specific. For example, some species of tachinid fly have been found to attack more than 100 different host insects. However, tachinids have not been used extensively in biological control programmes as yet.

Ichneumonidae. These include large, slender, black or reddish-coloured insects with extremely long ovipositors. They comprise 20 per cent of all parasitic insects and, therefore, are of great economic value. They are both external and internal parasitoids of the larvae of Lepidoptera, Coleoptera and Hymenoptera, and pupae of Lepidoptera. Many have varied habits, some being hyperparasitoids. Examples include *Isotomama javensis* on sugarcane top shoot-borer, *Scirpophaga nivella* and rice stem borer, *Scirpophaga incertulas* ; *Xanthopimpla punctata* on stem borer, *Chilo partellus; Gambroides javensis* on *Scripophaga excerptalis* and *Cremastus falvoorbitalis* on *Antigastra catalaunalis.*

Braconidae. These are small but stout-bodied insects found amongst flowers and on lights parasitising (externally or internally) the larvae of Lepidoptera, Coleoptera, Diptera and Hemiptera (aphids in particular). Pupation takes place inside a cocoon either on the body of the host or on foliage near the dead host, *e.g. Bracon brevicornis* on *Opisina arenosella* and *B. gelechidiphagus* on brinjal budworm, *Phthorimaea blapsigona. Cotesia flavipes* is a very common braconid parasitising the larvae of *Chilo partellw, Scirpophaga nivella, Sesamia inferens* and *Scirpophaga incertulas.*

Encyrtidae. These are small insects parasitic on aphids, whiteflies, scales, mealy bugs, etc. *Oencyrtus pyrillae* is an important parasitoid of the eggs of sugarcane pyrilla, *Pyrilla perpusilla.* Recently, a new parasitoid, *Aenasius bambawalei,* has been reported to feed on the nymphs of the mealy bug, *Phenacoccus solenopsis,* which is emerging as a serious pest of both Bt and non-Bt cotton. *A. bambawalei* has been recorded from Haryana, Delhi, Maharashtra and Punjab, and is spreading to other areas. The nymphal parasitoid has been known to cause 50-80 per cent parasitization in certain areas and kill the mealy bugs within a week after the attack. The mealy bugs turn into reddish dark brown mummies, which could be easily identified on the plants.

Eulophidae. By and large, these are the external parasitoids of stem borers and leaf miners belonging to Diptera, Hemiptera, Hymenoptera and Lepidoptera, and are important parasitoids of the woolly aphid, *Eriosoma lanigerum.* The eggs are laid by the female on the ventral side of the aphid and the larva feeds on the aphid through the puncture made for oviposition. *Trichospilus pupivora* on pupae of *Opisina arenosella* and *Tetrastichus* spp. on eggs of rice stem borer are the other two important parasitoids of this group.

Trichogrammatidae. This is one of the most important hymenopteran families, which contains very minute (0.3-1.0 mm) egg parasitoids of a large number of insects, especially those belonging to Lepidoptera. Majority of the trichogrammatids play a vital role in the natural control of a wide range of insect pests. More than 100 species of *Trichogramma* occur in agroecosystems throughout the world. Globally, approximately 20 species of *Trichogramma* are regularly used in biological control programmes on about 25 crops and trees. In India, the release of mass-produced egg parasitoids has been used for the control of several lepidopteran insect pests of various crops, *e.g.* rice stem borer, *Scirpophaga incertulas*; cotton bollworm, *Helicoverpa armigera*; maize borer, *Chilo zonellus* and sugarcane borers, *Chilo infuscatellus, Chilo auricilius* and *Emmalocera depresella.*

Tachinidae. The adults of tachinids resemble house flies, but somewhat larger in size and more bristly, and are often seen resting on foliage or flowers. They are endoparasitic on the larvae of Lepidoptera, Coleoptera, Hymenoptera, Diptera, Hemiptera, Dermaptera and Orthoptera. They have varied egg-laying habits; some cement their eggs to the skin of the host and the larvae on emergence bore their way into the former's body, some lay their eggs on plants which are then ingested by the host larvae while feeding, some viviparous forms deposit their larvae on the host's body, and in some cases the eggs are laid inside the body of the host with the help of spine-like apparatus.

The maggots feed upon the muscles and fat bodies of the host caterpillar. The caterpillar can transform into pupa, from which the adult parasitoid emerges, leaving behind the dead pupa, *i.e. Spoggosia bezziana* on *Opisina arenosella, Sturmia inconspicuella* and *Exorista civiloides.* Some other common tachinids are *Actia monticola* on *Spodoptera litura, Sturmiopsis inferens* on *Scirpophaga incertulas, Sesamia inferens* and *Chilo partellus,* and *Podomyia setosa* on *Achaea janata.*

WEED KILLERS

Weeds are unwanted plants and have been a menace in many countries by spreading to large areas of fertile land. Quite many insects feed upon the weeds, just as they do on cultivated plants. A successful weed killer insect (*i*) should not itself be a pest of cultivated plants and should not even at a later date turn to attack the useful crops ; (*ii*) should be effective in damaging and controlling the weed ; (*iii*) should preferably be a borer or internal feeder of the weed ; and (*iv*) should be able to multiply in good numbers without being affected by parasitoids and predators. In many cases, these insects have contributed much towards eradication of the weeds or at least keeping them under check.

Opuntia spp. (Prickly Pear)

Various species of *Opuntia,* which has its origin in the western hemisphere, have been transported for the purpose of human food (fruits), cattle food (pads) and food for the dye-producing insects. In Australia, it became an extremely aggressive weed, infestating some 25 million ha of cultivable land. A pyralid moth, *Cactoblastis cactorum* obtained from Argentina and introduced in Australia in 1925, was able to salvage huge areas of land from cactus by 1930. The most remarkable feature of this success story is that only 2750 *Cactoblastis* larvae were brought to Australia, of which only 1070 became adults. From these, however, more than 1,00,000 eggs were produced, and in February-March of 1926 more than 2.2 million eggs were released in the field. Additional releases and redistribution of almost 400 million feild-produced eggs until the end of 1929, ensured the project's success. The control was so drastic that the entomologists got concerned about the very survival of these insects themselves due to the shortage of food, *i.e. Opuntia.* The cochineal (scarlet dye-producing) insect, *Dactylopius ceylonicus,* a coccid or scale insect (Homoptera), has been successful in the prickly pear control in Kenya and *D. opuntiae* in the USA (California). In India, *O. dillenii* was a noxious weed and it has been practically eradicated by the cochineal insect, *D. tomentosus.* The insect is a native of Mexico and was introduced into India via Sri Lanka in about 1925. Within the next five or six years, the weed was almost exterminated.

Lantana camara

Lantana, a native of Central America, is extensively used throughout the world as an ornamental shrub. But in many countries, it has escaped civilisation and encroached upon vast areas of cultivable land. India shares this weed problem along with Hawaii, Fiji, and Australia. In India, two insects have been tried : a lace bug, *Teleonemia scrupulosa*, and a seedfly, *Ophiomyia lantanae* (both Central American in origin). In Uganda, Lantana has been controlled by *T. scrupulosa*.

Hypericum perforatum (St. John's Wort or Klamath)

This weed poses serious problems in the USA, Australia, Canada, New Zealand and Chile destroying thousands of hectares of land. Various species of the leaf-feeding beetle, *Chrysolina* have controlled this weed successfully.

Senecio jacobaeae (Tansy Ragwort)

This is another weed that has been causing a great damage to pastures in New Zealand, Australia, USA and Canada. The weed has been controlled to a great extent by the moth, *Tyria jacobaeae* and the seedfly, *Pegohylemyia seneciella*.

SOIL BUILDERS

Many insects during one or more of their life stages live inside the soil and some in the tunnels made by them. Members of almost all the orders of the insects have been observed in the soil and most important of these are the ants, beetles, bees, larvae of flies, crickets, cutworms, collembola and pupae of moths. They usually remain confined to the top 15 cm of soil, some of the insects like ants, termites, bees, beetles and crickets are also known to build nests. By their very habit, majority of the soil dwelling insects are ignored by humans. Only those that adversely affect our well-being, for example, termites, wireworms and cutworms, attract our attention. However, it seems probable that the damage done by such pests is greatly outweighed by the benefits that soil-dwelling insects confer.

During the process of making tunnels and burrowing into the soil, soil particles get disintegrated, subsoil is brought to the surface resulting in turning of the soil. Thus the burrowing activity facilitates aeration, drainage and turnover of the soil. Many species carry animal and plant material underground for nesting, feeding and/or reproduction, which has been compared to ploughing in a cover crop. The condition of the soil is improved by producing humus as a result of consuming organic matter and passing it out as waste. Soil is also enriched by the addition of insect saliva and decomposition of exuviae and dead bodies of the insects. Considering their vast numbers, the insects as a whole must equal or exceed the earthworms in building and improving the soil.

SCAVENGERS

Many insects feed on dead and decaying animal and plant matter, and thus accelerate the return of elements to food chains. Since these insects help to remove from the earth's surface the dead and decaying bodies, which would otherwise be a health hazard, they are referred to as scavengers. It is a common sight to see insects collecting over bodies of dead road-side animals and eating them. Such road-side deaths are much fewer than those occurring in inaccessible places like forests, deserts and mountains. If the carcases are not quickly eaten away by the insects, the environment of the entire Earth will get filled with stench of rotting making it impossible for humans to live. Linnaeus did not exaggerate when he had said that a dead horse can be devoured faster by hungry flies than a hungry lion. The insects, therefore, are the most efficient scavengers of nature and offer this service free to humans. In addition to cleaning filth from human habitations, these insects help to convert these bodies into simpler substances before returning them back to soil where they become easily available as food for growing plants. There are two groups of insects (Coleoptera and Diptera), which perform the major duties of scavengers. In addition, the termites (Isoptera) feed upon dead wood and ants (Hymenoptera) live upon dead animal or decaying vegetable matter.

Coleoptera

This group contains : (*i*) Dung or chafer beetles (Scarabaeidae). The larvae and adults of these beetles feed on dung or decaying vegetable matter. The larvae of many other species are generally found among wood, dead leaves and other plant refuse. (*ii*) Rove beetles (Staphylinidae). The larvae and adults abound wherever there is decaying animal and plant matter, including dung on the soil. (*iii*) Skin beetles (Dermestidae). Most of the members of this family, both in their larval and adult stages, feed on dead animal matter like skin, hides, wool and fur. (*iv*) Carrion beetles (Silphidae). Almost all the species of this family feed upon bodies of dead animals and a few on vegetable refuse. (*v*) Darkling beetles (Tenebrionidae). Some of these beetles live in dung and in dead animal matter and under bark.

The Australian dung beetle project has successfully exploited the use of dung beetles for dung disposal and preventing the use of the decaying material by pest insects, *e.g.* flies. In Australia, there are an estimated 22 million cattle and 162 million sheep that collectively produce 54 million tonnes of dung each year. The cattle dung especially provides food and shelter for many insects, including the larvae of two fly pests, the introduced buffalo fly (*Haematobia irritans exigua*) in northern Australia and the native bush fly (*Musca vetustissima*) in south-eastern and south-western areas of the country. In 1967, various species of tropical South African dung beetles were released in northern Australia. The beetles rapidly multiplied and spread over wide distances, while simultaneously achieving complete or partial disposal of dung for much of the year. Over the next 15 years, about 50 additional species of dung beetles, plus a few species of histerid beetles that prey on fly eggs, larvae, and puparia were imported, not only from southern Africa but also from southern Europe and Asia. Of the 50-odd species released, 25 dung beetles and 3 histerids have established breeding populations in the field. This project has resulted in saving farmers the cost of harrowing, accelerating the release of nutrients into the soil, and reducing the availability of fly breeding sites.

Diptera

In case of dipteran insects, it is only the larvae which feed upon decaying matter and serve as scavengers. This group includes : (*i*) Fungus gnats (Mycetophilidae). The larvae abound in decaying wood, manure, rotting fruits and vegetables, and fungus growth. (*ii*) Dady-long-legs (Tipulidae). The larvae usually live in moist soil, muddy waters or decomposing materials and feed upon decaying vegetable matter. (*iii*) Sand flies (Psychodidae). The larvae live in water or in moist organic matter. (*iv*) Midges or gnats (Chironomidae). These insects feed upon decayed organic matter in moist situations. (*v*) Hover flies (Syrphidae). This larvae of several species are scavengers on all kinds of decaying organic matter. (*vi*) House flies (Muscidae). The larvae of house flies and related insects develop in decaying animal or vegetable matter. (*vii*) Root maggot flies (Anthomyiidae). The larvae feed upon decaying vegetable matter.

INSECTS AS FOOD

Human Food

Insects and the products derived from them, are extremely rich source of high quality proteins, fats, minerals and vitamins. Hence these serve the purpose of human food, pet food and livestock feed. Insects play a key role in energy flow through the ecosystem, principally as herbivores but also as predators and parasitoids, which may themselves be consumed by higher level insectivorous vertebrates. In turn, some of these vertebrates, are eaten by humans. Frogs and many reptiles are well known for eating insects. Some highly prized game birds and fish depend upon insects for a large proportion of their food. Chickens and turkeys, so famous for their meat, can be raised almost exclusively on insects under proper conditions.

In many parts of the world, from ancient time to the present day, insects have been extensively consumed by man. The eating of insects by man or other animals is known as *entomophagy*. Insects are a rich source of essential nutrients including proteins, amino acids, fats, minerals and vitamins. Grasshoppers, crickets, beetles, caterpillars, pupae of moths and butterflies, termites, large ants, ant and aquatic insects' eggs, aquatic bugs, cicadas, and bee brood and pupae have been prized as food for most of the primitive races of the world including India.

Mexico

Of about 500 species of insects used as human food, approximately 40 per cent are utilized by the Mexicans. Their list of food insects includes bugs, beetles, ants and bees, and moths and butterflies. Maguey worms (*Aegiale hesperiaris*) are commonly eaten in Mexico and are exported as gourmet food to North America, France and Japan. Mexican caviar (eggs of many species of Hemiptera), locally called 'ahuahutle', is quite popular in Mexico. Both the maguey worms and ahuahutle were used to be exported to USA. However, shipment of ahuahutle to North America no longer occurs because of lake pollution. Nevertheless, it can still be found in many markets and restaurants in Mexico and is exported to Europe as bird and fish food. The other insects which are eaten in Mexico include the larvae of a butterfly (*Eucharia socialis*), locally called 'madrono' worms ; larvae of an ant (*Liomatopum apiculatum*), locally called 'escamoles' ; and a grasshopper (*Spherarium* spp.).

USA

Aboriginal people of the Great Basin region in the south western united states traditionally spent much time and effort harvesting a variety of insects, principally crickets, grasshoppers, shore flies (especially the pupae), caterpillars, ants (adults and pupae), though bees, wasps, stoneflies, aphids, lice and beetles were also consumed. Some of the insects were eaten raw though most were baked or roasted before consumption. Further, large quantities, especially of grasshoppers and crickets were dried and ground to produce that was stored for use in winter.

Australia

In parts of south eastern Australia, the Bogong moth (*Agrotis infusa*) would aestivate from December through February in vast numbers in the rock shelters. Hundreds of aborigines from different tribes would gather under the Bogong mountain of New South Wales to have a feast of these moths. Some tribes would make an annual trek over a considerable distance (up to 200 km) to take advantage of this seasonal food source, returning each year to the same area. Rocks covered with layers of these moths are scraped to dislodge them and collect them from the cave floors. In central Australia, the caterpillars of the Wutchery moth (*Xyleutes leuchmochla*) constitute a staple food for children and women.

Africa

In some African countries (including Botswana, South Africa, Zaire, and Zimbabwe), there is a thriving trade in mopanie caterpillars (*Gonimbrasia belina*), and when these are in season, beef sales may show a significant decline. Termites (both *Microtermes* spp. and *Macrotermes* spp.) are consumed in Angola, Uganda, Zaire, Zimbabwe and Kenya. The desert locust (*Schistocerca gregaria*) has been a favourite food in northern Africa for a long time.

Asia

The giant water bug (*Lethocerus indicus*) is a delicacy in Thailand. The males of the bug are preferred because of their having a unique flavour perhaps due to their sex pheromone glands. Large number of larvae and cocoons of silk worm (*Bombyx mori*) are imported from China for use in restaurants in Bangkok. In Korea, grasshoppers, and larvae and cocoons of silkworm are consumed. Giant water bugs and pupae of silkworm are exported to Asian community stores in USA from Thailand and South Korea, respectively.

In Japan, the rice grasshopper (*Oxya velox*), locally called 'inago', is the most widely eaten insect. Catching inago has a poetic charm in the country and some elementary schools arrange an inago hunt every year in which parents are also invited to participate alongwith their wards to collect the insects. Locusts have been eaten by farmers in India for a long time particularly when after a locust attack, nothing was left for them to eat. There are many tribes in different states of the country which eat insect eggs, caterpillars, termites, grasshoppers, etc.

Pet Food and Livestock Feed

Nutrients from live or dead insects or their products could help better survival of birds, lizards, fish, crocodiles, turtles and several other insectivorous pets. These days, it has become a lucrative business to rear and sell these insects to the stakeholders. Crickets are known to be marketed for consumption of a variety of pets, and Madagascar hissing roaches are being sold as reptile food.

Insects also provide a nutritious food source for livestock and domestic animals. Nutitive value of insects as major source of feed for fish, poultry, pig etc. is well recognized in China. Mealworm larvae. Housefly larvae and pupae and silk worm pupae are major contributors of insect-based diets.

EDUCATIONAL AND SCIENTIFIC VALUE

In view of their simple food and other requirements, short duration time, and high fecundity, many insects can be reared cheaply and easily under laboratory conditions. These attributes of insects make them ideal tools for use in teaching and research. In addition, the remarkable diversity of form and habits of insects, make even an important resource both in and outside the classroom. The fruit fly, *Drosophila melanogaster*, has played a key role as a test insect in advanced genetic research. The genetic experimentation with cumbersome and slow breeding guinea pigs, rats, peas and primroses was shifted to this insect. These tiny flies can be handled with ease, can be reared and maintained on fermenting banana in small vials in the laboratory. The space required and cost of maintenance of these flies are very much less when compared to peas or primroses. The flies have only four pairs of chromosomes in the cells and the large chromosomes of salivary glands reveal clearly the actual chromsomal segments and the flies are able to complete about 30 generations in a year. This enables on investigator to study a number of generations within a limited period. Studies on other insects have provided us with much of the basic knowledge of animal and cell physiology, particularly in the areas of nutrition, toxicology, metabolism, endocrinology, neuromuscular physiology and evolutionary biology. Studies on population dynamics of some pest insects have led to the formulation of some important concepts in population ecology.

Insects are being used for scientific detection of crimes. The presence of bugs, flies and other insects may be useful to solve the crimes from murder and rape to poaching of animals. The term *forensic entomology* is generally applied to the study of insects and other arthropods found in and on human bodies suspected of criminal action to help in the investigation and initiation of civil proceedings. Based on the species and stage of insects, entomologists are able to predict the time and location of crime. More importantly, they indicate whether a suspect is actually involved in the crime or not. In some of the countries like USA and Canada, where mapping of insect populations has been carried out over various seasons, forensic entomologists are routinely called upon to give evidence in cases of crime.

Insects provide useful indicators for assessing the status of biodiversity over time. Insects possess many of the desirable indicator attributes and respond to environmental changes more rapidly than do vertebrate indicators. Butterflies, for example, may be good indicators for climatic changes, as they are strongly influenced by local weather pattern, microclimate and light levels. In addition, insects can be good indicators of pollution of water bodies. Natural streams, canals, rivers, ponds and lakes are often polluted due to factory wastes and raw sewage discharged into them. The pollution results in death of fish useful to humans in these waters. The degree of pollution is measured by employing the insects. The number and kind of insects that are able to survive in the polluted waters will be an index of pollution; less the number of surviving insects, the more is the pollution of the water body.

HUMAN THERAPY

Several insects and their products have found their use to treat human ailments. Honey bees, fly maggots, ants and mosquitoes are known to be used in human therapy. The venom of honey bees is said to have remedial value in the treatment of arthritis and rheumatism. Cantharidin is a substance found in the blister beetle, *Lytta vesicatoria* and is useful internally treating certain urinary diseases and externally as a vesiccant and counter-irritant. Cantharidin is also probably the world's best known and most widely abused aphrodisiac. It is also known to be a tonic for hair. However, it has profound physiological effects on human body and its use in medicine is now banned because of its high toxicity.

Dr William Boric, a renowned homeopath, mentions two drugs in his *Materia Medica* that are prepared from cockroaches, *Blatta americana* and *Blatta orientalis*, the former for the treatment of tiredness and urinary ailments, and the latter for asthama. A specific medicine 'Apis' is extracted from the honey bees by digesting the excited bees in alcohol and is used against certain diseases like urinary irritation, diphtheria, etc.

Caterpillar fungus, prepared from caterpillars of *Cordyceps simensis*, is used as a tonic by the Chinese. Traditionally, this product was considered so precious that only nobles and emperors were able to use it. Now-a-days, it is used by the Chinese athletes for strengthening and rejuvenating the body, to relieve stress, protect lungs and strengthen the immune system.

Due to its legendry properties, it has been called the 'Chinese medicine for eternal youth'. The Aleppo gall of oak is a powerful astringent tonic and antidote for certain poisons, and has been used for about 25 centuries in Europe and West Asian countries.

Maggot therpay, *i.e.* the use of maggots of certain flies to clean wounds and promote healing, has been used for centuries in some societies and probably developed as a result of casual observations that the larvae of some flies had beneficial effects on infected wounds. Allantoin is a substance isolated from the secretions of fly maggots, which seems to have properties of healing deep wounds. With the development of microbial resistance to many antibiotics, there has been a revival in the use of maggot therapy. Myiasis, the infestation of animal tissues (living or dead) by maggots appears to have evolved in some dipteran families that were originally saprophagous, *i.e.* bred in carrion. Currently, it is mostly observed in three families, viz. Oestridae (all 150 species), Calliphoridae (about 80 species) and Sarcophagidae. However, most of these species are unsuitable for use in maggot therapy because they feed on healthy tissue and are highly host specific. Of about 10 species of the medicinal maggots, the most common are the larvae of the green bottle fly, *Lucilia sericata*. However, in UK, continental Europe and New Zealand, this fly is a major sheep pest, causing 'strike', which may prove fatal in heavy infestations. The live caterpillar ants of India, Africa and Mediterranean region are used to close surgical incisions. Though such live surgical instruments may not be used in modern hospitals but they have been used by native people for this purpose.

SOURCE OF DYES

The dead and dried bodies of certain insects and the galls produced by them are a source of natural dyes. The beautiful carmine red dye cochineal is obtained from the dried and powdered bodies of the cactus scale insects (also called the cochineal insects), *Dactylopius coccus* and *D. tomentosus*, which thrive on *Opuntia* spp. *D. coccus* is specially cultivated on *O. coccinellifera* in Mexico and other countries. In India, *D. tomentosus* occurs on *O. dillenii*. When the insects are fully developed, they are brushed off the host plant and killed by hot water or sun drying and marketed. Cochineal contains 10 per cent carminic acid and is used for colouring beverages, cakes and sweets, and for dyeing materials like wool, silk and leather where permanent colouring is required. With the advent of synthetic dyes, cochineal is now getting out of use.

Galls are tumourous outgrowths on the surface of plants induced by insect inflicted injuries. They yield valuable materials like tannic acid and dyes. Tannic acid occurs in high percentage (30-70%) in many of these galls which are the richest source of this material. It has been used for centuries for tanning animal skin. Dyes obtained from some galls make the finest and most permanent ink because of which in some countries the law requires that certain records be made only with ink compounded with gallnuts. Our own ancient sages, whose writings on palmleaves have survived to this day, possibly made use of gall inks. African Somali women use gall dyes for tattooing. The Turks obtain a fine scarlet colour from a reddish gall on oak. Turkey red is dyed from "mad apple" in Asia Minor. The ancient Greeks used the Aleppo gall for dying wool, hair and skin. More recently, great quantities of it have been used in dying leather and seal skin.

AESTHETIC VALUE

Insects have catered to the aesthetic needs of man for a long time. Some of the insects are extremely beautiful and they rivel flowers and beautiful birds in this respect. Their shapes, wing colour, and patterns have served as models for artists, florists, textile designers and interior decorators. They have been the subject matter of poems from times immemorial. The inimitable and almost endless variety found among insects and their curious habits have been a source of entertainment and diversion for humans. Because of their beauty, certain groups, especially butterflies, moths and beetles, are sometimes collected as a hobby. Some are embedded in clear materials from which jewellery, place mats, paper weights, etc. are made, others are simply used as models on which paintings and jewellery are made. Artists and designers have copied extensively from the beautiful colour pattern of butterflies. Ornaments like necklaces are made from whole bodies of some beautiful insects especially beetles. In South Africa and Australia, native people use strings made of beautiful shells of nymphs of certain scale insects. In western countries, several insect based games like Giant Cootie game, Ants in the Pants, Bedbugs, Wacko the Cockroach, Bizzy, Bizzy Bumble Bees, etc. provide enjoyment and fun to children. Insects also figure in several television and video shows like the Tick, Ant, Boy, the Queen Bee, Blue Beetle, Ambush Bug, etc. A movie titled, Them featured radiation-enlarged ants, and another one made in 1978, The Swarm, depicted killer bee invasion.

B. HARMFUL INSECTS

At a conservative estimate, insects arrived in this world some 300 million years ago and, therefore, when the first ancestor of man came a million years back, insects had already mastered the world and taken full possession of it. The result was that despite his superior intelligence and vast array of tools of destruction at his disposal, insects have defeated man at every stage and in all departments of the war of struggle for survival. If they have wanted our crops, they have taken them. If they have wanted to suck our or our animals' blood, they have pumped it out right under our eyes and if they have wanted to share our abodes, we have just not been able to oust them. These daring acts they have continued and will continue to do, man's relentless war against them notwithstanding, because both need the same things at the same time. Is it, therefore, not paradoxical that on the one hand the insects are so friendly that they have become indispensable to our existence itself, on the other, they form such formidable foes that we are always kept on tenterhooks to find ways and means to contain them.

Of an estimated 5-10 million species of insects, perhaps about 10,000 constitute pests which, either alone or in conjunction with microorganisms, cause significant damage to humans, agricultural or forest products, and manufactured goods. Insects directly feed on human beings, act as vectors of microorganisms that cause diseases in humans and domesticated animals, compete with us for food and other resources, and transmit diseases in valuable plants. Increasing human population and urbanization presented easy opportunities for the dissemination of insect parasites on humans and the diseases transmitted by them. Modern transportation also encourages the spread of pest insects and insect-borne diseases. Likewise, crop intensification has resulted in aggravation of insect pest problems in agriculture.

PLANT PESTS

Insects cause enormous damage to agricultural crops, forests as well as stored agricultural commodities. Almost every economically important plant is attacked by a variety of insect pests. Damage is caused either directly by insects as they feed (by chewing or sucking) or oviposition, or by bacterial, fungal or viral diseases, for which insects serve as vectors. Especially important for causing direct damage to plants are Coleoptera, Hemiptera, Lepidoptera and Orthoptera. Several hundred diseases of plants are known to be transmitted by insects, including about 300 that are caused by viruses. Especially important in disease transmission are Hemiptera, particularly aphids and leafhoppers. Worldwide, food and fiber losses caused by pests (principally insects, plant pathogens, weeds and birds) are generally estimated at about 40 per cent, of which about 12 per cent are attributed to insects and mites. These figures do not include post-harvest losses, estimated to be about 20 per cent, and these losses occur despite the application of about 3 million tonnes of pesticides. In India, the losses due to insect pests increased from 7.2 per cent in pre-green revolution era (early 1960s) to 23.3 per cent in post-green revolution era (2001-02). Subsequently, the losses decreased to 17.5 per cent (2007-08) (Table 1.2), primarily due to large scale adoption of IPM and introduction of Bt cotton. In terms of monetary value, the Indian agriculture suffers an annual loss of about ₹ 8,63,884 million due to insect pests.

Table 1.2 Crop losses caused by insect pests to major agricultural crops in India

Crop	Actual production (million tonnes)	Approximate estimated loss in yield due to insect pests		Hypothetical production in the absence of losses (million tonnes)	Monetary value of estimated losses (USD million)
		%	Total (million tonnes)		
Cotton	58.17	30	24.93	83.10	15767.69
Rice	106.65	25.00	35.55	142.20	8467.36
Maize	24.26	18.00	5.33	29.59	1268.41
Sugarcane	352.14	20.00	88.04	440.18	3160.25
Rapeseed- mustard	7.88	20.00	1.97	9.85	1026.70
Groundnut	9.71	15.00	1.71	11.43	1172.13
Other oilseeds	15.16	12.00	2.07	17.23	1215.55
Pulses	19.78	15.00	3.49	23.27	2285.29
Coarse cereals	19.03	8.00	1.65	20.68	378.20
Wheat	93.51	5.00	4.92	98.43	1135.75
Total/Average	**706.29**	**16.80**	**–169.66**	**–881.73**	**35877.33**

Source : Dhaliwal *et al.* (2015)

Chewing

Chewing is done with the help of well developed and strong mandibles. The external part of the plant (largely leaf, could also be stem, flower, etc.) is cut off, ground and swallowed — something like grazing by cows or horses. Insects that feed in this way are called phytophagous and belong to the orders Orthoptera (grasshoppers), Coleoptera (beetles) and Lepidoptera (caterpillars). Some of these insects can eat to the extent of skeletonising the leaves or even denuding the plants. In 1922, the grasshoppers (locusts) had denuded the crops so badly in Canada that trainloads of livestocks had to be shipped out of the country to let them survive.

Piercing and Sucking

In this case, the mouthparts (mandibles and labium) are modified into long, slender and sharply pointed beak (proboscis) which is thrust into plant to suck out the sap. The hole made by the beak is too small to be seen but the withdrawl of the sap results in either minute spottings of white, brown or red on the leaves, fruits or twigs or curling of leaves. Insects of the order Hemiptera (bugs, scale insects, aphids, leafhoppers, etc.) are the best known examples of piercing and sucking insects of plants and Diptera (mosquitoes) has such examples that suck blood of man and animals.

Boring

Insects that feed by getting inside the plant tissue are called borers. They gain entrance to the plants by having the egg thrust into the tissues by the sharp ovipositor of the mother insect or by eating their way in after they hatch from the eggs. Borers belong to insect orders Coleoptera, Lepidoptera and Diptera. Borers of fruits are called worms (Lepidoptera), of seeds and grains, weevils (Coleoptera) and leaves, leaf-miners (Diptera). Borers belonging to the first two orders, however, could also be boring into the stems (bark, cambium and heartwood) and roots. They make galleries as they feed upon the internal tissues, leave frass in them and make the plant very weak.

Gall Making

Some insects belonging to the orders Diptera (gall midges) or Hymenoptera (gall wasps) induce plants to produce external outgrowths or tumours of various shapes and sizes called galls. The formation of galls is initiated by oviposition carried out by the adult and its

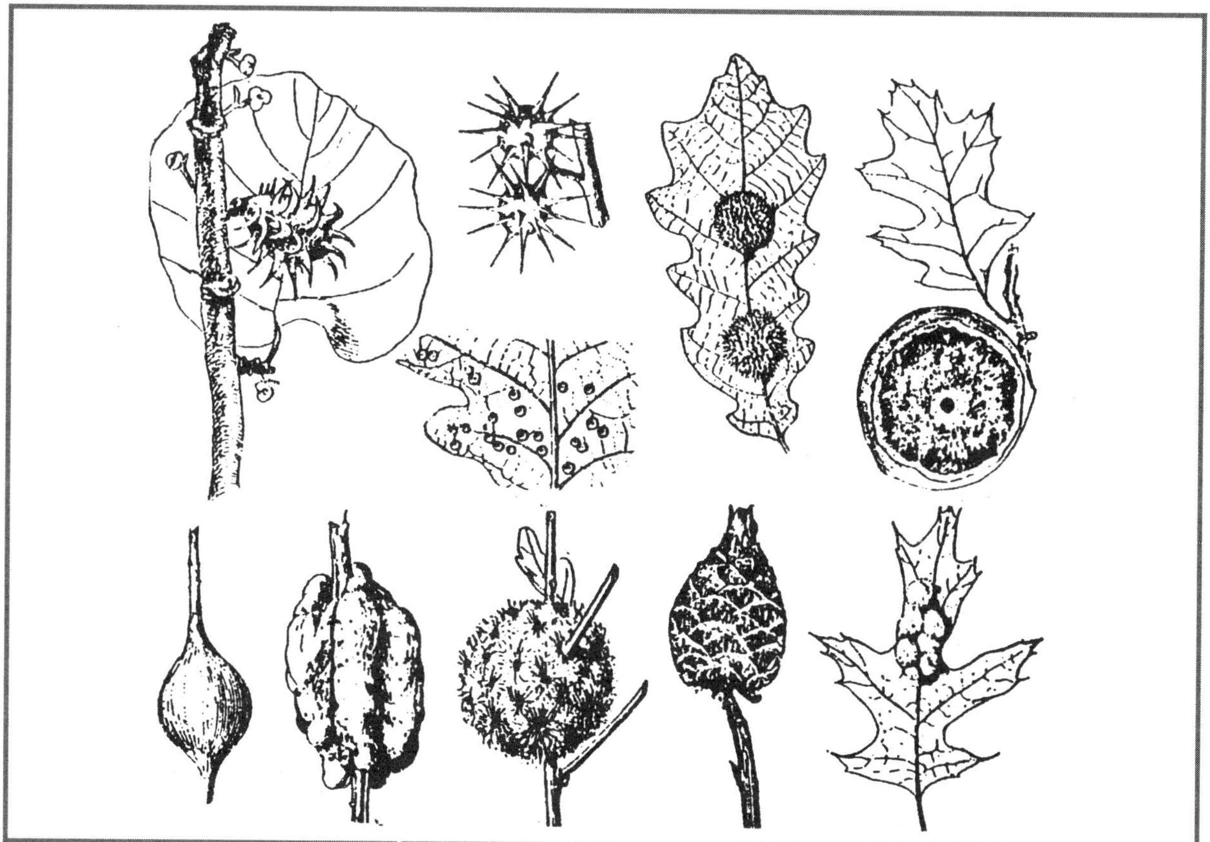

Fig. 1.1 Various forms of galls induced by injuries inflicted by insects

continued development results from the secretion of the developing larva. Galls provide both shelter and food for the larva and the strange features of the work of gall-insects is that in some cases, one species will produce similar galls on different plants but in some other cases, several species attacking the same plant produce galls that are greatly different in appearance. Although the gall is entirely a plant tissue, the insects in some unknown manner controls and directs the shape and size it shall take as it grows. There is a marvellous variety of such insect homes built by the "unwilling" but helpless plants (Fig. 1.1). Many of these galls seem to be practically harmless to the plants. However, the wheat jointworm, one of the worst pests of wheat, is a gall insect and the grape phylloxera (vine insect) has destroyed thousands of hectares of the most valuable vineyards in Europe and America.

Root Eating

These include sap suckers, root borers and gall insects whose attacks are very similar to the above-ground forms. Several examples of root feeders can be found later in this volume in chapters on crop pests. However, one important and interesting example of this category of insect is the woolly apple aphid, *Eriosoma lanigerum* whose two generations are passed as above-ground egg-laying and bud and leaf sucking alate forms whereafter winged forms are produced which migrate underground and produce most serious injuries by feeding on the roots. They give birth to young ones in summer which also feed upon roots and in winter develop into wingless males and females. When these mate, the progeny produced take to above ground living and become egg producing individuals. The damage caused by the underground adults and nymphs often kills the whole plant.

Injury by Egg Laying

Roughly 5 per cent of insects damage plants and trees by ovipositiong into them. Cicada female, for example, deposits its eggs in 1 year old fruit and forest trees by splitting the wood so severely that the entire twig beyond this point dies. The tree-hoppers and tree-crickets ruin the bark or twigs of their host plants. It may be pointed out that the emerging larvae of these insects, in majority of the cases, desert the trees or plants of their birth doing no further damage to them since their own food is some where else.

Injury by Nest Making

Many insects remove parts of plants for the construction of their nests, on the plant itself or elsewhere. An example of it is the leaf-cutter bee that nips out rather neat circular pieces of rose and other foliage, and fashions and cements them together into thimble-shaped cells one above the other in a tunnel previously made in the stem of plant. Each cell when completed contains a mass of nectar, pollen and eggs. The tropical leaf-cutting ants, *Atta* spp. carry millions of pieces of leaves into their nests where they are cut further into fine pieces and mixed with their own or other insects' excreta to make a medium on which grows a fungus that forms the only food for the larvae and adults of this insect.

Injury due to Mutualism

Mutualism is a relationship between two different insects which are mutually beneficial to each other. An example of this is the relationship between some ants and the aphids. Ants furnish a shelter and a feeding place to aphids while the aphids give them honeydew. Whereas, the ants are harmless to plants, the aphids are not. They cause severe injury to the roots. The cornfield ant, *Lasius alienus* collects the eggs of corn-root aphid, *Anuraphis maidiradicts,* during the winter and keeps them in their own nests. When during spring, the eggs hatch, the young nymphs are carried by the ant between their jaws to the roots of the host plants. The aphids are so much dependent on these ants that they themselves, even the adults, cannot by themselves search out their host plants. They have to be brought to the roots of the host plants by the ants only. In return for this service, aphids pass on honeydew, a modified form of plant sap from their anus into the mouth of the ants whenever they solicit by tickling the abdomen of the former with their antennae.

Dissemination of Plant Diseases

Insects are responsible for the transmission of several diseases caused by bacteria, fungi and viruses. The dissemination could be *passive* in which the role of the insect is only restricted to rupturing the protective epidermis during feeding or ovipositing and allowing pathogens, fungal or bacterial spores, already present in the air to enter the plant through the injury or it could be *active* in which the insects act as a mechanical carriers of the pathogens in or outside their body to pass them on to the plants by injection or through contact, contaminated saliva or mouthparts during feeding or contaminated ovipositor during laying eggs. Most of the insect vectors belong to the order Hemiptera (aphids, leafhoppers, whiteflies and mealy bugs), but a few belong to Thysanoptera (thrips), Coleoptera (beetles), Orthoptera (grasshoppers) and Dermaptera (ear, wigs). Homopteran insects alone are known to transmit about 90 per cent of the plant diseases.

HUMAN AND ANIMALS PESTS

A number of insects are external or temporary internal parasites of humans. Some of these are specific to humans, *e.g.* the human louse (*Pediculus humanus*), but most have a variable number of alternate hosts. Insect parasites usually weaken their hosts, making them more susceptible to diseases or cause irritation or sores which may then become infected. More importantly, insects serve as vectors of many important human diseases. Many insects, especially flies, act as mechanical vectors, contaminating human food with pathogens picked up during contact with faeces or other organic waste. Some insects especially bees and wasps may bite or sting, when disturbed accidentally or deliberately. Several caterpillars secrete poisonous substances through hairs on their dorsal surface. Generally, the effect of the bite or sting is temporary and nothing more than skin irritation, swelling or blister formation. In extreme cases, bee stings may cause death in some sensitive individuals. Several insect groups are parasites of domesticated animals. A majority of these are external feeders like bloodsucking flies (*e.g.* mosquitoes, horse flies, deer flies, black flies, and stable flies), biting and sucking lice, and fleas. Some of the insects like bot, warble and screwworm flies are internal parasites of animals for a part of their life history. Many of these insects act as vectors of important livestock diseases. In addition, almost all of them cause a reduction in the health of the infected animals. The quality of milk, meat, wool and other products obtained from such animals is adversely affected. In extreme cases, the infected animals may eventually die.

Annoy and Injure Man and Animals

There are several ways in which insects annoy and injure man and animals — both domesticated and wild. The monotonous sounds — droning, humming and buzzing — that the insects produce during flight is familiarly annoying to every one. The foul odour that some of them produce and the offensive taste that secretions and excretions of some of them leave on fruits, food and dishes are a cause of no less suffering. They pinch, chew or nibble our skin, produce irritating sensation when they crawl on our body and some of them (blister beetles) even cause painful and disfiguring blisters on any part of the body they may come in contact with. By accidentally entering the eyes, ears, nostrils, or alimentary canal, they cause *myiasis,* a painful muscle damage.

Inject Venoms

Many insects are venomous, which can be grouped into three categories, *viz.* stinging, biting and vesicating insects.

(*i*) The stinging insects include bees, wasps and ants, all belonging to the order Hymenoptera. In all these cases, the ovipositor has been modified to function as a stinging apparatus. The chief components of the bee venom are a protein (melittin) that has a powerful haemolytic (blood cell breaking) action as also the allergic reactions in sensitive persons and the enzymes, lecithinase (phospholipase A) and hyaluronidase. Lecithinase inhibits lactic dehydrogenases and citric acid cycle substrates, which is the cause of intense pain in the victim. The enzyme hyaluronidase helps spread other components to the tissues. The wasp venom is rich in serotonin (5-hydroxytryptamine) and hyaluronidase, and in some cases acetylcholine also. The constituents of ant venom vary with the species; myrmicine ants have a poison called iridomyrmecin and formicine ants contain formic acid.

(*ii*) The biting insects include the blood sucking bed bugs, mosquitoes, assasin bugs, stable flies, fleas and certain phytophagous insects turning blood-sucking such as thrips and some hemipterans. In these insects, the salivary glands are the source of venom, which in many cases (bed bugs, mosquitoes) also contain an anaesthetic, and an anticogulin besides the toxins.

(*iii*) Vesicating insects are those whose venom has the ability to produce some kind of skin eruption, *i.e.* urticarial caterpillars and blister beetles. The urticarial caterpillars belong to 10 families and over 50 species of Lepidoptera. Their hairs are hollow containing a toxin. By contact or through wind, these hairs or even the exuviae may come in contact with the skin of unexposed parts, hands, neck or face, producing severe dermatitis. Blister beetles produce a toxic substance called cantharidin, an anhydride of cantharidic acid. A contact with the blister beetle is bound to result in blisters full of a watery substance. If the blister ruptures, it will produce more blisters on areas where the fluid spills.

Make Home in and on Human and Animal Bodies

As external and internal parasites, many insect species make their homes on our body (lice) or on the body of some animals (bird lice) whereupon they lay their eggs and pass excreta. The larvae of some flies on hatching may tunnel into the muscles of any organ system— nose, ear, urinogenital passages, and alimentary canal causing mechanical injury and promoting infection. Horse bots are the larvae of the fly, *Gastrophilus intestinalis,* which develop in the stomach and rectum of horses, sometimes blocking these passages due to their large number and cutting off the nourishment leading to starvation and death.

Disseminate Diseases in Man and Animals

Some 150 diseases, some of them quite serious, are known to be exclusively transmitted by insects and their arthropod relatives. They transmit every disease producing pathogens like viruses, bacteria, spirochaetes, rickettsias, protozoa, nematodes and fungi to humans and animals. They do so mechanically through their bodies contaminated with filth, faeces, sputum, body excretions or exudations of infected wounds. The blood-sucking insects pick up the pathogens by biting diseased persons or animals or wild animals that act as reservoirs for some pathogens and transmit them when they bite healthy men and animals.

Destroyers of Useful Articles

Insects destroy almost every thing that is used by man; stored food, clothings, woollens, rugs, drugs, furnitures, bridges, telephone poles, animal and plant collections in museums, paper, books and so on. You name any thing and the insects are there to destroy or depreciate their value by eating them, contaminating them with their secretions, excretions, eggs, their own dead bodies or body-casts or simply by inhabiting them.

CONCLUSIONS

The insects provide us many useful products in the form of honey, royal jelly, silk, lac, wax, dyes, etc. The insects and their products are also eaten as delicacies in different parts of the world. In addition, they perform a valuable service of pollination of a number of field, vegetable and fruit crops. They also perform unique functions of soil builders, scavengers, killers of insect pests and weeds. They are of great educational, scientific and aesthetic value. However, a number of insects inflict heavy losses to crop plants and are also parasitic on humans and domesticated animals. In addition, they are also vectors of many bacterial, fungal and viral diseases. Hence it becomes difficult to decide whether to regard insects as our friends or foes because the benefits they provide are as important as the injuries they cause. However, if the verdict is to be given in favour of only one of the options, the rationale is to call the insects as one of the best friends of man. This is because we could reduce the injuries and treat the diseases they cause, but just cannot pollinate the plants and trees to retain their yield at the same level as with insects and also we cannot synthesise the useful products (honey, wax, silk, shellac, etc.).

*****

AGRICULTURAL ENTOMOLOGY

PART-II

- PESTS OF CEREALS AND MILLETS
- PESTS OF SUGARCANE
- PESTS OF PULSES
- PESTS OF OILSEEDS
- PESTS OF VEGETABLES
- PESTS OF FRUITS
- PESTS OF MUSHROOMS
- PESTS OF FIBRE CROPS
- PESTS OF PLANTATION CROPS
- PESTS OF SPICES
- PESTS OF ORNAMENTAL PLANTS
- POLYPHAGOUS PESTS
- NON-INSECT PESTS OF CROPS
- PESTS OF STORED PRODUCTS
- INSECT VECTORS OF PLANT DISEASES

2 CHAPTER

PESTS OF CEREALS AND MILLETS

Rice (*Oryza sativa*)

Stem borers

1. *Scirpophaga incertulas* (Walker) (Yellow stem borer, Lepidoptera : Pyralidae)
2. *Chilo suppressalis* (Walker) (Pale-headed striped borer, Lepidoptera : Pyralidae)
3. *Chilo polychrysus* (Meyrick) (Dark-headed striped borer, Lepidoptera : Pyralidae)
4. *Sesamia inferens* (Walker) (Pink stem borer, Lepidoptera : Noctuidae)
5. *Chilo infuscatellus* Snell (Sugarcane shoot borer, Lepidoptera : Pyralidae)

Leaf feeders

6. *Orseolia oryzae* (Wood-Mason) (Rice gall midge, Diptera : Cecidomyiidae)
7. *Nymphula depunctalis* Guenee (Rice caseworm, Lepidoptera : Pyralidae)
8. *Mythimna separata* (Walker) (Rice ear-cutting caterpillar, Lepidoptera: Noctuidae)
9. *Dicladispa armigera* (Olivier) (Rice hispa, Coleoptera : Chrysomelidae)
10. *Cnaphalocrocis medinalis* (Guenee) (Rice leaf-folder Lepidoptera : Pyralidae)
11. *Hieroglyphus banian* (Fabrcius) (Rice grasshopper, Orthoptera: Acrididae)
12. *Hieroglyphus nigrorepletus* Bolivar (Rice grasshopper, Orthoptera : Acrididae)
13. *Melanitis ledia ismene* (Cramer) (Rice butterfly, Lepidoptera : Nymphalidae)

14. *Hydrellia philippina* Ferini (Whorl maggot, Diptera : Ephydridae)
15. *Cofana spectra* (Distant) (White rice leafhopper, Hemiptera: Cicadellidae)
16. *Recilia dorsalis* (Motschulsky) (Zigzag leafhopper, Hemiptera: cicadellidae)
17. *Typhlocyba maculifrons* (Motschulsky) (Rice blue leaf hopper, Hemiptera: Cicadellidae)

Sap suckers

18. *Leptocorisa acuta* (Thunberg) (Rice bug, Hemiptera : Coreidae)
19. *Nephotettix virescens* (Distant) (Green leafhopper, Hemiptera: Cicadellidae)
20. *Nephotettix nigropictus* (Stal) (Green leafhopper, Hemiptera : Cicadellidae)
21. *Sogatella furcifera* (Horvath) (Whitebacked planthopper, Hemiptera : Delphacidae)
22. *Nilaparvata lugens* (Stal) (Brown planthopper, Hemiptera : Delphacidae)
23. *Cofana spectra* (Distant) (White rice leafhopper, Hemiptera : Cicadellidae)
24. *Recilia dorsalis* (Motschulsky) (Zig-zag leafhopper, Hemiptera: Cicadellidae)
25. *Typhlocyba maculifrons* (Motschulsky) (Rice blue leafhopper, Hemiptera: Cicadellidae)
26. *Ripersia oryzae* Green (Rice mealy bug, Hemiptera : Coccidae)
27. *Stenchaetothrips biformis* (Bagnall) (Rice thrips, Thysanoptera: Thripidae)
28. *Haplothrips ganglbauri* Schmutz (Panicle thrips, Thysanoptera : Phlaeothripidae)

Root feeder

29. *Echinocnemus oryzae* (Marshall) (Paddy root weevil, Coleoptera: Curculionidae)

Maize (*Zea mays*)

Stem borers

1. *Chilo partellus* (Swinhoe) (Maize stem borer, Lepidoptera : Pyralidae)
2. *Sesamia inferens* (Walker) (Pink stem borer, Lepidoptera : Noctuidae)
3. *Ostrinia furnacalis* (Guenee) (Asian maize borer, Lepidoptera: Pyralidae)
4. *Ostrinia nubilasis* (Hubner) (European corn borer, Lepidoptera : Pyralidae)

Shoot borer

5. *Atherigona soccata* Rondani (Sorghum shoot fly, Diptera : Muscidae)

Leaf feeders

6. *Hieroglyphus nigrorepletus* Bolivar (Phadka grasshopper, Orthoptera : Acrididae)
7. *Hieroglyphus banian* Fabricius (Rice grasshopper, Orthoptera: Acrididae)
8. *Colemania sphenarioides* Bolivar (Deccan wingless grasshopper, Orth. : Acrididae)
9. *Amsacta moorei* (Butler) (Red hairy caterpillar, Lepidoptera : Acrididae)

Sap suckers

10. *Rhopalosiphum maidis* Fitch (Maize aphid, Hemiptera : Aphididae)
11. *Pyrilla perpusilla* (Walker) (Sugarcane leafhopper, Hemiptera: Lophopidae)

Root feeders	12. *Holotrichia* spp. (White grub, Coleoptera : Scarabaeidae)
	13. *Tanymecus indicus* Faust (Gujhia weevil, Coleoptera : Curculionidae)

Sorghum (*Sorghum bicolor*)

Stem borers	1. *Chilo partellus* (Swinhoe) (Maize stem borer, Lepidoptera : Pyralidae)
	2. *Sesamia inferens* (Walker) (Pink stem borer, Lepidoptera : Noctuidae)
Shoot feeders	3. *Antherigona soccata* Rondani (Sorghum shoot fly, Diptera : Muscidae)
	4. *Peregrinus maidis* (Ashmead) (Sorghum shoot bug, Hemiplera : Delphacidae)
Grain (ovary) feeder	5. *Contarinia sorghicola* (Coquillett) (Sorgum midge, Diptera : Cecidomyidae)
Earhead feeders	6. *Calocoris angustatus* Lethiery (Sorghum earhead bug, Hemiptera : Miridae)
	7. *Helicoverpa armigera* (Hubner) (Gram pod borer, Lepidoptera : Noctuidae)
	8. *Mythimna separata* (Walker) (Armyworm, Lepidoptera : Noctuidae)
Root feeders	9. *Holotrichia* spp. (White grubs, Diptera : Scarabaeidae)
	10. *Tetraneura nigriabdominalis* (Sasaki) (Root aphid, Hemiptera : Aphididae)

Wheat (*Triticum* spp.)

Stem borer	1. *Sesamia inferens* (Walker) (Pink stem borer, Lepidoptera : Noctuidae)
Leaf feeders	2. *Chrotogonus trachypterus* (Surface grasshopper, Orthoptera : Acrididae)
	3. *Mythimna separata* (Walker) (Armyworm, Lepidoptera : Noctuidae)
Sap suckers	4. *Sitobion miscanthi* (Takahashi) (Wheat aphid, Hemiptera : Aphididae)
	5. *Anapothrips flavicinctus* Karny (Wheat thrips, Thysanoptera : Thripidae)
Seedling eater	6. *Tanymecus indicus* Faust (Ghujhia weevil, Coleoptera : Curculionidae).
Root eaters	7. *Microtermes obesi* (Holmgren) (Termite, Isoptera : Termitidae)
	8. *Odontotermes obsesus* (Rambur) (Termite, Isoptera : Termitidae).

India produced 279.5 million tonnes of foodgrains in 2017. Total foodgrain production in 2017-18 has been estimated at 284.83 million tonnes.

RICE

More than 100 insect species are associated with the rice crop at one stage or the other and 20 of these are pests of major economic significance.

1. *Scirpophaga incertulas* (Walker) (Yellow stem borer, Lepidoptera: Pyralidae) (Fig. 2.1A)

Distribution. The yellow stem borer is common in all the Asian countries. In India it is widespread in all paddy growing areas like Assam, West Bengal, Orissa, Uttar Pradesh, Punjab, Haryana, Andhra Pradesh and Tamil Nadu.

Identification. The adults have a wing expanse of 25-45 mm and are yellowish white with orange yellow front wings. The females have a prominent tuft of brownish yellow silken hair at the tip of their abdomen. The female moth is bigger than the male moth and has a centrally situated black spot on each of the fore wings. The females have a prominent tuft of brownish yellow silken hair at the tip of their abdomen. The caterpillars, when full-grown, measure about 20 mm and are dirty white or greenish yellow, having brown head and pronotum.

Life-history. In the northern regions of India, this pest is active from April to October and hibernates from November to March as a full-grown larva in rice stubble. The pupation starts sometimes in March and the emergence of moths begins in April. The moths become active after dusk when they mate and lay about 120-150 eggs on the underside of the leaves in 2-5 clusters of 60-100 eggs each. The eggs are covered with yellowish brown hair of the female tuft. They hatch in 6-7 days and the tiny black-headed caterpillars soon bore into the stem from the growing points downwards. The larva grows in 6 stages and is full-fed in 16-27 days. It then constructs an emergence hole which is always located above the water level and pupates inside the attacked plant. Within 9-12 days, it emerges as a moth. The life cycle is completed in 31-46 days. There are 3 broods in Bengal, 2 in Orissa, 4-5 in Punjab, Andhra Pradesh and Tamil Nadu.

Host plants. Paddy seems to be the only plant attacked by this pest, it does not have any alternative food.

Damage. The larva feeds inside the stem causing drying of the central shoot or 'deadheart' in young plant and drying of the panicle or 'white ear' in older plant. Basmati varieties suffer heavy damage than coarse varieties.

Management. (*i*) The removal and destruction of stubbles at the time of the first ploughing after harvesting the crop decreases the carry-over to the next crop. (*ii*) Ploughing and flooding the field is also effective in killing the larvae. (*iii*) Since the eggs of stem borer are laid near the tip of leaf, clipping of tips of seedlings before transplanting can reduce the carryover of eggs to the field. (*iv*) Simultaneous releases of *Trichogramma chilonis* and *T. japonicum* @ 100,000 ha^{-1} at 7 days interval, starting 30 days after transplanting, reduced borer damage and increased yield. (*v*) The fields showing more than 5 per cent dead hearts should be sprayed with 50 ml flubendiamide 480SC (green chemistry category insecticide) or 425 g of cartap hydrochloride 75SG or 875 ml of triazophos 40EC or 1.4 litre of monocrotophos 36SL or 2.5 litres of chlorpyriphos 20EC in 250 litres of water per ha. Application of any of these insecticides may be repeated if and when damage reaches ETL (Economic Threshold Level).

2. *Sesamia inferens* (Walker) (Pink stem borer, Lepidoptera : Noctuidae) (Fig. 2.1B)

Distribution. The pink stem borer is a polyphagous insect and is distributed throughout India and Pakistan.

Identification. The moths are straw-coloured and have a stout body. The caterpillars are pinkish brown and have a smooth cylindrical body, measuring about 25 mm.

Life-history. The pest breeds actively from March-April to November on rice and then migrates to the wheat crop. The moths are nocturnal and lay eggs on leaves or on the ground. The eggs hatch in 6-8 days and the young caterpillars bore into the epidermal layers of the leaf sheath. Later on, they bore into the stem as a result of which the growing shoot dries

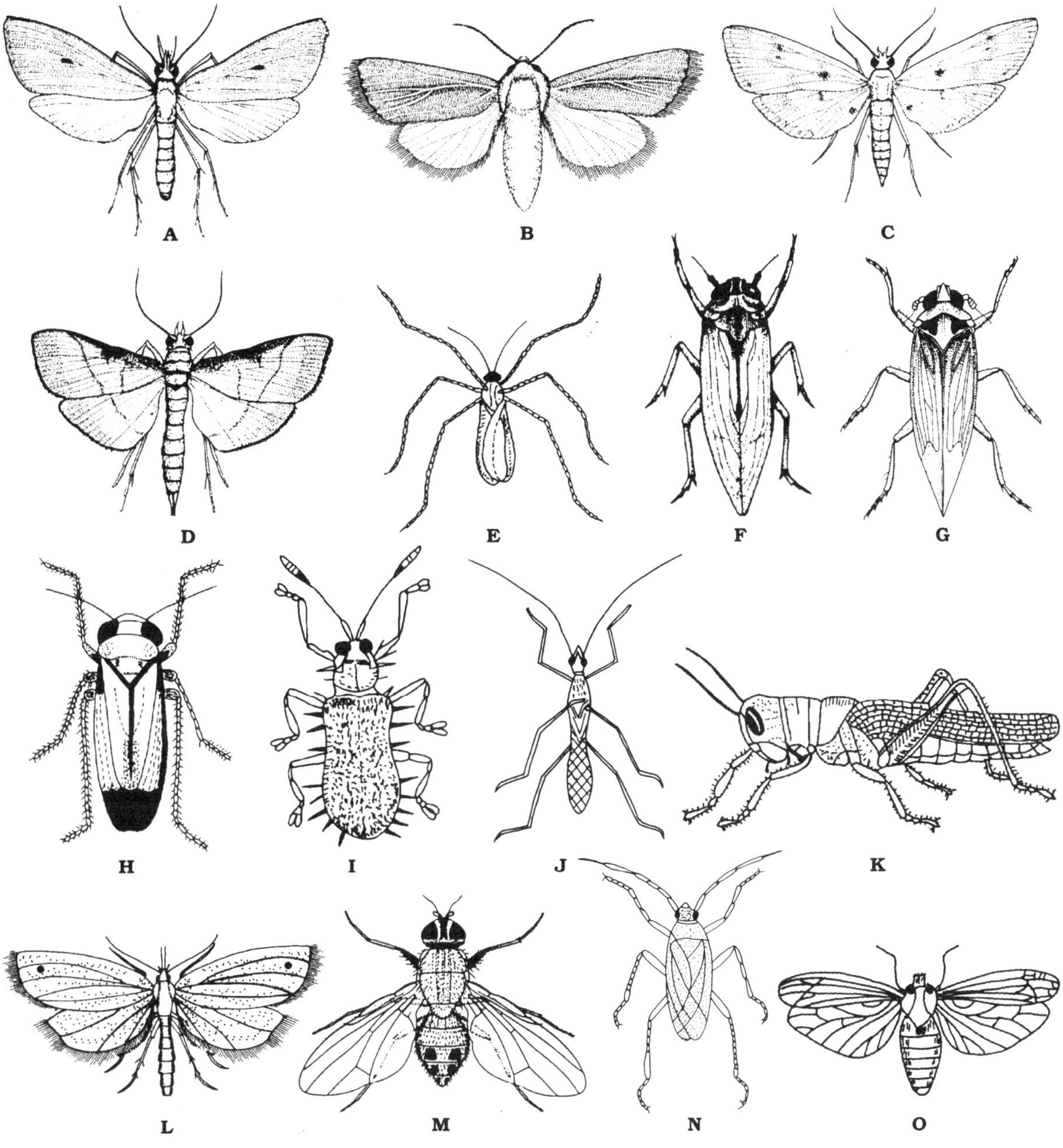

Fig. 2.1 Pests of cereals and millets. **A.** Yellow stem borer, *Scirpophaga incertulas*. **B.** Pink stem borer, *Sesamia inferens*. **C.** Rice case worm, *Nymphula depunctalis*. **D.** Rice leaf-folder, *Cnaphalocrocis medinalis*. **E.** Rice gall midge, *Orseolia oryzae*. **F.** Brown planthopper, *Nilaparvata lugens*. **G.** Whitebacked planthopper, *Sogatella furcifera*. **H.** Green leafhopper, *Nephotettix nigropictus*. **I.** Rice hispa, *Dicladispa armigera*. **J.** Rice bug, *Leptocorisa acuta*. **K.** Rice grasshopper, *Hieroglyphus banian*. **L.** Maize borer, *Chilo partellus*. **M.** Sorghum shoot fly, *Atherigone soccata*. **N.** Sorghum earhead bug, *Calocoris angustatus*. **O.** Sorghum shoot bug, *Peregrinus maidis*.

up producing dead-hearts. When the attacked plants die, the larvae move on to adjoining plants. They are full-fed in 3-4 weeks and pupate inside the stem or in between the stem and leaves. The pupal stage lasts about a week and the life-cycle is completed in 6-7 weeks. There are 4-5 generations of the pest in a year.

Host-plants. In some parts of the country, it is a minor pest of sugarcane whereas in others, it is common on *ragi* (*Elusine coracana*), and in still others on wheat. In northern India, it is recorded on rice, sugarcane, maize, sorghum and wheat, but its damage is significant on rice and maize only.

Damage. Same as in case of yellow stem borer.

Management. Same as in case of yellow stem borer.

3. *Chilo suppressalis* (Walker) (Pale-headed striped borer, Lepidoptera : Pyralidae)

Distribution. It is a serious pest in Japan, the Philippines, Southern Indonesia, Spain and China. It has also been recorded from Formosa, Korea, Malaysia, the Hawaii Islands, Northern Australia and India.

Identification. The moth is 12 mm long, with pale-yellow wings of 26 mm expanse. The male moth is smaller than the female. The newly emerged caterpillar is about 1.2 mm long and has five grey-brown linear dorsal stripes on its body. When full-grown, it is 26 mm long and 2.5 mm wide, and has a yellowish brown head.

Life-history. The insect passes through 1-4 generations, depending upon the climate of its habitat. In temperate regions of Japan, China and Korea, it has two broods and the full-grown larvae of the second brood remain dormant in the stubble during the winter.

A female lays about 300 eggs in masses of variable sizes on the leaf blades near the tip or on the leafsheath. The eggs hatch in 4-10 days, depending on the weather. The newly emerged larvae feed on the leafsheaths in groups. The 2nd and 3rd instar larvae disperse to the adjacent plants. They bore into the culm, through the nodes by the tenth day. As the larvae grow and plants wither, they disperse gradually to the neighbouring plants. The larvae of the second generation bore into the stem through the stalk of the panicle and travel downwards until they reach the lowermost part of the stem. The larva of the first generation becomes full-grown in 33-50 days after emerging from the egg. The mature larva pupates within the rice stalk either near the middle or in the basal internode. Pupation is completed in 5-10 days. The hibernating larvae remain in the stems or stubble when the crop is harvested. They resume development in the spring; their pupation being followed by the emergence of moths.

Host plants. Except for a few wild grasses, this borer is confined to the rice plant throughout its habitat.

Damage. The attacked leafsheaths first show transparent patches, and later turn yellow-brown and eventually dry up. The caterpillars, as a result of their feeding inside the stem around the nodes, weaken the stems which easily break. Seedlings which have been attacked at the base show dead-hearts, *i.e.* the drying up of the central shoot. Attacked plants bear white heads, indicating empty panicles or those with a few filled grains.

Two other allied species, namely, *Chilo indicus* (Kapur) and *Chilo infuscatellus* Snellen, have also been recorded infesting paddy in certain areas in India.

Management. Same as in case of yellow stem borer.

4. *Mythimna separata* (Walker) (Rice ear-cutting caterpillar, Lepidoptera : Noctuidae)

Distribution. The insect occurs in Andhra Pradesh, Assam, Orissa, Punjab, West Bengal and peninsular India.

Identification. The adult is pale-brown moth measuring 3.5-4.0 cm across stretched wings. The full grown caterpillar is about 39 mm long. The larvae are gregarious in habit and are commonly known as 'armyworm'.

Life-history. The eggs are laid in overlapping rows. The egg, larval and pupal periods have average durations of 2, 21 ad 10 days, respectively under field conditions during July-December when the pest is present in the fields. The full-grown larva pupates in clumps of paddy, in cracks and crevices in ground or in loose soil. The total life-cycle is completed in 48 days by female and 45 days by male. The longevity of the moth is 13 and 10 days for female and male, respectively. The insect completes two generations during July to December.

Host plants. Paddy, maize, wheat and some grasses.

Damage. The damage to the paddy leaves and ears is caused by the caterpillars. The newly hatched larvae feed on the epidermis of the tender leaves. The second and third instar larvae feed by cutting the leaf from the edge towards mid-rib. The fourth, fifth and sixth instar larvae, besides damaging leaves, also cut off the panicles mostly at the base and hence the name 'rice ear-cutting caterpillar'. This stage (4th-6th instar) of the insect causes serious loss to the paddy crop. The larvae are shy of sunlight, hide in the ground during day-time and generally feed at night. The damage to paddy crop is caused mostly during September to November.

Management. The insect can be controlled by spraying the crop with 1.0 litre of quinalphos 25EC or 1.4 litres of monocrotophos 36SL in 250 litres of water/ha. As the pest is noctural in behaviour, the spray should be done in the evening hours for getting better results.

5. *Nymphula depunctalis* Guenee (Rice caseworm, Lepidoptera : Pyralidae) (Fig. 2.1C)

Distribution. The insect is present in all the rice-growing tracts and may assume serious proportions in certain seasons in fields under swampy conditions.

Identification. The adult is a small white moth with a wing expanse of 16 mm with pale brown wavy markings. The larva is light green with a light brownish-orange head.

Life-history. The female lays about 50 eggs singly or in clusters of 4 on the undersurface of the leaves or grasses. The eggs hatch in 4-6 days. The young larvae feed by scraping the leaf surface. The larva makes a cylindrical tubular case out of a portion of the leaf cut out from it and remains inside it, moving with the case on the leaves. It feeds on the leaves and becomes full-grown in 18-22 days. It pupates inside the case which is attached to the base of the tiller and the adult moth emerges in 5-6 days. The life-cycle is completed in about 5 weeks.

Host plants. Paddy, but lives on grasses in off-season.

Damage. The caterpillars cause the damage by feeding upon the leaves. They lead a semi-aquatic life floating in their tubular cases on the surface of water or attached to the stems at or above the water level. The early stages of the crop are damaged by the pest. The leaf blades are eaten away completely leaving only the midribs. In case of severe attack, tillers become stunted and loose their vigour and often the plants are killed.

Management. (*i*) Drain-off the water from the field to kill the floating larvae. (*ii*) Put some kerosene in the field water and dislodge the leaf-cases by shaking the plants by passing rope or by branches of thorny plant. (*iii*) Chemical control measures are same as in case of rice ear-cutting caterpillar.

6. *Cnaphalocrocis medinalis* (Guenee) (Rice leaf-folder, Lepidoptera : Pyralidae) (Fig. 2.1D)

Distribution. The rice leaf-folder is distributed in Indonesia, Korea, Malaysia, the Philippines, Pakistan and India.

Identification. The moths are golden or yellowish brown and measure 8-10 mm in length and 16-20 mm in wing expanse. The wings have 2-3 wavy lines characterized by dark bands. Its greenish caterpillars are very agile and they feed inside the fold made by fastening together the edges of a leaf.

Life-history. The moths lay oval, creamy white eggs singly or in pairs on the undersurface of leaves and leafsheaths. The eggs hatch in 3-4 days. The pale yellowish brown larva becomes full grown in 15-25 days. Pupation takes place in loose silken webs in between the leaves or in the leafsheaths. The pupal stage lasts 6-8 days during the active season. The life-cycle is completed in 25-35 days.

Host plants. Rice and some grasses.

Damage. The young larvae feed on tender leaves without folding them. The older larvae fasten the longitudinal margins of leaf together with a sticky substance and feed inside the fold by scraping the green matter. The scraped leaves become membranous, turn white and finally wither. The heavily infested crop has streaks on the leaves and appears whitish from a distance. A single larva may damage a number of leaves as it migrates from one leaf to another.

Management. (*i*) Remove grass weeds from bunds around paddy fields. (*ii*) Light-trapping of adults helps to reduce the pest population. (*iii*) *Trichogramma japonicum* and *T. chilonis* when simultaneously released @ 1,00,000 ha at 7 days interval, starting one month after transplanting, prove very effective for the control of this insect. (*iv*) Spray any of the following insecticides at economic threshold level of 10 per cent damaged leaves : 50 ml of flubendiamide 480SC or 875 ml of triazophos 40EC or 2.5 litres of chlorpyriphos 20EC, 1.4 litres of monocrotophos 36SL, 625 ml of fenitrothion 50EC, 425 ml of fenthion 1000EC, 1.0 kg of carbaryl 50WP or 2.0 litres of quinalphos 20AF in 250 litres of water per ha.

7. *Orseolia oryzae* (Wood-Mason) (Rice gall midge, Diptera : Cecidomyiidae) (Fig. 2.1E)

Distribution. The paddy gall fly or gall midge is found in most of the paddy growing areas in the southern and eastern parts of India. The pest is also present in Pakistan, South-east Asia and Africa.

Identification. The fly is delicate mosquito-like insect with long and slender legs, hairy wings and beaded antennae. The female has bright red and stout abdomen; the male is darker.

Life-history. The tiny pink fly lays reddish elongated eggs about 0.5 mm in length, singly or in clusters, on the leaves or on stems. During August to November, they hatch in 1-3 days. The tiny maggots crawl down to the base of the shoot and enter a young bud where they feed for 10-13 days and then pupate. The pupa wriggles its way up with the help of abdominal spines and cuts a hole at the tip of the gall from which the fly emerges after 4-7 days. The life-cycle is completed in 15-23 days and the adults live for 3-4 days and lay upto 250 eggs. There are 3-5 overlapping generations on the same crop and 5-8 in a year.

Host plants. Paddy is the main host but some grasses like *Cynodon dactylon (doob)* or *Oryza barthi* (wild rice) form alternate hosts.

Damage. The maggot of this fly enters the stem and reaches the apical point of the central shoot or the tiller, where it develops. Owing to its feeding, some physiological changes take place which hamper the normal growth of the plant. The central leaf of an attacked tiller becomes hollow and deformed, and there is a swelling or gall formation on the basal portion. Its growth is stopped and the central leaf ultimately turns into a hollow outgrowth, giving a shining silvery colour called 'silver shoot'.

Management. (*i*) Careful timing of planting can avoid damage; once past the tillering stage, the plant is not suitable as a host. (*ii*) Considerable build up of midge population on grasses near the rice crop can be avoided by removing the grasses. (*iii*) For gall midge areas, seedling root dip in 0.02 per cent emulsion of ch1orpyriphos for 12 hours before transplanting protects the crop for 25-30 days. (*iv*) *Platygaster oryzae* (Platygasteridae) is the most important parasitoid of gall midge maggots, causing 50-90 per cent parasitization depending upon humidity and rainfall. (*v*) Apply insecticides at economic threshold level of 1 gall per m^2 in endemic areas or 5 per cent affected tillers in non-endemic areas. Spray 20-45 days after transplanting 625 ml of chlorpyriphos 20EC or 500 ml of quinalphos 20EC or fenitrothion 50EC in 750-1000 litres of water per ha. Alternatively, apply granules as mentioned for the control of yellow stem borer.

8. *Nilaparvata lugens* (Stal) (Brown planthopper, Hemiptera : Delphacidae) (Fig. 2.1F)

Distribution. The brown planthopper is the most destructive pest of rice in South and South-east Asia, China, Japan and Korea. In India, it has become very serious on the high-yielding varieties of paddy in many states including Uttar Pradesh, Madhya Pradesh, West Bengal, Punjab, Haryana, Andhra Pradesh and Tamil Nadu.

Identification. The brownish adults with brown eyes are 3.5-4.5 mm in length. The nymphs are brownish-black in colour and have greyish-blue eyes.

Life-history. The females start laying eggs within 3-10 days of their emergence and deposit eggs in masses, by lacerating the parenchymal tissue. The number of eggs per mass varies from 2 to 11 and a female lays, on an average, 124 egg masses. The eggs are somewhat dark and cylindrical, having two distinct spots. The incubation period ranges between 4 to 8 days. The nymphs, on emergence, start feeding on young leaves and after moulting 5 times, become adults in 2-3 weeks. The total cycle is completed in 18-24 days.

Host plants. Paddy

Damage. Both the nymphs and adults cause damage by sucking cell sap from the leaves which turn yellow. If the insect attacks during the early stages of growth, the entire plant may dry up. The population increases very rapidly and the rice fields start drying up in patches known as 'hopperburn'. The loss in yield may range from 10 to 70 per cent. This insect is known to transmit the grassy stunt virus disease of rice.

Management. (*i*) Closer spacing of 15 × 10 cm creates favourable microclimate in field for rapid development of hopper population. Hence, a spacing of 20 × 15 cm should be followed. (*ii*) Alternate drying and wetting the field during peak infestation, and draining out the standing water from the field 2-3 times checks the population of the hopper to a large extent. (*iii*) The releases of mirid bug, *Cyrtorhinus lividipennis* @ 100 bugs or 50-75 eggs/m^2 at 10-day intervals have been found effective for the control of brown planthopper. The presence of 3 predatory spiders, *Lycosa pseudoannulata*, per hill has been found to check the population of the pest. (*iv*) If minimum of 5 plant hoppers are seen floating in the water following tilting and tapping of the plants at the base, then spray 100 ml of imidacloprid 200SL, 625 g of carbaryl 50WP or 625 ml of fenthion 1000EC or 2.0 litres of quinalphos 25EC or 2.5 litres of chlorpyriphos 20EC or 1.4 litres of endosulfan 35EC or 1.4 litres of monocrotophos 36SL in 250 litres of water per ha. Repeat application if hopper population persists beyond a week after application. While spraying, nozzle should be directed at the basal portion of the plants. At hopper burn stage, treat the affected spots along with 2 to 4 meter periphery immediately since those spots harbour large population of the insect.

9. *Sogatella furcifera* (Horvath) (Whitebacked planthopper, Hemiptera : Delphacidae) (Fig. 2.1G)

Distribution. The whitebacked planthopper has assumed the status of a serious pest of rice in many Asian countries particularly India, Myanmar, Cambodia, Sri Lanka, China, Pakistan, Vietnam and the Philippines. It is widespread in many parts of India.

Identification. The adult is a straw-coloured, wedge-shaped insect, with white back . The nymph is greyish-white and turns dark grey when it nears maturity.

Life-history. The planthoppers breed continually in southern parts of India where paddy crop is available throughout the year. In northern parts, the planthopper becomes active in May in the paddy nursery, from where it shifts to the transplanted crop. The adults lay eggs generally on the leaf sheath. The eggs hatch in 3-5 days. The nymphs feed on leaves and are transformed into adults within 9-13 days. The life-cycle is completed in 12-18 days. The adult females live for about a week. There are several generations in a year.

Host plants. Paddy is its main food, grasses form the alternative food.

Damage. The nymphs and the adults suck cell-sap from the leaf surface and tend to congregate on the leaf-sheath at the base of the plant. The leaves of attacked plants turn yellow and later on rust red. These symptoms start from the leaf tips and spread to the rest of the plant. The attacked plants ultimately dry up without producing ears. The insect also excretes honeydew on which a sooty mould appears, imparting a smoky hue to the paddy fields.

Management. Same as in case of brown planthopper. The economic threshold level is 10 insects per hill.

10. *Nephotettix nigropictus* (Stal) (Fig. 2.1H) and *N. virescens* (Distant) (Green leafhoppers, Hemiptera: Cicadellidae)

Distribution. The green leafhoppers are found in all the rice growing regions of India, although they assume pest proportions only during certain years in Madhya Pradesh, Andhra Pradesh, Orissa and West Bengal. These species are also known pests of rice in Japan, the Philippines, Taiwan and Sri Lanka.

Identification. The female of *N. nigropictus* is green and a black tinge on pronotum is absent. The male, on the other hand, has two black spots extending up to the black distal portion on the forewings, a black tinge along the anterior margin of pronotum and a submarginal black band on the crown of the head. In *N. virescens,* black submarginal band on the crown is absent and the black spots on forewings do not extend up to the black distal portion.

Life-history. The females, after undergoing a pre-oviposition period of 6-9 days, lay eggs on the inner surface of the leaf-sheath in groups of 3-18. The eggs hatch in 3-5 days and the nymphal stage is completed in 12-21 days. The adults live for 7-22 days in summer. There are about six overlapping generations from March to November. The insect over-winters in the adult stage.

Damage. The nymphs and the adult suck sap from the leaves of plants, turning them yellow and ultimately brown. As a result of attack by this pest, the plants lose vigour. *N. virescens* is also known to be the vector of tungro virus.

Management. Same as in case of brown planthopper.

11. *Dicladispa armigera* (Olivier) (Rice hispa, Coleoptera:Chrysomelidae) (Fig. 2.1I)

Distribution. Rice hispa is distributed throughout India but often serious on young rice crop in parts of Andhra Pradesh, Tamil Nadu, West Bengal, Punjab, Haryana and Himachal Pradesh.

Identification. The adult is a small bluish black beetle, measuring 5 mm in length and is recognized by numerous short spines on the body. The legless, creamy-white larvae are not easily seen, because they are concealed inside the leaf tissue.

Life-history. The eggs are embedded in the leaf tissue towards the tip. On hatching, the young grubs feed as leaf-miners, between the upper and lower epidermis. The attacked leaves turn membranous, showing characteristic blisters or blotches. Later on, the attacked leaves wither and die. When the larvae are full-grown, they pupate inside and finally emerge as black beetles. The insect passes through about six generations in a year.

Host plants. Paddy, sugarcane and grasses

Damage. Apart from the damage caused by larvae as leaf-miners, the adults also feed on green matter and produce parallel whitish streaks on the leaves. The damage starts in nurseries and spreads to the rice fields. The infestation varies from 6 to 65 per cent.

Management. (*i*) The pest is suppressed if the infested leaf tips are clipped off and destroyed, while transplanting. (*ii*) If the nursery beds are flooded, the beetles float and can be swept together with brooms and then destroyed. (*iii*) In case the attack starts in the nursery, clip-off and destroy the leaf tips of affected seedlings before transplantation. (iv) Spray the transplanted crop at economic threshold level (1 adult or 1 or 2 damaged leaves per hill) with 300 ml methyl parathion 50EC or 1.6 litres of monocrotophos 36SL or 2.0 litres of quinalphos 25EC or 2.5 litres of chlorpyriphos 20EC in 250 litres of water per ha. Repeat spray after two weeks if attack continues.

12. *Echinocnemus oryzae* (Marshall) (Paddy root weevil, Coleoptera : Curculionidae)

Distribution. The paddy root weevil is a serious pest of rice in southern India. The insect was first reported to occur in Andhra Pradesh in 1954 and since then has spread to some other states like Tamil Nadu, Madhya Pradesh, Punjab Haryana, Orissa and Uttar Pradesh.

Identification. The adult weevils are black or piceous (pitch black), about 4 × 2 mm in size with dense clothing of scales and long rostrum. The grubs are translucent white and measure about 6 mm in length. There are six pairs of prominent tubercles on the dorsal side of the abdomen.

Life-history. The weevils emerge in July with the first shower of rain and are seen sitting in large numbers on rice plants at this time. The eggs which are laid on the plant hatch in a few days. The grubs lead an aquatic life and feed on the root-hairs. Grubs are full-grown by the middle of September when they bury themselves deep into the soil for pupation. The pupae emerge next year in July and, thus, the pest completes only one generation in a year.

Host plants. Paddy, but in its absence grasses act as alternative food.

Damage. The grubs feed on root hairs of the transplanted crop, thereby affecting plant growth. The infested crop remains stunted and a large number of plants are killed. The crop transplanted in July is more heavily attacked than the one transplanted in August.

Management. Apply 7.5 kg of phorate 10G per ha in standing water.

13. *Leptocorisa acuta* (Thunberg) (Rice bug, Hemiptera : Coreidae) (Fig. 2.1J)

The rice bug, commonly known as *gundhy* bug, is widely distributed in India, the Orient and Australia. It is a serious pest of rice in several parts of India.

Identification. The adults are slender, about 20 mm long and greenish brown. They have long legs and antennae with four joints. The newly hatched nymph is about 2 mm long and is pale green. However, as it grows, the green colour deepens. The grown up nymphs are very similar to the adults in colour and size, but they are wingless.

Life-history. The females lay 24-30 round yellow eggs in rows on the leaves. The eggs hatch in about 6 or 7 days and the nymphs grow to maturity in six stages within 2 or 3 weeks. The adult bugs live for 33-35 days. Many generations are completed in a year.

Host plants. Apart from rice, it also feeds on maize, millets, sugarcane and some grasses.

Damage. Rice fields severely attacked by this pest emit a repugnant smell which gives to this pest the name 'gundhy' bug. The nymphs and the adults suck juice from the developing grains in the milky stage, causing incompletely filled panicles or panicles with empty grains. Black or brown spots appear around the holes made by the bugs on which a sooty mould may develop.

Management. (*i*) The population can be suppressed by killing the bugs by using light traps, collecting the adults with nets and destroying the weeds and alternative hosts. (*ii*) Dust carbaryl 5 per cent or malathion 5 per cent @ 25 kg per ha.

14. *Hieroglyphus banian* (Fabricius) and *H. nigrorepletus* Bolivar (Rice grasshoppers, Orthoptera : Acrididae)

Distribution. Rice grasshoppers are sporadic pests of rice distributed throughout India.

Identification. *H. banian* and *H. nigrorepletus* are somewhat like locusts but are smaller. The adults are 40-50 mm long and are shining greenish yellow, having three black lines running across the pronotum. Nymphs are yellowish, with many reddish brown spots in the early stages, but become greenish as they grow older.

Life-history. *Hieroglyphus* spp. have one generation in a year and pass the winter and dry part of summer in the egg stage. The eggs are found in the soil and they hatch in June or in early July, a few days after the first shower of the monsoon. On emergence, the nymphs start feeding actively and complete their development in seven stages, within 3 weeks. The adults are seen feeding voraciously during August and September. When they are two months old, they mate. The female starts laying eggs by inserting her abdomen in the soil. The eggs are laid 5-8 cm deep, in pods, each containing 30-40 eggs. The egg-laying continues from September to November and the adults die soon after, sometime in the winter.

Host plants. They are polyphagous and feed on leaves of rice, maize, millets, sugarcane, grasses, sunnhemp, *arhar*.

Damage. The greatest amount of damage is caused during August-September when both adults and nymphs feed on paddy and other crops, causing defoliation. In certain years, they cause extensive damage, moving from field to field over large areas.

Management. Dust carbaryl 5 per cent or malathion 5 per cent @ 25 kg per ha.

15. *Cofana spectra* (Distant) (White rice leafhopper, Hemiptera: Cicadellidae) (Fig. 2.2A)

Distribution: The insect is widely distributed in the sub-tropical and tropical regions in South Asia

Identification: The adults are yellowish in colour and bear four black spots on the vertex; and have a rounded, rather swollen head. The adults are 5.7 – 7.4 mm long. The nymphs give paler appearance.

Life-history: The insect is active round the year. The adults mate after 1.8 – 6.8 days after emergence. The female lays greenish eggs in masses after lacerating the leaf sheath. During her life time spanning 30-35 days, the female deposits about 17 egg-masses, each containing 5-17 eggs. It takes about a week for the eggs to hatch. The newly emerged nymphs first feed inside the leaf sheath and later move to the leaf blade. There are 5 nymphal instars completed in about 18 days. The insect completes 12 generations in a year, in South India.

Host plants: Apart from paddy, other hosts include monocot plants including *Leersia hexandra* Sw., *Triticum aestivum* L., *Zea mays* L., *Cyprus rotundus* L., *Sorghum vulgare* L.,

Damage: The damaged leaves give yellowish appearance due to sucking of sap by the nymphs and adults. The leaves turn brown after heavy infestation and plants fail to produce ears.

Management: Same as in case of brown planthopper

16. *Recilia dorsalis* (Motschulsky) (Zigzag leafhopper, Hemiptera: Cicadellidae) (Fig. 2.2B)

Distribution: This is a serious pest of paddy in Japan, Korea, Philippines, Vietnam, Malaysia, Bangladesh, India, Sri lanka and several other coutries.

Identification: The whitish-grey adults of the hopper bear V-shaped and zig-zag brown lines on the forewings and measure 3.1-3.8 mm in length

Life-history: The insect breeds throughout the year in tropical parts of the world. After lacerating leaf surface with the help of ovipositor, the female deposits eggs in the exposed leaf tissue. The eggs, however, havc also been noticed scattered on the leaf sheaths. The adult female can lay up to 90 eggs during her life span of about 155 days. It takes about 6 days for eggs to hatch and the newly emerged nymphs feed on the leaf blades. The nymphal period of 5 instars is completed in 120 days. It takes about 180 days to complete the entire life-cycle from egg to adult stage. In the temperate climate of Southern Japan and Korea, the pest passes winter in egg satge.

Damage: The damaged leaves, due to sucking of sap by the insect, give orange appearance at the margins and subsequently become dry at the tips. In addition to acting as a pest, the female hoppers are also known to be vectors of the virus 'orange leaf' and 'yellow dwarf'.

Host plants Primarily the host plant is paddy

Management: Same as in case of brown planthopper

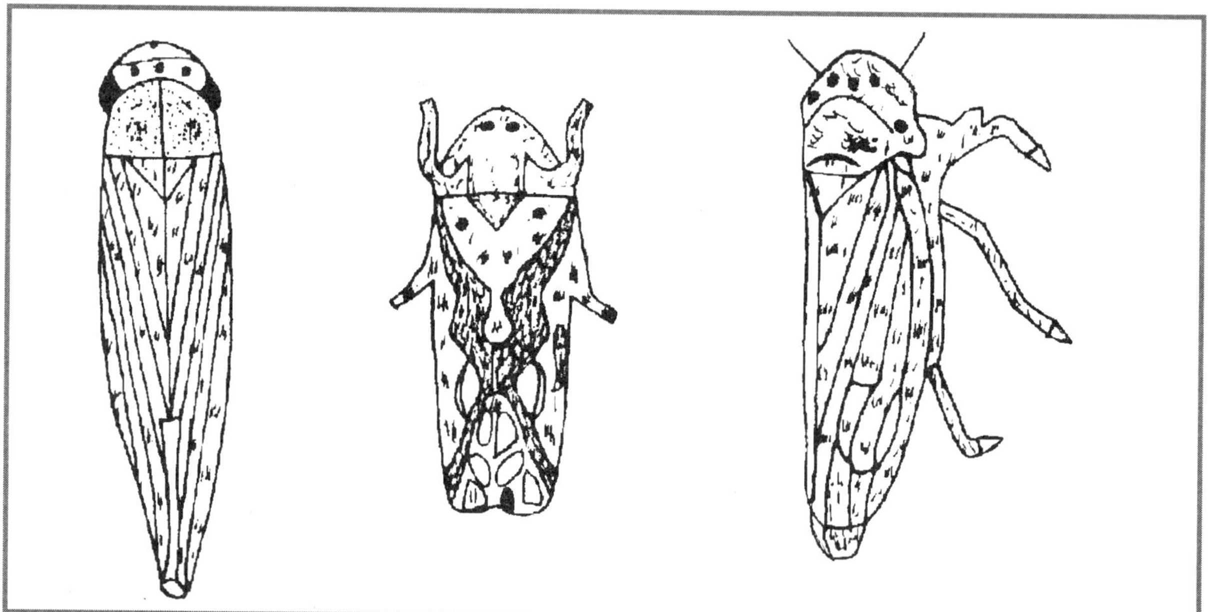

Fig. 2.2 Pests of cereals and millets. **A.** White rice leafhopper, *Cofana spectra.* **B.** Zigzag leafhopper, *Recilia dorsalis.* **C.** Rice blue leafhopper, *Typhlocyba maculifrons.*

17. *Typhlocyba maculifrons* (Motschulsky) (Rice blue leaf hopper, Hemiptera: Cicadellidae) (Fig. 2.2C)

Distribution: It is known to act as pest of rice nurseries in India and South-East Asia.

Identification: It is a small bluish coloured insect; the adults have a yellowish vertex with a black patch and black spot in the middle of the pronotum. The adults are 1.9-2.5 mm long.

Life-history: Though the insect is active throughout the year, but is more conspicuous in nurseries before the planting season. The female deposits eggs in batches of 2,3 or 4 after lacerating surface of the leaf blade. A female lays, on an average 48 eggs in its life of 45-50 days. It takes 6-12 days for the eggs to hatch and newly emerged nymphs start feeding inside the leaf sheath. Nymphal period, with 5 moults, extends to 11-20 days. The life-cycle is completed in 19-32 days.

Host plants: Apart from paddy it also feeds on maize, sorghum, ragi, sugarcane and wild grasses.

Damage: Both nymphs and adults inflict damage by sucking sap from the leaves and conseqyently leaves show symptoms of withering.

Management: Same as in case of brown planthopper

MAIZE

More than 130 insects have been recorded causing damage to maize in India. Among these, about half a dozen pests are of economic importance.

1. *Chilo partellus* (Swinhoe) (Maize stem borer, Lepidoptera : Pyralidae) (Fig. 2.1L)

Distribution. It is the most destructive pest of maize in Sri Lanka, India, Pakistan, Afghanistan, Uganda, Central and East Africa. It is found throughout India.

Identification. The adult moth is a medium sized insect with 3 cm wingspan. Its forewings are straw or light brown in colour with numerous shining brown spots on the margin, and the hind wings are white and papery. The grown-up caterpillars are about 20-25 mm long and dirty greyish white, with black head and four brownish longitudinal stripes on the back.

Life-history. The eggs are laid in clusters of 50-100 in rows on the undersurface of the leaves during April-May. A female lays over 300 eggs during its life-span of 2-12 days and the eggs hatch in 4-5 days in summer. The young larvae first feed on the leaves, making a few shot holes and then bore their way downwards through the central whorl as it opens. The larva becomes full-fed in 14-28 days, passing through six stages and after making a hole in the stem pupates inside it. The life-cycle is completed in about 3 weeks and there are probably 5 generations in a year. The full-grown caterpillars of the last generation hibernate in stubble, stalks, etc., and remain there till the next spring.

Host plants. Besides maize, this insect attacks *bajra* (*Pennisetum typhoides*), sugarcane, Sudan grass, *baru* (*Sorghum halepense*), *sarkanda* (*Saccharum munja*) and some other grasses.

Damage. The damage is done by the caterpillars by feeding inside the stem and producing 'deadhearts'. About 25-50 per cent of the plants are destroyed.

Management. (*i*) The potential for carry over may be reduced by destroying the stubble, weeds and other alternate hosts of the stem borer by ploughing the field after harvest. (*ii*) Removal and destruction of dead-hearts and destruction of infested plants showing early pin-hole damage has been found to be successful practice in reducing the pest incidence. (*iii*) Destruction of crop residues and chopping of stems harbouring diapausing larvae could be very effective in reducing borer population. (*iv*) Single release of *Trichogramma chilonis* @ 1,00,000 per ha after 10-15 days of sowing has proved quite effective. (*v*) (*a*) Spray the crop 2-3 weeks after sowing or as soon as borer injury to the leaves is noticed with any of the following synthetic pyrethroids using 125 litres of water per ha: fenvalerate 20EC @ 100 ml/ha, cypermethrin 10EC @ 100 ml/ha or deltamethrin 2.8EC @ 200 ml/ha. Usually, no additional spray or granular application is required after the spray with pyrethroids. (*b*) Alternatively, the crop should be sprayed with any of the following insecticides: endosulfan 35EC @ 250 ml/ha, monocrotophos 36SL @ 275 ml/ha, lindane 20EC @500 ml/ha, fenitrothion 50EC @ 440 ml/ha or carbaryl 50WP @ 250 g/ha. (*c*) After this spray, apply twice at 7-10 days intervals any of the following insecticides in the whorls of only infested plants that show fresh borer injury in the central leaves: fenitrothion or trichlorphon 5D or endosulfan 4G, lindane 6G, carbaryl 4G or trichlorphon 4G. In case of dust, mix it with equal quantity of moist soil before application. Apply a pinch of this mixture to the whorl of plants. Usually 1.5-2.5 kg of the insecticide would be required per ha for one application. Apply granules to the whorl of plants @ 0.5 -1.25 kg/ha per application through a bottle with a few holes in its cap.

2. *Ostrinia furnacalis* (Guenee) (Asian maize borer, Lepidoptera : Pyralidae)

Distribution. The pest is widely distributed in Sri Lanka, China, Taiwan, parts of India, Bangladesh, Indonesia, Japan, Korea, Vietnam, Laos, Cambodia, Malaysia, Myanmar, Thailand and the Philippines.

Identification. The female moth is yellow to light brown in colour, with a wing expanse of about 27 mm. The male is dark brown and has a tapering abdomen. The grown up larva is about 20 mm in length with dark brown head and is pinkish on the upper side of the body.

Life-history. The female moth lays 500-1500 eggs in flat masses on the underside of leaves. The eggs hatch in about 3 days and the newly hatched larvae feed within the leaf whorl, under a protective silken web. After about 9 days of feeding, they migrate downwards and bore into the stem. They feed there and complete five instars within 18 days. Normally, pupation takes place inside the tunnels made in the stem but the larvae may also pupate inside the maize ear, in-between the ear sheaths or in the ear stalk. The pupal stage lasts 6 days and one or more generations may be completed in a year.

Host-plants. It feeds on maize, sorghum, millets, Indian hemp, hops, *Artemisia* and many wild grasses.

Damage. Maize plants are usually attacked 3-4 weeks after sowing. The larvae first feed on leaf tissue, then tunnel into the midrib, and thereafter reach the tassels or bore into the stalks and the ears. The development of the plants, the production of tassels and of the ears may be affected. When the pest attack is towards the base of the stalk, the plant collapses, dries up and dies.

Management. Same as in case of maize borer.

3. *Ostrinia nubilasis* (Hubner) (European corn borer, Lepidoptera : Pyralidae)

Distribution: Though the insect does not occur in India, but is a serious pest of maize in Europe, earstwhile USSR, UAR, Japan and other countries of Far-East, Mexico and North America.

Identification: The female bears yellow to light brown wings with an expanse of 31.75 mm.The male is relatively smaller, slender and has darker wings. The full grown larva measures 25.4 mm in length giving flesh or cream-coloured appearance with a faintly dotted dorsum. The pupa is light to dark reddish brown measuring 12.7-19.05 mm in length.

Life-history: There are 1-5 generations of the insect depending upon the climatic conditions. The female lays around a total of 400-600 eggs in clusters of 3-50 on underside of the leaves. It takes 3-12 days for the eggs to hatch. The newly emerged larvae feed sparingly on surface of the leaves in a whorl. Third- and fourth instar larvae feed on the sheath and the mid-rib. Subsequently, the fifth- and sixth instar larvae bore into the sheath. The larvae become full grown in 25-44 days and pass winter in diapause inside tunnels made in the stalks, stubble and the cobs. Before pupation, the larvae make exits for the moths to escape in the late Spring or early Summer. Pupation occurs within tunnels made in the stalk, stubble or cobs. The pupal period is about 8-11 days. Life of female moth is 6-24 days depending upon the climatic condition.

Host plants: Besides maize, it also feeds on sorghum, potato, bean, celery, hump, cowpea, soybean, aster, dahlias and some weeds; the host range covering more than 200 species of plants.

Damage: As a result of larval attack, the plants become weak and the cobs get stunted. The attack by the first-generation larvae is severer than that by the second or the subsequent generations. The severe damage results in stalk breaking, ear-dropping and shrivelled ears resulting from tunneling by the larvae.

Management: Cultivate resistant or tolerant varities of maize to check damage by the borer. Besides, adoption of various sanitary measures and ploughing-under of the crop residue also helps to minimize infestation of the borer, since as a result of these practices overwintering larvae are destroyed to a great extent.

SORGHUM

More than 150 species of insects have been reported to damage sorghum. However, over a dozen species are very serious and constitute a major constraint in sorghum production.

1. *Atherigona soccata* Rondani (Sorghum shoot fly, Diptera : Muscidae) (Fig. 2.1M)

Distribution. The sorghum shoot fly, also known as the sorghum stem fly, is a widely distributed pest in Europe, Africa and Asia. In India, it is more serious in southern parts.

Identification. The insect resembles house fly but is much smaller. It is about 5 mm long, pale to dark grey with 3 pairs of black spots on the abdomen.

Life-history. The female fly lays approximately 40 eggs singly on the underside of the leaves during its life span of about one month. The eggs hatch in 1-2 days and the tiny maggots creep out and reach in between the sheath and the axis, and bore into the stem. They feed inside the main shoot for 6-10 days and, when full grown, they may pupate either inside the stem or come out and pupate in the soil. The pupal period in the summer lasts about a week. Several generations are completed in a year. In northern India, the pest over-winters in the pupal stage.

Host plants. Besides sorghum, it infests maize, wheat, broom corn, small millets (*Panicum* spp.) and grasses.

Damage. The insect attacks the young crop when it is in the six-leaf stage. As the maggots feed on the main shoot, the growing point is destroyed and by the time they pupate, the plant is almost dead. The young plants show typical dead-heart symptoms. When the attacked plants are somewhat older, tillers are produced, which mature later than the main crop. The total loss in yield is sometimes as high as 60 per cent.

Management. (*i*) Resistant varieties like CHS-7, CHS-8, Indian sorghum types IS-5566, 5285 and 5613 should be grown (*ii*) The early sown crop (early June to second week of July) escapes attack of the shoot fly, (*iii*) Seed coating with imidacloprid 600FS @15ml/Kg seed or isofenphos 5G @300g/Kg seed provides protection against shootfly up to two weeks. (*iv*) In case seed treatment has not been done, apply 12.5 Kg of carbofuran 3G or 10 Kg of phorate 10G per ha in furrows before sowing. (*v*) Alternatively, give two sprays, first at 4-leaf stage followed by second one after one week of the first spray with 625 ml of malathion 50EC or 250 g of carbaryl 50WP in 125 litres of water per ha.

2. *Calocoris angustatus* Lethiery (Sorghum earhead bug, Hemiptera: Miridae) (Fig. 2.1N)

Distribution. It is one of the most destructive pests of sorghum in southern states like Andhra Pradesh, Karnataka and Tamil Nadu and only sporadic elsewhere.

Identification. The adult is a small, slender, greenish yellow bug, measuring 5-8 mm in length and over 1 mm in width.

Life-history. The adults appear on sorghum crop as soon as the ears emerge from the leaf sheaths. The bug lays eggs under the glumes or in between anthers of florets, by inserting its ovipositor. The female lays 150-200 eggs which are cigar- shaped and measure about 1.5 mm.

The eggs hatch in 5-7 days and the nymphs start feeding on developing grains in the milk stage. The nymphs pass through 5 instars and develop into adults in about 3 weeks. The adults of the second generation are again ready to oviposit in the ears having developing grains which might be available on the same crop. As soon as the grains are ripe, the bugs stop multiplying on that crop. The insect completes its life-cycle in about one month and produces a number of generations in a year.

Host plants. This bug has been recorded feeding on a number of cereals, millets and grasses, but its breeding is mainly restricted to sorghum, on which it assumes the status of a pest.

Damage. Both the nymphs and the adults feed on the green earheads. As a result of feeding by the bugs, the grains remain chaffy or shrivelled. When a large army of tiny nymphs feeds, the whole ear may become blackened at first and may eventually dry up, producing no grains.

Management. Spray 625 ml of malathion 50EC or 200 ml of phosphamidon 80WSC or 3 kg of carbaryl 50 WP in 500 litres of water per ha.

3. *Peregrinus maidis* (Ashmead) (Sorghum shoot bug, Hemiptera: Delphacidae) (Fig. 2.10)

Distribution. It is pan-tropical in distribution and has been recorded in Barmuda, West Indies, Hawaii, Cuba, East Africa and the Philippines.

Identification. The adult hopper is yellowish brown, with translucent wings and measures 3.2-3.8 mm in length. The full-grown nymphs are light brown with prominent eyes and wing pads.

Life-history. The female bugs make slits in the midrib of the leaves with the help of their ovipositors and lay white, elongated and cylindrical eggs in groups of 1-4. Within the oviposition period of about 7 days, she can lay, on an average, 97 eggs. The eggs hatch in 7-10 days and the young nymphs feed at first within the leaf sheaths and the leaf whorls. As they grow, they spread out to wider areas; after undergoing 5 moultings, they become adults in 16-18 days. The total life-cycle is completed in 3-4 weeks.

Host plants. The nymphs and adults of this insect are serious pests of millets, sorghum and maize. The insect has also been reported feeding on sugarcane, oat and various species of grasses.

Damage. The nymphs and adults feed gregariously within the leaf whorls, the leaf sheaths and also on the leaves. As a result of their sucking the cell sap, the leaves become yellow and the growth of the plants is retarded. When the attack is severe, the ears fail to emerge. The adults also transmit the virus diseases, 'corn mosaic' and 'freckled yellow' of sorghum and other virus diseases of sugarcane and pearl millet.

Management. Same as in case of ear head bug.

4. *Contarinia sorghicola* (Coquillett) (Sorghum midge, Diptera : Cecidomyidae)

Distribution. This insect is distributed in all the sorghum growing tracts of the country.

Identification. The adult fly is a very small (2 mm) fragile mosquito-like insect with a bright orange abdomen and a pair of transparent wings, and a long conspicuous ovipositor.

Life-history. The female inserts the eggs singly into developing florets at the time pollen is being shed and lays about 30-100 eggs. The eggs hatch in 2-3 days and the maggot feeds inside the developing grain and pupates there itself. The larva has four instars with a total duration of 10-11 days. It emerges between the tip of the glumes leaving the white pupal case attached to the tip of the floret which is very characteristic. The pupal stage lasts about a week and the total life-cycle is completed in 14-22 days.

Host plant. Sorghum seems to be the only host plant of this insect.

Damage. The damage is caused by the maggots which feed on the ovaries and thus preventing the formation of grains. The infestation is dependent on humidity (more severe in low lying humid areas), initial infestation and duration of flowering of sorghum. The loss in yield varies from 20 to 50 per cent.

Management. (*i*) Both early and late maturing varieties of sorghum should not be grown in the same area as it would provide the pest a continuous supply of flowers. The varieties having the same flowering and maturity time would reduce midge damage considerably. (*ii*) Since the damaged and aborted seeds are the main source of carry over of the pest from one season to another, collect and burn the panicle and post-harvest trash. (*iii*) Spray 1 litre of malathion 50EC or endosulfan 35EC or 1.25 litres of lindane 20EC or 2.0 kg of carbaryl 50WP in 500 litres of water/ha. Only the earheads should be treated at 90 per cent panicle emergence followed by second spray after 4-5 days. (*iv*) Dusting the earheads with endosulfan 4% or carbaryl 5% or lindane 2% @ 12 kg/ha has also proved effective.

WHEAT

Wheat is comparatively less susceptible to insect pests in the field. However, in recent years, about half a dozen pests have become quite serious.

1. *Sitobion miscanthi* (Takahashi) (Wheat aphid, Hemiptera : Aphididae)

Distribution. Wheat aphid is widely distributed in India.

Identification. The insects are green, inert, louse like and appear on young leaves or ears in large numbers during the cold and cloudy weather. The nymphs and female adults look alike, except that the latter are larger.

Life-history. The wheat aphid breeds at fast rate during the cold weather and reaches the height of its population in February-March when the ears are ripening. The females give birth to young ones and are capable of reproducing without mating. During the active breeding season, there are no males and the rate of reproduction is very high. When the wheat crop is ripe and the summer is approaching, the winged forms of both males and females are produced and they migrate to other plants like *doob* grass (*Cynodon dactylon*). In October-November, the aphids again appear on wheat.

Host plants. Wheat, barley and millets.

Damage. These plant lice suck sap from the ears and tender leaves, and decrease yield of the crop. The damage is particularly severe in years of cold and cloudy weather. The losses due to aphids have been reported upto 36 per cent.

Management. Spray 100 ml of imidacloprid 200SL or 50 g of thiamethoxam 25WG or 30 g of clothianidin 50WDG or 375 ml of dimethoate 30EC or oxydemeton methyl 25EC in 250 litres of water per ha. Control measures should be initiated at economic theshold level of 5 aphids per ear head. Since, first the aphids appear on border of the crop, and hence initially the infected strips can be spayed to check further multiplication of the insect.

2. *Mythimna separata* (Walker) (Armyworm, Lepidoptera : Noctuidae)

Distribution. The armyworm is a pest of graminaceous crops all over the world.

Identification. Moths vary in colour from brick red to light brown to clay coloured, with wing span of 4.5-5.0 cm. Freshly emerged larva is dull white which later turns green.

Life-history. The adult moths of armyworm live for 1-9 days and lay eggs singly in rows or in clusters on dry or fresh plants or on the soil. In the Punjab, they hatch in 4-11 days from March to May, and in 19 days in December- January. In the spring, the larval stage is completed in 13-14 days, but in the winter it is prolonged to 88-100 days. In the pre-pupal stage, the insect spins a cocoon. The pre-pupal stage lasts 1-11 days during January to May. Pupation usually takes place in the soil at a depth of 0.5-5 cm, but it may also occur under dry leaves among the stubble or fresh tillers. The pupal stage is completed in 9-13 days in May and 36-48 days in the winter months. The survival of the pupae depends on the soil moisture.

Host plants. It is a sporadic pest of wheat, sugarcane, maize, sorghum, pearl millet and other graminaceous crops.

Damage. The freshly emerged larvae spin threads from which they suspend themselves in the air and then with the help of air currents reach from one plant to another. In the early stages, they feed on tender leaves in the central whorl of the plant. As they grow, they arc able to feed on older leaves also and skeletonize them totally. In the case of a severe attack by the armyworms, whole leaves, including the mid-rib, arc consumed and the field looks as if grazed by cattle.

Management. (*i*) The pest can be suppressed by collecting and destroying the caterpillars. (*ii*) Spray 500 ml of dichlorvos 85SL or 3 kg of carbaryl 50WP or one litre of quinalphos 25EC in 250 litres of water per ha.

3. *Tanymecus indicus* Faust (Ghujhia weevil, Coleoptera : Curculionidae)

Distribution. Ghujhia weevil is widely distributed in the Indian sub-continent.

Identification. Weevils are earthen grey and measure about 6.8 mm in length and 2.4 mm in width. Their fore wings arc oblong and hind wings are more or less triangular, but they cannot fly.

Life-history. The weevils lay 6-76 eggs in 5-11 instalments in the soil under clods or in crevices in the ground. The eggs hatch in 6-7 weeks and the young grubs enter the soil where they feed, probably on soil humus. They are full grown in 10-18 days and pupate in earthen chambers at a depth of 15-60 cm. The pupal stage lasts 7-9 weeks, and the adults emerge next year in June or July. The pest has only one generation in a year.

Host plants. It is a sporadic pest of considerable importance, feeding on germinating *rabi* crops, particularly wheat, barley, gram and mustard.

Damage. The adults feed on leaves and tender shoots of the host plants. The damage is particularly serious during October-November, when the *rabi* crops are germinating. Weevils cut the seedlings at the ground level and often the crop has to be resown.

Management. Dust carbaryl 5D or malathion 5D @ 25 kg per ha.

4. *Odontotermes obesus* (Rambur) and *Microtermes obesi* Holmgreen (Termites, Isoptera: Termintidae)

The wheat crop is damaged by termites soon after sowing and also near maturity. Plants attacked by the termites dry up and can be easily pulled out. White ears are produced in the plants due to damage by the termites at later stages (**see Chapter 13 for details**).

*****

3 CHAPTER

PESTS OF SUGARCANE

Stem borers

1. *Sciropophaga nivella* (Fabricius) (Sugarcane top borer, Lepidoptera : Pyralidae)
2. *Chilo infuscatellus* Snellen (Sugarcane shoot borer, Lepidoptera: Pyralidae)
3. *Chilo auricilius* Dudgeon (Stalk borer, Lepidoptera : Pyralidae)
4. *Acigona steniella* (Hampson) (Gurdaspur borer, Lepidoptera : Crambidae)
5. *Chilo sacchariphagus indicus* (Kapur) (Internode borer, Lepidoptera : Pyralidae)
6. *Sesamia inferens* (Walker) (Pink stem borer, Lepidoptera : Noctuidae)
7. *Raphimetopus ablutellus* Zeller (Green borer, Lepidoptera : Pyralidae)
8. *Chilo tumidicostalis* Hampson (Plassey borer, Lepidoptera: Pyralidae)

Leaf feeders

9. *Hieroglyphus nigrorepletus* Bolivar (Rice grasshopper, Orthoptera : Acrididae)
10. *Hieroglyphus banian* (Fabricius (Rice grasshopper, Orthoptera: Acrididae)
11. *Anomola biharensis* Arrow (Sugarcane beetle, Coleoptera : Scarabaeidae)
12. *Alissonotum simile* Arrow (Sugarcane beetle, Coleoptera : Scarabaeidae)

Sap suckers

13. *Pyrilla perpusilla* (Walker) (Sugarcane pyrilla, Hemiptera : Lophopidae).
14. *Aleurolobus barodensis* (Maskell) (Sugarcane whitefly, Hemiptera : Aleyrodidae)
15. *Neomaskellia bergii* (Signoret) (Sugarcane spotted fly, Hemiptera : Aleyrodidae)

16. *Saccharicoccus sacchari* (Cockerell) (Sugarcane mealy bug, Hemiptera : Pseudococcidae).
17. *Aulacaspis tegalensis* (Zehntner) (Sugarcane scale insect, Hemiptera : Diaspididae)
18. *Cavelerius excavatus* (Distant) (Sugarcane black bug, Hemiptera : Lygaeidae).
19. *Melanaphis sacchari (Zehtner).* (Sugarcane aphid, Hemiptera Aphididae).

Root feeders

20. *Emmalocera depressella* Swinhoe (Sugarcane root borer, Lepidoptera : Pyralidae)
21. *Holotrichia serrata* (Fabricius) (White grub, Coleoptera: Scarabaeidae)
22. *Holotrichia consanguinea* Blanchard (White grub, Coleoptera: Scarabaeidae
23. *Odontotermes obesus* (Rambur) (Termite, Isoptera : Termitidae)

Uttar Pradesh is the largest producer of sugarcane in India, followed by Maharashtra and Karnataka. It is estimated that cultivation of more productive short-duration canes are likely to boost total sugarcane production to 423 million tonnes on about 5.2 million hectares. As many as 200 species of insect pests have been reported to cause damage to the sugarcane crop at one stage or the other of crop growth. However, only a dozen are recognized as major pests.

1. *Scirpophaga nivella* (Fabricius) (Sugarcane top borer, Lepidoptera: Pyralidae) (Fig. 3.1A)

Distribution. This insect is one of the most destructive pests of sugarcane in India and Pakistan. It is also distributed in Myanmar, Sri Lanka, China, Taiwan, Japan, the Philippines and Thailand.

Identification. The moths are pure white. Males are considerably smaller than females. A female measures 25-40 mm across the spread wings and carries a brownish or reddish tuft of silken hairs at the tip of its abdomen. When full-grown, a caterpillar is 25-30 mm long, creamy white and rather sluggish.

Life-history. The female moths lay eggs on the lower surface of the leaves at the rate of about 150, in clusters of 30-60 eggs. These clusters are covered with a brown tuft of hairs and are quite prominent. Eggs hatch in 5-7 days and the young larvae bore into the mid-rib of a leaf, mining their way to the base. From there, they enter the spindle, feeding on the growing point and the soft portion of the cane. They grow to maturity in five stages within 4-5 weeks. When full-fed, a larva constructs a chamber with an emergence hole in the rind just above a node. It pupates inside the chamber and emerges as a moth within 7-9 days. The moths are short-lived; hardly live for more than 4-5 days. Four to five generations are completed during a year. Full-grown caterpillars of the last generation, however, do not pupate. They hibernate in the cane tops throughout the winter in northern India.

Host plants. Apart from sugarcane, it is also found on *jowar, bajra sarkanda (Saccharum munja), kahi (Saccharum spontaneum)* and some other grasses.

Damage. The first two broods of this pest attack young plants before the formation of canes. These plants are killed and are a total loss. In subsequent broods, the pest attacks the terminal portions of the canes, causing bunchy tops. Damage by the third and fourth broods may result in more than 25 per cent reduction in weight and a decrease in the quality of the juice. The loss in weight in different varieties may vary from 21 to 37 per cent and loss in sugar recovery from 0.2 to 4.1 units.

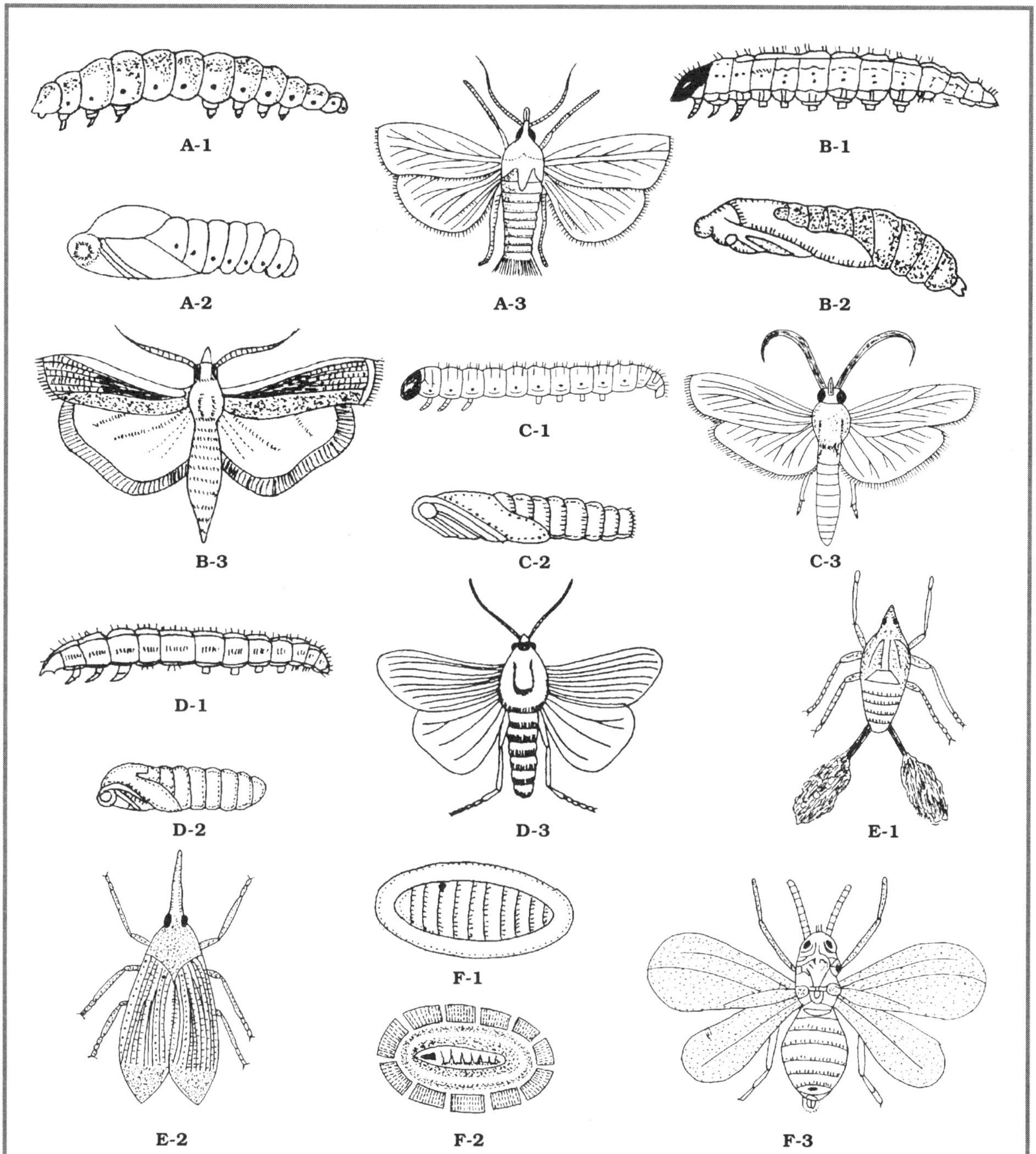

Fig. 3.1 Pests of sugarcane. **A.** Sugarcane top borer, *Scirpophaga nivella*; A-1. Larva, A-2. Pupa, A-3. Adult. **B.** Sugarcane shoot borer, *Chilo infuscatellus*; B-1. Larva, B-2. Pupa, B-3. Adult. **C.** Sugarcane root borer, *Emmalocera depressella*; C-1. Larva, C-2. Pupa, C-3. Adult. **D.** Gurdaspur borer, *Bissetia steniella*; D-1. Larva, D-2. Pupa, D-3. Adult. **E.** Sugarcane pyrilla, *Pyrilla perpusilla*; E-1. Nymph, E-2. Adult. **F.** Sugarcane whitefly, *Aleurolobus barodensis*; F-1. Nymph, F-2. Pseudo-pupa, F-3. Adult.

Management. (*i*) Collect and destroy moths and egg clusters. (*ii*) Cut the attacked shoots at the ground level from April to June. (*iii*) Since about one-third of the larvae remain in the underground portion of the stem, the sharp edge of a sickle should be inserted to kill them. (*iv*) Cutting and destroying cane tops which harbour the over-wintering larvae before mid-February, also reduce the incidence of this pest. (*v*) Release *Trichogramma chilonis* Ishii @50,000 per hectare at 10 days' interval from mid-April to end June. Generally 8 releases are considered enough. (*vi*) Apply 25 Kg of chlorantriniliprole 0.4GR or 30 kg of carbofuran 3G or phorate 10G per ha at the base of the shoots in the last week of June or first week of July only if the top borer damage exceeds 5 per cent. Earth up slightly to check the granules from flowing with irrigation water and irrigate the crop immediately. Before application, the granules should be mixed with moist soil to reduce chances of their falling in to eyes of the person applying these. Moreover, rubber gloves should be used during for application of the granules.

2. *Chilo infuscatellus* Snellen (Sugarcane early shoot borer, Lepidoptera: Pyralidae) (Fig. 3.1B)

Distribution. This is one of the very serious pests of sugarcane in India and Pakistan. It is also found in Afghanistan, Myanmar, Indonesia, Taiwan and the Philippines.

Identification. The moths have straw-coloured fore wings and whitish hind wings with apical light-buff areas. They measure 25-40 mm in wing expanse and are attracted to light at night. The caterpillars are dirty white and have five light-violet longitudinal stripes on the body. They measure 20-25 mm in length at maturity.

Life-history. The females lay creamy white scale like eggs in clusters of 11-36 on the lower surface of leaves. On an average, a female moth lays 300-400 eggs which hatch in 4-5 days. The larvae reach the plant base, bore into the shoot and feed there. They grow through five stages and complete their development in 3-4 weeks. Then each larva constructs a chamber for pupation in the cane and makes an exit from which it emerges as moth after 6-7 days. The moths live only for 2-4 days. The life-cycle is completed in 5-6 weeks and the pest breeds 4 or 5 times a year.

Host plants. In addition to sugarcane, it feeds on maize, *bajra, sarkanda, kahi, baru* and some other grasses.

Damage. The damage is done by the caterpillars maximally by those of the second, third and fourth generations by eating inside of the stems. The plants, which are attacked by this pest, produce dead-hearts from April to June, and completely dry up. A loss of 10-20 per cent of young shoots is not uncommon during this period and in years of serious infestation, it may be as high as 70 per cent. At harvest, losses of 22-33 per cent in yield, 12 per cent in sugar recovery, 2 per cent in commercial cane sugar (CCS) and 27 per cent in jaggery have been estimated.

Management. (*i*) Early planting of the crop (before the middle of March) helps to check the attack of the borer (*ii*) Release *Trichogramma chilonis* Ishii @50,000 per hectare at 10 days' interval from mid-April to end June. Generally 8 releases are considered enough (*iii*) Apply 25 Kg granules of fipronil 0.3G per ha, before the cane setts are covered with earth by planking (*iv*) Apply 25 Kg granules of cartap hydrochloride 4G or 25 Kg of fipronil 0.3G mixed in 50 Kg sand or 110 ml of imidacloprid 17.8SL or 5 litres of chlorpyriphos 20EC in 1000 litres of water per ha with sprinkling can along the rows at post-germination stage (about 45 days after planking). Earth up slightly and follow up with light irrigation.

3. *Chilo auricilius* Dudgeon (Stalk borer, Lepidoptera : Pyralidae)

Distribution. The stalk-borer, commonly known as the Tarai borer, is perhaps the most destructive pest of sugarcane in northern India. It is widespread in Bihar, the Tarai areas of Uttrakhand, and Haryana and Punjab.

Identification. The moth is straw-coloured and the female has a wing expanse of 22-30 mm and the male has a wing-span of 16-25 mm. The fore wings have golden spots and the hind wings are silvery white. The full-grown caterpillar is 25-30 mm long, with a light bluish pink body, and has a dark brown head and five longitudinal violet dorsal stripes.

Life-history. Eggs are laid in leafsheaths or on the underside of leaves of the late water-shoots and early ratoon sprouts. A female may lay 200-300 scale-like overlapping eggs in clusters of 60-70. The young larvae, measuring about 1 mm, emerge from these eggs in about a week. They feed on leafsheaths or on mid ribs for the next week or so and then bore into stalks by making circular holes in the rind. The larvae develop through 5 stages and are full-grown in 3-6 weeks. Then the mature larva constructs a chamber with an exit and begins pupation. Moths emerge in about one week and the life-cycle is completed in 5-9 weeks. In all, 5 or 6 over-lapping generations are completed in a year. The winter life-cycle is rather prolonged and is completed in 17-19 weeks, out of which 14-16 weeks are spent in the larval stage and 2-3 in the pupal stage.

Host plants. In addition to sugarcane, it feeds on paddy, wheat, oats and *baru.*

Damage. The damage is done by the larval stage by feeding inside the stem. The caterpillars have the habit of boring into one internode after another and moving from plant to plant, thus infesting up to 90 per cent of the canes in certain fields. According to one estimate, this pest causes, on an average, 16 per cent reduction in cane yield and a loss of 2.16 units in sugar recovery.

Management. (*i*) varieties resistant to stalk borer should be grown in the areas which is more prone to the damage (*ii*) Cane-seed from the infested fields should not be used (*iii*) Spread of the pest to uninfested areas may be prevented by restricting the movement of infested canes. (*iv*) The pest population can be suppressed by burning the trash in the fields after harvest and by removing and destroying the water-shoots over large areas during February-March. This practice also induces tillering and is useful (*v*) Do not ratoon a heavily infested crop; plough up the affected fields, collect the stubble and destroy them. (*vi*) Release *Trichogramma chilonis* Ishii @ 50,000 per ha from July to October at 10 days interval. Generally 10-12 releases are required. (*vii*) Avoid lodging of crop.

4. *Emmalocera depressella* Swinhoe (Sugarcane root borer, Lepidoptera : Pyralidae) (Fig. 3.1C)

Distribution. This is a very serious pest of sugarcane in eastern India but in Pakistan, Haryana and Punjab, it is of minor importance.

Identification. The moths are pale yellow-brown and have white hindwings. The female has a wing expanse of 30-35 mm. A full-grown caterpillar measures about 30 mm in length, creamy white with yellowish-brown head and a rather wrinkled body.

Life-history. A female lays, on an average, 277-355 scale-like, creamy-white eggs singly on the leaves, the stem or on the ground. The eggs hatch in 5-8 days and the young larvae bore into the stem below the soil surface. As they feed, they cut right across the stem, reaching the adjoining tillers. The larvae complete their development through five stages in about four weeks. When full-grown, they pupate inside the canes after making emergence holes just above the soil surface. The pupal stage lasts 9-14 days and moths emerge from these holes. The life-cycle is completed in 6-7 weeks. During a year, four generations are completed and the caterpillars of the fifth generation hibernate in winter.

Host plants. Apart from sugarcane, it feeds on *sarkanda (Saccharum munja), baru (Sorghum halepense),* Napier grass, etc.

Damage. The damage is done by the caterpillars by eating inside the lower stem. Central leaves of the attacked plants dry up and form deadhearts before the cane-forming stage. These deadhearts are not easily pulled out. This pest is primarily destructive to young plants and the attack is particularly severe from April to June. Plants attacked after the formation of canes are not killed, although their weight and sugar content are reduced. At harvest, a decrease in yield upto 10 per cent and reduction of sucrose in juice by about 0.3 unit have been reported.

Management. (*i*) The pest can be suppressed by ploughing up and burning the stubble in the fields not kept for ratooning. (*ii*) The canes should be harvested below the soil surface in order to kill the caterpillars. (*iii*) Chemical control is not feasible. (*iv*) Staple 40 Tricho-cards (5.0 cm x 2.5 cm hard paper piece glued with 7 days old eggs of laboratory host, *Corcyra cephalonica* parasitized by *Trichogramma chilonis)* to the under-sides of sugarcane leaves from July to October at 10 days intervals. Each card should have approximately 500 parasitized eggs and be spread uniformly at 100 spots per ha. Normally, 10-11 releases are required.

5. *Acigona steniella* (Hampson) (Gurdaspur borer, Lepidoptera : Pyralidae) (Fig. 3.1D)

Distribution. The Gurdaspur borer was considered the most destructive pest of sugarcane in Pakistan and India. It had also been recorded in Vietnam. It was noticed for the first time in District Sialkot in 1923 and was subsequently noticed as a pest at Gurdaspur (Punjab) in 1925. Later, it spread to newer sugarcane areas in Punjab, Haryana, Western Uttar Pradesh and the northern districts of Rajasthan. In the fifties and sixties it was considered to be the most destructive pest of sugarcane in northern India. Its importance as a pest started declining in the late sixties.

Identification. The moth is dull brown, 25-45 mm across the spread wings and has a number of dark spots along the outer margins of the fore wings. The hind wings are white. A full-grown caterpillar is 30-35 mm long, creamy white, with orange brown head. There are four prominent longitudinal violet stripes on the body.

Life-history. A female lays 90-300 flattened scale-like eggs in clusters of 3-22. The eggs are laid on the upper surface of the leaves along the mid-rib and they hatch in 4-9 days. In 4 or 5 hours, the young larvae enter the top portion of a cane through a single hole just above a node. There, they feed gregariously by making spiral galleries which run upwards. After about 7-10 days, when the cane top has dried up, the larvae (in the third stage) come out and enter the adjoining canes single or in twos. They may again come out of these canes and attack more plants. The larvae grow through five stages and are full-fed in 19-27 days. When mature, they make exit holes and pupate inside. The pupal stage lasts 6-12 days and, on emergence, the moths live for 4-5 days. The pest pupates in stubble and the life-cycle is completed in 5-6 weeks. It breeds two or three times in a year. In the beginning of September, the full-grown caterpillars start migration from the upper part by coming out and re-entering the cane near the base. They enter the stubble and hibernate there till June of the next year.

Host plant. Sugarcane

Damage. In the initial stages, the larvae feed gregariously in the top portion of the canes by making spiral galleries thus killing the plants. At about the time the larvae leave these canes and move on to new ones, the dried cane tops can be spotted in a field. Later on, large patches of dried canes appear. The pest destroys 20-25 per cent of the crop. In case of severe infestation, the loss may be as high as 70-75 per cent and sugar recovery from the affected crop is also greatly reduced.

Management. (*i*) Rogue out the canes showing withered tops in the afternoon every week from July to September and destroy. (*ii*) Do not ratoon heavily affected crop. (*iii*) Plough up the fields not meant for ratooning and destroy the stubble before June. (*iv*) Chemical control is not feasible.

6. *Raphimetopus ablutellus* Zeller (Green borer, Lepidoptera : Pyralidae)

Distribution. The green borer is a regular pest of sugarcane in Bihar, Uttar Pradesh, Haryana and Punjab. In certain years, it becomes quite a serious pest.

Identification. The insect is named after the caterpillar which is uniformly copper green and has a characteristic greyish prothoracic shield. The adult moths have ocherous fore wings and white hind wings.

Life-history. The pest is active in the sugarcane fields from February to June only and the rest of the year, it lives as a hibernating larva in the stubble. The moths appear from the pupae towards the end of February or early March. After mating, the females lay, on an average, 37 oval-shaped eggs, in small clusters, scattered in cracks and crevices in the soil or among loose soil particles. The dull white eggs are seen just below the surface of the ground, near the host plants.

The eggs hatch in 7-8 days in April. On emergence, the larvae bore into the soft cane shoots and feed inside. They undergo five moultings in 20-25 days during April and May. The total life-cycle is completed in 35-40 days. They pupate in the cane, leaving an exit hole and emerge as moths in about 7 days. Thus, the total life-cycle is completed in 35-40 days. There are three generations in a year, the larvae of the last generation undergo diapause for many months.

Host plant. Sugarcane

Damage. The damage by this borer is generally found in association with other shoot borers, e.g. *Chilo infuscatellus*, *Sesamia* sp. and *Emmalocera depressella*, during the summer months. The larvae attack the growing point of the plants, causing dead-hearts. In Uttar Pradesh, it has been found to kill 24-76 per cent of the mother shoots from April to June.

Management. Rake 35 kg of carbaryl 10 per cent dust per ha into the soil at the time of planting of sugarcane.

7. *Chilo sacchariphagus indicus* (Kapur) (Internode borer, Lepidoptera : Pyralidae)

Distribution. The insect is found throughout India and usually occurs on sugarcane late in its growing phase during June to December. It is a serious pest in Andhra Pradesh, Karnataka, Kerala, Tamil Nadu and Uttar Pradesh.

Identification. The moth is pale brown with white hind wings and the larva has a white body with dark spots and a brown head.

Life-history. The females lay white scale-like eggs in masses of 2-60 near the midrib of the leaves, on leaf sheaths and on stems. A maximum of 400 eggs are laid by a female. The incubation period is 5-6 days. The larva bores at the nodal region and enters the stem. The larva becomes full grown in 37-53 days and pupates in the leaf sheath. The pupal period lasts for 8-10 days and the adults survive for 3-4 days. The total life-cycle occupies 50-70 days and there are six broods of the insect in a year.

Host plant. Sugarcane.

Damage. The caterpillar bores into the canes near the nodes, the entry holes being plugged with excreta. A larva may attack 1-3 internodes and mostly the attack is seen in the top five internodes. Its feeding causes the tissues turn red. The loss to cane is more to its tonnage than to its quality. However, juice quality is affected if more than 10 per cent of the cane is affected.

Management. Same as in case of stalk-borer.

8. *Chilo tumidicostalis* Hampson (Plassey borer, Lepidoptera: Pyralidae)

Distribution. The borer is found in many parts of India, Nepal, Bangladesh and Thailand.

Identification. The adult moths measure about 16 to 20 mm from head to the tip of forewings which appear brown to pale brown with some dark marking. Hind wings in males are dirty white to light brown while those of females are white. The larva has dark brown head with creamy white body with big dark spots.

Life cycle. The adults live for about a week and are nocturnal in habit. Mating takes place at dusk and eggs are laid in batches on both sides of the leaves. Eggs appear oval shaped overlapping each other. The larval period is around 26 days and the pupal period lasts for about a week. Total life cycle is completed in 6 weeks.

Host plants. Sugarcane

Damage. As a result of damage by the borer, the central whorl of leaves dries up. The newly hatched larvae are gregarious feeders boring up to the top five internodes. As the larvae mature in to third and fourth instars they bore in the lower internodes of the same cane or can migrate to new canes as well.

Management. Same as in case of early shoot borer.

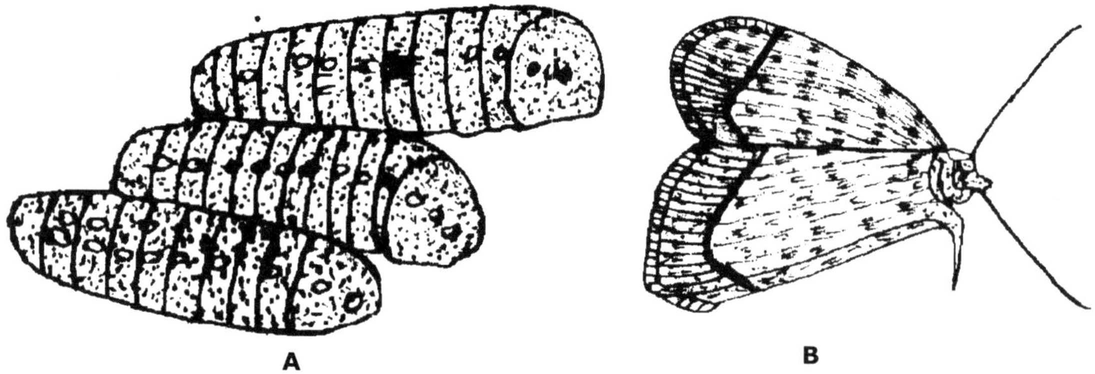

Fig. 3.2 Pests of sugarcane. Plassy borer, *Chilo tumidicostalis*. **A.** Pupae **B.** Adult.

9. *Pyrilla perpusilla* (Walker) (Sugarcane pyrilla, Hemiptera: Lophopidae) (Fig. 3.1E)

Distribution. Sugarcane pyrilla or the sugarcane leafhopper is distributed throughout India and appears periodically as a destructive pest of sugarcane in Uttar Pradesh, Uttarakhand, Punjab, Haryana and Rajasthan.

Identification. The adult is about 20 mm long and has a straw-coloured body with dark patches or spots on the wings. At the front end it has a snout like prolongation and prominent red eyes. When full-grown, a nymph is pale yellow, 10-15 mm long, and has two white prominent feather like filaments at the tail end of its body.

Life cycle. The adults lay 300-536 eggs in clusters on the underside of leaves during the summer and within the leafsheaths during winter. The clusters are covered with a white, fluffy material from the anal tufts of the females. As this fluff is removed, oval, pale-white eggs are seen in 3-5 longitudinal rows of 35-50 each. The eggs hatch in 8-10 days in summer and in about 3-4 weeks during November or December. The nymphs which hatch out from the eggs are pale brown in colour and 1.3 mm long. At this stage they do not possess snout, wings and tufts. Within a week they are characterized by the possession of two long tufts of waxy secretion at the end of the abdomen. They start sucking the sap of canes and grow to maturity through 5 stages within 8 weeks in summer and in 5-6 months in winter. The adults live for 27- 52 days in the summer and 18-20 weeks in the winter. In all, 3-4 generations are completed in a year.

Host plants. Apart from sugarcane, it feeds on wheat, barley, oats, maize, sorghum, *baru*, Guinea grass, *swank* and Sudan grass.

Damage. The damage is done by both nymphs and adults by sucking sap from the foliage. Owing to the loss of cell-sap the leaves turn pale-yellow and shrivel up later. Even the canes dry up and die when the attack is very severe. The insects excrete a thick transparent liquid, known as honeydew which falls on the leaves and makes a good medium for the growth of a black mould. Therefore, at times, the leaves acquire a sickly black appearance and the attacked crop can be spotted from a distance. The black coating interferes with photosynthesis and very little food is manufactured by the plants. The existing sucrose in the canes is also used up and about 35 per cent reduction in sugar yield is not uncommon.

Management. (*i*) ***Biological control.*** The release of parasitoid, *Epiricania melanoleuca* @ 4000-5000 cocoons or 4-6 lakh eggs per ha checks the multiplication of sugarcane pyrilla. Lower rates of cocoon releases are effective in areas where *E. melanoleuca* occurs naturally. (*ii*) ***Chemical control.*** Apply the following insecticides at an economic threshold level of 3-5 nymphs or adults per leaf: (a) *April to june.* Spray the crop with one litre of malathion 50EC or 875 ml of endosulfan 35EC or 565 ml of fenitrothion 50EC per ha in 250 litres of water with manually operated sprayer. (b) *August to October.* Spray 1.0-1.25 litres of endosulfan 35EC or 650-875 ml of fenitrothion 50EC per ha in 375 litres of water with a manually-operated sprayer. In case the crop is not very tall and thick, malathion LVC @ 1.0 litre per ha can be sprayed without adding water with the help of a motoized knapsack sprayer fitted with a special restrictor.

10. *Cavelerius excavatus* (Distant) (Sugarcane black bug, Hemiptera: Lygaeidae)

Distribution. This pest is widely distributed throughout India and Pakistan.

Identification. The adults are 6-7 mm long, black with white patches on the wings extending slightly beyond the abdomen. The shape and colour of nymphs is similar to those of the adults but are smaller in size.

Life-history. In summer, each bug lays 55-478 eggs in clusters of 14-67 on the inner side of the leafsheaths. The eggs are creamy white and hatch in 9-17 days. The nymphs grow through five stages and complete their development in 4-6 weeks. The adults are long-lived; males die earlier than the females. The insects complete approximately three generations in a year. In winter, the eggs are laid in the soil at a depth of 5-7 cm and they hatch during the next spring. Thus, in March-April the new nymphs and the old adults die and only the nymphs remain and they mature by June. From then on, the generations overlap and all stages are found in the field.

Host plants. Besides sugarcane, it has also been found feeding on rice, maize and a number of grasses.

Damage. On young plants, the nymphs and adults suck cell-sap from the central whorl. On the grown up plants they prefer to feed within the leaf-sheaths, and varieties having broad and loosely attached sheaths are preferred by this pest. The attacked leaves become paler and also show holes after feeding.

Management. (*i*) After harvesting of the crop, before the sprouting, in the fields meant for ratoon, do the stubble shaving, spread the dried up trash uniformly and burn, followed by irrigation. (*ii*) Spray 875 ml of chlorpyriphos 20EC in 1000 litres of water per ha. Direct the spray material into the leaf-whorl.

11. *Aleurolobus barodensis* (Maskell) (Sugarcane whitefly, Hemiptera: Aleyrodidae) (Fig. 3.1F)

Distribution. The whitefly of sugarcane is found throughout the Indian sub-continent and is a notorious pest in Punjab and Haryana.

Identification. The adults are small, delicate, pale-yellow insects about 3 mm long, and their wings have a white mealy appearance, mottled with black dots. The grown up nymphs are about 3 mm long, oval in outline but flattened and scale like in form. They are black and have a silvery grey waxy coating on the body.

Life-history. The female lays 60-65 creamy white conical eggs which are glued to the surface of the leaves. The eggs are found in groups of 15-20, arranged in a single file. Within a couple of hours, the eggs turn black and hatch in 8-10 days. On emergence, the young nymphs are pale yellow and they move away from the egg-shell to find a suitable place for feeding by the insertion of their piercing mouthparts. They complete their development in 25-30 days after passing through 4 instars. The pupal stage lasts 10-11 days and the adults, on emergence, live only for 24-48 hours. The insect completes 9 generations in a year and in March-April, they migrate from the old to the new sugarcane plants. Their life is prolonged in autumn when the nymphal and pupal stages are completed in 3-4 months.

Host plants. Sugarcane is the preferred crop but it can also attack other *Saccharum* plants.

Damage. Only the nymphs cause damage by sucking the cell-sap. Yellow streaks appear on the attacked leaves and the crop acquires a palish green appearance. The general vitality of the plants is reduced, and the quality and quantity of *gur* production is poor because of subnormal crystallization of sugar. Sugar recovery is reduced by about 15-25 per cent. A black mould develops on the honeydew excreted by the pest and it interferes with proper functioning of the leaves and renders them unfit as fodder.

Management. (*i*) Rati'o'ning of the crop in low lying and water logged areas should be avoided (ii) Detrash lower leaves containing the puparia. (iii) Spray 100 ml of imidacloprid 200SL or 1.5 litres of triazophos 40EC in 375 litres of water per ha.

12. *Saccharicoccus sacchari* (Cockerell) (Sugarcane mealy bug, Hemiptera.: Pseudococcidae)

Distribution. The mealy bug is widely distributed in Punjab, Uttar Pradesh, Bihar, Maharashtra, Karnataka and Tamil Nadu.

Identification. Mealy bugs are inert pink insects, having a rotund, sack-like, segmented body covered completely with a white mealy powder. The size, even among full-grown females, varies a great deal, but a large female measures about 5 mm in length and 2.5 mm in width. The males, whose only function is to fertilize the females, are sluggish having only one pair of wings and are short-lived.

Life-history. The females lay a large number of eggs at short intervals. Within few hours, the eggs become soft and elongated, and the crawlers emerge. The tiny young ones are transparent, pink and very active. They wander about for some time and spread all over the field or may even be blown away by the wind to the adjoining fields of sugarcane. Finding a suitable host plant, they force themselves underneath the leafsheaths near the basal nodes. As the canes grow taller, the older bugs remain at the lower end and the crawlers reach the higher nodes. The nymphs feed voraciously and pass through 6 stages before they are full-grown in 2-3 weeks. The life of a full-grown winged female is approximately 3-5 days. The entire life-cycle is completed in about a month during the summer. The pest completes several generations in a year.

Host plant. Sugarcane.

Damage. The damage is done by both nymphs and adults by continual sucking of sap. The bugs drain away large quantities of sap from the canes and befoul them by their mealy secretions and honeydew. A sooty mould develops on these secretions giving a blackish appearance to the canes. In severe cases of infestation, sucrose content decreases by 24 per cent and brix by 16 per cent.

Management. Spray 1.25 litres of malathion 50EC in 1250 litres of water per ha.

13. *Neomaskellia bergii* (Signoret) (Sugarcane spottedfly, Hemiptera : Aleyrodidae)

Distribution. The sugarcane aleyrodid is found in India, Sri Lanka, Java, the Philippines, Reno Manila, Mauritius and Fiji.

Identification. The adult flies are pale brown with black markings on the fore wings. The hind wings are short, thin and more or less transparent. The nymphs are pale brown to dark in colour and are covered with white wax.

Life-history. This pest is most active on sugarcane during September-October. The female lays 120-150 eggs in circular or semi-circular masses on the underside of the leaves during an oviposition period of 2-3 days. The freshly laid white egg is eliptical in shape and it turns black later on. The eggs hatch in 2-3 days. There are four moultings during larval period of 5-7 days. The pupal stage lasts 7-10 days and the life-cycle is completed in 15-18 days in September and 18-25 days from October onwards.

Host plants. Apart from sugarcane, it also attacks sorghum.

Damage. The nymphs suck plant sap and in case of severe attack, cause stunting of canes and drying of leaves.

Management. Same as in case of sugarcane whitefly.

14. *Aulacaspis tegalensis* (Zehntner) (Sugarcane scale insect, Hemiptera: Diaspididae)

Distribution. The sugarcane scale is commonly found on this crop in Malaysia, Thailand, Indonesia, Taiwan, the Philippines and Mauritius.

Identification. The adult female is sedentary having no legs or wings and lives inside a white covering or a white scale. It is about 1.8 mm long and 0.9 mm wide. The male is minute and is free living. It has a special sharp organ to penetrate the female's scale covering.

Host plants. Apart from sugarcane, it is also reported to feed on sorghum in Tanzania and on the wild grass, *Erianthus arundinaceus* in Java.

Life-history. The fertilized female lays eggs inside her scale and these hatch into mobile nymphs which escape from under the cover. They wander over the host plant and eventually fix themselves and secrete a scale cover. They moult many times and develop differentially according to the sex; the females remaining sedentary. Dry conditions are believed to favour survival and dispersion of the ineffective "crawler" stage.

Damage. The insects feed on stem parenchyma and by doing so prevent the accumulation of sucrose in the cane. Drying up of the canes may also result from heavy infestation. The infestation reduces germination by about 20 per cent, cane growth by 5.5 per cent, cane yield by 43 per cent, juice content by 0.30-41 per cent and jaggery production by 10 per cent.

Management. (*i*) Give hot water treatment at planting time. (*ii*) Dip setts for 15 minutes in 0.1 per cent malathion 50EC before planting. (*iii*) Spray 1.25 litres of malathion 50EC or 2.0 litres of dimethoate 30EC in 1250 litres of water per ha.

*****

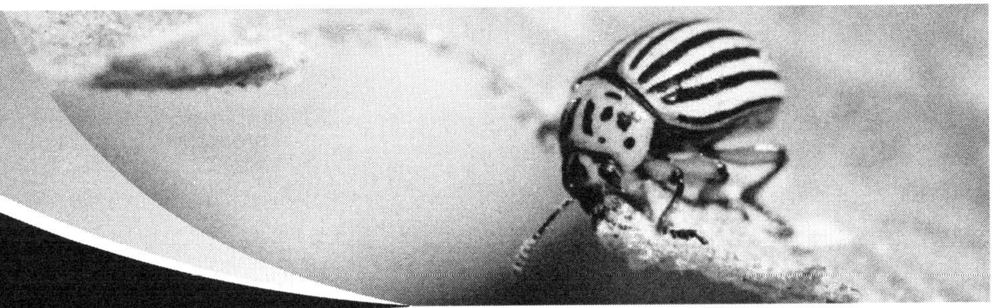

4 CHAPTER

PESTS OF PULSES

Bengal gram (*Cicer arietinum*)

1. *Helicoverpa armigera* (Hubner) (Gram pod borer, Lepidoptera: Noctuidae)
2. *Agrotis ipsilon* (Hufnagel) (Greasy gram cutworm, Lepidoptera : Noctuidae)
3. *Tanymecus indicus* Faust (Ghujhia weevil, Coleoptera : Curculionidae)
4. *Spodoptera litura* (Fabricius) (Tobacco caterpillar, Lepidoptera: Noctuidae)

Pea (*Pisum sativum*)

1. *Helicoverpa armigera* (Hubner) (Gram pod borer, Lepidoptera: Noctuidae)
2. *Etiella zinckenella* Treitschke (Pea pod borer, Lepidoptera : Pyralidae)
3. *Spodoptera exigua* (Hubner) (Beet armyworm, Lepidoptera : Noctuidae)
4. *Chromatomyia horticola* (Goweau) (Pea leaf miner, Diptera : Agromyzidae)
5. *Ophiomyia phaseoli* (Tryon) (Pea stem fly, Diptera : Agromyzidae)
6. *Acyrthosiphon pisum* (Harris) (Pea aphid, Hemiptera : Aphididae)

Black gram (*Phaseolus mungo*), green gram (*Phaseolus aureus*)

1. *Helicovera armigera* (Hubner) (Gram pod borer, Lepidoptera : Noctudiae)
2. *Spilosoma obliqua* Walker (Bihar hairy caterpillar, Lepidoptera: Arctiidae)
3. *Empoasca kerri* Pruthi (Leafhopper, Hemiptera : Cicadellidae)
4. *Exelastis atomosa* (Walsingham) (Plume moth, Lepidoptera : Pterophoridae

	5. *Amsacta moorei* (Butler) (Red hairy caterpillar, Lepidoptera : Arctiidae)
	6. *Maruca testulalis* (Geyer) (Spotted pod borer, Lepidoptera : Pyralidae)
Pigeon pea (*Cajanus cajan*)	1. *Helicoverpa armigera* (Hubner) (Gram pod borer, Lepidoptera : Noctuae)
	2. *Exelastis atomosa* (Walshingham) (Plume moth, Lepidoptera : Pterophoridae)
	3. *Adisura atkinsoni* Moore (Field bean pod borer, Lepidoptera : Noctuidae)
	4. *Melanagromyza obtusa* (Malloch) (Red gram pod fly, Diptera : Agromyzidae)
	5. *Clavigralla gibbosa* Spinola (Tur pod bug, Hemiptera : Coreidae)
	6. *Riptortus pedestris* (Fabricius) (Pod bug, Hemiptera : Coreidae)
	7. *Thosea aperiens* (Walker) (Green nettle slug caterpillar, Lepidoptera : Cochlidiidae)
	8. *Odontotermes* spp. (White ant, Isoptera : Termitidae)
Cowpea (*Vigna sinesis*), soybean (*Soja hispida*)	1. *Maruca testulalis* (Geyer) (Spotted pod borer, Lepidoptera : Pyralidae)
	2. *Ophimomyia phaseoli* (Tryon) (Bean fly, Diptera : Agromyzidae)
	3. *Thosea aperiens* (Walker) (Green nettle slug-caterpillar, Lepidoptera : Cochlidiidae)
	4. *Obereopsis brevis* (Gahan) (Girdle beetle, Coleoptera : Cerambycidae)
	5. *Helicoverpa armigera* (Hubner) (Gram pod borer, Lepidoptera : Noctuidae)

The total production of pulses in India was 14.76 million tonnes during 2007-08, which is estimated to decline to 14.66 million tonnes during 2008-09. About 250 insects have been recorded feeding on pulse crops, of which about a dozen including pod borers, stem borers, leaf-miners, foliage caterpillars, cutworms, etc. are of considerable importance.

1. *Helicoverpa armigera* (Hubner) (Gram pod borer, Lepidoptera : Noctuidae) (Fig. 4.1A)

Distribution. The gram pod borer or the gram caterpillar is cosmopolitan and is widely distributed in India.

Identification. The moth is stoutly built and is yellowish brown. There is a dark speck and a dark area near the outer margin of each fore wing. The fore wings are marked with greyish wavy lines and black spots of varying size on the upper side and a black kidney shaped mark and a round spot on the underside. The hind wings are whitish and lighter in colour with a broad blackish band along the outer margin. The caterpillars when full-grown, are 3.5 cm in length, being greenish with dark broken grey lines along the sides of the body.

Life-history. The females lay eggs singly on tender parts of the plants. A single female may lay as many as 741 eggs in 4 days. The eggs are shining greenish yellow and are round. They hatch in 2-4 days in April to October and 6 days in February and the young larvae feed on the foliage for some time and later bore into the pods and feed on the developing grains, with their bodies hanging outside. They move from pod to pod and are full-fed in 13-19 days and measure 35 mm in the last instar. The full-grown larvae come out of the pod and pupate in the soil. In the active season, the pupal period lasts 8-15 days, but in winter the duration

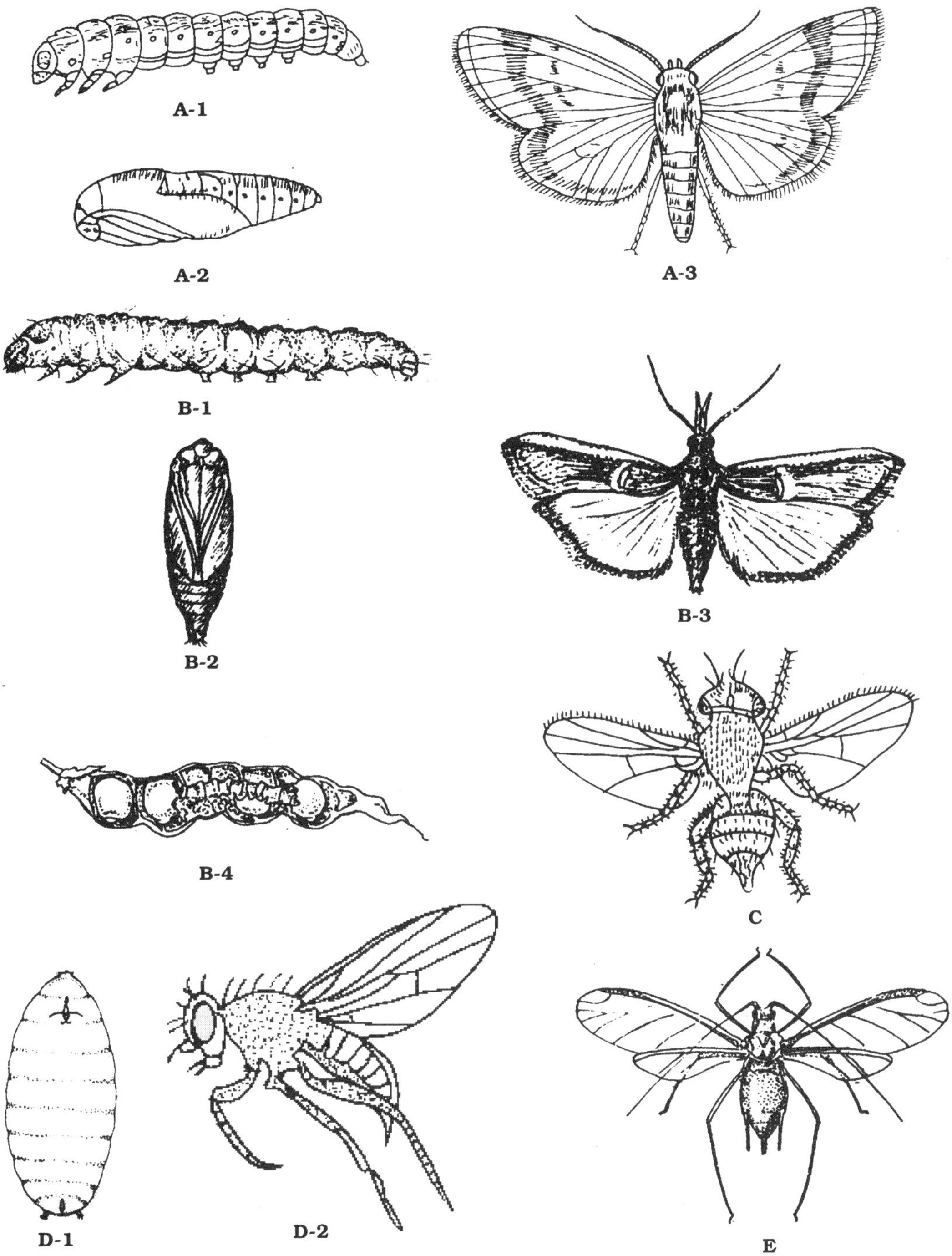

Fig. 4.1 Pests of pulses. **A.** Gram pod borer, *Helicoverpa armigera*; A-1 Larva, A-2, Pupa, A-3. Adult. **B.** Lentil pod borer, *Etiella zinckenella*; B-1. Larva, B-2. Pupa, B-3. Adult, B-4. Damaged pod. **C.** Red gram pod fly, *Melanagromyza obtusa*. **D.** Pea leaf-miner, *Chromatomyia horticola*; D-1. Pupa, D-2. Adult. **E.** Pea aphid, *Acyrthosiphon pisum*.

is prolonged, particularly in northern India. Some of the pupae remain in a facultative diapause during November – April in northern India. There may be as many as 8 overlapping generations in a year.

Host plants. It is a serious pest of chickpea, pigeon pea, pea, mungbean, urdbean, lentil, soybean and cowpea. The insect has also been found damaging cotton, sorghum, okra, maize, tomato, berseem, sunflower and lately wheat also.

Damage. Although they prefer food plants like gram and red gram, the larvae are polyphagous. They feed on the foliage, when young, and on the seed in later stages, and thus reduce yield. A single larva may destroy 30-40 pods before it reaches maturity.

Management. (*i*) Timely sowing, i.e upto mid October or growing early maturing cultivars which complete podding by first week of March in northern region helps in escaping peak activity period of *H. armigera.* (*ii*) Use of *Helicoverpa*-tolerant varieties like JG 315 and JG 74 for central zone and ICCV 7 for southern zone is recommended. (*iii*) Mixed intercropping with non-preferred host plants like barley, wheat, mustard and linseed should be preferred over sole crop. (*iv*) Hand picking of the older larvae during early hours of the day is helpful as these are less susceptible to insecticides. (*v*) Apply nuclear polyhedrosis virus (NPV) @ 250-500 larval equivalents/ha alone or alongwith half dose of endosulfan 35EC (1.25 litres/ha). Spraying should be carried out in the evening hours. (*vi*) The pod borer can be managed by spraying the insecticides at the economic threshold level of one larva per five plants at pod initiation stage. Use the recommended insecticides i.e. 500 ml of indoxacarb 14.5SC or 150 ml of spinosad 45SC or 250 ml of fenvalerate 20EC or 200 ml of cypermethrin 25EC or 400 ml of deltamethrin 2.8EC or 2 Kg of acephate 75SP in 200-250 litres of water per ha at the start of pod formation and repeat after two weeks, if necessary. Alternatively, apply malathion 5 per cent dust @ 25 kg/ha. For consuming any part of the raw gram plant, observe waiting period of 20 days after application of the insecticide.

2. *Exelastis atomosa* (Walsingham) (Plume moth, Lepidoptera : Pterophoridae)

Distribution. This insect is found in many parts of India, particularly in Andhra Pradesh, Assam, Madhya Pradesh, Punjab, Tamil Nadu, Haryana, Maharashtra and Karnataka.

Identification. The plume moth is delicate dry grass-coloured insect having deeply fissured wings with frilled edges to look like plumes. The full-grown caterpillar is greenish brown and measures 1.25 cm in length and has short hairs on the body.

Life-history. The female moths lay 17-19 eggs singly on tender parts of the plants. The eggs hatch in 2-5 days and the young larvae feed on the pods and become full-grown in 10-25 days. Pupation takes place outside the pod on its surface or in the entrance hole itself. The pupal period extends from 3 to 12 days. The life-cycle is completed in 17-42 days.

Host plant. Pigeon pea

Damage. The larvae first scrape the surface of the pods and finally make holes into them and feed on the seeds, reducing crop yield.

Management. Chemical control measures are same as in case of gram pod-borer.

3. *Clavigralla gibbosa* Spinola (Tur pod bug, Hemiptera : Coreidae)

Distribution. This insect is widely distributed in the Indian sub-continent and adjoining countries. In India, it has been recorded from Delhi, Orissa, Tamil Nadu, Uttar Pradesh, Maharashtra, Madhya Pradesh, Andhra Pradesh, Karnataka, Haryana and Bihar.

Identification. The adult bugs are greenish brown in colour, having a spined pronotum and the femur swollen at the apical end. The bugs are about 20 mm long. The young nymphs are reddish and show prominent lateral spines on the prothoracic and abdominal segments.

Life-history. The eggs are usually laid on pods and, less frequently, on leaves or the floral buds, in clusters of 5-25 each. A female, on an average, lays 60 eggs during an oviposition period of 15 days. The eggs hatch in about 8 days and the newly-hatched nymphs move away from the egg shells within 10-15 minutes and gather together at a suitable feeding spot. They are gregarious in nature and are seen feeding in groups. The nymphs take about 17 days to complete development, after passing through five nymphal stages. The pest is active from the middle of October to the end of May and completes six overlapping generations during this period.

Host plants. The insect feeds on pigeon pea, lablab and cowpea.

Damage. Both the nymphs and the adults suck cell sap from the stem, leaves, flower-buds and pods. As a result of this damage, the pods show pale yellow patches and later on shrivel up. The grain inside remains small in size and the yield may be reduced significantly.

Management. Spray 1.25 litres of monocrotophos 36SL or one litre of trichlorphon 50EC in 625 litres of water per ha. Two sprays during flowering and three during pod formation are quite effective.

4. *Etiella zinckenella* Treitschke (Lentil pod borer, Lepidoptera : Phycitidae) (Fig. 4.1B)

Distribution. The pest is widely distributed in India, particularly in Assam, Orissa, Bihar, Uttar Pradesh, Punjab, Karnataka, Andhra Pradesh and Tamil Nadu.

Identification. The moths are grey with a wing expanse of 25 mm. The fore wings have dark marginal lines and are interspersed with ochreous scales. The full-grown larvae are rosy, with a purplish tinge.

Life-history. The eggs are laid both singly and in clusters on various parts of the plant, including the pods. The newly emerged larvae feed on floral parts and subsequently, they bore into the pods to feed on the seeds. The larval stage is completed in 10-27 days. Pupation takes place in the soil at a depth of 2-4 cm and the pupal development is completed in 10-15 days. The pest breeds throughout the year and passes through 5 generations.

Host plants. It is a serious pest of lentil and green peas in northern India and is also found on a variety of other pulses in various parts of the country,

Damage. The larvae consume floral parts, newly formed pods and seeds inside the developing pods. The reduction in yield may be up to 5 per cent.

Management. At flower initiation, spray the crop with 2.25 kg of carbaryl 50WP in 250 litres of water per ha and repeat the treatment after three weeks, if necessary. Carbaryl should be used if the husk is to be fed to the cattle.

5. *Melanagromyza obtusa* (Malloch) (Red gram pod fly, Diptera : Agromyzidae) (Fig. 4.1C)

Distribution. This pest occurs wherever pigeon pea is grown in India like West Bengal, Assam, Bihar, Uttar Pradesh, Punjab, Tamil Nadu and Madhya Pradesh.

Identification. It is a small metallic-black fly, whose tiny maggots bore into the pods and feed on seeds.

Life-history. The adult female fly thrusts its minute eggs into the shell of a tender pod. They hatch in 2-4 days. The maggots feed under the epidermis for some time and then enter the seed. They arc full-grown in 5-10 days. Pupation takes place inside the damaged pods and the pupal period lasts 4-13 days. The adults emerge by cutting holes. The life-cycle is completed in 11-27 days and several generations are produced in a year.

Host plants. Mainly pigeon pea.

Damage. The maggots eat away only a part of the seed and the partially damaged seed becomes subject to bacterial and fungal infections. The damaged grains are thus, rendered unfit for human consumption.

Management. Spray 1.75 kg of carbaryl 50WP in 200 litres of water on dwarf varieties and 300 litres on tall varieties per ha at the time of 50 per cent flowering. Repeat the spray after 15 days.

6. *Ophiomyia phaseoli* (Tryon) (Bean fly, Diptera : Agromyzidae)

Distribution. Bean fly is widely distributed in Sri Lanka, India, China, Indonesia, Malaysia, the Philippines, Singapore and many African countries.

Identification. It is a very minute insect, body length of the male being about 1.9 mm and that of the female 2.2 mm. The maggot is creamy in colour and apodous in form.

Life-history. The slender, white eggs are laid singly in holes made on the upper surface of young leaves, especially near the petiole end of the leaf. On hatching, the maggot forms a short linear leaf mine and further on it tunnels underneath the epidermis of the leaf until it reaches one of the veins which leads it to the midrib and then to the leaf stalk and the stem. Pupation takes place inside the stem. The total life cycle takes 2-3 weeks. As many as seven generations of this pest have been reported during the active season of the pest infestation.

Host plants. The bean fly has been found to infest the streak bean, cowpea, lima bean, soybean, *Cajanus, Canavalia* and *Dolichos.*

Damage. As a result of severe infestation, the leaves turn yellow, giving the plants a dry appearance. The stems turn brown, become swollen and break down. The attacked plants bear less pods which are mostly empty or else their seeds may be very small.

Management. (*i*) Apply 625 ml of monocrotophos 36SL or 750 ml of oxydemeton methyl 25EC in 625 litres of water per ha at 15-day intervals during flowering stage. (*ii*) Soil application of 10 kg of phorate 10G is effective upto 40 days of sowing.

7. *Chromatomyia horticola* (Goureau) (Pea leaf-miner, Diptera : Agromyzidae) (Fig. 4.1D)

Distribution. This pest is widely distributed in northern India.

Identification. The adults are two-winged flies having greyish black mesonotum and yellowish frons.

Life-history. The pest is active from December to April or May and is believed to pass the rest of the year in soil, in the pupal stage. The adults emerge at the beginning of December and after mating, start laying eggs singly, in leaf tissues. The eggs hatch in 2-3 days and the larvae feed between the lower and upper epidermis by making zig-zag tunnels. They are full-grown in about 5 days and pupate within the galleries. The adults emerge from the pupae in

6 days and the life-cycle is completed in 13-14 days. The pest passes through several broods from December to April-May.

Host plants. It feeds on a large number of cruciferous plants, antirrhinum, nasturtinum, pea, linseed (*Linum usitatissimum* L.) and potato (*Solanum tuberosum* L.).

Damage. The large number of tunnels made by the larvae interfere with photosynthesis and proper growth of the plants, making them look unattractive.

Management. Spray one litre of dimethoate 30EC in 250 litres of water per ha and repeat spray at 15-day interval. A waiting period of 20 days should be observed for picking of pods.

8. *Acyrthosiphon pisum* (Harris) (Pea aphid, Hemiptera : Aphididae) (Fig. 4.1E)

Distribution. Pea aphid is cosmopolitan in distribution in both Palaearctic and Nearctic regions and has been recorded from practically all the areas where the peas are grown.

Identification. Adult aphids are soft-bodied, long legged, pear-shaped, green yellow or pink in colour with long conspicuous cornicles.

Life-history. Both alate as well as apterous forms are present and these are generally females; males are rare. Winged and wingless males have been reported from Europe and USA but not from India. Reproduction is parthenogenetic and viviparous. It takes about a week to complete one generation and there are several overlapping generations in a year.

Damage. Both nymphs and adults suck the sap from young shoots, ventral surface of tender leaves, inflorescence and even on stems. There is curling of leaves, which become irregularly distorted, while the shoots become stunted and malformed. The leaves turn pale and dry. Honeydew secreted by the aphids encourages growth of sooty mould and this superficial black coating on leaves and stems hinders the photosynthetic activity of the plants, which become weak, thus affecting adversely the pod formation. Aphids are carriers of pea mosaic.

Host plant. Pea

Management. Spray 1·0 litre of dimethoate 30EC in 250 litres of water per ha when the attack starts and repeat after 15 days if necessary.

9. *Maruca testulalis* (Geyer) (Spotted pod borer, Lepidoptera : Pyralidae)

Distribution. This pest is wide spread in tropical and sub-tropical regions of the world.

Identification. The moth has a white cross band on the dark brown forewings and a dark border on the white hind wings. The larva is green with a brown head, short dark hairs and black warts on the body.

Life-history. The eggs are laid singly in the flowers or buds or on the pods of the host plants. After hatching, the young caterpillar enters the bud, flower or the pod. It feeds on the seeds within pods. The entrance hole is plugged with excreta. It pupates within debris or near surface of the ground. The moths shelter among lower leaves.

Host plants. It is an important pest of cowpea, lablab, green gram, black gram, pigeon pea, soybean, etc.

Damage. The larvae web together the flowers and feed on them and also bore into pods and feed on the seeds resulting in appreciable loss in yield of seeds.

Management. Chemical control measures are same as in case of gram pod borer.

10. *Adisura atkinsoni* Moore (Field bean pod borer, Lepidoptera : Noctuidae)

Distribution. This is a cold weather pest of lablab and red gram having a wide distribution in India.

Identification. The adult is a pale yellowish-brown moth, with V-shaped specks on fore wings and pale brown markings on hind wings. The full-grown larva is brownish-green and about 2.5 cm in length.

Life-history. The eggs are laid in the setting flowers and very young pods. A female may lay as many as 290-950 eggs. The eggs hatch in 2-3 days and the larvae bore into the pods and feed on the seeds. The larval stage lasts 14-15 days and pupation takes place in the soil. The pupal period is 8-16 days. During February to November, it hibernates in the pupal stage.

Host plants. This is mainly a pest of lab lab and red gram.

Damage. The larvae feed on flower buds and bore into the pods feeding on the developing seeds and cause considerable loss.

Management. Chemical control measures are same as in case of gram pod borer.

11. *Thosea aperiens* (Walker) (Green nettle slug–caterpillar, Lepidoptera: Cochlidiidae)

Distribution. This insect is widely distributed in India and Sri Lanka.

Identification. Fore wings of the adult moths are dark, cinereous-brown, whereas the hind wings are palish in colour. The wing expanse may vary from 30 to 35 mm. The greenish larvae which are 30 mm in length, feed on leaves. They have stinging hairs on their body and are thus a nuisance to the field workers, in addition to damaging the plants.

Life-history. The moths are active during October-November and lay eggs on host plants. The caterpillars on emergence feed on leaves till the end of December. When full-grown, they bore into the soil, construct a cocoon and hibernate there in the larval stage. During the following August-September, they pupate and subsequently emerge as moths. The period from the onset of pupation and the emergence as moths takes about 30 days. Normally, one life-cycle is completed in a year.

Host plants. In India, this insect is a pest of sorghum, pigeon pea, *Eleusine coracana* (finger millet), *Cassia auriculata* (Tanner's cassia), cowpea and tamarind. In Sri Lanka, it is reported to feed on *Dunbaria heynei,* an herbaceous climber.

Damage. The larvae defoliate the plants. The field workers when accidentally touch the stinging hair of the caterpillars may develop painful rashes on their hands and arms.

Management. Chemical control measures are same as in case of gram pod borer.

12. *Obereopsis brevis* (Gahan) (Girdle beetle, Coleoptera : Cerambycidae)

Identification. The adult is a small black beetle with hard shell-like exterior and rather long antennae. The freshly emerged adult is yellow, red, brown on the head, thorax and bases of elytra. The larva is white, soft-bodied worm with a dark head.

Life-history. The ovipositing female beetle girdles the stem twice and makes 3 punctures just above the lower ring before inserting a single egg through the largest whole into the pith. This results in dropping of the upper part of the stem. A female beetle lays 7-13 eggs and they hatch in 4-5 days. The larva tunnels upwards and downwards within the stem and a single larva can destroy the whole plant. The larval period lasts 34-47 days. Over-wintering takes place as the full- grown larva within the feeding tunnel in a gall-like chamber near the base of the plant in the girdled portion of the stem which has fallen out or under plant debris. The pupal period is 8-11 days.

Host plants. This is an important pest of soybean and also attacks cowpea and lablab.

Damage. The attack of this insect begins initially in the last week of July to first fortnight of August. The female of this insect feeds on the xylem of the stem. The larvae further damage the stem and make tunnels inside and fill these with excreta. The leaves and the growing points dry up. In later stages, the plant is cut at about 15-25 cm above the ground and broken stems can be seen in the field.

Management. Same as in case of bean fly.

13. *Riptortus pedestris* (Fabricius) (Pod bug, Hemiptera : Coreidae)

Distribution. This insect is widely distributed in pulse growing regions of India.

Identification. The adult is a dark-brown bug measuring 15 mm long.

Life-history. The adults mate 2-3 days after emergence and repeat it throughout life. Egg laying starts 12-14 days after emergence. A female lays, on an average, 115 eggs during on ovipositional period of 30 days. Eggs are laid singly on pods at their base and hatch in 3-4 days. There are 5 nymphal instars in about 16 days. The adult lives for 45-47 days.

Host plants. This is a pest of red gram, cowpea, lablab, soybean and other pulses.

Damage. The damage is caused by nymphs and adults by sucking juice from seeds piercing the pods in the process. The seeds within the pods become rough and rugged. Tender pods when attacked do not develop.

Management. Same as in case of tur pod bug.

*****

5

CHAPTER

PESTS OF OILSEEDS

Groundnut (*Arachis hypogaea*)

1. *Aphis craccivora* Koch (Groundnut aphid, Hemiptera: Aphididae).
2. *Stomopteryx nertaria* Meyrick (Groundnut leafminer, Lepidoptera : Gelechiidae)
3. *Holotrichia consanguinea* Blanchard (White grub, Coleoptera: Scarabaeidae)
4. *Sphenoptera perotetti* Guenee (Groundnut stem borer, Coleoptera : Buprestidae)
5. *Amsacta moorei* (Butler) (Red hairy caterpillar, Lepidoptera : Arctiidae)
6. *Aproaerema modicella* Deventer (Groundnut leaf-miner, Lepidoptera : Gelechiidae).
7. *Elasmolomus sordidus* (Fabricius) (Pod bug, Hemiptera : Lygaeidae)
8. *Odontotermes obesus* (Rambur) (Termite, Isoptera : Termitidae).

Mustard (*Brassica campestris*)

1. *Lipaphis erysimi* Kaltenbach (Mustard aphid, Hemiptera : Aphididae)
2. *Athalia lugens* (Klug) (Mustard sawfly, Hemiptera : Tenthredinidae)
3. *Bagrada hilaris* (Burmeister) (Painted bug, Hemiptera : Pentatomidae)
4. *Pieris brassicae* (Linnaeus) (Cabbage butterfly, Lepidoptera : Pieridae)
5. *Myzus persicae* (Sulzer) (Green peach aphid, Hemiptera : Aphididae)

Castor (*Ricinus communis*)

1. *Achaea janata* (Linnaeus) (Castor semilooper, Lepidoptera : Noctuidae)
2. *Dichocrocis punctiferalis* (Guenee) (Castor capsule borer, Lepidoptera : Pyralidae)
3. *Trileurodes ricini* Misra (Castor whitefly, Hemiptera : Aleyrodidae).

	4. *Euproctis lunata* Walker (Castor hairy caterpillar, Lepidoptera: Lymantriidae)
	5. *Asphondylia ricini* Mani (Gall fly, Diptera : Cecidomyiidae)
	6. *Parasa lepida* Cramer (Castor slug, Lepidoptera : (Limacodidae)
Sesame (*Sesamum indicum*)	1. *Antigastra catalaunalis* (Duponchel) (Til leaf and pod caterpillar, Lepidoptera : Pyralidae)
	2. *Acherontia styx* (Westwood) (Till hawk moth, Lepidoptera : Sphingidae)
	3. *Asphondylia sesami* Felt. (Sesame gall fly, Diptera : Cecidomyiidae)
	4. *Dasineura sesami* Grover (Til gall fly, Diptera : Cecidomyiidae)
Linseed (*Linum usitatissimum*)	1. *Dasineura lini* Barnes (Linseed gall midge, Diptera : Cecidomyiidae)
	2. *Spodoptera exigua* (Hubner) (Beet armyworm, Lepidoptera : Noctuidae)
Safflower (*Canthamus tinctorius*)	1. *Acanthiophilus helianthi* (Rossi) (Safflower bud fly, Diptera : Tephritidae)
	2. *Uroleucon compositae* (Theobold) (Safflower aphid, Hemiptera.: Aphididae)
	3. *Perigaea capensis* (Guenee) (Safflower caterpillar, Lepidoptera.: Noctuidae)
	4. *Eublemma rivula* Moore (Safflower semilooper, Lepidoptera : Noctuidae)
	5. *Uroleucon compositae* (Theobald) (Safflower aphid, Hemiptera: Aphididae)
Sunflower (*Helianthus annuus*)	1. *Helicoverpa armigera* (Hubner) (Head borer) Lepidoptera : Noctuidae)
	2. *Spilosoma obliqua* Walker (Bihar hairy caterpillar, Lepidoptera: Arctiidae)
	3. *Agrotis* spp. (Cutworms, Lepidoptera : Noctuidae)

The total oilseed production in India was 297.55 lakh tonnes during 2007-08, which is estimated to be 281.57 lakh tonnes during 2008-09. The production of oilseeds is estimated at 152.33 lakh tonnes during 2009-10, which is about 15 per cent lower than the production during 2008-09. All the oilseed crops are attacked by a variety of insect pests, which cause considerable loss in yield.

GROUNDNUT

1. *Aphis craccivora* Koch (Groundnut aphid, Hemiptera : Aphididae) (Fig. 5.1A)

Distribution. Groundnut aphid is distributed throughout India. It has also been recorded in Africa, Argentina and Chile.

Identification. The winged adults are soft-bodied insects with black wings.

Life-history. Even without fertilization, the females may produce 8-20 young ones in a life span of 10-12 days. The young nymphs are brownish and they pass through four moults to become adults in 5-8 days. The apterous females start producing brood within 24 hours of attaining that stage. Breeding occurs almost throughout the year and both alatae and apterae are present.

Host plants. This is one of the most serious pests of groundnut. It also attacks peas, beans, pulses, safflower and some weeds.

Damage. The nymphs and adults suck the sap, usually from the underside of leaves. Infestation in the early stages causes stunting of the plants as well as reducing their vigour. When the attack occurs at the time of flowering and pod formation, the yield is reduced considerably. Infestation on the groundnut crop usually occurs 4-6 weeks after sowing. The aphid is also vector of rossette disease of groundnut.

Management. (*i*) The coccinellid beetles, *Menochilus sexmaculatus* and *Ischiodon javana* are the main predators of this aphid pest. (*ii*) As soon as the pest appears on growing points, spray 625 ml of malathion 50EC or 425 ml of dimethoate 30EC or 425 ml of oxydemeton methyl 25EC in 200 litres of water per ha.

2. *Aproaerema modicella* (Deventer) (Groundnut leaf-miner, Lepidoptera: Gelechiidae)

Distribution. This pest is distributed all over India, Pakistan, Sri Lanka, Myanmar, China, Indonesia, Malaysia, the Philippines and Thailand. In India, it is most serious in Tamil Nadu, Karnataka and Andhra Pradesh as well as Maharashtra and Gujarat.

Identification. The adult is a small bronze moth with a wing expanse of about 1 cm and a small distinct white spot on fore wings. The larva is small and green, and has a conspicuous dark head.

Life-history. The female moth lays upto 470 eggs singly on leaves and on shoots. The eggs hatch after about 3 days. The newly hatched larva measures about 1.5 mm in length. After wandering about for some time, it mines into the leaves and, later on, bites its way out. It then webs together a number of leaflets and feeds inside the chamber, thus formed. The larvae pass through 3 instars and are full grown in 9-17 days, when they measure 6-8 mm in length and turn dirty green. They prepare silken cocoons to pupate. The pupal period lasts about 4 days. The adults may live for 5-20 days. There are 6-10 generations during a year.

Host plants. Besides groundnut, the insect also attacks soybean and pigeonpea.

Damage. As a result of the mining, skeletonizing and webbing together of the leaves, the crop suffers serious losses. In badly infested fields, the plants present a look as if the crop has been scorched.

Management. (*i*) Crop rotation with non-leguminous crops and intercropping with cowpea are reported to reduce the severity of attack. (*ii*) Light traps placed at ground level early in the season to collect and destroy the moths have been reported to reduce pest incidence; (*iii*) As the attack is more severe under drought conditions, it can be reduced by irrigation. (*iv*) Spray 2.0 kg of carbaryl 50WP or 350 ml of oxydemeton methyl 25EC in 250 litres of water per ha.

3. *Holotrichia consanguinea* Blanchard (White grub, Coleoptera : Scarabaeidae)

Distribution. The insect appeared as a pest of groundnut in 1957 in the Gujarat state and is now distributed in Uttar Pradesh, Bihar, Haryana, Himachal Pradesh, Rajasthan and Punjab.

Identification. The adult beetles are dull brown and measure about 18 mm in length and 7 mm in width. The grubs when full-grown are about 35 mm long and are white, having a brown head and prominent thoracic legs.

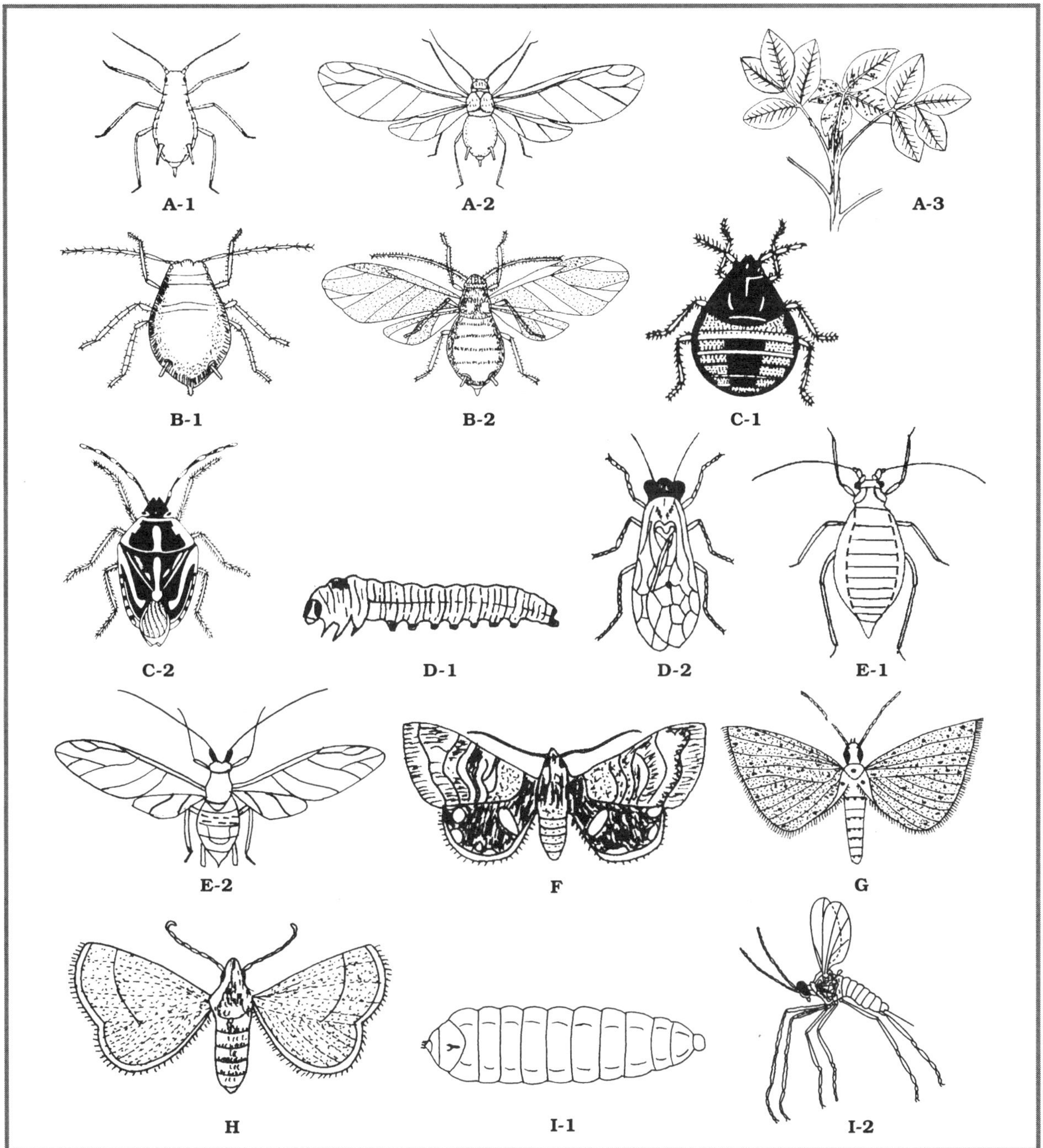

Fig. 5.1 Pests of oilseeds. **A.** Groundnut aphid, *Aphis craccivora*; A-1. Nymph, A-2. Adult, A-3. Infested plant **B.** Mustard aphid, *Lipaphis erysimi*; B-1. Wingless adult, B-2. Winged adult. **C.** Painted bug, *Bagrada hilaris*; C-1. Nymph, C-2. Adult. **D.** Mustard saw fly, *Athalia lugens*; D-1. Larva, D-2. Adult **E.** Green peach aphid, *Myzus persicae*; E-1 Apterus female adult, E-2. Alate female adult. **F.** Castor semilooper, *Achaea janata*. **G.** Castor capsule borer, *Dichocrocis punctiferalis*. **H.** Castor slug, *Parasa lepida*. **I.** Sesame gall fly, *Asphondylia sesami*; I-1. Larva, I-2. Adult.

Life-history. The adult beetles lay eggs singly up to a depth of 10 cm. The eggs hatch in 7-10 days. The newly hatched grubs measure about 12 mm in length and their development is completed in 8-10 weeks. After the monsoon, the full-grown larvae migrate to a considerable depth in the soil for pupation. The pupa is semicircular and creamy white and the pupal stage lasts about a fortnight. The beetles remain in the soil at a depth of 10-20 cm and come out for feeding at night. Adults formed in November remain in soil till next June. Their population is maximum in the rainy season and there seems to be only one generation in a year.

Host plants. Groundnut and all types of oilseed plants, vegetables, sugarcane, pulses, cereals, etc.

Damage. The grubs eat away the nodules, the fine rootlets and may also girdle the main root, ultimately killing the plants. At night, the beetles feed on foliage and may completely defoliate even trees like *neem (Azadirachta indica)* and banyan *(Ficus bengalensis).*

Management. (*i*) Plough the fields twice during May-June. It would help in exposing the beetles resting in the soil. (*ii*) Treat the seed before sowing with 12.5 ml of chlorpyriphos 20EC per kg of kernels. (*iii*) Collect and destroy the beetles continuously for 2-3 days after the first monsoon rains during the late evening hours. (*iv*) Kill the beetles by spraying 500 g of carbaryl 50WP in 250 litres of water per ha on the preferred host plants like *ber, guava, rukmanjani,* grapevines, almond, etc. The spray should be carried out in the afternoon and repeated after every rainfall till the middle of July. (*v*) Apply 10 kg of phorate 10G or 33 kg of carbofuran 3G per ha in the soil at or before sowing.

4. *Sphenoptera perotetti* Guenee (Groundnut stem borer, Coleoptera : Buprestidae)

Distribution. This pest infests the groundnut crop in Andhra Pradesh, Bihar, Delhi, Gujarat, Kerala, Tamil Nadu, Madhya Pradesh, Maharashtra and Karnataka. It has not been recorded anywhere outside India.

Identification. The adult is a small jewel-like beetle, 10-12 mm in length with a striking metallic shine over a dark brown background. The full-grown grub is whitish in appearance.

Life-history. The beetles lay scale like eggs and glue them on to the branches. The slender, creamy white grubs bore into the branches and travel down the main stem and ultimately reach the tap-root. When full-grown, the larvae pupate inside the tunnels. The pupal period lasts 7-10 days. The beetles emerge from the tunnels by cutting their way out and they start the next generation. The infested plants receive a set-back and are killed when the borer reaches the tap-root.

Host plants. Besides groundnut, it attacks sesamum, gram and other pulses.

Damage. As a result of the larvae boring into the stems and because of the feeding injury to the roots, some plants are killed. The damage appears in patches.

Management. The pest can be suppressed by cutting and destroying the infested branches thus preventing the grubs from entering the tap-root. No chemical control is possible.

MUSTARD

1. *Lipaphis erysimi* (Kaltenbach) (Mustard aphid, Hemiptera : Aphididae) (Fig. 5.1B)

Distribution. The mustard aphid is worldwide in distribution and found throughout India.

Identification. The aphids are minute, soft-bodied and light green insects having a pair of short tubes called cornicles on the postero-dorsal region of the abdomen.

Life-history. The insect breeds parthenogenetically and the females give birth to 26-133 nymphs. They grow very fast and are full-fed in 7-10 days. About 45 generations are completed in a year. The winged forms are produced in autumn and spring, and they spread from field to field and from locality to locality.

Damage. Both the nymphs and adults suck cell-sap from leaves, stems, inflorescence or the developing pods. Due to the very high population of the pest, the vitality of plants is greatly reduced. The leaves acquire a curly appearance, the flowers fail to form pods and the developing pods do not produce healthy seeds. The honeydew excreted by the aphids provides congenial conditions for the growth of sooty mould on the plant. In case of severe infestation, the crop yield may be reduced by even 80 per cent or more.

Host plants. The mustard aphid is a serious pest of cruciferous oilseeds like *toria, sarson, raya, taramira* and *Brassica* vegetables like cabbage, cauliflower, knol-khol, etc

Management. (*i*) Early sowing reduces the incidence of mustard aphid at many locations in India. (*ii*) Three rounds of manual removal (clipping) of aphid infested twigs at 15 day intervals starting with the first appearance of the pest has been found effective if cheap labour is available. (*iii*) Apply any one of the following insecticides when the population of the pest reaches 50-60 aphids per 10 cm terminal portion of the central shoot or when an average of 0.5-1.0 cm terminal portion of central shoot is covered by aphids or when plants infested by aphids reach 40-50 per cent: **(*a*) *Foliar sprays*.** 625-1000 ml of oxydemeton methyl 25EC, dimethoate 30EC, quinalphos 25EC, malathion 50EC; 940-1500 ml of chlorpyriphos 20EC, 100 g of thiamethoxam 25WG in 200-315 litres of water per ha depending on the stage of the crop. **(*b*) *Granular insecticides*.** 10 kg of phorate 10G or 33 kg of carbofuran 3G per ha followed by a light irrigation.

2. *Bagrada hilaris* (Burmeister) (Painted bug, Hemiptera : Pentatomidae) (Fig. 5.1C)

Distribution. The painted bug is a serious pest of cruciferous crops and is widely distributed in Myanmar, Sri Lanka, India, Iraq, Arabia and East Africa.

Identification. The adult bugs are 3.71 mm long and 3.33 mm broad. They are sub-ovate, black and have a number of orange or brownish spots. The full-grown nymphs are about 4 mm long and 2.66 mm broad. They are black with a number of brown markings.

Life-history. These bugs lay oval, pale-yellow eggs singly or in groups of 3-8 on leaves, stalks, pods and sometimes on the soil. A female bug may lay 37-102 eggs in its life-span of 3-4 weeks. The eggs hatch in 3-5 days during summer and 20 days during December. The nymphs develop fully in five stages and transform themselves into adults in 16-22 days during summer and 25-34 days during winter. The entire life-cycle is completed in 19-54 days and it passes through 9 generations in a year.

Host plants. Besides cruciferous crops, it has also been observed feeding on rice, sugarcane, indigo and coffee.

Damage. The painted bug appears at two stages of crop growth, i.e. seedling and maturity, and many times infestation is carried even to threshing floor. Both nymphs and adults suck cell sap from the leaves and developing pods, which gradually wilt and dry up. Severe attack at seedling stage may even kill the plants. The nymphs and adult bugs also excrete a sort of resinous material which spoils the pods.

Management. (*i*) Give first irrigation 3-4 weeks after sowing as it reduces the bug population significantly (*ii*) Spray one litre of malathion 50EC or 625 ml of quinalphos 25EC in 150-200 litres of water per ha once in October and again in March-April.

3. *Athalia lugens* (Klug) (Mustard sawfly, Hymenoptera : Tenthredinidae) (Fig. 5.1D)

Distribution. The mustard sawfly is widely distributed in Indonesia, Taiwan, Myanmar and the Indian sub-continent.

Identification. The adults are small orange yellow insects with black markings on the body and have smoky wings with black veins. The larvae are dark green and have 8 pairs of abdominal prolegs. There are five black stripes on the back, and the body has wrinkled appearance. A full-grown larva measures 16-18 mm in length.

Life-history. The adults lay 30-35 eggs singly, in slits made with saw like ovipositors along the underside of the leaf margins. The eggs hatch in 4-8 days and the larvae feed exposed in groups of 3-6 on the leaves during morning and evening. They pass through seven stages and are full-grown in 16-35 days. The full-fed larvae descend the plant and enter the soil to a depth of 25-30 mm. There, they pupate in water proof oval cocoons made of silk and emerge from them as adults in 11-31 days. Thus, the life-cycle is completed in 31-34 days. The pest completes 2-3 generations from October to March.

Host plants. It feeds on various cruciferous plants like mustard, *toria,* rapeseed, cabbage, cauliflower, knol-khol, turnip, radish, etc.

Damage. It is a serious pest of all crucifers at the seedling stage. The grubs alone are destructive. They bite holes into leaves preferring the young growth and skeletonize the leaves completely. The older plants, when attacked, do not bear seed.

Management. Same as in case of painted bug.

4. *Myzus persicae* (Sulzer) (Green peach aphid, Hemiptera : Aphididae) (Fig. 5.1E)

Distribution. This insect is distributed throughout India.

Identification. The aphids are minute (2.0-2.5 mm long), delicate, pear-shaped, yellowish-green winged or wingless insects.

Life-history. The green peach aphid remains active from December to March with peak activity during February. The nymph undergoes 4-5 instars taking 4-7 days for apterous and 5-8 days for alate forms. Apterous adults produce 5-92 young ones per female while the alate forms produce 8-49 nymphs. Longevity of adult is 15-27 days for alate and 10-25 days for apterous forms.

Damage. Both nymphs and adults damage plants by actively sucking their sap. After the appearance of inflorescence, the aphid congregates on terminal buds and feeds there. As a result, there is flower shedding, poor-pod formation and shrivelling of grains. The insect also transmits virus diseases. The honeydew attracts sooty mould.

Host plants. Besides mustard and other cruciferous plants, the pest also attacks peaches, beans, potato, tobacco, etc.

Management. (*i*) Sow the crop in first week of October. (*ii*) Spray 500 ml of dimethoate 30EC or 625 ml of oxydemeton methyl 25EC in 250 litres of water/ha when aphids start congregating on top flower buds. Only one spray is needed.

CASTOR

1. *Trialeurodes ricini* Misra (Castor whitefly, Hemiptera : Aleyrodidae)

Distribution. The castor whitefly has been reported from India and Pakistan.

Identification. The adults are pale yellow with white wings covered with waxy powder. The nymphs are translucent, light yellow in colour and are covered with thick waxen filaments.

Life-history. This pest is active from February to November. The eggs are laid in small clusters on the undersurface of tender leaves. The incubation period is 3-5 days. On emergence, the nymphs attach themselves to leaves and become full-grown after four moultings. The life-cycle is completd in 19-21 days during July, August and September.

Host plants. It is primarily a pest of castor but the nymphs also feed on the leaves and stems of *Breynia rhamnoides* and *Achras zapota.*

Damage. As a result of sucking of sap by the nymphs, the leaves show yellow patches initially. Later on, there is a gradual drying of the leaves and ultimately the plants die.

Management. Spray one litre of malathion 50 EC or 625 ml of dimethoate 30 EC or oxydemeton methyl 25 EC or formothion 25 EC or 200 ml of phosphamidon 100 EC in 625 litres of water per ha and repeat at 2-3 week intervals.

2. *Achaea janata* (Linnaeus) (Castor semilooper, Lepidoptera : Noctuidae) (Fig. 5.1F)

Distribution. This is a serious pest of castor in all parts of India and Pakistan, and has also been reported from Sri Lanka and Thailand.

Identification. The adult is a pale reddish brown moth with a wing expanse of 6-7 cm. The wings are decorated with broad zig-zag markings, a large pale area and dark brown patches. The full-grown larva is dark and is marked with prominent blue-black, yellow and reddish stripes. It has a pair of reddish processes and also a dorsal hump near the head end of the body. There is a characteristic white mark on the head.

Life-history. A female lays up to 450 eggs during its life span. The egg, being about 1 mm in length, is fairly large and also has on its surface a few ridges and furrows which radiate from the circular depression at the apex. The larva emerges by cutting a hole in the egg-shell in 2-5 days and devours it immediately. The larva feeds and moults 4-5 times and becomes full-grown in 15-20 days. The grown-up larva prepares a loose cocoon of coarse silk and some soil particles, and pupates under the fallen leaves on the soil, usually at the edge of the field. In some cases, pupation also takes place within the folded leaves on the plant itself. The pupal stage lasts 10-15 days and the moths, on emergence, feed on the soft fruits of citrus, mango, etc. There are 5-6 generations in a year.

Host plants. Besides castor, the insects feed on *Zizyphus*, accacia, pomegranate, rose, euphorbid, etc.

Damage. The caterpillars feed voraciously on castor leaves, starting from the edges inwards and leaving behind only the midribs and the stalks. With the excessive loss of foliage, the seed yield is reduced considerably.

Management. Apply 625 ml of methyl parathion 25EC in 625 litres of water per ha.

3. *Dichocrocis punctiferalis* (Guenee) (Castor capsule borer, Lepidoptera: Pyralidae) (Fig. 5.1G)

Distribution. This borer is distributed throughout India wherever castor is grown such as Uttar Pradesh, Bihar, Orissa, Maharashtra, Gujarat, Karnataka, Andhra Pradesh and Tamil Nadu.

Identification. The moths are orange yellow, with black markings on both the wings. The full-grown caterpillar measures 25-30 mm in length, is reddish brown, with black blotches all over the body and a pale stripe on the lateral side.

Life-history. The moths lay eggs on leaves and other soft parts of the plant. The eggs hatch in about a week. The larvae pass through 4-5 instars and are full-fed in 2-3 weeks. Pupation takes place inside the seed or sometimes in the frass that collects after feeding. The pupal stage lasts about one week. The life-cycle is completed in 4-5 weeks and 3 generations are completed in a year.

Host plants. It is a polyphagous pest attacking besides castor many other plants.

Damage. The attack by this borer is recognized from a distance by the webbed capsule heads. The yield is reduced considerably since the capsules and the seeds within are damaged.

Management (*i*) It is advisable that the infested shoots and capsules may be collected and destroyed. (*ii*) Spray 2.5 kg of carbaryl 50WP in 625 litres of water per ha and repeat at 15-day intervals.

4. *Euproctis lunata* Walker (Castor hairy caterpillar, Lepidoptera: Lymantriidae)

Distribution. The castor hairy caterpillar is widely distributed in India particularly in Uttar Pradesh, Orissa, Haryana, Madhya Pradesh, Andhra Pradesh, Karnataka and Tamil Nadu.

Identification. The moths are pale yellow. Full-grown larvae measure 35-40 mm and are dark grey, with a wide white dorsal stripe, and have long hair all over body.

Life-history. Moths lay a large number of eggs in clusters on the underside of leaves. The eggs are covered with the female anal tuft of brown hair. They hatch in 5-7 days and the young larvae feed gregariously for the first few days. Later on, they disperse and feed individually. They pass through six stages and are full-fed in 2-3 weeks. The full-grown caterpillars make loose, silken cocoons in the plant debris lying on the ground and pupate inside. The pupal stage lasts about one week in the summer. During the winter months, the egg, larval and pupal stages may last 10, 85 and 20 days, respectively. The pest passes through several generations in a year.

Host plants. Besides castor, it has also been observed feeding on linseed, groundnut and grapevine.

Damage. Caterpillars feed on the leaves of various host plants and in case of severe infestation, they may cause complete defoliation. The attacked plants remain stunted and produce very little seed.

Management. Spray 625 ml of methyl parathion 50EC in 625 litres of water per ha.

5. *Parasa lepida* Cramer (Castor slug, Lepidoptera : Limacodidae) (Fig. 5.1H)

Distribution. The insect is of common occurrence in India, Malaysia and Sri Lanka.

Identification. The moth is short and stout with fore wings predominantly green in the middle and brownish at the end. The full-grown larva is flat, fleshy and greenish in colour with white lines on the body. It is covered with spines having red or black tips.

Life-history. The female moths lay flat shining eggs in batches of 15-35 on the under surface of the leaves of host plants. The eggs hatch in 7 days and the young larvae start feeding in clusters on the under surface of leaves. The larva passes through five instars and is fully developed in 40-42 days. It then pupates in a hard shell-like greyish cocoon on the tree trunk. The pupal stage lasts 20-28 days and the life cycle is completed in about 10 weeks. The pest remains active throughout the year.

Host plants. It is a serious pest of sporadic occurrence on castor, mango, pomegranate, citrus, coconut, palm, rose, wood apple, country almond, etc.

Damage. The young caterpillars feed gregariously by scraping the undersurface of the leaves. The loss of sap from plant tissue reduces the vitality of plants and the leaves dry up. As the larvae grow, they get scattered and feed on the entire leaf and cause defoliation.

Management. Same as in case of castor hairy caterpillar.

SESAME

1. *Antigastra catalaunalis* (Duponchel) (Til leaf and pod caterpillar, Lepidoptera : Pyralidae)

Distribution. The sesame leaf and pod caterpillar is distributed throughout India. This species has also been reported from Europe, Africa, Cyprus, Malta, Indonesia and South-east Africa.

Identification. The moth is a small insect with a wing span of about 2 cm having dark brown markings on the wing-tips. The caterpillars are pale yellow, when young, but gradually become green and develop black dots all over the body. The full-grown larva measures 14-17 mm.

Life-history. Females lay up to 140 eggs singly on the tender portions of plants at night. The eggs are shiny, pale-green and they hatch in 2-7 days, depending upon the season. On emerging, the young larva, which measures about 2 mm in length, feeds for a little while on the leaf epidermis or within the leaf tissue. Soon after, it binds together the tender leaves of the growing shoot with the help of silken threads and continues to feed in the webbed mass. The size of this rolled mass increases gradually as the caterpillar grows older. It becomes full-grown in about 10 days in summer, but the period may be prolonged to 33 days in winter. The grown-up larvae creep to the ground and pupate in silken cocoons in soil. Sometimes, pupation also takes place in the plant itself. Pupal development is completed in 4-20 days, depending upon the season. In summer, a generation is completed in about 23 days but in the winter it takes about 67 days.

Host plants. Til (*Sesamum indicum* and *S. orientale*)

Damage. Young caterpillars feed on leaves. They also bore into the shoots, flowers, buds and pods. An early attack kills the whole plant, but infestation of the shoots at a later stage hampers further growth and flowering.

Management. (*i*) Collect and destroy the webbed leaves and infested pods (*ii*) Spray the crop twice (first at pest appearance and then at flowering stage) with 250 ml of fenvalerate 20EC or 375 ml of deltamethrin 2.8 EC or thrice with 500 ml of cypermethrin 10EC at pest appearance, flowering and pod formation in 250 litres of water per ha.

2. *Acherontia styx* (Westwood) (Til hawk-moth, Lepidoptera : Sphingidae)

Distribution. This pest of sesamum is common in India and is also distributed in Indonesia, Sri Lanka, the Philippines and Myanmar.

Identification. The adult is a large reddish brown, robust thick-set moth with a wing span of about 10 cm. The forewings are decorated with a mixture of dark-brown and grey patterns with dark or black wavy markings and a prominent yellow spot on each wing. There is a prominent Death's head mark on the thorax. The full-grown caterpillar measures about

5 cm in length and 1 cm in width. It often retracts some of its anterior body segments and looks like a sphinx. The horn-like projections on the hind end of the abdomen are conspicuous. The body of the larva is plump and is decorated with a pleasant mixture of soft colours.

Host plants. Besides sesamum, it has been reported on potato, brinjal, lablab and ornamental plants such as balsam.

Life-history. The moths lay globular eggs singly on the underside of leaves of food plants. The eggs are conspicuous since they are fairly large. They are greenish white when freshly laid but turn yellow later on. The pale-yellow larvae emerge in 2-5 days and start feeding on leaves. The larval period is usually long and may last two months or more. The pupal stage lasts 2-3 weeks in summer and about 7 months in winter. There are 3 generations in a year.

Damage. The larvae feed voraciously on leaves and defoliate the plants. The insect is capable of inflicting heavy damage at times, but generally it is not a very serious pest in India. However, it draws our attention because of its peculiar characteristics.

Management. The pest can be suppressed by hand-picking and destroying (by immersing in kerosene oil) the larvae in the initial stages of attack and also by ploughing up the soil in winter.

3. *Asphondylia sesami* Felt. (Sesame gall fly, Diptera : Cecidomyiidae) (Fig. 5.1l)

Distribution. The sesame gall fly, also known as the sesamum gall-midge, occurs all over India and sometimes assumes serious proportions, particularly in southern India. It has been recorded in Tamil Nadu, Andhra Pradesh, Kerala, Madhya Pradesh, Gujarat, Maharashtra and Rajasthan.

Identification. The adult is mosquito-like fly with bright coloured wings.

Life-history. The female lays eggs singly in buds, flowers and developing capsules. The eggs hatch in 2-4 days. The young maggots feed on floral parts and cause malformation of the buds which fail to develop into seeds. The larvae complete their development in 14-21 days and pupate inside the galls. The moths emerge from the galls in 7-12 days. The life-cycle is completed in 23-37 days. There are several generations in a year.

Host plant. Sesame

Damage. As a result of feeding by maggots, the buds develop into galls and produce no fruits and seeds. When infestation is severe, the crop may be a total failure.

Management. (*i*) Clip the galls; pick and burn the shed buds (*ii*) Spray 2.5 kg of carbaryl 50WP in 625 litres of water per ha.

LINSEED

Dasineura lini Barnes (Linseed gall midge, Diptera : Cecidomyiidae)

Distribution. This insect appears as a serious pest of linseed in some parts of India., including Andhra Pradesh, Madhya Pradesh, Bihar, Uttar Pradesh, Delhi and Punjab.

Identification. The adult is small delicate, mosquito like orange coloured insect.

Life-history. The female lays 29-103 smooth, transparent eggs in the folds of 8-17 flowers or in tender green buds, either singly or in clusters of 3-5. The eggs hatch in 2-5 days. Just after emergence, the larvae are transparent, with a yellow patch on the abdomen. These larvae feed inside flower buds and eat the contents. They pass through four instars in 4-10 days and when full-grown, become deep pink and measure about 2 mm in length. The full-grown maggots drop to the ground, prepare a cocoon and pupate in the soil. The pupal period lasts 4-9 days. A generation is completed in 10-24 days. There are four overlapping generations during the season.

Host plant. Linseed.

Damage. Damage is the result of feeding by maggots on buds and flowers. Consequently, no pod-formation takes place.

Management. (*i*) The adult flies can be killed by using light traps. The flies are also attracted in day-time to molasses or *gur* added to water. (*ii*) As the incidence of this pest is more on the late-sown crop as compared with the normal-sown crop, the practice of normal-sown crops should be adopted if possible.

SAFFLOWER

1. *Acanthiophilus helianthi* (Rossi) (Safflower bud fly, Diptera : Tephritidae)

Distribution. This pest has been reported from Delhi, Uttar Pradesh, Haryana and Madhya Pradesh in India.

Identification. The adult fly is ash coloured with light brown wings.

Life-history. The females lay eggs in clusters of 6-24 within the flower buds or the flowers. The eggs hatch in about one day in April and young maggots start feeding on the florets and the thalamus. Within one week they grow to the full and attain a size of 5×1.5 mm. They pupate inside the buds. The pupal stage lasts 7 days. The adults emerge out of the bud through the holes made by the larvae before they pupate. Three generations are completed during a crop season.

Host plant. Safflower.

Damage. The injury is caused by the maggots which feed upon the floral parts including the thalamus. The infested buds begin to rot and an offensive smelling fluid oozes at the apices giving a soaked appearance to the buds. The pest causes reduction in the yield of safflower seed.

Management. The early removal and destruction of infested buds is helpful in checking the spread of the pest.

2. *Uroleucon compositae* (Theobald) (Safflower aphid, Hemiptera: Aphididae) (Fig. 5.2.)

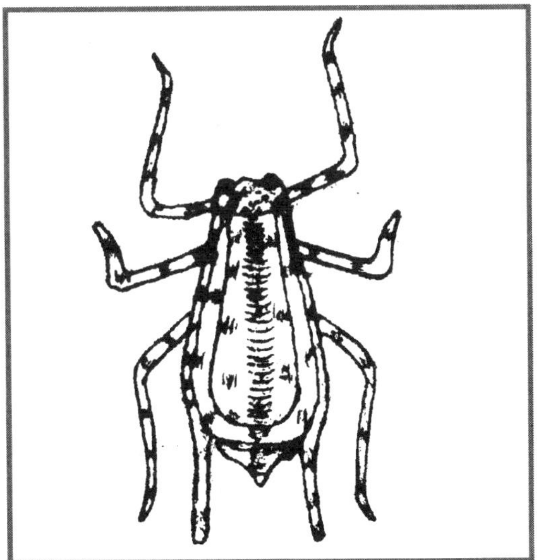

Fig. 5.2 Pests of oilseeds. Sawflower aphid, *Uroleucon compositae*

Distribution. The pest is known to be distributed in Punjab, Haryana, Uttar Pradesh, Madhya Pradesh and Karnataka.

Identification. The adults are small, soft bodied and appear shining black. Tiny nymphs are reddish brown in colour.

Life-history. The aphid is active from December

to April and total life cycle is completed in about 15 to 25 days. It reproduces parthenogenetically and there are four nymphal instars. Average fecundity was recorded to be nearly 32 numphs.

Host plant. Safflower.

Damage. Both nymphs and adult aphids cause damage by sucking sap from leaves, twigs and capsules resulting in to weak and stunted plants which may ultimately dry up. Initially the infestation is in lower plant parts but as the plants reach maturity infestation reaches inflorescence and capsules, Black sooty mould develops due to honeydew excreted by the aphids.

Management. To check damage by the aphid, spray 250 ml of dimethoate 30EC or 625 ml of chlorpyriphos 20EC in 250 litres of water per ha; the spray may be repeated after two weeks depending upon the infestation.

SUNFLOWER

1. *Helicoverpa armigera* (Hubner) (Head borer, Lepidoptera: Noctuidae)

The head or capitulum borer causes considerable damage to developing grains in the head capsule. The young larvae first attack the tender parts like bracts and petals, and later on shift to reproductive parts of the flower heads. Bigger larvae mostly feed on seeds by making tunnels in the body of the flower heads and often remain concealed. They may also shift to the backside of the heads and even leaves, and feeding may continue upto maturity. Star bud stage of the crop is most vulnerable and suffers maximum yield loss. The detailed account of life-history of the pest has been given in chapter 4.

Management. (*i*) Early sown crop usually suffers lower attack of the pest. (*ii*) The natural enemy complex on the crop is quite rich. The use of conventional insecticides should, therefore, be avoided. (*iii*) The pest may be controlled by 2-3 weekly sprays of NPV @ 375 LE/ha. (*iv*) In case of severe attack, especially on late sown crop, spray 2.5 kg of carbaryl 50WP or 2.0 kg of acephate 75SP or 2.5 litres of chlorpyriphos 20EC in 250 litres of water per ha at the initiation of starbud stage, and repeat after two weeks if necessary.

2. *Agrotis* spp. (Cutworms, Lepidoptera : Noctuidae)

The cutworms may be serious during March-April in fields where sunflower follows potato. Caterpillars cut the seedlings at the ground level. The pest has been described in chapter 13.

Management. (*i*) Sow the crop in ridges to avoid cutworm damage in the germinating seedlings. (*ii*) Where flat sowing is practiced, apply 5 litres of chlorpyriphos 20EC per ha before sowing. The insecticide should be mixed in 10 kg fine soil and broadcasted uniformly in the field after last ploughing before planking.

*****

6 CHAPTER

PESTS OF VEGETABLES

Solanaceous Vegetables

Brinjal (*Solanum melongena*)

1. *Leucinodes orbonalis* Guenee. (Brinjal shoot and fruit borer, Lepidoptera : Pyralidae)
2. *Henosepilachna dodecastigma* (Wiedemann) and *H.vigintioctopunctata* (Fabricius) (Hadda beetles, Coleoptera.: Coccinellidae)
3. *Eublema olivacea* Walker (Brinjal leaf roller, Lepidoptera : Noctuidae)
4. *Euzophera perticella* Rag. (Brinjal stem borer, Lepidoptera : Pyralidae)
5. *Urentius sentis* Distant (Brinjal lace-wing bug, Hemiptera : Tingidae)

Potato (*Solanum tuberosum*)

1. *Phthorimaea operculella* (Zeller) (Potato tuber moth, Lepidoptera : Gelechiidae)
2. *Agrotis ipsilon* (Hufnagel) (Greasy cutworm, Lepidoptera : Noctuidae)
3. *Henosepilachna vigintioctopunctata* (Fabricius) (Hadda beetle, Coleoptera: Coccinellidae)
4. *Myzus persicae* (Sulzer) (Green peach aphid, Hemiptera : Aphididae)
5. *Bemisia tabaci* (Gennadius) (Cotton whitefly, Hemiptera : Aleyrodidae)
6. *Globodera rostochinensis* Wollenweber (Golden nematode of potato, Tylenchida : Heteroderidae).
7. *Amrasca bigutulla bigutulla* Ishida (Jassid, Hemiptera: Cicadellidae)

Sweet potato (*Ipomea batatas*)

1. *Cylas formicarius* (Fabricius) (Sweet potato weevil, Coleoptera: Apionidae)
2. *Aspidomorpha miliacis* (Fabricius) (Tortoise beetle, Coleoptera: Cassididae)

	3. *Spodoptera litrua* (Fabricius) (Tobacco caterpillar, Lepidoptera: Noctuidae)
	4. *Spilosoma obliqua* Walker (Bihar hairy caterpillar, Lepidoptera: Arctiidae)
Tomato (*Lycopersicum esculentum*)	1. *Euzophera perticella* Rag. (Brinjal stem borer, Lepidoptera : Pyralidae)
	2. *Helicoverpa armigera* (Hubner) (Tomato fruit borer, Lepidoptera : Noctuidae)
	3. *Spodoptera litura* (Fabricius) (Tobacco caterpillar, Lepidoptera: Noctuidae)
	4. *Liriomyza trifolii* (Burgess) (Diptera : Agromyzidae)

Malvaceous Vegetables

Okra (*Abelmoschus esculentus*)	1. *Earias insulana* (Boisduval) and *E. vittella* (Fabricius) (Spotted bollworms, Lepidoptera : Noctuidae)
	2. *Dysdercus koenigii* (Fabricius) (Red cotton bug, Hemiptera : Pyrrhocoridae)
	3. *Amrasca biguttula* (Ishida) (Cotton jassid, Hemiptera: Cicadellidae)
	4. *Bemisia tabaci* (Gennadius) (Cotton whitefly, Hemiptera : Aleyrodidae)
	5. *Oxycarenus hyalinipennis* Costa (Dusky cotton bug, Hemiptera.: Lygaeidae)
	6. *Sylepta derogata* (Fabricius) (Cotton leaf-roller, Lepidoptera : Pyralidae)

Cruciferous Vegetables

Cabbage (*Brassica oleracea* var. *capitata*), cauliflower (*Brassica oleracea* var. *botrytis*)	1. *Thysanoplusia orichalcea* (Fabricius) (Cabbage semilooper, Lepidoptera : Noctuidae)
	2. *Trichoplusia ni* (Hubner) (Cabbage green semilooper, Lepidoptera : Noctuidae)
	3. *Plutella xylostella* (Linnaeus) (Diamond back moth, Lepidoptera : Yponomeutidae)
	4. *Pieris brassicae* (Linnaeus) (Cabbage butterfly, Lepidoptera : Pieridae)
	5. *Spodoptera litura* (Fabricius) (Tobacco caterpillar, Lepidoptera: Noctuiidae)
	6. *Hellula undalis* (Fabricius) (Cabbage borer, Lepidoptera : Pyralidae
	7. *Crocidolomia binotalis* Zeller (Crucifer leaf-webber, Lepidoptera : Pyralidae)
	8. *Phyllotreta cruciferae* (Goeze) (Cabbage flea beetle, Coleoptera: Chrysomelidae)
Radish (*Raphanus sativus*)	1. *Bagrada hilaris* (Burmeister) (Painted bug, Hemiptera : Pentatomidae)
	2. *Hellula undalis* (Fabricius) (Cabbage borer, Lepidoptera : Pyralidae)
Turnip (*Brassica rapa*)	1. *Chromatomyia horticola* (Goureau) (Pea leaf-miner, Diptera : Agromyzidae)

	2. *Chaetocnema basalis* Bally (Flea beetle, Coleoptera : Alticidae)
Carrot (*Dacus carota*)	1. *Chromatomyia horticola* (Goureau) (Pea leaf-miner, Diptera : Agromyzidae) 2. *Chaetocnema basalis* Bally (Flea beetle, Coleoptera : Alticidae)

Cucurbitaceous Vegetables

Gourds (*Momordica charantia, Trichosanthes anguina, Lagenaria siceraria, Cucurbita pepo*)	1. *Aulacophora foveicollis* (Lucas) (Red pumpkin beetle, Coleoptera : Chrysomelidae) 2. *Bactrocera cucurbitae* (Coquillett) (Melon fruit fly, Diptera : Tephritidae) 3. *Thrips tabaci* Lindeman (Onion thrips, Thysanoptera : Thripidae) 4. *Epilachna* spp. (Hadda beetles, Coleoptera : Coccinellidae)

Lilliaceous Vegetables

Onion (*Allium cepa*), garlic (*Allium sativum*)	1. *Thrips tabaci* Lindeman (Onion thrips, Thysanoptera : Thripidae) 2. *Delia antiqua* (Meigen) (Onion maggot, Diptera : Anthomyiidae) 3. *Caliothrips indicus* (Bagnall) (Thrips, Thysanoptera : Thripidae) 4. *Spodoptera litura* (Fabricius (Tobacco caterpillar, Lepidoptera: Noctuidae)

Trapaceous Vegetables

Water-nut (*Trapa bispinosa*)	1. *Galerucella birmanica* (Jacoby) (Singhara beetle, Coleoptera : Chrysomelidae)

India is the second largest producer of vegetables in the world (ranks next to China) and accounts for about 15 per cent of the world's production of vegetables. India occupies the prime position in the production of cauliflower, second in onions and third in cabbage in the world. The total production of vegetables in India was 169.1 million tonnes during 2015-16. Five vegetables, viz. potato, tomato, onion, cabbage and cauliflower account for about 60 per cent of the total vegetable production in the country. Insect pests are a major threat to production of vegetables and cause considerable loss in terms of quality and quantity.

I. SOLANACEOUS VEGETABLES

BRINJAL

1. *Leucinodes orbonalis* Guenee (Brinjal shoot and fruit borer, Lepidoptera : Pyralidae) (Fig. 6.1A)

Distribution. This pest of brinjal fruits and shoots is widely distributed in Malaysia, Myanmar, Sri Lanka, India, Pakistan, Germany and East Africa.

Identification. The moth is white but has pale brown or black spots on the dorsum of the thorax and abdomen. Its wings are white with a pinkish or bluish tinge and are ringed with small hair along the apical and anal margins. The fore wings are ornamented with a number of black, pale and light brown spots. The moth measures about 2.0-2.2 cm across the spread wings. The caterpillars are creamy white when young, but light pink when full-grown. The measue about 1.8-2.3 cm in length.

Life-history. The female moths lay 80-120 creamy white eggs, singly or in batches of 2-4 on the underside of leaves, on green stems, flower buds or the calyces of fruits. The eggs hatch in 3-6 days and the young caterpillars bore into tender shoots near the growing points into flower buds or into the fruits. The larvae grow through 5 stages and are full-fed in 9-28 days. The mature larvae come out of their feeding tunnels and pupate in tough silken cocoons among the fallen leaves. The pupal stage lasts 6-17 days and the life-cycle is completed in 20-43 days during the active season. There are five overlapping generations in a year.

Damage. The caterpillar when attack the terminal shoots, the growing-points are killed. Damage to the fruits, particularly in the autumn, is very severe and it is not uncommon to see the whole of the crop destroyed by the borers.

Host plants. Besides brinjal, it has also been recorded feeding on many other solanaceous plants and occasionally on the green pods of peas also.

Management. (*i*) Cultivate resistant varieties like SM17-4, PBr 129-5, Punjab Barsati and ARU-2 among long-fruited types and Pusa Purple Round and Punjab Neelam among round-fruited types. (*ii*) Remove and destroy all the affected shoots and fruits with borers inside. (*iii*) Avoid continuous cropping of brinjal crop. (*iv*) Spray 3-4 times at 2-week interval using 250 - 300 litres of water per ha with anyone of the following insecticides as the attack starts: (*a*) ***Organochlorine***. Two litres of endosulfan 35EC. (*b*) ***Organophosphates***. Two litres of quinalphos 25EC, 1.4 litres of monocrotophos 36EC, 1.25 litres of triazophos 40EC. (*c*) ***Carbamate***. Two kg of carbaryl 50WP. (*d*) ***Synthetic pyrethroids***. 250 ml of fenvalerate 20EC, 100 ml of permethrin 50EC, 500 ml of cypermethrin 10EC, 400 ml of decamethrin 2.8EC.

2. *Urentius sentis* Distant (Brinjal lace-wing bug, Hemiptera : Tingidae) (Fig. 6.1B)

Distribution. The lace-wing bug is distributed in the north-western parts of the Indian sub-continent and is common in the plains.

Identification. The adult bugs measure about 3 mm in length and are straw coloured on the dorsal side and black on the ventral side. On the pronotum and wings, there is a network of markings and veins. The full-grown nymphs are about 2 mm long and 1.35 mm broad. They are pale ochraceous, and are stoutly built, with very prominent spines.

Life-history. The bugs lay 35-44 shining white nipple-shaped eggs singly in the tissues on the underside of the leaves. The eggs hatch in 3-12 days and the young nymphs feed gregariously on the lower surface of the leaves, but the fully-developed nymphs are found feeding and moving about individually on thc lower surface as well as on the upper surface. They grow through five stages and transform themselves into adults in 10-23 days. The insect passes through 8 overlapping generations in a year.

Host plant. Except for brinjal, it has not been recorded feeding on any other plant.

Damage. The nymphs and the adults suck the sap from leaves and cause yellowish spots which, together with the black scale-like excreta deposited by them, impart a characteristic mottled appearance to the infested leaves. When the attack is severe, about 50 per cent of the crop may be destroyed.

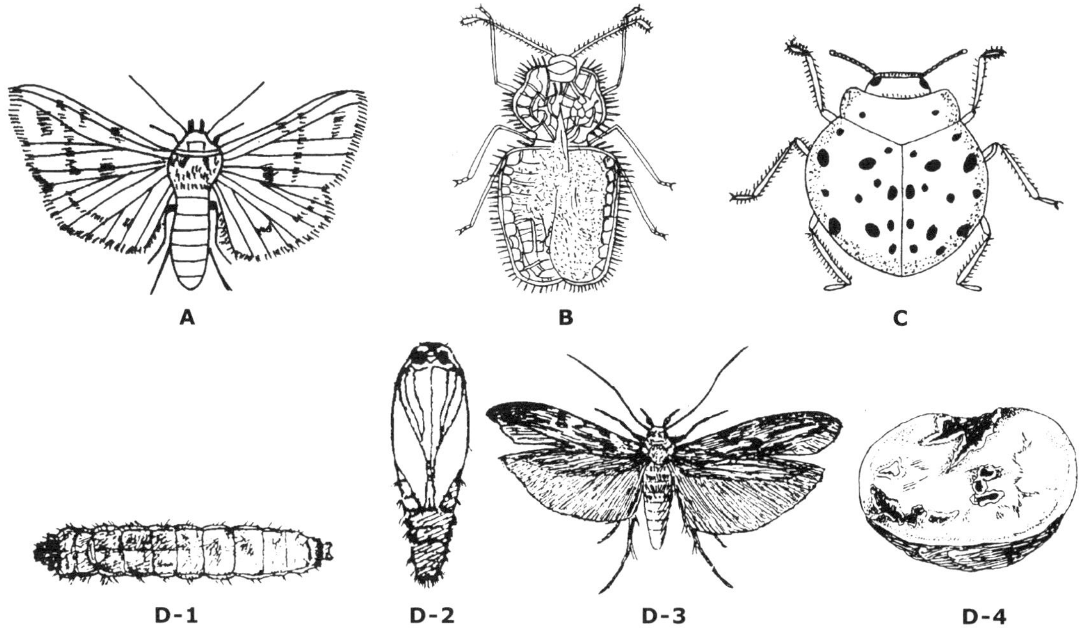

Fig. 6.1 Pests of solanaceous vegetables. **A.** Brinjal shoot and fruit borer, *Leucinodes orbonalis*. **B.** Brinjal lace-wing bug, *Urentius sentis*. **C.** Brinjal hadda, *Henosepilachna vigintioctopunctata*. **D.** Potato tuber moth, *Phthorimaea operculella*; D-1. Larva, D-2, Pupa, D-3. Adult, D-4. Damaged potato.

Management. Apply 625 ml of diazinon 20EC or one litre of dimethoate 30EC in 250-300 litres of water per ha.

3. *Henosepilachna dodecastigma* (Wiedemann) and *H. vigintioctopunctata* (Fabricius) (Hadda beetles, Coleoptera: Coccinellidae) (Fig. 6.1C)

Distribution. This pest is prevalent throuhout India.

Identification. *H. vigintioctopunctata* beetles are deep red and usually have 7-14 black spots on each elytron whose tip is somewhat pointed. Beetles of *H. dodecastigma* are deep copper-coloured and have six black spots on each elytron whose tip is more rounded. The grubs of both the species are about 6 mm long, yellowish in colour and have six rows of long branched spines.

Life-history. The female beetle lays yellow cigar-shaped eggs, mostly on the underside of leaves, in batches of 5-40 each. A single female can lay upto 400 eggs in her lifetime. The eggs hatch in 2-3 days. The grubs feed on the lower epidermis of leaves and are full-grown in 11-15 days. The pupae are darker and are found fixed on the leaves, stems and most commonly, at the base of the plants. The pupal stage lasts 5-7 days. The pest passes through several broods from March to October and its population is at a maximum at the end of April or in early May.

Host plants. The hadda beetles attack different solanaceous vegetables like brinjal, tomato and potato.

Damage. Both the grubs and the adults cause damage by feeding on the upper surface of leaves. They eat up regular areas of the leaf tissue, leaving parallel bands of uneaten tissue in between. The leaves, thus, present a lace-like appearance. They turn brown, dry up and fall off, and the plants are completely skeletonized.

Management. Spray 625 ml of malathion 50EC or diazinon 20EC or 2.5 kg of carbaryl 50WP in 250-300 litres of water per ha as soon as the hadda beetle appears

4. *Euzophera perticella* Rag. (Brinjal stem borer, Lepidoptera : Pyralidae)

Distribution. The stem borer is widely distributed in India.

Identification. The moths measure about 32 mm across the spread wings and have pale-yellow abdomens. The head and thorax are greyish, the fore wings are pale straw-yellow and the hind wings are whitish. The caterpillars measure about 20-22 mm in length, when full-grown. They are creamy white and have a few brislty hairs. Their bodies taper posteriorly.

Life-history. This pest is active from March to October and passes the winter as a hibernating caterpillar in the stems of old plants. The overwintered larvae pupate at the beginning of March and emerge as moths in the second half of the month. The moths are active at night when they mate and lay cream-coloured scale like eggs singly or in batches on the underside of young leaves or in the axils of young branches. A single female may lay 104-363 eggs in its life span of about a week. The eggs hatch in 3-10 days and the young larvae feed for a few minutes on exposed parts of plants before boring into the stem where they feed on the pith by making longitudinal tunnels. They pass through 4 or 5 stages and are full-fed in 26-58 days. When full-grown, they make silken cocoons within the feeding galleries or in the cracks and crevices in the soil. After pupation, they transform themselves into adults in 6-8 days. The life-cycle is completed in 35-76 days and the pest has 5-6 overlapping generations in a year.

Host plants. Besides brinal, it may also attack chillies (*Capsicum annum* L.), potato and tomato plants.

Damage. The caterpillars feed exclusively in the main stem and have never been observed to bore into the fruits. As a result of their attack in the field, stray plants are seen withering and drying up.

Management. (*i*) When the attack of this borer is serious, the ratooning of brinjal plants should be discontinued. The withered plants should be uprooted and burnt. (*ii*) Four sprays of 500 ml of malathion 50EC or 315 ml of dichlorvos 100EC in 250-300 litres of water per ha should be given at 15-day intervals.

POTATO

1. *Phthorimaea operculella* (Zeller) (Potato tuber moth, Lepidoptera: Gelechiidae) (Fig. 6.1D)

Distribution. The pest is distributed in all potato growing areas, hills and plains of Uttarakhand in particular, and very serious in Himachal Pradesh.

Identification. The adult is very small narrow-winged nocturnal moth, about 13mm across the wings when spread. It is greyish brown with mottling of dark brown. The caterpillars are about 2.0 cm in length, pinkish-white or greenish with mottling of dark brown.

Life-history. A female, on an average, lays 150-200 eggs singly on the underside of leaves or on exposed tubers. The larvae first produce blotch mines on leaves but subsequently they work their way into the stems. The larval stage in summer lasts 2-3 weeks and the mature larva pupates in a greyish silken dirt-covered cocoon, which is about 13 mm in length. The moths emerge in 7-10 days. They complete their life-cycle in about one month and there are usually 5-6 generations in a year.

Host plants. This pest is destructive to potato and also attacks tobacco, tomato, brinjal and solanaceous weeds.

Damage. The damage is caused by the caterpillars by boring into the tubers, eating away the pulp and destroying the eye-buds. In warm dry climates extensive damage may be done to the crop; but the potato tubers kept in cold stores escape damage. Later generations in the field infest the tubers also. In storage, 30 to 70 per cent of tubers are damaged by the larvae.

Management. (*i*) All the infested tubers should be removed and destroyed. (*ii*) Cold storage of tubers also helps in suppressing the pest. (*iii*) The pest can be checked by spraying 2.5 kg of carbaryl 50WP in 625 litres of water per ha or by dusting seed potato with 150 g of malathion 2 per cent per 100 kg. Repeat spraying 2-3 times at fortnightly intervals and do not dust the edible potatoes. (*iv*) If potato tubers in the stores get infested, fumigation with carbon disulphide @ 2-3 litres per 100 m^3 should be done.

2. *Amrasca bigutulla bigutulla* Ishida (Jassid, Hemiptera: Cicadellidae

(See Chapter 9)

SWEET POTATO

Cylas formicarius (Fabricicus) (Sweet potato weevil, Coleoptera : Apionidae)

Distribution. This weevil is a serious pest of sweet potato in India.

Identification. The adult weevils are small, 5.0-6.5 mm in length, bluish black in colour, with reddish brown prothorax and a long snout. The apodous grub is whitish with a brown head and is 8.22 mm long.

Life-history. The female weevil lays 97-216 eggs in cavities made on the vines or the tubers. The oviposition period of the adults may range from 51 to 102 days. The eggs hatch in 3-7 days. The grubs feed both on vines and the tubers, and the larval development is completed in 21-26 days. The pupation also takes place either in the vine or in the tuber. The pupal stage lasts 7-11 days and the life-cycle is completed in 36-43 days. More than one geneations are completed in a year.

Damage. The weevils feed on leaves, vines and tubers, whereas the grubs bore into tender vines and tubers, making the latter unfit for makreting and consumption. Up to 60 per cent damage may be caused by the pest.

Host plant. Sweet potato.

Management. (*i*) No infested or rotting tuber should be left in the field after harvest of the crop. (*ii*) Spray 2.5 kg of carbaryl 50WP followed by 2.0 litres of malathion 50EC in 625 litres of water per ha.

TOMATO

Helicoverpa armigera (Hubner) (Tomato fruit borer, Lepidoptera: Noctuidae)

Tomato fruit borer is one of the most destructive pests of tomato. The adults lay majority of the eggs on the upper and lower leaf surfaces of the first four leaves in the top canopy. The larvae scrape the tomato foliage until early or late second instar stage. Thereafter, the larva bores into the fruit making it unfit for marketing. In severe cases of infestation, more than 80 per cent fruits get damaged. Tall African marigold may be grown as a trap crop in tomato to attract ovipositing *H. armigera* moths. This results in 80-90 per cent reduction in damage to tomato crop. The detailed account of the pest has been given in chapter 4.

For control of tomato fruit borer, give three sprays at 3 weeks intervals starting from the initiation of flowers with any of the following insecticides using 250 litres of water per ha: 2 litres of malathion 35EC, 2 kg of carbaryl 50WP, 250 ml of fenvalerate 20EC, 500 ml of cypermethrin 10EC, 400 ml of deltamethrin 2.8EC, 1.5 litres of profenophos 50EC, 75 ml of flubendiamide 480SL, 500 ml of indoxacarb 14.5SC.

II. MALVACEOUS VEGETABLES

OKRA

1. ***Amrasca biguttula* (Ishida) (Cotton leafhopper, Hemiptera : Cicadellidae)**
2. ***Bemisia tabaci* (Gennadius) (Cotton whitefly, Hemiptera : Aleyrodidae)**
3. ***Oxycarenus hyalinipennis* Costa (Dusky cotton bug, Hemiptera : Lygaeidae)**
4. ***Earias insulana* (Boisduval) and *E. vittella* (Fabricius) (Spotted bollworms, Lepidoptera : Noctuidae)**
5. ***Sylepta derogata* Fabricius (Cotton leaf-roller, Lepidoptera : Pyralidae)**

The details of the above pests have been given in chapter 9. Spraying once or twice at fortnightly interval with 1.4 litres of malathion 50EC in 250-300 litres of water per ha will control the sucking pests of okra. As soon as flowering starts, give three sprays at fortnightly interval with 175 g emamectin benzoate 05SG or 1.25 kg of carbaryl 50 WP or 875 ml of endosulfan 35EC or 250 ml of fenvalerate 20EC or 200 ml of cypermethrin 25EC in 250-300 litres of water per ha to control the leafhopper as well as spotted bollworms.

For seed crop, apply 20 kg of phorate 10G at sowing in furrows or spray twice at fortnightly interval, starting 15 days after sowing with 625 ml of dimethoate 30EC in 250-300 litres of water per ha for control of leafhopper. For the control of spotted bollworms, spray the crop when 20-30 per cent shoots show borer damage with any of the following insecticides using 250-300 litres of water per ha: one litre of fenitrothion 50EC, one litre of monocrotophos 36SL, 250 ml of fenvalerate 20EC, 200 ml of cypermethrin 25EC, 400 ml of deltamethrin 2.8EC.

III. CRUCIFEROUS VEGETABLES

CABBAGE, CAULIFLOWER, RADISH, TUNIP AND CARROT

1. ***Plutella xylostella* (Linnaeus) (Diamondback moth, Lepidoptera: Yponomeutidae) (Fig. 6.2A)**

Distribution. This pest is distributed world wide.

Identification. The moths measure about 8-12 mm in length and are brown or grey, with conspicuous white spots on the fore wings, which appear like diamond patterns when the wings lie flat over the body. When full-grown, the larvae measure about 8 mm in length and are pale yellowish green with fine black hair scattered all over the body.

Life-history. Yellowish eggs of the size of pin-heads are laid singly or in batches of 2-40 on the underside of leaves. A female may lay 18-356 eggs in her life-time. The eggs hatch in 3-6 days. The newly hatched caterpillars bore into the tissue from the underside of leaves and feed in these tunnels. Third and fourth instar larvae feed from the underside of leaves, leaving intact a parchment-like transparent cuticular layer on the dorsal surface. They become full-grown in 14-21 days. Before pupating, the larva constructs a barrel-shaped silken cocoon which is open at both ends and is attached to the leaf surface. The pupal stage lasts 4-5 days and the moths may live for as long as 20 days. The life-cycle is completed in 15-18 days during September-October and there are several generations in a year.

Host plants. This is a serious pest of cauliflower and cabbage, but also feeds on many other cruciferous, solanaceous and liliaceous plants.

Damage. Caterpillars damage the leaves of cauliflower, cabbage and rape-seed particularly in the heart of the first two. Central leaves of cabbage or cauliflower may be riddled and the vegetables rendered unfit for human consumption.

Management. (*i*) *Apanteles plutellae* effectively checks the population of diamondback moth on cabbage in Gujarat and Karnataka under favourable environmental conditions. In the hill regions of Tamil Nadu, *Diadegma semiclausum* exercises 70 per cent parasitization of diamondback moth in winter months. (*ii*) Remove and destroy all the remnants, stubble, debris, etc. after the harvest of the crop and plough the fields. (*iii*) Tomato, when intercropped with cabbage, inhibits or reduces egg laying by diamondback moth. (*iv*) Bold seeded Indian mustard, which attracts 80-90 per cent diamondback moths for colonisation, can be used as a trap crop. To control the pest on the trap crop, 4 per cent neem seed kernel extract (NSKE) is applied at the primordial or head initiation stage and repeated at 10-15 day intervals. (*v*) Spray 750 ml of Dipel 8L or 750 g of Halt WP (*Bacillus thuringiensis* var. *kurstaki*) in 200-250 litres of water per ha in the evenings at one week interval. (*vi*) Spray 625 ml of spinosad 2.5 SC or 175 g emamectin benzoate 0.58G or 325 ml indoxacarb 15.8EC or 500 g cartap hydrochloride 50 SP or quinalphos 35EC or 250 ml of fenvalerate 20 EC in 250 litres of water per ha. Repeat sprays at 10-day intervals, if necessary.

2. *Spodoptera litura* (Fabricius) (Tobacco caterpillar, Lepidoptera: Noctuidae) (Fig. 6.2B)

Distribution. The tobacco caterpillar is found throughout the tropical and sub-tropical parts of the world. It is widespread in India.

Identification. The moths are about 22 mm long and measure 40 mm across the spread wings . The fore wings have beautiful golden and greyish brown patterns. The caterpillars are velvety black with yellowish-green dorsal stripes and lateral white bands.

Life-history. The female lays about 300 eggs in clusters. These clusters are covered over by brown hair and they hatch in about 3-5 days. The larvae feed gregariously for the first few days and then disperse to feed individually. They pass through 6 stages and are full-fed in 15-30 days. The full-grown larvae enter the soil where they pupate. The pupal stage lasts 7-15 days and the moths, on emergence, live for 7-10 days. The life- cycle is completed in 32-60 days and the pest completes eight generations in a year.

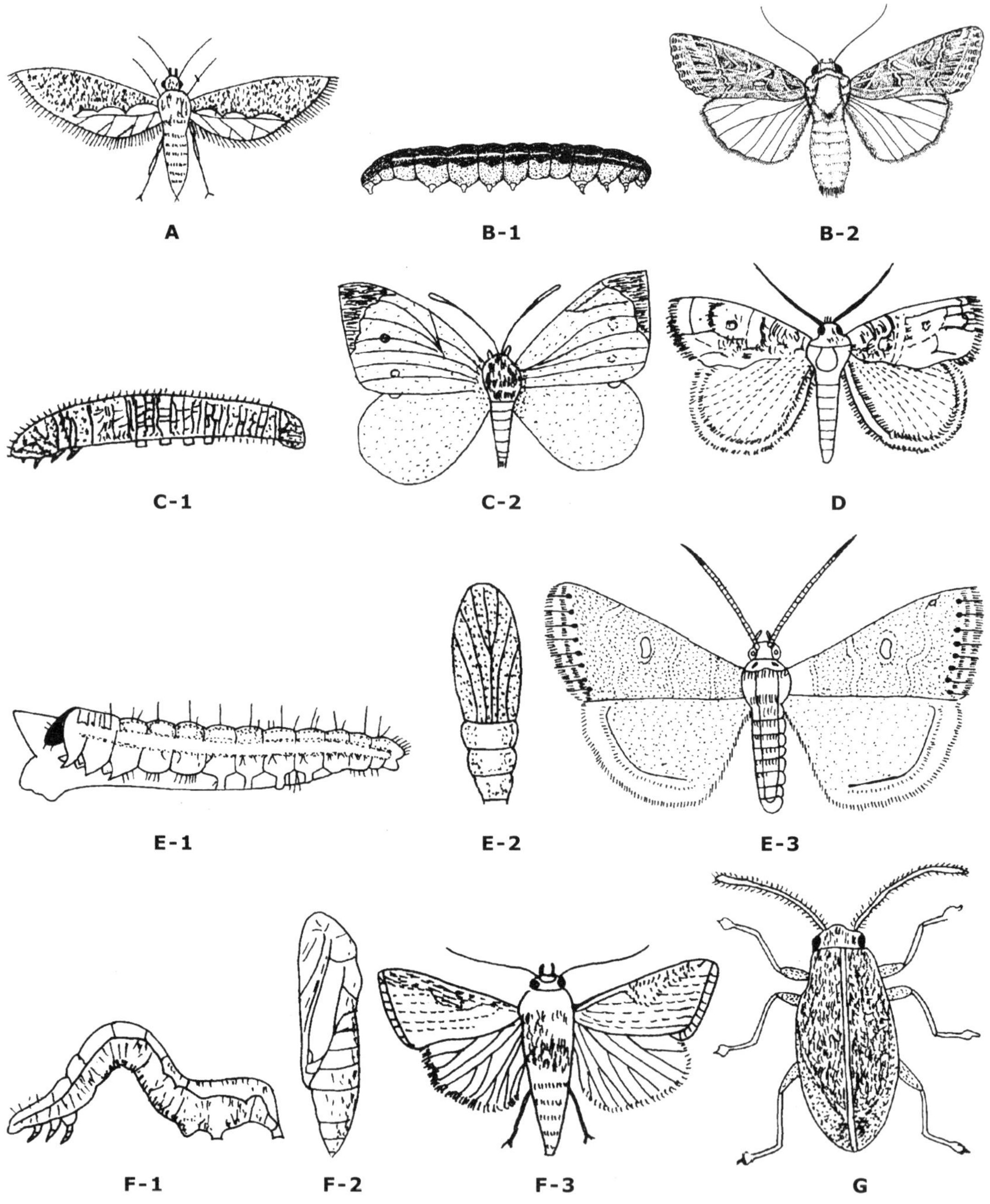

Fig. 6.2 Pests of cruciferous vegetables. **A.** Diamond back moth, *Plutella xylostella*. **B.** Tobacco caterpillar, *Spodoptera litura*; B-1. Larva, B-2. Adult. **C.** Cabbage caterpillar, *Pieris brassicae*; C-1, Larva, C-2. Adult. **D.** Crucifer leaf-webber, *Crocidolomia binotalis*. **E.** Cabbage stem borer, *Hellula undalis*; E-1. Larva, E-2. Pupa, E-3. Adult. **F.** Cabbage semilooper, *Thysanoplusia orichalcea*; F-1. Larva, F-2. Pupa, F-3. Adult. **G.** Cabbage flea beetle, *Phyllotreta cruciferae*.

Host plants. Besides tobacco, it feeds on castor, groundnut, tomato, sunflower, cabbage and various other cruciferous crops.

Damage. The larvae feed on leaves and fresh growth. They are mostly active at night and cause extensive damage, particularly in tobacco nurseries.

Management. Same as in case of cabbage caterpillar.

3. *Pieris brassicae* (Linnaeus) (Cabbage caterpillar, Lepidoptera : Pieridae) (Fig. 6.2C)

Distribution. The cabbage caterpillar is world-wide and is found wherever cruciferous vegetables are grown.

Identification. It is a large 5.6-6.6 cm white coloured butterfly with black fore wing tips and 2 prominent black spots on the fore wings of females alone. The young larvae are pale yellow, and become greenish yellow later on. The head is black and the dorsum is marked with black spots. The body is decorated with short hair. When full-grown, they measure 4.0-5.0 cm in length.

Life-history. The butterflies lay, on an average, 164 yellowish conical eggs in clusters of 50-90 on the upper or the lower side of a leaf. The eggs hatch in 11-17 days in November-February and 3-7 days in March-May. The caterpillars feed gregariously during the early instars and disperse as they approach maturity. They pass through five stages and are full-fed in 15-22 days during March-April and 30-40 days during November- February. The larvae pupate at some distance from the food plants, often in barns or on trees. The pupal stage lasts 7.7-14.4 days in March-April and 20-28 days in November-February. The butterflies live for 2.5-12.5 days and the pest breeds four times during October-April.

Host plants. It is a serious pest of cabbage, cauliflower, knol-khol and it may also attack turnip, radish, *sarson, toria (Brassica campestris)* and other cruciferous plants.

Damage. The caterpillars alone cause damage. The first instar caterpillars just scrape the leaf surface, whereas the subsequent instars eat up leaves from the margins inwards, leaving intact the main veins. Often, entire plants are eaten up.

Management. (*i*) The larvae of this insect are parasitized by *Apanteles glomeratus* in the natural populations. (*ii*) Handpicking and mechanical destruction of caterpillars during early stage of attack can reduce infestation. (*iii*) Spray one litre of malathion 50EC or 925 ml of endosulfan 35EC in 625 litres of water per ha. Repeat spraying at 10-day intervals if necessary. Do not spray the crop at least one week before the harvest.

4. *Crocidolomia binotalis* Zeller (Crucifer leaf-webber, Lepidoptera : Pyralidae) (Fig. 6.2D)

Distribution. It is a serious pest of cruciferous plants in India, Myanmar, Sri Lanka, Kenya and Uganda.

Identification. Moths are light brown with a wingspan of about 2 cm. The caterpillars are dark green with a light brown head, and dark and yellowish white light stripes on the body. When full-grown, the larva measures 1.6-2.0 cm in length.

Life-history. The moth lays eggs on the underside of leaves in masses of 40-100 each. The eggs hatch in 5-15 days. In the early stages, the larvae feed gregariously on the leaf parenchyma. As they grow, they spread out and start webbing the leaves and feeding on them. The larval stage is completed in 24-27 days in the summer and about 50 days in winter. When full-grown, the larva descends to the ground and pupates in the soil after making an earthen cocoon. The adult moth emerges in 14-40 days and the life-cycle is completed in 43-82 days. More than one generation may be completed in the season.

Host plants. Cabbage, radish, mustard and other curciferous plants.

Damage. The caterpillars cause considerable damage to the crops by webbing the leaves together and feeding on them. They also feed on flower buds and bore into the pods.

Management. (*i*) Remove and destroy the webbed leaves with larvae within. (*ii*) Spray 940 ml of malathion 50EC or 320 ml of dichlorvos 100EC in 250 litres of water per ha.

5. *Hellula undalis* (Fabricius) (Cabbage stem borer, Lepidoptera : Pyralidae) (Fig. 6.2E)

Distribution. The cabbage stem borer is one of the serious pests of cruciferous crops, having a world wide occurrence.

Identification. The adult moth is slender, pale yellowish-brown, having grey wavy lines on the fore wings. The caterpillar (1.2-2.5 cm long) is creamy yellow with a pinkish tinge and has seven purplish brown longitudinal stripes.

Life-history. The female moths lay eggs singly but more often in clusters, on the under surface of the leaves or some other parts of the plant. The eggs hatch in 2-3 days. The caterpillars feed in the heart of the cabbage and become full-grown in 7-12 days, after undergoing four moultings. The full-grown caterpillar spins a cocoon among the leaves touching the ground or even inside larval burrows. The pupal period is about 6 days and the life cycle is completed in 15-25 days.

Host plants. The larvae attack cabbage, cauliflower, radish, knol-khol and beet-root.

Damage. The caterpillars first mine into the leaves. Later on, they feed on the leaf surface, sheltered within the silken passages. As they grow bigger, they bore into the heads of cauliflower and cabbage. When the attack is heavy, the plants are riddled with worms and outwardly the heads look deformed.

Management. (*i*) Collection and mechanical destruction of caterpillars in early stage of attack helps to check the infestation. (*ii*) Since the attack is mostly in the nursery and on young plants in the field, spray 375 g of carbaryl 50WP in 150 litres of water per ha. Repeat spray at 10-day interval, pick all flowering heads before spraying and observe 7 days waiting period after spray for the next picking.

6. *Thysanoplusia orichalcea* (Fabricius) (Fig. 6.2F) and *Autographa nigrisigna* (Walker) (Cabbage semi-looper, Lepidoptera : Noctuidae)

Distribution. These two species are widely distributed in north-western India.

Identification. The adults of *T. orichalcea* are light palish brown with a large golden patch on each fore wing. They measure about 4.2 cm across the spread wings. The adults of *A. nigrisigna* are darker and have dark-brown and dirty-white patches on the fore wings. The caterpillars are plump and polish green.

Life-history. These insects are active during the winter and it is not known how they survive the heat of summer. During the active period, they lay eggs on leaves of host plants and the caterpillars feed individually, biting holes of varying size according to the stage of their development. When full-grown, they pupate in the debris lying on the ground. The moths are very active at dusk on flowers in gardens and public parks, where they are seen in hundreds during the spring season.

Host plants. They are minor pests of cabbage, cauliflower and other winter vegetables. They are polyphagous and attack a number of plants, including groundnut and sunflower.

Management. Same as in case of cabbage caterpillar.

7. *Phyllotreta cruciferae* (Goeze) (Fig. 6.2G), *P. chotanica* Duviv., *P. birmanica* Harold, *P. oncera* Maulik and *P. downesi* Baly (Cabbage flea beetles, Coleoptera : Chrysomelidae)

Distribution. The cabbage flea beetles attack almost all the cruciferous plants in Europe, erstwhile USSR, North and South America, Australia, Japan and India.

Identification. The dorsum of the adult beetle, *P. cruciferae,* is metallic blue in colour, with a greenish hue. The body is elongate narrow in front but broad distally. The beetle is round at the anal end. The head is finely punctate and the antennae extend beyond the middle of elytra. The female beetle measures 2.0 mm in length while the male beetle measures 1.8 mm. The larva is dirty white in colour with pale white head and measures about 5 mm in length.

Life-history. This pest is active throughout the year except during the winter months, when it hibernates in the soil or among plant debris. The over-wintered adult beetles emerge in the last week of February or in the beginning of March and settle on the growing cruciferous plants. The female beetle lays 50-80 creamy white eggs singly in the soil around the host plants, during the oviposition period of 25-30 days. The incubation period ranges between 5-10 days. The larva is very active and feeds on the tender roots of the host plant. It moults thrice during a total larval period of 9-15 days. The larva before entering into the pre-pupal stage wriggles out of the mined roots and prepares an earthern cell, 0.5 mm long, in the vicinity of the infested plants. There it pupates. The pre-pupal period is 2-4 days and the pupal stage lasts 8-14 days. There are 7-8 generations of this pest in a year.

Host plants. The common field crops like mustard, *raya, taramira, toria* and vegetables like radish, turnip, cabbage, cauliflower and knol-khol are severely damaged by adult beetles. Some winter flowering plants, namely dahlia, sweet sultan, antirrhinum and sweet peas also provide food for the beetles.

Damage. The adults mostly feed on the leaves by making innumerable round holes in the host plants. The stem, the flowers and even pods may also be attacked. The old, eaten away leaves dry up, while the young leaves are rendered unfit for consumption. A special kind of decaying odour is emitted by the cabbage plants attacked by this pest.

Management. Spray 2.5 kg of carbaryl 50WP or 2.0 litres of endosulfan 35EC in 250 litres of water per ha.

IV. CUCURBITACEOUS VEGETABLES

1. *Bactrocera cucurbitae* (Coquillett) (Melon fruit fly, Diptera : Tephritidae) (Fig. 6.3A)

Distribution. This is the commonest and most destructive fruit fly of cucurbits throughout India. It is also found in Pakistan, Myanmar, Malaysia, China, Taiwan, Japan, East Africa, Australia and the Hawaiian Islands.

Identification. The adult flies are reddish brown with lemon-yellow markings on the thorax and have fuscous areas on the outer margins of their wings. The maggots are legless and appear as headless, dirty-white wriggling creatures, thicker at one end and tapering to a point at the other. A full-grown maggot is 9-10 mm long and 2 mm broad in the middle.

Life-history. The adult females puncture fruits by its ovipositor to lay eggs, singly or in clusters of 5-12, inside the pulp. The eggs hatch in 1-9 days and the maggots bore into the pulp, forming galleries. The attacked fruits decay because of secondary bacterial infection. The larvae are full-grown in 3 days during summer and 3 weeks during winter. The mature larvae come out of the rotten fruits and move away in jumps of 12-20 cm. After reaching a suitable place, they bury themselves about 5 mm deep in the soil and pupate. The pupae are barrel-shaped, light brown and they transform themselves into winged adults in 6-9 days in the rainy season and 3-4 weeks in the winter. There are several generations in a year.

Host plants. In addition to melons, it has been found feeding on tomato, chillies, guava, citrus, pear, fig, cauliflower, etc.

Damage. The maggots destroy fruits by feeding on the pulp. The damage caused by this fruit fly is most serious in melons and after the first shower of the monsoon, the infestation often reaches 100 per cent. Other cucurbitaceous fruits may also be infested up to 50 per cent.

Management. (*i*) The regular removal and destruction of the infested fruits helps in the suppression of this pest. (*ii*) Frequent raking of the soil under the vine or ploughing the infested field after the crop is harvested can help in killing the pupae. (*iii*) Apply the bait spray containing 50 ml of malathion 50EC + 0.5 kg of gur/sugar in 50 litres of water per ha. When the attack is serious, it should be repeated at weekly intervals. (*iv*) Spray the bait on lower surface of the leaves of maize plants grown as trap crop at a distance of about 10 cm.

2. *Aulacophora foveicollis* (Lucas) (Red pumpkin beetle, Coleoptera: Chrysomelidae) (Fig. 6.3B)

Distribution. The red pumpkin beetle, is widely distributed in Asia, Australia, southern Europe and Africa.

Identification. The adult beetles are 6-7 mm long brilliant orange red and ventral surface is black, being clothed in short white hair. The grubs are creamy white, with a slightly darker oval shield at the back.

Life history. The beetles in their life span of 60-85 days lay about 300 oval yellow eggs singly or in batches of 8-9 in moist soil, near the base of the plants. The eggs hatch in 6-15 days and the grubs remain below the soil surface feeding on roots, underground stems of creepers and on fruits lying in contact with the soil. They are full-grown in 13- 25 days and pupate in thick-walled earthen chambers in the soil, at a depth of about 20-25 cm. The pupal stage lasts 7-17 days and the beetles, on emergence, begin to feed and breed. The life-cycle is completed in 26-37 days and the pest breeds five times from March to October.

Host plants. It is a serious pest of cucurbitaceous vegetables such as ash gourd, pumpkin, *tinda, ghia, tori,* cucumber and melon.

Damage. The beetles are very destructive to cucurbitaceous vegetables, particularly during March-April when the creepers are very young. The grubs damage the plants by boring into the roots, underground stems and sometime into the fruits touching the soil. The beetles

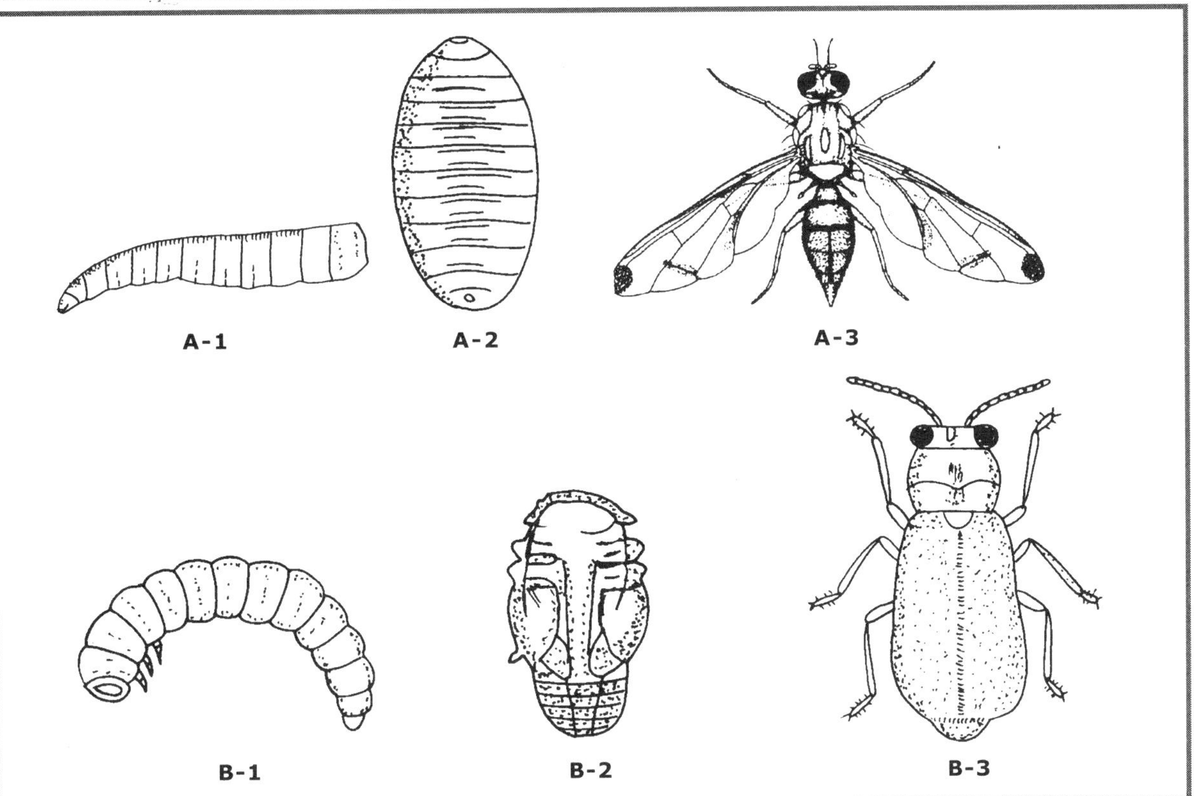

Fig. 6.3 Pests of cucurbitaceous vegetables. **A.** Melon fruit fly, *Bactrocera cucurbitae;* A-1. Larva, A-2. Pupa, A-3. Adult. **B.** Red pumpkin beetle, *Aulacophora foveicollis*; B-1. Larva, B-2. Pupa, B-3. Adult.

injure the cotyledons, flowers and foliage by biting holes into them. The early sown cucurbits are so severely damaged that they have to be resown.

Management. (*i*) After harvesting the infested fields, plough deep to kill the grubs in the soil. (*ii*) Sow the crop in November to avoid damage by this pest. *(iii)* Apply 7.0 kg of carbofuran 3G per ha 3-4 cm deep in the soil near the base of the plants just after germination and irrigate or spray 375 g of carbaryl 50WP in 250 litres of water per ha.

V. LILLIACEOUS VEGETABLES

ONION AND GARLIC

1. *Thrips tabaci* Lindeman (Onion thrips, Thysanoptera : Thripidae)

Distribution. Onion thrips is world-wide and is found throughout India.

Identification. The adults are slender, yellowish brown and measure about 1 mm in length. The males are wingless whereas the females have long, narrow strap-like wings, which are furnished with long hair along the hind margins. Nymphs resemble the adults but are wingless and slightly smaller.

Life history. The adult female lays 50-60 kidney-shaped eggs singly in slits which are made in leaf tissue with its sharp ovipositor. The eggs hatch in 4-9 days and the nymphs start feeding on plant juices by lacerating the leaf tissues. The nymphs pass through four stages and are full-fed in 4-6 days, after which they descend to the ground and pupate at a depth of about 25 mm. The pre-pupal and pupal stages last 1-2 and 2-4 days, respectively. Several generations are completed in a year.

Host plants. It is a major pest of onion and garlic It also feeds on many other plants, including cotton, cabbage, cauliflower, potato, tobacco, tomato, cucumber, etc.

Damage. Both nymphs and adults suck plant sap and the leaves of attacked plants become curled, wrinkled and gradually dry up. The plants do not form bulbs nor do the flowers set seed.

Management. Spray 625 ml of malathion 50EC in 250 litres of water per ha as soon as the pest appears. Add some sticker for better control. A waiting period of 7 days should be observed before harvest.

2. *Delia antiqua* (Meigen) (Onion maggot, Diptera : Anthomyiidae) (Fig. 6.4A)

Distribution. The onion maggot is widely distributed in France, Germany, Canada, USA, Japan, erstwhile USSR and England. This pest also attacks onions in northern India.

Identification. The flies are slender, greyish, large-winged, rather bristly and about 6 mm in body length. The maggots are small, white and about 8 mm in length.

Life-history. The female lays elongate, white eggs near the base of the plant, in cracks in the soil. The eggs hatch in 2-7 days. The maggots crawl up to the plant, and enter the inside of the leaf sheath and reach the bulb. They feed there and become full-grown in 2-3 weeks. The maggots then crawl out of the bulb and pupate in the soil. After 2-3 weeks, the adults emerge and start the new generation. In the third generation, the pest often attacks the onions shortly before the harvest. It initiates the process of rotting of the onions in storage.

Host plant. Onion and garlic

Damage. The maggots bore into the bulbs, causing the plants to become flabby and yellowish. They mine through the small bulbs completely, leaving only the outer sheath and thus causing a thin stand of the crop. The larger bulbs are attacked by several maggots at a time, making cavities.

Management. Apply 10 kg of carbaryl 4G or lindane 6G or phorate 10G per ha to the soil followed by light irrigation.

VI. TRAPACEOUS VEGETABLES

WATER-NUTS

Galerucella birmanica (Jacoby) (Singhara beetle, Coleoptera: Chrysomelidae)

Distribution. The *singhara* beetle is widely distributed in Pakistan, Sri Lanka, Myanmar and India, and is a serious pest of water-nuts.

Identification. The beetles are about 6 mm long and 3 mm broad and are yellowish brown to dark brown, with black eyes and a large hump in the middle of the body. The full-grown grubs are about 6 mm in length, the upper surface of the body being black and the lower surface being yellow.

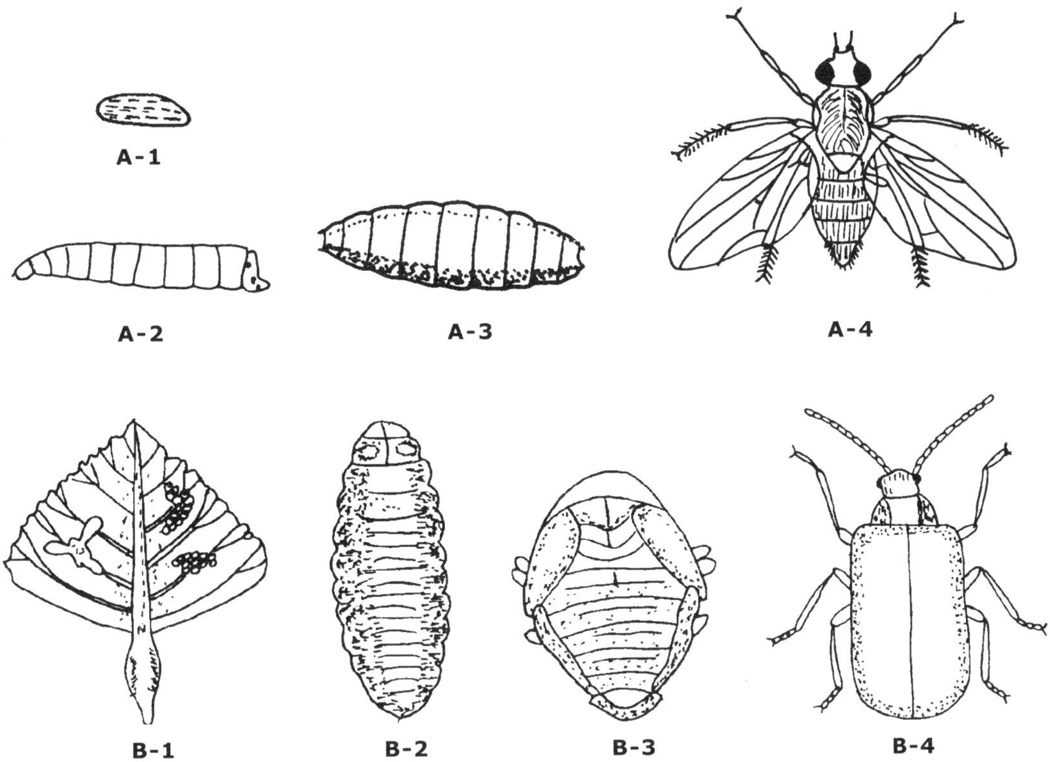

Fig. 6.4 Pests of lilliaceous and trapaceous vegetables. **A.** Onion maggot, *Delia antiqua*; A-1. Egg, A-2. Larva, A-3. Pupa, A-4. Adult. **B.** Singhara beetle, *Galerucella birmanica*; A-1. Eggs on a leaf, A-2. Larva, A-3. Pupa, A-4. Adult.

Life-history. The beetles lay reddish-brown rounded eggs on the upper surface of leaves, in clusters of 6-10. The eggs are securely glued to the leaves. A beetle may lay, on an average, 254 eggs which hatch in 7-8 days and the grubs start feeding on the upper epidermis of the leaves. They grow through 3 stages and become mature in 7- 22 days. Pupation takes place on the leaf surface and, like the eggs, the pupae are also firmly glued to the leaves. The pupal stage lasts 3-7 days and the adult beetles live for about a month; although some of them live up to three months. The life-cycle is completed in 17-37 days and there may be as many as 12-17 overlapping generations in a year.

Damage. Both the grubs and adult beetles feed on leaves. Hence, there is an untimely drying up of the plants. The integument of the *singhara* fruits at the surface of the water may also be damaged and this results in rotting of the fruits.

Management. The pest can be controlled by dusting the crop with carbaryl 5 per cent or malathion 2 per cent @ 25 kg per ha.

*****

7 CHAPTER

PESTS OF FRUITS

Tropical and Sub-tropical Fruits

Mango (*Mangifera indica*)

1. *Amritodus atkinsoni* (Lethiery) (Mango hopper, Hemiptera : Cicadellidae)
2. *Idioscopus clypealis* (Lethiery) (Mango hopper, Hemiptera : Cicadellidae)
3. *Drosicha mangiferae* (Green) (Mango mealy bug, Hemiptera : Margarodidae)
4. *Sternochaetus mangiferae* (Fabricius) (Mango stone weevil, Coleoptera : Curculionidae)
5. *Batocera rufomaculata* DeGeer (Mango stem borer, Coleoptera : Cerambyciade)
6. *Bactrocera dorsalis* (Hendel) (Oriental fruit fly, Diptera : Tephritidae)
7. *Chlumetia transversa* Walker (Mango shoot borer, Lepidoptera : Noctuidae)
8. *Apsylla cistella* (Buckton) (Mango gall psyllid, Hemiptera : Psyllidae)

Citrus (*Citrus* spp.)

1. *Papilio demoleus* Linnaeus (Citrus caterpillar, Lepidoptera : Papilionidae)
2. *Diaphorina citri* Kuwayana (Citrus psylla, Hemiptera : Aphalaridae)
3. *Indarbela quadrinotata* (Walker) (Bark caterpillar, Metarbelidae)
4. *Ophideres conjuncta* Cramer (Fruit-piercing moth, Lepidoptera : Noctuidae)
5. *Dialeurodes citri* (Ashmead) (Citrus whitefly, Hemiptera : Aleyrodidae)
6. *Aleurocanthus woglumi* Ashby (Citrus blackfly, Hemiptera : Aleyrodidae)

7. *Phyllocnistis citrella* Stainton (Citrus leafminer, Lepidoptera : Phyllocnistidae).
8. *Icerya purchasi* Maskell (Cottony cushion scale, Hemiptera : Margarodidae)
9. *Aonidiella aurantii* (Maskell) (Citrus red scale, Hemiptera : Diaspididae)
10. *Pseudococcus filamentosus* Cockrell (Citrus mealy bug, Hemiptera : Pseudococcidae).
11. *Dasineura citri* Grover (Citrus blossom midge, Diptera : Cecidomyidae)
12. *Psorosticha zizyphi* (Stainton) (Citrus leaf-folder, Lepidoptera: Oecophoridae)

Grapevine (*Vitis vinifera*)

1. *Rhipiphorothrips cruentatus* Hood (Grapevine thrps, Thysanoptera : Heliothpidae)
2. *Sylepta lunalis* Guenee (Leaf-roller, Lepidoptera : Pyralidae)
3. *Scelodonta strigicollis* Motschulsky (Flea-beetle, Coleoptera: Chrysomelidae)
4. *Sthenias grisator* Fabricius (Grapevine girdler, Coleoptera : Cerambycidae)
5. *Sinoxylon anale* Lense (Grapevine beetle, Coleoptera : Bostrychidae)

Guava (*Psidium guajava*)

1. *Indarbela tetraonis* Moore (Bark caterpiller, Lepidoptera : Metarbelidae).
2. *Bactrocera dorsalis* (Hendel) (Oriental fruit fly, Diptera : Tephritidae)
3. *Chloropulvinaria psidii* (Maskell) (Guava mealy scale, Hemiptera : Coccidae)
4. *Dichocrocis punctiferalis* (Guenee) (Castor capsule borer, Lepidoptera : Pyralidae)
5. *Saissetia coffeae* (Walker) (Helmet scale, Hemiptera : Coccidae)

Banana (*Musa paradisiaca*)

1. *Nacoleia octasema* (Meyrick) (Banana scale moth, Lepidoptera : Pyralidae)
2. *Cosmopolites sordidus* (Germar) (Banana weevil, Coleoptera: Curculionidae)
3. *Odoiporus longicollis* (Olivier) (Banana stem borer, Coleoptera: Curculionidae)
4. *Bactrocera dorsalis* (Hendel) (Oriental fruitfly, Diptera : Tephritidae)
5. *Pentalonia nigronervosa* Coquerel (Banana aphid, Hemiptera: Aphididae)
6. *Nodostoma subcostatum* Jacoby (Leaf beetle, Coleoptera : Eumolpidae)

Ber (*Ziziphus mauritiana*)

1. *Carpomyia vesuviana* Costa (Ber fruit fly, Diptera : Tephritidae)
2. *Adoretus pallens* Arrow (Ber beetle, Coleoptera : Scarabaeidae)
3. *Indarbela tetraonis* Moore (Bark caterpillar, Lepidoptera : Metarbelidae)
4. *Kerria lacca* (Kerr) (Lac insect, Hemiptera : Lacciferidae)
5. *Meridarches scyrodes* Meyr. (Fruit borer, Lepidoptera : Carposinidae)

Pomegranate (*Punica granatum*)

1. *Virachola isocrates* (Fabricius) (Pomegranate or 'anar' butterfly, Lepidoptera : Lycaenidae)
2. *Indarbela quadrinotata* (Walker) (Bark caterpillar, Lepidoptera : Metarbelidae)

	3. *Bactrocera zonata* (Saunders) (Oriental fruit fly, Diptera : Tephritidae) 4. *Othreis fullonica* (Linnaeus) (Fruit-sucking moth, Lepidoptera : Noctuidae)
Fig ***(Ficus carica)***	1. *Batocera rufomaculata* DeGeer (Mango stem borer, Coleoptera : Cerambycidae) 2. *Bactrocera dorsalis* (Hendel) (Mango fruit fly, Diptera : Tephritidae) 3. *Anjeerodiplosis peshawarensis* Mani (Fig midge, Diptera : Cecidomyiidae)
Jock-fruit ***(Artocarpus heterophyllus)***	1. *Ferrisia virgata* (Cockerell) (White-tailed mealy bug, Hemiptera : Pseudococcidae) 2. *Ceroplastes rubens* Maskell (Pink waxy scale, Hemiptera : Coccidae) 3. *Perina muda* Fabricius (Jack-fruit leaf-webber, Lepidoptera : Lymantriidae) 4. *Batocera rufomaculata* DeGeer (Mango stem borer, Coleoptera : Cerambycidae)
Loquat ***(Eriobotrya japonica)***	1. *Indarbela quadrinotata* (Walker) (Bark caterpillar, Lepidoptera : Pyralidae) 2. *Bactrocera dorsalis* (Hendel) (Mango fruit fly, Diptera : Tephritidae)
Pineapple ***(Ananas comosus)***	1. *Thrips tabaci* Lindeman (Pineapple thrips, Thysanoptera : Thripidae) 2. *Parasa lepida* (Cramer) (Slug caterpillar, Lepidoptera : Limacodidae)
Date plam ***(Phoenix dactylifera)***	1. *Aspidiotus destructor* Signoret (Date palm scale, Hemiptera : Scarabaeidae) 2. *Oryctes rhinoceros* (Linnaeus) (Black palm beetle, Coleoptera : Scarabaeidae) 3. *Rhynchophorus ferrugineus* (Olivier) (Red palm weevil, Coleoptera : Curculionidae)
Jamun ***(Syzigium cuminii)***	1. *Indarbela tetraonis* (Moore) (Bark caterpillar, Lepidoptera : Metarbelidae) 2. *Acrocercops phaeospora* Meyrick (Jamun leaf miner, Lepidoptera : Gracilliariidae)
Tamarind ***(Tamarindus indica)***	1. *Aspidiotus destructor* Signoret (Coconut scale, Hemiptera : Diaspididae) 2. *Nipaecoccus viridis* (Newstead) (Citrus mealy bug, Hemiptera : Pseudococcidae) 3. *Phycita orthoclina* Meyrick (Tamarind fruit borer, Lepidoptera : Phycitidae). 4. *Virachola isocrates* (Fabricius) (Anar butterfly, Lepidoptera : Lycaenidae) 5. *Dichocrocis punctiferalis* (Guenee) (Castor capsule borer, Lepidoptera : Pyralidae) 6. *Holotrichia insularis* Brenske (White grub, Coleoptera : Scarabaeidae)
Litchi ***(Litchi chinensis)***	1. *Chrysocoris stolii* Wolff. (Litchi bug, Hemiptera : Pentatomidae) 2. *Aceria litchi* Keifer (Leaf curl mite, Acari : Eriophyidae)

Papaya (*Carica papaya*)

1. *Poekilocerus pictus* (Fabricius) (Ak grasshopper, Orthoptera : Acrididae)
2. *Tetranychus urticae* Koch (Red spider mite, Acari : Tetranychidae)

Sapota (*Manilkara achras*)

1. *Nephopteryx eugraphella* Ragonot (Sapota leaf-webber, Lepidoptera : Pyralidae)
2. *Metanastria hyrtaca* Cramer (Sapota hairy caterpillar, Lepidoptera : Lasiocampidae)

Phalsa (*Grewia asiatica*)

1. *Euproctis fraterna* (Moore) (Plum hairy caterpillar, Lepidoptera : Lymantriidae)
2. *Drosicha mangiferae* (Green) (Mango mealy bug, Hemiptera : Margarodidae)
3. *Indarbela tetraonis* (Moore) (Lepidoptera : Metarbelidae)

Temperate Fruits

Apple (*Pyrus malus*)

1. *Quadraspidiotus perniciosus* (Comstock). (San Jose scale, Hemiptera : Diaspididae)
2. *Malacosma indicum* Walker (Tent caterpillar, Lepidoptera : Lasiocampidae)
3. *Eriosoma lanigerum* (Hausmann) (Woolly apple aphid, Hemiptera : Aphididae)
4. *Cydia pomonella* (Linnaeus) (Codling moth, Lepidoptera : Tortricidae)
5. *Apriona cinerea* Cheverlot (Apple stem borer, Coleoptera : Cerambycidae)
6. *Dorysthenes hugelii* Redtenbacher (Apple root borer, Coleoptera : Cerambycidae).
7. *Cacopsylla mali* (Schmidbergerer) (Apple psylla, Hemiptera: Psyllidae).

Pear (*Pyrus communis*)

1. *Quadraspidiotus perniciosus* (Comstock) (San Jose scale, Hemiptera : Diaspididae)
2. *Malacosma indicum* Walker (Tent caterpillar, Lepidoptera : Lasiocampidae)
3. *Dacus dorsalis* (Hendel) (Oriental fruit fly, Diptera : Tephritidae)

Peach (*Prunus persica*)

1. *Bactrocera zonata* (Saunders) (Peach fruit fly, Diptera : Tephritidae)
2. *Sphenoptera lafertei* Thompson (Peach stem borer, Coleoptera: Buprestidae)
3. *Brachycaudus helichrysi* (Kaltenbach) (Peach leaf curl aphid, Hemiptera: Aphididae).
4. *Anarsia lineatella* Zeller (Twig borer, Lepidoptera : Gelechiidae)

Walnut (*Juglans regia*)

1. *Alcidodes porrectirostris* Marshall (Walnut weevil, Coleoptera : Curculionidae)
2. *Chromaphis juglandicola* (Kaltenbach) (Walnut aphid, Hemiptera : Aphididae).
3. *Batocera horsfieldi* Hope (Long-horned walnut beetle, Coleoptera : Cerambycidae)

India is one of the leading producers of fruits in the world, as its diverse agro-climatic conditions allow production of a wide range of tropical, sub-tropical and temperate fruits. Production of fruits is estimated to be about 97 million tonnes which is about 4.5% higher than previous year.

I. TROPICAL AND SUB-TROPICAL FRUITS

Fruit production in India is largely dominated by tropical and sub-tropical fruits; banana, mango and citrus production alone accounts for more than 70 per cent. About 39.5 per cent of the world's mangoes and 11 per cent of the world's bananas are produced in India.

MANGO

There are a number of insect pests of this fruit and over 175 species of insects have been reported damaging mango tree but the most abundant and destructive at the flowering stage are the mango hoppers.

1. *Amritodus atkinsoni* (Lethiery) (Mango hopper, Hemiptera : Cicadellidae) (Fig. 7.1A)

Distribution. The mango hoppers are widely distributed in India, Malaysia, Indonesia and Taiwan.

Identification. It is a small, about 5 mm long, light greenish-brown wedge-shaped insect with small yellow and black marking, broad head and tapering body. The nymphs are pale yellow, elongated and more active. The other two species of mango hoppers are *Idioscopus clypealis* (Lethiery) and *I. niveosparus* (Lethiery).

Life-history. The overwintering adults lay eggs by inserting the ovipositor in the shoot and flower stalks. A female deposits, on an average, 200 eggs within 4-7 days, the eggs hatch and the newly emerged nymphs are first seen at the end of February or in early March. They commence feeding on the inflorescence, quickly suck the cell-sap and excrete honeydew. The nymphs become full-grown in three stages in 8-13 days. The full-fed nymphs then moult and give rise to winged hoppers. The life cycle, from the time eggs are laid to the time the adults appear, takes 15-19 days and during the flowering season, two or more broods of the pest may occur.

Host plants. Only mango of all varieties.

Damage. Mango hoppers are the most destructive pests of fruit trees. Injury to the inflorescence and young shoots is caused by egg laying and feeding. The voracious feeding nymphs are particularly harmful. They cause the inflorescence to wither and turn brown. Even if the flowers are fertilized, the subsequent development and fruit-setting may cease. In thick and protected gardens where the atmosphere is humid, a sooty mould develops on patches of honeydew exuded by the nymphs. As the wind blows, young fruits and dried inflorescence break off at the axil and fall to the ground. The growth of young trees is much retarded and the older trees do not bear much fruit. Damage to the mango crop may be as high as 60 per cent.

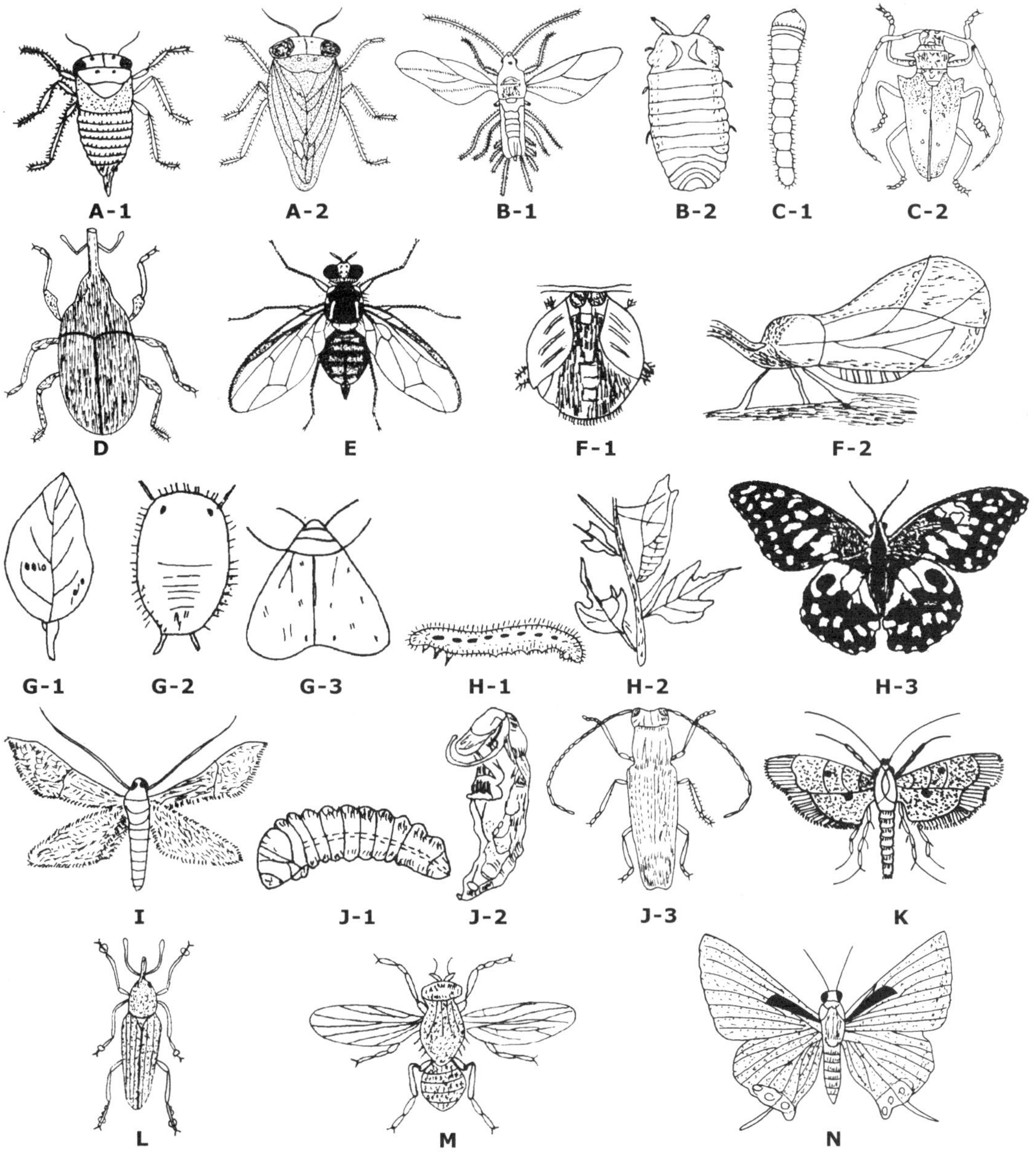

Fig. 7.1 Pests of tropical and sub-tropical fruits. **A.** Mango hopper, *Amritodus atkinsoni*; A-1. Nymph, A-2. Adult; **B.** Mango mealy bug, *Drosicha magiferae*; B-1. Male, B-2. Female. **C.** Mango stem borer, *Batocera rufomaculata*; C-1. Grub, C-2. Adult. **D.** Mango stone weevil, *Sternochetus mangiferae*. **E.** Oriental fruit fly, *Bactrocera dorsalis*. **F.** Citrus psylla, *Diaphorina citri*; F-1. Nymph, F-2. Adult. **G.** Citrus whitefly, *Dialeurodes citri*; G-1. Eggs on leaf, G-2. Nymph, G-3, Adult. **H.** Citrus caterpillar, *Papilio demoleus*; H-1 Larva, H-2. Pupa on a twig, H-3. Adult. **I.** Citrus leaf miner, *Phyllocnistis citrella*. **J.** Grapevine gridler, *Stethnias grisator*; J-1. Larva, J-2. Pupa, J-3. Adult. **K.** Banana scale moth, *Nacoleia octasema*. **L.** Banana stem borer, *Odoiporus longicollis*. **M.** Ber fruit fly, *Carpomyia vesuviana*. **N.** Pomegranate butterfly, *Virachola isocrates*.

Management. (*i*) Do not go for high density planting as it provides favourable habitat for hopper multiplication. (*ii*) Do not encourage plants to put intermittant flushes by regular irrigation and split doses of nitrogenous fertilizers. (*iii*) Avoid waterlogged or damp conditions. (*iv*) In case of old dense orchards, prune some of the branches during winter to have better light interception. (*v*) Spray 2.5 kg of carbaryl 50WP or 2 litres of malathion 50EC in 1250 liters of water, once in February and again in March.

2. *Drosicha mangiferae* (Green) (Mango mealy bug, Hemiptera: Margarodidae) (Fig. 7.1 B)

Distribution. The mango mealy bug is widely distributed in the Indo-Gangetic plains from Punjab to Assam.

Identification. The wingless females are oval, flattened and have body covered with a white mealy powder. The males have one pair of black wings and are crimson red.

Life-history. The eggs are generally deposited in April-May in soil up to 15 cm within silken purses. The dead body of the female is often found sticking to them. They hatch at the end of December or in January and, in a given locality, continue to hatch for about one month. Thus, the nymphs appear before the fresh growth of flowers on mango trees. The young nymphs ascend the trees and congregate on the panicles where they feed on the cell-sap and pass through three stages. At the time of moulting the younger nymphs wander away from the original feeding places in search of suitable shelters such as cracks and crevices in trunks. After moulting, they again seek suitable feeding-sites. The third-stage nymphs, however, stick to their original feeding places and those destined to be females, continue feeding.

Mating takes place soon after emergence of the males at a time when the females are not fully developed. The males fly about in large numbers, apparently in search of their mates. They have a very strong sex instinct and during the life-span of about one week they mate frequently. The females mature after 15-35 days and lay eggs for 22-47 days during April-May.

Host plants. Besides mango, it also attacks 62 other plants, including such trees as the jack-fruit, banyan, guava, papaya, citrus fruits and *jamun*.

Damage. The nymphs and adult females are destructive and they suck plant juice, causing tender shoots and flowers to dry up. The young fruits also become juiceless and drop off. The pest is responsible for causing considerable loss to the mango growers and when there is a serious attack, the trees retain no fruit at all.

Management. (*i*) Remove weeds from orchards which act as additional hosts for mealy bug. (*ii*) Ploughing of orchards during summer exposes eggs to natural enemies and extreme sun heat. (*iii*) Nymphs should be prevented from crawling up the trees by applying 15-20 cm wide sticky bands with alkathene or plastic sheets around the trunk about one meter above the ground level during second week of December. (*iv*) The nymphs found congregating below the lower edge of alkathene band should be killed mechanically or by applying 50 g of methyl parathion 2 per cent dust.

3. *Batocera rufomaculata* DeGeer (Mango stem borer, Coleoptera : Cerambycidae) (Fig. 7.1C)

Distribution. Mango stem borer has a wide range of distribution in north-western parts of the Indian sub-continent.

Identification. The adults are longicorn beetles, well built, large and pale greyish, measuring about 5 cm in length and 2 cm in breadth. The beetle is provided with long legs and antennae and a dirty white band, extending from the head to tip of the body on each side. A number of dirty yellowish spots are present on the elytra. The full-grown larva is a stout, yellowish-white, fleshy grub, measuring about 6 cm in length.

Life-history. The adults deposit eggs under the loose bark in a wounded or diseased portion of the trunk or a branch. The grubs are equipped with strong biting mouthparts and they penetrate into the stem or even the roots, feeding on woody tissues. Winter is passed in the grub stage in that very burrow. They again start feeding as soon as the weather warms up in spring and during the feeding process, they bore through the wood by cutting large galleries. The full-grown larvae then hollow out a cell for pupation. The larval stage probably lasts more than a year and the pupal stage lasts about one month. The life-cycle may be completed in 1-2 years.

Host plants. Besides mango, it also attacks jack fruit, rubber, fig., eucalyptus, etc.

Damage. Although the borer is not very common, yet whenever it appears in the main trunk or a branch, it invariably kills the host. Though the external symptoms of attack are not always visible, the site can be located from the sap or frass that comes out of the hole.

Management. (*i*) Cut and destroy the infested branches with grubs and pupae within. (*ii*) Remove frass near the holes on main stem and inject 4 ml of methyl parathion 50EC mixed in one litre of water into the hole and plug it with mud. If the holes open, these may be treated again.

4. *Sternochetus mangiferae* (Fabricius) (Mango stone weevil, Coleoptera: Curculionidae) (Fig. 7.1D)

Distribution. This pest is widely distributed in Uttar Pradesh, Orissa, West Bengal, Assam, Tripura, Karnataka and Andhra Pradesh.

Identification. This is a stoutly built, ovoid, dark brown weevil measuring about 6 mm.

Life-history. The weevils lay eggs in the skin of ripening fruit. The wound caused by the ovipositor heals soon after and the fruit does not exhibit any outward sign of infestation. On a fruit 12-36 eggs may be deposited. On emergence from the egg, the grub moves further inwards, eating its way through the unripe tissue until it bores into the embryo of the mango stone. When full-grown, the larva forms a cell inside the stone in which it pupates. The weevil cuts its way through the stone and the pulp comes out. The generation is completed in 40-50 days, but the emerging adults become inactive and resume breeding only in the next season. Thus, there seems to be a single generation of this pest in one year.

Host plants. Only mango

Damage. The insect attacks mango varieties with a relatively soft flesh. The injury caused by the larvae feeding in pulp sometimes heals over but a certain number of fruits always get spoiled when the weevils make an exit through ripe or near-ripe mangoes.

Management. (*i*) The pest can be suppressed by destroying all fallen fruits, weeviled mangoes and by disposing off refuse, stone, debris, etc. (*ii*) The weevil, being an internal feeder throughout its development, is not amenable to control with any of the insecticides. (*iii*) Raking of soil below the tree in October/November and March can also partially check infestation by the weevil.

5. *Bactrocera dorsalis* (Hendel) (Oriental / mango fruit fly, Diptera : Tephritidae) (Fig. 7.1E)

Distribution. The Oriental fruit fly or mango fruit fly, is the most serious of all fruit-flies and is widely distributed in India and South-east Asia. It has also been recorded in Malaysia, Indonesia, Taiwan, the Philippines, Australia and the Hawaii Islands.

Identification. The adult is stout, a little larger than the house fly, is brown and has transparent wings and yellow legs and dark rust-red and black patterns on the thorax. It measures 1.4 cm across the wings and 0.7 mm in body length. The legless maggots are yellow and opaque; when full-grown, measure 8-9 mm long and 1.5 mm across the posterior end.

Life-history. The adult flies emerge in April and start laying eggs under the rind of the ripening fruits and vegetables of the season (such as guava, loquat, apricot, plum, brinjal, etc.) and later shift to mango. They lay 2-15 eggs at a time in clusters. A female lays, on an average, 50 eggs but under favourable conditions, 150-200 eggs are laid in one month. The eggs hatch in 2-3 days in March-April and 1-1.5 days in the summer, and 10 days during winter. As the maggots develop they pass through 3 stages in the ripening pulp and are full-grown in 6-29 days. They leave the fruit and move away by jumping in little hops. On reaching a suitable place, they bury themselves into the soil and pupate 8-13 cm below the surface. In 6-44 days, they emerge as flies and reach the ripe fruit for further multiplication. The life-cycle is completed in 2-13 weeks and many generations are completed in a year.

Host plants. Apart from mango, the pest also feeds on guava, peach, apricot, cherry, pear, *chiku, ber,* citrus and other plants, totalling more than 250 hosts.

Damage. The damage is caused both by maggots and adults. The adults feed on exudation of ripe fruits and honeydew of various insects. The punctures for egg laying made by the females attract fermenting microorganisms. The maggots destroy the pulp making it foul smelling and discoloured. The fruits develop brown rotten patches on them and fall to the ground ultimately. The infested fruits become unmarketable and at times almost all of them contain maggots.

Management. (*i*) Avoid infestation of fruit flies by early harvesting of mature fruits. (*ii*) To prevent the carryover of the pest, collect and destroy all fallen infested fruits twice in a week. (*iii*) Plough round the trees during winter to expose and kill the pupae. (*iv*) Monitor the fruit fly population in orchards by using methyl eugenol traps. (*v*) Spray 1.25 litres of malathion 50EC + 12.5 kg *gur* or sugar in 1250 litres of water per ha and repeat sprays at 7-10 days interval if infestation continues or fix PAU fruit fly trap @ 40 per ha in the 3rd week of May. Recharge the trap after 30 days, if needed. (*vi*) After harvest, dip the fruits in 5 per cent sodium chloride solution for 60 minutes to kill the eggs, if any and also to decontaminate them of insecticide residue if at all present.

CITRUS

There are a large number of insect pests of citrus which cause considerable damage to different parts of the trees. The insects alongwith nematodes were responsible for citrus decline observed in various parts of India and other adjoining countries.

1. *Diaphorina citri* Kuwayana (Citrus psylla, Hemiptera : Aphalaridae) (Fig. 7.1F)

Distributon. The citrus psylla is distributed throughout the Orient and has been reported from India, China, Taiwan, Japan, Myanmar, Sri Lanka, the East Indies and New Guinea.

Identification. The adult is small, 3 mm in length and rests on the leaf surface with closed wings, the tail end of the body being turned upwards. The nymphs are flat, louse-like and orange yellow.

Life-history. The female adults lay, on an average, 500 almond-shaped, orange and stalked eggs on tender leaves and shoots of citrus trees. The lower end of the egg stalk is embedded in plant tissue. The eggs are laid either singly or in groups of two or three and are arranged in straight line, there being as many as 50 eggs in one place. The eggs hatch in 10-20 days in winter and 4-6 days in summer. On emerging, the light-yellow nymphs have a tendency to stick close to the egg-shell. They are found congregated on young half-open leaves, but in the later stages of development they may also migrate to the older leaves. There are five nymphal stages and the development is completed in 10-15 days in summer and 34-36 days in winter. There are 8-9 overlapping generations in a year.

Host plants. This pest it has been recorded on all species of citrus and a number of other plants of the family Rutaceae.

Damage. Both the nymphs and adults suck the cell-sap in millions with the help of their sharp, piercing mouthparts. The vitality of the plants deteriorates, and the young leaves and twigs stop growing further. The leaf buds, flower buds and leaves may wilt and die. Whatever little fruit is formed in the spring, falls off prematurely. Moreover, the nymphs secrete drops of a sweet thick fluid on which a black fungus develops, adversely affecting photosynthesis. This insect is also responsible for spreading the greening virus.

Management. (*i*) *Tetrastichus radiatus* is an important parasitoid of nymphs and is distributed in all the citrus grooves. A number of lady bird beetles, viz. *Coccinella septempunctata, Menochilus sexmaculatus* and *Brumoides suturalis,* and *Chrysoperla carnea* larvae also feed on nymphs. (*ii*) Pest population may be reduced to a great extent by conserving these natural enemies which are quite abundant in citrus ecosystem. (*iii*) Spray 400 g of thiamethoxam 25WG or 500 ml of imidacloprid 17.8SL or 3.125 litres of of dimethoate 30EC or 2.5 of oxydemeton methyl 25EC or 15.625 litres HMO (Horticulture Mineral Oil) in 1250 litres of water per ha during March with appearance of the pest and again in the first week of September.

2. *Dialeurodes citri* (Ashmead) (Citrus whitefly, Hemiptera : Aleyrodidae) (Fig. 7.1G)

Distribution. The pest is very widely distributed in America, India, Pakistan, Vietnam and China.

Identification. The adult is a minute insect, measuring 1.02-1.52 mm, the males being smaller than the females. The nymph is pale yellow, with purple eyes and its body is marginally fringed with bristles.

Life-history. The female adults lay eggs singly on the underside of soft young leaves. The eggs are oval, pale yellow and rest on small stalks. A single female may lay 200 or more eggs during its life which may last from 7 to 10 days. When there is severe infestation, there may be as many as 2,000 eggs on a single leaf. It may take 10-20 days for the eggs to hatch. The young larva, on emergence, crawls about for a few hours and then inserts its proboscis into the succulent portion of a twig. The larvae remain there in a stationary state and transform themselves into pupae at the same spot. A nymph is full-fed in 25-71 days and then changes into a pupa. The pupal stage is of the longest duration during the hottest part of summer and the coldest part of the winter, when it lasts 114-159 days.

Host plants. Although is a pest of citrus, the insect prefers to feed on certain deciduous plants such as persimmon and *dharek* (*Melia azedarach*).

Damage. The pest causes damage in the larval and adult stages. It sucks the cell-sap from leaves which curl over and fall off. The honeydew excreted by the nymphs is a very good medium for the growth of a sooty mould, which interferes with photosynthesis. Thus, the trees infested with this pest deteriorate further.

Management. (*i*) *Encarsia lahorensis* and *E. citufila* are the major parasitoids of this insect. A number of predators are recorded feeding on the eggs as well as nymphs of this insect, viz. *Brumoides suturalis*, *Cryptognatha flavescens* and *Verania cardoni* ; a predatory thrips, *Aleurothrips fasciatipennis* and a lacewing, *Chrysopa* sp. (*ii*) For effective management of flies, close planting, water logging or any other stress condition should be avoided. (*iii*) In case of localized infestation, the affected shoots should be clipped off and destroyed. (*iv*) Spary 2.5 litres of ethion 50EC or 3.125 lires of triazophos 40 EC in 1250 litres of water per ha during April-May and again during September-October.

3. *Pseudococcus filamentosus* Cockerell (Citrus mealy bug, Hemiptera : Pseudococcidae)

Distribution. The citrus mealy bug is more common in southern India than in the north.

Identification. The adult female is wingless, with a flattened body and short, waxy filaments along the margins. The nymphs are amber with a whitish waxy coating and filaments.

Life-history. The females lay eggs in clusters on citrus plants, which are found in protective cotton-like masses. There may be 300 eggs or more in one mass. The eggs hatch in 10-20 days and the nymphs crawl out and start feeding by inserting their mouthparts in the lower surface of the leaves. A waxy white covering is soon formed on their bodies. A female nymph is full-grown in 6-8 weeks. The male nymphs spin cotton-like cocoons, two or three weeks after hatching, and pupate before transforming themselves into winged adults.

Host plants. The mealy bugs are known to feed on a number of plants, often not closely related to citrus.

Damage. The insects feed on cell-sap and the plants become pale, wilted and the affected parts eventually die. The insects also excrete honeydew on which a black mould grows, which interferes with photosynthesis. In severe cases of infestation, the citrus flowers do not set fruit.

Management. (*i*) For effective management of these coccids, orchard sanitation is extremely important. Weeds act as additional hosts and these must be removed. (*ii*) The infested shoots should be pruned and destroyed. (*iii*) The coccinellid beetle, *Cryptolaemus montrouzieri*, should be released @ 10 beetles per plant, to control mealy-bugs. Inoculative releases of an exotic parasite, *Leptomastix dactylopii*, are also recommended. (*iv*) Spary 4.5 litres of chlorpyriphos 20EC in 1250 litres of water per ha. Repeat the spary after 15 days, as per need.

4. *Papilio demoleus* Linnaeus (Citrus caterpillar, Lepidoptera: Papilionidae) (Fig. 7.1H)

Distribution. The citrus caterpillar or the lemon butterfly, is found in Africa, greater part of Asia as far as Taiwan and Japan. It has been reported all over India.

Identification. The adult is a large beautiful butterfly, 2.8 cm in length and 9.4 cm in wing expanse. Its head and thorax are black, there being a creamy-yellow coloration on the underside of the abdomen. Its wings are dull black; ornamented with yellow markings. The full-grown caterpillar is yellowish green, has a horn-like structure on the dorsal side of the last body segment, and is 4.0 cm long and 6.5 mm wide.

Life-history. The butterflies lay eggs on tender shoots and fresh leaves, mostly on the undersurface. They hatch in 3-5 days. The young larva emerges by cutting a round hole through the egg-shell, which forms the first food of the larva. The larval life lasts 13-21 days. The larvae show preference for young and shiny leaves of citrus. The first four larval instars mimic the colouration of bird's dropping. The mature larva spins a supporting girdle around its body and pupates on a twig, a dry stick or any other raised structure. The pupal stage lasts about 8-11 days. The pest passes through three or four generations in a year.

Host plants. It can feed and breed on all varieties of cultivated or wild citrus and various other species of the family Rutaceae.

Damage. The young larvae feed only on fresh leaves and terminal shoots. Habitually, they feed from the margin inwards to the midrib. In later stages, they feed even on mature leaves and sometimes the entire plant may be defoliated. The pest is particularly devastating in nurseries and its damage to foliage seems to synchronize with fresh growth of citrus plants in April and August-September. Heavily attacked plants bear no fruits.

Management. (*i*) Hand picking of various stages of the pest and their destruction especially in nurseries and new orchards helps to suppress the population of the pest. (*ii*) Spraying of entomogenous fungus, *Bacillus thuringiensis*, nematode DD-136 strain or neem seed extract (3%) also gives quite high mortality of caterpillars. (*iii*) In severe infestation, spray 1.5 litres of quinalphos 25EC or 2.0 kg of carbaryl 50WP in 1250 litres of water per ha during April (after fruit set) and October (after rainy season).

5. *Phyllocnistis citrella* Stainton (Citrus leaf miner, Lepidoptera : Phyllocnistidae) (Fig. 7.1l)

Distribution. This insect is widely distributed in the Orient, northern Australia and India, and is known to be a serious pest of citrus nurseries in Tamil Nadu, Madhya Pradesh, Assam, Uttar Pradesh, Punjab, Haryana and in Pakistan.

Identification. The adult is a tiny moth, measuring 4.2 mm across the wings. On the front wings there are brown stripes and prominent black spots along the tips. The hind wings are pure white and both pairs are fringed with hairs. The full-grown larva measures 5.1 mm is length and is pale yellow or pale green with light brown well developed mandibles.

Life-history. The moths lay minute, flattened, transparent eggs on young leaves or tender shoots, usually on the lower surface, particularly near the midrib. The eggs which are laid singly, generally two or three per leaf, hatch in 2-10 days, giving rise to legless larvae. Soon after emerging, the larvae mine into the leaf tissue and form galleries within which they remain confined for the rest of their immature life. Larvae are full-fed in 5-30 days, and when mature, they settle down in enlargements of the galleries near the leaf margin. By the time they spin cocoons for pupation, the leaves get twisted or folded over. The pupal stage lasts 5-25 days. The life-cycle is completed in 12-55 days and several overlapping generations are produced in a year.

Host plants. Apart from citrus, the insect also feeds on a variety of other plants such as pomelo, willow and cinnamon.

Damage. The damage is caused by the larvae due to their mining habit. The injured epidermis takes the shape of twisted silvery galleries. On older leaves, brownish patches are formed which serve as focii of infection for citrus canker. The attacked leaves remain on the plants for a considerably long time and the damage gradually spreads to fresh leaves. Heavily attacked plants can be spotted from a distance and young nurseries are most severely affected; the young plants of orange and grape fruit may not even survive. In larger trees, the photosynthesis is adversely affected, vitality is reduced and there is an appreciable reduction in yield.

Management. (*i*) On nursery plants, spary 125 ml of fenvalerate 20EC or 250 ml of cypermethrin 10EC or 875 ml of decamethrin 2.8EC or 370 ml of monocrotophos 36SL in 250 litres of water per ha at fortnightly intervals. (*ii*) Spray of 2 per cent neem seed extract has also been found quite effective and safe. (*iii*) In full- grown orchards, spray 400 g thiamethoxam 25WG or 500 ml of imidacloprid 17.8SL or 1.25 litres of fenvalerate 20EC or 2.5 litres of cypermethrin 10EC or 3.125 litres of triazophos 40EC or 4.5 litres of chlorpyriphos 20EC in 1250 litres of water per ha during April-May and August-September. Avoid use of synthetic pyrethroids on full-grown trees.

6. *Indarbela quadrinotata* (Walker) (Bark caterpillar, Lepidoptera: Metarbelidae)

Distribution. The pest is widely distributed in Myanmar, Bangladesh, Sri Lanka and India.

Identification. The adults are pale brown moths with rufous head and thorax. The fore wings are pale rufous with numerous dark rufous bands. Their hind wings are fuscous. The freshly hatched larvae are dirty brown, while the full-grown caterpillars (5-6 cm) have pale brown bodies with dark brown heads.

Life-history. The females lay eggs in clusters of 15-25 each, under the loose bark of the trees. As many as 2000 eggs may be laid by a single female. The eggs hatch in 8-10 days and the freshly hatched larvae nibble at the bark and after 2-3 days bore inside. The larvae have the habit of making webs along the feeding galleries and above the holes where they bore deeper into the wood. The galleries and the webs above them have a zig-zag shape and contain wooden frass and excreta. The larvae take as many as 9-11 months to complete development. When full-grown, they make a hole into the wood and pupate inside. The pupal stage lasts 3-4 weeks. The moths emerge in summer and they are short lived. Only one generation is completed in a year.

Host plants. The bark-eating caterpillars feed on citrus, mango, guava, *jamun,* loquat, mulberry, pomegranate, *ber,* drumstick, litchi, *amla,* rose and a number of forest and ornamental trees.

Damage. Thick, ribbonlike, silken webs are seen running on the bark of the main stem especially near the forks. The larvae also make holes and as many as 16 holes may be seen on a tree, one caterpillar or pupa occupying each hole. A severe infestation may result in the death of the attacked stem but not of the main trunk. There may be interference with the translocation of cell sap and thus arrestation of growth of the tree is noticed with the resultant reduction in its fruiting capacity.

Management. (*i*) Remove the webbing and inject kerosene oil into the holes during September-October and again in January-February. Treat all the alternate host plants in the vicinity. (*ii*) The insecticides for 100 litres of water are 40 g carbaryl 50WP or 2 ml dichlorvos 76EC or 5 ml methyl parathion 50EC or 10 ml monocrotophos 36SL. These chemicals should be applied after removing webbings.

GRAPEVINE

A large number of insect pests attack the grapevine and over 85 species have been reported in India. However, only about half a dozen pests require attention for their management.

1. *Rhipiphorothrips cruentatus* Hood (Grapevine thrips, Thysanoptera: Heliothripidae)

Distribution. This is the most destructive pest of grapevine in India.

Identification. The adults are minute, being 1.4 mm long, blackish brown, with yellowish wings. The nymphs are yellowish brown, just visible to the unaided eye as minute fast-moving streaks on the underside of leaves or in the centre of various flowers, particularly the rose.

Life-history. The adults lay eggs on the undersurface of leaves by making small slits in the plant tissues, placing one egg in one slit. A female, on an average, lays 50 eggs which are dirty white, bean-shaped. The eggs hatch in 3-8 days and young nymphs appear as reddish active creatures which become yellowish brown, as they grow older. They feed on the underside of leaves by rasping the surface and sucking the oozing cell-sap. They are full-fed in 9-20 days and during the season of active breeding, they pupate on leaves. In 2-5 days, they change into adults which also feed like the nymphs. The females can reproduce with or without fertilization; the fertilized eggs hatch into females and unfertilized eggs hatch into males. The insect hibernates as a pupa in the soil from December to March and, during the active period, many generations are completed.

Host plants. Besides grapes, this pest also feeds on rose, *jamun* and *ak*.

Damage. Plants suffer because of constant feeding by large number of insects. The attacked leaves take a whitish hue, acquire a withered appearance, and then turn brown. The leaves ultimately curl up and drop off the plant. Such vines either do not bear fruit or the fruit drops off prematurely.

Management. (*i*) Remove grasses from orchard and prune infested leaves. (*ii*) Spray 500 ml of malathion 50EC in 500 litres of water per 100 vines, once before flowering and again after the fruit set.

2. *Sylepta lunalis* Guenee (Grapevine leaf roller, Lepidoptera : Pyralidae)

Distribution. The leaf roller is a serious pest of grapevine in Andhra Pradesh, Tamil Nadu, Karnataka, Maharashtra, Punjab and U.P.

Identification. The adults are dirty brown, with white spots on the fore and hind wings.The abdomen is light brown, the terminal segment being dark brown. The wing span of the male moth is 2.2-2.4 cm, whereas that of the female is 2.5-2.8 cm. The full-grown caterpillars are cylindrical and measure 2.6 cm, The body is covered with hairs and the head is brownish-black.

Life-history. The moths lay creamy white oval (1.4 mm across) eggs on the lower surface of the leaves. The number of eggs laid by a female varies from 98 to 120. The eggs hatch in

2-3 days. The first instar larva is tiny, dirty green and measures 3-5 mm in length. After 2 days, it changes to the second instar, which also lasts 2-3 days. There are five larval instars and pupation takes place inside the leaf-rolls. Later on, the pupa falls to the ground on fallen leaves and debris. The pupal stage lasts 6-7 days.

Host plants. Besides grapevine, this pest can also survive on some other species of the family Vitaceae.

Damage. The young caterpillars (1-3 instars) feed on the lower epidermis of the leaves and skeletonize them. The grown-up larvae (4th and 5th instars) roll up the leaf margins towards the mid-rib with one caterpillar in each roll.

Management. (*i*) In the initial stage of attack, remove the rolled up leaves and destroy them with larvae/pupae within. (*ii*) Spray 1.25 litres of endosulfan 35EC or 1.25 litres of malathion 50EC in 1250 litres of water as soon as the attack starts.

3. *Sinoxylon anale* Lesne (Grapevine beetle, Coleoptera : Bostrychidae)

Distribution. In India, the grapevine beetle is commonly known as 'ghun' and is one of the most important pests of grapevine. Its distribution covers France, Italy, erstwhile USSR, Japan and China.

Identification. The adult is sturdy, walks slowly and flies rarely. Typically, it is dark brown and measures 4.25 mm in length and 1.8 mm in breadth. The diagnostic three-bladed antennae and a pair of spines on the posterior elytral extremity are present. The full-grown larvae are thick yellowish-white curved grubs, often found feeding alongwith the adults, when the infested vises are split open.

Life-history. This pest is active on dormant vines. After winter sets in, the adult beetles bore into the living woody stems and branches. Eggs are laid in galleries constructed by adult beetles inside the attacked portions. After hatching, the grubs continue feeding inside. The activity of the pest is accompanied with a peculiar crackling noise, followed by the ejection of a dusty material from the exits of the feeding-galleries. The multiplication of the pest continues in the dead vines throughout the year.

Host plants. It is primarily a pest of grapevine but also feeds on *sal* (*Shorea robusta*), teak (*Ouglinia dalbergioides, Boswellia serrata*), *shisham* (*Dalbergia sissoo*), wooden packing cases, etc.

Damage. Damage is done only to the dormant grapevine. The adult beetle constructs a circular hole, extending to the centre of the stem and then makes longitudinal galleries and forms a number of exits. The damage is always found about 30 cm above the ground level. Both adults and grubs cause damage by feeding inside the vine-stem. All plant parts above the point of attack dry up completely. The pest prefers the late sprouting varieties, such as Anab-E-Shahi and Selection 7 and its incidence varies from 26.6 to 63.5 per cent

Management. (*i*) Clean cultivation including removal of loose bark coupled with careful pruning and destruction of infested parts prove very helpful to prevent infestation by the beetle. (*ii*) Spray the vines with 1.5 litres of monocrotophos 40EC or 2.5 kg of carbaryl 50WP in 1250 litres of water.

4. *Sthenias grisator* Fabricius (Grapevine girdler, Coleoptera : Cerambycidae) (Fig. 7.1J)

Distribution. The grapevine girdler is a serious pest throughout the grape growing areas in India, particularly Uttar Pradesh, Bihar, Maharashtra and Andhra Pradesh.

Identification. The adult is a greyish brown beetle with the elytra bearing an eye-spot near the tips.

Life-history. The adults deposit eggs in clusters of 2-4 underneath the bark of girdled branches. A slight bulge on the bark adjacent to the transverse cut indicates the location of eggs underneath. Each egg is enveloped in a white parchment-like covering and hatches in 8 days. On hatching, the tiny grubs (2-4 mm in length) immediately tunnel into the wood. Their head is dark brown and the mouth has a pair of prominent mandibles, each with two teeth. The most conspicuous part of the grub is the globular thorax, having a few chitinous spines on top. These probably aid in tunnelling into the wood. The full-grown grub is 10-12 mm long. The life- cycle is completed in more than a year. The adults appear again late in summer, but they hibernate during winter.

Host plants. Beside grapes, the stem girdler, feeds on rose-bushes, mulberry, various garden shrubs, creepers, crotons, etc.

Damage. The girdling of green branches is an essential event before egg-laying. This results in considerable damage to the vines, as they dry up above the point of girdling. The bark and wood are cut right upto the centre and, at times, even the branches are cut into two bits.

Management. (*i*) Cutting and burning of attacked branches below girdling point, and hand collection and destruction of beetles may help in mitigating the beetle. (*ii*) Chemical control measures are same as for grapevine beetle.

5. *Scelodonta strigicollis* Moltschulsky (Flea beetle, Coleoptera : Chrysomelidae)

Distribution. This is one of the most destructive pests of grapevine in India and is found throughout the country particularly in Uttar Pradesh, Bihar, Maharashtra and Andhra Pradesh.

Identification. The adult is a shining beetle with metallic bronze colour and 6 dark spots on the elytra and is about 4.5 mm long.

Life-history. The female oviposits in the bark or in the soil and eggs may be laid singly or in groups of 20-40. A female lays 200-600 eggs during its life of 8-12 months. Eggs hatch in 4-8 days and the grubs feed on the roots and the larval period lasts 35-45 days. The full-grown grubs pupate 6-8 cm deep in the soil and emerge as adults in 7-10 days. The life-cycle is completed in about two months.

Host plants. Grapevine

Damage. Both the adults and the grubs cause damage, the former being voracious feeder, are very destructive. The adults eat up and bore into the buds, nibble the leaves making a number of holes on them, scratch the tendrils and eat the epidermis of the branches. The affected buds or sprouts soon dry up. The grubs feed on the cortex of the roots and cause considerable damage.

Management. (*i*) Remove the loose bark after pruning. (*ii*) Adult beetles may be collected and killed. (*iii*) Spray 2.5 kg of carbaryl 50WP or 3.5 litres of chlorpyriphos 20EC in 1250 litres of water/ha, after pulling out the loose bark.

GUAVA

More than 80 species of insects and mites have been recorded on guava trees affecting the growth and yield. However, the major pests are fruit flies, bark eating caterpillars and scales.

1. *Bactrocera dorsalis* (Hendel) (Oriental fruit fly, Diptera : Tephritidae)

Guava fruits are attacked by five species of fruit flies, viz., *B. dorsalis, B. diversus* (Coquillett), *B. cucurbitae* (Coquillett), *B. nigrotibialis* (Perkins) and *B. zonata* (Saunders). However, among these, the former two are most common and serious pests of guava. The details are given under 'Mango'.

2. *Indarbela tetraonis* (Moore), *I. quadrinotata* (Walker) (Bark eating caterpillar, Lepidoptera: Metarbelidae)

The details are given under 'Citrus'.

3. *Chloropulvinaria psidii* (Maskell) (Guava mealy scale, Hemiptera: Coccidae)

Distribution. The guava mealy scale is widely distributed throughout the tropical regions of the world including India, Bangladesh and Sri Lanka. In India, it is a major pest of guava in Punjab, Uttar Pradesh, Maharashtra, Andhra Pradesh, Karnataka and Tamil Nadu.

Identification. The adult scales are shield-shaped, oval, yellowish green and measure 3 mm in body length.

Life-history. Eggs are laid beneath the body of mature female in a conspicuous egg-sac and later the female dies. The first instar nymphs or crawlers are the active dispersive phase responsible for starting new infestation.

Host plants. Apart from guava, the scale feeds on coffee, tea, citrus, mango, *gular,* jack-fruit, *jamun,* litchi, loquat, sapota and many other shrubs and trees.

Damage. The scale insects are found in large numbers sticking to leaves on ventral side, tender twigs and shoots. They suck sap from ventral side of leaves, petioles, tender shoots and occasionally from fruits. They cause leaf distortion and growth disturbance. The females feed voraciously and also exude copious quantity of honeydew. The honeydew excreted by the scales encourages the development of sooty mould on foliage which interferes with photosynthetic activity of plants and spoils the market value of fruits. Severe infestation could kill the branches.

Management. (*i*) Prune and destroy the infested shoots at initial stage of infestation. (*ii*) In case of severe attack, spray 1.25 litres of monocrotophos 40EC in 1250 litres of water per ha. (*iii*) After two weeks, release 20 *Cryptolaemus montrouzieri* beetles per tree.

4. *Dichocrocis punctiferalis* (Guenee) (Castor capsule borer, Lepidoptera: Pyralidae)

The damage is done by the caterpillars which bore into the fruits and render these unfit for consumption. The details of this pest are given under 'Castor'.

5. *Saissetia coffeae* (Walker) (Helmet scale, Hemiptera : Coccidae)

The details of this pest are given under 'Coffee'.

BANANA

There are more than 182 insect pests of banana in India.

1. *Nacoleia octasema* (Meyrick) (Banana scale moth, Lepidoptera: Pyralidae) (Fig. 7.1K)

Distribution. This pest occurs in Indonesia, eastern Australia, New Guinea, Solomon Islands, Fiji, Tonga, Samoa and Queensland.

Identification. The moth has a wing span of 2.2 cm and its colour varies from light brown to dark brown.

Life-history. The female moths lay pale greenish-white eggs on or near the flag leaf of banana plant just before the bunch emerges. The eggs hatch in about 4 days and the small transparent yellow caterpillars crawl under the closed bracts of the young banana bunch and begin feeding there. After completing this development, the larvae may pupate right on the plant or more often in the debris near the base.

Host plants. Besides banana, this insect can also develop on Manila hemp, maize and some wild plants.

Damage. The gregarious caterpillars feed on the young female flowers and leave scale-like scars on the young fruits. They feed so voraciously that the inflorescence is soiled with frass and refuse of the larvae, and gives an ugly appearance.

Management. Spray 2.5 kg of carbaryl 50WP in 1250 litres of water per ha directing the spray towards the bracts of the inflorescence.

2. *Cosmopolites sordidus* (Germar) (Banana weevil, Coleoptera: Curculionidae)

Distribution. This species although native to South-east Asia, has attained wide distribution on cultivated bananas of the world. Its present distribution, in addition to India and South-east Asia, covers parts of Australia, the Hawaii Islands, tropical and South Africa and tropical America.

Identification. The adults are shiny black with elongated and slightly curved snout.

Life-history. The female weevil bites a small hole in the corm, lays a single egg and continues this activity on other plants throughout the year. A female can lay 10-50 eggs during its life of a few months. The larvae emerge from the eggs in about a week and bore into the corm, where they feed, making a tunnel. When full-grown in 2-6 weeks, the larvae pupate in the same tunnel. The pupal stage lasts about a week. The adults, on emergence, remain in the soil for sometime, feeding on the underground parts of the plants. Later on, they visit the growing point for oviposition.

Host plant. Banana rhizone.

Damage. The damage done by the weevil is through the destruction of the corm tissue. The seedlings are killed as a result of the borer attack when the larvae approach the growing-point. The tunnelled corms sometimes break out, since the weevils do not attack the roots, they do not cause toppling over.

Management. (*i*) The cultural operations consist of destroying the sheltering and feeding places of the adult weevils. The pseudostems, from which the bunches have been cut, are chopped up and scattered in the plantation so that they rot quickly. Also, the pesudostems should be cut close to the ground and the infested suckers should not be used for planting. (*ii*) Suckers should be dipped in 0.1 per cent quinalphos emulsion before planting. In case of attack, spray 315 ml of phosphamidon 100 or 625 ml of dimethoate 30EC in 625 litres of water per ha, around the base of the plants or clumps.

3. *Odoiporus longicollis* (Olivier) (Banana stem borer, Coleoptera : Curculionidae) (Fig. 17.1L)

Distribution. It is a serious pest of banana in North-east India.

Identification. The adult is a robust reddish brown weevil about 1.5-2.0 cm long. The grub is apodous, yellowish with reddish head.

Life-history. The eggs are laid in small burrow in the rhizome or within leaf sheaths just above the ground. Eggs hatch in 3-5 days in summer and 5-8 days in winter. The larva bores into pseudostem making tunnels within and cutting holes on its outer surface. The larval duration is 26 days in summer and 68 days in winter with five larval instars. It pupates in tunnel towards the periphery. The pupal period lasts 20-24 days in summer and 37-44 days in winter. The adult lives for a period of upto two years.

Host plant. Banana

Damage. Both the grubs and adults cause the damage. Grubs bore into the rhizome and make tunnels within it. Adults also tunnel within the stem, feeding on its internal tissues as a result of which the internal shoot is killed. Infested plants show premature withering, leaves become scarce, fruits become undersized and their suckers are killed outright.

Management. (*i*) Uproot and burn the infested plants. (*ii*) Spray 2.5 kg of carbaryl 50WP in 1250 litres of water/ha.

4. *Pentalonia nigronervosa* Coquerel (Banana aphid, Hemiptera : Aphididae)

Distribution. The pest is found in most of the banana growing areas in India.

Identification. The aphid is brownish in colour and has black-veined wings.

Life-history. The aphid lives in colonies within the leaf-axils, or tender leaves and at base of the culm at the ground level. Young ones are given birth by alate and apterous females by parthenogenetic development. An aphid is capable of producing 30-50 nymphs in its life time of 27-37 days. The nymph undergoes four instars of 2-3 days duration each. Total life-cycle is completed in 8-9 days. About 30 to 40 generations are completed during a year under South Indian conditions.

Host plants. Apart from banana, it also attacks cardamom, large cardamom and *Colocasia antiquorum*.

Damage. Both nymphs and adults suck the sap from the tender leaves. The pest is very important because it transmits the bunchy top virus.

Management. Spray 1.70 litres of dimethoate 30EC or 1.25 litres of oxydemeton methyl 25EC in 1250 litres of water/ha.

BER

In India, as many as 80 insect species feeding on *ber* tree have been reported, out of which fruit fly, -*ber* beetle and lac insect are important.

1. *Carpomyia vesuviana* Costa (Ber fruit fly, Diptera : Tephritidiae) (Fig. 7.1M)

Distribution. This pest is widely distributed in India, Pakistan and southern Italy.

Identification. The adults, smaller than the house fly, are brownish yellow, with brown longitudinal stripes on the thorax, being surrounded on the sides and the back with black spots. There are greyish brown spots on the wings and bristly hair on the tip of the abdomen. The larvae are creamy white and slightly smaller than those of the other fruit flies.

Life-history. The flies make cavities in the skin of fruit and lay one or two spindle-shaped creamy-white eggs, 1 mm below the skin, leaving behind a resinous material. The eggs hatch in 2-3 days and the maggots feed on the flesh of the fruit, making galleries towards the centre. The larvae are full-grown in 7-10 days and they come out of the fruit by cutting one or two holes in the skin. They move away, and reach a suitable place to pupate generally 6-15 cm below the soil surface. The pupal stage lasts 14-30 days and the shortest life-cycle, from egg to the emergence of the adult, is completed in 24 days. There are 2-3 broods in a year.

Host plant. Ber

Damage. The damage is caused by the maggots which eat away the pulp. Since the area around the puncture made by the female for oviposition stops growing, the fruits become deformed. Fleshy varieties of ber are more seriously damaged than the less fleshy ones. The attacked fruits are rotten near the stones and emit a strong smell. Late maturing fruits are destroyed almost entirely.

Management. (*i*) Collect and destroy the fallen infested fruits at alternate days. (*ii*) Rake the soil around the trees during summer to expose the pupae to heat and natural enemies. (*iii*) To escape egg laying on fruits, do not allow the fruits to ripe on the trees, harvest at green and firm stage. (*iv*) Spray 1.25 litres of dimethoate 30EC in 750 litres of water per ha during February-March, and repeat sprays at 10 days interval. Stop spraying at least 15 days before fruit picking.

2. *Adoretus pallens* Arrow (Ber beetle, Coleoptera : Scarabaeidae)

Distribution. This defoliating beetle is widely distributed in northern India and Pakistan.

Identification. The adult beetles are bright yellow with yellowish-brown wings.

Life-history. The adults lay white, smooth, elongate eggs, singly in the soil near the host plants. Egg laying continues at irregular intervals from May to August and the eggs hatch in 6-9 days in that season. The whitish grubs feed on soil humus, roots of grasses and other vegetable matter found under or near the ber trees. When full-grown, the grubs measure 15 mm in length and are creamy white. They make an earthen cell in the autumn and hibernate through the whole of winter. Pupation takes place sometimes during next April and the adults emerge after 11-12 days. There is only one generation in a year.

Host plants. The beetle is polyphagous, but prefers the ber tree and the grapevine.

Damage. Damage is characterized by round holes cut in the leaves by beetles during the night. The ber trees are sometimes so heavily attacked that the entire foliage may disappear and such trees do not bear any fruit. The attack starts early in the spring and continues up to August.

Management. (*i*) Light traps are quite effective in trapping the adult beetles. (*ii*) Raking around the trees is useful in exposing the hibernating grubs and killing them. (*iii*) Spray 2.5 kg of carbaryl 50WP in 750 litres of water per ha in the evening as soon as the damage starts. If the damage continues, repeat the spraying after one week.

3. *Kerria lacca* (Kerr) (Lac Insect, Hemiptera : Kerriidae) (Fig. 7.2)

Distribution. Apart from India, the insect is also found in Pakistan, Bangla Desh, Sri Lanka, Myanmar, Malaysia, Thailand and China.

Identification. The newly hatched nymphs are pinkish in colour about 0.60 mm long. Males appear pinkish-red in colour and are both winged and wingless. There is only a single pair of translucent membranous forewings in winged males. The female is wingless (apterous) pinkish in colour and measuring 1.5 mm in length; dorsal surface of the body is convex while ventral surface is flat.

Life-history. A female lays eggs ranging from 200 to 500 in lac encrustation underneath its body. Since embryos are fully developed hence the eggs hatch within a few hours. The first instar nymphs known as "crawlers" emerge in large numbers from the lac encrustations and crawl along the branches of their host plants and feed on the *phloem*. As the nymphs pierce the branches to reach the phloem, they cover the holes with their wax secretions. Upon getting settled on the twigs, the nymphs do not move. After few days they start secreting resin from glands located all over the body under cuticle except mouth parts, two breathing pores and anus. With the growth of the insect, there is simultaneous increase in size of the resinous covering. Females produce more quantity of the commercial lac than males. The nymphs undergo three moultings before reaching adult stage. The maximum activity of the lac insect has been recorded in January-February and June-July.

Host plants. Apart from four major host plants i.e. *ber, kusum, palas and khair*, it is also found on grapevine, pomegranate, *amla, litchi,* sugar apple, tamarind etc.

Damage. Sucking of sap by the lac insect leads to reduction of vitality and vigour of the infested trees resulting in substantial loss in yield and quality. Black mould develops on the honeydew giving sooty and ugly appearance to the trees.

Management. (*i*) Prune all severely infested branches when the trees are in dormancy and burn these. (*ii*) Scrap off the infested twigs and spray 250 ml dimethoate 30 EC by diluting it with 250 litres of water in April and repeat the spray in September.

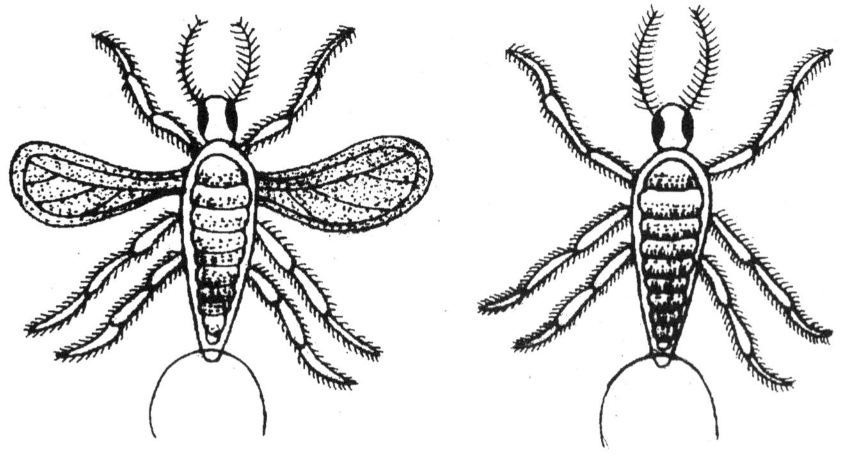

(*a*) Winged male (*b*) Wingless male

Fig. 7.2. Pests of tropical and sub-tropical fruits **A.** Lac insect, *Kerria lacca*

POMEGRANATE

Pomegranate is attacked by several insect pests among which pomegranate butterfly is the most serious.

1. *Virachola isocrates* (Fabricius) (Pomegranate butterfly, Lepidoptera: Lycaenidae) (Fig. 7.1N)

Distribution. This insect is widely distributed all over India and the adjoining countries. In India, it is commonly found in Uttar Pradesh, Bihar, Orissa, Himachal Pradesh, Haryana, Punjab, Rajasthan, Madhya Pradesh, Andhra Pradesh, Karnataka and Tamil Nadu.

Identification. The adult butterflies are glossy-bluish violet (males) to brownish violet (females) in colour with an orange patch on the forewings. The wing expanse is 4-5 cm. The full-grown caterpillars (1.7 – 2.0 cm) are dark brown in colour and have short hair and whitish patches all over the body.

Life-history. The female butterfly lays shiny white, oval shaped eggs singly on the calyx of flowers and on small fruits. The eggs hatch in 7-10 days and the young larvae bore into the developing fruits. They feed there for 18-47 days till they are full-grown. Then they pupate inside the fruit but occasionally may pupate outside even, attaching themselves to the stalk of the fruit. The pupal stage lasts 7-34 days. There are four overlapping generations in a year.

Host plants. It is a polyphagous pest having a very wide range of host plants including *Aonla,* apple, ber, citrus, guava, litchi, loquat, mulberry, peach, pear, plum, pomegranate, sapota and tamarind.

Damage. The caterpillars damage the fruit by feeding inside and riddling through the ripening seeds of pomegranate. The infested fruits are also attacked by bacteria and fungi which cause the fruits to rot. The affected fruits ultimately fall off and give an offensive smell. This pest may cause 40 to 90 per cent damage to the fruits.

Management. (*i*) Bagging of fruits before maturity will help in checking damage. (*ii*) Collection and destruction of fallen infested fruits prevents build up of the pest. (*iii*) Removing flowering weeds, particularly of compositae family helps to check multiplication of the pest *(iv)* Spray young fruits with 2.5 Kg of carbaryl 50WP in 1250 litres of water per ha during May-June at 15 days interval

2. *Indarbela quadrinotata* (Walker) (Bark caterpillar, Lepidoptera : Metarbelidae)

The pest has been described under 'Citrus'.

II. TEMPERATE FRUITS

The share of temperate fruits in total fruit production in India is about 3 per cent. Since temperate fruits are grown universally, some of the serious cosmopolitan pests, namely San Jose scale and the woolly aphis, have been introduced accidently in India. Another dreaded world-wide pest of apple, the codling moth, was recorded in Ladakh in 1964, but its further spread has not been reported.

1. *Eriosoma lanigerum* (Hausmann) (Woolly apple aphid, Hemiptera: Aphididae) (Fig. 7.3A)

Distribution. This insect is most common in India and Pakistan.

Identification. The aphids are minute, 1.0 mm long and purplish coloured insects concealed underneath a white cottony mass.

Life-history. The aphids reproduce parthenogenetically and the progeny, thus produced, consists of females only. Each female may produce up to 116 young ones in her lifetime. There are four nymphal instars and the duration of each varies according to the season. The total duration of the nymphal period is 35-42 days in February, 29.5 days in August-November, and 10.5-19.5 days in April-July. There may be 13 generations in a year. In December, there is a partial migration from aerial parts to the roots of infested plants and the reverse migration from the roots to the aerial parts takes place in May.

Host plants. It is a serious pest of apple, pear and crab apple.

Damage. The aphids suck cell-sap from the bark of the twigs and from the roots underground. Swellings or knots appear on the roots which hinder the normal plant functions. Owing to the loss of cell-sap, the twigs also shrivel and the young nursery plants, which are affected the worst, may die quickly.

Management. The management of woolly aphid in apple orchards is a difficult task because of the waxy covering on the body and reinfestation due to local migration from roots. However, good success can be achieved if following strategies are followed : (*i*) Use of resistant root stock seems to be the only answer for subterranean aphid population. Use resistant root stock like Golden Delicius, Northern Spy and Morton Stocks 778, 779, 789 and 793. (*ii*) In Himachal Pradesh, the woolly aphid has been controlled by using natural methods by introducing a parasite, *Aphelinus mali* which attacks the 4th and 5th stage nymphs. The parasite has to be maintained on cut twigs fixed in moist soil inside wire-gauze cages. (*iii*) As the main source of infestation in the orchard is infested plant material from nurseries, select healthy plants from nursery and then before planting in the orchard, treat them with chlorpyriphos 0.05 per cent. (*iv*) During leaf-fall, spray the plants with 2.0 litres of chlorpyriphos 20EC in 1250 litres of water per ha against aerial forms. For controlling the root forms, apply one litre of oxydemeton methyl 25EC in 1250 litres of water per ha. These chemicals should be sprayed during winter months. (*v*) For checking this pest during summer, spray 2.0 litres of malathion 50EC in 1250 litres of water per ha. The insecticidal spray should be avoided where the parasite, *A. mali,* is present. (*vi*) Carry out fumigation against root forms with paradichlorobenzene granules in a 15 cm deep trench dug round the infested tree, about 2 metres from it.

2. *Quadraspidiotus perniciosus* (Comstock) (San Jose scale, Hemiptera: Diaspididae) (Fig. 7.3B)

Distribution. This insect is world-wide and is the most serious pest in temperate regions. In India, it is most common in Jammu and Kashmir, Himachal Pradesh, Uttarakhand and Tamil Nadu.

Identification. The adults are greyish tiny insects showing sexual dimorphism the females being rounded 2 mm across and wingless, the males are elongated and winged (bear 2 wings instead of 4).

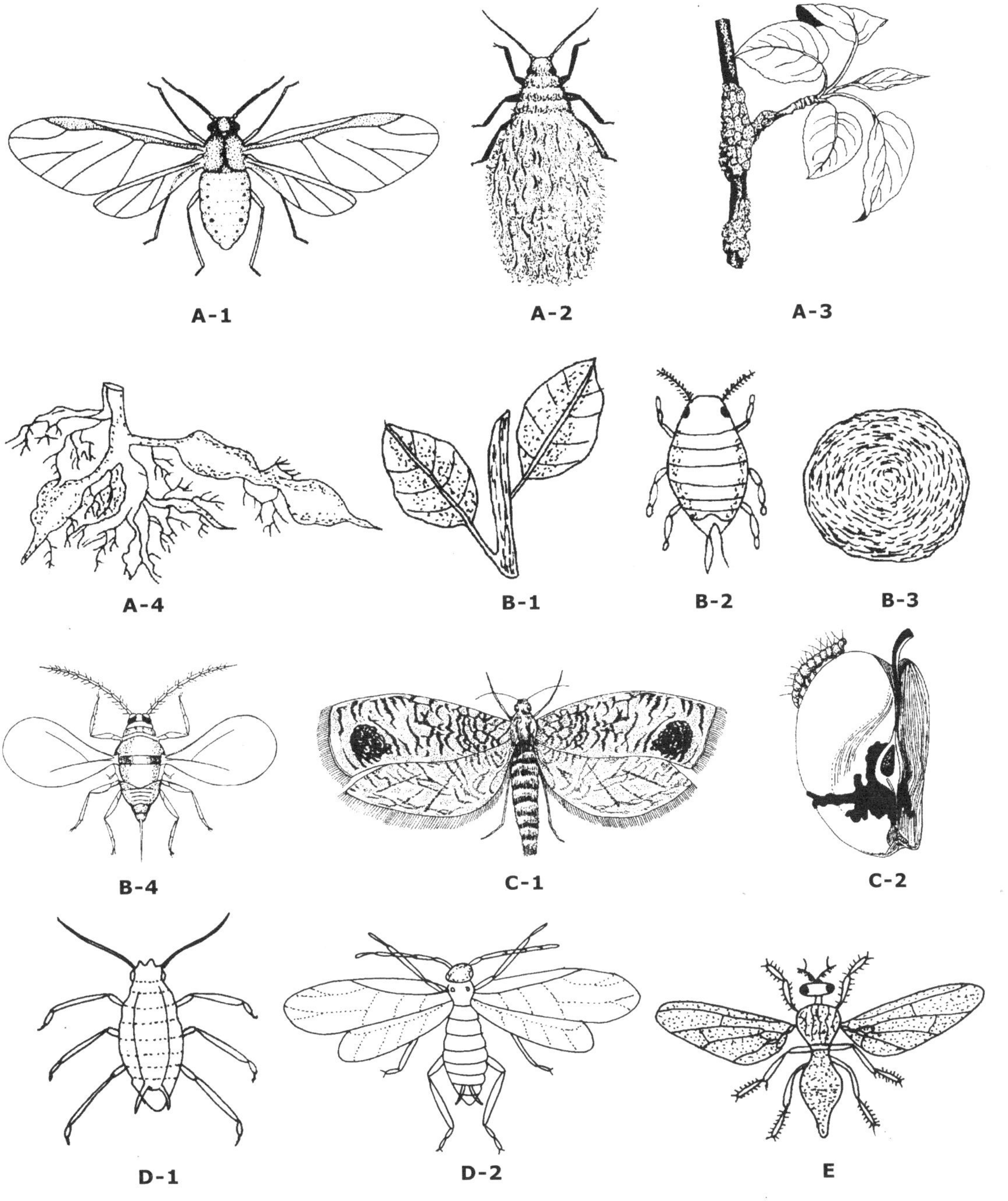

Fig. 7.3 Pests of temperate fruits. **A.** Woolly apple aphid, *Eriosoma lanigerum*; A-1. Winged male, A-2. Wingless female, A-3. Affected twig, A-4. Affected root. **B.** San Jose scale, *Quadraspidiotus perniciosus*; B-1. Affected twig, B-2. Crawler, B-3. Wingless female, B-4. Winged male. **C.** Codling moth, *Cydia pomonella*; C-1. Adult C-2. Mature larva on damaged apple. **D.** Peach leaf curl aphid, *Brachycaudus helichrysi*; D-1. Nymph, D-2. Adult. **E.** Peach fruit fly, *Bactrocera zonata*.

Life-history. The San Jose scale gives birth to young ones, which hatch from the eggs developed within the body of the female. Each female may give birth to 200-400 nymphs. The newly-born nymphs crawl out of the parental scale and lead a free life for 12-24 hours. On finding a suitable place, they insert their mouth-parts into the plant tissue and begin to feed by sucking the cell-sap. They become full-grown in 30-40 days and the females again start giving birth to young ones within the next 10-14 days. The gravid mothers live for about 50-53 days. The male nymph has an elliptical or oval scale and develops into a winged adult in 25-31 days. The life of the male adult is short and hardly exceeds 24-32 hours, during which it fertilizes the non-winged females. Four overlapping generations are completed in a year and the fifth-generation nymphs overwinter.

Host plants. It usually prefers plants belonging to the Rosaceae such as apple, plum, pear, peach, etc.

Damage. Adult females and nymphs suck sap from twigs, branches and fruits. At first, the growth of the infested plants is checked, but as the scales increase in number, the infested plants may die.

Management. (*i*) For effective management of San Jose scale, orchard sanitation should be given priority. Infested pruned material should be collected immediately and burnt. (*ii*) Augmentative and inoculative releases of two exotic parasitoids, *Encarsia perniciosi* and *Aphytis* sp. *proclia* group have given promising results for the suppression of San Jose scale on apples. The Russian strain of *E. perniciosi* proved effective in Himachal Pradesh while Chinese and American strains proved better in Uttar Pradesh. (*iii*) Spray diesel oil emulsion + Bordeaux mixture (diesel oil 68 litres + copper sulphate 15 kg + unslacked lime 3.75 kg) to be emulsified and diluted 5-6 times before spraying or spray 7.5 litres of ESSO tree spray oil emulsion in 250 litres of water per ha during the winter season when the trees are in dormant stage and completely defoliated. (*iv*) Severe scale infestation under neglected orchard management requires additional summer sprays with 1.25 litres of diazinon 20EC or 625 ml of methyl demeton 25EC in 1250 litres of water per ha. (*v*) To protect the plants in nursery, apply carbofuran granules @ 0.75-1.0 g a.i. per plant.

3. *Malacosoma indicum* Walker (Tent caterpillar, Lepidoptera.: Lasiocampidae)

Distribution. The insect is common in north-western India, being more serious in Himachal Pradesh and Jammu and Kashmir.

Identification. The male moth is light reddish and the female moth is light brown, with a wing expanse of 2.9-3.2 cm and 3.5-3.7 cm, respectively. When full-grown, the larva is 4.0-4.5 cm long, with black head and abdomen.

Life-history. The eggs are laid in bands of 200-400 around branches from mid-March to May and remain dormant during the next 9 months. The eggs hatch by about the middle of March when buds appear on the plants. The larvae live gregariously and, soon after emerging, each spins a silken nest at a convenient and sheltered place on the tree. As the caterpillars grow, the nest is also enlarged until it is 0.3 -0.5 metre across. During the day, the caterpillars rest in their nests and at night they feed on the leaves. The larval stage lasts 39-68 days and when full-fed, they spin oval, white and compact cocoons, each about 2.5 cm in length. The pupal stage lasting 8-22 days is passed inside these cocoons in some protected place. The moths begin to emerge some time in the 3rd week of May and continue to do so till the beginning of June. The moths are short-lived and a female in captivity may survive for 3-5 days. The life-cycle is completed in one year.

Host plants. Bsides apple, it also damages the pear, apricot, walnut, etc.

Damage. The caterpillars alone do the damage by defoliating the trees. In case of severe infestation, the entire plant may be defoliated and subsequently the caterpillars may feed even on the soft bark of twigs. When there is serious infestation, 40-50 per cent of the apple plants in an orchard may be defoliated producing a poor harvest.

Management. (*i*) The caterpillars can be killed by mopping up the 'tents' with a pole and some rags dipped in kerosene tied on its end. The best results are obtained when the operation is carried out from 12 noon to 3 p.m. on clear sunny days. Kerosenized water in an open vessel should be placed below the tree so that the larvae that fall may also be killed readily. (*ii*) Destroy all egg bands at the time of pruning in December-January. (*iii*) Spray 2.0 kg of carbaryl 50WP in 500 litres of water. The pest can also be controlled by spraying 0.5% malathion.

4. *Cydia pomonella* (Linnaeus) (Codling moth, Lepidoptera : Tortricidae) (Fig. 7.3C)

Distribution. It is widely distributed throughout Europe, North America, Australia, Baluchistan and Ladakh region of India.

Identification. The adult moth is small, about 1.2-1.4 cm in wing span and is 6-8 mm long. The fore wings are dark greyish and are marked with wavy lines and a copper coloured metallic eye like circle towards the outer margin. The hind wings are pale grey. The full-grown larvae are 1.6-2.2 mm long and are pinkish or creamy-white in colour with a brown head and eight pairs of legs.

Life-history. The adult moths appear from the end of May to June. They fly at dusk and spend the day at rest on the trunk, branches or leaves of the apple trees. Being cryptic in colour they are difficult to detect. The females, after pairing, lay white coloured eggs singly on young fruits, leaves and the twigs. The eggs are small, 1 mm in diameter, oval and very flat, appearing, in fact, more like small shining scales than the eggs of an insect. A single female may lay about 100 eggs in her life time. After a period of 4-12 days the young larvae emerge from the eggs and enter the fruit usually through the calyx. Having penetrated into the apple fruit, the larva attacks the core and the flesh around, burrowing further to the centre and the tips, which may also be eaten. After a period of three weeks to one month, the larva is full-fed. At this stage the larva burrows its way out of the apple fruit and falls to the ground. It seeks shelter in cracks or crevices in the bark of the apple trees and having chosen a proper position, it spins a silken cocoon in which it transforms into a yellowish-brown pupa. The pupal period is completed in 8-14 days.

The second brood moths give rise to larvae that attack the apples in the same way as the first brood, though they usually enter the fruit through the side instead of through the calyx. Like the first brood, they spin cocoons in which to pass the winter, pupating the following spring and producing moths in due course. In cooler regions, there is only one generation, but in warmer areas there are two generations in a year.

Host plants. In addition to apple, the pear fruits sometimes suffer rather severely from the attack of the larvae. The fruits of quince, walnut and of many wild species of *Pyrus* may also be damaged.

Damage. Damage is caused by the larvae which burrow into the fruit and feed on the pulp. The infested fruits lose their shape and fall off prematurely. These fruits cannot be marketed for human consumption.

Management. The control measures are same as in case of tent-caterpillar. Strict quarantine measures should be adopted to check the spread of this pest to other apple growing areas of the country.

5. *Apriona cinerea* Cheverlot (Apple stem borer, Coleoptera : Cerambycidae)

Distribution. The insect has been recorded from Pakistan, Afghanistan, Kashmir, Himachal Pradesh and Uttar Pradesh.

Identification. The adult beetles are 3.5-5.0 cm long, grey in colour and have antennae larger than the body.

Life-history. The beetles appear in July-August after the start of the monsoon and mate soon after. The female when ready to lay eggs excavates an oval patch on a shoot and lays eggs inside the cavity. Thus, she moves from tree to tree and lays a number of eggs. The grubs emerge in 7-8 days and start feeding by boring inside the stem. As autumn approaches, the feeding activity of the grubs becomes very slow and by October stops altogether. It remains quiscent during the winter and resumes feeding in March. As it feeds, it makes a tunnel towards the thicker side of the stem and thus by September-October it reaches close to the tree trunk. As winter sets in, the grubs remain quiscent. As the summer season comes, it starts activity and when full-fed it pupates inside a tunnel made in the woody tissue. The pupal stage lasts more than a month and the adults emerge in July-August to start procreation. The life-cycle is completed in about two years.

Host plants. The grubs of this pest are destructive stem borers of apple, peach, fig and other fruit trees.

Damage. As a result of feeding by the grubs, the affected trees may not die for many years, but their vitality and productivity is greatly impaired. The adult beetles feed on bark and have an unusual habit of cutting more than they acually consume.

Management. (*i*) Prune and burn all attacked shoots and branches during winter. (*ii*) Location of live holes and injection of carbon disulphide or chloroform or petrol and sealing them with mud will kill the pest. (*iii*) The borers can be effectively controlled by inserting cotton wick soaked in insecticide solution of about 10 ml of dimethoate 30EC or oxydemeton methyl 25EC or dichlorvos 100EC inside the hole and plugging it by moist soil or mud. (*iv*) Placing of 0.2 g aluminium phosphide tablets inside the hole and then plugging with moist soil will also ensure control of the pest.

6. *Dorysthenes hugelii* Redtenbacher (Apple root borer, Coleoptera : Cerambycidae)

Distribution. The grubs of this beetle are very damaging root borers of apple in the Kumaon region of Himalayas.

Identification. The adult beetles are chestnut in colour with head and thorax darker than the elytra. The full-grown grub is creamy-white with black head and mandibles, and may be 7.5-10.0 cm long.

Life-history. Adult beetles emerge from the soil with the advent of monsoon, around the end of June and some of them continue to emerge upto the middle of July. Immediately after emergence, they start mating and the males die soon after. The females also live for 10-12 days only, during which time they lay eggs to progenerate. A female lays, on an average, 300 ovoid shaped, yellow-white eggs, 8-12 mm below the soil surface. The eggs hach in 30-40 days.

The grubs, on emergence from the eggs, go down into the soil, 10-25 cm deep and feed on organic matter and also on the roots of a number of plants and trees. The legless, slow moving creatures feed and move gradually, under the soil surface among the root system of host plants. It takes up to 3.5 years for them to mature and become full-grown, storing huge quantities of food reserves. If the grubs are confined without food they can survive for 24-90 days. When full-grown they pupate inside the earthen cocoons and then emerge as beetles after the first shower of monsoons.

Host plants. Besides apple, it also attacks the roots of apricot, cherry, peach, pear, walnut and a number of forest trees.

Damage. As a result of the grubs feeding on roots, the small as well as the major roots are severed from the base. The trees, if young, die immediately whereas the older ones become weak and fall down eventually owing to the action of strong winds.

Management. (*i*) Avoid dry sandy soils for planting apple orchards. (*ii*) Remove and destroy the grubs from the affected trees. (*iii*) Inter-culturing in the soil under the trees helps in killing the grubs. (*iii*) Once the infestation has occurred, it is imperative to treat the tree basins with phorate granules @ 100 g a.i. per tree soon after monsoon.

7. *Brachycaudus helichrysi* (Kaltenbach) (Peach leaf curl aphid, Hemiptera : Aphididae) (Fig. 7.3D)

Distribution. This world-wide aphid is prevalent both in the plains and in the mountainous areas of India, up to an altitude of 2,200 metres.

Identification. This plant louse is very small and is generally yellow, with dark stripes on the head. Its colour varies according to the host plant. For example, on peach, it is light green and on golden-rod, it is greenish yellow.

Life-history. The females produce eggs without fertilization and these hatch inside the body of the mother. Thus, the females give birth to young ones instead of laying eggs. Each viviparous female produces about 50 young aphids in her short lifetime of about 13 days. Three or four generations are completed on the fruit plants. With the warming up of the season, winged males and females are also produced. They migrate to other alternative host plants, such as golden-rod, and again start reproducing. Four or five generations are completed on golden-rod from June to October. Early in November, the winged females are produced again. They migrate back to peach, plum and other fruit-trees. The old foliage has been shed by that time, therefore, the females lay eggs at the base of the buds. Egg-laying is completed by the middle of December, when the females die.

Host plants. It is a very destructive pest of peach, plum, almond and other temperate fruits.

Damage. The nymphs and females suck the sap from young leaves and cause them to curl. The severely attacked plants have only small crumpled or twisted leaves and bear very little fruit. In the plains, another species, *Myzus persicae* (Sulzer), has been recorded as a serious pest of peach trees.

Management. (*i*) For effective management of aphid, removal of weeds which act as secondary hosts is essential. (*ii*) Spray 2.0 litres of malathion 50EC or dimethoate 30EC in 1250 litres of water per ha. One pre-bloom and a post-bloom spray at 10-day interval should be given.

8. *Bactrocera zonata* (Saunders) (Peach fruit fly, Diptera : Tephritidae) (Fig. 7.3E)

Distribution. The peach fruit fly is widely distributed in the Indian sub-continent.

Identification. The fly is a small insect about the size of a house fly and is reddish brown with yellowish cross bands on the abdomen. The wings are transparent and have a small brown spot on the tip of each wing. The maggots found inside the fruits are dirty white, headless and legless. They are elongated wriggling creatures about 1 cm in length.

Life-history. The adult flies lay white, cylindrical eggs just under the skin of a fruit, in groups of 2-9. A single female may lay, on an average, 137 eggs in her life-time. The place of oviposition is marked by a resinous secretion. The eggs hatch in 2-4 days in May-June and the maggots feed on the fruit pulp by making galleries. These larvae are full-fed in 4-16 days and, at the same-time, the fruits also fall from the tree. The larvae crawl out of the rotting fruits and by jumping movements, reach a suitable place for pupation in the soil at a depth of 2.5-7.6 cm. The flies emerge from these pupae in about one week and the life-cycle is completed in 13-27 days. Many generations are completed in a year.

Host plants. It feeds on a number of fruits, viz. peach, fig, guava, ber, citrus, apple, cucurbits, tomato, brinjal and pear.

Damage. The peaches, apricots or other fruits attacked by this pest are malformed, mis-shaped, undersized and are rotten within. The damage caused is very heavy and the fruits become unmarketable.

Management. (*i*) Plant early maturing cultivars i.e. Prabhat, Partap, Florida Prince, Earli Grande, Flordasun and Shan-i-Punjab. (*ii*) Regularly remove of fallen fruits from the ground and bury the infested fruits atlaest 60 cm deep. (*iii*) Hoe the orchard in May-June to expose the pupae which are present mostly at 4-6 cm depth. (*iv*) Apply bait spray of yeast hydrolysate (250 g), crude sugar (2.5 kg) and malathion 50EC (250 ml) in 250 litres of water per ha. Spraying should be started two weeks before harvesting or use PAU fruit fly traps @ 40 traps per ha in the first week of May. Recharge the traps after 30 days, if needed. (*v*) In orchards with history of severe infestation, spray 3.125 lires of fenvalerate 20EC in 1250 litres of water per ha, in mid May and repeat after one week if required. Fruits should be harvested at least on third day after the spray.

9. *Sphenoptera lafertei* Thompson (Peach stem borer, Coleoptera: Buprestidae)

Distribution. This beetle is widely distributed in Afghanistan, Pakistan and India.

Identification. The beetles are blackish-bronze and are 1.0-1.3 cm long. The grubs are smoky dark or black, club-shaped and attain 1.8-2.4 cm body length.

Life-history. The beetles lay small, spherical, white eggs singly, scattered all over the tree trunk and the main branches. The eggs hatch in 20 days. The grubs on emergence feed on the bark and as they grow they bore inside. The larval stage is completed in two months in summer, but those which over-winter take 6 months. The larva makes a small chamber in the woody tissue about 10 mm deep from the surface. The pre-pupal and pupal periods last 1-2 and 8-12 days, respectively in summer. The winter is passed in the grub stage. Three generations of this pest are completed in a year.

Host plants. The insect feeds on peach, almond, apricot, cherry, loquat, pear and plum trees.

Damage. The grubs feed under the bark as well as bore deep into the wood. Gum globules ooze out of the entrance holes. Leaves of the attacked plants turn pale and their growth is arrested. The attacked branches dry up and do not bear fruits. With continued damage, the tree dies ultimately.

Management. (*i*) The dead or heavily gummed branches should be cut and destroyed. (*ii*) Swab the entire trunk and main branches with 2.5 litres of chlorpyriphos 20EC in 1250 litres of water per ha during June after harvesting the crop and in October.

10. *Alcidodes porrectirostris* Marshall (Walnut weevil, Coleoptera : Curculionidae)

Distribution. This is the most destructive pest of walnuts in the Himalyan region at altitudes of 1,000-2,450 metres and has been reported as a serious pest in Kumaon, Kulu and Kashmir.

Identification. The adult weevil is about 1 cm long, pitch black when young, and turns dark brown with age. There is a prominent snout in front which is somewhat straight and is directed downwards. The grub is legless, with a pale brown head and measures 1.5 cm in length.

Life-history. The egg laying, which starts in April, coincides with the appearance of flower buds. As the fruits are formed, the weevils puncture them, laying more than one egg. As many as 15 eggs have been noticed in one fruit. The punctures on the young fruits are circular and on older fruits, they are crescent or irregular. The eggs hatch in one week and the creamy white tiny grubs bore deeper, feeding on the kernels. The grub is full grown in 13-22 days and pupates inside the fruit. The pupa is creamy white and is transformed into an adult in 9-17 days. The adults emerge from the fruits by biting roundish holes. There are two generations in a year.

Host plant. Only walnut

Damage. The grubs feed exclusively on walnut kernel and reduce it to a useless black mass, but the weevils feed on green twigs, petioles, flowers and young fruits also. The grubs are far more destructive than the adults and as a result of their attack, more than 50-70 per cent of the fruits drop off and even those which remain on the trees may be unmarketable.

Management. (*i*) Collect and destroy the fallen fruits in May-June to check the population build up of the pest. (*ii*) Spray 2.0 kg of carbaryl 50 WP in 1250 litres of water per ha at fortnightly intervals when the young fruits are being formed.

11. *Batocera horsfieldi* Hope (Long-horned walnut beetle, Coleoptera: Cerambycidae)

Distribution. The grubs of this beetle are a serious pest of walnut in Darjeeling, Kumaon hills, Kulu valley and Shimla hills.

Identification. The beetles are 4.5-6.5 mm long, black in colour with fine ashy or yellow-grey pubescence. Their elytra have numerous shining black tubercles at the base and several rounded white marks extending up to the apex. The grubs are 9-15 cm long and pale yellow in colour.

Life-history. The beetles emerge in June and July, and live for about 4 months during which period they mate and find suitable sites and lay eggs. The eggs are brown and oval, and are laid singly in the bark of the walnut tree. A female may lay 55-60 eggs in her life time.

The egg stage lasts 8-15 days. The grubs at first feed on the bark and then bore inside the wood, completing their development in 20-25 months. There they remain in the pre-pupal stage for 50-182 days and make puparia. Once it pupates, the insect remains in that stage for 40-90 days. The life-cycle is completed in 23-32 months which is spread over 2-3 winters.

Host plant. Walnut only

Damage. The young grubs feed on the inner side of the bark making zig-zag tunnels. Later on, the grubs bore down to the surface of sap wood and go even further into the centre of the wood. The attacked timber trees become useless except as fire wood, which hardly fetches the cost of cutting and marketing the wood.

Management. (*i*) Hand picking and mechanical destruction of grubs and adults checks the population of the beetle. (*ii*) Plug the live holes with cotton soaked in kerosene, petroleum or EDCT mixture and then plaster them from outside with mud.

12. *Aeolesthes holosericea* Fabricius (Cherry stem borer, Coleoptera : Cerambycidae)

Distribution. This polyphagous defoliating beetle is widely distributed in India, Sri Lanka, Bangladesh, Myanmar, Malaysia and Thailand.

Identification. The adults are dark brown, 3.8-4.5 cm long, having short mottled yellowish pubescence on the elytra. Antennae of the male are 1.5 times their body length, while those of the female are about the same length as the body. The flabby grubs are yellowish in colour and are clothed with fine bristles, and measure 7-8 cm, when full-grown.

Life-history. The beetles emerge out of the tunnels in the host trees from May to October and are active throughout the summer. After mating, the females start laying eggs on the dry woody portions of the host trees in the cuts or in cracks and crevices of the bark. A female, on an average, lays about 100 eggs. The eggs are white, elliptical in shape and are about 2.5 mm in length. They hatch in 7-12 days and the young grubs on emergence feed first on the bark and, as they grow in size, they bore deeper inside the woody portions of a tree branch. In summer, they feed at a fast rate, throwing frass from the exit holes. As a result of their feeding and cutting into the wood, sap flow in that portion of the branch or the trunk becomes restricted. It gradually causes death of that portion. In the winter time, the rate of feeding of the grubs is very slow and it is seen quite often that the full-fed grubs may just rest in the tunnels without feeding.

The larval period is completed in 27-32 months. The pre-pupal period varies from 3 to 150 days and pupation takes place either in October-November or in March-April. The pupal stage lasts from 40 to 100 days. The beetles that emerge from puparia formed in October, remain within the tunnels throughout the winter and the spring, while those beetles that emerge from the puparia formed in April, rest for only 6 weeks. Thus, the life-cycle is completed in three years.

Host plants. The grubs of the beetle are the most destructive pests of cherry and they also attack apple, guava, apricot, crab apple, mulberry, peach, pear, plum, walnut and other trees.

Damage. The newly hatched grubs first feed on bark and make zig-zag galleries. They bore inside and feed on sap wood. As a result of their feeding and the consequential damage to the woody tissue, the vitality of the trees is reduced. Parts of the attacked tree start drying till it becomes unproductive. Within a few years, the tree is dead. The pest can be located from the frass that comes out of the holes in the branches or in the main trunk. There may be more than one such hole, indicating multiple damage.

Management. (*i*) Collect and destroy the grubs and beetles. (*ii*) Since the pest feeds inside the woody portions, no insecticide spray can be effective. The only sure way to get rid of this pest is to locate the feeding holes, clear the passage and inject contact poisons or even diluted phenyle. Insert in the holes cotton wicks soaked in dichlorvos (0.1%) or dimethoate (0.03%) or phosphamidon or thiometon (all at 0.025%) and seal with mud.

13. *Myllocerus lactivirens* Marshal (Almond weevil, Coleoptera : Curculionidae)

Distribution. Almond weevil is found in most of the almond growing regions of India.

Identification. The weevils are small 3-4 mm long and pale metallic green in colour. The full-grown grubs are creamy white, 4 mm long, are stout in body which is without legs. They have short erect setae which help them in locomotion.

Life-history. The adults appear in May and lay eggs from the end of July till the beginning of September in the soil in batches of 40-50 each. The eggs are broadly oval in shape, creamy-yellow, smooth, transparent and shiny. They hatch in 4-5 days and the grubs burrow deep in the soil up to 20-30 cm. They feed on roots of the host plants. When full-grown, they come up on soil surface to pupate in the upper 2.5 cm of the soil. The grub stage is completed in 10 months and the pupal period lasts 4-5 days. The pest passes winter in the pupal stage in the soil.

Host plants. The almond weevil is polyphagous and besides almond, it has been reported to feed on apple, apricot, ber, citrus, falsa, loquat, mango, peach, plum and pomegranate. Almond and pear are its preferred hosts.

Damage. The weevils congregate on ventral surface on leaves, nibble irregular holes and gradually eat away the entire leaf laminae, leaving only the mid-ribs. The tender leaves are eaten first and then the older leaves are also skeletonized. The pest causes the maximum damage to foliage during the rainy season.

Management. Soil application of lindane 2 per cent dust @ 30 kg per ha will effectively control grubs.

*****

8 CHAPTER

PESTS OF MUSHROOMS

Sciarid flies (Diptera : Sciaridae)	1. *Bradysia tritici* (Coquillet) 2. *Lycariella mali* (Fitch) 3. *Lycariella auripila* (Winnertz)
Phorid flies (Diptera : Phoridae)	1. *Megaselia halterata* (Wood) 2. *Megaselia agarici* (Disney) 3. *Megaselia scalaris* (H. Loew) 4. *Megaselia sandhui* Disney
Cecid flies (Diptera : Cecidomyiidae)	1. *Heteropeza pygmaea* Winnertz 2. *Mycophila speyeri* (Barnes)
Springtails (Collembola : Entomobryidae)	1. *Seira iricolor* Tosii & Ashraf 2. *Lepidocyrtus* spp.
Nitidulid beetle (Coleoptera : Nitidulidae)	*Cyllodes indicus* Grouvelle
Mushroom mites	1. *Pigmophorus* spp. (Prostigmata : Pyemotidae) 2. *Tarsonemus* spp. (Prostigmata : Tarsonemidae) 3. *Tyroglyphus* spp. (Stigmata : Acaridae) 4. *Tyrophagus* spp. (Astigmata : Acaridae) 5. *Tetranychus* spp. (Prostigmata : Tetranychidae) 6. *Hypoaspis* spp. (Mesostigmata : Laelapidae) 7. *Lasioseius* spp. (Mesostigmata : Phytoseiidae)

8. *Uroobovella* spp. (Mesostigmata : Uropodidae)
9. *Urosternella* spp. (Mesostigmata : Uropodidae)
10. *Scheloribatid* spp. (Cryptostigmata : Oribatidae)
11. *Epilohmmania* spp. (Cryptostigmata : Oribatidae)

In India, mainly three species of edible mushroom, viz. white button mushroom (*Agaricus* spp.), paddy straw mushroom (*Volvariella* spp.) and oyster mushroom (*Pleurotus* spp.) are commercially cultivated. The annual production of mushroom in India is about 1,00,000 tonnes. About 20 insect and mite pests are reported to attack mushroom all over the world. In India, the dipteran flies, viz. sciarid fly, phorid fly and cecid fly have been found causing considerable damage.

1. *Bradysia tritici* (Coquillet) (Sciarid fly, Diptera : Sciaridae) (Fig. 8.1A)

Identification. The adults are small, delicate, greyish black, two winged insects measuring 2.5-3.0 mm is length with conspicuous bead-like antennae. Females have a pointed abdomen that is frequently swollen with eggs, while males have prominent claspers at the end of their abdomen. The larvae (maggots) are dirty white with black head and are 6.5 mm long.

Life-history. The females lay eggs on compost, casing and mushroom in clusters of chain. The eggs are small, 1.5 mm long, oval and translucent white. The larvae hatch from the eggs after about 4-6 days. The larvae feed on decaying organic matter, mycelial attachments below casing and at the spawning surface. The larvae transform into pupae after about 20 days and pupation generally lasts about a week. The insect completes its life-cycle in 26-28 days. There are five generations during the cropping period.

Damage. The larvae feed on mushroom, enter from the stem end and move towards the cap portion, The most serious injury is, however, caused to the developing pin-heads, which turn yellowish brown and never develop into normal mushrooms. Very high numbers of larvae feeding in the compost during spawn run can also inhibit fruit body production through destruction of the compost and the mycelium. The incidence of this pest starts in the first week of February and reaches its peak in the second week of March, with an overall average infestation of 40 per cent.

Management. (*a*) ***Preventive measures.*** (*i*) Compost should not be prepared directly on soil surface. (*ii*) Sterilization of compost should be done at 60°C to kill insects which come through compost. (*iii*) Screen room exteriors or interiors with nylon net of 35-40 mesh size. (*iv*) The trap consisting of 15 watt bulb and polythene sheet (50 × 75 cm) coated with white grease and then hanged over the wall below bulb during second fortnight of January in mushroom houses is most efficient in reducing the fly population. (*v*) Mix the compost thoroughly at last turning after spraying 15-20 ml of chlorpyriphos 20EC or 100 ml of Nimbecidine 0.003% in 20 litres of water. This quantity is used for the compost prepared from 100 kg of wheat/paddy straw. If the flies are present in the mushroom house before casing, mix thoroughly 10 ml of chlorpyriphos 20EC in 4-5 litres of water in 100 kg of ready to use casing material before its use. (*b*) ***Remedial measures.*** Spray premises with dichlorvos 100EC at the rate of 6 ml per 10 litres of water on window panes, walls and ceiling of mushroom house. After spraying, close the mushroom house for 2 hours. Observe an interval of 48 hours between spraying and picking of mushrooms. Direct spraying on beds should be avoided.

2. *Megaselia halterata* (H. Loew) (Phorid fly, Diptera : Phoridae) (Fig. 8.1B)

Identification. The adult flies are small, hump-backed and light to brown in colour. The adults are two winged flies, measuring 2-3 mm in length and the bristle like antennae are incospicuous. They appear stockier than sciarid flies, and are very active, running and hopping with quick and jerky movements. The larvae are dirty white maggots, 3.5 mm long with narrow head and visible blackish mouth hooks.

Life-history. The female flies lay about 50 eggs, which are very small, elongated, cylindrical and whitish. They prefer spawned compost and gills of opened mushrooms for egg laying. The larvae after hatching directly bore into the mushroom cap, whereas those hatching from the eggs laid on spawn-run compost or casing, tunnel through the lower end of the mushroom stalk. Mature larvae come out of the mushroom and pupate in the casing or compost or sometime in mushrooms. The pupae are about 2-3 mm long and gradually turn from cream coloured to dark brown as they mature. The development from egg to adult takes 14-16 days. The insect becomes active during September to November and again from second half of February till the end of the cropping period. The severe winter is passed as hibernating pupae when pupal period is prolonged upto 50 days.

Damage. The maggots feed gregariously on mushroom, starting from the stalk and moving upward into the cap forming tunnels in the stalk. The attacked mushrooms turn yellowish brown to brownish, and when attacked at pin-head stage, the development is restricted. The adult flies are capable of transmitting fungal and bacterial diseases. Since they are active fliers, phorid flies can be a significant irritant to picking crews.

Management. Same as in case of sciarid fly.

3. *Heteropeza pygmaea* Winnertz (Cecid fly, Diptera : Cecidomyiidae) (Fig. 8.1C)

Identification. These are tiny flies and orange black in colour. The cecid fly larvae are white legless maggots, about 2 mm long and bluntly pointed at both ends. The head and tail are not easily distinguished except by the direction of travel.

Life-history. The adults of cecid flies are rarely seen because under most conditions, larvae become 'mother larvae' giving birth directly to 10-30 daughter larvae. This species usually does not become a pupa and subsequent adult that must mate before laying eggs. Reproduction is accomplished without mating and gives rise to daughter larvae directly (paedogenesis). When conditions are optimal, this method of reproduction can result in very rapid multiplication of this pest, leading to very large number of larvae, tens of thousands per square metre.

Damage. Larvae are the damaging stage which feed on mycelium and cause damage to stalk and gills. Brown coloured stripes can be seen on the stipe and gills. Initial infestation of cecid fly may take place by transport of infested peat or substrate. As the maggots are sticky, they might spread through trays, tools, clothes, shoes, etc. of the workers. Small infestations may not be readily apparent at first. If large populations develop, the larvae may mass together on the floor and disperse in large groups. Larvae can also be found on mature mushroom caps packed for market. This species has the potential to significantly reduce yield, when it becomes established on a farm. Damage to mushrooms has been recorded to be as high as 50 per cent due to this pest.

Management. Same as in case of sciarid fly.

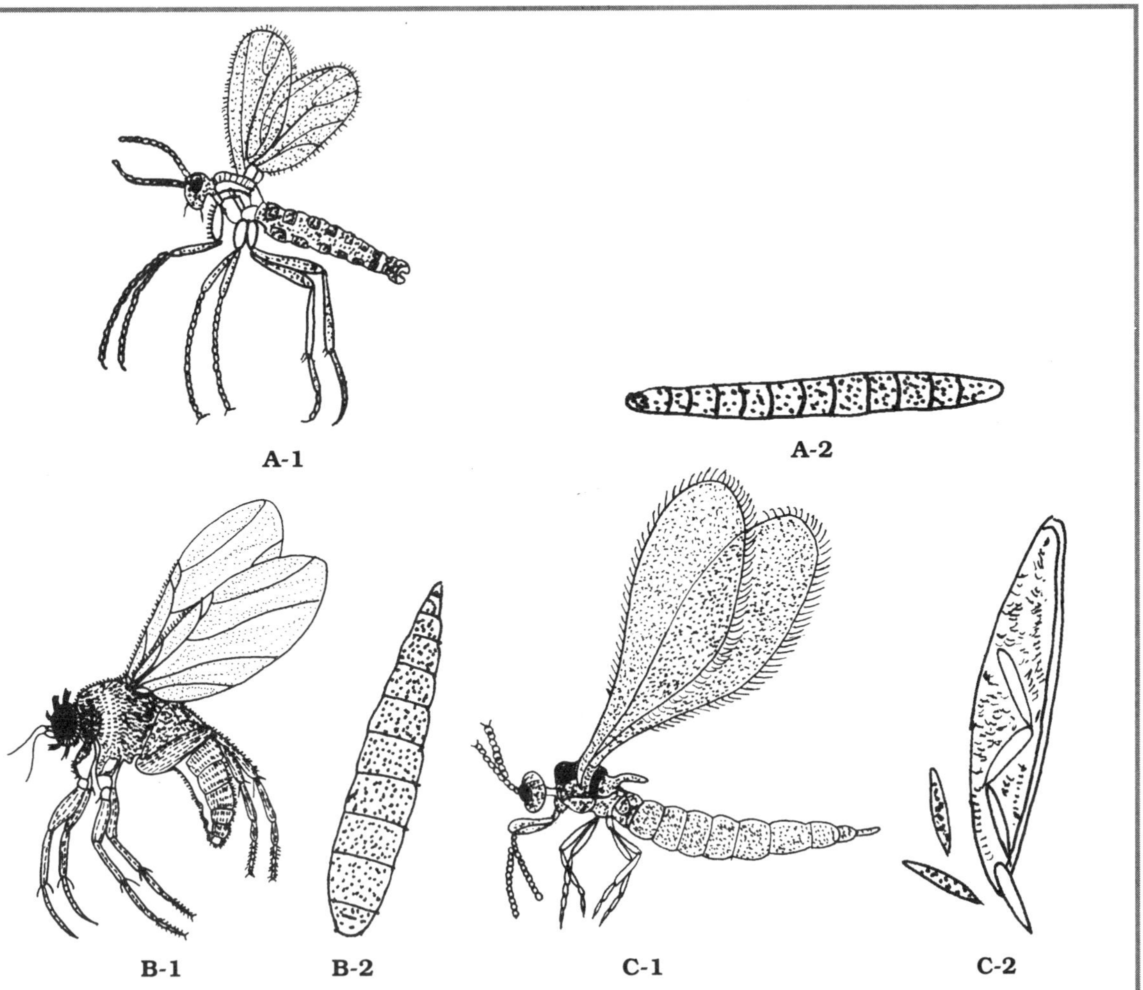

Fig. 8.1 Pests of mushrooms. **A.** Sciarid fly, *Bradysia tritici*; A-1. Adult, A-2. Larva. **B.** Phorid fly, *Megaselia halterata*; B-1. Adult, B-2. Larva. **C.** Cecid fly, *Heteropeza pygmaea*; C-1. Adult, C-2. Larvae.

4. *Seira iricolor* Tosii & Ashraf (Springtails, Colembolla : Entomobryidae)

Identification. Springtails are tiny, 1 mm long, silver coloured, stout, having long tails and move by jumping.

Life-history. Eggs are laid singly or in small groups on paddy straw pieces. A female lays 9-16 eggs which hatch in 5-20 days. The pre-reproductive period is 10-15 days and adult longevity is between 22-30 days. *S. iricolor* is active throughout the year on button, oyster and paddy straw mushrooms. Maximum activity occurs during July-August on tropical mushroom (*Volvariella volvacea*). In the absence of mushrooms, *S. iricolor* survives on moist organic matter near mushroom houses.

Damage. Both nymphs and adults feed on mycelium and destroy planted spawn. They also attack stalks and caps. They are found in straw, compost and casing layer. Oyster mushroom in most preferred.

Management. (*i*) Follow proper sanitation and pasteurization. (*ii*) Crop should be raised above the ground level. (*iii*) Never use spent compost. (*iv*) Spray malathion 50EC at 0.05% on the infested place. (*v*) Use diazinon 20EC @ 15 ml in 100 kg wheat straw compost.

5. *Cyllodes indicus* Grouvelle (Nitidulid beetle, Coleoptera : Nitidulidae)

This is a serious pest of oyster mushroom. Female lays eggs singly between the gills. Grubs are the damaging stage which feed between gills and then on stipes of mushroom making them hollow.

Management. (*i*) Over matured mushroom should not be left unharvested. (*ii*) Apply bleaching powder to repel these beetles.

6. *Pigmophorus* spp. (Prostigmata : Pyemotidae), *Tarsonemus* spp. (Prostigmata : Tarsonemidae), *Tyroglyphus* spp. (Stigmata : Acaridae) (Mushroom mites)

Sixty species of mites have been found associated with mushrooms world wide. However, in India only 8 species have been identified to be economically important. The mushroom mites are 0.3 to 0.5 mm long, *i.e.* pin head size and varying in colours. They are present in compost and migrate to casing material. Female lays about 100-200 eggs. Fertile eggs develop into females and unfertile ones into males. Life-cycle lasts for 10 days at 20-30°C. Prolonged summer temperature increases the population. They feed on mycelium and damage sporophores that result in shrunk caps and brown rusted spots on buttons. Buttons are sometimes hollowed out or cavities appear in/on stalks and caps.

Management. (*i*) Disinfect mushroom houses by kelthane 50EC at 0.1%. (*ii*) Sterilize compost at 60°C to kill pests which come through compost. (*iii*) Burn sulphur in empty mushroom houses. (*iv*) All infested and decaying mushrooms should be removed and destroyed to prevent further increase of pest population.

*****

9 CHAPTER

PESTS OF FIBRE CROPS

Cotton (*Gossypium* spp.)

1. *Pectinophora gossypiella* (Saunders) (Pink bollworm, Lepidoptera : Gelechiidae)
2. *Earias insulana* (Boisduval), *E. vittella* (Fabricius) (Spotted bollworms, Lepidoptera : Noctuidae)
3. *Helicoverpa armigera* (Hubner) (American bollworm, Lepidoptera : Noctuidae)
4. *Spodoptera litura* (Fabricius) (Tobacco caterpillar, Lepidoptera : Noctuidae)
5. *Sylepta derogata* (Fabricius) (Cotton leaf roller, Lepidoptera : Pyralidae)
6. *Tarache notabilis* (Walker) (Cotton semilooper, Lepidoptera.: Noctuidae)
7. *Anomis flava* (Fabricius) (Green semilsooper, Lepidoptera: Noctuidae)
8. *Phycita infusella* (Meyrick) (Bud moth, Lepidoptera : Pyralidae)'
9. *Bemisia tabaci* (Gennadius) (Cotton whitefly, Hemiptera.: Aleyrodidae)
10. *Amrasca biguttula* (Ishida) (Cotton leafhopper, Hemiptera.: Cicadellidae).
11. *Aphis gossypii* Glover (Cotton aphid, Hemiptera : Aphididae)
12. *Phenacoccus solenopsis* Tinsley (Cotton mealy bug, Hemiptera : Pseudococidae)

13. *Oxycarenus hyalinipennis* Costa (Dusky cotton bug, Hemiptera : Lygaeidae)
14. *Dysdercus koenigii* (Fabricius) (Red cotton bug, Hemiptera: Pyrrhocoridae)
15. *Pempherulus affinis* (Faust) (Cotton stem weevil, Coleoptera : Curculionidae)
16. *Myllocerus undecimpustulatus* Faust (Cotton grey weevil, Coleoptera: Curculionidae)

Jute (*Corchorus capsularis, C. olitorius*)

1. *Anomis sabulifera* (Guenee) (Jute semi-looper, Lepidoptera: Noctuidae)
2. *Nupserha bicolor postbrunnea* Dutt (Jute stem girdler, Coleoptera : Lamidae)
3. *Apion corchori* Marshall (Jute stem weevil, Coleoptera : Apionidae)
4. *Spodoptera exigua* (Hubner) (Indigo caterpillar, Lepi-doptera : Noctuidae)
5. *Phenacoccus hirsutus* Cr. (Jute mealy bug, Hemiptera Pseudococcidae)

Sunnhemp (*Crotalaria juncea*)

1. *Utetheisa pulchella* (Linnaeus) (Sunnhemp hairy caterpillar, Lepidoptera : Arctiidae)
2. *Enarmonia pseudonectis* Meyr. (Sunnhemp stem borer, Lepidoptera: Tortricidae)
3. *Plusia eriosoma* Distant (Leaf caterpillar, Lepidoptera : Noctuidae)
4. *Ragmus importunitas* Distant (Sunnhemp capsid, Hemiptera : Miridae)
5. *Bemisia tabaci* (Gennadius) (Cotton whitefly, Hemiptera : Aleyrodidae)

Mesta (*Hibiscus cannobinus*)

1. *Agrilus acutus* Thunberg (Spiral borer, Coleoptera : Buprestidae)
2. *Dysdercus cingulatus* (Fabricius) (Red cotton bug, Hemiptera : Pyrrhocoridae)
3. *Nezara viridula* Linnaeus (Green potato bug, Hemiptera.: Pentatomidae)
4. *Earias insulana* (Boisduval) (Spotted bollworm, Lepidoptera : Noctuidae).

Fibre crops play a vital role in the Indian economy. Cotton production in India was 258.84 bales (170 kg each) in 2007-08, which decreased to 231.56 bales in 2008-09. However, production in 2009-10 is estimated at 236.57 bales. Total production of jute and mesta was 112.11 lakh bales (180 kg each) in 2007-08, which decreased to 104.07 lakh bales in 2008-09. The production is estimated to further decrease to 102.43 lakh bales in 2009-10.

COTTON

More than 1326 species of insects have been reported attacking cotton in the world. However, in India, only 162 species have been recorded, among which only 15 may be called as major pests due to their occurrence in serious proportions almost every year.

1. *Pectinophora gossypiella* (Saunders) (Pink bollworm, Lepidoptera.: Gelechiidae) (Fig. 9.1A)

Distribution. The pink bollworm is one of the most destructive pests of cotton and is found in America, Africa, Australia and Asia. It is highly destructive in India and Pakistan.

Identification. The adult is a deep brown moth, measuring 8-9 mm across the spread wings. There are blackish spots on the fore wings, and the margins of the hind wings are deeply fringed. The larvae are pink and measure 8-10 mm when full-grown, and are found inside flower buds, panicles and bolls of cotton.

Life-history. The females lay whitish, flat eggs singly on the underside of the young leaves, new shoots, flower buds and the young green bolls. The eggs hatch in one week and the caterpillars, on emergence, are white and turn pink as they grow older. Soon after emergence, the larvae enter the flower-buds, the flowers or the bolls. The holes of entry close down, but the larvae continue feeding inside the seed kernels. They become full-grown in about two weeks and come out of the holes for pupation on the ground, among fallen leaves, debris, etc. Within one week, the moths emerge to start the life-cycle all over again. By October-November, 4-6 generations are completed.

Full-grown larvae of the last generation do not, however, pupate. Just a few of them reach the ground, but the great majority keep feeding inside the bolls and connecting to produce what are known as the 'double seeds'. The hibernating larvae lie curled in double seeds for many months and after passing the winter, they emerge as moths. The last life-cycle is very long covering 5-10 months, although during the active season, the life cycle is short, taking only 3-4 weeks. The pest passes through several broods during its active period.

Host plant. Cotton

Damage. There is excessive shedding of the fruiting bodies. The attacked squares, buds, flowers (called rosetted flowers) and young bolls fall off pre-maturely and those which do mature do not open properly. The damaged seed-cotton is difficult to pick, discoloured and gives a lower ginning percentage, lower oil extraction and inferior spinning quality. The infestation ranges from 40 to 85 per cent.

Management. ***(a) Cultural and mechanical control.*** The carryover and multiplication of this pest can be appreciably reduced by the following cultural and mechanical control measures: (*i*) Pick the seed cotton completely. Partially unpicked loculi *(burs)* should not be left on the plants. (*ii*) After the last picking, sheep, goats and other animals should be let into the cotton fields to feed on the plant debris and unopened bolls. Goats are most effective as they can browse even on the standing plants. (*iii*) The leftover, unopened and partially picked bolls should be dislodged by beating against the ground or by plucking them. The *burs* and bolls so collected should be burnt immediately. (*iv*) Cut the cotton sticks 5-6 cm below ground level to prevent their re-growth. (*v*) Do not keep the cotton sticks in the fields. Stack them in the village premises. This would reduce the number of focal points from which initial infestation spreads to the fields. (*vi*) Plough the cotton fields deep by the end of February, preferably with a furrow-turning plough. (*vii*) Crushing of cotton seed should be completed before sowing of cotton begins in the area and seed left uncrushed should be sun-dried in thin layers for three consecutive days in the middle of April or fumigated to kill the diapausing larvae of the pink bollworm. For fumigation one 3-g aluminium phosphide (Celphos) tablet should be used per cubic metre of space giving an exposure period of 48 hours or 2 tablets per cubic metre of space

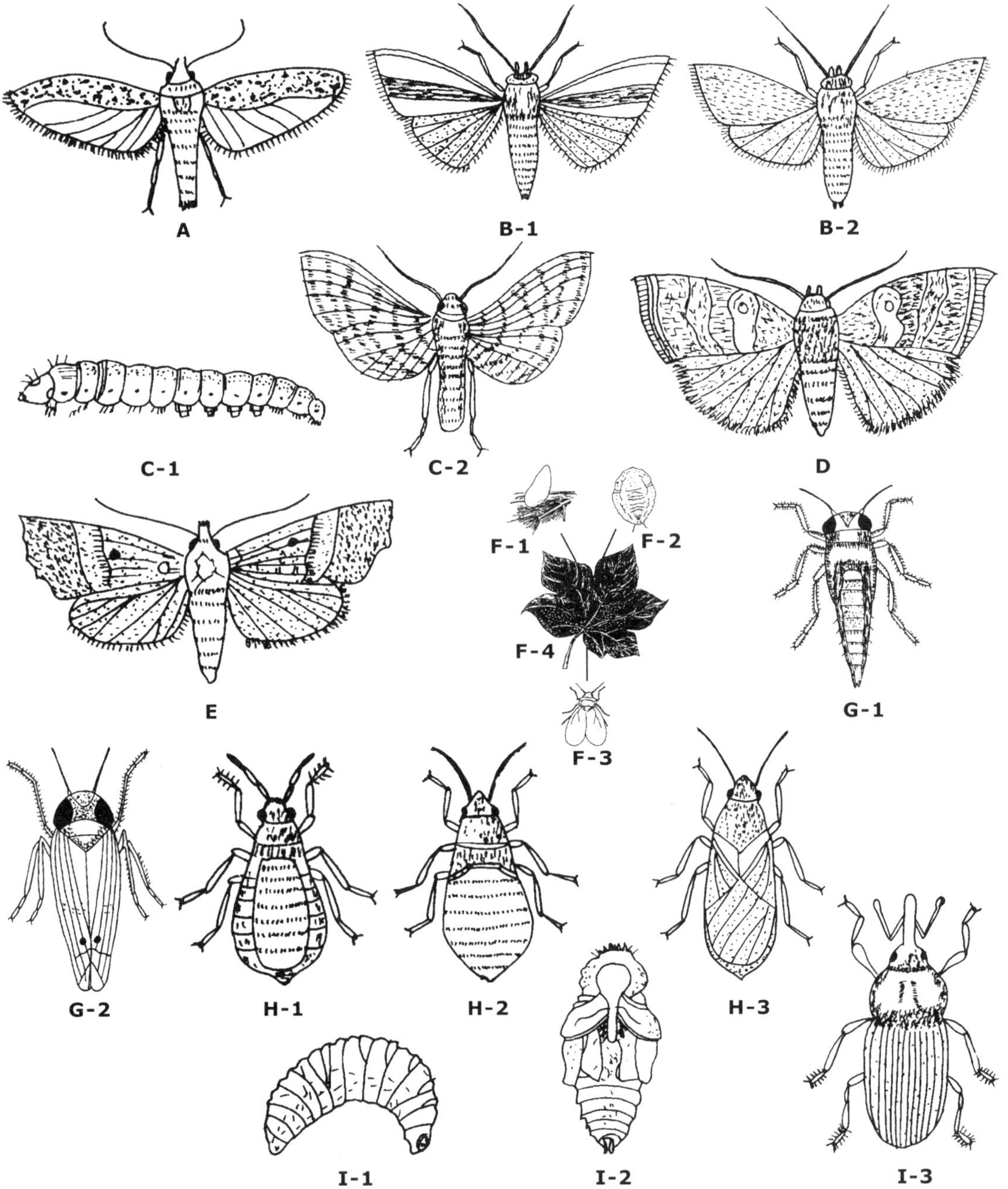

Fig. 9.1 Pests of cotton. **A.** Pink bollworm, *Pectinophora gossypiella*. **B.** Spotted bollworms; B-1. *Earias vittella*, B-2. *Earias insulana*. **C.** Cotton leaf roller, *Sylepta derogata*, C-1. Larva; C-2. Adult. **D.** Cotton semi-looper, *Tarache notabilis*, **E.** Green semi-looper, *Anomis flava*. **F.** Cotton whitefly, *Bemisia tabaci*. F-1. Egg, F-2. Pupa, F-3. Adult, F-4. Infested leaf. **G.** Cotton leafhopper, *Amrasca biguttula*; G-1. Nymph, G-2. Adult. **H.** Dusky cotton bug, *Oxycarenus hyalinipennis*; H-1. Young nymph, H-2. Grown-up nymph, H-3. Adult. **I.** Cotton grey weevil, *Myllocerus undecimpustulatus*; I-1. Larva, I-2. Pupa, I-3. Adult.

with an exposure of 24 hours. (*viii*) The seed should be acid-delinted or fumigated before sowing. (*ix*) Replace the cotton seed by seed-cake for feeding the animals. (*x*) The damage of the pest can be reduced by sowing short-duration varieties and by early termination of last irrigation to the crop.

(*b*) ***Biological control.*** The releases of *Trichogramma* spp. @ 1,50,000 parasitized eggs ha^{-1} at weekly intervals have proved promising for bollworm control.

(*c*) ***Chemical control.*** In case the bollworm damage exceeds 5 per cent, the crop should be sprayed immediately and thereafter at 10-day interval with any of the following insecticides in 315-375 litres of water per ha.

(*i*) *Organophosphates.* 2.0 litres of quinalphos 25EC, 1.25 litres of monocrotophos 36SL, 5.0 litres of chlorpyriphos 20EC, 1.5 litres of triazophos 40EC, 2.0 litres of ethion 50EC, 2.0 kg of acephate 75SP, 1.25 litres of profenophos 50EC. (*ii*) *Carbamates.* 2.5 kg of carbaryl 50WP, 625 g thiodecarb 75WP (*iii*) *Synthetic pyrethroids.* 500 ml of cypermethrin 10EC, 200 ml of cypermethrin 25EC, 400 ml of deltamethrin 2.8EC, 275 ml of deltamethrin 4EC, 250 ml of fenvalerate 20EC, 750 ml of β-cyfluthrin 0.25SC, 250 ml of alphamethrin 10EC, 750 ml fenpropathrin 10EC (*iv*) Miscellaneous. 150 ml spinosad 48SC, 100 ml flubendiamide 48SC, 500 ml indoxacarb 15SC, 375 ml novaluron 10EC, 750 ml pyridalyl 10EC, 150 ml chlorantraniliprole 18.5SL. At least 5-6 sprays are required for effective control of bollworms. Same insecticide should not be sprayed repeatedly to avoid the development of pesticide resistance and appearance of secondary pests. Also, avoid using insecticides of the same group in more than three sprays.

2. *Earias insulana* (Boisduval) and *E. vittella* (Fabricius) (Spotted bollworms, Lepidoptera : Noctuidae) (Fig. 9.1B)

Distribution. These two species of bollworms are widely distributed in North Africa, India, Pakistan and other countries and are serious pests of cotton.

Identification. The moths are yellow green and measure about 2.5 cm across the wings. *E. vittella* moths are of the same size and have a narrow light longitudinal green band in the middle of the fore wing. The full-grown dull-green caterpillars are 2 cm long having tiny stout bristles and a series of longitudinal black spots on the body.

Life-history. The female moths lay 200-400 eggs at night, singly on flower buds, brackets and tender leaves of okra or cotton plants. The eggs hatch in 3-4 days and the caterpillars pass through 6 stages, becoming full-grown in 10-16 days. They pupate either on the plants or on the ground (during November – December) among fallen leaves and the moths emerge in 8-14 days in summer and 18-23 days in winter. The life cycle is completed (usually August to October) in 17-29 days. Several overlapping generations are completed in a year.

Host plants. Several malvaceous plants like cotton, okra, hollyhock, sunnhemp, China rose, etc.

Damage. When cotton plants are young, the larvae bore into the terminal portions of the shoots, which wither away and dry up. Later on, they cause shedding of the fruiting bodies. The green bolls attacked by spotted bollworm are often infected by fungi which causes bolls to rot and dry up without opening. The infested bolls called aborted bolls open prematurely and produce poor lint, resulting in lower market value.

Management. (*i*) The pest can be suppressed with clean cultivation and the destruction of alternative food plants (*Abutilon indicum, Malvastrum tricuspidatum, Sida* spp.), particularly when cotton or okra is not growing in that locality. (*ii*) The withering tops of the plants damaged by the spotted bollworm during June-July should be removed and destroyed to check the multiplication of the pest in the initial stage. (*iii*) Chemical control measures are same as in case of pink bollworm. The economic threshold level is 10 per cent incidence in shoots or reproductive parts.

3. *Helicoverpa armigera* (Hubner) (American bollworm, Lepidoptera: Noctuidae)

The American bollworm has become a serious pest of cotton in northern parts of India. It was first reported on cotton in 1977 in Punjab. In 1983, it appeared in serious form in the northern cotton growing belt and reduced yield by 40-50 per cent. Again in 1990, it caused severe losses to cotton in Haryana, Punjab and Rajasthan. However, its incidence has declined after the introduction of Bt cotton. This pest has been discussed in chapter 4.

Damage. The extent of its damage depends upon the time of attack and the relative length of the effective growing season. The squares, buds, flowers and young bolls are pierced and shed to the ground. The older bolls are perforated and contents partially eaten resulting in rotting. The growing points of the plants are damaged by young larvae. In case of severe attack, even the leaves are eaten up.

Management. In case of *H. armigera* attack, prefer to use acephate/chlorpyriphos/ fenitrothion from the insecticides recommended against the pink bollworm. The economic threshold level is 10 per cent incidence in fruiting bodies. Cultivation of berseem, tomato, sunflower and groundnut favours the survival of this pest during hot summer months of April-June. Growing of *arhar* and *moong* in and around cotton fields increases the overwintering population.

4. *Spodoptera litura* (Fabricius) (Tobacco caterpillar, Lepidoptera : Noctuidae)

This pest has been described in detail in chapter 6. Tobacco caterpillar is a polyphagous pest and the larvae cause serious loss to cotton from August to November. The young larvae feed gregariously and skeletonize the foliage. The grown up larvae disperse and feed singly. Besides leaves, they also damage the buds, flowers and green bolls.

Management. (*i*) Avoid growing castor, *moong, dhaincha (Sesbania aculeata)* and okra in and around cotton as these are the most preferred hosts of tobacco caterpillar and help the pest to multiply before shifting to cotton. (*ii*) Plough the *dhaincha* crop immediately when it has attained reasonable height and bury the larvae alongwith the straw deep into the soil. (*iii*) Keep the fields free from the weed *itsit (Trianthema portulacastrum)*, as it acts as an alternate host of the insect. (*iv*) Collect and destroy the egg masses and young larvae feeding gregariously on the cotton crop. (*v*) Spray 2·5 litres of endosulfan 35EC or 2·0 kg of acephate 75SP or 5·0 litres of chlorpyriphos 20 EC or 2·0 litres of quinalphos 25EC or 625 g thiodicarb 75WP or 375 ml of novaluron 10EC or 750 ml of pyridalyl 10EC or 150 ml of chlorantraniliprole 18.5SL in 250 litres of water per ha.

5. *Sylepta derogata* (Fabricius) (Cotton leaf roller, Lepidoptera: Pyralidae) (Fig. 9.1C)

Distribution. The cotton leaf-roller is widely distributed in the Orient and Africa. In India, it occurs in all the cotton-growing tracts and is an important sporadic pest.

Identification. Moths are yellowish-white, with black and brown spots on the head and the thorax. They measure about 2.8-4.0 cm across the spread wings and have a series of dark brown wavy lines on the wings. The caterpillars are greenish grey or pink and measure 2.5-3.0 cm when full-grown.

Life-history. The female moths lay 200-300 eggs singly on the underside of the leaves. The eggs hatch in 2-6 days and the young caterpillars feed first on the lower surface of the leaves. The older larvae roll leaves from the edges inwards up to the midrib and feed on leaf tissues from the inside. The larvae grow through seven stages and are full-fed in 15-35 days. They pupate either on the plant, inside the rolled leaves or among plant debris in the soil. They emerge as moths in 6-12 days and live for about a week. The life-cycle is completed in 23-53 days. and the pest passes through 5 or 6 generations.

Host plants. Besides cotton, it has also been recorded on various other malvaceous plants like okra, *gulkhaira, kanghi buti* and some forest trees.

Damage. The larvae feed on cotton leaves. In severe infestation, the plants may be completely defoliated. Young larvae feed on the lower epidermis of leaves while older larvae roll up the leaves from the edges towards mid-rib.

Management. Same as in case of pink bollworm.

6. *Tarache notabilis* (Walker) (Cotton semi-looper, Lepidoptera: Noctuidae) (Fig. 9.1D)

Distribution. This insect is found throughout the plains of Pakistan and India as a minor pest of cotton, but in certain years, it assumes a serious form.

Identification. The adults arc stoutly built, white moths with prominent grey and brown spots on the wings, measuring 3.0-3.2 cm across. The full-grown larvae are about 4 cm long and dark green, having six pairs of black and bright-yellow spots on the back. As they move, they bend the body, forming half loops and hence the name semi-looper.

Life-history. The females lay green, rounded eggs singly, on the underside of leaves. The eggs hatch in 2-4 days and the larvae immediately start feeding voraciously. They are full-fed in 9-16 days and then descend to the ground, where they construct earthen cells at a depth of 3 cm for pupation. They emerge as moths in 5-14 days and are short-lived. The life-cycle is completed in 16-34 days. By October-November, they complete 4-5 generations.

Host plants. Besides cotton, it also feeds on the leaves of *sonchal (Malva parviflora),* brinjal, etc.

Damage. The larvae feed on cotton leaves and skeletonize them altogether. In years of heavy infestation, the plants may be completely denuded of leaves.

Management. (*i*) The incidence of pest on the next crop can be minimized by ploughing the fields soon after cotton harvest or by growing clovers in rotation with this crop. (*ii*) Chemical control measures are same as in case of pink bollworm.

7. *Anomis flava* (Fabricius) (Green semi-looper, Lepidoptera : Noctuidae) (Fig. 9.1E)

Distribution. The green semi-looper is widely distributed throughout the cotton growing areas of Africa, Asia and Australia. In India, it is a sporadic pest of cotton and sometimes causes a serious damage to the crop particularly in Gujarat and Rajasthan.

Identification. The adult is an attractive, small moth with reddish-brown fore wings traversed by two darker zig-zag bands. The hind wings are pale brown. The full-grown larva is 2.5-3.00 cm long and is pale-yellowish green with five white lines arranged longitudinally on the dorsal surface.

Life-history. The emergence of moths coincides with the warming up of the season. The female lays up to 600 eggs on leaves during an oviposition period of 8-12 days. The eggs hatch in 4-5 days. The larvae which move around with a characteristic semi-loop crawl and feed on leaves. They complete development by passing through 5 instars within a period of 18-20 days. They make a loose cocoon before pupation, either within the leaf folds or among debris in the soil. The pupal period lasts 8-9 days. The moths have a life-span of 12-13 days and the life-cycle is completed in 4-6 weeks. More than one generation is completed in a crop season.

Host plants. Besides cotton, the larvae also feed on *Hibiscus esculentus, Hibiscus cannabinus* and *Phaseolus radiatus* among the cultivated plants and on *Hibiscus rosasinensis, Sida cardifolia, Althaea rosea, Bombyx malabaricum* and *Malachra capitata* among the forest trees.

Damage. The young larvae congregate in small groups and move actively and feed on leaf lamina making small punctures. The grown-up larvae feed voraciously on the entire leaves, leaving only the main veins. The caterpillars also eat the tender shoots, buds and bolls. Sometimes, the attack is heavy and the plants may be completely defoliated.

Management. Same as in case of pink bollworm.

8. *Phycita infusella* (Meyrick) (Bud moth, Lepidoptera : Pyralidae)

Distribution. This insect is found throughout India as a minor pest of cotton and is more serious on *desi* than on the American varieties. It is sporadic in occurrence and becomes serious in certain localities only.

Identification. The adult is a greyish-yellow moth, speckled with fuscous, and measures 2.0 cm across the wing expanse. The front wings are faint yellow at the base with red wavy lines and the hind wings are white, with brown marginal lines. The full-grown caterpillars are 1.3-1.6 cm long, having a black front and faint brown stripes on the rest of the body.

Life-history. The pest is active from April to October and passes winter as a hibernating caterpillar in debris on the ground. The moths appear in April and lay small rounded eggs on tender leaves of cotton or other host plants. The eggs hatch in about 7 days and the young larvae start feeding on bud or young leaves. As the larvae grow, they web together the terminal leaves with silken threads and feed inside. They are full-fed in 21 days and make silken cocoons in the midst of twisted leaves. The pupal stage lasts 11 days and the moths, on emergence, live for a few days only. The life-cycle is completed in 5-6 weeks and the pest completes 4-5 generations in a year. *Bracon brevicornis* and *B. kitcheneri* are associated with larvae of this pest.

Host plants. Apart from cotton, it also feeds on okra and other allied plants.

Damage. Due to the webbing of leaves and feeding by the caterpillars, further growth of the plants is inhibited. The attacked leaves wither away, dry up and drop off. The flowering and fruiting are very poor and the reduction in yield is considerable.

Management. Spray 2.0 kg of carbaryl 50WP in 315-375 litres of water per ha.

9. *Bemisia tabaci* (Gennadius) (Cotton whitefly, Hemiptera : Aleyrodidae) (Fig. 9.1F)

Distribution. This pest is distributed throughout the northern and western regions of the Indian sub-continent and is a very serious pest of American cotton, particularly in the dry areas.

Identification. In the winged stage, they are 1.0-1.5 mm long and their yellowish bodies are slightly dusted with a white waxy powder. They have two pairs of pure white wings and have prominent long hind wings.

Life-history. The females lay stalked eggs singly on the underside of the leaves, averaging 119 eggs per female. The eggs hatch in 3-5 days during summer, 5-33 days in winter. The nymphs feed on cell-sap and grow into three stages to form the pupae within 9-14 days in summer and in 17-81 days in winter. In 2-8 days, the pupae change into whiteflies. The total life-cycle is completed in 14-122 days and 11 generations are completed in a year.

Host plants. Apart from cotton, this insect also feeds on various other plants such as cabbage, cauliflower, *sarson, toria,* melon, potato, brinjal, okra and some weeds.

Damage. The damage is caused by both the nymphs and the adults by sucking the sap from the leaves. Insects exude honeydew which attracts sooty mould. Therefore, in severe infestation, the plants not only become weak, but the mould interferes with the normal photosynthesis resulting in poor growth and yield of cotton. *B. tabaci* is known to transmit a number of virus diseases including the cotton leaf curl, the leaf curl disease of tobacco, the vein clearing disease of okra and the leaf curl of sesame.

Management. Insecticidal treatment against the whitefly should be initiated when population reaches six adults per leaf in the upper canopy of the plants before 10 AM or when honey dew appears on 50 per cent of the plants. Spray 500 g of diafenthiuron 50WP or 500 ml of spiromesifen 240SC or 1.5 litres of triazophos 40EC or 2.0 litres of ethion 50EC in 250 litres of water per ha.

10. *Amrasca biguttula* (Ishida) (Cotton leafhopper,Hemiptera : Cicadellidae) (Fig. 9.1G)

Distribution. The cotton leafhopper is widely distributed in India and is the most destructive pest of American cotton in the north-western regions.

Identification. Adults are about 3 mm long and greenish yellow during the summer, acquiring a reddish tinge in the winter.

Life-history. The females lay about 15 yellowish eggs on the underside of the leaves, embedding them into the leaf veins. The eggs hatch in 4-11 days and give rise to nymphs which are wedge-shaped and are very active. They suck cell-sap from the underside of the leaves and pass through six stages of growth in 7-21 days. On transformation into winged adults, they live for 5-7 weeks, feeding constantly on the plant juice. The pest completes seven generations in a year.

Host plants. Besides cotton, it also feeds on okra, potato, brinjal and some wild plants, like hollyhock, *kangi buti,* etc.

Damage. Injury to plants is caused both by the nymphs and the adults which suck sap from the foliage and probably also due to the injection of toxins into the plant tissues. The attacked leaves turn pale and then rust-red. With change in appearance, the leaves also turn downwards, dry up and fall to the ground. Owing to the loss of plant vitality, the cotton bolls also drop off, causing upto 35 per cent reduction in yield.

Management. (*i*) Grow American cotton varieties which are resistant or tolerant to leafhopper attack. In Punjab, recommended varieties are F1861, F1378, F846, LH1556 and hybrid LH144, all of which are moderately resistant or tolerant to leafhopper attack. (*ii*) Spray against leafhopper should be done only at economic threshold level of 1-2 nymphs per leaf or when second grade injury symptoms (yellowing and curling at margins of leaves) appear in 50 per cent of the plants. Any one of the following insecticides can be used in 250 litres of water per ha: 100 ml of imidacloprid 200SL, 100 ml of imidacloprid 555, 100 ml of imidacloprid 17.8SL, 100 g of thiamethoxam 25WG, 200 g of flonicamid 50WG. At the time of sowing, smear the cotton seed with imidacloprid 75WS @ 5g/kg seed or thiamethoxam 30FS @ 7g/Kg seed.

11. *Aphis gossypii* Glover (Cotton aphid, Hemiptera : Aphididae)

Distribution. The cotton aphid is world wide in distribution and is known as a potential pest of cotton.

Identification. The adults are small, greenish brown and soft-bodied insects found in colonies on the tender parts of the plants and under surface of the leaves.

Life-history. The adults exist in both winged and wingless forms. The alate as well as apterous females multiply parthenogenetically and viviparously. In a day, a female may give birth to 8-20 nymphs. The nymphs moult four times to become adults in 7-10 days. The coccinellid beetles, *Menochilus sexmaculatus* and *Coccinella septempunctata* are some common insects found to be predaceous on the aphid.

Host plants. Though it is a polyphagous pest infesting a variety of plants, it is of more significance on crops like lady's finger, brinjal, guava, gingelly, etc.

Damage. The damage is caused both by the nymphs and adults by sucking plant sap. Severe infestation results in curling of leaves, stunted growth and gradual drying and death of young plants. Black sooty mould develops on the honeydew of the aphids which falls on the leaves. Dry conditions favour rapid increase in pest population and the younger plants are more susceptible than the older ones.

Management. Chemical control measures are same as in case of cotton leafhopper.

12. *Phenacocus solenopsis* Tinsley (Cotton mealy bug, Hemiptera : Pseudococcidae)

Distribution. Cotton mealy bug has recently emerged as a serious pest of cotton in several Asian countries including India and Pakistan. This insect severely infected the cotton crop in the cotton growing provinces (Sindh and Punjab) of Pakistan in 2005 The infestation was recorded from 11 out of 18 cotton-growing areas, covering 45,000 km^2, on both Bt and non-Bt cotton. In India, mealy bug appeared in serious proportions in 2006 in cotton growing areas of Punjab, Haryana, Rajasthan, Maharashtra and Gujarat, and caused widespread damage to cotton. It struck in epidemic form in 2007 and 2008, and at many places, farmers had to plough down their badly infested crop.

Identification. The adult is pink and elongated oval (about 3 mm in length), flattened and covered with a white mealy powder. The female adults are wingless, however, male adults are having one pair of wings. The nymphs are pale yellow with reddish eyes, which are later on covered with white powdery mass.

Life-history. A female lays 150-600 eggs usually in a cotton like ovisac beneath her body.The embryonic development of the young ones takes place within the body of the female (ovoviviparity). The eggs hatch in 6-9 days. The newly emerged nymphs (crawlers) crawl out and start feeding on young plants. They prefer the growing shoot of the plant which is soft and juicy. Later on, they attack the older lower portion of the cotton plant. Its population increases tremendously and soon a colony is formed. Mature females are relatively sessile with a large, outpocketing cottony pouch from the posterior end, stuffed with its offspring. In case of severe infestation, the mealy bug occurs in the form of clusters with white cottony crawler sacs protruding from the anal region of their body. Thus, unspecified protective layers are formed due to the overlapping and clinging of one mealy bug over another. The female mealy bugs pass through four instars in 10-15 days. The longevity of the adult is 7-14 days. The total life cycle is completed in 25-30 days and there may by 14-15 generations in a year.

Host plants. The mealy bug has been recorded from 55 host species in 18 plant families. Besides cotton, it also feeds on tomato, mustard, sorghum, *bakain* (*Melia azedarach*) trees, and several weeds like congress grass*(Parthenium hysterophorus), kanghi buti (Abutilon theophrasti), peeli buti (Abutilon indicum), puthkanda (Achyranthes aspera), gutputna (Xanthium strumarium), bhakhra (Tribulus terrestris), itsit (Trianthema portulacastrum)* and *tandla* (*Digera arvensis*).

Damage. The mealy bug first attacks the alternate hosts growing in outer region of the cotton fields and then shifts to the cotton crop. Both nymphs and adults suck the sap from leaves, flower buds, petioles, twigs, internodes and even from the stem of the cotton plants. The insect heavily sucks the sap from the plant and renders it weak, feeble and dehydrated. In severe cases, defoliation takes place by the development of sooty mould on honeydew produced by crawlers. The sooty mould reduces the photosynthetic ability of the plants. In addition, mealy bug also injects toxins into the host tissues.

The flower buds, flowers, immature bolls and even the leaves fall down, and the growth of the plant is retarded. The infested plants bear fewer bolls of smaller size and there is incomplete opening of bolls. The entire plant remains stunted and shoot tips develop a bushy appearance. The cotton plant exhibits a die-back of growing shoots and twigs, ultimately reducing the yield. This damage of the pest is initiated from the borders and spreads to the main cotton crop. White cottony heads appear on the infested plants where intensive infestation of all the stages can be observed. Its infestation starts in patches and in case of severe infestation, the infested plants give the appearance of a field sprayed with a defoliant or herbicide.

Management. (*i*) To check the spread of mealy bug, remove regularly the weeds growing adjacent to road sides, pathways, water channels and waste lands. (*ii*) Destroy the infested host plants alongwith the pest very carefully, preferably by burning/deep ploughing, but never throw in open water channels. (*iii*) Avoid growing cotton near the fields of tomato, sorghum and *bakain* trees, as they serve as alternate hosts of mealy-bug. (*iv*) The hymenopterous parasitoid, *Aenasius bambawalei* is very effective against mealy bug ; as high as 70-80 per cent parasitization has been recorded in certain areas. The parasitoid kills the mealy bugs within a week, which turn into dark reddish brown mummies. The parasitoid population should be augmented in cotton through collection of mealy bug mummies from various host plants and releasing them onto the cotton plants. (*v*) In case of severe infestation, spray any one of the following insecticides in 300-400 litres of water per ha : (*a*) ***Carbamates***. 2.5 kg of carbaryl 50WP or 625 g of thiodicarb 75WP. (*b*) ***Organophosphates.*** 1.25 litres of profenophos 50EC or 2.0 litres of quinalphos 25EC or 2.0 kg of acephate 75SP or 5.0 litres of chlorpyriphos 20EC.

(*c*) ***Insect Growth Regulators***. 1.25 litres of buprofezin 25EC. (*d*) The first spray should preferably be done with buprofezin since it is safe for natural enemies. (*e*) Since damage of mealy bug is normally localised to border rows, treat only these rows with the above pesticides.

13. *Oxycarenus hyalinipennis* Costa (Dusky cotton bug, Hemiptera : Lygaeidae) (Fig. 9.1H)

Distribution. This insect is found in all the cotton growing regions in India.

Identification. The adults are 4-5 mm in length, dark brown and have dirty white transparent wings. The young nymphs have a rotund abdomen and, as they grow older, they resemble the adults, except for being smaller and having prominent wing pads instead of wings.

Life-history. The cigar-shaped eggs are laid in the spring on *Hibiscus* and then on okra and finally on cotton during the monsoon. Initially, they are whitish turning pale and finally becoming light pink before hatching. The eggs are usually laid in the lint of half-opened bolls, either singly or in small clusters of 3-18 each. The egg stage lasts 5-10 days and the nymphs, on emerging, pass through 7 stages, completing the development in 31-40 days. The life-cycle lasts 36-50 days and a number of generations are completed in a year.

Host plants. Besides cotton, it also feeds on okra, hollyhock and other malvaceous weeds.

Damage. The nymphs and adults suck the sap from immature seeds, whereupon these seeds may not ripen, lose colour and remain light in weight. The adults found in the seed cotton are crushed in the ginning factories, thus staining the lint and lowering its market value.

Management. Same as in case of cotton leafhopper.

14. *Dysdercus koenigii* (Fabricius) (Red cotton bug, Hemiptera: Pyrrhocoridae)

Distribution. This insect is widely distributed in India and is a minor pest of cotton in the Punjab and Haryana.

Identification. The bugs are elongated slender insects, crimson red with white bands across the abdomen. The membraneous portion of their forewings, antennae and scutellum is black.

Life-history. The bug lays, on an average, 100-130 eggs in moist soil or in crevices in the ground in clusters or in loose irregular masses of 70-80 eggs each. They hatch in 7-8 days and the young nymphs have flabby abdomens, but as they grow older, they become more slender and develop black markings on the body. There are 5 nymphal stages and the development is completed in 49-89 days.

Host plants. Apart from cotton, it also feeds on okra, maize, pearl millet, hollyhock, wheat, maize, pearl-millet, clovers, etc.

Damage. The insects suck cell-sap from leaves and green bolls of cotton. Heavily attacked bolls open badly and the lint is of poor quality. The seed produced may also have low germination and less oil. Moreover, the bugs stain the lint with their excreta or body juices as they are crushed in the ginning factories.

Management. Same as in case of cotton leafhopper.

15. *Pempherulus affinis* (Faust) (Cotton stem weevil, Coleoptera : Curculionidae)

Distribution. The cotton stem weevil is widely distributed in India, Myanmar, Thailand and the Philippines. In India, it occurs in Tamil Nadu, Andhra Pradesh, Karnataka, Kerala, Bihar, Orissa, Rajasthan, Uttar Pradesh, Gujarat and Assam.

Identification. The adult is a dirty brown or greyish black weevil, about 3 cm in length. The grub is slightly curved, creamy white, with a distinct head.

Life-history. During an oviposition period of 60-80 days, a female may lay up to 121 eggs visiting from plant to plant. The eggs hatch in 6-10 days and the grubs feed inside the soft stem tissue. They continue to feed inside till the development is completed in 35-57 days. The pupation takes place inside the stem and this stage lasts from 25 to 30 days. Three generations are completed in a year from October to April.

Host plant. Cotton

Damage. As the grubs tunnel within the stem, that portion swells, and such symptoms are generally seen at the base of the plant. The younger plants when attacked succumb, while the older plants may survive but suffer in vigour. Under strong winds, the affected plants may break at the swellings. The pest causes plant mortality upto 25 per cent, especially during the early stages of growth.

Management. (*i*) Collection and destruction of affected plants is recommended for the control of this pest (*ii*) Apply 5 litres of chlorpyriphos 20EC in 315-375 litres of water per ha at 15 days interval commencing 3 weeks after sowing.

16. *Myllocerus undecimpustulatus* Faust (Cotton grey weevil, Coleoptera.: Curculionidae) (Fig. 8.1l)

Distribution. This insect is found throughout India.

Identification. The weevils are grey and are 3-6 mm long. The grubs are white, legless, cylindrical and are about 8 mm in length.

Life-history. The pest is active from April to November and passes winter in the adult stage hidden in debris. The weevils appear in April-May and lay ovoid, light yellow eggs in the soil. A female lays, on an average, 360 eggs over a period of 24 days. The eggs hatch in 3-5 days in May-September and the young grubs feed on the roots of cotton and other plants. The grubs complete their development in 1-2 months. They pupate in the soil inside earthen cells, forming creamy-white pupae, which change into adults in about one week. The adults live for 8-11 days in the summer and 4-5 months in the winter. During the active period, the life-cycle is completed in 6-8 weeks and the pest probably breeds 3-4 times in a year.

Host plants. It is a minor pest of cotton, particularly of the *desi* cotton varieties. It also feeds on a number of other cultivated plants such as *bajra* (*Pennisetum typhoides*), maize, sorghum, guava, *arhar* (*Cajanus cajan*), groundnut, etc.

Damage. Both adults and grubs cause damage. The grubs feed underground on the roots of cotton seedlings and destroy them. One grub can destroy 9 seedlings in 40 days. The adults which feed on leaves, buds, flowers and young bolls cut prominent round holes.

Management. (*i*) The pest can be suppressed by disturbing the soil up to a depth of 7.5 cm and destroying the eggs, grubs and pupae. (*ii*) Spray 2.5 kg of carbaryl 50 WP in 375 litres of water per ha.

JUTE

As many as 32 insect pests have been reported damaging jute in India, but only a few are of major significance.

1. *Anomis sabulifera* (Guenee) (Jute semi-looper, Lepidoptera: Noctuidae)

Distribution. This is the most destructive pest in the jute tracts of India, Bangladesh, Myanmar and Sri Lanka.

Identification. The adult is a stoutly built moth with brownish wings bearing dark brown patches on the apex of the fore wings. Being green in colour, caterpillars camouflage but are easily noticed when they crawl by producing a loop in the middle.

Life-history. The adults lay eggs singly on the underside of young leaves; a female may lay more than 150 eggs which look like water droplets. The egg stage lasts about two days. The tiny caterpillars, on emerging, start feeding on the apical leaves and buds. They attain a full length of about 4 cm after 5 moults, in about 17 days. The pupation may take place on the plant or in the soil. In summer, the pupae emerge in about a week, but those, which diapause, spend the entire winter in that stage. The life-cycle is completed in about one month and several generations are completed in a year.

Host plant. Jute

Damage. The attack is severe on half-grown plants which are one metre high. The second generation is the most damaging and sometimes up to 90 per cent of the leaves may be eaten up. Generally, the top 7-9 leaves are damaged and plant growth is adversely affected, resulting in a considerable reduction in the yield of fibre.

Management. (*i*) The pest can be suppressed by ploughing the infested fields after harvest and thus killing the pupae. (*ii*) The caterpillars can be dislodged into kerosenized water by drawing a rope across the young crop. (*iii*) Spray 500 ml of fenitrothion 50EC in 500 litres of water per ha. Repeat the treatments three times at 15-day interval from mid June or at first appearance of the pest.

2. *Nupserha bicolor postbrunnea* Dutt (Jute stem girdler, Coleoptera: Lamiidae)

Distribution. The pest is distributed throughout the jute belt in India and Bangladesh.

Identification. The adult is medium-sized, bright coloured and cylindrical bodied beetle. When full-grown, the larvae measure about 1.4 cm.

Life-history. The female beetle makes two rings by cutting a strip, the space in between the rings being 1.0-1.4 cm. In this area, a slit is made, which reaches as far as the pith, where the beetle deposits one egg. Since a female lays, on an average, 35 eggs, many jute plants are damaged within 2-3 weeks. The eggs hatch in 3-4 days and the emerging larvae start feeding and travelling downwards along the central hollow of the stem, feeding on the pith.

The larvae become full-grown in 30-50 days. During the active season, the larvae pupate in a chamber made in the hollow of the stem. With the advent of winter, the larvae cut out small portions of the stem in which they encase themselves and diapause. These encasements are detached from the main stem and when the jute plants are placed under water, they float, carrying with them, the larvae. Thus, the diapausing larvae escape drowning. The females prefer stems of 2.5-5.0 mm in diameter, which are available at different heights of the jute stem, depending on the age of the crop. The larval stage continues up to the next spring and pupation takes place only after the rains have started. There is only one generation in a year.

Host plants. Originally, this pest was confined to a number of host plants, among which *Sesbania aegyptiaca (dhaincha)* was the most important. However, in the past three decades, it has become a major pest of only one species of jute *(Corchorus olitorius* L.) and also of mesta, an allied fibre crop.

Damage. The main damage occurs because of oviposition, resulting in the breakage of fibre length at several places. Thus, both the quality of fibre and the yield suffer. The damage is estimated at 6-30 per cent, being more in younger plants than in the older ones. Not much damage is caused by the feeding of larvae or adults.

Management. (*i*) In areas where the girdler is a severe pest, the growing of resistant species of jute *(capsularis)* is useful. (*ii*) Mix 25 kg of phorate 10G per ha in the top soil followed by light irrigation.

3. *Apion corchori* Marshall (Jute stem weevil, Coleoptera : Apionidae)

Distribution. The jute stem weevil has been recorded in all the jute-growing parts of India and Bangladesh.

Identification. The small weevil is only 1.8 mm in length and 0.8 mm in breadth, brown or dull black and has small whitish setae on its body. The full-grown larvae measure 2.8 mm is length and about 1 mm is breadth.

Life-history. In the active season, the weevils make holes in the stem and lay eggs which are about 0.4 mm in length and 0.3 mm in breadth. A single female may lay as many as 675 eggs during its life-span of about 120 days. The eggs are generally laid at the base of the petiole, in which the larvae bore and damage the top leaves. In older plants, the weevils prefer to oviposit in the basal region and the lower part of the stem is damaged. The larvae emerge after 3-5 days and start feeding on the surrounding tissues. They are full-fed in 8-11 days and make a rough chamber in the stem and pupate.

The pupal stage is completed in 4-6 days and the weevil emerges from the pupal case through an exit which is either made by the larva before pupation or by the weevil itself. Although the adults may live for about 200 days, the normal life-cycle is completed in 15-24 days. A number of overlapping generations are completed during the jute season.

Host plants. Jute, particularly *capsularis* variety and some allied plants.

Damage. The main damage to the quality of fibre is caused by weevils making oviposition holes. A female may make a number of holes before laying an egg and damages numerous stems in her life time.

Management. (*i*) The pest may be suppressed by the removal and destruction of infested plants at the time of thinning the crop and by collecting and destroying the stubble after harvest. (*ii*) Spray 2.5 kg of carbaryl 50WP in 625 litres of water per ha.

4. *Spodoptera exigua* (Hubner) (Indigo caterpillar, Lepidoptera : Noctuidae)

Distribution. Geographically, this pest is found in Europe, South Africa, America and the Orient. In India, USA, Canada and other countries, it has been recorded as a minor pest of lucerne (*Medicago sativa*) and hence, is also known as the lucerne caterpillar.

Identification. The moths have dark spotted fore wings and white hind wings. They are active at night but remain hidden under various shrubs in the day time. The colour of larvae depends on the crop on which they feed.

Life-history. The pest passes winter as a pupa, which is enclosed in webbings, forming a rough pupal cocoon. Some of them emerge as moths in February, but a number of them continue in that state till the beginning of the monsoon. A female lays up to 200 eggs in clusters. The eggs are spherical and resemble poppy seeds in shape and size, having lines radiating from the centre. The egg-clusters are covered with buff hairs. The eggs hatch in 1-3 days and the young caterpillars start feeding in groups. They feed voraciously on the epidermis and also make webs. Within 2-3 days, the gregarious larvae spread out and hide under various shelters, from where they come out in the morning and evening to feed on the leaves.

The larval stage is completed in 15-20 days and the full-grown larvae seek shelter in debris, on the ground. They spin silken webbings and prepare rough cocoons with bits of leaves and other material. The pupal stage lasts 5-7 days and the life cycle is completed in about 30 days. From November onwards, the pest hibernates in the pupal stage. During the active season, a number of generations are completed.

Host plants. This polyphagous insect is a serious pest of young jute plants and at one time, was a major pest of indigo (*Indigofera arrecta*) and hence called indigo caterpillar. Also, it is a minor pest of chillies, onion, binjal, sweet pepper, gram, linseed, lentil, cabbage, maize, cotton, safflower (*Carthamus tinctorius*), sunflower, etc.

Damage. The damaged crop, on which larvae have fed, gives a webbed appearance. The older caterpillars, which feed in the morning and evening, have a voracious appetite and strip off quite large patches on the foliage. However, the young jute plants, less than two months of age, suffer the most. The early sown *capsularis* varieties suffer greater losses than those sown later.

Management. (*i*) The pest can be suppressed by collecting and destroying the egg masses and the caterpillars which are feeding within the webs. (*ii*) Spray 625 ml of fenitrothion 50EC in 625 litres of water per ha.

5. *Maconellicoccus hirsutus* Green (Jute mealy bug, Hemiptera : Pseudococcidae)

Distribution. The pest is distributed in jute tracts of India and Bangladesh.

Identification. The female is a rotund, sack-like, light pink creature and measures about 3 mm in length. The males are slender and have a pair of delicate wings.

Life-history. The mated females lay pink cylindrical eggs which are rounded at the ends. The eggs are laid on plants inside the ovisacs and measure 0.3 mm in length and 0.2 mm in breadth. The incubation period varies from 7 to 14 days in different seasons. On completion of the incubation period, the emergence of the nymphs starts from the ovisacs in batches, corresponding with the sequence of egg-laying. The tiny nymphs crawl out on the host and select a suitable spot to settle down. They are light pinkish and secrete both a white mealy powder and honeydew. They develop distinctive sex characters after undergoing a few early moultings. The full-grown larva secretes fine white mealy fibres with which it forms a cocoon and then pupates in it. The females remain wingless, and on maturity, they develop ovisacs in which eggs are laid. The bugs suck sap from the stem and leaves. *Scymnus pallidicollis* is the most efficient predator and feeds vigorously on the eggs, nymphs and adult females.

Host plants. Besides jute, this sap-sucking mealy bug attacks the roselle fibre crop (*Hibiscus sabdariffa*), an important fibre allied to jute, and is responsible for an appreciable decrease in the yield of fibre.

Damage. The nymphs and females feed on the apical parts of a plant which becomes stunted and shows bushy-top symptoms. The petiole becomes shortened, the lamina crumples and the internodal length is reduced, resulting in fibre deterioration and yield reduction.

Management. Spray 1.25 litres of dimethoate 30EC in 625 litres of water per ha.

SUNNHEMP

Sunnhemp is attacked by about a dozen of insect pests but only hairy caterpillar and stem borer are important.

1. *Utetheisa pulchella* (Linnaeus) (Sunnhemp hairy caterpillar, Lepidoptera: Arctiidae)

Distribution. This insect is the most important pest of sunnhemp in Tamil Nadu, Andhra Pradesh, West Bengal, Orissa, Bihar, U.P. and Maharashtra.

Identification. The adult moth is pale, whitish with red black spots on the upper wings and black marginal blotches on the lower wings. The full-grown caterpillar is about 20 mm in length and has red, dark and white markings on its body and a brownish head.

Life-history. The moths lay small whitish eggs on the tender leaves and shoots. On emergence from the eggs, the larvae feed on leaves. As the crop matures and pods appear, the caterpillars feed by thrusting the head in and leaving the rest of the body exposed. Pupation takes place either in the leaf folds or in the soil. The life-cycle is completed in about 5 weeks and a number of generations are completed in a year.

Host plant. Sunnhemp

Damage. The caterpillars defoliate the crop and cause a decrease in seed production.

Management. (*i*) The pest can be suppressed by hand picking and killing the caterpillars as well as by collecting the moths with nets during the day time. (*ii*) Spray 1.25 litres of endosulfan 35EC or 2.5 kg of carbaryl 50WP in 625 litres of water per ha.

2. *Enarmonia pseudonectis* Meyrick (Sunnhemp stem borer, Lepidoptera : Tortricidae)

Distribution. Same as in case of sunnhemp hairy caterpillar.

Identification. It is a dusky grey or greyish-brown moth

Life-history. The eggs are laid on the leaves which hatch in 4-7 days. Young larvae first feed on the leaves and then bore into the stem. They are full-grown in 15-18 days. Pupation occurs in the galls produced by the injuries inflicted by the larvae. The pupae become adults in 4-7 days.

Host plant. Sunnhemp.

Damage. The damage is caused by the caterpillars by feeding on the leaves and occasionally on the pods. The injuries caused by the larvae induce formation of small swellings or galls which can be easily seen.

Management. Same as in case of sunnhemp hairy caterpillar.

3. *Ragmus importunitas* Distant (Sunnhemp capsid, Hemiptera: Miridae)

Distribution. The pest is widely distributed in southern India.

Identification. This is a small, active, green bug which sucks plant sap and when present in large swarms, causes appreciable damage.

Life-history. The bugs lay white cylindrical eggs in the plant tissue, generally under the surface layer of leaves. The young nymphs, on emergence, begin to feed on the plants. All stages of the insect may be found simultaneously. When the population is high and the attack is severe, the plants become pale and appear unhealthy.

Management. (*i*) The population of the pest can be suppressed by collecting the bugs with nets or sticky boards. (*ii*) Spray 2.5 kg of carbaryl 50WP or 625 ml of malathion 50EC in 625 litres of water per ha.

MESTA

Mesta is attacked by several species of insects among which spiral borer is the most important.

Agrilus acutus Thunberg (Spiral borer, Coleoptera : Buprestidae)

Distribution. The pest is distributed in the states of Bihar, Uttar Pradesh and Madhya Pradesh.

Identification. It is a minute bronzy or metallic blue coloured beetle with cylindrical body.

Life-history. The eggs are laid on the stem preferably on the nodal region below the leaf-base. The eggs hatch in 12-14 days and the newly hatched larvae start feeding inside the stem. There are 3-4 larval instars and the larval stage lasts for 25-30 days. Pupation takes place inside the stem and the adults emerge in 8-10 days.

Host plant. Mesta

Damage. The damage is caused by the grubs by feeding inside the stem on woody tissue. During feeding, the grub travels throughout the entire length of the stem in a spiral manner. A portion of the infested region swells up considerably to form an elongated gall, the portion of the stem above the gall dries up and breaks.

Management. Swabbing the stem with 2.5 per cent metasystox controls the pest.

*****

10 CHAPTER

PESTS OF PLANTATION CROPS

Coconut
(*Cocos nucifera*)

1. *Oryctes rhinoceros* (Linnaeus) (Rhinoceros beetle, Coleoptera : Scarabaeidae)
2. *Rhynchophorus ferrugineus* (Olivier) (Red palm weevil, Coleoptera : Curculionidae)
3. *Opisina arenosella* Walker (Black-headed caterpillar, Lepidoptera : Xyloryctidae)
4. *Leucopholis coneophora* Burmeister (Coconut white grub, Coleoptera: Melolonthidae)
5. *Aspidiotus destructor* Signoret (Coconut scale, Hemiptera: Diaspididae)
6. *Diocalandra frumenti* (Fabricius) (Coconut weevil, Coleoptera : Curculionidae)

Tea
(*Camellia* spp.)

1. *Helopeltis theivora* Waterhouse (Tea mosquito-bug, Hemiptera : Miridae)
2. *Zeuzera coffeae* Nietner (Coffee red borer, Lepidoptera : Cossidae)
3. *Andraca bipunctata* Walker (Bunch caterpillar, Lepidoptera.: Bombycidae)
4. *Spatulicraspeda castaneiceps* Hampson (Humped slug caterpillar, Lepidoptera : Cochlidiidae)

Coffee
(*Coffea* spp.)

1. *Ferrisia virgata* (Cockerell) (Striped mealy bug, Hemiptera.: Pseudococcidae)
2. *Xylotrechus quadripes* Chevrolat (Coffee stem borer, Coleoptera : Cerambycidae)

3. *Coccus viridis* (Green) (Soft green scale, Hemiptera.: Coccidae)
4. *Xylosandrus campactus* Eichhoff (Coffee shot-hole borer, Coleoptera: Scolytidae)
5. *Hypothenemus hampei* (Ferrari) (Coffee berry-borer, Coleoptera : Scolytidae).
6. *Saissetia coffeae* (Walker) (Helmet scale, Hemiptera : Coccidae)
7. *Zeuzera coffeae* Nietner (Coffee borer, Lepidoptera : Cossidae)

Cashewnut (*Anacardium occidentale*)

1. *Plocaederus ferrugineus* (Linnaeus) (Cashew tree borer, Coleoptera : Cerambycidae)
2. *Acrocercops syngramma* Meyrick (Cashew leaf-miner, Lepidoptera : Gracillariadae)
3. *Helopeltis antonii* Signoret (Tea mosquito-bug, Hemiptera: Miridae)
4. *Cricula trifenestrata* Hubner (Leaf caterpillar, Lepidoptera: Saturnidae)
5. *Chelaria haligramma* Meyrick (Shoot-tip and inflorescence caterpillar, Lepidoptera : Gelechiidae)
6. *Rhipiphorothrips cruentatus* Hood (Cashew thrips, Thysanoptera : Thripidae)
7. *Parasa lepida* Cramer (Slug caterpillar, Lepidoptera : Limacodidae)

Arecanut (*Areca catechu*)

1. *Carvalhoia arecae* Miller & China (Arecanut mirid bug, Hemiptera: Miridae)
2. *Odontotermes obesus* (Rambur) (Termite, Isoptera : Termitidae)
3. *Rhynchophorus ferrugineus* (Olivier) (Red palm weevil, Coleoptera : Curculionidae)
4. *Rhipiphorothrips cruentatus* Hood (Thrips, Thysanoptera.: Thripidae)

Rubber (*Ficus elastica* and *Havea brasiliensis*)

1. *Aestherastis circulata* Meyrick (Rubber bark caterpillar, Lepidoptera: Yponomeutidae)
2. *Aspidiotus destructor* Signoret (Rubber scale, Hemiptera.: Coccidae)
3. *Apoderus chrysochlorus* Wiedemann (Weevil, Coleoptera.: Curculionidae)
4. *Comocritis pieria* Meyrick (Rubber bark caterpillar, Lepidoptera : Yponomeutidae

The total production of plantation crops was 9.84 million tonnes in 2004-05, which increased to 11.26 million tonnes in 2005-06, 12.08 million tonnes in 2006-07 and more than 15 million tonnes in 2011-12. Among plantation crops, coffee has made significant contribution to the Indian economy during the last 50 years. The production of coffee in 2009-10 is estimated at 2.90 lakh tonnes, comprising 0.95 lakh tonnes of *arabica* and 1.95 lakh tonnes of *robusta*.

COCONUT

1. *Aspidiotus destructor* Signoret (Coconut scale, Hemiptera : Diaspididae)

Distribution. The coconut scale is one of the most dangerous pests of coconut palm in most of the coconut growing regions of India. It also occurs in Iran, Japan, USA, South Africa and Australia.

Identification. The scale of the female is circular, flat, transparent, whitish to grey white and about 1.8 mm in diameter. The scale of the male is oval and much smaller than that of the female.

Life-history. The female deposits about 20-25 yellow, tiny eggs under her scale. Incubation takes 7-8 days. On hatching, the crawler takes up a position on the leaf and starts feeding. The male nymph moults three times and the female twice. The larval development takes 24 days. The total life-cycle is completed in 31-35 days and there are about 8-10 generations per year.

Host-plants. In addition to coconut, this pest also feeds on other palms, bananas, avocado, cocoa, citrus, ginger, guava, *Artocarpus, Pandanus,* papaya, rubber, sugarcane, yam and many wild plants.

Damage. The damage is caused by both nymphs and adults by sucking plant sap. The scale affected leaves first show a yellow discoloration around areas of the sucking activity, followed by brown necrosis. In extreme cases, the leaves dry up, entire fronds drop off, the crown dies and the whole crop is lost.

Management. Spray 500 ml of malathion 50EC in 250 litres of water per ha.

2. *Opisina arenosella* Walker (Black-headed caterpillar, Lepidoptera: Xyloryctidae) (Fig. 10.1A)

Distribution. This is one of the most important pests of coconut palm in Kerala as well as along the western coast of India, Sri Lanka and Myanmar.

Identification. The moth is ash grey. It is medium-sized, measuring 1.0-1.5 mm, with a wing expanse of 2.0-2.5 cm.

Life-history. A female moth lays 125 scale like eggs in small batches on the underside of the tips of the old leaves. Freshly laid eggs are creamy white and turn pink on completion of embryonic development. The incubation period lasts about 3-5 days in summer and 10 days in winter. The larva feeds on green matter and simultaneously constructs a silken gallery in which it feeds and voids frass. When full-grown in about 40 days, the larva transforms itself into a brownish pupa inside the gallery. Within about 12 days, a whitish moth emerges and starts the life-cycle all over again. The caterpillar is parasitized by *Apanteles taragammae, Bracon brevicornis* and *Elasmus nephantidis.*

Host plants. Coconut and other plams.

Damage. As a result of the numerous galleries made by the feeding caterpillars, the foliage dries up. Infested trees can be recognized from the dried up patches in the fronds. In case of severe attack due to large scale drying of leaflets, the whole plantation presents a burnt up appearance from a distance, resulting in a considerable reduction in yield.

Management. (*i*) Inundative releases of native parasitoids, *Goniozus nephantidis* and *B. brevicornis* at 3000 and 4500 ha^{-1}, respectively have given encouraging results for management of black-headed caterpillar. (*ii*) Apply 2.5 litres of chlorpyriphos 20EC in 625 litres of water per ha.

3. *Oryctes rhinoceros* (Linnaeus) (Rhinoceros beetle, Coleoptera: Scarabaeidae)

Distribution. The rhinoceros beetle is one of the most important pests of the coconut in all coconut growing states of India like Assam, West Bengal, Orissa, Maharashtra, Karnataka, Kerala, Tamil Nadu, Andaman and Nicobar islands. It is found throughout South-east Asia, the Philippines and southern China.

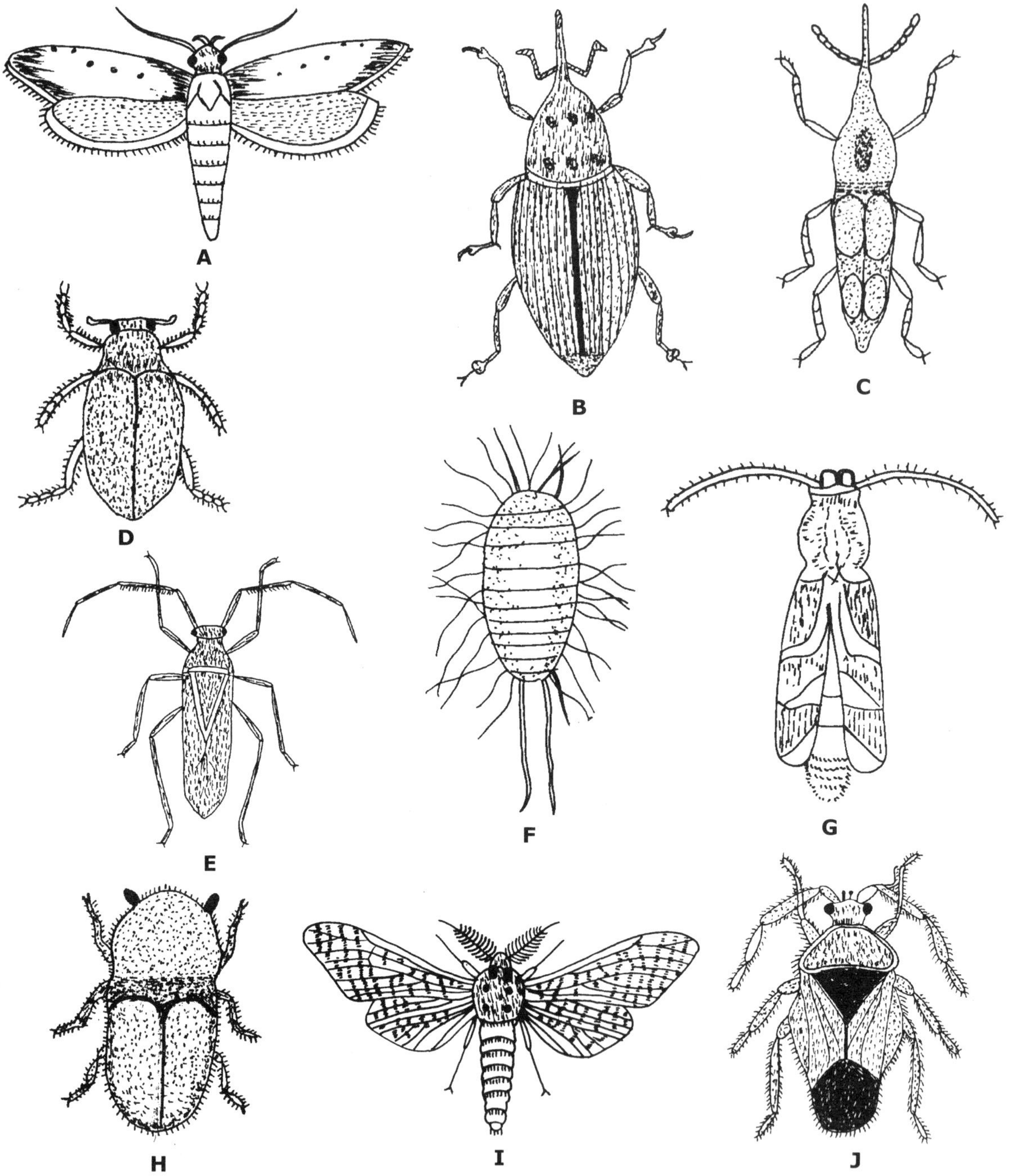

Fig. 10.1 Pests of plantation crops. **A.** Black-headed caterpillar, *Opisina arenosella*. **B.** Red palm weevil, *Rhynchophorus ferrugineus*. **C.** Coconut weevil, *Diocalandra frumenti*. **D.** Coconut white grub, *Leucopholis coneophora*. **E.** Tea mosquito-bug, *Helopeltis theivora*. **F.** Striped mealy bug, *Ferrisia virgata*. **G.** Coffee stem borer, *Xylotrechus quadripes*. **H.** Coffee berry borer, *Hypothenemus hampei*. **I.** Coffee red borer, *Zeuzera coffeae*. **J.** Arecanut mirid bug, *Carvalhoia arecae*.

Identification. The stoutly built beetle has a pointed horn on its head, is elongate and cylindrical and measures about 4-5 cm.

Life-history. The oval, white, seed-like eggs are laid 5-15 cm below the soil surface in decaying organic matter. The early stages of the beetle are generally passed in manure pits and decomposing vegetable matter, chiefly in the dead palm trunks. The female lays 100-150 eggs, 5-15 cm below the soil surface in decaying matter. The eggs hatch in 8-18 days and the grubs start feeding on the decaying matter found in the vicinity. The larvae pass through three instars to complete their development in 80-130 days. Pupation takes place in chamber at a depth of about 30 cm and the beetles emerge after 10-25 days. They remain in the pupal cell for about 11-20 days before coming out of the soil and, on emergence, they are soft-bodied creatures. Soon, they fly to the nearest palm-tree and start the attack. They lay eggs after 20-60 days. The adults can live for more than 200 days. Generally, one generation is completed in a year.

Host plants. Coconut and other palms such as date-palm, sago-palm, palmyra, etc.

Damage. The damage is done by adults alone since grubs feed on decaying matter. The beetles throw out a fibrous mass while feeding in the burrows made in the young fronds. The injury is seen as a series of holes on the fronds when they open out. As a result, the growing point is soon cut off and the tree dies. The damage caused by this beetle is more serious on young trees.

Management. (*i*) Plant legumes as cover crops to conceal the potential breeding sites of the beetle. (*ii*) Treat the breeding places of the beetle with the fungus *Metarhizium anisopliae*. (*iii*) Leave some dead standing palms to promote the spread of non-occluded virus (orv) which kills the beetles (*iv*) Increase the prevalence of the orv by releasing virus-infected beetles. (*v*) The exotic predatory bug, *Platymeris laevicollis* has shown considerable promise against this pest. The frogs, toads, birds, rats and squirrels also prey upon grubs of this pest. (*vi*) Drench the manure heaps upto a depth of 60 cm at quarterly intervals. (*vii*) Treat the breeding places with 2.0 kg of carbaryl 50WP in 250 litres of water per ha.

4. *Rhynchophorus ferrugineus* (Olivier) (Red palm weevil, Coleoptera: Curculionidae) (Fig. 10.1B)

Distribution. The pest is distributed in India, Pakistan, Bangladesh, Sri Lanka, Malaysia, the Philippines and New Guinea. It is one of the most destructive pests of coconut palm in Maharashtra, Assam, Kerala, Tamil Nadu, Mysore and Orissa.

Identification. This weevil is reddish-brown, cylindrical, with a long curved snout. The male has tuft of hairs along the dorsal surface of the snout, whereas the female is without it. The full grown grub is yellowish.

Life-history. The mother weevil scoops out a small hole with its snout in the soft tissues of the trees or in the existing wounds, in the crown or trunk and lays an oval, whitish egg. A weevil may lay up to 200-500 eggs in its life span of 3-4 months. The eggs hatch in 2-5 days and the soft whitish grubs on hatching, feed on the soft tissues and tunnel into the tree trunk. The larval period ranges from 2 to 4 months. The grub changes into a pupa after spinning a cocoon. The weevil emerges from this cocoon on the completion of the pupal stage in about 14 days. The adults remain within the case for 11-18 days out of life-span of 50-113 days, the male surviving for a longer period than the female. The adult is capable of flight and is diurnal in habits.

Host plants. Coconut and other palms.

Damage. The larvae feed on the soft tissue of trees and often cause very severe damage, especially when a large number of them bore into the soft growing parts. The borer attacks all palms, including the coconut, the date-palm and the sago-palm (*Metroxylon* spp.). The weevil is attracted to the trees by the smell of palm juice, which flows as a result of the wounds caused by man or other agents. The dead palms also attract these insects. The pest multiplies quickly in young coconut plantations.

Management. (*i*) Destroy the infested, dead or dying plants (*ii*) Cutting petioles about 120 cm away from the trunks helps to check entry of the weevil. (*iii*) Inject emulsion of dimethoate 30EC @ 400 m1 or chlorpyriphos 20EC @ 2.0 litres or carbaryl 50WP @ 250 g in 25 litres of water into the live holes and plaster them with mud after application of chemicals. (*iv*) Apply 2.0 litres of chlorpyriphos 20EC in 250 litres of water to the damaged trunks or spray on crowns after every three months.

5. *Diocalandra frumenti* (Fabricius) (Coconut weevil, Coleoptera : Curculionidae) (Fig. 10.1C)

Distribution. The pest is recorded from Sri Lanka, Myanmar, South India, Malaysia, Thailand, Indonesia and the Philippines.

Identification. The adults are small weevils (6-8 mm in length) shiny blackish with four large reddish spots in the elytra.

Life-history. Eggs are laid in crevices at the base of the adventitious roots at the foot of the trunk, flowers, petiole or at the base of the peduncle. The eggs hatch in 4-9 days. Larval development takes 8-10 weeks and the pupal period lasts 10-12 days. The life-cycle is completed in 10-12 weeks.

Host plants. This weevil attacks coconut palm, date-palm, oil and nipa-palms, and sorghum.

Damage. The grubs attack all parts of the coconut palm particularly the roots, the leaves, and the fruit stalks. As a result of this attack, there is premature fruit-fall and the loss of yield is appreciable.

Management. Spray 2.0 kg of carbaryl 50WP in 500 litres of water per ha.

6. *Leucopholis coneophora* Burmeister (Coconut white grub, Coleoptera : Melolonthidae) (Fig. 10.1D)

Distribution. It is a major pest of coconut in South India, particularly in Kerala.

Identification. The beetles are chestnut coloured and measure 1.6 cm in length and grubs are white.

Life-history. The eggs are laid in the soil at a depth of 7-15 cm. The eggs hatch in 20 days and the grubs start feeding on roots. They moult a number of times and when full-grown, they pupate within a period of 10 months or so. The pre-pupal period is 9-12 days and the pupal stage lasts 25 days. The insect completes one generation in a year.

Host plants. Besides coconut, it also feeds on tapioca, yam, colocasia, sweet potato, banana, etc.

Damage. The beetles defoliate the host plants. As a result of continued feeding of the grubs on roots, the vitality of the palms is reduced and their colour becomes yellowish. In the end, trees become very weak and show the symptoms of premature falling of the nuts.

Management. (*i*) Deep tilling, particularly in areas of high rainfall and sandy soil, helps to check the pest. (*ii*) Dust the soil with chlorpyriphos 2 per cent @ 30 kg per ha.

7. *Aceria guerreronis* Keifer (Coconut Eriophyid mite, Acarina : Eriophyidae)

Distribution. It is a serious pest of coconut in Tamil Nadu and Kerala

Identification. The minute mite cannot be seen without a 10X hand lens; the adult female mite is 205 to 255 μm long and 36 to 52 μm wide. Like typical eriophyid mites , these are elongate and have two pairs of legs, instead of four pairs as is typical of most mites. They are white and translucent.

Life-history. Nearly 18 eggs are laid by a single female and it takes 9-12 days to complete a generation. Ess laid by non-fertised females produced only male offspring.

Host plants. Coconut palm appears to be the only host of coconut mite

Damage. The mites suck sap from the tender meristematic mesocarp tissue and can be seen living in colonies in the perianth of developing nuts where they live in the white tender portion covered by the inner bracket of perianth. The nuts maturing up to nine months, harbor the mites. As a result of damage by the mite, warts and numerous longitudinal fissures develop on the husk of nuts.

Management. (*i*) Monocrotophos 36 WSC @ 10 ml in 10 ml of water per palm should be used to root feed it. (*ii*) Give combination treatment with 500 ml of 0.03 % azadirachtin oil formulation and 100 g talc based product containing the fungus *Hirsutella thompsonii* (having spore count of 1×10^7) in 200 litres of water.

TEA

1. *Helopeltis theivora* Waterhouse (Tea mosquito-bug, Hemiptera : Miridae) (Fig. 10.1E)

Distribution. This pest is widely distributed in southern India and has also been recorded in Sri Lanka, Vietnam and Indonesia.

Identification. The adult is slender, 6-8 mm long, agile and a good flier. The female bug is orange across the shoulders and the male is almost black.

Life-history. The female bug lays up to 500 eggs in the buds and axils of the leaves or often in the broken end of the plucked shoot. The eggs hatch in 5-17 days. A freshly emerged nymph is wingless. In summer, it completes its development in about two weeks after passing through five moults. In winter, the nymphal stage is prolonged to eight weeks or more.

Host plant. Tea

Damage. The damage is done by both nymphs and adults by puncturing the leaf frequently to suck the juice. While feeding, the saliva is injected and the tissues around the site of feeding are necrosed, becoming brownish or black. By the coalescence of a large number of such patches, the entire leaf may become black and shrivelled, and may fall off eventually.

Management. (*i*) Collect nymphs and adults with hand nets early in the morning or in the evening and destroy them. (*ii*) Spray the bushes with 500 ml of malathion 50EC in 500 litres of water per ha.

2. *Andraca bipunctata* Walker (Bunch caterpillar, Lepidoptera : Bombycidae)

Distribution. The pest is widespread in India, Indonesia, Taiwan and Vietnam.

Identification. The brown moths have a wing span of 4-5 cm and the fore wings have wavy cross lines with two white spots near the outer margins.

Life-history. The female moth lays up to 500 yellowish eggs in linear clusters on the underside of leaves. The larvae emerge in about ten days and are light yellow. At first they eat up their egg-shell and later on, they start feeding on the leaf tissues. The larvae pass through five instars and complete their development in 20-30 days. The full-grown larvae descend to the ground and spin cocoons among dry leaves. The pupal period is completed in 15-30 days. In the north-eastern region, the pest passes through four generations in a year.

Host plant. Tea

Damage. The caterpillars feed on leaves and cause considerable damage. Due to their gregarious nature, caterpillars can destroy several bushes before pupation.

Management. (*i*) The pest can be suppressed by collecting the caterpillars manually and destroying them. (*ii*) Spray 500 ml of malathion 50EC in 500 litres of water per ha.

3. *Spatulicraspeda castaneiceps* Hampson (Humped slug caterpillar, Lepidoptera : Cochlidiidae)

Distribution. This caterpillar is quite common on tea in Sri Lanka and India.

Identification. The male moth is dark brown with bipectinate antennae and has a wing expanse of 1.5-1.7 cm. The female moth has chestnut brown fore wings and smoky black hind wings with a wing expanse of 2.0-2.2 cm. The full-grown caterpillars are small, dark brown or pale brown with a reddish band.

Life-history. The female moth lays 190-200 pale yellow and oval eggs on the under surface of leaves. The incubation period of eggs is 5-6 days. The young larvae start feeding on tender leaves. The larval stage is completed in 20-22 days. The larva pupates in a broadly oval globular cocoon attached to the plant. The pupation is completed in 13-14 days. The duration of life-cycle from egg to adult stage ranges from 38 to 42 days.

Host plants. Tea, castor and coconut.

Damage. The caterpillars mainly feed on the young leaves of tea which are the primary commercial product. Hence, the pest causes a significant damage to the crop.

Management. (*i*) Handpicking and destruction of the caterpillars helps to check the pest. (*ii*) Spray 625 g of malathion 50WP in 625 litres of water per ha.

4. *Zeuzera coffeae* Nietner (Red borer, Lepidoptera : Cossidae) (Fig. 10.2)

Distribution. This borer is distributed almost in all the tea growing parts of the world

Identification. Larvae appear purplish brown with brown head. The moth is

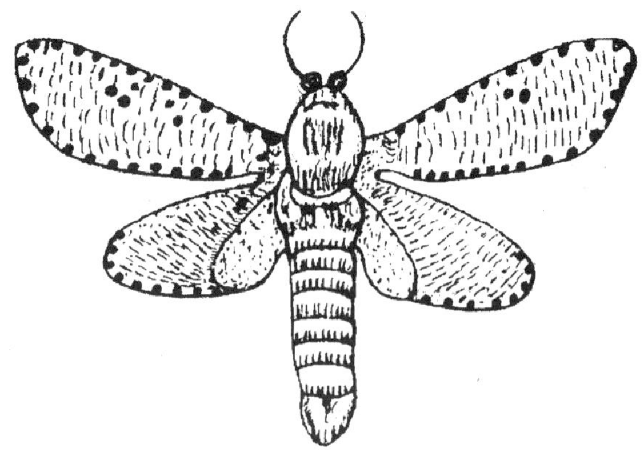

Fig. 10.2 Pests of plantation crops
A. Red borer, *Zeuzera coffeae*

white, measuring 28-40 mm with fully stretched wings, and there are small black spots on forewings and marginal dots on hindwings.

Life-history. The female moth deposits eggs on leaves, bark or even in soil. It takes about 10 days for the eggs to hatch and then larvae start boring into the bark. Subsequently the larvae tunnel down the main trunk, reach up to the tap root in young plants. During a period of 4-5 months, a larva becomes fully grown and pupation takes place within its tunnel for about 3-4 weeks. The moths emerge in April-May and August-September.

Host plant. Main host plants are tea and coffee.

Damage. Attack of the borer results in withering of leaves on the damaged branches which eventually die. Pinkish exreta emerging out of holes on the the stem, can be seen in attacked plants.

Management. (*i*) The danmaged branches should be pruned and/or removed. (*ii*) Chemical control recommendations are the same as for red palm weevil.

COFFEE

1. *Ferrisia virgata* (Cockerell) (Striped mealy bug, Hemiptera.: Pseudococcidae) (Fig. 10.1F)

Distribution. This bug is found in India, Pakistan, Bangladesh, Myanmar, Sri Lanka, Malaysia, the Philippines, Java and New Guinea.

Identification. The adult female is a distinctive mealy bug with a pair of conspicuous longitudinal submedian dark stripes and long glossy wax threads and a pronounced tail.

Life-history. The sessile female lays 300-400 eggs, which hatch in a few hours and the young nymphs move away quite rapidly. The nymphs feed by sucking cell sap. They become full-grown in six weeks and the life cycle is completed in about 40 days. This pest multiplies in large numbers and becomes abundant during drought conditions.

Host plants. It is a polyphagous pest on many crops like coffee, cocoa, citrus, cotton, jute, groundnut, beans, cassava, sugarcane, sweet potato, cashew, guava, tomato, etc.

Damage. The mealy bugs suck plant sap from the young shoots, berries and leaves, resulting in the withering and yellowing of plants. It is also reported to act as a vector of virus which causes the swollen shoot disease of cocoa.

Management. Spray 500 ml of quinalphos 25EC or fenitrothion 50EC in 250 litres of water per ha.

2. *Coccus viridis* (Green) (Coffee green bug, Hemiptera : Coccidae)

Distribution. The soft green scale is found in India, Sri Lanka, Bangladesh, Myanmar, Thailand and Malaysia. It is a major pest of coffee in Kerala, Andhra Pradesh, Karnataka and Tamil Nadu.

Identification. The crawlers are flat, ovate, slightly convex, pale-green to yellowish-green in colour. When mature, they are 2-3 mm long.

Life-history. The scales are ovoviviparous and the males are very rare. The female lays 300-500 eggs in her life time of 2-5 months. The hatching of eggs occurs within a few hours but the young ones remain under the scale for a few days and then crawl out. They get fixed at some succulent spot for feeding. There are three nymphal instars and then they become adults. A generation is completed in 1-2 months and there are many generations in a year.

Host plants. In addition to coffee, this scale also feeds on citrus, guava, loquat, mango and other plants.

Damage. The scales are present on the under surface of leaves, crowding along the midribs and veins. Tender branches and developing fruits are also attacked. As a result of heavy feeding, the leaves and fruits become discoloured and malformed, and drop off. The plants become very weak and unproductive.

Management. Spray 750 ml of malathion 50EC or 500 ml of dimethoate 30EC or 375 ml of methyl parathion 50EC or 200 ml of phosphamidon 85WSC in 500 litres of water per ha.

3. *Xylotrechus quadripes* Chevrolat (Coffee stem borer, Coleoptera : Cerambycidae) (Fig. 10.1G)

Distribution. This insect is considered as one of the important pests of coffee in India. It is now distributed in southern India as well as in Assam. Besides India, the pest has been reported in Myanmar, Sri Lanka, Thailand, Indonesia and the Philippines.

Identification. The adult is a blackish-brown beetle, about 1.25 cm long with prominent antennae, There is a characteristic pattern of yellowish bands on the elytra.

Life-history. A female beetle lays about 100 eggs in 3-4 weeks in the cracks and crevices of trunk bark or primary branches. They hatch in about 10 days and after feeding on soft bark for sometime, the grubs start boring into the woody tissue. The borer continues to feed and tunnel in all directions for about ten months. When full-grown, it cuts an exit hole and pupates near it, inside the tunnel. The pupal stage is completed in about one month after which the beetle emerges. Although only one generation is completed during the year, there are two distinct periods during which the adults emerge, one occurring in April-May and the other during September-December.

Host plant. Coffee

Damage. The damage is done both by the grubs and the adults by tunnelling into the stem and branches. The branches tunnelled by larvae wilt and break easily and the young plants often succumb to this injury. When infestation is severe, the plantation may have to be abandoned or replanted.

Management. (*i*) The pest can be suppressed by removing and destroying the affected shoots along with borers. (*ii*) The incidence can also be reduced by catching and killing the beetles, especially during their egg-laying period. (*iii*) Dislodging the eggs and young borers with tough brushes of coconut husk is also useful. (*iv*) Carry out swabbing of the main stem and thick primary branches with chlorpyriphos 20EC emulsion @ 1.25 litres mixed in 125 litres of water per ha, once during April-May and twice during September-January.

4. *Xylosandrus compactus* (Eichhoff) (Coffee shot-hole borer, Coleoptera.: Scolytidae)

Distribution. This borer may sometimes acquire serious proportions in coffee growing regions of India.

Identification. The adult is a cylindrical, dark-brown beetle.

Life-history. The female beetle bores into the bark of tertiary branches and lays eggs in the tunnels so formed. Many tunnels are made by a female which lays up to 50 eggs. These hatch in about one week. The white apodous larvae feed on ambrosia, a fungal growth developed on the beetle excreta inside the tunnel. The larval development is completed in about 20 days and the full-grown larvae make cocoons near the exits. The pupal period lasts about 10 days and the life-cycle is completed in 35-40 days. There are several generations during a year.

Damage. The tunnelling by larvae and adults results in wilting, defoliation and dieback of the plant. The area around a shot-hole becomes discoloured and secondary infection due to micro-organisms hastens the death of the affected shoots.

Host plant. Coffee, particularly *robusta* coffee.

Management. (*i*) The pest can be suppressed by removing and destroying the affected shoots harbouring the borers, early in the season. (*ii*) Apply 2.5 litres of malathion 50EC or 1.5 litres of methyl parathion 50EC in 250 litres of water per ha.

5. *Hypothenemus hampei* (Ferrari) (Coffee berry borer, Coleoptera.: Scolytidae) (Fig. 10.1H)

Distribution. This pest has been recorded from tropical Africa, Sri Lanka, South-east Asia and Indonesia.

Identification. These are dark coloured beetles, the female being about 2.5 mm long and the male about 1.6 mm. The females are winged while the males are wingless. The grubs are white, leg-less and brown-headed.

Life-history. The females lay 30-60 eggs in batches of 8-12 on the maturing coffee-beans during an oviposition period of 3-7 weeks. The eggs hatch in 8-9 days. The grubs feed by tunnelling into the beans. The larval period is completed in 2-3 weeks, after undergoing 2-3 moultings. The pupal stage lasts 7-8 days and is spent in the larval galleries.

Host plants. Coffee, both *robusta* and *arabica* varieties.

Damage. A number of beetles at a time make one or more round holes near the apex of green or the ripe berries. The damaged bean contains upto 20 larvae of different sizes. The damage caused by this pest makes the coffee beans unfit for marketing.

Management. Spray 1.25 litres of quinalphos 25EC in 625 litres of water per ha.

6. *Saissetia coffeae* (Walker) (Helmet Scale, Hemiptera : Coccidae)

Distribution. The helmet scale is a cosmopolitan pest. It is widely distributed in the tropics and in some sub-tropical areas.

Identification. The scale is green in colour when young but becomes dark brown later on. Mature scales are about 2 mm long.

Life-history. The mature female may lay upto 600 eggs beneath her helmet. The newly hatched crawlers are flat and oval in shape. They get fixed at suitable spots and may feed on leaves, berries, or the green shoots. The nymphs undergo three moultings and then they become adults. The immature females have an H-shaped yellow mark on their body. The dark brown adult females have a strongly convex helmet-shaped carapace and are immobile. The males are unknown. It takes six months to complete one generation.

Host plants. It attacks both *arabica* and *robusta* coffee. It has a wide range of alternative hosts including tea, citrus, guava, mango and many other plants, both wild and cultivated.

Damage. The scales cluster on the shoots, leaves and green berries. Because of their feeding, the chlorotic leaves and fruits begin to drop.

Management. Same as in case of coffee green bug.

7. *Zeuzera coffeae* Nietner (Coffee red borer, Lepidoptera : Cossidae) (Fig. 10.1I)

Distribution. The pest is distributed in all coffee and tea growing states of India.

Identification. These are white moths with many small black spots on the fore wings and marginal dots on the hind wings.

Life-history. The female lays about 600 eggs, which are deposited in rows on the surface of leaves, cracks and crevices of the bark or even in the soil. The larva bores into the stem and may take a period ranging from a few months to over a year to become full-grown. Pupation occurs in the tunnels during late spring and pupal stage lasts for 20-50 days. The adults emerge in June-July.

Host plants. Normally coffee, but being polyphagous also attacks tea, pomegranate, cotton, cocoa, etc.

Damage. The damage is done by the caterpillars which feed by tunnelling the stem. Pinkish frass (excreta) can be seen coming out of holes in the stem and smaller branches dryup.

Management. (*i*) Pruning and destruction of the affected branches, and spiking the larvae inside their burrows are helpful to check the pest. (*ii*) Inject a mixture of chloroform and creosate or a fumigant like CS_2 to control the pest.

CASHEWNUT

1. *Plocaederus ferrugineus* (Linnaeus) (Cashew tree borer, Coleoptera: Cerambycidae)

Distribution. This pest is the most important pest of the cashew tree in south India.

Identification. The adult is a medium-sized dark-brown beetle. When full-grown, the larva measures 7.5 cm.

Life-history. The beetle lays eggs under the loose bark on the trunk. The newly emerged grubs bore into the bark and feed on soft tissues, making tunnels in all directions. The grown-up grubs may also feed on wood. When full-grown, the larva tunnels its way to the root region, where it forms a calcareous shell for pupation. The life-cycle is completed in more than a month and there are several overlapping generations in a year.

Host plants. Cashew

Damage. The borers damage the cambial tissues and hence the flow of sap is arrested. The tree is weakened and if infestation continues it may die.

Management. (*i*) Collect and destroy the eggs, and fell and burn the badly infested trees. (*ii*) Drench the basal trunk and the root region with 2.0 litres of chlorpyriphos 20EC in 250 litres of water per ha. (*iii*) Inject carbon disulphide into the tunnels and plaster them with mud (iv) Uproot and burn the severely infested trees.

2. *Acrocercops syngramma* Meyrick (Cashew leaf-miner, Lepidoptera : Gracillariadae)

Distribution. The leaf-miner is distributed in all the cashew growing areas.

Identification. It is a small silvery-grey moth with pale-white larva turning reddish-brown when full-grown (5-6 mm in size).

Life-history. The eggs are laid on very tender leaves, which hatch in 2-3 days. On hatching, the larva mines into one leaf eating its material as it mines. When full-grown, the larva falls to the ground to pupate. The duration of larval and pupal stages is 14 and 7-9 days, respectively.

Host plant. Cashew.

Damage. The damage is done by the caterpillar by mining through the leaves. A single leaf could be infested by as many as 8 caterpillars. The thin epidermal peel swells up in the mined areas, which appear as whitish blistered patches on the leaf surface. The symptoms on older leaves are big holes due to drying and crumbling of mined areas.

Management. Apply 2.0 Kg of carbaryl 50WP or 1.25 litres of malathion 50EC or 1.0 litre of methyl parathion 50EC in 625 litres of water per ha.

3. *Helopeltis antonii* Signoret (Tea mosquito-bug, Hemiptera : Miridae)

Distribution. It is a major pest of cashew in Kerala, Karnataka, Goa, Maharashtra and Tamil Nadu.

Identification. Adult bug has black head, red thorax, and black and white abdomen with a knobbed process mid-dorsally on the thorax.

Life-history. The female lays 30 eggs by inserting them in the epidermis of the tender shoots, axis of inflorescence and nuts.

Damage. The damage is caused by the adults and nymphs by sucking plant sap from petioles, tender shoots and leaf-veins causing necrotic lesions on these regions. Resin exudes from the feeding punctures, blossom-blight and die-back symptoms appear. Widespread drying of shoots, inflorescence and shedding of the nuts takes place causing loss to the yield to the extent of 30 per cent.

Management. Spray 2.0 kg of carbary 50WP at the time when new flush and panicles appear.

4. *Cricula trifenestrata* Hubner (Leaf caterpillar, Lepidoptera : Saturnidae)

The adult is medium-sized reddish-brown moth with 3 clear spots on the wings. It is a sporadic pest but when present, causes extensive defoliation of cashew trees. The caterpillars are beset with poisonous hairs and spines. Pupation occurs in dark cocoons amongst the leaves. The pest can be controlled by spraying 1.25 litres of methyl parathion 50EC in 250 litres of water per ha.

5. *Chelaria haligramma* Myer. (Shoot-tip and inflorescence caterpillar, Lepidoptera : Gelechiidae).

The adult is tiny dark moth and the caterpillar is small yellowish or greenish brown. The larvae feed on the shoot-tips and inflorescence, they pupate inside the folded leaves or in small holes made on the shoot-tips or floral branches. Control measure is same as for leaf-caterpillar.

6. *Rhipiphorothrips cruentatus* Hood (Cashew thrips, Thysanoptera : Thripidae)

The cashew plants are attacked by many genera of thrips which weaken the plants and so affect the yield by sucking the sap of leaves and flowers which fade as a consequence. Infestation is heavy during March to May and the tender plants suffer more. They can be effectively controlled by spraying 1.25 litres of lindane 20 EC or 1.0 litre methyl parathion 50EC in 250 litres of water per ha.

7. *Parasa lepida* (Cramer) (Slug caterpillar, Lepidoptera : Cochlidiidae)

Distribution. The pest is distributed in cashew and coconut growing regions of India.

Identification. It is stout moth having 1.5 cm long body and 4.0 cm wing-expanse and green wings fringed with brown patches. The caterpillar is fleshy and slug-like with yellowish-green body bearing greenish-blue stripes dorsally, yellowish-green strips laterally and highly irritating nettle hairs (hence also called nettle grub).

Life-history. The female lays about 170 flat scale-like eggs on the undersurface of the tender leaves. The incubation period is 7 days. The larva passes through 7 instars and is full-grown in 35-42 days. Pupation occurs in hard shell-like cocoon on the tree trunk. The pupae become adults in 28-30 days.

Host plants. Cashew and coconut.

Damage. Damage is caused by the caterpillars by feeding on the leaves, gregariously in the beginning and in a dispersed state later. Young trees, 6-10 years old, are more susceptible to the attack. In severe infestation, defoliation can occur.

Management. (*i*) Handpicking and destruction of caterpillars and cocoons proves useful to check the pest. (*ii*) Dust with lindane 2 per cent @ 25 kg per ha.

ARECANUT

1. *Carvalhoia arecae* Miller & China (Arecanut mirid bug, Hemiptera.: Miridae) (Fig. 10.1J)

Distribution. This bug is one of the important pests of arecanut in south India.

Identification. The adult is a red and black bug measuring 6 mm long and 2.5 mm wide. The nymphs are greenish with reddish brown patches.

Life-history. The female bug lays eggs singly into the tissues of the tender unopened leaves of the palm. The eggs are oval, with two-bristle like structures arising from the operculum. The eggs hatch in nine days and the young nymphs suck cell sap from tender parts. The nymphs become adults in 2-3 weeks after undergoing 5 moultings.

Host plant. Arecanut

Damage. The nymphs and the adults suck sap from the tender leaves of arecanut palm. The bugs remain clustered together within the top-most of the leaf axils. In case of severe infestation, the leaves get shredded and stand erect. Continued attack over a number of years results in stunted growth of the palm and the yield is also reduced.

Management. Spray 250 ml of monocrotophos 36SL or 375 ml of quinalphos 25EC in 250 litres of water per ha at monthly intervals especially on the spindles and young fronds.

2. *Rhynchophorus ferrugineus* (Olivier) (Red palm weevil, Coleoptera : Curculiridae)

The pest has been discussed under Coconut in this chapter.

3. *Rhipiphorothrips cruentatus* Hood (Thrips, Thysanoptera : Thripidae)

The pest has been described under Cashew in this chapter.

RUBBER

1. *Aestherastis circulata* Meyrick (Rubber bark caterpillar, Lepidoptera : Yponomeutidae)

Distribution. The pest is distributed in the rubber growing areas like Tamil Nadu and Karnataka.

Identification. The adult is white and black spotted moth. The larva is bright red flat caterpillar, measuring about 2.5 cm when full-grown.

Life-history. The eggs are laid on the bark of the rubber tree, which hatch in 2-4 days. The larvae feed on the dead bark and are full-grown in 10-12 days. Pupation takes place under the dead bark and the adults emerge in 8-10 days.

Host plant. Rubber trees.

Damage. The damage is done by the caterpillars by feeding on the bark of the tree, either on the renewing bark or any other part of the tree but generally at a height of 90 cm from the ground and up to the region of the first branch. Usually, the caterpillar feeds on the dead bark, but when it feeds on the renewing bark or tapping surface, it becomes troublesome.

Management. (*i*) Application of tar on bark surface prevents the attack (*ii*) Brush away the caterpillars with a stiff brush and then kill them. (*iii*) Application of a persistent organochlorine insecticide is helpful to control the pest.

2. *Aspidiotus destructor* Signoret (Rubber scale, Hemiptera : Diaspididae).

These insects infest twigs and leaves sucking their sap. As a result of sap sucking, the leaves become weak and drop prematurely. The pest has been discussed under Coconut in this chapter.

3. *Comocritis preia* Meyrick (Rubber bark caterpillar, Lepidoptera : Yponomeutidae)

The caterpillars construct galleries on the bark and feed on the bark surface. A considerable portion of the stem may be covered by the galleries. Pupal chambers are made at the bottom of the galleries.

*****

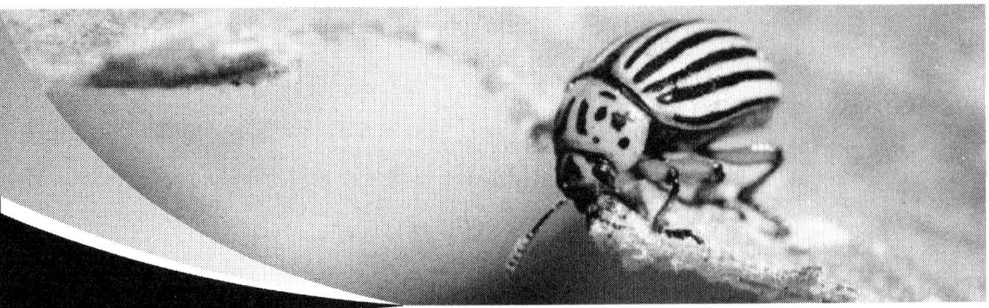

11 CHAPTER

PESTS OF SPICES

Cardamom (*Elletaria cardomomum*)

1. *Pentalonia nigronervosa* Coquerel (Banana aphid, Hemiptera : Aphididae)
2. *Sciothrips cardamomi* (Ramakrishna Ayyar) (Cardamom thrips, Thysanoptera : Thripidae)
3. *Prodioctes haematicus* Chevrolat (Rhizome weevil, Coleoptera : Curculionidae)
4. *Eupterote cardamomi* Ranga Ayyar (Cardamom hairy caterpillar, Lepidoptera : Bombycidae)
5. *Kanakarajiella cardamomi* (David & Subramaniam) (Cardamom whitefly, Hemiptera : Aleyrodidae)

Large cardamom (*Amomum subulatum*)

1. *Pentalonia nigronervosa* Coquerel (Banana aphid, Hemiptera : Aphididae)
2. *Rhipiphorothrips cruentatus* Hood (Grapevine thrips, Thysanoptera : Heliothripidae)

Chillies (*Capsicum annuum*)

1. *Bemisia tabaci* (Gennadius) (Cotton whitefly, Hemiptera : Aleyrodidae)
2. *Scirtothrips dorsalis* Hood (Chillies thrips, Thysanoptera.: Thripidae)
3. *Holotrichia consanguinea* Blanchard (White grubs, Coleoptera : Scarabaeidae)

Black pepper (*Piper nigrum*)

1. *Longitarsus nigripennis* (Motschulsky) (Pollu beetle, Coleoptera : Chrysomelidae)
2. *Cydia hemidoxa* Meyrick (Pepper shoot borer, Lepidoptera.: Tortricidae)

Turmeric (*Curcuma longa*)	1. *Udaspes folus* Cramer (Skipper butterfly, Lepidoptera : Hesperidae)
	2. *Dichocrocis punctiferalis* (Guenee) (Castor capsule borer, Lepidoptera: Pyralidae)
	3. *Spilarctia obliqua* Walker (Bihar hairy caterpillar, Lepidoptera : Arctiidae)
Ginger (*Zingiber officinale*)	1. *Aspidiotus hartii* (Cockerell) (Scale, Hemiptera : Diaspididae)
	2. *Dichocrocis punctiferalis* (Guenee) (Castor capsule borer, Lepidoptera: Pyralidae)
	3. *Udaspes folus* Cramer (Skipper butterfly, Lepidoptera : Hesperidae)
Coriander (*Coriandrum sativum*)	1. *Bemisia tabaci* (Gennadius) (Cotton whitefly, Hemiptera.: Aleyrodidae)
	2. *Hyadaphis coriandri* (Das) (Coriander aphid, Hemiptera.: Aphididae)
Cinnamon (*Cinnamomum zeylanicum*)	1. *Chilasia clytia* Linnaeus (Cinnamon butterfly, Lepidoptera : Papilionidae)
	2. *Phyllocnistis chrysophthalina* Stainton (Cinnamon leaf-miner, Lepidoptera : Phyllocnistidae)

The production of spices in India was 4.07 million tonnes in 2004-05, which decreased to 3.92 million tonnes in 2005-06 and 2006-07. Since spices come from different parts of plants, belonging to a number of families, the pests that have adopted themselves to feeding on these aromatic plants are also of different types. Apart from the field pests of the spice plants, a number of insect pests of stored products also damage spices in storage.

CARDAMOM

About 56 species of insects and mites have been reported to attack cardamom in India, among which banana aphid, cardamom thrips and rhizome weevil are quite important.

1. *Pentalonia nigronervosa* Coquerel (Banana aphid, Hemiptera : Aphididae) (Fig. 11.1)

Distribution. The banana aphid is more or less pantropical in distribution and is of common occurrence in southern parts of India, Sri Lanka and Australia.

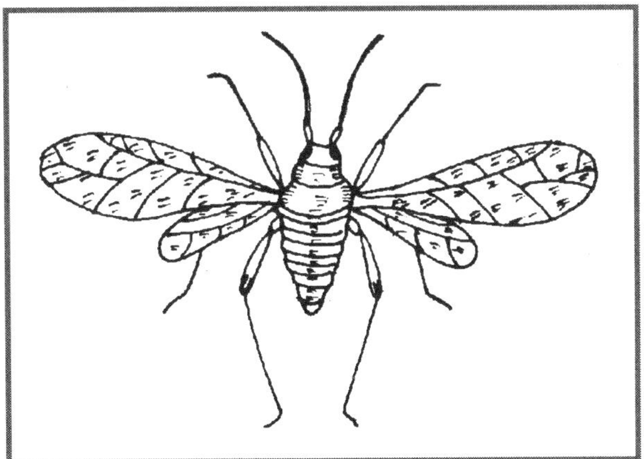

Fig. 11.1 Banana aphid, *Pentalonia nigronervosa*. Adult

Identification. The wingless aphid is dark brown pyriform measuring 1.34 mm in length and with six segmented antennae which are longer than the body. The winged form is dark brown, elongated and pyriform. They are longer than the wingless forms but with less body width.

Life-history. The reproduction takes place parthenogenetically. The longevity of adult varies from 8 to 26 days with an average of 14 days. A single female lays 8-28 offsprings with an average of 14. A single female may produce as many as four offsprings in 24 hours. The development is completed through three and four moults taking 13 and 15 days, respectively from November till January. There are 21-24 generations in a year.

Host plants. Banana, small and large cardamom.

Damage. The aphids feed on the leaf sheath and pseudostem. The insect causes little direct damage but is of considerable significance being vector of cardamom mosaic *(Kattle* disease), *Amomum* mosaic and *Foorky* disease of large cardamom.

Management. Spray 875 ml of dimethoate 30EC or 300 ml of phosphamidon 85WSC in 250 litres of water per ha at an interval of two weeks.

2. *Sciothrips cardamomi* (Ramkrishna Ayyar) (Cardamom thrips, (Thysanoptera: Thripidae)

Distribution. The cardamom thrips is the most destructive pest of cardamom in South India and was first discovered in 1933 in a cardamon estate at Valparai on Annamalai Hills.

Identification. The adult is greyish-brown and measures 1.25-1.50 mm in length.

Life-history. The female lays 5-71 eggs at random on all the feeding areas of the plant. The young nymphs emerge from the eggs in 9-12 days. The first two nymphal instars are active and grow by feeding on the plant sap. Life-cycle is completed in 25-30 days.

Host plant. Cardamon.

Damage. The thrips cause damage by sucking cell sap. It feeds on tender blossoms and the bunch pods of cardamom. The attack on the flower stalk results in shedding of flowers. The panicle stalks also become stunted and do not bear flowers.

Management. Spray 875 ml of dimethoate 30EC or 1.0 litre of quinalphos 25EC in 250 litres of water per ha.

3. *Prodioctes haematicus* Chevrolat (Rhizome weevil, Coleoptera: Curculionidae)

Distribution. The rhizome weevil is found widely distributed in various parts of South India.

Identification. The adult is a brown weevil measuring 1.2 cm in length, with three dark lines on pronotum.

Life-history. The weevils emerge in large numbers in April, soon after an early shower of the monsoon. The eggs are laid in cavities made on rhizomes. The young grubs come out of the eggs in 8-10 days and bore into the rhizome, making tunnels. The larvae feed inside the rhizomes and become full-fed in three weeks. They pupate within the feeding tunnels for another 3 weeks. On emergence, the adult weevils live for 7-8 months. There is only one generation in a year.

Host plant. Cardamom

Damage. The severe tunnelling and feeding by grubs inside the rhizomes results in the death of entire clumps of the cardamom plants.

Management. (*i*) Destroy affected plants/seedlings. (*ii*) If the grub population is more in the soil, drench the base of the clamp with 1.25 litres of malathion 50EC or 1.25 kg of carbaryl 50WP in 625 litres of water per ha.

4. *Eupterote cardamomi* Ranga Ayyar (Cardamom hairy caterpillar, Lepidoptera: Bombycidae)

Distribution. It is a sporadic pest of cardmom in South India.

Identification. The adults are large moths, ocherous in colour, with post medial lines on the wings. They measure 7-8 cm in wing expanse. The larvae are hairy, dark grey in colour with pale brown head, bearing conical tufts of hairs on the dorsal side of the body. When full-grown, the caterpillar measures 9 cm in length.

Life-history. The moths emerge with the commencement of the south-west monsoon rains in June and July. The female moths lay 400-500, yellowish and dome-shaped eggs in flat masses on the undersurface of leaves. Each egg mass contains about 50-160 eggs. The hatching of eggs occurs in 15-17 days. The larva passes through ten instars in 140-151 days. It pupates in the soil in a silken cocoon at a depth of 5-8 cm for 7-8 months. The moth lives for about 20 days. There is only one generation in year.

Damage. The larvae feed on leaves of the shade trees up to the 6th or 7th instar and then they drop down on the cardamom plants growing underneath, with the help of silken threads. They start feeding on the leaves voraciously and defoliate the cardamom plants causing heavy reduction in the yield.

Management. Spray 500 ml of malathion 50EC or 500g of carbaryl 50WP in 250 litres of water per ha.

5. *Kanakarajiella cardamomi* (David & Subramaniam) (Cardamom whitefly, Hemiptera : Aleyrodidae)

This whitefly was first reported infesting cardamom in 1975. The nymphs and adults suck the sap from leaves and cause chlorotic patches. Heavy infestation causes development of black sooty mould on the honeydew excreted by the nymphs. The adult whitefly inserts the eggs into tissue by a pedicel. There are four nymphal instars, the last being the pupal stage. Life-cycle is completed in 2-3 weeks depending on weather.

Management. Spray application of ethion (0.1%) or acephate (0.075%) or neem oil (5%) has been found to be effective for the control of this pest.

LARGE CARDAMOM

Although there is no major pest attacking large cardamom, but aphids and thrips are considered to be quite important.

1. *Pentalonia nigronervosa* Coquerel (Banana aphid, Hemiptera : Aphididae)

For the details on its life cycle, see under 'Cardamom'.

2. *Rhipiphorothrips cruentatus* Hood (Grapevine thrips, Thysanoptera : Heliothripidae)

This thrips infests the leaves, which turn brown and wither gradually. For full account of the life cycle of this pest, see chapter 7.

CHILLIES

More than 20 insect species have been recorded attacking both leaves as well as fruits of chilli. However, cotton whitefly and chillies thrips cause considerable damage.

1. *Bemisia tabaci* (Gennadius) (Cotton whitefly, Hemiptera : Aleyrodidae)

For full details on the life cycle of this pest, see chapter 8.

2. *Scirtothrips dorsalis* Hood (Chillies thrips, Thysanoptera : Thripidae)

Distribution. The chillies thrips is a polyhagous pest and is widely distributed in India.

Identification. The adults are slender, yellowish brown in colour, having apically pointed wings, and they measure about 1 mm in length. The females possess long, narrow wings with the fore margin fringed with long hairs. The nymphs resemble the adults in shape and colour but are wingless and smaller in size.

Life-history. The female thrips lays 45-50 eggs inside the tissues of the leaves and shoots. The eggs hatch in 5 days. The larvae feed for 7-8 days and pupate in 2-4 days. The adult thrips lives for about 31 days. There are several over-lapping generations of this pest in a year.

Host plants. It feeds on a number of plants including chillies, tomato, castor, sunflower, mango, cotton and citrus.

Damage. Damage is caused by the adults as well as by the nymphs. They suck the cell sap from tender regions and cause the leaves to shrivel. In case of severe infestation, there is malformation of leaves, buds and fruits, which may damage half the crop. The attacked plants are stunted and may finally dry up. The insect is also responsible for transmitting the virus causing leaf curl disease of chillies.

Management. Spray 1.0 litre of malathion 50EC or 1.0 kg of carbaryl 50WP in 250 litres of water per ha.

3. *Holotrichia consanguinea* Blanchard and *H. insularis* (Brenske) (White grubs, Coleoptera : Scarabaeidae)

The chillies crop is seriously damaged by these insects in Rajasthan. Damage is caused by the grubs that feed on the roots. A full account of the life-cycle is given in chapter 5.

BLACK PEPPER

About 20 insect species have been recorded damaging pepper plantations among which pollu beetle and pepper shoot borer are quite important.

1. *Longitarsus nigripennis* (Motschulsky) (Pollu beetle, Coleoptera : Chrysomelidae) (Fig. 11.2)

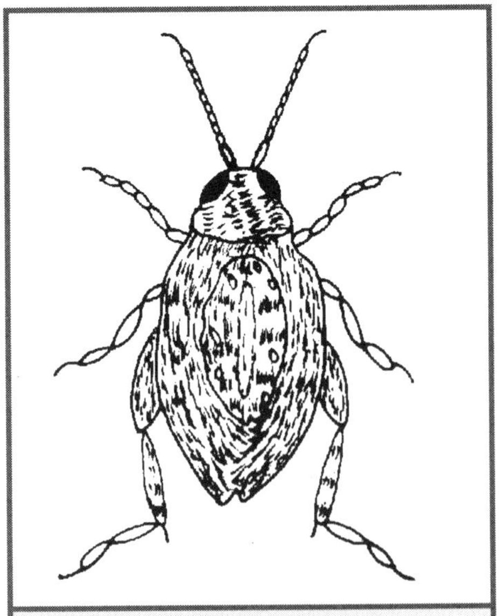

Fig. 11.2 Pollu beetle, *Longitarsus nigripennis*. Adult

Distribution. The pollu beetle is a specific pest of black pepper in India occurring regularly in the plantations.

Identification. The adult is a small shining, yellow and blue flea-beetle with stout hind legs. The full-grown grub is yellowish with a black head and it measures 5 mm in length.

Life-history. The females make shallow holes on the berries and lay 1-2 eggs in each hole. A female, on an average, lays about 100 eggs. The eggs hatch in 5 -8 days and the young grubs bore into the berry and feed for

20-32 days. Then they drop to the ground and pupate in an earthen cell in the soil at 5.0-7.6 cm depth. The adults emerge in 6-7 days after pupation. The total life-cycle is completed in 39-50 days. The insect completes four overlapping generations in a year.

Host plant. Black pepper.

Damage. The grubs cause damage by boring into the berries and eating the contents completely in about 10 days. Each grub destroys at least 3-4 berries during the larval period. The attacked berries appear dark in colour, are hollow inside and crumble when pressed. The grubs may also eat into the spike and cause the entire distal region to dry up. The adults feed voraciously on tender leaves and make holes in them.

Management. (*i*) Tilling the soil at the base of vines at regular intervals can reduce the population considerably. (*ii*) Spray 1.5 litres of dimethoate 30EC or 2.0 litres of quinalphos 25EC in 500 litres of water per ha in late July and again in early October.

2. *Cydia hemidoxa* Meyrick (Pepper shoot borer, Lepidoptera : Tortricidae)

The larvae of the crimson and yellow moth bore into tender terminal shoot and cause drying. Its attack is severe during August-September and the total life-cycle takes about a month.

TURMERIC

Skipper butterfly, capsule borer and hairy caterpillar are important pests of turmeric.

1. *Udaspes folus* Cramer (Skipper butterfly, Lepidoptera : Hesperidae) (Fig. 11.2)

This is a common pest of turmeric. The adult is brownish-black butterfly with 8 white spots on fore wings and one large patch on hind wing. The full-grown larva is dark-green and measures 3.6 cm in length. A female lays about 50 eggs on leaves which hatch in 3-4 days. The larva undergoes 5 instars during 12-21 days and pupates in leaf-fold for 6-7 days. The larva which pupates in December emerges only in March. The insect is abundant during August to October. The damage is caused by the larvae which fold the leaves and feed on them.

Fig. 11.3 Skipper butterfly, *Udaspes folus.* Adult

Management. (*i*) The pest can be kept under check by collecting the butterflies with the help of net and destroying them. (*ii*) In case of severe infestation, spray 1.5 litres of quinalphos 25EC in 500 litres of water per ha.

2. *Dichocrocis punctiferalis* (Guenee) (Castor capsule borer, Lepidoptera.: Pyralidae)

The caterpillar enters into the aerial stem killing the central shoot which results in the appearance of 'dead heart'. For details on the life-cycle of this insect, see chapter 15.

3. *Spilarctia obliqua* Walker (Bihar hairy caterpillar, Lepidoptera : Arctiidae)

This pest damages the turmeric plants extensively in Bihar and Bengal. The life-cycle of the Bihar hairy caterpillar has been described in chapter 13.

GINGER

Ginger is attacked by several insect pests both in field and in storage, among which scale and capsule borer are quite important.

1. *Aspidiotus hartii* (Cockerell) (Scale, Hemiptera : Diaspididae)

This is a small circular hard scale which infests the rhizome in large numbers. A female lays about 180 eggs under the scale which hatch within a day. The nymph takes about 30 days for its development. The male forms a pupa before emergence as the winged adult. The insect multiplies in large numbers on stored ginger rhizomes which shrink and dry up. Rhizomes in the field are also attacked by the scale and the infested plants look pale and dry up.

Management. Spray 750 ml of malathion 50EC or 500 ml of dimethoate 30EC in 500 litres of water per ha.

2. *Dichocrocis punctiferalis* (Guenee) (Castor capsule borer, Lepidoptera: Pyralidae)

The caterpillar bores into the aerial stem and kills it. For detailed account, see chapter 5.

3. *Udaspes folus* Cramer (Skipper butterfly, Lepidoptera : Hesperidae)

The leaves are rolled by the larvae of the skipper butterfly.

CORIANDER

The important pests of coriander are whitefly and coriander aphid.

1. *Bemisia tabaci* (Gennadius) (Cotton whitefly, Hemiptera : Aleyrodidae)

The nymphs suck sap of the plants and adversely affect their growth. The life-cycle of this pest has been described in chapter 9.

2. *Hyadaphis coriandri* (Das) (Coriander aphid, Hemiptera : Aphididae)

It infests the shoot and inflorescence, and sucks the juice.

CINNAMON

The cinnamon crop is attacked by a number of insect pests, but only cinnamon butterfly is considered to be the most destructive.

1. *Chilasia clytia* Linnaeus (Cinnamon butterfly, Lepidoptera: Papilionidae) (Fig. 11.4)

Distribution. Cinnamon butterfly is widely distributed in the cinnamon tracts of Sri Lanka and South India.

Identification. The upper side of adult moth is rich velvety brown, while on underside of the body, the colour varies from soft pale brown to rich dark velvety brown. Freshly hatched larvae are jet black in colour with white patches which later undergo various changes in colour pattern.

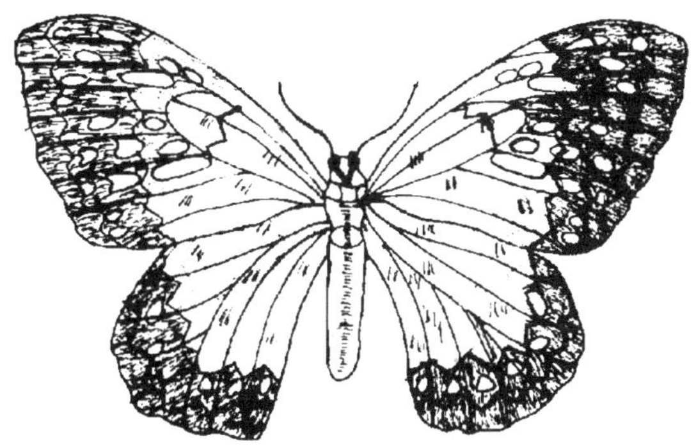

Fig. 11.4 Cinnamon butterfly, *Chilasia clytia.* Adult

Life-history. The female butterfly lays eggs singly on the upper and lower surface of young leaves, petioles and even tender shoots. Eggs are small round and pale yellow in colour. The larvae hatch out in 3-5 days. The larva moults five times to complete its development in 12-18 days. The pupation takes place in rough silken padding on the stem prepared by the larva. The pupal period is completed in 11-13 days. The adults live for 3-5 days and the total life-cycle is completed in 24-36 days.

Host plants. The insect has been reported to feed on a number of wild species of cinnamon and other forest plants.

Damage. After hatching, the first instar larva starts feeding on the lamina of the freshly emerged leaves. The later instars feed voraciously on the tender leaves leaving only the mid rib with portion of veins. In case of severe infestation, the growth of the plant is adversely affected.

Management. Same as in case of skipper butterfly.

2. *Phyllocnistis chrysophthalina* Stainton (Cinnamon leaf-miner, Lepidoptera : Phyllocnistidae)

The larvae make mines in the growing parts and cause defoliation.

*****

12

CHAPTER

PESTS OF ORNAMENTAL PLANTS

1. *Macrosiphum rosaeformis* Das (Rose aphid, Hemiptera : Aphididae)
2. *Nausinoe geometralis* (Guenee) (Jasmine leaf webworm, Lepidoptera : Pyraustidae)
3. *Elasmopalpus jasminophagus* Hampson (Jasmine gallery worm, Lepidoptera: Pyralidae)
4. *Hendecasis duplifascialis* Hampson (Jasmine budworm, Lepidoptera : Pyraustidae)
5. *Plytela gloriosae* Fabricius (Lily moth, Lepidoptera : Noctuidae)
6. *Cadmilos retiarius* Distant (Sunflower lacewing bug, Hemiptera : Tingidae)
7. *Urentius euonymus* Fabricius (Hollyhock tingid bug, Hemiptera : Tingidae)
8. *Mylabris phalerata* Pallas (Banded blister beetle, Coleoptera : Meloidae)
9. *Lygaeus civilies* Wolff. (Milkweed bug, Hemiptera : Lygaeidae)
10. *Thrips orientalis* Bagnall (Jasmine thrips, Thysanoptera : Thripidae)
11. *Aphis gossypii* Glover (Cotton aphid, Hemiptera : Aphididae)
12. *Bemisia tabaci* (Gennadius) (Cotton whitefly, Hemiptera : Aleyrodidae)
13. *Oxycarenus halinipennis* Costa (Dusky cotton bug, Hemiptera : Lygaeidae)
14. *Dysdercus koenigii* (Fabricius) (Red cotton bug, Hemiptera : Pyrrhocoridae)
15. *Diaphorina citri* Kuwayana (Citrus psylla, Hemiptera : Aphalaridae)

India has made noticeable advancement in the production of flowers. During 2006-07, the country produced 886000 metric tonnes of loose and 27.23 million cut flowers. Various species of thrips, aphids, leafhoppers, scale insects, mealy bugs, leaf-miners, caterpillars, cutworms and chaffer beetles attack the common ornamental plants including rose, chrysanthemum, hibiscus, hollyhock, sunflower, iris, jasmine, etc.

1. *Macrosiphum rosaeiformis* Das (Rose aphid, Hemiptera : Aphididae)

Distribution. This aphid has been recorded in Punjab, Delhi, Karnataka, Andhra Pradesh and the Nilgiri Hills.

Identification. The non-winged rose aphid has an elongated body measuring 2.5-2.6 mm, large red eyes, black cornicles and a yellowish green tip of the abdomen.

Life-history. Nymphal development is completed in 11-14 days of the non-winged forms and 14-19 days of the winged forms, the growth being the quickest in March. In northern India, the insect appears in the middle of November. The population increases progressively and is the highest in March, declining early in April as the season warms up. The winged forms are present throughout the period from November to April, but there is an increase in their number from December onwards, reaching the peak in March, when about 90 per cent of the adults become winged. The aphid multiplies most rapidly in late spring but cannot withstand the summer heat. Consequently, its population declines.

Damage. The aphid sucks cell sap from the tender leaves, buds and twigs. It is particularly injurious to tender buds, resulting in the disfigurement and withering of flowers. Each aphid makes several punctures, producing wounds, which leave their mark as the flower opens. A black fungus may also develop on the honeydew excreted by these insects, giving an ugly appearance to the plant.

Management. Spray 500 ml of malathion 50EC or methyl demeton 25EC in 500 litres of water per ha. The treatment may be repeated at the reappearance of the pest.

2. *Nausinoe geometralis* (Guenee) (Jasmine leaf webworm, Lepidoptera: Pyraustidae)

Distribution. This pest is widely distributed in West Africa, India, Pakistan, Sri Lanka, Myanmar, Java, Taiwan, China and Australia.

Identification. The moths are brown with hyaline patches on the wings. Their abdomen is purplish brown, which is interspersed with lateral patches of lighter shades on each segment. The young caterpillars are light yellow in colour but as they grow they become darker.

Life-history. This pest is most active during the rainy season. The moths are seen resting on the lower surface of leaves on the periphery of the plants, thus avoiding the inner shaded portions. The female lays 15-20 eggs singly on the leaf lamina. The eggs are greenish yellow in colour which hatch in 3-4 days. The larvae become full-grown in 12-15 days after passing through five instars. The larvae spin extensive webbings in the shaded portion of the plant around the leaves on which they feed and pupate within that area. The pupal stage lasts 6-7 days and the life-cycle is completed in 22-24 days during July-August.

Damage. During the rainy season, the caterpillars attack leaves of the plant mostly in the lower bushy and shaded portions. During the dry and sunny weather the terminal shoots are attacked. The leaves are webbed in an open and loose manner. The silk threads are seen as a cobweb on the surface of leaves. The larvae skeletonize the leaves by eating away the parenchyma. As a result of the gregarious attack of the caterpillars, the vitality of the plant is reduced which tells upon its further growth and the production of buds, which are so important for getting a good commercial crop of jasmine flowers.

Management. Spray 500 ml of dimethoate 30EC in 500 litres of water per ha.

3. *Hendecasis duplifascialis* Hampson (Jasmine budworm, Lepidoptera: Pyraustidae)

Identification. The moth is pale white. The larva is yellowish green in colour with a distinct black head and prothoracic shield.

Life-history. The freshly laid eggs are round, creamy and glued to the flower buds. The eggs hatch in 2.6-3.5 days and the larva passes through five instars. The total larval duration varies from 11.5 to 17.0 days depending on the jasmine species. The pupal stage lasts 6.5-9.0 days and the life cycle is completed in 21-29 days.

Damage. The larva bores into immature bud and feeds on the internal contents. The larva feeds voraciously on the corolla leaving only the corolla tube in mature buds. In the case of younger buds, the larva remains outside the buds and feeds on the inner floral whorl through a small hole in the corolla tube. The infested flower turns violet and eventually dries out. A single larva may damage upto 6 flower buds. During heavy infestation, the adjacent buds along the inflorescence are webbed together by silken thread.

Management. Spray 500 ml of dimethoate 30EC or 200 ml of cypermethrin 25EC in 500 litres of water per ha.

4. *Plytela gloriosae* Fabricius (Lily moth, Lepidoptera : Noctuidae)

Distribution. The lily moth is a sporadic and specific pest of lilies in India and Sri Lanka.

Identification. The moth has mosaic patterns of red, yellow and black on fore wings, with a row of black and yellow dots on the apical margins. The hind wings are black. The full grown larva measures 3.9-4.2 cm and possesses black, white and red mosaic patterns on the body.

Life-history. The adult moths emerge from the hibernating pupae after the first heavy shower during July. The female moth lays round, yellowish eggs on the apical portion of the undersurface of leaves in clusters of 13-42. The larvae emerge from eggs after 3-6 days and they feed on leaves for 16-20 days. When full fed, they pupate in the soil in an earthen cocoon and the adults emerge within 15-20 days. The insect has two generations in a year and the pupae of second generation hibernate.

Damage. The larvae feed on green matter of leaves which may result in complete defoliation of the lily plants.

Management. Spray 500 ml of malathion 50EC in 500 litres of water per ha.

5. *Cadmilos retiarius* Distant (Sunflower lacewing bug, Hemiptera : Tingidae)

Identification. The sunflower lacewing bug is a small insect measuring about 4 mm, with transparent, shiny, reticulated wings and black body.

Life-history. The pest appears during July and remains active up to September. The adult female bugs lay eggs mainly on the upper surface of leaves of the host plants. The eggs are inserted slantingly into plant tissue leaving the opercula exposed, which appear like white or brown dots. The eggs hatch in 5-7 days and the young nymphs moult five times during nymphal period of 2-3 weeks. Then they become adults.

Damage. Both nymphs and adults cause damage to many garden plants like sunflower, *Gaillardia*, daisy, *Chrysanthemum*, marigold, vernonia, launea and the weed, *Argemone mexicana*. They suck plant sap and the infested leaves turn yellowish-brown and finally dry up.

Management. Spray 500 ml of malathion 50EC in 500 litres of water per ha.

6. *Urentius euonymus* Fabricius (Hollyhock tingid bug, Hemiptera : Tingidae)

Identification. The bugs are easily recognized by their densely reticulate body and wings, and measure about 5-6 mm in length. The nymphs are spiny in appearance.

Life-history. The hollyhock tingid bug appears on hollyhock plants from March to June. The adult female lays eggs on the upper surface of leaves. The incubation period of the eggs is 8-10 days. There are five nymphal instars and development is completed in 15-27 days. The full developmental cycle is completed on a single leaf. The pest overwinters in egg stage.

Damage. The tingid bug infests the garden hollyhock, *Althaea rosea, Abutilon indicum, Sida cordifolia* and *Chrozophora rottleri*. Both nymphs and adults suck plant sap from the under-surface of leaves. The infested leaves become pale-yellow and turn brown. Ultimately they shrivel and dry up.

Management. Spray 500 ml of dimethoate 30EC in 500 litres of water per ha.

7. *Mylabris phalerata* Pallas (Banded blister beetle, Coleoptera : Meloidae)

This prominent large beetle has six alternating, bright orange and black bands, against the general dark background of the body. It is 3 cm in length. The adult beetles attack the flowers of *H. rosa-sinensis* and *Ruellia indica* and other plants from July to September, and devour them completely. In August, the population becomes high and they appear to be more prominent than the flowers.

Management. (*i*) Handpick and destroy the beetles. (*ii*) Spray 1.25 kg of carbaryl 50WP in 625 litres of water per ha.

8. *Lygaeus civilies* Wolff. (Milkweed bug, Hemiptera : Lygaeidae)

It is a red bug with black spots on corium and clavus, and three white spots on the black membrane of the hemelytra. The adults of this species are found feeding on plant sap of *H. rosa-sinensis, Asclepias curassavica, Carissa carandas, Dombeya spectabilis* and *D. natalensis* througout the year. The maximum population is observed in May-June on its most preferred host plant, *A. curassavica.*

Management. Spray 500 ml of malathion 50EC in 500 litres of water per ha.

9. *Aphis gossypii* Glover (Cotton aphid, Hemiptera : Aphididae)

The adults are small soft and greenish-brown insects. They are parthenogenetic and viviparous giving birth to 8-20 nymphs per female per day. The nymphs moult 4 times to become adults in 7-10 days. Both adults and nymphs suck plant sap of many ornamental plants like *Hibiscus rosa-sinensis, Cassia glauca, Tecoma capensis* and *Rosa* spp. from September to April in northern India. The maximum population is observed in *H. rosa-sinensis* during March-April. On *Rosa* spp., it is also observed in September-October and on *C. glauca* in March-Apri1. As a rcsult of its attack, a sooty mould develops which results in a blackened look of the plants.

The details of this insect have been described in chapter 9.

10. *Oxycarenus hyalinipennis* Costa (Dusky cotton bug, Hemiptera.: Lygaeidae)

The nymphs and adults of this pest species are commonly found feeding on *H. rosa-sinensis, Dambeya natalensis, D. spectabilis, Malvaviscus arboreus, Bougainvillea* spp., *Jasminum grandiflorum, J. multiflorum, J. humile, Bauhinia acuminata* and *Plumeria acuminata* throughout the year except during winter months. The host plant, *H. rosa-sinensis* is most preferred by this bug. The maximum population of the insect is found from March to May. The flower buds of *Hibiscus* plants become pale as a result of its feeding and fall down without opening. The adults usually feed on the terminal portions. They hide in the clusters of dry leaves and flowers during December-January. The life-cycle of this pest has been mentioned in chapter 9.

11. *Aphis craccivora* Koch (Groundnut aphid, Hemiptera : Aphididae)

This black coloured aphid species attacks *Bougainvillea* spp. from December to February. Both nymphs and adults infest flowers, tender leaves and the terminal portions of the plant and suck cell sap. Its attack results in the premature fall of the flowers and the downward cupping of the leaves. The details of its life-cycle are given in chapter 4.

12. *Dysdercus koenigii* (Fabricius) (Red cotton bug, Hemiptera.: Pyrrhocoridae)

It is a bright red bug 15 mm long, having black spots on the wings. Both adults and nymphs feed on *Hibiscus rosa-sinensis, Dombeya spectabilis, D. natalensis* Sind., *Carissa carandas, Buddleia madagascariensis* and *Jasminum sambac* from April to December. Out of all its host plants, *H. rosa-sinensis* is the most preferred one. As a result of severe sucking of sap from the leaves and flower buds, vitality of the plants and their flowering capacity is reduced. The details about the life cycle have been discussed in chapter 9.

13. *Diaphorina citri* Kuwayana (Citrus psylla, Hemiptera : Aphalaridae)

The citrus psylla is a serious pest of *Murraya paniculata* from April to July. It also feeds on *Plumeria acuminata, Dombeya spectabilis* and *Duranta plumieri*. The nymphs and adults suck sap of the fresh leaves and tender parts of the plants, and thus vitality of infested plants is reduced, giving them a sickly appearance. For details on the life-cycle, see chapter 7.

14. *Bemisia tabaci* (Gennadius) (Cotton whitefly, Hemiptera : Aleyrodidae)

The cotton whitefly is found feeding on *Euphorbia pulcherima, Hibiscus rosa-sinensis, Lantana camara, Dombeya spectabilis* and *Poinciana pulcherima* from May to October. The maximum population is found in August-September on all these host plants. The attack of the whitefly results in downward cupping of the leaves. A sooty mould develops on the leaves which gives blackish look to the plants. With excessive sap sucking, the leaves fall down. Full account of the life-history of this pest has been given in chapter 9.

15. *Rhipiphorothrips cruentatus* Hood (Grapevine thrips, Thysanoptera : Thripidae)

The grapevine thrips attacks many ornamental plants like *Rosa* spp., *Lagerstroemia indica* and *Punica granatum* from August to January. The infestation becomes heavy on *P. granatum* and *Rosa* spp. during September-October. As a result of severe feeding, the leaves turn rusty brown, particularly from the undersurface and ultimately they fall down. For details about the life cycle, see chapter 7.

16. *Thrips orientalis* Bagnall (Jasmine thrips, Thysanoptera : Thripidae)

The dark coloured jasmine thrips is mainly found on *Jasminum multiflorum* from February to April. Both nymphs and adults feed on flowers. The attacked flowers give a decayed look and fall off prematurely. Another thrips species, *Taeniothrips traegardhi* Tryban, also attacks the flowers of *Nerium indicum* and *Daedolacanthus nervosus* in the months of March-April. The insects are light brown in colour and are found in flowers, giving them a decayed look caused by feeding.

Management. Same as in case of grapevine thrips.

17. *Spilarctia obliqua* Walker (Bihar hairy caterpillar, Lepidoptera : Arctiidae)

The caterpillars of this polyphagous insect attack the ornamental plant, *Barleria cristata* during October-November and December-January. They feed on leaves and floral parts of the plant. In many cases, the whole leaf is eaten away by the caterpillars. Full account of the life-history of this pest is given in chapter 13.

18. *Euproctis lunata* Walker (Castor hairy caterpillar, Lepidoptera: Lymantriidae)

The castor hairy caterpillar, in addition to castor, is also found on *Lagerstroemia indica, Punica granatum, Hibiscus rosa-sinensis* and *Rosa* spp. during September-October. The young larvae eat the leaf margins of the host plants. The full-grown caterpillars, however, feed on the entire leaf lamina and cause maximum damage during these months. The life-cycle of this pest has been given in chapter 5.

19. *Danais chrysippus* Linnaeus (*Ak* butterfly, Lepidoptera: Nymphalidae)

The caterpillars of the *Ak* butterfly feed on *Asclepias curassavica* from September to December. Their population becomes high during the months of October and November. The larvae feed on the leaves and flowers of this plant, and in many cases, the entire leaves are eaten up.

Management. Spray one litre of methyl parathion 50EC in 625 litres of water per ha.

20. *Chromatomyia horticola* (Goureau) (Pea leaf-miner, Diptera : Agromyzidae)

The pea-leaf-miner is a polyphagous pest. It feeds on a large number of cruciferous plants, antirrhinum, nasturtium, pea, linseed and potato. The larvae of this pest are very destructive and make prominent whitish tunnels in the leaves. The details of the life-cycle are given in chapter 4.

21. *Myllocerus undecimpustulatus* Faust (Cotton grey weevil, Coleoptra : Curculionidae)

The cotton grey weevil is commonly found from July to September on *H. rosa-sinensis, Lagerstroemia indica, L. speciosa, Bauhinia acuminata, Dombeya spectabilis, D. natalensis, Thuja occidentalis* and *Malvaviscus arboreus.* The adults feed on the leaves of these host plants in an irregular fashion, starting from the leaf margins. For details on the life cycle, see chapter 9.

22. *Holotrichia consanguinea* Blanchard (Groundnut white grub, Coleoptera : Scarabaeidae)

The adults of the white grub feed on *Acalypha tricolor, Bauhinia acuminata, Jatropha intergrima, Lagerstroemia indica, L. speciosa, Punica granatum, Rosa* spp. and *Thuja occidentalis* during the period June to August and they completely defoliate the host-plants. Full account of the life cycle has been given in chapter 5.

*****

13 CHAPTER

POLYPHAGOUS PESTS

Locusts

1. *Patanga succincta* Linnaeus (Bombay locust, Orthoptera.: Acrididae)
2. *Locusta migratoria* (Linnaeus) (Migratory locust, Orthoptera : Acrididae)
3. *Schistocerca gregaria* (Forskal) (Desert locust, Orthoptera.: Acrididae)

Grasshoppers

1. *Oxya nitidula* Walker (Sporadic grasshopper, Orthoptera.: Acrididae)
2. *Chrotogonus trachypterus* (Blanchard) (Surface grasshopper, Orthoptera.: Acrididae)

Termites

1. *Odontotermes obesus* (Rambur) (Isoptera : Termitidae)
2. *Microtermes obesi* Holmgren (Isoptera : Termitidae)

Hairy caterpillars

1. *Amsacta moorei* Butler (Red hairy caterpillar, Lepidoptera.: Arcitiidae)
2. *Spilarctia obliqua* Walker (Bihar hairy caterpillar, Lepidoptera : Arctiidae)

Cutworms

1. *Ochropleura flammatra* Denis & Schiffermuller (Gram cutworm, Lepidoptera : Noctuidae).
2. *Agrotis ipsilon* (Hufnagel) (Greasy cutworm, Lepidoptera.: Noctuidae)

Aphids

1. *Aphis gossypii* Glover (Cotton aphid, Hemiptera : Aphididae)
2. *Aphis craccivora* Koch (Groundnut aphid, Hemiptera : Aphididae)
3. *Myzus persicae* (Sulzer) (Green peach aphid, Hemiptera : Aphididae
4. *Lipaphis erysimi* (Kaltenbach) (Mustard aphid, Hemiptera.: Aphididae)

Thrips	1. *Thrips tabaci* Lindeman (Onion thrips, Thysanoptera : Thripidae) 2. *Rhipiphorothrips cruentatus* Hood (Grapevine thrips, Thysanoptera : Heliothripidae) 3. *Scirtothrips dorsalis* Hood (Chillies thrips, Thysanoptera.: Thripidae)
Miscellaneous insects	1. *Helicoverpa armigera* (Hubner) (Gram pod borer, Lepidoptera : Noctuidae) 2. *Spodoptera litura* (Fabricius) (Tobacoo caterpillar, Lepidoptera : Noctuidae) 3. *Mythimna separata* (Walker) (Armyworm, Lepidoptera : Noctuidae) 4. *Holotrichia consanguinea* Blanchard (White grub, Coleoptera : Scarabacidae) 5. *Bemisia tabaci* (Gennadius) (Cotton whitefly, Hemiptera : Aleyrodidae) 6. *Phenacoccus solenopsis* Tinsley (Cotton mealy bug, Hemiptera : Pseudococcidae)

LOCUSTS

Locusts are grasshoppers that belong to the order Orthoptera, family Acrididae. Such species of grasshoppers that congregate in large numbers as larvae (nymphs) and swarm to fly long distances as adults destroying vegetation on their way are called locusts; those that do not have this ability are simply called grasshoppers. Thus all locusts are grasshoppers but all grasshoppers are not locusts. There are some 5000 species of grasshoppers (acridids) found in the world but only 9 are recognised as locusts of which 3 belong to the Indian sub-continent. These 9 locusts are as follows:

1. Italian locust, *Calliptamus italicus* : Occurs in Italy, France, Northern Africa, Iran, Southern Russia.
2. Moroccan locust, *Dociostaurus moroccanus* Thunberg : Occurs in Southern Europe, Northern Africa, Iraq, Iran, Afghanistan.
3. Red locust, *Nomadacris septemfasciata* (Serville) : Occurs in Tanganyika, Souther Africa.
4. Brown locust, *Locustana pardalina* (Walker) : Occurs in Southern Africa.
5. South American locust, *Schistocerca paranensis* (Burmeister) : Occurs in Argentina to Mexico.
6. Australian locust, *Chortoicetes terminefera* (Walker) : Occurs in Australia.
7. Bombay locust, *Patanga succincta* (Linnaeus) : Occurs in India, Sri Lanka, Malaysia.
8. Migratory locust, *Locusta migratoria* (Linnaeus) : Occurs in India, Europe, Africa, Pakistan, East and South Asia, Australia.
9. Desert locust, *Schistocerca gregaria* (Forskal) : Occurs in India, Pakistan, Arabia, North African countries.

Among the 3 locusts belonging to the Indian sub-continent, *S. gregaria* is the most destructive.

1. *Patanga succincta* Linnaeus (Bombay locust, Orthoptera : Acrididae)

In India, the activities of this locust are generally confined to the area extending from Gujarat in the North to Tamil Nadu in the South. The adult is smaller than the desert locust, bears an acute (pointed) ventral (prosternal) tubercle, 8 eye-stripes and conspicuous yellowish stripes laterally on its pronotum. The fore wings (elytra) have oblique dark markings and the hind wings become rose coloured basally after the insect has spent a month as a fledgeling. It breeds during monsoon in the Western Ghats and has only one brood a year. Its plague occurred during 1835-45, 1864-66 and 1901-08.

2. *Locusta migratoria* (Linnaeus) (Migratory locust, Orthoptera : Acrididae)

This species occurs in India in Rajasthan and Gujarat. The distinguishing features are the absence of ventral tubercle and eye strips, hind wings are hyaline in the young and yellow in the old adult. Unlike Bombay locust, it breeds twice; winter-spring breeding occurs in Baluchistan (Pakistan) and summer-monsoon breeding in Rajasthan and Gujarat. It may, therefore, have many broods a year. The swarms of this species were observed in India in 1878 in Tamil Nadu, in 1954 in Bangalore and concentrated breeding occurred in Gujarat during September-October of 1959.

3. *Schistocerca gregaria* (Forskal) (Desert locust, Orthoptera : Acrididae) (Fig. 13.1A)

This is the most destructive of all locusts. It invades 30 million square kilometer areas spreading over 60 countries from the west and north of Africa to Assam in India and in 50 per cent of this area, breeding can occur.

Identification. The desert locust is found in two phases, *i.e.* the solitary phase and the gregarious phase. Individuals having characteristics in between the two are often placed under the transient phase. The nymphs of the gregarious phase are yellow or pink, with distinct black markings, whereas the colour of the solitary hoppers varies according to the colour of the surrounding vegetation. The gregarious adults are pink on emergence, gradually turning grey and ultimately yellow, when sexually mature. The adults of the solitary phase remain greenish grey throughout their life (Table 13.1).

Life-history. A single female may lay up to 11 egg-pods, each pod containing up to 120 eggs. A female normally lays 500 eggs in about 5 pods. Before egg laying, the female, with the help of her ovipositor, bores a hole into the loose sandy soil, 5-10 cm deep. Having laid a pod, she secretes a frothy material over the eggs, which hardens on drying and makes the pod water-proof. While laying eggs, the females may be sitting very close to one another and as many as 5,000 eggs may be laid in one square metre. The egg, resembling grain of rice, is lightly curved and 7-9 mm long. The duration of the egg stage depends upon the soil conditions, temperature and moisture. The eggs laid in February and March hatch in 3-4 weeks and those laid in May-September hatch in 12-15 days. The nymphs, at the time of emerging, break the egg-shell and creep out of the holes. The duration of the nymphal (hopper) stage lasts 6-8 weeks in spring and 3-4 weeks in summer.

Host plants. Locusts eat all kind of vegetation except a few namely, neem (*Azadirachta indica*), *ak* (*Calotropis procera*), *dhatura* (*Datura stramonium*), jamun (*Psidium cuminii*), sheesham (*Dalbergia sissoo*) and anjeer (*Ficus carica*).

Table 13.1 Distinguishing features of solitary and gregarious phases of the desert locust

Sr. No.	Feature	Solitary phase	Gregarious phase
Hoppers			
1.	Colour	Green as of vegetation on which they live, no black marking.	Black with pink markings when young, black with yellow markings when grown up; never green.
2.	Behaviour	Remain scattered on vegetation.	Form groups or bands and march long distances.
3.	No. of moults	5 to 6 (occasionally 4 or 7).	5
Adults			
1.	Colour	Greenish or grey throughout.	Pink when immature, yellow when sexually mature.
2.	Behaviour	Fly during nights as isolated individuals.	Generally fly during day in swarms.
3.	Pronotum	Short, convex and crested.	Longer, concave (saddle-shaped) and without a crest.
4.	Antenna	27-30 jointed.	26-jointed.
5.	Eye stripes	6-7	6
6.	Femoral spines	Both strong and weak.	Only weak.

Damage. The locust is harmful in both the hopper and the adult stages. These gregarious and voracious feeders eat almost any vegetation. When in swarms, they can consume all the green vegetation and cause a famine. In addition to the damage to crops, orchards, forests, etc., the locust can be nuisance in houses, as these creatures climb over the walls, invade kitchens, store-rooms and even enter into the beds. They fall into wells by the million and thus make water unfit for drinking. If an army of hoppers or adults marches on to the railway lines, all traffic is suspended because the crushed hoppers cause slippery rails.

Management. Management operation can be carried out against all stages of the locust, the most practicable and effective measures are against the nymphs.

(*a*) Eggs. If eggs are laid in a well-defined area, a trench may be dug around it, so that the young nymphs on emerging drop into it and can be buried alive, filling the ditch with soil. If these trenches are heavily dusted with lindane, it may not be necessary to bury the nymphs.

(*b*) Nymphs. The hopper stage is the most vulnerable and control measures are most effective before the second moult. The nymphs may be destroyed either with chemicals or by using mechanical methods: (*i*) The principal mechanical method of control lies in digging trenches in front of the moving army of nymphs and driving them into these trenches, with brooms or with twigs of trees and then, buried alive. The nymphs can also be guided to the trenches along metal or canvas barriers, 45 cm high. Two barriers, one on each side of the army of the marching hoppers, are so fixed that they converge on a narrow gap that leads to a trench in which they drop. The trench should be deep enough to accommodate a large

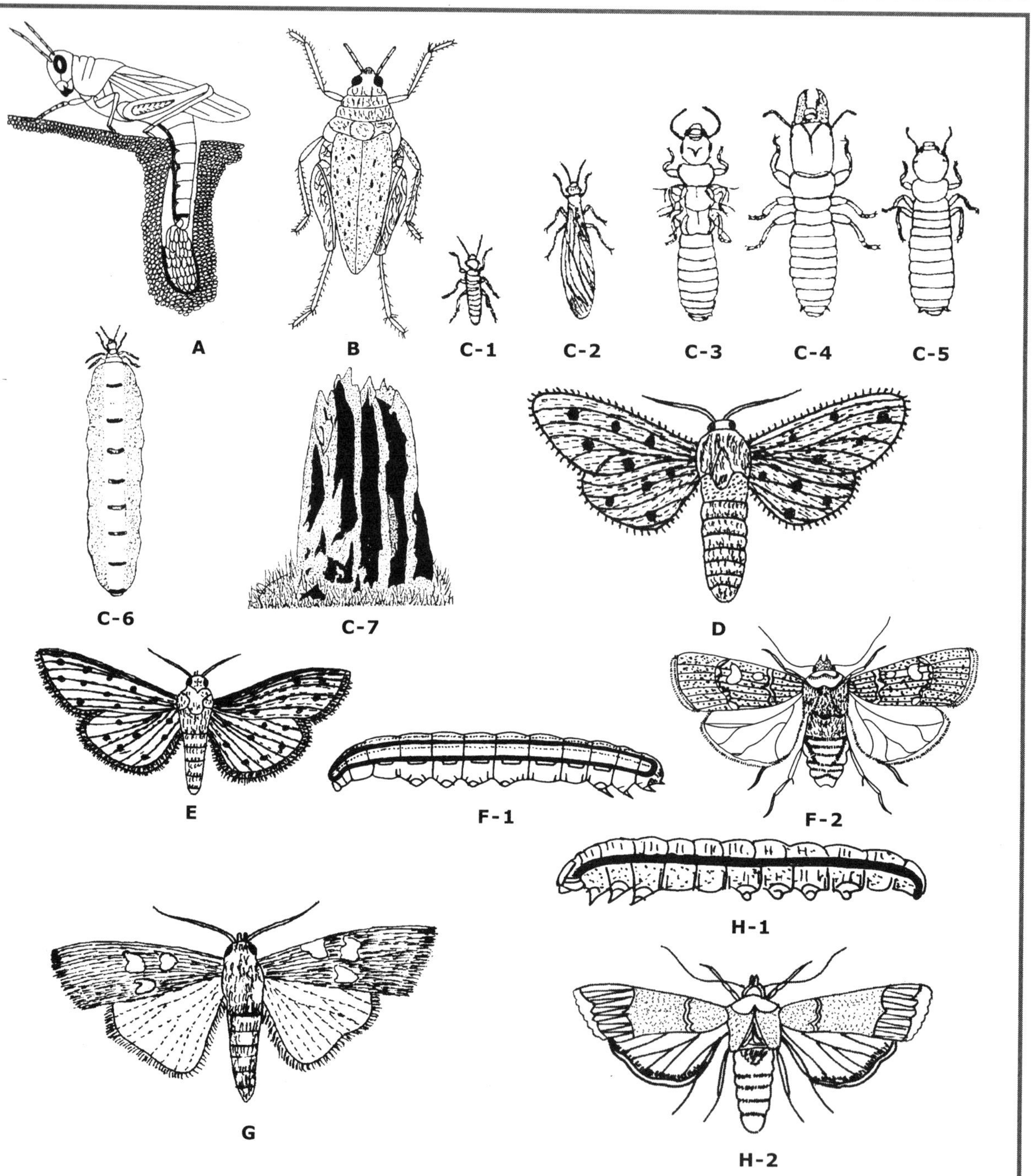

Fig. 13.1 Polyphagous pests. **A.** Desert locust, *Schistocerca gregaria*. **B.** Surface grasshopper, *Chrotogonus trachypterus*. **C.** Termite, *Odontotermes obesus* ; C-1. Nymph, C-2. Winged female, C-3. King, C-4. Soldier, C-5. Worker, C-6. Queen, C-7. Termitarium. **D.** Red hairy caterpillar, *Amsacta moorei*. **E.** Bihar hairy caterpillar, *Spilarctia obliqua*. **F.** Common cutworm, *Agrotis segetum*; F-1. Larva, F-2. Adult. **G.** Gram cutworm, *Ochropleura flammatra*. **H.** Greasy cut worm, *Agrotis ipsilon*; H-1. Larva, H-2. Adult.

number of hoppers, most of which would then die under the weight of their own fellow-creatures. Later, the trench can be filled with earth. In the early stages, a trench, 30-45 cm wide and 60 cm deep, is sufficient but when the hoppers are older, the width should be 75 cm and the depth more than 60 cm. (*ii*) At night when the hoppers rest on bushes, they can be burnt with flame-throwers. (*iii*) Poison baits such as the poisoned bran mash or sawdust, if scattered in the early morning or in the evening, are effective. During day, the bait dries quickly so the hoppers do no eat it. The poison used is a sodium fluosilicate or Paris green. (*iv*) Diazinon dust and diazinon spray (0.2%) are very effective. (*v*) Diazinon as a spray can also be applied shortly before the emergence of the hoppers, so that as soon as they come out, they come into contact with the insecticide and die. (*vi*) Spraying the crop with neem seed kernel powder suspension (1%) has been found to be very promising. (*vii*) A number of birds attack locusts and of these, the common *mynah* and the *tiliar* (starling) are the most important. During the locust cycle, if practicable, these birds should be protected.

(*c*) Adults. (*i*) The adults can be beaten to death with thorny sticks, brooms or can be swept together and buried underground in heaps. (*ii*) Diazinon 2 per cent, if dusted on crops, trees and the ground, is very effective. (*iii*) Diazinon (2%), in an oil medium, is also effective when sprayed with an aeroplane on top of a flying swarm. Diazinon 25EC in water suspension, can also be sprayed on locusts, on the ground.

Anti-Locust Organization

The Anti-Locust Organisation in India consists of (*a*) The Central Anti-Locust Organization, and (*b*) the State Anti-Locust Organizations.

(*a*) Central Anti-Locust Organization. This organization is handled by the Plant Protection Adviser to the Government of India, who is also the Director of Locust Control, having his headquarters at Faridabad (Haryana). The Directorate is required to :

- Record the weekly density of locusts per unit area in the breeding areas located in India and to carry out control operations there.
- Interpret the records and pass on the information on locust movements to the various State Locust Control and Warning Officers and to the revenue authorities of the concerned districts before the locust reaches there so that arrangements for control can be made in advance.
- Keep watch on the coming swarms of extra-Indian origin, their direction and size.
- Give technical and material assistance to the various states.
- Coordinate the anti-locust work in India by issuing a fortnightly bulletin on the locust situation both in India and in foreign countries.

In India, the work of this organization extends both to the scheduled desert areas where locusts breed and to the cultivated areas where they do the damage. In the scheduled desert areas, the Central Anti-Locust Organization operates over an area of 2,05,785 square kilometers in the states of Rajasthan, Haryana, Maharashtra and Gujarat. This area is divided into 10 zones which are grouped into 4 circles with headquarters at Bikaner, Jodhpur, Barmer and Palanpur (Gujarat). The responsibility of the control work is entrusted to the Locust Entomologist in-charge of the circle.

(*b*) State Anti-Locust Organizations. In the scheduled area of the desert as well as in the adjoining states where locusts cause damage, there are State Anti-Locust Organizations to take suitable measures against the swarms. The state organization is headed by the Locust Control and Warning Officer, who is well connected with the local revenue authorities, from the Deputy Commissioner to the Tehsildar and Patwari. When the latter official receives information from district headquarters warning him of a locust invasion, he alerts the villagers to be ready with machines and insecticides, kerosene, flame-throwers, spades, etc. When the swarm actually arrives, the farmers try to kill it as well as they can and then the Patwari intimates the Locust Control Officer and his own Deputy Commissioner of the extent of success achieved. In case the swarm settles down to lay eggs, the Locust Control Officer or his staff visits the place to devise suitable control measures.

GRASSHOPPERS

1. *Oxya nitidula* Walker (Sporadic grasshopper, Orthoptera : Acrididae)

Distribution. Sporadic grasshopper is widely distributed in the Orient and is a pest of sporadic occurrence. In Punjab, it is serious in the low-lying areas of Amritsar, Gurdaspur and Hoshiarpur which are flooded occasionally.

Identification. The nymphs are shiny green and have a broad, black band extending from the base of the eyes to the wing pads. The legs are greenish-yellow and the full-grown nymphs measure about 1.5-2.5 cm in length. The adults are similar in body colour but are larger (about 2.5-3.0 cm) and have green wings.

Life-history. The pest is active from March to December and passes winter in egg stage in the soil. The over-wintered eggs hatch in March and the emerging nymphs feed on *berseem* (*Trifolium alexandrinum*), *khabbal* grass (*Cynodon dactylon*) and other available crops. They moult 6 or 7 times by June and are transformed into winged adults in 60-64 days. The adults also feed on various *kharif* crops and live for 40-49 days. They lay brown eggs in clusters on the underside of leaves of various food plants, particularly sugarcane. A female may lay 29-143 eggs, which hatch in 16-24 days. The nymphs of the second generation developing during July-August are transformed into winged adults in 46-57 days. These adults live for about 60-71 days and lay eggs in the soil instead of plants. Some of these eggs hatch in October and give rise to third-generation nymphs which never complete their development and eventually die of cold in December. A majority of eggs, however, do not hatch and remain in the soil till next March. Thus, the pest completes two broods in a year.

Host plants. The insects feed on various *kharif* crops, such as maize, sorghum, rice, berseem, bajra, sugarcane, etc.

Damage. The nymphs and adults feed on various crops. When there is a serious infestation, the plants may be completely defoliated and the crops, such as *berseem*, may be wiped out.

Management. Dust the crop with fenvalerate 0.4 per cent @ 25 kg per ha.

2. *Chrotogonus trachypterus* (Blanchard) (Surface grasshopper, Orthoptera : Acrididae) (Fig. 13.1B)

Distribution. This species of surface grasshoppers is widely distributed in the Orient and Africa. In India, it is common in the north whereas *C. oxypterus* occurs in the southern regions.

Identification. The adults are stoutly built, about 2.0 cm long and 8 mm broad, with a rough brownish appearance. There are two longitudinal rows of black dots on the underside of the white body. The nymphs are similar in body form but are smaller and have wing pads instead of wings.

Life-history. *C. trachypterus* remains active throughout the year but its activity is considerably reduced during winter when only eggs and adults are found. A female may lay 36-434 eggs in 2-15 egg pods, at a depth of 3-6 cm in the soil. There are generally 16-46 eggs in a pod. In summer, the eggs hatch in 19-33 days whereas in winter they hatch in about 5 months. The developing nymphs feed on grasses or other soft foods. They moult 5-7 times and are full-fed in 40-70 days. Adults are long-lived, the female for about three months and the male about 1.5 months. There are two complete generations in a year and sometimes the eggs laid in October also hatch giving rise to a third partial brood, which dies in the nymphal stage during the winter.

Host plants. The grasshoppers are polyphagous and, besides cotton and wheat, they feed on a number of other cultivated crops such as *berseem* (*Trifolium alexandrinum*), sugarcane, *kharif* fodders, barley, etc.

Damage. Both nymphs and adults feed on leaves by cutting germinating plants of cotton, wheat, etc. particularly in areas adjoining the waste-lands. Often the damaged fields have to be resown. Unlike *Oxya* sp., the attack by this grasshopper is more serious in low-rainfall areas.

Management. Same as in case of sporadic grasshopper.

TERMITES

The termites, commonly called white ants, are among the common insect pests belonging to the order Isoptera. They are found abundantly and widely in tropical and sub-tropical regions of the world. They live in large communities, mostly in underground nests and are familiar because of their depredations. They make small earthen mounds or earthen passages that are visible above the ground. On opening a portion of an earthen passage, greyish white, wingless insects are seen moving towards or away from the centre of their nest, where the queen of the colony resides. They belong to many families and their nesting behavior is characteristic of every group.

The following four families of the order Isoptera are economically important: (*i*) Kalotermitidae (exclusively inhabit dead, dying and living wood, have no connection with the soil, e.g. *Neotermes, Cryptotermes*); (*ii*) Hodotermitidae (live in arid zones of India, attack grasses and stored grains, live and breed wholly underground, e.g. *Acanthotermes*); (*iii*) Rhinotermitidae (largely sub-terranean, some invade wood works in buildings, e.g. *Heterotermes, Rhinotermes, Captotermes, Reticulotermes*); and (*iv*) Termitidae (largest and economically most important, both under and above ground dwellers, e.g. *Odontotermes, Microtermes, Hypotermes, Nasutitermes*). Although about 270 species of termites from South Asia are injurious to economic plants, principal among them are *Microtermes obesi* Holmgren and *Odontotermes obesus* (Rambur).

The termites are social insects and their colony organization is based on a caste-system. In a colony, there are numerous workers, lots of soldiers, one queen, a king and a good number of complementary or the colonizing forms of true but immature males and females (Fig. 13.1C). The various castes and their duties are described as under.

A. Productive Castes

1. **Colonizing individuals.** These are winged individuals of both sexes and are produced in large numbers during the rainy season. When the temperature and moisture

conditions are optimum, they emerge from the parent colony and hover over street lamps early in the evening, usually after a shower of rain. The wings are meant for the nuptial flight only and when they have mated, the wings usually drop off. Most of the winged insects are eaten up by frogs, lizards and snakes. A pair that happens to escape may start a new colony in a crevice in the soil as the queen and the king of a colony. To start with, they themselves attend to the foraging and other duties which, later on, are performed by the workers.

2. **Queen.** This is the only perfectly developed female in the colony. She develops either from colonizing individuals described above or from the wingless forms (complementals) present in an established colony. She attains a much larger size when developed from the former caste. Her reproductive system occupies almost the entire abdomen. She is a phenomenal 'egg-laying machine', laying one egg per second or 70,000-80,000 eggs in 24 hours. There is only one queen in a colony and normally she lives from 5 to 10 years. The queen is fed by the workers on the choicest food, and is housed in a special area referred to as the 'royal chamber' which is situated in the centre of the nest, at a depth of about 0.5 metre below the ground surface.
3. **King.** A king develops from an unfertilized egg and becomes fully developed by consuming a superior diet. He is the father of the colony and is a constant companion of the queen, living with her in the 'royal chamber'. He is much smaller than the queen and is slightly bigger than the colonizing individuals. He mates with the queen from time to time and, thus, aids her in laying fertilized eggs from which the colonizing forms and workers develop. The king's life is much shorter than that of the queen and, when he dies, he is replaced by a new one.
4. **Complementary castes.** They are short-winged or wingless creatures of both sexes and lead a sub-terranean life. In the event of the untimely death of the king or queen in a colony, the complementary castes replace them. They are induced by the workers to undergo sexual development.

B. Sterile Castes

5. **Workers.** The workers develop from the fertilized eggs but remain stunted as they are reared on ordinary food. Numerically, they are the most abundant in a colony but are smaller than the soldiers. Except for the reproduction and defence of the community, practically all other duties are performed by the workers. They take care of the eggs and the young ones and remove them to safe places at the time of danger. They also tend and feed the queen, collect food and cultivate a fungus food (ambrosia) in underground gardens.

   When a new colony is established, the earlier broods of workers construct a hemispherical chamber for the queen and it is connected with innumerable galleries. In certain species, the workers also construct a high mound above the ground, which is known as the *termitarium.* Since the workers have to collect all provisions for the colony, they are notoriously destructive.
6. **Soldiers.** The soldiers develop from unfertilized eggs and remain comparatively underdeveloped. They are the most specialized members of the community and can be readily recognized by the large head and strongly chitinized sickle-shaped mandibles.

Distribution. Termites abound in tropical and sub-tropical countries. They live in colonies which may be small or large containing from few thousand to a million or above insects.

Identification. Termites are medium-sized, soft-bodied, cream to light or dark brown insects.

Life-history. In the rainy season when atmospheric conditions are favourable, the colonizing forms leave their parent colony. As they are weak fliers, they do not travel a long distance unless aided by wind. As a rule, a particular species swarms at about the same time of season. The members of the swarm comprise individuals of both sexes. They are attracted to light where they mix with individuals of the neighbouring swarms. A great majority of them fall prey to many types of predators and only a few individuals survive in the end. Sooner or later the survivors fall down and cast their wings and mate before or after shedding them. Both the male and female participate in the early operations of forming a nest by excavating small burrows or galleries or the nuptial chambers. In the beginning, only a few eggs are laid and are looked after by them and the newly hatched nymphs are fed by the parents themselves. They develop into workers and then take over all the brooding. During the first season, the reproductive castes are usually not produced. Gradually, the queen grows in size and the number of eggs laid increases.

The eggs hatch after one week during the summer and within 6 weeks the larvae develop to form soldiers or workers, as the case may be. The reproductive castes, when produced, mature in 1-2 years. The queen is capable of laying millions of eggs during her life, which is very difficult to estimate, but probably 6-9 years is the approximate span. The nests of many termites grow fungus gardens in the centre, near about the 'royal chamber'. The fungus grows into a comb-like structure and is fed to the royal pair and the larvae.

Host plants. Since the termites are wood-feeding insects, they can eat away the roots of any plant.

Damage. The damage is largely done by the workers who are responsible for feeding of the entire community. The large number of workers is responsible for the inflicting of the damage. The termites live on cellulose which they obtain from dead and living vegetable matter. Besides all kinds of crops, termites damage wood works in the buildings, furniture, bridges, poles, airfields, books in archives and clothes. (Table 13.2)

Table 13.2 Different categories of commodities damaged by termites

Sr. No.	Category	Commodities
1.	Agricultural crops	Wheat, barley, oat, maize, millets, paddy, pulses, cotton, groundnut, sugarcane, castor, poppy, sunflower, vegetables, grasses, etc.
2.	Plantation crops	Tea, coffee, rubber, coconut, cocoa, jute, sunnhemp, etc.
3.	Fruit trees	Mango, apple, ber (*Zizyphus*), citrus, mulberry, guava, custard apple, cashew, pomegranate, peach, cheeku (Sapota), grapevine, etc.
4.	Other economic trees	Bamboo, eucalyptus (in surseries), mahua, neem, oak, palm, chir pine, willow, semal, sal, teak, sheesham, etc.
5.	Garden plants	Chrysanthemum, rose, bouganvillea, etc.
6.	Seeds	
7.	Ordinance stores	Wooden ammunition boxes, wooden cable and wire rope drums, tents (wooden and bamboo pegs and tents themselves), textiles, boots, saddlery, other leather goods, matting stored timber. The more common species damaging ordinance stores are : *Heterotermes indicola, Captotermes heimi* and *Odontotermes obesus*. What the termites cannot eat, they spoil by sticking eathern pellets to the surfaces.

Management of Termites

1. When a colony is established, it is not so easy to eradicate the pest. The only sure method is to reach the centre of the nest and kill the queen and the complementary forms. Since the termite tunnels run for hundreds of metres, it is often difficult to locate the royal chamber. However, in the mound-forming species of termites, it is much easier to locate the centre which lies in the mound or just below it.
2. Stubbles of the previous crops and other dead decaying matter should be removed since they attract termites.
3. To avoid the attack of white-ants in cultivated fields, care should be taken not to use green manure or raw farmyard manure.
4. Insecticidal control for different situations is as follows :
   (*a*) **Fruit trees.** (*i*) In new plantations, the pits should be treated with 0.2 per cent lindane emulsion or crude-oil emulsion before planting the trees. This is done by thoroughly mixing 0.25 kg of crude-oil emulsion and a little arsenic in about 4 baskets of subsoil taken from the pit. The treated soil is returned to the pit. (*ii*) To protect the tree trunks, spraying them with 1 per cent lindane is effective. (*iii*) To protect the roots, 0.5 per cent chlorpyriphos or lindane or 3 per cent sanitary fluid in the irrigation basin should be applied.

   (*b*) **Field crops.** (*i*) For protecting chillies in small plots, 3 per cent sanitary fluid should be applied to the soil. When large areas are to be treated, the sanitary fluid is put in a canvas bag at the rate of 25-35 litres per hectare. The bag is suspended in the irrigation channel. (*ii*) Soaking the sugarcane setts in 0.5 per cent chlorpyriphos suspension or 0.25 per cent chlorpyriphos emulsion in furrows at the time of planting, saves them from termite attack. Alternatively, 25 Kg of fipronil 0.3G can be applied after mixing with 50 Kg sand per ha, in the furrows and then cover the sugarcane setts by planking. (*iii*) Treat one kg of wheat seed with 3 ml of imidacloprid 600FS or 4 ml chlorpyriphos 20EC or 6 ml of fipronil 5SC. After spreading 100 kg of seed in thin layers on cemented floor or tarpaulin or plastic sheet, spray 300 ml of imidacloprid 600FS or 400 ml of chlorpyriphos 20EC or 600 ml of fipronil 5SC dissolved in 2.5 litres of water.

   (*c*) **Buildings.** (*i*) A galvanised sheet of iron with its outer edge turned downwards when placed just above the damp-proof layer makes the house white-ant-proof. Wooden structures such as doorframes should not directly touch the ground and should be raised on a cement layer. (*ii*) An insecticidal barrier between the ground and woodwork in building should be made by treating the soil beneath the building and around foundations with 0.5 per cent chlorpyriphos. The solution should be applied at the rate of 5 litres per m^2.
5. To protect wood-work, paint it with solignum. The cupboards, almirahs, shelves, etc. should be sprayed with chlorpyriphos frequently. The place from where the galleries originate in the house should be either sprinkled over or injected with 0.5 per cent chlorpyriphos suspension in water. If wooden structures have already been attacked, injection of 0.5 per cent chlorpyriphos emulsions with a hypodermic needle into the wood and in the crevices is the only remedy. For a lasting relief, the nests should be located in the vicinity and destroyed by flooding them with the insecticide emulsions.
6. Mounds of termite, if any, in the area should be treated with 0.5 per cent chlorpyriphos after breaking open the earthen structure, and making holes with an iron bar. The insecticidal emulsion should be used at the rate of 4 litres per m^3 of the mound.

HAIRY CATERPILLARS

1. *Amsacta moorei* (Butler) (Red hairy caterpillar, Lepidoptera : Arctiidae) (Fig. 13.1D)

Distribution. The red hairy caterpillar or *kutra* is widely distributed in the Orient, including India. In India, it is more common in Andhra Pradesh, Tamil Nadu, Karnataka, Maharashtra, Gujarat, Punjab, Madhya Pradesh and Uttar Pradesh.

Identification. The moths are stoutly built and have white wings with black spots. The outer margins of the fore wings, the anterior margin of the thorax and the entire abdomen are scarlet red. There are black bands and dots on the abdomen. The full-grown caterpillars are reddish-amber to olive green and the body is covered with numerous long hairs arising from the fleshy tubercles.

Life-history. The female moths lay light-yellow spherical eggs in clusters of 700-850 each on the under surface of the leaves of host plants. A single female may lay up to 1,500 eggs, which hatch in 2-3 days. The young caterpillars feed gregariously and, as they grow older, they march in bands destroying field after field of various *kharif* crops. The caterpillars grow through six stages and complete their development in 15-23 days. They enter the soil, shed their hair and make earthen cocoons at a depth of about 23 cm. Here they pupate and remain in this stage for many months till they emerge next year from the cocoons. In a given population, probably more than one generation is completed in a year.

Host plants. It is a polyphagous insect and feeds practically on all kinds of vegetation growing during the *kharif* season. Its attack is particularly serious on sunnhemp, cotton, groundnut, maize, sorghum, *guara, mung, moth* and sesamum.

Damage. The young *kutra* caterpillars prefer to eat the growing points of plants. The older ones have no such discrimination and they feed voraciously on all vegetation resulting in severe defoliation. Field after field is devastated by the moving army of caterpillars.

Management. (*i*) The moths are strongly attracted to artificial light. Therefore, light traps of electric or petromax lamps placed just above a broad flat basin full of kerosenized water, should be put on the night following the first shower of the monsoon and continued throughout the period of emergence for about one month. (*ii*) Young larvae can be destroyed by pulling out the infested plants and burying them under-ground. (*iii*) The grown-up caterpillars may be destroyed by crushing them under feet or picking and putting them into kerosenoized water. (*iv*) In case of serious attack, spray quinalphos 25EC or 500 ml of dichlorvos 100EC in 500 litres of water per ha.

2. *Spilarctia obliqua* Walker (Bihar hairy caterpillar, Lepidoptera : Arctiidae) (Fig. 13.1E)

Distribution. The Bihar hairy caterpillar is a sporadic pest and is widely distributed in the Orient. In India, it is very serious in Bihar, Madhya Pradesh, Uttar Pradesh and the Punjab.

Identification. The moth measures about 5.0 cm across the spread wing and is dull yellow. The full-grown caterpillars are profusely covered with long greyish hair.

Life-history. The female lays 410-1240 light green, spherical eggs in clusters on the underside of leaves. The eggs hatch in 8-13 days and during the first two stages, the tiny caterpillars feed gregariously, but afterwards they disperse widely in search of food. They grow to maturity through 7 stages, within 4-8 weeks. When full-grown, larva spins a loose silken cocoon in which pupation takes place in plant debris or in the soil. The pupal stage lasts 1-2 weeks in the active period and the moths live for about a week. The life-cycle is completed in 6-12 weeks and the pest passes through 3 or 4 broods in a year.

Host plants. The pest is polyphagous feeding on sesamum, *mash, mung,* linseed, mustard, sorghum, cotton, jute, groundnut, sunflower and some vegetables.

Damage. The caterpillars eat leaves and soft portions of stems and branches. In severe infestation, the plants may be completely denuded of leaves.

Management. (*i*) The young caterpillars can be killed easily by dusting the infested crop with malathion 5 per cent @ 25 kg/ha.(*ii*) When they are full-grown, it is difficult to kill them and very high doses of the pesticides are needed. The chemical control measures are same as in case of red hairy caterpillar.

CUTWORMS

The term cutworm or surface caterpillar is applied to the larvae of several species of noctuid moths which have, in common, the habit of biting through the stems of seedlings at ground level and eating the leaves or the entire seedlings. The various species of cutworms have a wide range of food plants, both cultivated and wild. The majority of cutworms found in India fall under the genera *Agrotis* and *Euxoa.* Of the recorded species, only four are widespread in the plains and have considerable economic importance. *Agrotis ipsilon* (Hufnagel) (Fig. 13.1F) is the commonest and *Ochropleura flammatra* (Denis & Schiffermuller) is occasionally abundant in India, the latter being particularly destructive in the north. *Agrotis segetum* (Denis & Schiffermuller) and *A. biconica* Kollar are also quite common in India, being more so in the south.

1. *Ochropleura flammatra* (Denis & Schiffermuller) (Gram cutworm, Lepidoptera: Noctuidae) (Fig. 13.1G)

Distribution. The gram cutworm is one of the most important pests of chickpea or gram in northern India, particularly in the Punjab, Haryana and in the sub-Himalayan region. Its distribution extends to Europe, Syria, Iran, western Siberia and Pakistan.

Identification. The adult is a heavy bodied, greyish-brown or wheat-coloured insect which measures 5.0-6.2 cm in wing expanse. Its fore wings have characteristic markings and smoky patches. The caterpillars are dark grey or dull green and their skin is smooth and greasy.

Life-history. The female moths lay yellowish-white eggs on the under surface of leaves, on shoots, stems, or in the soil, within 5-9 days of their short life span of 7-13 days. A female lays up to 980 eggs in its life time. The eggs hatch in 4-7 days during summer and 10-14 days during winter. The larvae remain hidden in soil during the day time and feed at night on young shoots or underground tubers. They are full-grown in 4-7 weeks and then make earthen cells in the soil for pupation. The pupal stage lasts 12-15 days but during winter it extends up to 5 weeks. The life-cycle is completed in 7-11 weeks and there are generally two generations in a year.

Host plants. It is a polyphagous pest and besides gram, it feeds on the seedlings of many vegetables and other plants such as potato, cucurbits, peas, okra, wheat, tobacco, opium, poppy, etc.

Damage. This cutworm is a sporadic pest of major importance. In some years, 50 per cent of the gram crop may be destroyed. The caterpillars spend the day hiding near and about the plant bases. They remain in the top 5-10 cm of the soil near the plants that might have been cut the night before. At night, they come out and become active, cutting down the young plants of gram, potato, vegetable seedlings, etc. just above or slightly below the surface of the soil. They seem to be very voracious eaters and they cut more plants than they can consume.

Management. The pest can be controlled with fenvalerate 0.4per cent dust @ 25 kg per ha or spray 80 ml fenvalerate 20EC or 50 ml cypermethrin 25EC or 150 ml decamethrin 2.8EC in 100 litres of water per ha. Alternatively, drench the soil around the plant and ridges with chlorpyriphos 20EC @ 2.5 litres in 1000 litres of water per ha, on appreance of the pest.

2. *Agrotis ipsilon* (Hufnagel) (Greasy cutworm, Lepidoptera : Noctuidae) (Fig. 12.1H)

Distribution. This is a pest of worldwide occurrence and is found in America, Europe, North Africa, Syria, Japan, China, Indonesia, Australia, New Zealand, Hawaii, Sri Lanka, Myanmar and India. It has been reported from almost all the potato growing regions of northern India, forming a continuous belt from the Punjab in the west to Bengal in the east and Madhya Pradesh in the south.

Identification. The adult moth measures about 2.5 cm from the head to the tip of the abdomen and looks dark or blackish with some greyish patches on the back and dark streaks on the fore wings. The slightly yellowish caterpillar, on emergence, is 1.5 mm long with a shiny, black head and a black shield on the prothorax. The full-grown larva is about 4.2-4.5 mm long and is dark or dark-brown with a plump and greasy body.

Life-history. The pest is active from October to April and probably migrates to the mountains for further breeding during summer. The moths appear in the plains in October and come out at dusk and fly about until darkness sets in. They oviposit at night and lay creamy-white, dome-shaped eggs in clusters of about 30 each, either on the undersurface of the leaves of food plants or in the soil. The number of eggs laid by a female varies from 199 to 344. Oviposition continues from 5 to 11 days and the duration of the egg stage varies from 2 days in summer to 8-13 days in winter. The newly hatched larvae feed on their egg shells and move like a semilooper. The larval stage varies from 30 to 34 days in February-April. The advanced-stage larvae may become cannibalistic. The caterpillars are found throughout the winter and become active at night when they cut off and fell the young plants. During the day, they hide in cracks and crevices in the soil. When full-grown, they make earthen chambers in the soil and pupate underground. The pupal stage varies from 10 days in summer to 30 days in winter. The moths usually emerge at night. The life-cycle is completed in 48-77 days and generally three generations are completed in a year. It is a cold-weather pest and is active from October to March in the plains. It suddenly disappears with the onset of summer during April and is not traceable during the off-season, from April to August-September.

Host plants. This polyphagus pest has been reported feeding on gram, potato, tobacco, peas, wheat, lentil, mustard, linseed, maize, sugarcane, cucurbits, *bhang (Cannabis sativa)*, vegetable seedlings and several weeds.

Damage. The young larvae feed on the epidermis of the leaves. As they grow, their habit changes. During the daytime they live in cracks and holes in the ground and come out at night and fell the plants by cutting their stems, either below the surface or above the ground. The cut branches are sometimes seen to have been dragged into the holes where the leaves are eaten at leisure. The larvae may also bore into cabbages. Damage to the *rabi* crops may go as high as 37 per cent and to the potato crop may be as high as 80 per cent.

Management. Same as in case of gram cutworm.

*****

14
CHAPTER

NON-INSECT PESTS OF CROPS

Mammals

Rodents

1. *Rattus rattus* L. (House rat)
2. *Rattus meltada* Gray (Soft-furred field rat)
3. *Rattus norvegicus* (Berkenhout) (Brown rat/Norway rat)
4. *Mus musculus* L. (House mouse)
5. *Mus booduga* Gray (Field mouse)
6. *Bandicota bengalensis* Gray (Mole-rat/Lesser bandicoot)
7. *Bandicota indica* Bechstein (Large bandicoot rat)
8. *Nesokia indica* Gray (Short-tailed field rat)
9. *Golunda ellioti* Gray (Bush rat)
10. *Tatera indica* Hardwicke (Indian gerbil)
11. *Meriones hurrianae* (Jerdon) Indian desert gerbil)
12. *Funambulus pennanti* Wroughton (Five-striped pam squirrel)
13. *Funambulus palmarum* L. (Three-striped palm squirrel)
14. *Hystrix indica* Kerr (Indian crested porcupine)

Other mammals

1. *Rhesus macaque* (Red-faced monkey)
2. *Macaca mulatta* Zimmerman (Monkey)
3. *Semnopithecus entellus* Dufresne (Langur)
4. *Lepus nigricollis* Cuvier (Rabbit)
5. *Lepus ruficaudatus* Geoff (Hare)

6. *Pteropus giganteus* Brunnich (Flying-fox/Fruit bat)
7. *Canis aureus* L. (Jackal)
8. *Boselaphus tragocomelus* (Pallas) (Blue bull/Neelgai)
9. *Sus scrofa cristatus* Wagner (Wild boar)
10. *Elephas maximus* (Wild elephant)
11. *Cervus unicolor* Kerr. (Sambhar)
12. *Antelope cervicapra* L. (Black-buck/Indian antelope)
13. *Hemiechinus auritus* Gmelin (Long-eared hedge hog)
14. *Malursus ursinus* (Shaw) (Sloth bear)
15. *Axis axis* Erxleben (Chital/Spotted deer)

Birds

1. *Corvus splendens* Vieillot (Common house crow)
2. *Corvos macrorhynchos* Wagner (Jungle crow)
3. *Psittacula krameri* Scopoli (Rose-ringed parakeet/Tota)
4. *Passer domesticus* L. (House sparrow)
5. *Pycnonotus cafer L.* (Red-vented bulbul)
6. *Ploceus philippinus* L. (Weaver bird/Baya)
7. *Acridotheres tristis* L. (Common myna)
8. *Columba livia* Gmelin (Blue rock pigeon)
9. *Pavo cristatus* L. (Peacock)
10. *Terroides terricolor malabaricum* (Seven sisters)

Molluscs

Snails

1. *Helix* spp.
2. *Achatina fulica* Ferussac (African land snail)
3. *Macrochlamys indica* Godwin-Austin (Large common garden snail)
4. *Opeas gracilis* Hutton (Green house snail)

Slugs

1. *Limax* sp.
2. *Laevicaulis alte* Ferrusac
3. *Arion reticulatus*
4. *Arion hartensis* Fer.

Mites

Graminaceous crops (wheat, barley, rice, maize, sorghum, sugarcane)

1. *Oligonychus indicus* (Tetranychidae)
2. *Schizotetranychus andropogoni* (Tetranychidae)
3. *Petroiba latens* (Tetranychidae)

Fruits	1. *Eutetranychus orientalis* (Tetranychidae)
	2. *Eutetranychus hirsti* (Tetranychidae)
	3. *Panonychus citri* (Tetranychidae)
	4. *Aceria mangiferae* (Eriophyidae)
	5. *Aceria litchii* (Eriophyidae)
	6. *Aceria cajani* (Eriophyidae)
Vegetables and ornamentals	1. *Tetranychus ludeni* (Tetranychidae)
	2. *T. cinnabarinus* (Tetranychidae)
	3. *T. neocaliedonicus* (Tetranychidae)
	4. *Larvacarus transitans* (Tenuipalpidae)
	5. *Brevipalpus phoenicis* (Tetrancychidae)
	6. *Polyphagotarsonemus latus* (Tenuipalpidae)
Plantation crops (tea, coffee, coconut, arecanut)	1. *Oligonychus coffeae* (Tetranychidae)
	2. *O. indicus* (Tetranychidae)
	3. *Calcarus carinatus* (Eriophyide)
Cotton	1. *Tetranychus cinnabarinus* (Tetranychidae)
	2. *Acalitus gossypii* (Eriophyidae)

Nematodes

Order Tylenchida	1. *Meloidogyne* spp.
	2. *Heterodera rostochinensis*
	3. *Tylenchulus semipenetrans* Cobb
	4. *Pratylenchus* spp.
	5. *Anguina tritici*
Order Dorylamida	1. *Xiphinema* spp.
	2. *Longidorus* spp.
	3. *Trichodorus* spp.

RODENTS

Rodents are omnivorous and feed on grains, vegetables, fruits, meat and other products in the houses or in the field. Rodents are responsible for causing enormous losses to crops and stored grains. Besides feeding on these products, they destroy a substantial quantity by spillage and contamination with their droppings, urine, body hair, etc. Rats daily consume food equal to about 10 per cent of their body weight, damage about 20 times the amount they actually consume, by their gnawing activity and by polluting the foodgrains. It has been estimated that there are about 2500 million rats in India. They inflict, on an average, about 5-10 per cent loss in food production alone. Of the 84 species of rodents in India, 10 are of major significance.

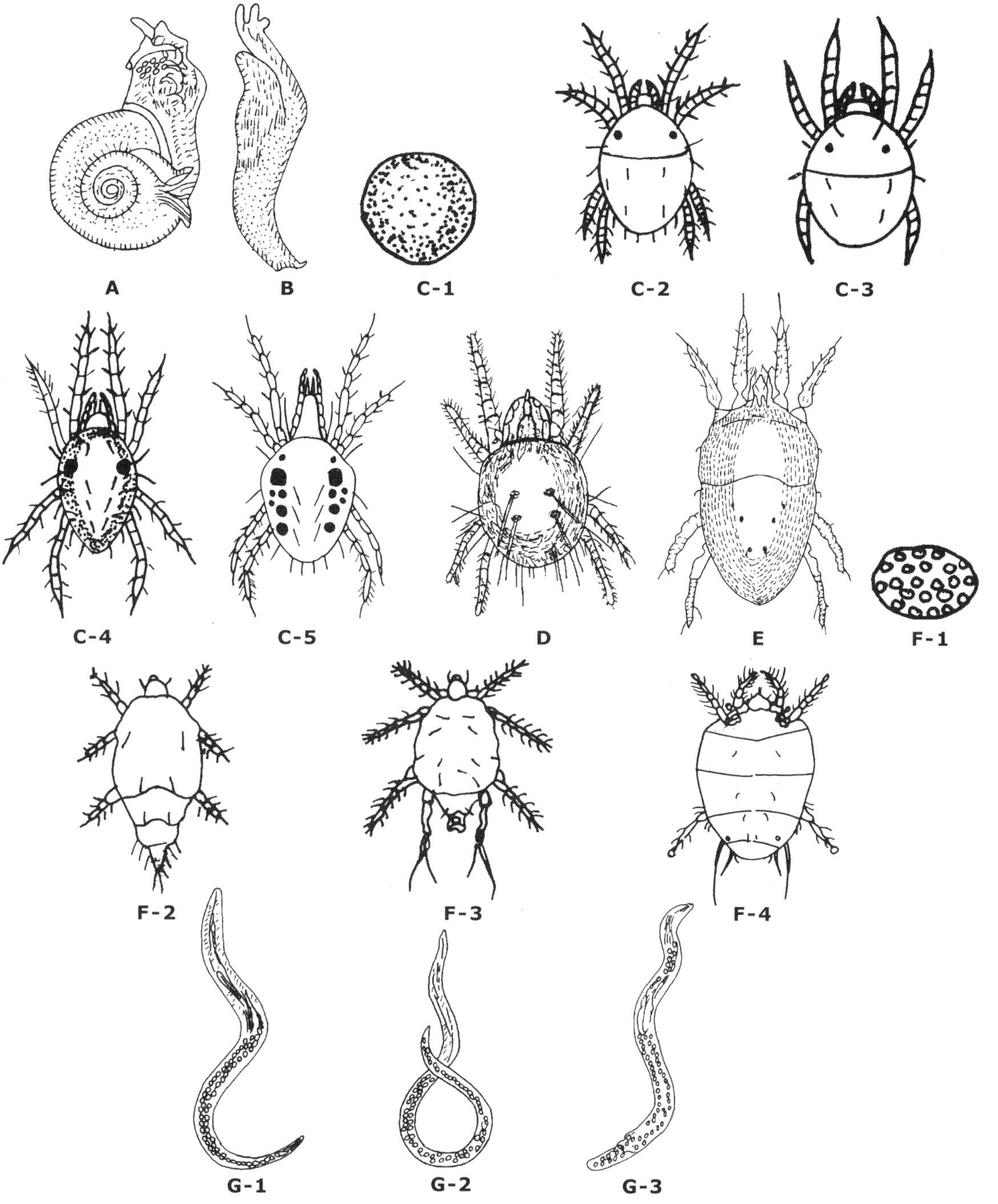

Fig. 14.1 Non-insect pests of crops. **A.** Snail, *Helix* sp. **B.** Slug, *Limax* sp. **C.** Red spider mite, *Tetranychus cinnabarius*; C-1. Egg, C-2. Larva, C-3. Nymph, C-4. Male adult, C-5. Female adult. **D.** Citrus mite, *Panonychus citri*. **E.** Red crevice tea mite, *Brevipalpus phoenicus*. **F.** Chilli mite, *Polyphagotarsonemus latus*; F-1. Egg, F-2. Larva, F-3. Nymph, F-4. Adult. **G.** Citrus nematode, *Tylenchulus semipenetrans* ; G-1. Larva, G-2, Male, G-3. Young female.

The commonest rats found in our houses are *Rattus rattus* and *Mus musculus* which along with *Rattus norvegicus* and bandicoots are instrumental in spreading *bubonic plague*, a disease which only a few decades ago used to kill millions of people every year.

1. Rattus rattus *L.*

It is the commonest house rat distributed all over India and the world. Its body (head and trunk together) measures 10-12 cm, tail slightly longer and weighs 150-200 g. Its colour has shades of brown and black on the upperside and off-white to grey on the underside. It is nocturnal in habit, does not burrow but can make nests on trees. It can occur in fields, coconut field in particular, and has a denser population in villages because of the availability of harbourage.

2. Rattus meltada *Gray*

It is the common field rat found all over India, Nepal and Sri Lanka. It is 12-15 cm long with equal or shorter tail and about 60 g in weight. It bears large rounded ear lobes and soft coat of fur which is light brownish-grey on the upper side and greyish-white on the underside. It is mostly found in irrigated fields, bunds, hedges and grasslands. Nocturnal in habit, it lives in simple burrows whose openings are often hidden in bushes.

3. Rattus norvegicus *(Berkenhout)*

Called brown or Norway rat, it is found mainly at ports in tropical countries and in cities and farmlands in temperate (European) countries. Its body measures 18-20 cm with 16-18 cm long tail and 200-450 g weight. Its dorsum is brown to dark brown and venter greyish, occasionally black. It is distinguished from *R.. rattus* by its blunt muzzle, smaller ears and tail shorter than the body length. It is predominantly a burrower and in big cities, it is specially found in sewers and so often called *sewer rat*.

4. Mus musculus *L.*

The common house mouse and a miniature replica of *R. rattus* in looks, it measures 5-7 cm with an equally long tail and 18 g weight. Its dorsum is dark brown on sandy brown and venter off-white, grey or dark brown. It is cosmopolitan in distribution, nocturnal and fossorial (burrowing) in habit, can live indoors and in fields and is a close associate of *R. rattus* in houses and godowns, and a great destroyer of textiles, sacs, paper, etc.

5. Mus booduga *Gray*

It is the common Indian field mouse found in Peninsular India to Kutch, Punjab, U.P., Bihar, Orissa and Bhutan. It measures 5-7 cm with slightly shorter tail. Its colour varies from pale-sandy in desert zone to brown or dark greyish-brown in moisture regions with off-white venter. Nocturnal in habit, it dwells in shallow burrows with 1 or 2 openings, the main opening sometimes plugged with earth. It lives in association with *R. meltada* and *Tatera indica*.

6. Bandicota bengalensis *Gray*

This Indian mole rat is distributed all over India (except perhaps the desert of Rajasthan), Nepal, Burma, Thailand, Sri Lanka, Java and Sumatra, and Vietnam. It is a robust rodent measuring 15-22 cm with and 12-15 cm tail, 300 g weight, rounded head, and broad muzzle. Its fur is coarse, dark greyish brown speckled with buff on the top and pale on the underside. Like bandicoots, they have the habit of erecting piles of long hairs and grunting on being excited. Noctunal and fossorial, they live in extensive burrows which may lie at a depth of 1 m and may have as many as 12 openings. It is a great destroyer of crops at every stage of their growth.

7. Gerbils

Gerbils, also called antelope rats differ from rats in having their tails clothed in fur (not naked like rats) and ending in a tassle. Their hind feet are much longer than rats of equal size that enable them to run by bounds. There are two species of gerbils : *Tatera indica* (Indian gerbil, 15-18 cm long tail and reddish-brown to fawn or greyish-fawn dorsum and white underside; it is noctunal in habit and lives in simple burrows with 3-10 openings, a central chamber and a few bold runs), and *Meriones hurrianae* (the Indian desert gerbil, 17-18 cm long with equally long tail, 65 g weight and sandy-yellow to brownish-grey dorsum and dirty white venter; it is diurnal in habit and lives in extensive but unplanned burrow).

8. Squirrels

There are a number of genera of squirrels found in India but the genus *Funambulus* with two species *F. pennanti* (five-striped palm squirrel) and *F. palmarum* (three-striped palm squirrel) are important from our (control) point of view. Five-striped squirrels are predominant in the North and three-striped ones are predominant in the South. Both are diurnal and arboreal with their peaks of activity in the morning and early evening depending on man for food but also supplementing it with fruits, seeds, vegetables, crops, occasionally insects (acridids in particular) and eggs of birds. Their damage to fruit gardens is severe.

9. Porcupines

The Indian crested porcupine, *Hystrix indica* is the largest rodent found in our country. It occurs from the Russian Turkestan, Syria to India and Sri Lanka. It measures 65-75 cm, weighs about 10-18 kg and is covered with quills of deep brown to black and white bands alternating with each other. A long crest of bristles is present on the head and white rattling quills on its short tail. It likes to inhabit rocky habitats (in caves) but is also found in stabilised sand dunes (in long burrows). It breeds from March to October with peak period during monsoon months. Its litter size is 1-3. It is mostly destructive to tuberous crops like sweet potato, potato, onions, and carrots but can also damage forest trees by girdling them.

Management of Rodents

The various techniques to manage rodents include cultural, mechanical, biological and chemical control practices.

Cultural control. Deep ploughing upto 45 cm, reduction of size and trimming of field bunds at the time of land preparation would certainly go a long way in controlling rodents Weed management and removal of burrows reduce availability of alternative food and shelter.

Mechanical control. Guarding of rat attacks by means of rodent-proof containers and plastering storage structures help in checking rodent infestation. Trapping is an economical and effective way of reducing rodent population. Trapped rats should be killed by drowning cages in ponds and dead rats should be buried deep in the soil. The trapped rats should not be released in the fields as they usually come back to their original place.

Biological control. A number of predators like snakes, owls, eagles, mangooses, etc. contribute to natural regulation of rodent population. Keeping cats in houses also checks the rat population.

Chemical control. The two most commonly employed chemical control measures include poison baits and fumigation.

(*i*) ***Poison baits.*** The most effective method of controlling rats is the use of poison baits. The poisons used in the baits are of two types: (*a*) acute poisons which are used in a single dose, e.g. strychnine hydrochloride, zinc phosphide, norbormide (Raticate), sodium fluoro-acetate, thallium sulphate, ANTU (Alphanaphthyl thiourea); and (*b*) chronic poisons which act as blood anticoagulants and are used in multiple doses. They include hydroxy coumarins (Warfarin, Fumarin, Tomarin, Recumin) and indandions (Pival, Radione, Valone). These poisons are lethal when consumed for several days, as they cause external and internal haemorrhage. The other anticoagulant rodenticides (Brodicacoum, Bromadiolane) are lethal in a single dose but the rats die after several days of poisoning.

Zinc phosphide (2% bait) is the most commonly used rodenticide in India. The bait is prepared by mixing 1 part of zinc phosphide with 40 parts of whole or cracked grains of wheat, gram, maize, *bajra* or sorghum smeared with vegetable oil. Racumin bait (0.0375% bait) is more effective against the bandicoot rat than other species. The bait is prepared by mixing 50 g of 0.75 per cent racumin powder, 20 ml of groundnut or sunflower oil and 20 g of powdered sugar in 1 kg of cracked wheat or any other cereal. Another bait (0.005% Bromadiolone bait) can be prepared by mixing 20 g of 0.25 per cent Bromadiolone powder, 20 g of oil and 20 g of powdered sugar in 1 kg of any cereal flour. The mixture is wrapped in paper packets which are distributed in the field at 10-15 m distance. For better results in the field, the poison operations with zinc phosphide should be preceded by careful prebaiting, i.e. false baiting with non-poisoned bait for 1-2 days. Field operations with zinc phosphide result in 70-80 per cent reduction of rodent population. The rest of the population acquires bait shyness after a single exposure to the bait. Poison baiting with zinc phosphide should not be repeated within 2-3 months. The residual population should be controlled by the fumigation of burrows or by baiting with warfarin.

(*ii*) ***Fumigation of burrows.*** Another effective method of rat control is killing them inside the burrows by fumigation. Aluminium phosphide tablets (2 tablets of 0.6 g or half tablet of 3 g per burrow) have been found to be very effective and safe. After introducing a tablet into a live burrow, the opening is closed tight with soil. The chemical reacts with soil moisture and deadly phosphine gas is generated.

Environmental control. Rat infestations get encouragement from several environmental factors such as delapidated conditions of the buildings/godowns, collection of refuse on streets, neglect of any patch of land/field, high bunds around fields, etc. If these factors are removed, rats will not find the surrounding congenial for their living and survival. Therefore, new buildings should be designed appropriately, old structures (doors, etc.) repaired, refuse quickly and correctly disposed, bunds made lowest and thinnest, and animal yards kept scrupulously clean.

It is desired to initiate control measures against the rats at large scale covering large continuous area, in the form of a campaign, to achieve the worthwhile results; otherwise they breed so fast that the population reaches the same level within a few months.

OTHER MAMMALS

1. Monkeys

Monkeys are found all over India, macaques living in villages near temples, often in towns also ; langurs (*Seminopithecus*) in forests or rocky cliffs sometimes coming to human habitations. Both live in troups. Macaques feed on human food, fruits and insects while langurs are strictly vegetarians feeding on leaves, fruits and young shoots. Macaques are mischievous and a nuisance destroying fruits in orchard, entering houses, damaging clothes and biting. Monkeys could be rabid and so their bites should not be ignored. Due to religious sentiments of the people and hence for fear of public reaction, monkeys are not shot or poison baited. They are usually trapped and supplied to laboratories within the country and abroad for research purposes. Male chemosterilization and castration are also suggested to keep their numbers down.

2. Hares and Rabbits

Distributed all over India, they do not burrow but hide under bushes preferring open bushy plains or cultivated fields, and are nocturnal in habit. They destroy crops like sorghum, millets, sesame and bark of young tress. They could be brought about by strychnine treated carrots, apples, grains or green hays.

3. Flying Fox

These are found in tropical India roosting during the day on big trees like banyan, peepal and tamarind. Nocturnal in habit, they feed and damage all kinds of fruits, even young coconut, except citrus. Explosives are strung on the tree roosts to kill or stun them (but this can be done in non-residential areas), noise repellents are used extensively and trapping with prickly bushes held on long poles to disturb the animals is also possible.

4. Jackals, Wolves and Wild Dogs

Jackals are found in hilly and mountaineous regions but are quite common in plains near towns and villages. They live in holes, on ground, in unused buildings and dense grasses, and are nocturnal feeding on carcases, sugarcane, maize cobs, melons, fallen ber (*Zizyphus*) fruits, etc. Wolves live in mountains and rock caves or burrow in sand-dunes of desert. They hunt deer, rodents, wild sheep, antelopes and even domesticated animals and man. Hunting is carried out both during the night and day. Wild dogs are confined to forests living in caves and hunting animals even larger than themselves like deer, buffalo, bear and tiger. Domesticated animals that stray into jungles are also attacked. Jackals could be poison-baited with meat treated with strychnine, wolves can be dealt with the help of dogs of Gaddi breed and all the three could be controlled by shooting.

5. Nilgai

They occur from the Himalayas to Karnataka except Bengal, Assam and Malabar coast. They avoid dense forests and roam about in the hills or in the plains covered with grass or shrubs with few trees around. They live in herds and feed on grasses, carrot, *mahua* flowers, leaves/fruits like ber (*Zizyphus*), crops of sorghum, millets, sesame and wheat. Shooting during the day is the most effective method but their numbers have already dwindled due to indiscriminate killing.

6. Wild Boar

Found all over India, it lives in scant jungles or grasses in herds. It is omnivorous feeding on crops, tuberous roots, carrions, and insects. Its habit of uprooting the trees does considerable damage to crops and plantations. It is, however, very intelligent and bold with acute sense of smell. Shoot at sight is the best method of control but due to their meat being a delicacy, their numbers have already greatly declined due to poaching.

7. Elephant

Elephas maximus (=*indicus*) found in India and *Loxodonta* (=*Elephas*) *africana* occurring in Africa are the only two extant species of the huge herbivors. The animals inhabit jungles feeding on bark, tender shoots and leaves of the trees. But sometimes they also stray into the neighbouring crop fields when they destroy more than they eat. While these animals are a protected species, their numbers have been kept down by poaching carried out for their tusks.

8. Sambhar

Found in Assam and Kumaun and up to the peninsular India, it lives in herds in forests and feeds on grasses, cultivated crops and fruits. It is a great destroyer of crops. Shooting, fencing (two parallel fences 3-4 m apart and 3 m high), use of metal and wooden guards around trees; exploders and fireworks are some of the other methods of controlling these animals.

9. Antelope

Found in the plains of India, these animals live in herds of 20-30 and feed on grasses and cereal crops which they damage by grazing and trampling. Fencing by laying thorny bushes and sharpened bamboo stakes are the best protection. Noise repellent may be of some value.

10. Hedgehog

These are confined to dry western and north-western parts of India. They live underneath thorny bushes, grasses or sand holes feeding from dusk to dawn on insects, worms, lizards, rats and roots of tuber crops. Fumigation with phosphine (placing 3 g tablet of $AlPO_4$ in the burrow and closing its mouth) is a good method of control.

11. Sloth Bear

It occurs in the forests of Himalayan base up to Sri Lanka and is recognised from black bears by its longer muzzle and white V breast mark. Omnivorous, it feeds on insects, carrions, fruits, roots, sugarcane, maize and honey combs which are its most prized food items procured by laborious climb or vigorous shaking of trees. Human voice, fire and strong light frighten it away. While passing through jungles, men move in groups carrying torches and talking loudly. Shooting, of course, is the best method of controlling it.

12. Chital

Also found in the forests at the foot of Himalayas up to Sri Lanka (absent in north-west deserts), it lives in large herds eating grasses, fruits, barks and crop. Its number has already greatly declined by indiscriminate killing for its beautiful hide. However, its control method is similar to that of sambhar.

BIRDS

It is interesting to note that only 25 of about 1200 species of birds found in India (*i.e.* only 2.1%) have been reported to inflict damage to crops and fruits. Certain pestiferous bird species have shown a tremendous increase in their populations. It would appear that, in general, grainivorous birds became abundant with the increase in area under grain crops and the subsequent storage of grains in godown or bulk storage.

1. Crow

Found up to a height of 1200 m, this bird is a great parasite of man. It builds its nests on trees and telephone poles and is famous for its stupidity of bringing up the young ones of cuckoo. It feeds on any thing and every thing, *i.e.* eggs, crops (groundnut, maize, sorghum, any grain), fruits and flesh (carrion). Slow poisoning with thallium sulphate is useful since quick death with strong poisons makes them abandon the area. Trapping and acetylene exploders are other methods.

2. Parrot

Found up to 1200 m, this bird is a great destroyer of fruits and crops (peas, gram, maize, grains), wasting more than eating. Its holes in the trees can be fumigated with phosphine. Bird catchers catch it with 'lassa' (a strong glue) rubbed on the tip of a long pole and orchard keepers try to protect their fruits by sounding empty tins and cannisters.

3. House Sparrow

Occuring up to a height of 200 m, this bird is also a great parasite of man living in homes. Principally grainivorous, it can also feed on insects and kitchen scraps and is a great destroyer of grain crop. Poison-baiting is a good method of its control. Spray of thiurum (0.6%) on crops at milk-seed stage acts as a repellent to this bird.

4. Baya

Occurring in the plains, this bird is famous for its meat and nests which it builds with woven grass in the form of retorts hanging from trees by the hundreds. It lives in huge colonies and feeds on seeds as adults and insects as nestlings. It damages crops like paddy, sorghum and millets, the damage becoming serious because of their sheer numbers. The reed beds near water stretches where they prefer to build their nests should be destroyed or treated with a strong contact insecticide.

5. Myna

This bird can be found up to 2,700 m height. It builds its nests in tree holes with feather, twigs, rags and rubbish. The bird is known for its sharp chattering calls that are annoying to the ears. Being omnivorous, it feeds on insects, earthworms, fruits, kitchen scraps and crops like maize and wheat when their grains are about to mature. It could be poison-baited with bread crumbs or trapped.

6. Pigeon

It has been recorded up to 4000 m in the Himalayas. It makes its rather crude nests with coarse twigs on rocks but prefers tall buildings like churches, temples, uninhabited historical buildings, minarets, power houses, stations, etc., where it becomes a nuisance by its droppings and noise. Individually or in large groups, it destroys grain crops like wheat, bajra, sorghum, maize, etc. It can be killed by offering poisoned grains. Wire-netting around strategic places could prevent their entry into buildings. Its meat being tasteful, it is generally hunted.

7. Peakcock

It is found up to 1500 m and makes its nests in shallow scrape on the ground, in a dense thicket, in boundary walls or on thatched roof-tops. It is a national bird of India, is also considered sacred and, therefore, not killed. But it does considerable damage to grains, vegetables (pepper, brinjal, tomato) and other crops. It also feeds on isnects and reptiles. It is illegal to kill this bird, trapping is done for its beautiful feathers, Chemical repellents can be tried on sown seeds and acoustal repellent in the fields.

8. Seven Sisters

Found every where in India, it lives in groups of seven and so its name. It is very destructive to germinating seeds, seedlings due to its constant habit of pecking in the soil and fruits. Being intruders in homes, they are a source of great nuisance due to their sharp and unmusical noise. It can be easily trapped and poison-baited.

MANAGEMENT OF BIRDS

(*i*) **Cultural methods.** These include deep sowing of seeds, covering the seeds with soil, pre-and post-dating of sowing, growing of trap crops near the main one and use of plant varieties that are physically and gustatorily unattractive to birds. It has been observed that in some plants, morphological features such as shed layer of anthers or awns (hybrid *bajra*), tight spathe (maize) grain size, compact or loose earheads (pearl millet), large glumes (bracts), loose panicles and gooseneck-shaped (pendant) heads (sorghum) and gustatory features such as an extra quantity of tannins in the grains (sorghum) make the crop unacceptable (resistant) to birds.

(*ii*) **Use of nylon nets.** Spreading a nylon net over the crops and orchards can offer protection against bird attacks.

(*iii*) **Habitat manipulation.** A preferred bird-habitat can be made unpreferred by removing food, water and shelter.

(*iv*) **Electrified perches.** Bird perches could be electrified to disperse the birds or kill them by regulating the voltage.

(*v*) **Use of deterrents.** (*i*) A conventional deterrent commonly used by farmers is 'scare crow', a human figure erected in the fields, may scare some birds like crows, (*ii*) acetylene gun, a device by which loud bangs are produced by the action of water on calcium carbide can offer some protection to orchards, (*iii*) use of bioacoustics in which bird's stress or alarm signals are recorded and played in the fields at intervals which should be kept changing to prevent the birds getting used to them, (*iv*) use of repellents like some insecticides (lindane, malathion) or an effective avian feeding deterrent (tetra methyl thiuram disulphite, TMDT) can repel birds, and (*v*) use of baits of some immoblising agents such as alpha chloralose (1-2%) that has been found to immobilise and stupefy birds like pigeons and sparrows.

(*vi*) **Fumigation.** Fumigation of nests with phosphine tablets could be used in case of such birds only which make their nests on trees or in wall holes (like mynas, parrots).

(*vii*) **Trapping.** Various trapping devices such as flood light trap, decoy trap, nets, cages, etc. can be used to trap the birds. Bird catchers often used a very sticky glue, 'lassa' on the tip of a pole; the bird just cannot rid itself if it comes in contact with it.

(*viii*) **Destruction of birds.** The birds could be destroyed by shooting. But the method should be resorted to only in rare cases and with the knowledge whether or not the bird belongs to the protected list.

(*ix*) **Destruction of nests.** This has a limited use in view of their scattered distribution and often inaccessibility due to being located on heights.

(*x*) **Poison baiting.** Bajra (*Pennisetum typhoides*) seeds soaked in fenthion (2%) emulsion and dried, are placed in small cups and hung from the rafters or branches of trees to control house sparrow. A piece of *chapatti* dipped in methyl parathion (0.3%) or fenthion (2%) placed on top of a roof is a good bait for house crow.

SNAILS AND SLUGS

Snails and slugs (Fig. 14.1 A, B) belong to the invertebrate phylum Mollusca (class Gasteropoda, sub-class Pulmonata). Both these animals are amphibious capable of living on land and water. Snails differ from slugs in having a spirally coiled shell over their body which in slugs is reduced and completely hidden under the mantle. The snails that do a lot of damage to our crops are the common garden snails, *Helix, Macrochlamys indica,* the green-house snail, *Opeas gracilis* and the giant African snail, *Achatina fulica,* the last named having migrated from Africa has established itself in the Andaman islands, coastal regions of Assam, Bengal, Tamil Nadu and Kerala. The common Indian slugs are *Limax* sp., *Laevicaulis alte, Arion* sp., etc.

Life-history. The common snail breeds in the spring and the summer. It makes a hole of 1.24 cm in diameter and 3 cm in depth in damp soil, in which it lays eggs in a loose mass of about 60. The eggs hatch within two weeks and the young snails start feeding upon tender plants. The shell increases in size with age and the snail is full-grown in about two years. Snails are seen at all hours, except during mid day when it is hot and dry. In winter, they stay in colonies and are found among rockeries, loose boards of fences, at the bottom of hedges, in rubbish heaps, etc. The slugs feed at night in damp places and destroy young shoots of various plants. Under dry conditions, their population is reduced considerably.

Damage. The snails live in humid environment under bushes, stones, pots, uncared wooden logs, etc. They are active from spring up to the onset of winter and hibernate/aestivate in very cold/very hot and dry months. They are nocturnal, carnivorous, pestiferous and scavengers feeding on the dead bodies of their kind and carrions in agriculture, they do a lot of damage to vegetables (ipomea, beans, lady's finger, cucurbits, etc.) and garden plants (violets, marygold, papaya), the damage being more serious in the seedling stage. African giant snails even damage plantation crops like arecanut, rubber buds and coffee.

Management. (*i*) They could be handpicked and then killed by immersing in 10 per cent solution of common salt or in boiling water and buried in the fields away from the popoulated area. (*ii*) Snails and slugs can be managed by biological methods. (*a*) Snails predatory on other snails are *Euglandina rosea* and *Gonaxis quadrilateralis* but they are not found in India, (*b*) larvae of Indian glow-worm, *Lamprophorus tenebrosus,* lacerate flesh and feed on the slime secreted by the snails; larvae of another insect belonging to dipteran family Sciomyzidae (genus *Tetanocera*) attack aquatic and terrestrial snails, slugs and their eggs; hermit crab

Coenobita enter the shell of *Achatina* to feed on it and the millipede *Orthomorpha* secrete hydrocyanic acid that instantly immobilises the snails, and (*c*) snails are known to suffer from a leukoderma like diseases; pathogens of this disease can be water extracted and sprayed on snail colonies to spread the same. (*iii*) Metaldehyde (5%), copper sulphate solution (1%) and insecticides (arsenates, persistent organochlorines, etc.) are employed as molluscicides of which metaldehyde spray or dust (sold as *Metadex*) in 5% dilution has been found to be the most effective. Since slugs secrete a lot of slime that prevent contact with the irritants, repeat treatment will be needed in their case. A bait of 30% bran + 2% metaldehyde proves a good killer for the slug, *Laevicaulis*; for *Achatina*, a mixture of cut pieces of papaya stem (or fallen yellow leaves) + 5% metaldehyde acts as good poison-bait (these snails are attracted to papaya stem pieces, its yellow leave or more strongly to marygold plants which singly or in mixture can be used as attractant ; likewise freshly powdered lime sprinkled around the plants acts as a deterrent.

MITES

Mites belong to the order Acarina of the class Arachnida. They are the pests of both animals and plants. Plant pests belong to the families Tetranychidae (spider mites, so called because some of them weave webs on the plants), Tenuipalpidae (false spider mites), Tarsonemidae (tarsonemids), Eriophyidae (blister or gall mites) and Eupodidae (eupodids). Of these, the spider mites are the most important and prevalent. Some of these mites (*e.g. Tetranychus urticae*) produce considerable amounts of fine silken webbing on the plant surface but others produce little or no webbing.

The presence of mites may go unnoticed because of their minute size. However, symptoms of attack are often apparent before the mites themselves can be seen. For control, it is important to be able to recognise mite injury at an early stage. Mites normally feed on the undersurface of the leaves but the symptoms are more easily seen on the uppersurface. Two kinds of symptoms are produced by mites. While feeding carried out by tetranychids produce blotchings on the leaf-surface, that by tarsonemids and eriophyids produce distortion, puckering or stunting of leaves and other parts of the plant. Some species of eriophyids produce distinct galls or blisters.

Tetranychidae

1. ***Tetranychus ludeni* (Zacher)**. This is a very important pest of many vegetable crops like cowpea, brinjal, bhindi, etc. It generally prefers to live on the underside of the leaves but as the population increases, it spreads over the entire leaf and eventually over the entire plant. Initially the leaves take a stippled appearance due to formation of pale yellow spots which finally become brown. Moderate population may reduce the yield while severe infestation could kill the entire plant. In eastern U.P., it severely damages the cowpea crop.
2. ***Tetranychus cinnabarinus* (Boisduval).** (Fig. 14.1C). This species has a world-wide distribution. Its infestaion has been recorded on vegetables, fruits, cotton and ornamental plants. Brinjal, cotton and the lady's finger (bhindi) are the worst sufferers. The mite is more troublesome during periods of warm dry weather. As a result of its attack, leaves get covered with strands of webbing which affect photosynthesis and so the yield. Eventually, the leaves dry up and fall off. Growth, flowering and fruit setting in the plants are greatly affected.

3. ***Tetranychys neocaledonicus* (Andre).** It is one of the more serious pests of brinjal besides other vegetables. The mites in all stages remain confined to the undersurface of the leaves covered with their webs where dust particles get entangled. The continuous sucking from leaves produces yellow spots on them which ultimately turn brown. The leaves wither and fall, and the plants lose vitality which affects their yield.
4. ***Eutetranychus orientalis* (Klein).** This is a serious pest of fruits, ornamental and medicinal plants. They are generally found on the uppersurface of the leaves. The affected leaves turn yellowish brown which afterwards dry up and fall off. The species is serious citrus, *Zizyphus* (ber), peach, fig and castor.
5. ***Eutetranychus hirsti* (Prichard Baker).** This is a serious pest of fig in whole of North India. Due to the infestation of these mites, light green patches are produced which turn yellowish green, then brown with rough and dry texture. Such leaves along with the fruits drop-off prematurely, often resulting in complete defoliation of the plants. The infested fruits get shrivelled, fail to ripen and ultimately fall off.
6. ***Panonychus citri* (McGregor).** (Fig. 14.1D). It is an important pest of citrus. The infested leaves are speckled with whitish spots which later turn silvery or brown and drop prematurely. Fruits are also attacked which turn grey or yellow.
7. ***Oligonychus indicus* (Hirst).** It is a serious pest of sugarcane, arecanut, coconut palm and some cereals. When infested, the lower fronds of the leaves show burning discolouration.
8. ***Oligonychus coffeae* (Nietner).** It is a major pest of coffee, tea and also jute in both North-East and South India. Damage is caused by scraping of the surface of the leaves and sucking the sap. Attacked leaves become bronzed and fall.
9. ***Petrobia latens* (Miller).** During recent years, this species has emerged as a serious pest of wheat, barley and coriander in the drier regions of Madhya Pradesh, Rajasthan, Delhi, Haryana and Punjab. It is active during the winter months with peak activity during February-March. Heavily infested wheat crops show drying of leaves, chlorosis and formation of no or only shrivelled seeds.
10. ***Schizotetranychus andropogoni* Hirst.** It causes serious damage to sugarcane in Tamil Nadu and Andhra Pradesh. The damage is done by scraping the leaf-surface and sucking of cell sap that leads to withering. Plants in shade have larger populations of this mite.
11. ***Brevipalpus phoenicis* (Geijskes).** (Fig. 14.1E). It is an important pest of many fruits, ornamental and plantation crops. It causes first yellowing and then browning of leaves, brownish patches appear on the fruits as well, specially in guava. Sometimes, the fruits may split up.
12. ***Larvacarus transitans* (Ewing).** It is a serious pest of *Zizyphus* (ber) in Rajasthan. It causes soft minute galls on the twigs. Yield due to its infestation may go down by as much as 30 per cent.

Tarsonemidae

13. ***Polyphagotarsonemus latus* (Banks).** (Fig. 14.1F). These are pests of chilli that cause great losses throughout the country, more particularly in Tamil Nadu, Andhra Pradesh, Maharashtra and West Bengal. It attacks tea and potato also. Infested leaves show crinkling and curling, often leading to defoliation. The yield is considerable reduced.

Eriophyidae

14. ***Aceria guerreronis*** **(Keifer).** This mite pest has been reported as a serious pest of coconut in Kerala and Tamil Nadu. The mites are seen in colonies in the perianth of developing nuts and live in the white tender portion covered by the inner bract of perianth and suck the sap from the tender meristematic mesocarp tissues. Maturing nuts up to nine months old harbour the mites. The feeding results in warts and numerous longitudinal fissures on the husk of developing nuts.

15. ***Aceria mangiferae*** **(Sayed).** This species is associated with the mango malformation disease. The disease has assumed an alarming magnitude in North India and it is threatening the very existence of mango industry. It causes floral and vegetation malformations.

16. ***Aceria litchii*** **(Keifer).** It is one of the devastating pests of litchi especially in Bihar and West Bengal. As a result of the mite infestation, the undersurfaces of the leaves show abnormal growths of epidermal cells in the form of hair-like velvety layer of chocolate brown color erineum (abnormal growth of leaf hair).

17. ***Aceria cajani*** **(Channa Basavanna).** This mite has been associated with the sterility disease in pigeonpea. It is believed to be the carrier of a virus that causes this disease. It is a widely spread mite found all over the country.

18. ***Calacarus carinatus*** **(Green).** It is a major pest of tea both in the North and South India. Fields affected by this mite can be recognised from a distance by the bronzed, coppery-brown or smoky colouration of the leaves. Severe attack leads to suppression of the growth of the shoot and defoliation.

19. ***Acalitus gossypii*** **(Banks).** It is a serious pest of cotton, particularly in Bihar and Gujarat. In Bihar, it is commonly known as leaf-blister mite, and in Gujarat, as cotton-woolly mite. It attacks also balls to cause greater losses.

20. ***Aceria jasmini*** **Channa Basavanna.** It is a serious pest of jasmine in Tamil Nadu causing felt-like white hairy outgrowths on the surface of leaves, tender stem and flower buds. Growth is stunted and flower production is affected.

Management of Mite Pests

(*i*) **Cultural control.** The following cultural methods can be adoped to keep mite populations down : (*a*) monoculture cropping should be avoided, (*b*) intercropping using non-host crops should be done, (*c*) destruction of mite-damaged parts particularly in the case of mango malformation and litchi erineum formation will minimise mite attack, and (*d*) clean culture.

(*ii*) **Biological control.** (*a*) ***Mites***. Some of the predatory mites provide an effective control over the phytophagous mites by voraceously feeding on them. Their examples are *Amblyseius longispinosus* and *A. alstoniae* (Phytoseidae), *Agistemus industani* (Stigmaeidae), and *Hemicheyletia balkeri* (Cheyletidae) (*b*) ***Insects***. The insects which are voraceous feeders on mites are *Stethorus pauperculus*, the coccinellid beetles that cannot survive without mite (food); *Scolothrips indicus and Chrysopa* sp. also feed on mites.

(*iii*) **Chemical control.** Till recently, the problem of controlling phytophagous mites was successfully coped with organophosphorus insecticides, *e.g.* dimethoate, oxydemeton methyl, malathion, phosalone, etc. But it was found that after prolonged use of these substances, group resistance to organophosphorus compounds appeared very rapidly in the mites. The need, therefore, arose to develop new chemicals with somewhat different mode of action. And thus were born the specific acaricides capable of killing phytophagous mites in all stages of their development. The important properties of these compounds are that they are persistent in action, slightly or moderately toxic to man and animals, and cause no serious side effects to environment. Some of these compounds are tetradifon, chlorbenzalite and dicofol.

NEMATODES

Nematodes belong to class Nematoda of the Phylum Nemathelminthes. They are minute worm-like animals without true body cavity (coelom) and with unsegmented, bilaterally symmetrical and externally cuticularised body. They are found all over the world in salt and fresh water, soil, animals and plants. In plants, they are either endoparasites or ectoparasites. The mouthparts of nematodes are armed with a hollow protrusible stylet or spear used to puncture plant cells for extracting the sap. The stylet is a structure of taxonomic value being characteristic of different groups. Of the 10 orders of the class Nematoda, only 2 namely Tylenchida and Dorylamida contain plant-parasitic nematodes. Of these two, while the former are parasitic to plants (largely roots), the latter are vectors of plant viruses and may be free living, migratory or ectoparasitic. The important genera of Tylenchida are described herein.

1. *Meloidogyne* spp.

These are called root-knot nematodes as they produce galls on the roots which may appear as string of beads on smaller root branches or a heavily knotted root-mass. With the formation of galls, the flow of water and food through the roots is blocked and plants starve and die. The eggs are deposited in a mass within the root-galls. The first stage larva lies within the egg-shell while the second stage larva is free-living and is the infective stage that enters new roots to feed on it. Two important species of this genus are *M. incognita* and *M. javanica* which attack solanaceous (tomato, brinjal, etc.), leguminous, malvaceous and cucurbitaceous plants.

2. *Heterodera* spp.

These are cyst-forming nematodes. Here also the second stage larva is the free-living infective stage. The first stage larvae or eggs may remain dormant in the soil in the form of cysts for years. The infested roots proliferate into a shallow bushy system and the infected field can be recognised by circular or oval patches of plant showing very poor growth. An important species is the golden nematode of potato, *H. rostochinensis*.

3. *Globodera* spp.

The golden cyst nematode, *G. rostochiensis* is a notorious pest of potato in the Niligiri and Simla hills, but it also infests tomato, brinjal and chillies. The infested plants, when pulled out, show clusters of white and golden spherical bodies attached to the roots and tubers, about the size of a sand grain. These are the cysts of mature female bodies and generally appear when the potato crop is 2-3 months old. The larvae feed on the juice sucked from the roots. The attacked plants remain stunted and give a dull and unhealthy appearance. The lower leaves turn yellow, wither and drop off. The root system is poorly developed and the size of the tubers is reduced, resulting in considerable reduction in yield.

4. *Aphelenchoides* spp.

The white tip nematode, *A. besseyi,* is widely distributed in rice growing areas. In the pre-adult stage, it is carried by the paddy grains beneath the hull and at this stage it can remain alive for about two years. When nematode carrying seeds are sown, the immature forms become active, move up the plant along a thin film of moisture and feed on the foliage ectoparasitically. The adults lay eggs in the foliage and the larvae move to the panicle when formed and some larvae enter the grain. The leaf tips of the affected rice plant turn yellow, brown and finally white for 2-5 cm, which then dries up and hangs down. Tips of developing leaves become twisted and crinkled. The kernels are distorted and in extreme cases become chaffy.

5. *Tylenchulus* spp.

The citrus nematode, *Tylenchulus semipenetrans* (Fig. 14.1G) is an example of this genus. Its body remains partly outside the root. The exposed part of the larva that is destined to become a female after moults, enlarges to become sac-like or saccate. At maturity the female deposits eggs in a jelly-like mass. The males remain wormlike, small and non-feeding, and they are also not necessary for reproduction. The symptoms of the affected plants are early wilting, death of terminal buds and death of foliage and twigs.

6. *Pratylenchus* spp.

These are root-lesion nematodes. The nematodes are endoparasitic in fibrous roots and are the most important destroyers of roots. They move from root to root feeding and laying eggs. The eggs may also be laid in the soil.

7. *Anguina* spp.

These nematodes are obligate plant parasites which produce galls in stems, leaves and flowers of a number of graminaceous crops. *A. tritici,* which causes ear-cockles in wheat is the well-known species of this genus. The hard round galls containing nematodes replace the seeds in the ears. The second stage larvae liberated from the galls in moist soil, infest wheat seedlings at an early stage. For sometime, they live as ectoparasites on the young leaves and as the flowers appear, they enter their tissues. After pairing, the females lay hundreds of eggs in the galls.

Management of Nematodes

Various methods have been employed for suppression of nematodes; the choice of method largely depends on the nematode-crop combination and value of the crop.

Cultural control. (*i*) Intercropping of okra with sesame reduces the attack of root-knot nematode on the former. (*ii*) The spread of golden cyst nematode can be checked by avoiding the cultivation of potato, brinjal, tomato and chillies in infested fields; adjusting the crop rotation so that potato and related crops in the same field are sown after 4 years and using uninfested potato as seed. (*iv*) Nematodes can be suppressed by sowing clean seed in uninfested soil. (*v*) Summer following with periodical raking up the soil through ploughing or harrowing and flooding the field are some of the practices used for controlling nematodes, especially the root-knot nematodes.

Physical control. (*i*) The seed-borne white tip nematode of rice is controlled by dipping paddy seeds in hot water at 52-55°C for 15 minutes. (*ii*) Blowing hot air at 50°C for four hours into chambers containing sweet potato tubers kills the tuber-borne nematodes. (*iii*) The wheat gall nematode can be controlled by separating the galls from the wheat seed by floating them on water in a tub. After skimming off the lighter floating galls, seed should be dried before sowing.

Chemical control. (*i*) Dip the roots of nursery plants in dimethoate (0.03%) for six hours before transplanting to control root-knot nematodes. (*ii*) Citrus nematode can be controlled by using dibromochloropropane @ 25 litres per ha. Pulverise the soil in the basin area around a plant and mix the chemical thoroughly followed by flood irrigation. (*iii*) Golden cyst nematode can be controlled by using 450 litres of DD mixture or 25 kg of dibromochloropropane per ha.

*****

15 CHAPTER

PESTS OF STORED PRODUCTS

Grains

Major pests

1. *Sitotroga cerealella* (Olivier) (Angoumois grain moth, Lepidoptera : Gelechiidae)
2. *Plodia interpunctella* (Hubner) (Indian meal moth, Lepidoptera : Pyralidae)
3. *Cadra cautella* (Walker) (Almond moth, Lepidoptera : Pyralidae)
4. *Corcyra cephalonica* (Stainton) (Rice moth, Lepidoptera : Gelechiidae)
5. *Trogoderma granarium* Everts (Khapra beetle, Coleoptera.: Dermestidae)
6. *Sitophilus granarius* Linnaeus (Grain weevil, Coleoptera.: Curculionidae)
7. *Sitophilus oryzae* (Linnaeus) (Rice weevil, Coleoptera : Curculionidae)
8. *Tribolium castaneum* Herbst (Rust red flour beetle, Coleoptera : Tenebrionidae)
9. *Tribolium confusum* Duval (Flour beetle, Coleoptera : Tenebrionidae)
10. *Rhyzopertha dominica* (Fabricius) (Lesser grain borer, Coleoptera : Bostrichidae)

Minor pests

11. *Oryzaephilus surinamensis* (Linnaeus) (Saw-toothed grain beetle, Coleoptera : Silvanidae)
12. *Cryptolestes pusillus* (Schonherr) (Flat grain beetle, Coleoptera : Cucujidae)
13. *Latheticus oryzae* Waterhouse (Long-headed flour beetle, Coleoptera: Tenebrionidae)

14. *Tenebrio molitor* Linnaeus (Meal worm, Coleoptera : Tenebrionidae)
15. *Tenebroides mauritanicus* (Linnaeus) (Cadelle, Coleoptera: Trogosositidae)
16. *Lasioderma serricorne* (Fabricius) (Cigarette beetle, Coleoptera : Anobiidae)

Pulses

1. *Callosobruchus chinensis* (Linnaeus) (Gram dhora, Coleoptera : Bruchidae)
2. *Callosobruchus analis* (Fabricius) (Mung dhora, Coleoptera.: Bruchidae)

The total production of foodgrains in India is about 233 million tonnes. Since the cereals and pulses are the staple food of people in India, a substantial quantity is stored by the producers in their homes and by traders and government agencies in godowns for a year or so. When the grains are harvested in the field, they are practically free from insect infestation. The insects reach the grains either through the infested gunny bags or receptacles and through the storage of fresh grains in godowns already having infested grains. Almost all the insect pests of stored grains have a remarkably high rate of multiplication and within one season, they may destroy 7-10 per cent of the grains and contaminate the rest with undesirable odours and flavours. Although about 1000 species of insects have been associated with stored products in various parts of the world, about a dozen insect pests are important in India.

1. *Sitotroga cerealella* (Olivier) (Angoumois grain moth, Lepidoptera : Gelechiidae) (Fig. 15.1A)

Distribution. This pest is world-wide in distribution. In the Indian sub-continent, the pest is more abundant in the mountaineous areas or where the climate is rather mild.

Identification. The moth takes its name 'Angoumois' after the province of Angoumois in France where it was first reported in 1736 as a pest of wheat. The moth is buff-coloured with pointed hind wing bearing a heavy fringe of hairs and measures 1.0-1.2 cm in wing expanse. The full-grown larva is 5 mm long, white in colour with yellowish-brown head capsule.

Life-history. Breeding takes place from April to October. The insect overwinters as a hibernating larva and as the season warms up, it pupates in early spring. After emergence, moths mate within 24 hours and the females start laying eggs singly or in batches on or near the gain. The eggs are small and white, when freshly laid, turning reddish later on. A single female lays, on an average, 150 eggs, usually within a week after mating. The incubation period is about 4-8 days in summer. Newly emerged larvae bore into the grains and feed on the kernel. The larval stage may last about 3 weeks. Pupation occurs within cocoon inside the cavity made in the grains and the adult emerges from the hole bored by the larva before pupation. There are several generations in a year.

Host. Wheat, maize, sorghum, barley and other grains.

Damage. The damage is done by the larvae, maximally during the monsoon months, by boring into and feeding inside the grains. Upper layers of the heaps are most seriously infested where 50-100 per cent grains could be consumed. The infested grains give out an unpleasant smell and present an unhealthy appearance. The grains get covered with scales shed by the moths. In a heap of grain, it is the upper layers that are most severely affected.

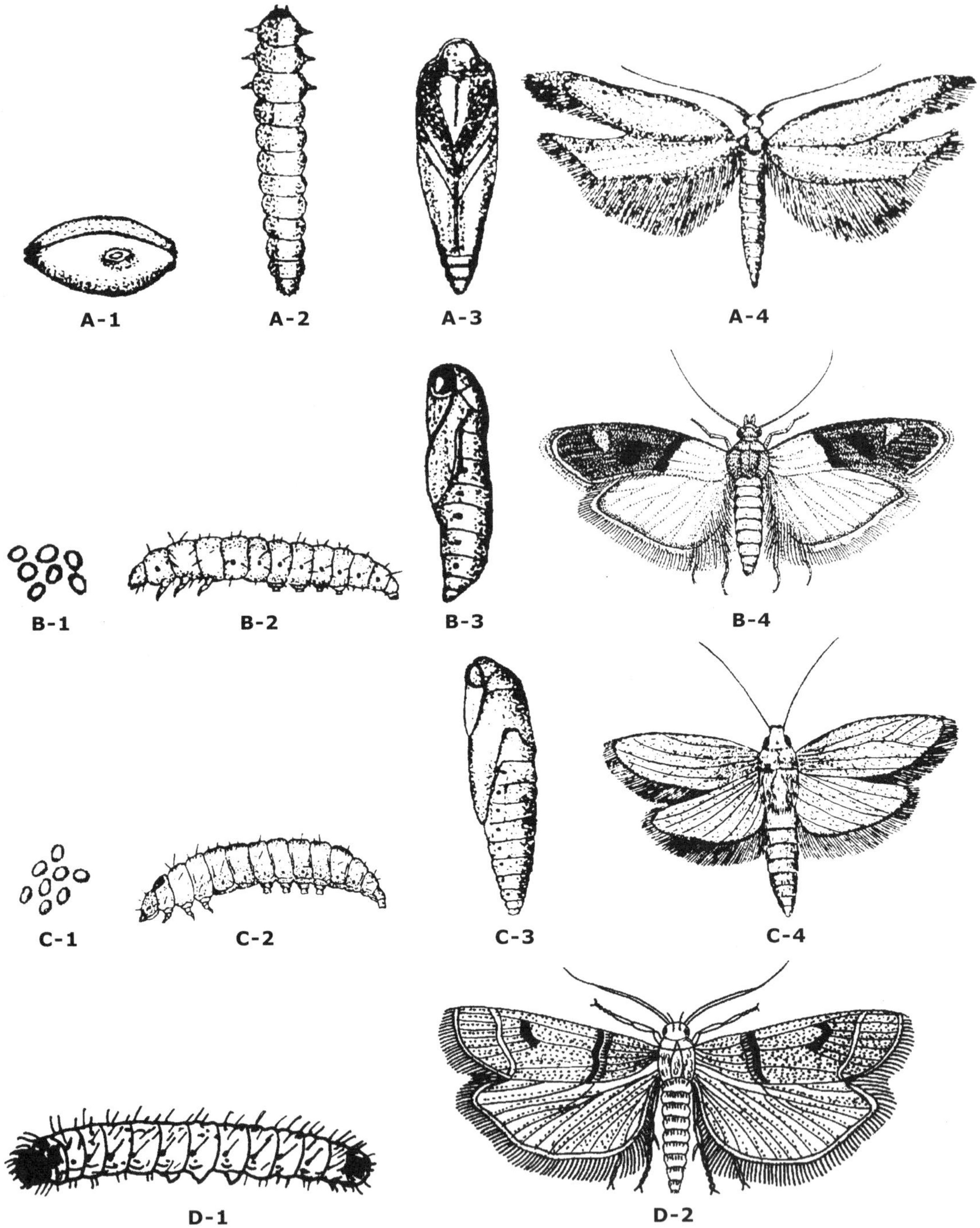

Fig. 15.1 Lepidopteran pests of stored grains. **A.** Angoumois grain moth, *Sitotroga cerealella* ; A-1. Egg on grain, A-2. Larva, A-3. Pupa, A-4. Adult. **B.** Indian meal moth, *Plodia interpunctella* ; B-1. Eggs, B-2. Larva, B-3. Pupa, B-4 Adult. **C.** Rice moth, *Corcyra cephalonica* ; C-1. Egg, C-2. Larva, C-3. Pupa, C-4. Adult. **D.** Almond moth, *Cadra cautella* ; D-1. Larva, D-2. Adult .

2. *Plodia interpunctella* (Hubner) (Indian meal moth, Lepidoptera : Pyralidae) (Fig. 15.1B)

Distribution. The insect is cosmopolitan in distribution.

Identification. The moth, 1.3-2.0 cm in wing-expanse, is partly copper coloured and partly whitish-grey with hind wing light coloured and fore wing partly dark coloured. The larva is a small whitish caterpillar (often tinged with green or pink) in early stages, a light-brown head, a prothoracic shield and an oval plate. On reaching maturity, it measures 8-13 mm in length.

Life-history. Breeding continues throughout the year under favourable warm conditions, however, in cold weather or in unheated buildings, the insect overwinters in the larval stage. The female moth lays 300-500 minute whitish ovate eggs, singly or in clusters, on or in clusters on or near the appropriate foodstuffs. The incubation period is 2-14 days depending upon weather. The larvae feed upon the grains of other foods and become full-grown in 30-35 days. They crawl up to the surface of the food material and pupate within a thin silken cocoon. The pupal stage lasts for 4-35 days. In summer, the life-cycle is completed in 5 or 6 weeks and there are 4-6 generations in a year.

Host. Grains, meals, soybean, dry fruits, herbs, nuts, dead insects, etc.

Damage. The damage is done by the caterpillars which feed covered under a silken web. The adults fly about from one bin to another spreading the infestation.

3. *Corcyra cephalonica* (Stainton) (Rice moth, Lepidoptera : Gelechiidae) (Fig. 15.1C))

Distribution. The rice moth is distributed in Asia, Africa, North America and Europe.

Identification. It is a pale greyish brown moth, a little larger than the Angoumois grain moth.

Life-history. The rice moth is active from March to November when all stages are noticed. It passes winter in the larval stage and the overwintered larvae pupate sometimes during February. The moths emerge in March. They are active at night and lay eggs singly or in groups of 3-5 each on the grains, bags and on other objects in the godowns. A single female may lay 62-150 eggs during its life-span of 2-4 days. The eggs hatch in 4-7 days and the larvae feed under silken web-like shelters, preferring the partially damaged grains. They grow in five stages and are full-fed in 21-41 days, after which they make silken cocoons among the infested grains for pupation. The pupal stage lasts 9-14 days and the adults live for over one week. They complete their life-cycle in 33-52 days and the pest completes approximately 6 generations in a year.

Host. Rice but can be also found in various grains like sorghum, maize, gram, groundnut and also cotton seeds.

Damage. The larvae alone damage the grains of rice and maize by feeding under silken webs. When infestation is high, the entire stock of grains may be converted into a webbed mass. Ultimately, a characteristic foul odour develops and the grains are rendered unfit for human consumption.

4. *Cadra cautella* (Walker) (Almond moth, Lepidoptera : Pyralidae (Fig. 15.1D))

Distribution. The distribution of the pest is world wide.

Identification. The moth, 1.2 cm in wing-expanse, is greyish in colour with transverse stripes on grey coloured wings.

Life-history. The female lays whitish eggs indiscriminately in cracks and crevices of the receptacles or on the food stuff. While feeding, the larvae spin tubes in the food material and are full-grown in 40-50 days. The full-grown larva is white with pinkish tinge and measures 1.5 cm. The larvae pupate inside the cocoons and pupal stage lasts for about 12 days. The life-cycle is completed in about two months and there are 5-6 generations in a year.

Host. Cereals, dry fruits like currants, dates, berries, figs, almonds, walnut, tamarind seed, even mango-pulp and dry garlic bulbs.

Damage. The damage is done by the caterpillars which tunnel into food material. The number of silken tubes is sometimes extremely high and these clog the mill machinery where the infested grains have been sent for milling.

5. *Trogoderma granarium* Everts (Khapra beetle, Coleoptera : Dermestidae) (Fig. 15.2A)

Distribution. It is distributed all over India and also in many other countries like UK, USA, Germany and Israel. In the Indian sub-continent, it is very destructive pest of wheat and other grains, particularly in the north-western dry regions of Pakistan, Rajasthan, Haryana and Punjab.

Identification. These are small (2-3 mm), dark-brown beetles with retractile head and clubbed antennae. Full-grown larva is 4 mm long, brownish with yellowish-brown bands across the body which is bristled and hairy. Males are half of the females in size and adults cannot fly.

Life-history. The insect breeds from April to October and hibernates in the larval stage from November to March in cracks and crevices of walls and floor or in other sheltered places. The eggs are laid singly or in groups on the grains. A female may lay 30-40 eggs in 1-7 days at the rate of 1-25 eggs per day. The incubation period varies from 4 to 10 days. The larva is full-fed in 24-40 days. Pupation takes place in the last larval skin among the grains and this stage lasts for 4-6 days. There are 4-5 generations in a year.

Host. Apart from wheat, the insect has been recorded on sorghum, oats, rice, barley, gram, maize, poppy, pulses, pistachio, linseed, walnut and other dried fruits.

Damage. The damage is done both by the grubs and adults, maximally during July-October. The grubs eat near the embryo region of the grains and are very destructive. They usually confine to the upper (50 cm) layers of the heap and are resistant to temperature, humidity, starvation (can survive without food for more than 4 years) and are, therefore, difficult to control.

6. *Sitophilus oryzae* (Linnaeus) (Rice weevil, Coleoptera : Curculionidae) [Fig. 15.2B]

Distribution. The pest is world-wide and is found practically throughout India.

Identification. Both the species (*S. oryzae* and *S. granarius*) are of the same size and colour. They are small (3 mm) reddish brown beetles with cylindrical body and a long curved rostrum. The elytra bears four reddish or yellowish spots and thorax is fitted with round depressions. The grubs (5 mm) are white with yellowish brown head. Unlike *S. granarius*, meta-thoracic wings of this insect are well developed.

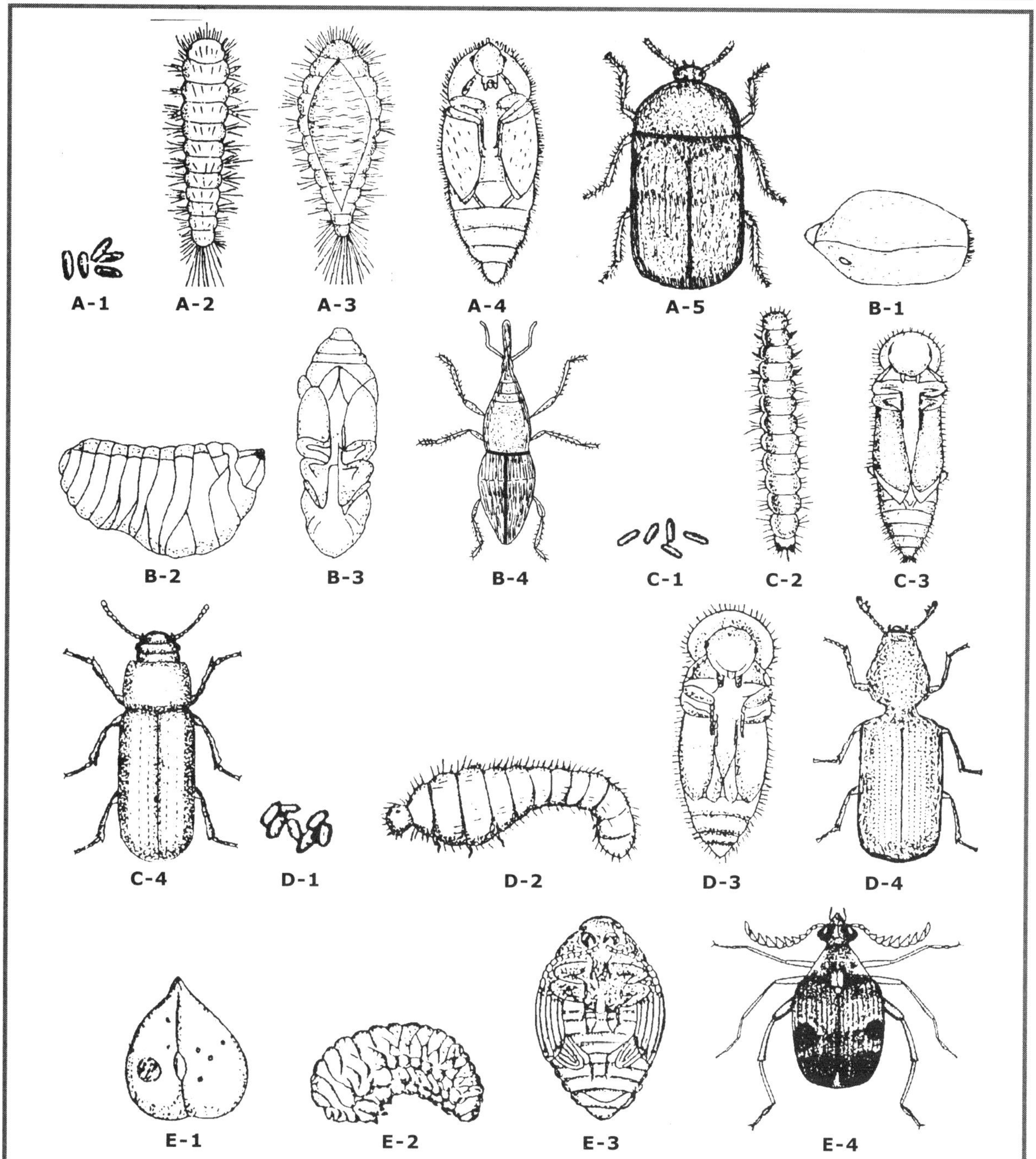

Fig. 15.2 Coleopteran pests of stored grains. **A.** Khapra beetle, *Trogoderma granarium*; A-1. Eggs, A-2. Larva, A-3. Pupa in larval skin, A-4. Pupa, A-5. Adult. **B.** Rice weevil, *Sitophilus oryzae*; B-1. Egg on grain, B-2. Larva, B-3. Pupa, B-4. Adult. **C.** Red flour beetle, *Tribolium castaneum;* C-1. Eggs, C-2. Larva, C-3. Pupa, C-4. Adult. **D.** Lesser grain borer, *Rhyzopertha dominica*; D-1. Eggs, D-2. Larva, D-3. Pupa, D-4. Adult.**E.** Gram dhora, *Callosobruchus chinensis*; E-1. Eggs or grain, E-2. Larva, E-3. Pupa, E-4. Adult.

Life-history. The rice weevil breeds from April to October and hibernates in winter as an adult inside cracks and crevices or under wheat bags in the godowns. During the active season, the females lay eggs on the grain by making a depression with the help of the mandibles. After an egg has been laid, the hole is sealed with a gelatinous secretion. A single female may lay as many as 400 eggs. The eggs hatch in 6-7 days and the young larvae bore directly into grain, where they feed and grow to maturity in 20-35 days. Then they pupate inside the grain and the pupal stage lasts for 6-14 days. On emergence, the adult weevil cuts its way out of the grain and lives for about 4-5 months. At least 3-4 generations are completed in a year.

Host. While the rice weevils prefer rice, they can be found feeding together with *S. granarius* on rice, wheat, maize and other grains. The rice weevil may also be found in the paddy fields.

Damage. The damage is done by both the grubs and adults by breaking and hollowing the grains. They destroy more than they eat.

7. *Tribolium castaneum* Herbst (Rust red flour beetle, Coleoptera : Tenebrionidae) (Fig. 15.2C)

Distribution. The insect is world-wide in distribution.

Identification. The two species (*T. castaneum* and *T. confusum*) are reddish brown beetles, found in wheat flour with more or less similar life-cycles but with varying physical attributes (Table 15.1). *T. castaneum* adult measures about 3.5 mm in length and 1.2 mm in width. Its antennae are bent and bear a distinct club formed by three enlarged terminal joints. The last antennal segment is transversely rounded. The young larva is yellowish white and measures 1 mm in length. As it matures, it turns reddish yellow, becomes hairy and measures over 6 mm in length.

Table 15.1 Differences between the two species of *Tribolium*

Sr. No.	*T. castaneum*	*T. confusum*
1.	Larger	Smaller
2.	Antennae enlarge gradually towards the tips	Enlarge abruptly
3.	Wings are non-functional	Functional (can fly)
4.	Eeggs smaller	Larger

Life-history. The insect breeds from April to October and passes the winter mostly in the adult stage. In the active season, the adults copulate one or two days after emergence. The females lay white, transparent, cylinderical eggs in the flour or in the frassy material among the grains and other foodstuff. The surface of freshly laid eggs is sticky and, therefore, flour or dust particles easily adhere to them. A single female may lay as many as 327-956 eggs. The incubation period lasts 4-10 days. The worm like larvae undergo 6-7 moultings and they are full-grown in 22-25 days at 30°C. Pupation takes place in the flour. The pupa is yellowish and hairy. The pupal stage lasts for 5-9 days. The development period from egg to the adult stage is 26-30 days in summer.

Host. Preferably wheat flour but can be also found in wheat, cereal products, pulses, dry fruits, etc.

Damage. The damage is done by both adults and grubs but less damaging than *Sitophilus* and *Rhizopertha* in whose company it may be found. Adults are incapable of feeding on whole grains but feed on damaged ones or pick up pieces broken by the co-existing pests. Like other stored grain pests, damage is more serious during the humid (monsoon) season. In severe infestation, the flour turns greyish and mouldy, and has a pungent odour, making it unfit for human consumption.

8. *Rhyzopertha dominica* (Fabricius) (Lesser grain borer, Coleoptera : Bostrichidae) [Fig. 15.2D]

Distribution. Originating in India, it has now spread to all over the world. It has been reported as a pest from Algeria, Greece, USA, Australia, Japan and China.

Identification. The adult is metallic (shining) dark brown or black, about 3 mm long beetle, head covered by hood-shaped pronotum. The antennae are 10-jointed and terminate in a prominent tripartite club, the first two segments of which are triangular and the apical segment oval. Adults are powerful fliers, flying from godown to godown. The larva is about 3 mm long, dirty white, with a light-brown head and a constricted elongated body.

Life-history. The insect breeds from March to November and enters hibernation in December as an adult or as a larva. It resumes activity in March and the female begins to lay eggs by the first week of April. A single female can lay 300-400 eggs in 23-60 days at the rate of 5-20 eggs per day. The eggs are laid singly in the frass or glued to the grain in batches. The incubation period is about 5-9 days. The grubs on hatching crawl about feeding on the particles broken by the boring adults or enter the damaged grains to feed inside. The larva moults 4-5 times and is full-fed in 28-56 days. The pupal stage is passed within the grain or in the grain dust for 7-8 days. The adult, on emergence, remains inside the grain for a few days and then cuts its way through the side of the grain and comes out. The period from egg to adult stage is completed in 30 days in summer. There are 5-6 generations in a year.

Host. Primarily wheat but can also be seen in other grains (rice, sorghum, maize, barley, lentils, food products, tamarind seed, etc.).

Damage. The adults are more harmful than the grubs and they destroy more than they eat. The grubs eat upon the kernel leaving the husk behind. The first instar grubs being straight in outline can bore inside the grains while the later instars get curved and are unable to bore and depend mainly on flour produced by the adults. The grains at times are reduced to mere shells and the milled products into tangled mass of excreta.

9. *Oryzaephilus surinamensis* (Linnaeus) (Saw-loothed grain beetle, Coleoptera: Silvanidae)

Distribution. It is distributed throughout the world.

Identification. It is dark brown, much flattened, slender about 0.25 cm long beetle. Observed under a lense, 6 saw-toothed projections can be seen on each side of the prothorax.

Life-history. The female lays 50-300 eggs on or near the food. The incubation period is 3-17 days. The larvae are brown headed, elongate, white, 6-legged grubs with posteriorly tapering abdomen. When full-grown, the grubs form a protective covering by sticking together some bits of food material under which they pupate. The pupal stage lasts for 6-21 days. The adults almost never fly and can survive for 3 years. There are 4-6 generations in a year.

Host. Like *Tribolium*, this insect feeds on great variety of products, like all grains, grain products, dry fruits, nuts, seeds, yeast, sugar, candy, tobacco, snuff, dried meat, etc.

Damage. The damage is caused by both adults and grubs. Being incapable of attacking sound grains, the insects attack seeds damaged by other insects. Feeding consists of scarring the roughing of surface of the grains. Infested material will show many slender, much flattened small darkened beetles hurrying over the surface of the food. Its flattened shape enables this species to work into packages of food that are apparently tightly sealed.

10. *Tenebroides mauritanicus* (Linnaeus) (Cadelle, Coleoptera : (Trogossitidae)

Distribution. It is cosmopolitan in distribution.

Identification. The adult beetles are black or nearly black about 1 cm long with head and prothorax distinctly separated from rest of the body to which it is attached by a rather loose prominent joint. The larvae are soft-bodied white to greyish-white in colour with prominent black head, black spots on the 3 thoracic segments and 2 short hooks at the end of the abdomen.

Life-history. The egg are laid in clusters of 10-60 on or near the food but preferentially in the crevices and cracks, under flaps of cartons or in some such protected situations. A female may lay 1000-3000 eggs, which hatch in 1-2 weeks. The larvae are full-grown in 70-90 days. Full-grown larvae and adults have the habit of boring into wooden structures in the grainaries, store rooms and grain ships where they remain hiding for months ready to attack the next consignment of foods. Pupal stage, which lasts for 10-19 days, is passed in such cavities or in other secluded places.

Host. This insect could be sometimes though not always an important pest of the grainaries. The damage it causes is to some extent counter-balanced by its being also predaceous on other insects.

Damage. As usual for the beetles, the damage is caused by both adults and grubs not only by feeding on the grains and grain-products but also by cutting holes in the grain bins, flour sacks, cartons of packaged food and cloth used in machinery. It generally attacks embryos eating out only the softer parts of the grain.

11. *Lasioderma serricorne* (Fabricius) (Cigarette beetle, Coleoptera : Anobiidae)

Distribution. It is cosmopolitan in distribution.

Identification. It is rounded, light brown 0.02-0.25 cm long beetle with head and prothorax bent downwards so as to give the insect a strongly humped look.

Life-history. The creamy white oval eggs are laid in and around the substance on which the insects feeds. A female lays about 100 eggs and the incubation period is 6-10 days. Ths grubs are yellowish with light brown head. Pupation occurs in silken cocoon covered with bits of food. The grubs and pupal periods range from 30-50 and 8-10 days, respectively. There are 6 generations in a year.

Host. Tobacco products, specially cigarette tobacco with high sugar content and its dried leaves, are its main food though it can also feed on seeds and dried plant products specially used as drugs, black and red pepper.

Damage. The damage is caused both by adults and grubs by boring holes into tobacco products, *i.e.* cigarettes, cheroots and chewing tobacco. It also damages uphostry of furnitures, materials used in stuffing furnitures and as mentioned above some plant products.

12. *Callosobruchus chinensis* (Linnaeus) (Gram dhora, Coleoptera : Bruchidae) (Fig. 15.2E)

Distribution. The gram *dhora* or pulse beetle has been reported from the USA, Mauritius, Taiwan, Africa, China, the Philippines, Japan, Indonesia, Sri Lanka, Myanmar and India.

Identification. The adult beetle measuring 3-4 mm in length, is oval, chocolate or reddish brown and has long serrated antennae. There is a pair of white elongate prominences in the middle of the hind margin of the thorax, a spine on each of the inner and outer edges of the end of the hind femur and truncate elytra, not covering the pygidium. The larva is whitish with a light brown head in the early stages and acquires a creamy hue later on. The full-grown larva measures 6-7 mm.

Life-history. The pest breeds actively from March to the end of November. It hibernates in winter in the larval stage. At the end of March, the adults appear and copulate immediately after emergence. The eggs are laid singly but as many as 8 eggs could be glued to a single seed. A single female may lay 34-113 eggs at the rate of 1-37 per day. The eggs hatch in 4-6 days. The young larva bores into the grain and completes its development inside. The larval stage is completed in 14-21 days. The full-grown larva migrates towards the periphery and comes to lie next to the seed coat where it turns into an oval white pupa. The pupal stage lasts 4-28 days, depending upon the season. The adult escapes by cutting a circular hole in the seed coat. The average life-span of an adult is 5-20 days. The insect passes through 7-8 overlapping generations in a year.

Host. It is a notorious pest of gram, *mung (Phaseolus aureus), moth (Phaseolus aconitifolius),* peas, cowpeas, lentil and *arhar (Cajanus cajan).* It has also been reported on cotton seed, sorghum and maize.

Damage. The damage is at caused by the grubs alone which could eat away the entire seed content leaving only the shell. Damage to the pulses infested with this insect is very high and quite often each and every grain is infested so that the pulses become unfit for human consumption. Infested grain is often converted by the traders into flour which has a characteristic off-flavour and should not be marketed.

13. *Callosobruchus analis* (Fabricius) (Mung dhora, Coleoptera : Bruchidae)

Distribution. The distribution of *mung dhora* or pulse beetle is comparatively limited. So far, it has been recorded from Germany, Rhodesia, Myanmar and India.

Identification. The adult is an oval beetle, somewhat smaller than *C. chinensis.* The female is of chocolate colour with a black trapezoidal area surrounded by white streaks on three sides. The exposed pygidium is black with a central longitudinal white streak. The male is uniformly chocolate with a tinge of straw. The larva is recognized by its creamy-white, oval, flabby body.

Life-history. The insect breeds from March to December and then over-winters in the larval stage within the infested grain. In the first week of March, the adults escape by cutting out a circular hole in the seed coat. The females lay oval, white eggs singly or in batches but only one egg is laid on a grain. The eggs are glued to the grain and the number laid in 2-22 days by a female varies from 11 to 150. The incubation period is 3-6 days. The young larva, on emergence, bores into the grain and feeds there. The development is fast during the summer but during the winter larvae take as long as 95-145 days to complete their development.

When full-grown, the larvae pupate inside the grain. The life of adults varies from 5 to 10 days, the male having longer life. The insect completes 9-19 overlapping generations.

Host. It is a pest of *mung (Phaseolus aureus), mash (Phaseolus mungo), moth (Phaseolus aconitifolius),* peas, cowpeas and other pulses.

Damage. This pest causes the maximum damage from April to August, when all stages of development are present. The larvae feed and breed inside the grain, consuming the entire contents. When the infested grain happens to be in a poorly aerated receptacle, a foul smelling fungus also develops.

Management of Storage Pests

The effective management of storage pests may be ensured by drying the grains properly before storage, storing new grains in the clean godowns or receptacles and plugging all cracks, crevices and holes in the godowns thoroughly. If infestation of grain has already taken place or is imminent on account of a peculiar situation in which the grain is stored, then application of chemicals becomes necessary. The chemical control measures to be practiced under different situations are variable.

1. **Surface treatment.** The grain kept in jute bags can be protected by spraying insecticides on the surface of the stack. The godowns are disinfested before storing the grain and new infestation can be prevented by surface treatment. Disinfect old gunny bags by dipping them in 0.0125 per cent fenvalerate or cypermethrin for 10 minutes and drying them in shade before filling with grains or use new gunny bags. Disinfect empty godowns or receptacles by spraying 0.05 per cent malathion emulsion on the floor, walls and ceiling.
2. **Seed treatment.** The grain meant for seed can be protected by mixing dusts with it. At present, mixing of malathion 5 per cent dust at the rate of 250 g per quintal of seed is recommended. The grains may also be treated with 25 ml of Cythion 50EC (malathion premium grade) or 2 ml of fenvalerate 20EC or 1.5 ml of cypermethrin 25EC or 14 ml of deltamethrin 2.8EC per quintal of seed by diluting in 500 ml of water. Before treatment, the grains should be spread in thin layer on *pucca* floor or polythene sheet. After treatment, the grains should be mixed thoroughly and then put into the containers. Against pulse beetle *(dhora),* cover the pulses stored in bulk with 7 cm layer of sand or sawdust or dung ash.
3. **Fumigation.** Fumigation is a process of creating lethal concentration of a toxic gas for the time necessary to destroy insect infestation in a closed space. If there is any sign of infestation in the grain, whether stored in receptacles or in godowns, it is best to fumigate it with one of the poisonous gases available for the purpose and then to sieve and dry it before returning to the receptacles. To ensure a complete mortality of the infesting pests, it is advisable to repeat the fumigation after one month. Since the fumigants are highly poisonous to human-beings and animals, fumigation should be carried out only if the godowns are away from the residential buildings and only if it is possible to make them air-tight. If the godowns are in an awkward position and these conditions are not met with, the grain, whether in bags or in bulk, should be taken out in the open and fumigated under a gas-proof tarpaulin or a tent. Metalic drums or wooden boxes can also be used for fumigating small quantities of grain.

The chemicals used are available as liquids, gases or solids. In India, ethylene dichloride and carbon tetrachloride mixture, has been recommended for fumigation of foodgrains in storage at farm level, and hydrogen phosphide in the form of aluminium phosphide. Suitable fumigant which can be used under ordinary conditions of storage is the mixture of ethylene dichloride and carbon tetrachloride at the rate of 1 litre for 20 quintals of grain or 35 litres per 100 m^3 of space with exposure period of 4 days. This fumigant-mixture is comparatively safe. The fumigant, hydrogen phosphide (aluminium phosphide), is currently used for large scale fumigation of foodgrains in those storage structures which are away form living premises. It is available in tablet form and can be used at the rate of one to two tablets (3 g each) per metric tonne or 25 tablets per 100 m^3 of space with an exposure period of 7 days.

Procedure for fumigation. It is desirable to do mud plastering of storage structures in advance leaving only exit door or openings in the wall. The aluminium phosphide tablets when used, are inserted into the grain kept in bulk or distributed uniformly among bagged grains. The opening is then immediately sealed with mud plaster and polythene sheet. The storage structures thus sealed should be left undisturbed for a period of seven days or as long as the grain is not wanted. After the required period of exposure to the fumigant, grain should be aerated well for a few hours until no smell of the fumigant is left. The treated grains should be cleaned and sieved properly before they are consumed.

Precautions. The following precautions should be strictly followed during fumigation:

- The fumigants should be used only in airtight stores or under tarpaulins in the open by specially trained persons, because these compounds are deadly poisonous.
- Inhalation of fumigant vapours should be avoided by wearing gas masks and protective clothing.
- The fumigants should be applied at the recommended dosages.
- Splashing of the liquid fumigants over hands and face should be avoided.
- Aluminium phosphide must not be used in living quarters. Its use in a godown next to the living rooms may also be hazardous.

4. Use of improved storage receptacles. The grains can be best protected by using improved insect-proof receptacles of various types.

A. *Indoor Bins*

(*i*) *Domestic metal bins.* Several types of domestic designs of metal bins have been developed, the capacities of which range from 3 to 27.5 quintals. These are indoor bins and may be kept in a room or verandah under a roof. The bins are made from galvanized iron sheets and are moisture, rodent and insect-proof. These are found suitable for storage of wheat, paddy, maize, pulses and seed grains.

(*ii*) *Gharelu theka.* This type of storage structure consists of rat-proof metal base, rubberized cloth containers and bamboo posts, having different storage capacities ranging from 2 to 3 metric tonnes.

(*iii*) *Pucca kothi.* The improved structure called 'Pucca kothi' is constructed using burnt bricks plastered with cement mortar. The structure is constructed in two compartments with a capacity of 1 metric tonne.

(*iv*) *Welded wire-mesh bin.* The bin is fabricated using wire-mesh with hessian cloth lining inside so that the air may circulate freely through it. The structure is mounted on pre-fabricated steel elevated base to prevent the entry of rodents. The storage capacity of bin is 2.8 metric tonnes. The foodgrains like maize and paddy can be stored in this bin even at slightly higher moisture level without deterioration in quality.

(*v*) *Reinforced cement ring bins.* This design consists of pre-fabricated RCC rings placed one over the other with gripping joints at the edges.

(*vi*) *Paddy straw-mud structure.* The improved paddy straw-mud structure of 400 kg capacity is made from paddy straw rope plastered on both sides with specially prepared mud. Externally, the structure is further plastered with water proof mud to prevent the entry of moisture. The structure is mounted on a raised brick masonary platform to prevent the entry of rats. It is commonly used for paddy storage.

B. *Outdoor Bins*

(*i*) *Flat and hopper bottom-metal bins.* These bins are fabricated using either steel or aluminium metal sheets of different capacities ranging from 2.0 to 10.5 metric tonnes. The bin can be either erected on brick masonary base, brick masonary columns or pre-fabricated steel elevated base. These bins are suitable for storage of wheat, paddy and maize under different climatic conditions.

(*ii*) *Composite bins.* These are the outdoor flat bottom storage bins fabricated with steel and timber in combination with varying storage capacities ranging from 3 to 14.5 metric tonnes.

(*iii*) *Partly underground and above ground structures.* A prototype structure of 10 m^3 or 7.5 metric tonnes capacity which is partly underground and partly above ground has been constructed. The underground part of the structure is of RCC or brick, while the above ground part of the structure is of galvanized iron sheet. This bin is suitable for construction in areas where water table is low.

(*iv*) *Seed storage bins.* Quite popular in rural areas, these bins are either circular or square in shape with storage capacities ranging from 1 to 15 quintals.

(*v*) *Ferro-cement bins.* The bins are constructed by using rich cement mortar and closely spaced chicken wire mesh. The bin is cylindrical in shape and has flat bottom and a dome-shaped roof. It is treated on the outside with suitable moisture proofing paint like bituminous aluminium paint. The capacity of the ferrobins ranges from 0.6 to 3.0 metric tonnes. They are lighter in weight than the cement concrete structure.

(*vi*) *Pusa bin.* This design consists of two brick walls of 10 cm thick each using sun-dried bricks with polythene sheet sandwitched in between. The structure is constructed on a brick masonary platform plastered with cement mortar. A mud slab is provided as the top on a wooden frame structure. The polythene sheet is also provided at the top and the base to make the structure completely moisture-proof and airtight.

(*vii*) *Improved godowns.* For larger bag storage of foodgrains, it is advisable to construct improved godowns, specifications for which are available from the Bureau of Indian Standards, New Delhi. The bag storage structures are conventional type godowns either with angle iron trusses, tubular trusses, raiser type trusses, pre-cast trusses, wooden trusses or godowns with RCC flat roof or shell type roof.

(*viii*) *Bulk storage installations.* In addition to these godowns, large scale storage installations with adequate storage and mechanical grain handling facility are used by grain handling authorities in the country like Food Corporation of India, Marketing

Cooperative Federations, Central and State Warehousing Corporations, etc. The storage bins or silos have a capacity of 10,000 tonnes each and provide for bulk storage of grain. The elevators are provided with mechanical operations for receiving and issuing out grain with the help of a mechanical system on scientific lines.

(*ix*) *Vacuum process storage.* The vacuum process storage (VPS) is a modern concept in storage system. Under the VPS system, the PVC containers, manufactured for the purpose, are filled with foodgrains and air is sucked out of them instantly. Thus, vacuumised containers could be operated like stone boxes and stacked like gunny bags in the open field. The foodgrains in such containers never get infected or catch fungus in the absence of air. Besides, the foodgrains thus stored never get discoloured and suffer damage in quality even though the stocks are kept for 3-4 years.

*****

16
CHAPTER

INSECT VECTORS OF PLANT DISEASES

A vector is an organism capable of transmitting pathogens from one host to another. The insects, besides directly damaging the crops, sometimes become responsible for the spread of pathogens in plants. All those insects which acquire the disease causing organisms by feeding on the diseased plants or by contact and transmit them to healthy plants are known as insect vectors of plant diseases. Plant pathogens are transmitted either through contact, by contamination through soil or other biological agencies. Majority of the plant diseases are transmitted by insects and a few by other arthropods like mites and only a small percentage by mechanical means or contamination of the soil.

Insects having both piercing and sucking mouthparts, and biting and chewing mouthparts are associated with disease transmission. Most of the insect vectors belong to the order Hemiptera (aphids, leafhoppers, whiteflies and mealy bugs), but a few others belong to Thysanoptera (thrips), Coleoptera (beetles), Orthoptera (grasshoppers) and Dermaptera (earwigs). Homopteran insects alone are known to transmit about 90 per cent of the plant diseases. The salient features of homopterans (aphids and leafhoppers), which make them efficient vectors are as follows :

- They make brief but frequent probes with their mouthparts into host plants.
- As the population density reaches a critical level, winged migratory individuals are produced.
- In many species, winged females deposit a few progeny on each of the many plants.
- These insects do not cause wholesome destruction of cells during feeding and viruses require living cells for their subsistence and multiplication.

A number of plant diseases caused by viruses, phytoplasmas, bacteria and fungi are transmitted by insects.

VIRUSES

A virus is a set of one or more nucleic acid molecules, normally encased in a protective coat or coats of protein or lipoprotein that is able to organize its own replication only within suitable host cells. It is ultramicroscopic in size and can be seen only with the aid of an electron microscope. It is spherical or rod-shaped, nucleoproteinaceous (chief constituents being ribonucleic acid 5–35% and proteins 65–95% by weight) in composition, and can live and multiply only in living cells. Viruses are responsible for many diseases in man (influenza, measles, mumps, polio, pox, etc.) and plants (mosaic, leaf curl, etc.).

Plant virus diseases have become more prevalent and destructive in recent years. This is mainly because of better recognition of the virus diseases, exchange of plant material from region to region facilitating spread of the virus to new areas, and distribution of many insect vectors in new regions in the world. There are over 850 described plant virus species. About half of the insect vectors are aphids, a third are the leafhoppers. Mealy bugs and whiteflies transmit some viruses, and six are transmitted by thrips. The main aphid vectors are *Myzus persicae, Aphis gossypii* and *Aphis craccivora* (Table 16.1). In addition, whitefly, *Bemisia tabaci* and leafhoppers are also responsible for transmission of plant viruses. Whitefly mostly transmits mosaics and leaf curls in pulses, vegetables and other crops like cotton, tobacco and papaya. The leaf- and planthoppers transmit tungro, yellow-orange leaf, grassy stunt and ragged stunt in rice. Tomato spotted wilt is known to be transmitted by thrips. Mandibulate insects like grasshoppers, earwigs and chrysomelid beetles transmit turnip yellow mosaic. Several species of mites are also responsible for transmission of viruses of cereals and fruit crops (Table 16.2).

Table 16.1 List of important insect vectors of plant viruses

S.No.	Insect vector(s)	Virus(es)	Host(s)
1.	*Acyrthosiphon pisum*	Alfalfa mosaic	Alfalfa
	(Hemiptera : Aphididae)	Bean mosaic	Beans
		Onion yellow dwarf	Onion
		Pea mosaic	Peas
		Soybean mosaic	Beans, peas
2.	*Aphis craccivora*	Alfalfa mosaic	Alfalfa
	(Hemiptera : Aphididae)	Cowpea mosaic	Cowepa
		Onion yellow dwarf	Onion
		Papaya mosaic	Papaya
3.	*Aphis fabae*	Alfalfa mosaic	Alfalfa
	(Hemiptera : Aphididae)	Beet yellows	Spinach, sugarbeet
		Dahlia mosaic	Calendula, dahlia, zinnia
		Onion yellow dwarf	Onion
		Pea mosaic	Peas
4.	*Aphis gossypii*	Alfalfa mosaic	Alfalfa, potato
	(Hemiptera : Aphididae)	Chilli mosaic	Chillies
		Cucumber mosaic	Cucumber

S.No.	Insect vector(s)	Virus(es)	Host(s)
		Dahlia mosaic	Dahlia, zinnia
		Lettuce mosaic	Lettuce, sweet pea
		Papaya mosaic	Papaya
		Sugarcane mosaic	Sugarcane
5.	*Aphis rumicis* (Hemiptera : Aphididae)	Bean common mosaic	Beans
		Pea mosaic	Broadbean, garden pea, sweet pea
6.	*Bemisia tabaci* (Hemiptera : Aleyrodidae)	Cotton leaf curl	Cotton
		Dolichos yellow mosaic	Dolichos
		Okra yellow vein mosaic	Okra
		Papaya leaf curl	Papaya
		Sesame leaf curl	Sesame
		Tobacco leaf curl	Tobacco
		Tomato leaf curl	Tomato
7.	*Brevicoryne brassicae* (Hemiptera : Aphididae)	Cauliflower mosaic	Cabbage, cauliflower
8.	*Chorthippus bicolor* (Orthoptera : Acrididae)	Turnip yellow mosaic	Cabbage, cauliflower, turnip
9.	*Forficula auricularia* Linnaeus (Dermaptera : Forficulidae)	Turnip yellow mosaic	Cabbage, cauliflower, turnip
10.	*Frankliniella schultzei* *F. fusca*, *F. occidentalis* (Thyanoptera : Thripidae)	Tomato spotted wilt	Dahlia, pineapple, tobacco, tomato
11.	*Laodelphax striatellus* (Hemiptera : Delphacidae)	Rice streaked dwarf	Rice
		Rice stripe	Rice
12.	*Leptophyes punctatissima* (Orthoptera : Acrididae)	Turnip yellow mosaic	Cabbage, cauliflower, turnip
13.	*Macrosiphum euphorbiae* (Hemiptera : Aphididae)	Alfalfa mosaic	Alfalfa
		Lettuce mosaic	Garden pea, lettuce, sweet pea
		Potato virus Y	Potato, tobacco, tomato
14.	*Macrosiphum granarium*, *M. miscanthi* (Hemiptera : Aphididae)	Barley yellow dwarf	Barley, oat, rye, wheat
15.	*Myzus persicae* (Hemiptera : Aphididae)	Alfalfa mosaic	Alfalfa
		Beet yellows	Spinach, sugarbeet
		Cabbage black ring spot	Cabbage
		Cauliflower mosaic	Cabbage, cauliflower
		Cucumber mosaic	Cucumber

S.No.	Insect vector(s)	Virus(es)	Host(s)
		Dahlia mosaic	Calendula, dahlia, zinnia
		Lettuce mosaic	Garden pea, lettuce, sweat pea
		Onion yellow dwarf	Onion
		Pea mosaic	Broadbean, garden pea, sweet pea
		Potato virus Y	Potato, tobacco, tomato
		Soybean mosaic	Soybean
		Sugarcane mosaic	Maize, sorghum, sugarcane
16.	*Nephotettix nigropictus*, *N. virescens* (Hemiptera : Cicadellidae)	Tungro Yellow-orange leaf	Rice Rice
17.	*Nilaparvata lugens* (Hemiptera : Delphacidae)	Grassy stunt Ragged stunt	Rice Rice
18.	*Pentalonia nigronervosa* (Hemiptera : Aphididae)	Banana bunchy top Cardamom mosaic	Banana Cardamom
19.	*Phaedon cochleariae* (Coleoptera : Chrysomelidae)	Turnip yellow mosaic	Cabbage, cauliflower, turnip
20.	*Phyllotreta* spp. (Coleoptera : Chrysomelidae)	Turnip yellow mosaic	Cabbage, cauliflower, turnip
21.	*Recilia dorsalis* (Hemiptera : Cicadellidae)	Yellow-orange leaf	Rice
22.	*Rhopalosiphum maidis* (Hemiptera : Aphididae)	Barley yellow dwarf Onion yellow dwarf Sugarcane mosaic	Barley, oat, rye, wheat Onion Maize, sorghum, sugarcane
23.	*Schizaphis graminum* (Hemiptera : Aphididae)	Sugarcane mosaic	Maize, sorghum, sugarcane
24.	*Sogatodes orizicola* (Hemiptera : Delphacidae)	Hoja blanca	Rice
25.	*Thrips tabaci* (Thysanoptera : Thripidae)	Tomato spotted wilt	Dahlia, pineapple, tobacco, tomato

Source **:** Modified from Gillot (2005)

Table 16.2 List of important mite vectors of virus diseases of plants

S.No.	Mite vector(s)	Virus	Host(s)
1.	*Abacarus hystrix* (Acari : Eriophyidae)	Agropyron mosaic	Wheat, switch grass
2.	*Aceria ficus* (Acari : Eriophyidae)	Fig mosaic	Fig

S.No.	Mite vector(s)	Virus	Host(s)
3.	*Aceria tulipae* (Acari : Eriophyidae)	Wheat streak mosaic	What, oats, barley, maize
4.	*Aculus fockeui* (Acari : Eriophyidae)	Prunus necrotic ring spot	Plum, peach, cherry
5.	*Eriophyes inaequalis* (Acari : Eriophyidae)	Cherry leaf mottle	Sweet cherry
6.	*Eriophyes insidiosus* (Acari : Eriophyidae)	Peach mosaic	Peach, nectarine

Types of Viruses

On the basis of the method of transmission and persistence in the vector, viruses may be classified into three categories :

(*i*) Non-persistent viruses. These are those viruses which are believed to be transmitted as contaminants of the mouthparts. Such viruses are also called stylet-born viruses and the type of transmission is mechanical. The vector is able to acquire the virus from a disease source and transmit to a healthy plant by feeding for a few seconds. These viruses do not persist longer within the insect vectors which can transmit them soon after feeding on infected plant but the ability to transmit fresh infection soon disappears after the insect feeds on healthy or immune plants. The efficiency of transmission of non-persistent virus is greatly affected by modifying the time of feeding and by starving the vectors before and after feeding. Aphids are the vectors of a great majority of such viruses which are carried only in their stylets.

The following are the main features of the non-persistent viruses :

- Vectors are optimally infective when they have fed for approximately 30 seconds on the infected plant.
- Transmission is improved if vector is starved for a period before an infection feed.
- If the vector is starved after an acquisition, it begins to lose ability to transmit within 2 minutes.
- After acquisition feeding, infectivity is rapidly lost when the vectors feed on healthy plants.

(*ii*) Semi-persistent viruses. These viruses are carried in the anterior regions of the gut of a vector, where they may multiply to a certain extent. Vectors do not normally remain infective after a molt, presumably because the viruses are lost when the foregut intima is shed. Several of the leafhopper-transmitted viruses fall under this category.

(*iii*) Persistent viruses. Persistent viruses are those that persist longer within the infective agent, *i.e.* vector. These viruses, when acquired by a vector, pass through the midgut wall to the salivary glands from where they can infect new hosts. In case of these viruses, the insect has to feed on the source of virus for comparatively longer periods. The insect, after such acquisition of virus, becomes infective only after a certain period, ranging from several hours to 10-20 days, which is called the *incubation period* or *latent period*. Such viruses may multiply within tissues of a vector, which retains the ability to transmit the virus for several days and in some instances the rest of its life. Therefore, the vector need not feed on the virus source again and again to retain its infective capacity.

Thus, the vector insect feeds on the diseased plant (acquisition feed), requires some time after acquisition feed to transmit the virus (latent or incubation period), feeds on healthy plant (inoculation feed) and in the process transmits the virus acquired earlier. Such viruses are also called circulative or circulative-propagative viruses and the type of transmission as non-mechanical. Many of the leafhopper-transmitted viruses belong to this category.

Mechanism of Transmission

For inoculation of virus into a plant by sucking insects, the puncture is initiated by a number of forward and backward movements of the inner pair of stylets. During the forward movements, the fluid flows into them, during the backward movements, saliva is ejected. Generally, an insect injects by feeding on any part of the plant, but in some cases the virus is only found in the phloem and has to be injected into the phloem, the movement of which is perhaps controlled by the pH gradient between the mesophyll and the phloem. Some viruses are concentrated in the epidermal cells and others in the mesophyll or xylem.

The mandibulate insects like grasshoppers and beetles regurgitate during feeding. The regurgitated fluid containing the virus is brought into contact with the healthy plant, thus transmitting the virus.

Virus-Vector Relationship

Irrespective of the type of transmission, virus-vector relationship is highly specific. Generally, one type of virus disease is transmitted only by insects belonging to one particular group, *i.e.* mosaics by aphids and leaf curls by whiteflies. In case of leafhoppers, among 110 species known to be vectors, about 100 species transmit only one virus. Similarly, there are viruses which are transmitted by a particular species of an insect and not by others of the same genus. For instance, cabbage ring spot is transmitted only by *M. persicae* and not by *M. ornatus*. A vector can also acquire and transmit more than one virus to the respective hosts. For example, the aphid, *Pentalonia nigronervosa*, transmits banana bunchy top and cardamom mosaic. Similarly, the whitefly, *Bemisia tabaci* transmits okra yellow vien mosaic, dolichos yellow mosaic, tomato leaf curl, papaya leaf curl, etc. Onion yellow dwarf is known to be transmitted by 60 insect vectors.

For transmission of viruses, activity of insect vectors is more important rather than their number. In case of aphids, it is the activity and number of migrant insects that is important in the efficiency of virus transmission rather than the number of apterous individuals which are, of course, important in respect of their direct injury to the crop.

PHYTOPLASMAS

Phytoplasmas (originally called mycoplasma-like organisms) are non-culturable degenerate gram-positive prokaryotes closely related to mycoplasmas and spiroplasmas. They are without a visible cell wall, whose place is taken by a thin elastic cytoplasmic membrane which cannot withstand osmotic pressure. Phytoplasmas are pleomorphic and may be spherical or oval, varying from 80 to 800μ in diameter.

Phytoplasmas are important insect-transmitted pathogenic agents causing more than 700 diseases in plants. The single most successful order of insect phytoplasma vectors is the Hemiptera. This group collectively possesses several characteristics that make its members efficient vectors of phytoplasmas.

- They are hemimetabolous, thus nymphs and adults feed similarly and are in the same physical location-often both immatures and adults can transmit phytoplasmas.
- They feed specifically and selectively on certain plant tissues, which makes them efficient vectors of pathogens residing in these tissues.
- Their feeding is non-destructive, promoting successful inoculation of the plant vascular system without damaging the conductive tissues and eliciting defensive responses.
- They have a propagative and persistent relationship with phytoplasmas. They have obligate symbiotic prokaryotes that are passed to the offspring by transovarial transmission, the same mechanisms that allow the transovarial transmission of phytoplasmas.

Mechanism of Transmission

Phytoplasmas are phloem-limited, therefore, only phloem-feeding insects can potentially acquire and transmit the pathogen. Most phytoplasma vectors are members of the family Cicadellidae (Table 16.3). Phloem-feeding insects acquire phytoplasmas passively during feeding in the phloem of infected plants. The feeding duration necessary to acquire a sufficient titer of phytoplasma (acquisition access period), may range from a few minutes to several hours; the longer the period, the greater the chance of acquisition. The time that elapses from initial acquisition to the ability to transmit the phytoplasmas (latent period or incubation period) is temperature dependent and ranges from a few to 80 days.

During the latent period, phytoplasmas move through and replicate in the vector's body. They can pass intracellularly through the epithelial cells of the midgut and replicate within a vesicle or they can pass between two midgut cells and through the basement membrane to enter the hemocoel. Phytoplasmas circulate in the haemolymph, where they may infect other tissues such as the Malpighian tubules, fat bodies and brain or reproductive organs. The replication in these tissues, albeit not essential for transmission, may be indicative of a longer coevolutionary relationship between host and pathogen. To be transmitted to plants, phytoplasmas must penetrate specific cells of the salivary glands and high levels must accumulate in posterior acinar cells of the salivary gland before they can be transmitted.

Vector-Phytoplasma Relationship

The interaction between insects and phytoplasmas is complex and variable. The complex sequence of events required for an insect to acquire and subsequently transmit phytoplasmas to plants suggests a high degree of specificity of phytoplasmas to insects. However, numerous phytoplasmas are transmitted by several different insect species. In addition, a single vector species may transmit two or more phytoplasmas, and an individual vector can be infected with dual or multiple phytoplasma strains. Vector-host plant interactions also play an important role in determining the spread of phytoplasmas. Polyphagous vectors have the potential to inoculate a wider range of plant species, depending on the resistance to infection of each host plant.

S.No.	Insect vector(s)	Mycoplasma(s)	Host(s)
1.	*Aphrodes albifrons* (Hemiptera : Cicadellidae)	Clover phyllody	Most clovers
2.	*Cestius phycitis* (Hemiptera : Cicadellidae)	Brinjal little leaf	Brinjal
3.	*Dalbulus elimatus, D. maidis* (Hemiptera : Cicadellidae)	Corn stunt	Maize
4.	*Euscelis lineolatus, E. plebeja* (Hemiptera : Cicadellidae)	Clover phyllody	Most clovers
5.	*Graminella nigrifrons* (Hemiptera : Cicadellidae)	Corn stunt	Maize
6.	*Gyponana hasta* (Hemiptera : Cicadellidae)	Aster yellows	Aster, barley, carrot, celery, cucumber, wheat
7.	*Macrosteles cristata, M. viridigriseus* (Hemiptera : Cicadellidae)	Clover phyllody	Most clovers
8.	*Macrosteles quadrilineatus* (Hemiptera : Cicadellidae)	Aster yellows	Aster, barley, carrot, celery, cucumber, wheat
9.	*Nephotettix nigropictus, N. virescens* (Hemiptera : Cicadellidae)	Yellow dwarf	Rice
10.	*Orosius albicinctus* (Hemiptera : Cicadellidae)	Sesame phyllody	Sesame
11.	*Recilia dorsalis* (Hemiptera : Cicadellidae)	Yellow dwarf	Rice
12.	*Scaphytopius acutus, S. irroratus* (Orthoptera : Gryllotalpidae)	Aster yellows	Aster, barley, carrot, celery, cucumber, wheat
13.	*Stephanitis typica* (Hemiptera : Tingidae)	Coconut root wilt	Coconut

Source **:** Modified from Gillot (2005)

It has been found that leafhoppers are not able to acquire equally phytoplasmas from different infected plant species. Chrysanthemum yellows (CY) phytoplasma is successfully transmitted by three leafhoppers, viz. *Euscelidius variegatus, Macrosteles quadripunctulatus* and *Euscelis incisus.* All three species acquire from and transmit to CY-infected chrysanthemum and uninfected chrysanthemum, respectively. However, only *M. quadripunctulatus* and *E. variegatus* acquire CY after feeding on CY-infected periwinkle and subsequently transmit CY to uninfected plants. None of the leafhoppers acquires the phytoplasma from CY-infected celery, a dead-end host. *Dead-end hosts* are plants that can be inoculated and subsequently become infected with phytoplasma, but from which insects can not acquire phytoplasma.

BACTERIA

Bacteria are microscopic single celled organisms increasing by fission, they have a cell membrane, a rigid cell wall and often one or more flagella. Of the total about 1800 known bacterial species, most are saprophytes living on dead plant or animal tissues or organic wastes. There are about 200 species of bacteria which are parasitic on plants and many of them consisting of numerous pathovars. Bacterial diseases fall into three categories : (*i*) Wilting, due to invasion of the vascular system or water-conducting vessels, e.g. cucumber wilt. (*ii*) Necrotic blights, rots and leaf spots, where the parenchyma is killed, e.g. fire blight. (*iii*) Hyperplasia or over growth, e.g. crown gall.

Pathogenic bacteria apparently cannot enter plants directly through unbroken cuticle but get in through insect or other wounds, stomata, hydathodes, lenticels and flower nectaries. The fact that the plant pathogenic bacteria are unable to penetrate plant tissue without a court of entry has led to the realization of significance of the role of insects in transmission. The insect contributes through feeding and oviposition wounds, as a mechanical carrier of the organism on its body and in some cases, by virtue of a mutualistic relationship between the organism and the insect which ensures a continuing association among pathogen, insect and the host plant.

A number of plant diseases caused by bacteria are known to be transmitted by insects (Table 16.3). Fire blight of apple and pear, caused by *Erwinia amylovora* is carried by aphids, leafhoppers, etc. Potato blackleg, caused by *Erwinia carotowora,* is transmitted by seedcorn maggot, *Hylemyia cilicrura*. Bacterial wilt of cucurbits, caused by *Erwinia tracheiphila* is transmitted by cucumber beetle, *Diabrotica duodecimpunctata*. Bacterial wilt of maize, caused by *Xanthomonas stewarti* is transmitted by the flea beetle, *Chaetocnema pulicaria*. Black rot of crucifers, caused by *Xanthomonas campestris* is transmitted by several insects and slugs.

Table 16.3 List of major vectors of bacterial diseases of crop plants

S.No.	Insect vector(s)	Disease	Host(s)
1.	*Chaetocnema pulicaria*, *C. denticulata* (Coleoptera : Chrysomelidae)	Bacterial wilt (or Stewart's bacterial wilt)	Maize
2.	*Diabrotica duodecimpunctata*, *D. vittata* (Coleoptera : Chrysomelidae)	Cucurbit wilt	Cucumber, muskmelon
3.	*Diaphorina citri* (Hemiptera : Aphalaridae)	Citrus canker	Citrus
4.	*Hylemya cilicrura*, *H. trichodactyla* (Diptera : Anthomyiidae)	Potato blackleg	Potato
5.	Wide range of species of bees, wasps, flies, ants and aphids	Fire blight	Apple, pear, quince, etc.

FUNGI

Fungi are organisms having no chlorophyll, reproducing by sexual and asexual spores, not by fission like bacteria and typically possessing a mycelium or mass of interwoven threads (hyphae) containing well marked nuclei. There are about 4300 valid genera of fungi and about 70,000 species living as parasites or saprophytes on other organisms or their residues. More than 8,000 species are known to cause plant diseases.

There are several insects associated with the spread of fungal diseases (Table 16.4). Many flies mechanically transmit the ergot of cereals caused by *Claviceps purpurea*. The ergot disease of *bajra*, caused by *Sphacelia microcephala*, is mechanically carried by insects that visit the flowers attracted by the sugary secretion found on the fungus infected earheads. The cotton wilt, caused by *Fusarium vasinfectum*, is transmitted through the faecel pellets of many grasshoppers like *Melanoplus differentialis*, after they have fed upon infected plants. The common sooty mould fungus (*Capnodium* spp.) grows on the honeydew excreted by several homopteran insects like aphids, leafhoppers, mealy bugs, whiteflies, etc.

Table 16.4 List of principal vectors of fungal diseases of crop plants

S.No.	Insect vector(s)	Disease	Host(s)
1.	*Hylurgopinus rufipes* (Coleoptera : Scolytidae)	Dutch elm disease	Elm
2.	*Melanoplus differentialis* (Orthoptera : Acrididae)	Cotton wilt	Cotton
3.	*Scolytus multistriatus, S. scolytus* (Fabricius) (Coleoptera : Scolytidae)	Dutch elm disease	Elm
4.	About 40 species of insects especially flies, beetles and aphids	Ergot of cereals	Cereals
5.	Several species of insect visiting flowers	Ergot of *bajra*	*Bajra*

MANAGEMENT OF VECTORS AND DISEASES

Among the various types of plant diseases transmitted by insects, virus diseases are considered to be the most serious. Hence a multi-pronged strategy needs to be adopted to manage the vectors and virus diseases. Some of the important components of such a strategy should involve selection of healthy seed, cultural practices, biological measures, resistant varieties and use of chemicals.

Healthy Seed

Management of virus diseases starts with obtaining healthy seed, cuttings or plants. Care should be taken to obtain only certified seed, *i.e.* seed obtained from the plants which have been inspected during growing season and found free of certain diseases. Virus-free foundation stock can be built up by heat treatment, *i.e.* growing plants at high temperatures for weeks or even months. The production of virus-free stocks can also be achieved by taking advantage of the fact that some plants grow and elongate faster than the virus can occupy the new tissue. Therefore, the virus can be eliminated by using meristem or tip cultured plants. Virus free stock is tested by indexing (growing a part of the cutting or plant in a pot or greenhouse and recording its condition with respect to disease symptoms), bioassays and/or serological assays.

Cultural Control

Several cultural practices have proved to be helpful in reducing the incidence of vectors and vector-borne diseases. Intercropping with a barrier crop has provided encouraging results to reduce the incidence of several diseases. For example, the incidence of yellow vein mosaic of okra is reduced by intercropping with soybean. Similarly, intercropping of tomato with coriander and lobiabean reduces the incidence of tomato leaf curl virus in tomato. Plant spacing such as close spacing reduces the incidence of French bean crinkle stunt disease. Manipulation in planting dates is another way of reducing the disease incidence. Rogueing also helps the removal of the source of disease causing organism. Removal of weeds and alternate hosts of viruses and vectors helps to reduce the incidence of diseases.

Resistant Varieties

Growing resistant/tolerant varieties is another effective way of managing vectors and vector-transmitted diseases. A number of genotypes have been identified under various All India Coordinated Research Projects, sponsored by the Indian Council of Agricultural Research and various State Agricultural Universities, which have resistance against virus borne diseases in pulses, tomato, cotton, etc.

Biopesticides

The use of biopesticides such as parasitoids and predators, microbials and plant extracts is an eco-friendly approach to manage the vectors and vector born diseases. A fungus, *Paecilomyces farinosus* has been found parasitic on *Bemisia tabaci*. Several neem-based formulations have provided effective control of *B. tabaci* on cotton. Aqueous extracts of leaves of *Clerodendron frageans* and *Aerva anguinolenta* and roots of *Boerhavia diffusa*, sprayed at 4 per cent concentrations at 3-4 days starting from germination, was found to reduce yellow mosaic incidence in blackgram and mungbean.

Chemical Control

The control of insect vectors by application of insecticides appears to be a difficult task as few survivors would be able to transmit the disease. Still insecticidal control of insect vectors is the most practicable method of control of plant viruses. The timely application of insecticides restricts the spread of the disease by reducing the vector population. Several systemic and non-systemic insecticides have been reported to control the insect vectors. The prominent insecticides reported to be effective are sprays of oxydemeton methyl, malathion, dimethoate, carbaryl, dichlorvos, fenitrothion, phosphamidon, monocrotophos, triazophos and ethion in doses ranging from 300 ml to 1·5 litres per ha. The soil application of carbofuran and phorate granules @ 10-12 kg per ha has also proved useful.

*****

FOREST ENTOMOLOGY

PART-III

- PESTS OF FOREST TREES

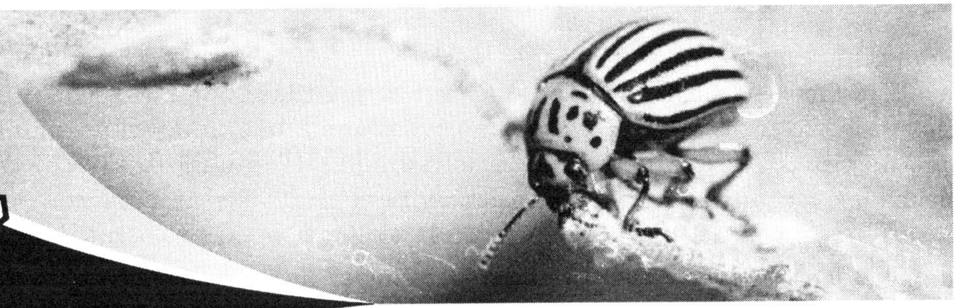

17 CHAPTER

PESTS OF FOREST TREES

Defoliators

Teak	1. *Hapalia machaeralis* Walker (Lepidoptera : Pyralidae)
(*Tectona grandis*)	2. *Eutectona machaeralis* Walker (Lepidoptera : Pyraustidae)
	3. *Hyblaea puera* Cramer (Lepidoptera : Hyblaeidae)
Poplar	1. *Clostera cupreata* Butler (Lepidoptera : Notodontidae)
(*Populus* spp.)	2. *Clostera fulgurita* (Walker) (Lepidoptera : Notodontidae)
Sheesham (*Dalbergia sisoo*)	1. *Plecoptera reflexa* Guenee (Lepidoptera : Noctuidae)
Gamhar (*Gmelina arborea*)	1. *Calopepla leayana* Latreille (Coleoptera : Chrysomelidae)
Deodar (*Cedrus deodara*)	1. *Ectropis deodarae* Prout (Lepidoptera : Geometridae)
Willows	1. *Lymantria obfuscata* Walker (Lepidoptera : Lymantriidae)
Sal (*Shorea robusta*)	1. *Lymantria mathura* Moore (Lepidoptera : Lymantriidae)
Ailanthus (*Ailanthus excelsa*)	1. *Atteva fabriciella* Swederus (Lepidoptera : Yponomeutidae)

Sap Suckers

1. *Heteropsylla cubana* Crawford (Hemiptera : Psyllidae)
2. *Urostylus puntigera* Westwood (Hemiptera : Penta-tomidae)
3. *Cinara cupressi* (Buckton) (Hemiptera : Aphididae)

4. *Pineus pini* (Macquart) (Hemiptera : Adelgidae)
5. *Nipaecoccus viridis* (Newstead) (Hemiptera : Pseudococcidae)
6. *Tingis beesoni* Drake (Hemiptera : Tingidae)
7. *Helopeltis* spp. (Hemiptera : Miridae)

Borers

Sal (*Shorea robusta*)	1. *Haplocerambyx spinicornis* Newman (Coleoptera : Cerambycidae)
Babool (*Acacia arabica*)	1. *Coelosterna scabrator* Fabricius (Coleoptera : Cerambycidae)
Teak (*Tectona grandis*)	1. *Dihammus cervinus* Hope (Coleoptera : Cerambycidae) 2. *Aleterogystia cadambae* (Moore) (Lepidoptera : Cossidae)
Mahogany (*Swietenia macrophylla*)	1. *Hypsiphla robusta* Moore (Lepidoptera : Pyralidae) 2. *Pagiophloeus longiclavis* Marshall (Coleoptera : Curculionidae)
Poplar (*Populus* spp.)	1. *Apriona cinerea* Cheverlot (Coleoptera : Cerambycidae)
Oak (*Quecrus incana*)	1. *Aphrodisum hardiwickionum* White (Coleoptera : Cerambycidae)
Bamboo (*Bambusa* spp.)	1. *Dinoderus* spp. (Coleoptera : Bostrychidae) 2. *Lyctus* sp. (Coleoptera : Lyctidae)

Soil Insects

1. Termites (Isoptera : Termitidae)
2. Cockchafers (Coleoptera : Scarabaeidae)

Forests are not only the most important natural resource for mankind but also the best protector of our climate and our earth's ecology. According to 2009 State of Forest Report of the Forest Survey of India, the total forest cover in the country is 698,899 km^2, which is 21.02 per cent of the geographical area. This cover comprises of very dense forest (2.54%), moderately dense forest (9.71%) and open forest (8.77%). Next to man, the greatest destroyer of forests are insects which damage almost all parts of the forest trees. The annual loss caused by insects to seeds, transplants, standing trees, wood and finished products has been estimated to be about 10 per cent of the total revenue of the forests.

DEFOLIATORS

The foliage of trees provides food to a large varieties of insects such as the leaf-miners, leaf rollers, leaf feeders, sap suckers, gall producers, etc. The overall effects of all these insects on the health of the trees are the same, namely, a serious attack may kill the trees, a moderate one debilate them and adversely affect the quality of wood they produce.

1. Teak is defoliated by the caterpillars of two species of moths, ***Hapalia machaeralis* (Lepidoptera : Pyralidae)** (Fig. 17.1A) and ***Hyblaea puera* (Lepidoptera : Hybacidae)**

(Fig. 17.1B). The insects derive their destructive power by their sheer numbers. A female lays from 500-1000 eggs per year and the short life-histories of these insects produce several generations so that one can easily imagine what the vast populations of them must be feeding upon the leaves of the trees every year. The caterpillars, being voracious feeders skeletonise the leaves or even completely defoliate the trees in no time.

2. **Teak skeletonizer, *Eutectona machaeralis* (Lepidoptera : Pyraustidae)** has a wide distribution in India. The moth lays 250-500 eggs singly on leaves and the incubation period is 2-3 days. The grown up larva is green with brown or yellow longitudinal bands laterally. The larva skeletonizes the leaf uniformly. The larva becomes full-grown in 18-27 days and pupates on the leaf itstelf or on fallen leaves. The pupal period is 4-11 days. There are 10-12 generations in a year.
3. **Sheesham defoliator, *Plecoptera reflexa* (Lepidoptera : Noctuidae)** (Fig. 17.1C) female lays 400 eggs, the larval period lasts 14-21 days and pupal period, 5-12 days, pupation occurring amongst the fallen leaves. The caterpillars flourish on young leaves and during an epidemic, when the foliage has been completely destroyed, masses of larvae can be seen moving on the ground in search of food.
4. Gamhar (*Gmelina arborea)* trees grow up to 18 metres. Its wood is similar to teak lasting well under water. The juice of the leaves of these trees is said to provide relief in gonorrhoea, cough and ulcers. The plants are also used as an antidote for snake-bite and scorpion sting. **Gamhar defoliator, *Calopepla leayana* (Coleoptera.: Chrysomelidae)** (Fig. 17.1D), causes serious damage to these trees in Assam and Bengal. They are active from July to October, going in hiding for the remaining eight months in the cracks, holes, under fallen leaves, under dead bark, in hollow bamboos and in grass heaps.
5. **Deodar defoliator, *Ectropis deodarae* (Lepidoptera : Geometridae)** (Fig. 17.1E) occurs in an epidemic form in cycles that last 2-3 years at intervals of 7-10 years. The pest is found at higher altitudes above 1500 m and most injurious to deodar forests in Punjab and U.P. Females with poorly developed wings climb up the trees to lay their eggs on the needles of deodar. The caterpillars emerge in spring, eat up the needles by end of summer and climb down to pupate under a layer of humus or amongst fallen needles before the rains start. The rest of the year is passed in pupal stage.
6. **Willow defoliator, *Lymantria obfuscata* (Lepidoptera : Lymantriidae)** (Fig. 17.1F), is the most serious pest in Kashmir and N-W Himalayas. Eggs hatch in early April and the larvae feed for 6 weeks during cooler hours of the morning; in the afternoon they congregate on the bark of the trees, on the undersurface of the branches and under the debris and stones. Larvae pupate in similar places in June and emerge as adults by June-end or July. Willows yield wood with which sports goods like cricket bats, hockey sticks etc. are made
7. Ailanthus (*Ailanthus excelsa*) is deciduous tree planted on a large scale in the Nimar Forest division of M.P. Its wood is in great demand for the paper industry and various species of *Ailanthus* yield drugs that are considered anti-amoebic and even anti-cancer. ***Atteva fabriciella* (Lepidoptera : Yponomeutidae)** is a serious defoliator of *Ailanthus* in South India. It undergoes a series of nine overlapping generations in a year.

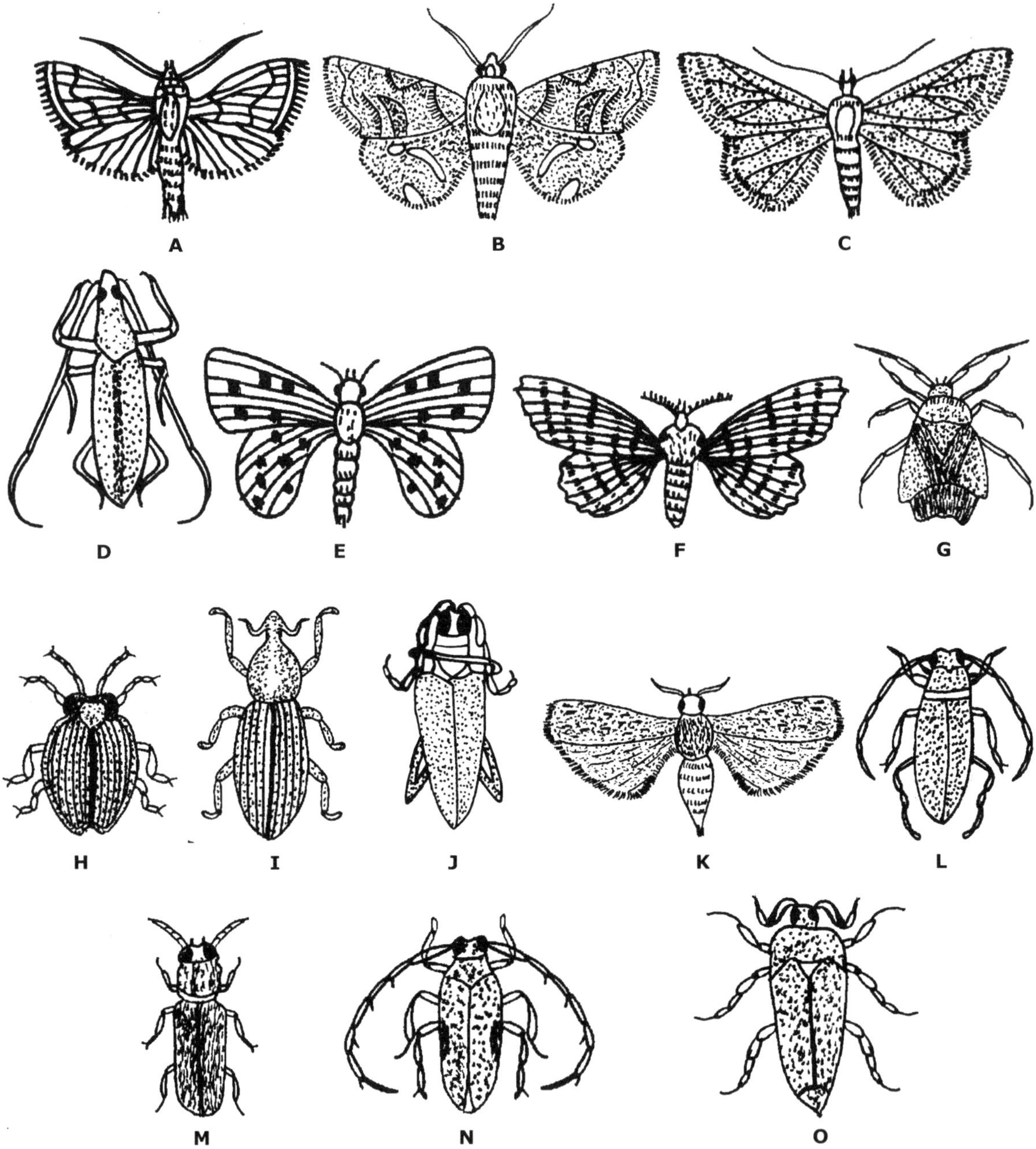

Fig. 17.1 Pests of forest trees. **A.** Teak moth, *Hapalia machaeralis*. **B.** Teak moth, *Hyblaea puera*. **C.** Sheesham defoliator, *Plecoptera reflexa*. **D.** Gamhar defoliator, *Calopepla leayana*. **E.** Deodar defoliator, *Ectropis deodarae*. **F.** Willow defoliator, *Lymantria* spp. **G.** Pentatomid bug, *Urostylus puntigera*. **H.** Sal heartwood borer, *Haplocerambyx spinicornis*. **I.** Babul borer, *Coelosterna scabrator*. **J.** Teak borer, *Dihammus cervinus*. **K.** Mahogany shoot borer, *Hypsiphla robusta*. **L.** Mahogany collar borer, *Pagiophloeus longiclavis*. **M.** Oak heart- wood borer, *Aphrodisum hardiwickionum*. **N.** Bamboo beetle, *Lyctus* spp.. **O.** Bamboo beetle, *Dinoderus* spp.

SAP-SUCKERS

1. **The psyllid, *Heteropsylla cubana* (Hemiptera : Psyllidae)**, is a serious pest of widely planted, multipurpose tree, *Leucaena leucocephala*. Females lay eggs on young unopened leaves, eggs being attached to the leaf surface by stalk. A female may lay 400 eggs in her life time. Nymphs hatch in 2-3 days and there are five nymphal instars lasting about 9 days. The total life-cycle is about 14 days. Both nymphs and adults feed on foliage, causing leaflets to turn yellow, curl and wilt. Massive populations can cause shoot necrosis, defoliation and death of the tree. The deposition of honey dew encourages the growth of sooty moulds which can interfere with the development of adjacent leucaena leaflets.
2. **The pentatomid bug, *Urostylus puntigera* (Hemiptera : Pentatomidae)** (Fig. 17.1G) destroys *champa* forests in Bengal and Assam by sucking plant sap. A female can lay up to 450 eggs and the pest having five generations, hibernates in winter.

BORERS

The larvae of many beetles and moths cause considerable damage to forest trees by boring into the trunks and feeding on their living tissues. They bore holes and tunnels of various sizes, thus reducing the vitality of the trees and often causing their decay and death. In any case, the quality of the timber is affected and the value of the plantation goes down.,

1. **Sal heartwood borer, *Haplocerambyx spinicornis* (Coleoptera : Cerambycidae)** (Fig. 17.1H), is on record to have destroyed 60 lakh sal trees in a single epidemic in North and Central India. The female of this dark brown beetle lays 100-300 eggs. The grubs on hatching first feed under the bark, then on the sapwood and finally on the heartwood, where they pass the winter and spring in tunnels packed with woodfibres and emerge during May-June.
2. **Babul borer, *Coelosterna scabrator* (Coleoptera : Cerambycidae)** (Fig. 17.1I) is a very serious pest of babul in M.P. The larvae bore into the stem and roots hollowing them out. Adult beetles feed during night on the bark of young shoots in irregular patches, thus girdling and eventually killing them
3. **Teak borer, *Aleterogystia cadambae* (Lepidoptera : Cossidae)** is an important pest of standing teak trees in Kerala, Tamil Nadu and Karnataka. It causes extensive bark injury and riddling of the bark with numerous holes. Initially, the caterpillar feeds on bark and sap wood in the axis of side shoot and then tunnels into the heart wood. The larval stage lasts for about eight months and the larvae pupate in the soil. The presence of borer holes affects the commercial value of the converted teak.
4. **Teak borer or canker grub, *Dihammus cervinus* (Coleoptera : Cerambycidae)** (Fig. 17.1J), is an injurious pest of both teak and *Gmelina arborea* in Northern India. Its feeding causes irritation that induces the formation of cankers twice the diameter of the stem. Tunneling and canker formation is more extensive in teak than in Gmelina.
5. **Mahogany shoot borer, *Hypsiphla robusta* (Lepidoptera : Pyralidae).:** (Fig. 17.1K), and Mahogany collar-borer, *Pagiophloeus longiclavis* (Fig. 17.1L) do a lot of damage to the precious Mahogany trees, the former being more serious in the south (Coimbatore region) and the latter also in Assam and Bengal and is attracted by the flowing sap from trees injured by the former.

6. **Oak heartwood borer, *Aphrodisum hardiwickionum* (Coleoptera : Cerambycidae)** (Fig. 17.1M), is a metallic green beetle whose grubs tunnel into the heartwood of the stem, frass ejecting from the holes. The tunneling is so extensive that despite girth, the weight of the stem is greatly reduced which is a loss to the growers who sell the wood by weight for fuel.
7. Two important timber trees Nangu (*Mesua ferrea*) and Vayal (*Poeciloneuron indicum*) which constitute the evergreen forests of the Western Ghats and South India are attacked by the beetle ***Chrysochroa* spp. (Coleoptera : Buprestidae)**. The wood of these trees is used for making railway sleepers, bridges and buildings. 8. Bamboos which provide multipurpose wood (for scaffolding, tentpoles, ladders, poles for boat masts, support for beetle vines, umbrella, sticks, furniture, basket, etc.) are attacked by the beetles, ***Lyctus* spp. (Coleoptera : Lyctidae)** (Fig. 17.1 N) and ***Dinoderus* spp. (Coleoptera : Bostrichidae)** (Fig. 17.1O). The beetles bore through the cut-ends, abrasions and injuries on culm surfaces and make galleries for egg-laying. The larvae excavate long tunnels up and down, and the adults escape after boring several holes. The pest has 3-4 generations a year.

SOIL INSECTS

The important soil dwelling insects that cause appreciable damage to our forest trees are termites and cock-chafers. Termites cause damage to forest nurseries and young plantations by attacking the roots. The common genera injurious to forests are ***Captotermes, Odontotermes*** and ***Cryptotermes* (Isoptera : Termitidae)**. Termites also attack felled trees if they are left uncared for a long time and timber used in the construction of buildings, bridges and furniture. The cock-chafers or white grubs which cause injury to seedlings are ***Holotrichia consanguinea, Granida albosparsa*** and ***Melolontha* spp. (Coleoptera : Scarabaeidae)** Typically, the adult female burrows into the soil to lay her legs, larvae live in the soil, feeding on decaying organic matter when young and later on plant roots. They migrate through the soil profile, burrowing deeper in very cold or very hot, dry weather, and coming close to the surface in wet conditions. They pupate in the soil often in a smooth-walled cell. New adults may remain in the soil for a period until stimulated to emerge by heavy rain. Some species feed on leaves of trees and can cause occasionally severe damage. The life-cycle of most species lasts 1-2 years.

MANAGEMENT OF FOREST INSECT PESTS

Control of forest pests is much more difficult than the control of agricultural pests because it is more costly, detection of incipient infestation is difficult and it needs highly skilled labour. Following methods, however, can be adopted for keeping the forest pest populations under check.

- Regular patrolling of forests should be carried out to detect infestations as also to fell and remove the infested trees from the forest areas.
- Manual collection of eggs, larvae, diapausing pupae and adult beetles for being killed in kerosenised water or by insecticides.
- Adoption of clean culture to remove alternate host plants of pests.
- Maintenance of natural mixed undergrowth flora to encourage breeding of parasitoids and predators of the forest pests.

- Banding of trees with grease or coal-tar in the case of deodar defoliator whose females, being unable to fly, climb the stems to reach foliage for oviposition. If the branches of banded trees could be shaken strongly, the larvae feeding on leaves will be forced to fall on the ground; they will then not be able to climb the trees beyond the band.
- Search and introduction of biocontrol agents (parasitoids, predators and pathogens) is the most rewarding method of forest pest control because of their self-sustaining ability.
- Many insect pests undergo diapause for which they look for protected places. Artificial shelter traps could be provided to collect such insects for being destroyed.
- Pheromones could be employed either to collect one of the sexes in pheromone-baited traps or to disrupt chemical communication between sexes and thus prevent mating. The advantages of pheromonal control are : (*i*) the insects are forced to come to the chemicals (pheromones) and the chemicals are not to be carried to insects as in the case of insecticides, and (*ii*) for disruption of chemical communication, pheromone dispensers are now available for being scattered over forests by aircrafts, thus saving both labour and time.
- In many cases (*e.g.* sal heartwood borer), insects are attracted to the trees by the smell of their sap. Therefore, if an infested tree is felled and logged and the logs scattered in infested areas, fresh sap would attract the pests to the logs sparing to a great extent the trees.
- Felled trees have to be removed from the forest to storage depots as quickly as possible to minimize exposure to pests. The cut-end may also be swabbed with creosote to give further protection. In the storage depots also, the logs should be sold or exported as soon as possible.
- Use of chemical toxicants, in general, has not been considered advisable in forestry practices because of certain inherent problems, such as environmental pollution, disturbance in species diversity, pesticide resistance, and above all economic viability. However, in situations where other methods have not been successful, pesticides have been employed, including aerial spraying on a limited scale.
  - Foliar sprays of fenitrothion (0.04%), and monocrotophos and quinalphos (0.05%) have been found effective against poplar defoliators.
  - Aerial spraying of fenitrothion 50EC @ one litre per ha is very effective against deodar defoliator.
  - Inject 5 ml of paradichlorobenzene in kerosene per tree from lower most hole and plug the hole with clay, to kill the grub population of babool borer and poplar stem borer.
  - Drench the soil with chlorpyriphos 20EC @ 50 ml per 5 litres of water for the control of termites.
  - For protection against soil insects in the nursery, general application, of 0.03 per cent water solution of any insecticide, *e.g.* chlorpyriphos 20EC (75 ml) or lindane 20EC (75 ml) in 50 litres of water on the surface of nursery beds should be carried out before sowing.

*****

HOUSEHOLD, VETERINARY AND MEDICAL ENTOMOLOGY

PART-IV

- HOUSEHOLD PESTS
- PESTS OF FARM ANIMALS
- PESTS OF PUBLIC HEALTH IMPORTANCE

18 CHAPTER

HOUSEHOLD PESTS

1. *Periplaneta americana* (Linnaeus) (Cockroach, Dictyoptera : Blattidae)
2. *Blatella germanica* (Linnaeus) (Cockroach, Dictyoptera : Blatellidae)
3. *Grylloids sigillatus* Linnaeus (House cricket, Orthoptera : Gryllidae)
4. *Acheta domesticus* (Linnaeus) (House cricket, Orthoptera : Gryllidae)
5. *Monomorium indicum* Forel (Brown ants, Hymenoptera : Formicidae)
6. *Camponotus compressus* Fabricius (Black ants, Hymenoptera : Formicidae)
7. *Polistes hebraeus* (Fabricius) (Yellow wasp, Hymenoptera : Vespidae)
8. *Vespa orientalis* Linnaeus (Brown wasp, Hymenoptera : Vespidae)
9. *Tinea pellionella* (Linnaeus) (Clothes moth, Lepidoptera : Tinaeidae)
10. *Lepisma sachharina* Linnaeus (Silverfish, Thysanura : Lepismatidae)
11. *Anthrenus flavipes* Le Conte (Carpet beetle, Coleoptera : Dermestidae)
12. *Attagenus piceus* (Olivier) (Carpet beetle, Coleoptera : Dermestidae)
13. *Lyctus africanus* Lesne (Powder-post beetle, Coleoptera : Lyctidae)
14. *Liposcellis transvaalensis* Enderlein (Book louse, Psocoptera : Liposcelidae)
15. *Lasioderma serricorne* (Fabricius) (Cigarette beetle, Coleoptera : Anobiidae)

Many of the household pests are cosmopolitan in distribution because wherever human beings went, they took these pests alongwith their belongings. There are two main types of pests in the houses, *viz.* those which are generally observed flying in the houses and those which are seen crawling on the ground, furniture, clothes and other belongings. The flying type of insects are particularly annoying to man as they disturb his well-being, sleep and comfort apart from acting as vectors of various diseases. The crawling type of insects breed, feed and live in the houses, and damage various types of goods, including food articles.

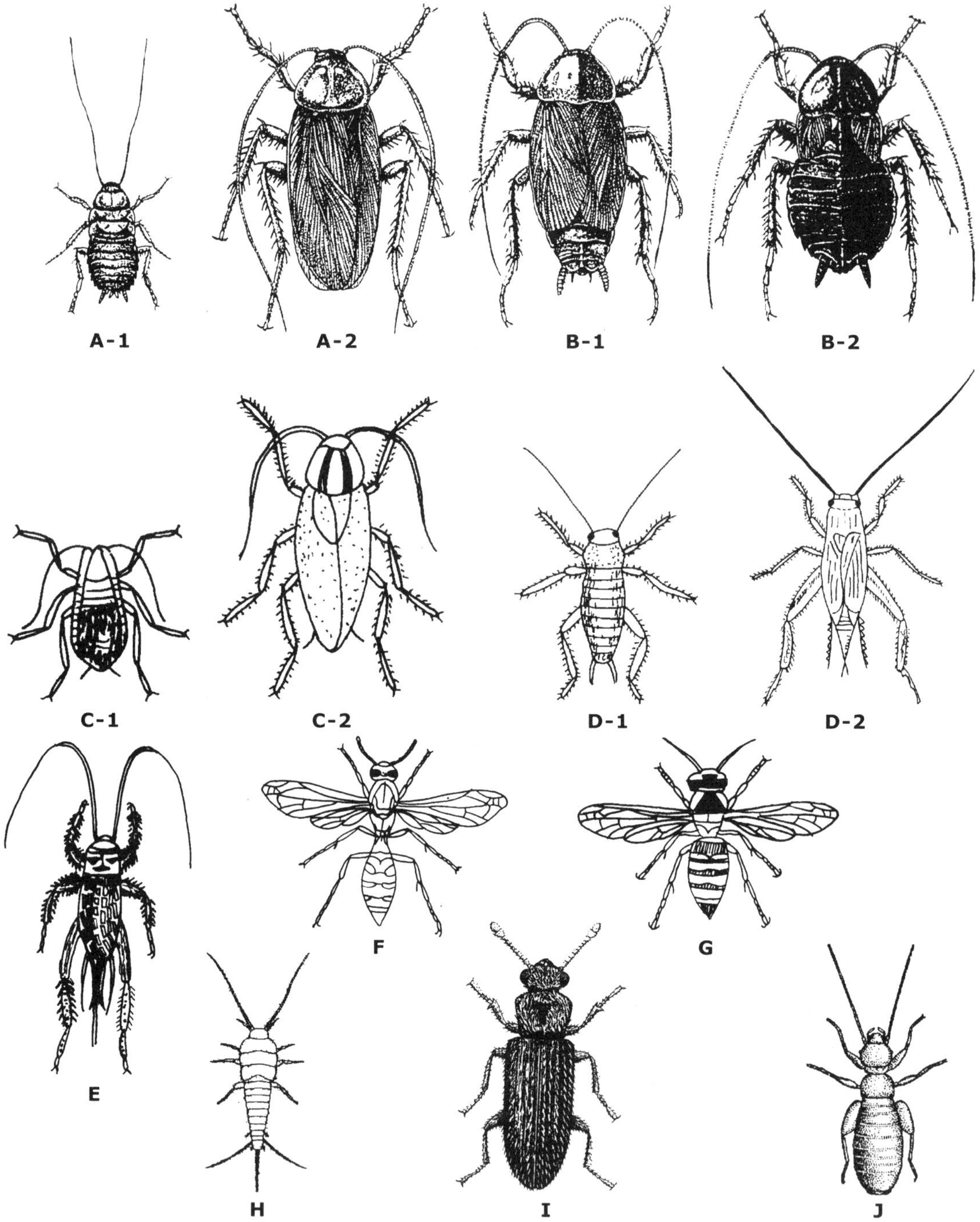

Fig. 18.1 Household pests. **A.** Cockroach, *Periplaneta americana*. A-1. Nymph, A-2. Adult. **B.** Cockroach, *Blatta orientalis*; B-1. Male, B-2. Female. **C.** Cockroach, *Blatella germanica*; C-1. Nymph, C-2. Adult. **D.** House cricket, *Grylloides sigillatus*; D-1. Nymph, D-2. Adult. **E.** House cricket, *Acheta domesticus*. **F.** Yellow wasp, *Polistes* spp. **G.** Brown wasp, *Vespa* spp. **H.** Silverfish, *Lepisma succharina*, **I.** Powder-post beetle, *Lyctus* spp. J. Book louse, *Liposcellis transvaalensis*.

1. *Periplaneta americana* (Linnaeus) (Fig. 18.1A), *Blatta orientalis* Linnaeus (Fig. 18.1B) (Cockroaches, Dictyoptera : Blattidae), *Blatella germanica* (Linnaeus) (Fig. 18.1C) and *Supella longipalpa* (Fabricius) (Cockroaches, Dictyoptera : Blatellidae).

Distribution. Cockroaches are cosmopolitan in distribution but they thrive in tropical and sub-tropical climates. While the above species of cockroaches are more commonly found in India, there are some other species too that are restricted to some regions of the country.

Identification. *P. americana* is the largest and dark brown in colour, *B. orientalis* is dark brown to black coloured, *B, germanica* is small and pale ochraceous coloured and *S. longipalpa* is also small but brown and white banded cockroach.

Life-history. In case of *P. emericana*, 25-30 eggs are laid in bean-shaped or lady's purse-shaped dark brown chitinous capsules called ootheca which is carried protruding at the end of the female abdomen for several days before being deposited at any warm sheltered and dark place (neglected containers, boxes, cupboards, corners of the roofs, walls or even clothes in wardrobes). The female cockroach produces an ootheca once in 4 or 5 days and 15-90 oothecae may be laid. Each ootheca contains 14-16 eggs and the incubation period ranges from 15 to 100 days. The nymphal period occupies 10-16 months. Generally, there is only one generation.

Damage. Both nymphs and adults do the damage. Being omnivorous, they eat and contaminate all kinds of food with their excreta. They eat away bookbindings and leather articles for the sake of starchy glue, and leave unacceptable roachy odour wherever they go. The cockroaches are a common sight in trains, unclean kitchens and restaurants, in old musty buildings and other filthy places. They are also suspected of transmitting some diseases by contaminating food with germs.

Management. (*i*) Cockroaches inhabit dark moist places like crevices, boxes, underboxes, cupboards, drains etc.; therefore, clean house-keeping leaving no place neglected can keep cockroach numbers low. (*ii*) The cockroaches can be killed by spraying the room with malathion/ chlopyriphos (0.5%) or by repeated dustings with malathion, carbaryl (5%) at night in the corners on the floor along the walls, taking care that food materials are not contaminated with insecticides. (*iii*) Dichlorvos (0.5%) spray may also be used in situations where a rapid knock-down effect is desired. The combined application of dichlorvos and a persistent insecticide can be made for getting both the knock-down and the residual effects.

2. *Grylloides sigillatus* Linnaeus (Fig. 18.1D) and *Acheta domesticus* (Linnaeus) (Fig. 18.1E) (Crickets, Orthoptera : Gryllidae)

Distribution. Two species of crickets, *Gryllodes sigillatus* and *Acheta domesticus* are commonly found throughout India, the former being more aburdant in the houses and the latter more abundant in the fields.

Identification. The house cricket (*G. sigillatus*) is dull straw coloured insect with deep brown spots on the body. The female is apterous (wingless) and bears long ovipositor in addition to a pair of cerci. The male, on the other hand, is winged with anterior wings hardened into tegmina and the posterior ones reduced to pads. The field cricket (*A. domesticus*) is dark brown in colour with wings in both sexes, the anterior pair being tegmina and the posterior pair, thin, papery long and folded in the form of a tail in between the cerci.

Life-history. These insects breed in late summer and autumn. A female lays eggs in batches of 30 in holes in dark moist soil, crevices or even on fabrics. The eggs hatch in about a week and give rise to tiny active nymphs which resemble the adults except that they are smaller and wingless. They are full-grown in 3-4 months. There is only one generation in a year.

Damage. Due to their shrill, monotonous chirping noise during the night, they are a great nuisance in the house. They are omnivorous feeding on all kinds of materials ranging from cereals to cotton, silken and woollen clothes. They also damage crops in the fields by eating away roots and underground stems of various crops and fruits.

Management. Crickets can be killed by dusting the corners and floors of the house with malathion/carbaryl (5%) at night, taking care that the food-stuffs are placed at a safe height.

3. *Monomorium indicum* Forel and *Camponotus compressus* Fabricius (Ants, Hymenoptera : Formicidae)

Distribution. Ants are cosmopolitan in distribution; the above species being found all over India.

Identification. *M. indicum* are brown and smaller, while *C. compressus* are large and black ants.

Life-history. The winged sexual forms of ants appear at the first rains. Like other social insects, they have a nuptial flight during which they mate, the male usually dying after the mating. The fertilised female seeks a suitable site for nest making where it sheds its wings, seals itself in a small chamber and starts laying eggs. In the beginning, the larvae are fed by the female (queen) with a secretion from its mouth but late when a population of adult (workers) have developed, they take over the function of taking care of all the duties of the nest, keeping it clean, feeding the larvae and transferring pupae to safer corners of the nest.

Damage. Ants bite and some even sting causing pain and burning sensation. They are attracted to sweet substances in great numbers, eating and spoiling them. There are also some species which are injurious because they build nests in the sills and wood work of the houses. The species that are found in lawns and walks in our house gardens throw mounds of earth about the entrance to their nests and thus disfigure the lawn. Some species feed on seeds, fats, dead insects, etc.

Management. (*i*) Nests situated outside the buildings can be destroyed by injecting CS_2, petrol or kerosene or lindane (5%) through holes punched at several places, (*ii*) Use of barriers such as dipping legs of cupboards in dishes containing a mixture of water and kerosene or sticking 'ant tapes' on the legs made from lamp-wick soaked in a saturated solution of corrosive sublimate or applying a paste of corrosive sublimate dissolved in ethyl alcohol and orange shellac added to it helps to keep the ants away. (*iii*) Dusting carbaryl 10 per cent or spraying 0.5 per cent solution of chlorpyriphos in deodorized kerosene in infested area may afford relief. (*iv*) Poison baiting with thallium sulphate bait for sweet loving ants and thallous sulphate bait for protein loving ants may be useful.

4. *Polistes hebraeus* (Fabricius) (Fig. 18.1F) and *Vespa orientalis* Linnaeus (Fig. 18.1G) (Wasps, Hymenoptera : Vespidae)

Distribution. *P. hebraeus* and *V. orientalis* are found in the plains of India.

Identification. *P. hebraeus* is uniformly yellow and *V. orientalis* is larger and deep brown with yellow bands in the abdomen. Both the species make their nests in protected places in houses, on the walls or ceilings or in the hollows of trees.

Life-history. The wasps are active in summer months and hibernate as fertilised females during the winter months. The first batch of brood is raised in spring either in new nests or old ones by the female alone. The later broods take over the brood-rearing work. The young larvae are fed on masticated animal tissue obtained by predation on insects or by biting off bits from the dead animals. Some sugary foods are also given. The full-grown larvae pupate in the cells which are capped by the workers. The adults on emergence bite their way out of these cells. During the cold season (winter), all workers and males die leaving the fertilised females (queens) of the last brood to survive till the next spring.

Damage. All wasps feed on ripe sweet fruits sometimes causing heavy damage. The mountain species (*Vespa magnifica*) is a serious pest of honey bees and becomes a hurdle in beekeeping in certain regions. The wasp sting is not just painful but it could even cause death of more sensitive victims.

Management. (*i*) Wasps can be warded off from their nests by smoke and then the nests could also be burnt (*ii*) They can be baited by hanging sugar baits containing trichlorphon as the poison in the houses or orchards.

5. *Tinea pellionella* (Linnaeus) and *Tinea pachyspila* Meyr. (Clothes moths, Lepidoptera : Tineidae)

Distribution. Both species are found all over India, *T. pellionella* being the more common one.

Identification. These moths are straw-coloured and tiny (less than 1.25 cm across the wings) in size.

Life-history. A female lays about 75 eggs on fabrics. The eggs hatch in 4-5 days.The pale-yellow larvae make a parchment like silken case around them which they drag along as they move. Larval stage lasts for about 5 days. Pupation occurs in these (larval) cases and adults start copulating soon after emergence.

Damage. The larvae feed on fabrics and articles made of wool, hair, feather, fur, dried skin, animal and fish meals, milk powders, and even dried insects. Numerous holes are made in the articles so that they become useless.

Management. (*i*) Materials should be thoroughly dried under the sun before storage; they should be preferably packed in polythene bags. (*ii*) Fumigation of boxes, wardrobes and houses if left vacant for some time with paradichlorobenzene and naphthalene balls spread on papers is useful.

6. *Lepisma saccharina* Linnaeus (Fig. 18.1H) and *Thermobia domestica* Packard (Silverfish, Thysanura : Lepismatidae)

Distribution. These insects occur all over the world.

Identification. *Lepisma* is wingless, silvery white and small (1-3 cm) insect with carrot-shaped body. *Thermobia* is like *Lepisma* but with upper surface mottled with black patches.

Life-history. These pests are active throughout the year in the warmer climates. All stages may be found throughout the year and the number of generations may vary according to the temperature and humidity of a locality. The female lays a few whitish oval eggs in warm and damp places, and the incubation period may be about a week. The young ones resemble the adults except that they are smaller. The development is slow and an indefinite number of moultings take place. The insects reach maturity in 7-9 months and the generations overlap.

Damage. The silverfishes live amongst neglected books, papers, files, behind picture hangings and on the walls of the pantries. They prefer starch materials (glue and starched cotton, clothings, bookbindings, wall paper, etc.), occasionally causing considerable damage to fabrics and libraries.

Management. (*i*) The population of the pest may be checked by regular cleansing and ventilation of the places. The cracks, if any, should be sealed. (*ii*) Poisoned glue pasted on small cardboard pieces to be placed on the books, serves an effective bait against these insects. The bait may be prepared by mixing wheat flour (200 parts), sodium fluoride or white arsenic (16 parts), powdered sugar (10 parts) and powdered common salt (5 parts). (*iii*) Dusting the haunts of the pest with malathion (5%) is also useful. Alternatively, naphthalene balls may also be kept in boxes.

7. *Anthrenus flavipes* Le Conte and *Attagenus piceus* (Olivier) (Carpet beetles, Coleoptera : Dermestidae)

Distribution. All these species are found throughout India and many other countries.

Identification. *Anthrenus flavipes* is oval and 3 mm long with red, yellow, white and black mottled markings. *Attagenus piceus* is uniformaly dull-black and 3-4 mm long.

Life-history. The eggs are laid on the food material of the larva or in secluded dark places. The eggs hatch in about 7 days. The newly hatched larvae are creamy-white and clothed with dark hairs. The larvae, unlike their parents, shun light and feed voraciously in the dark secluded folds of their food. Their cast-off skin (exuviae) closely resemble and are often mistaken for the living larvae. The larval period lasts for 18 days and pupae may take 24 days to become adults. The entire life-history may be completed in as long as 1-3 years depending on temperature, humidity and nature of the food.

Damage. The damage is done by the larvae alone, the adults feeding on pollens and nectar in the outdoor. The larvae can feed on any animal product such as wool, hair, fur, leather, skin, feather, horn, bristles, dry insects, and also on silk rayon, linen and jute. Feeding in between the folds of the fabrics, they make irregular holes.

Management. (*i*) Woollen articles, *i.e.* carpets, blankets and woollen clothes should be occassionally exposed to strong sun, beaten or frequently brushed; in off-season, they could be stored along with naphthalene balls or packed in polythene bags which act as barriers to insects; (*ii*) Stuffed skin specimens could be painted with turpentine oil containing 10-12% orthodichlorobenzene; horns and bones could be cleaned with turpentine oil and boxes storing insect and plant specimens could carry a mixture of naphthalene powder, creosote, chloroform and petroleum (6 : 1 : 1 : 4 parts) in small cloth sacs or simply a mixture of napthalene powder and paradichlorobenzene. (*iii*) In the case of widespread infestation, the entire house could be fumigated with CS_2 or the cracks and crevices sprayed with lindane or pyrethrum (1%) mixed in deodorized kerosene.

8. *Heterobostrychus aequalis* (Waterhouse) and *Dinoderus ocellaris* Stephens (Furniture beetles, Coleoptera : Bostrichidae), and *Lyctus africanus* Lesne (Powder-post beetle, Coleoptera : Lyctidae) (Fig. 18.1I)

Distribution. The furniture beetles occur all over India.

Identification. *H. aequalis* is a small black and cylindrical beetle with its prothorax acting as a hood over the head and the elytra bearing curved projections at the hind margins.

D. ocellaris is 3-4 mm long, brownish beetle and *L africanus* is 2-4 mm long, light-brown coloured beetle.

Life-history. *H. aequalls* is a very common borer of packing cases, boxes, plywood chests, panels, fittings and furniture. The adult beetle lays eggs in small tunnels excavated by it in the timber or even on its surface. The newly ecdysed larvae bore into the wood making deep irregular tunnels packing the holes with fine food dust. The full-grown larva pupates in a cell at the end of a tunnel. The freshly emerged beetle continues to feed and bore for some time before it finally escapes by making a hole on the surface. The life-history may be completed in 1-6 years depending on the environmental conditions.

D. ocellaris is a serious pest of bamboo furniture and articles and felled bamboo plants. The eggs laid in pores and depressions on the surface of the wood, hatch in 5-6 days. Like the adults, the newly hatched larvae also bore into the interior of the wood, packing the tunnels with fine powdery frass; the adult frass, however, is in the form of pellets. Pupation occurs at the end of a tunnel and the adult stays inside for a while feeding and boring before escaping by cutting a hole or by travelling back through the existing passage (tunnel).

L. africanus, popularly known as the 'powder-post' beetle due to its attacking telegraphic and other wooden poles (posts) and rendering them into powder, also attacks packing cases, planks, board furniture, plywood, tool-handles, etc. The eggs are laid in the open pores on the surface of the sawn timber. Hatching occurs in 1-2 weeks and newly hatched larva tunnels into the wood widening the tunnel as it goes deeper. The powdery frass excreted by the larva is packed closely in the tunnels. The adult beetle cuts its way out of a circular hole and may have 1-3 generations in a year in favourable conditions but in unfavourable conditions, even one generation may last as long as 8 years.

Damage. All the three species of beetles do a lot of damage to wooden structures. The insects cut the hard and dry wood tunnelling through timbers in successive generations until the interior is completely reduced to fine packed powder. Small shot holes are visible externally. They are often responsible for destruction of timbers of buildings, log cabins, furniture, tool handles, etc.

Management. (*i*) Unpolished furnitures may be painted with benzene or CCl_4 mixed with naphthalane while polished products should be frequently polished or varnished to protect them from the beetles. (*ii*) For protection against *Lyctus,* timber should be impregnated with $CuSO_4$ or $ZnCL_2$ solution. (*iii*) Infested wood should be sprayed with lindane (1%). (*iv*) Bamboo articles should be painted with crude creosote oil.

9. *Liposcellis transvaalensis* Enderlein (Fig. 18.1J) (Book louse, Pscopotera : Liposcelidae)

Distribution. Book lice or psocids are cosmopolitan in distribution; they are active and gregarious insects found in bookbindings, paper, wall-paper, boxes, libraries, museums, dark, damp and dingy places inside houses, mills, warehouses and food-stores.

Identification. They are small about 1.0 mm long insects, light-brown, grey or pale yellow in colour.

Life-history. The eggs are laid singly or in masses at damp places near their food. The number of nymphal instars depends on the weather conditions. In favourable warm conditions, they may breed throughout the year.

Damage. Psocids are not usually injurious unless their breeding place is not disturbed for a long time and they are allowed to increase in large numbers. They eat away starchy (glued) materials like bookbindings. They can also damage zoological and botanical museum specimens.

Management. (*i*) The best way to eliminate the pest is to dry out the houses and provide ventilation. (*ii*) The old books and paper files should be brushed regularly. (*iii*) The articles likely to be infested should be kept in tight containers. (*iv*) The paste meant for binding books should contain 5 per cent copper sulphate. (*v*) The almirahs and shelves containing books and paper records should be treated with 5 per cent carbaryl dust. (*vi*) Heavily infested libraries should be made airtight and fumigated with carbon disulphide or phosphine.

10. *Lasioderma serricorne* (Fabricius) (Cigarette beetle, Coleoptera : Anobiidae)

Distribution. It is cosmopolitan in distribution.

Identification. The adult beetle is about 2.5 mm long, roundish and reddish-brown in colour. The head and prothorax are strongly bent downwards.

Life-history. The eggs are laid on the food the grubs feed on. The grubs are curved, cream-coloured and hairy. They are full-grown in 30-35 days. Pupation occurs in silken cocoon and lasts for 10 days. Six generations may be passed in a year.

Damage. Cigarette beetle is a very serious pest of stored tobacco in cigarette and cigar factories. The attack may start at the time of the harvest itself and continue up to the factory. These insects can also attack spices like turmeric, black and red pepper.

Management. (*i*) Heating the godown to 57.2°C or cooling the tobacco bales to 4°C for a week kills all stages of the pest. (*ii*) Fumigation of the entire room or vacuum fumigation of the tobacco bales with ethylene oxide and carbon dioxide is helpful (*iii*) Spraying godown with lindane (1%) or chlorpyriphos (0.5%) helps to control the insects.

*****

19 CHAPTER

PESTS OF FARM ANIMALS

Blood-sucking Flies (Diptera)

1. *Phlebotomus argentipes* Annandale & Brunetti
2. *Phlebotomus papatasi* (Scopoli) (Sand fly, Psychodidae)
3. *Tabanus striatus* Fabricius (Horse fly, Tabanidae)
4. *Stomoxys calcitrans* (Linnaeus) (Stable fly, Muscidae)
5. *Haematobia irritans* (Linnaeus) (Horn fly, Muscidae)
6. *Glossina palpalis* (Robineau-Desvoidy) (Tsetse fly, Muscidae)
7. *Simulium aureohirtum* Brunetti (Black fly, Simuliidae)
8. *Hippobosca maculata* Leach (Louse fly, Hippoboscidae)
9. *Siphona exigua* (de Meijere) (Buffalo fly, Tachinidae)

Myiasis Flies (Diptera)

Bot flies

1. *Gastrophilus intestinalis* (De Geer) (Horse bot fly, Oestridae)
2. *Oestrus ovis* Linnaeus (Sheep bot fly, Oestridae)
3. *Cephalopina titillator* (Clark) (Camel nasal bot fly, Oestridae)
4. *Hypoderma lineatum* (Villers) (Warble fly, Oestridae)

Blow flies

5. *Chrysomya bezziana* Villeneuve (Indian screwworm, Calliphoridae)
6. *Cochliomyia hominivorax* (Coquerell) (American screwworm, Calliphoridae)
7. *Calliphora erythrocephala* (Meigen) (Common blue bottle, Calliphoridae)

8. *Calliphoira vicina* Robineau-Desvoidy (Blue flies, Calliphoridae)
9. *Lucilia cuprina* (Wiedemann) (Green fly, Calliphoridae)
10. *Phormia regina* (Meigen) (Blue fly, Calliphoridae)

Flesh flies
11. *Sarcophaga* spp. (Flesh fly, Sarcophagidae)

Lice (Phthiraptera)

Sucking lice
1. *Haematopinus eurysternus* Denny (Cattle louse, Haematopinidae)
2. *Linognathus vituli* (Linnaeus) (Blue lice of cattle, Linognathidae)

Biting lice
3. *Menopon gallinae* (Linnaeus) (Shaft louse, Menoponidae)
4. *Columbicola columbae* (Linnaeus) (Pigeon louse, Philopteridae)
5. *Menacanthus stramineus* (Nitzsch). (Chicken body louse, Monoponidae).
6. *Bevicola* spp. (Animal lice, Trichodectidae)
7. *Trichodectis canis* (DeGeer) (Dog louse, Trichodectidae)

Fleas (Siphonaptera)

1. *Echidnophaga gallinaeca* (Westwood) (Stickfast flea, Hectosyllidae)
2. *Ctenocephalides canis* (Curtis) (Dog flea, Pulicidae)

Arachnids (Acarina)

Ticks
1. *Boophilus microplus* (Canestrini) (Cattle tick, Ixodidae)
2. *Hyalomma anatolicum* Koch (Cattle tick, Ixodidae)
3. *Argas persicus* (Oken) (Fowl tick, Argasidae)
4. *Rhipicephalus sanguineus* (Latreille) (Dog tick, Ixodidae)

Mites
5. *Demodex canis* Leydig (Dog mite, Demodicidae)
6. *Sarcoptes scabiei* (DeGeer) (Mange mite, Sarcoptidae)
7. *Psoroptes communis* (Furstenberg) (Scabies mite, Psoroptidae)

Pests of farm animals fall into two categories, *viz.* direct pests that damage the host animal by feeding on its blood or tissues, and indirect pests that act as vectors or intermediate hosts (or both) of parasites or pathogens, caushing disease. Some of the major diseases of livestock transmitted by insects and mites are listed in Table 19.1. The more important species to be regarded as veterinary pests are described herein.

BLOOD-SUCKING FLIES

1. *Phlebotomus* spp. (Sand fly, Diptera : Psychodidae)

There are 3 species of this genus found in India : *P. papatasi* (Fig. 19.1A), distributed all over northern India; *P. argentipes* occurring in Bengal and Assam; and *P. minutus* found in several parts of the country. These insects are small, about 3 mm long, slender and yellowish or buff-coloured with a hairy body.

Life-history. The flies live in damp and dark places and breed in sandy soil (so the name, sand flies), loose dirt, rubbish, damp cracks and crevices of ruined masonary. The egg laying

Table 19.1 Some animal diseases transmitted by insects and mites

Vector	Disease	Parasite	Transmission	Distribution
Musca domestica	Anthrax	*Bacillus anthracis*	Contamination	Worldwide
Culicoides spp.	Blue tongue of sheep	Virus	Bite	S. Africa
Simulium ornatum, etc.	Cattle filariasis	*Onchocerca gutturosa*, etc.	Bite	Europe, N. America
Simulium venustum	(Ducks)	*Leucocytozoon anatis*	Bite	N. America
Glossina spp.	Nagana	*Trypanosoma* spp.	Bite	Africa
Tabanidae	Surra	*Trypanosoma evansi*	Bite	India, South East Asia
Tabanidae	(Cattle)	*Trypanosoma theileri*	Bite	Cosmopolitan
Stomoxys calcitrans	Mal de Caderas	*Trypanosoma equinum*	Bite	S. America
Ctenocephalides felis	Dog tapeworm	*Dipylidium caninum*	Eating flea	Cosmopolitan
Dermanyssus gallinae	Fowl spirochaetosis	*Borrelia anserina*	Bite	Australia
Argas persicus	Duck tick paralysis	*Anaplasma marginale*	Bite	USA
	Poultry piroplasm	*Aegyptianella pullorum*	Bite	USA
	Fowl spirochaetosis	*Borrelia anserina*	Bite	Europe, Asia
Ixodes ricinus	Pyaemia of lambs	*Staphylococcus aureus*	Bite	Britain
	Redwater of Cattle	*Babesia bovis*	Bite	Africa
Boophilus annulatus	Texas cattle fever	*Babesia bigemina*	Bite	USA
Rhipicephalus spp.	East Coast fever (of cattle)	*Theileria parva*	Bite	E. and S. Africa
	Redwater of cattle	*Babesia bigemina*	Bite	Africa
Amblyomma hebraeum	Heartwater of cattle	*Rickettsia ruminantium*	Bite	Africa

Source : Hill (1997)

starts after 30-36 hours of blood meal. A female lays 30-35 eggs which hatch in 6-12 days, undergo 4 moults in 25-35 days to become pupa which moults in 6-14 days, into adult.

Damage. Both males and females suck blood, preferably of cattle but can feed also on horses, birds, man, dogs and hogs in that order. The insect's bite is a sharp painless incision with oozing accompanied by itching and formation of red pustule. In addition to debilating (weakening) effect and reduction of milk yield, these insects also transmit pathogens of diseases such as anthrax in animals, an acute viral "three day fever" (caused by *P. papatasii*), visceral (or Kala azar) and *cutaneous leishmaniasis* in man.

Management. (*i*) Elimination of breeding grounds, cracks and crevices from the walls and floors has a satisfactory control due to the flies' inability to move to other breeding places on account of their having a short flight-range. (*ii*) The flies are attracted to light at night and, thus, may be killed on the wall around lamps. (*iii*) Dust the dark corners in and around sheds with malathion 5 per cent dust. (*iv*) Spray the sheds to the point of run-off, using water based sprays @ 5-10 litres per 100 m^3 containing 0.5 per cent diazinon or 1 per cent malathion or 1 per cent ronnel.

2. *Tabanus* spp. (Horse flies, Diptera : Tabanidae)

Tabanids are known by many common names such as horse flies, gad flies, deer flies, green-headed flies, etc. Three genera of the insect, *viz. Tabanus, Chrysops* and *Haematopota* are found in this country of which the first one is most widely distributed. These insects are larger than the common house fly with a thick-set body, large head and big brilliantly coloured eyes that meet in the middle in the males but are separated in the females. The genus *Tabanus* has several species such as *T. rubidus, T. viva, T. striatus* (Fig. 19.1B), *T. macer* and *T. ditaeniatus*, all of which live in marshy places (rice fields, marshes, banks of ponds and pastures) and prefer sunlight.

Life-history. A female deposits 200-500 eggs in masses on aquatic and sub-aquatic vegetation as well as on logs of wood near water. The egg-masses are enclosed in a transparent and water-proof material. Hatching occurs in 5-8 days, and the larvae fall in mud. The carnivorous larvae nocturnally feed on small crustaceans, insects, snails, worms, etc., and moult 6 times to become pupae in 5-6 months time but before pupation, they move to drier places. Pupation takes place at a depth of 3 cm or more in the soil. The imago emerges in 10-18 days.

Damage. Only females are blood suckers, the males being nectar feeders. They bite during the day and fly along running animals as they attack. They feed on horse, cattle, camel, elephant and occasionally on man. The three genera have their preferences for feeding sites : *T. rubidens* feeds on the lower part of the back of the hind legs, *Chrysops dispar* on the inner side of the fore legs and *Haematopota javana* on the hump and neck. The animals may lose as much as 3 ounces of blood per day in areas where the flies abound. This weakens them and reduces their milk production. Besides, the tabanids transmit pathogens of anthrax (a contagious disease of cattle in which malignant pustule or *corbuncle* develops), equine anemia and surra in hoofed animals in India (in which the hoofs start rotting) and trypanosomal infections in animals in Africa. *Chrysops* spp. transmits tularemia (in which suppuration or pus formation occurs at the site of bite followed by inflammation and fever) in man and animals and loasis (a kind of filaria caused by the microfliariae named *Loa loa*) in Africa and other western countries.

Management. (*i*) Stagnant water in the area should be drained away to prevent breeding of the pest. (*ii*) Door nets or cloth covers can give some protection to farm and domestic animals. (*iii*) Oiling pools of water can kill adult females who dive to lay eggs. (*iv*) The application of sprays containing 0.1 per cent pyrethrins + 1 per cent piperonyl butoxide @ 1-2 litres per animal, twice or thrice a week is effective.

3. *Stomoxys calcitrans* (Linnaeus) (Stable fly, Diptera : Muscidae) (Fig. 19.1C)

Called stable flies, storm flies and stinging flies, these insects are cosmopolitan in distribution. They are somewhat oval, 6-8 mm long greyish insects resembling common house fly but differing in being more robust and darker with proboscis longer than the head and

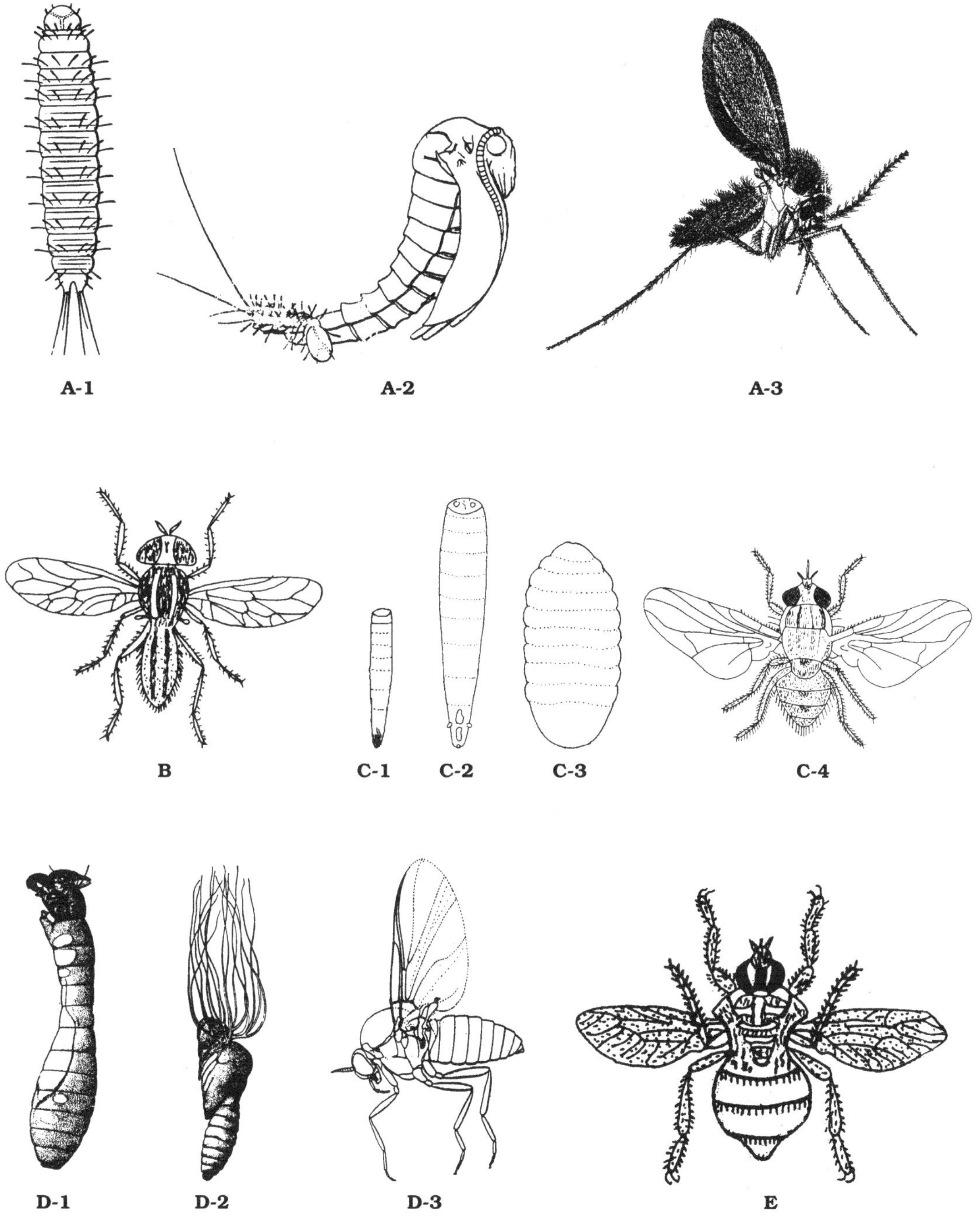

Fig. 19.1 Pests of farm animals : Blood sucking-flies. **A.** Sand fly, *Phlebotomus papatasi*; A-1. Larva, A-2. Pupa, A-3. Adult. **B.** Horse fly, *Tabanus striatus*. **C.** Stable fly, *Stomoxys calcitrans*; C-1. Egg, C-2. Larva, C-3. Pupa, C-4. Adult. **D.** Black fly, *Simulium* sp., D-1. Larva, D-2. Pupa, D-3. Adult. **E.** Louse fly, *Hippobosca maculata*.

wings more divergent. The fly frequents stables and farm yards attracted by the animals and moist decaying urine-mixed straw, hay and other vegetable matter. Besides animals, they also feed on fruits, straw and manure.

Life-history. Breeding takes place in moist decaying organic matter in the barnyard, stables, gardens, marshy ground and the banks of streams. The female burrows 5-7 cm the decyaing matter to lay 20-50 eggs or even more (maximum eggs reported is 278-820 per female). Oviposition starts in the evening after taking 3 blood meals. The larvae hatch in 7-21 days, move to drier grounds for pupation. Pupal stage lasts for 6-26 days and the life-cycle is completed in 4-5 weeks.

Damage. Both sexes bite to suck blood from the legs of horses and dairy cattle and from ankle of man if they happen to get inside the house specially in stormy weather. Terror and restlessness are caused to animals in the case of mass attack by the flies; horses get wild, animals lose weight and milk yield in cattle goes down. Besides, the flies also transmit viruses causing *poliomyeletis* (infantile paraylsis) and leprosy in man and anthrax, surra, swamp fever (infectious anemia of horses), trypanosomiasis and leishmaniasis in animals.

Management. (*i*) Straw/hay after harvest should be piled up in bales and not scattered in stables and barns. (*ii*) Destroy by burning of the possible breeding places like garbage, manure, wheat hay, straw, etc., and prompt disposal of dung and all other fermenting organic matter (vegetable residues, lawn clipping, etc.). (*iii*) Animals may be covered, their sheds wire-netted and brushes/sac-cloth suspended from shed/stable doors so that the flies accompanying the animals are brushed off as the animals enter. (*iv*) Chemical treatment of manure (equal parts of a mixture of borax and crude calcium borate dissolved in water) would kill the larvae in the manure. (*v*) The animal can be sprayed with 0.05 per cent pyrethrins + 0.5 per cent piperonyl butoxide (1-2 litres per head) once or twice a week. Alternatively, the animal may be treated with malathion 5 per cent dust @ 50 g per dairy cattle. (*vi*) The pest can be controlled by spraying diazinon (1%) on the surfaces in the cattle sheds.

4. *Siphona exigua* (de Meijere) (Buffalo fly, Diptera : Muscidae)

This fly is yellowish grey and is smaller than the stable fly. The proboscis is very slender and projects downwards. Though normally a pest of cattle and buffaloes, it may attack other species of livestock when the latter are moving with cattle and buffaloes. When feeding or resting on the host, the wings of this fly are held at an angle from its body.

Life-history. The fly lays eggs only on freshly dropped dung of cattle and buffaloes. About 20 eggs are laid by a female, which hatch within a day. The larvae feed for 3-5 days and pupate in the bottom layer of the dropping or in nearby soil. The adult emerges after a pupal period of 3-5 days.

Damage. The fly is active during the day and feeds on the flank and neck of the cattle. The bite of this fly is painful. The fly sucks considerable amount of blood of the host. A constant attack of hundreds of flies seriously affects milk production and work efficiency of the animals.

Management. Same as in case of stable fly.

5. *Haematobia irritans* (Linnaeus) (Horn fly, Diptera : Muscidae)

This fly has come to India from Africa. It is dark or yellowish-grey in colour, half the size of the house flies and stable flies. But unlike them, these remain on their hosts all the time.

When not feeding, they roost around the base of the horns forming a black ring (so the name horn flies) but they do not damage the horns.

Life-history. A female lays 300-400 eggs in fresh manure, dashing from the droppings of one animal to those of another. Within 2 minutes, the dung loses attraction to the female. The eggs hatch into maggots in a day or two, which feed on dung, moult and become full-grown in 3-5 days, pupate in dung or soil as brown seeds and the pupa hatches into adult in 6-8 days.

Damage. Both sexes suck blood chiefly from the cattle, but also from goats, horses, dogs and sheep. Being constantly in company of the host, they cause great annoyance and interference with the feeding of animals they parasitise. They bite on the flanks and neck producing weakness and reduction in milk yield. Man is rarely attacked. In animals, they are suspected of transmitting anthrax.

Management. (*i*) Darken the stables/cattle sheds since the insects are active in the light. (*ii*) Hang brushes/sac cloth on doors to brush the flies off as the animals enter (*iii*) Scatter or rake the dung/manure to make them dry and unattractive to insects, the hogs and chicken that run along with the cattle; scatter the dung and destroy the maggots.

6. *Glossina palpalis* (Rabineau-Desvoidy) (Tsetse fly, Diptera : Muscidae)

These insects are almost entirely confined to equatorial Africa. Nevertheless, a knowledge of them would be desirable because of their being of great medical importance both to man and animals. In Africa, there are 22 known species of these flies of which only 2, *viz. G. palpalis* and *G. morsitans* are of importance in transmitting the African sleeping sickness disease. They are yellow, yellowish-brown, dark brown or black flies, 6-13 mm in size prefering to live in moist habitat.

Life-history. It is viviparous, chooses sandy beaches and loose soil near water for larviposition. A female can deliver 10 fully developed larvae, one at a time at an interval of 10 days. The larvae burrow soon after they are born to a depth of 5 cm and immediately pupate. Pupal period lasts for 35-37 days.

Damage. While most species of *Glossina* are capable of transmitting trypanosomiasis in animals (which in animals is called *Nagana* of horse and cattle), only *G. palpalis* and *G. morsitans* spread African sleeping sickness in man due to their habit of sucking blood, which is done by both sexes. Most species bite only during the day time.

Management. (*i*) Destroy the habitat by cutting away trees along the river bank in the fly-belt. (*ii*) Create barrier-screen to prevent passage of the flies along the river course. (*iii*) Handpick and trap adult flies. (*iv*) Destroy game animals that act as reservoirs for the pathogen, *Trypanosoma* whose effectiveness is, however, debatable since the flies could take to smaller animals such as birds, reptiles and rodents as a source of food. (*v*) Spray pyrethrum on habitats, barrier screens and breeding grounds.

7. *Simulium aureohirtum* Brunetti (Black fly, Diptera : Simuliidae) (Fig. 19.1D).

These flies are cosmopolitan in distribution. They are small, 2-3 mm long and robust insects living in forests near running streams and breeding in moderately running water.

Life-history. The eggs, 300-500, are laid in masses enveloped in a gelatinous material on sub-merged plants, rocks, stones, leaves and debris. They hatch in 3-4 days, the larvae feed on algae and small animals, moult 7 times in 13 days to pupate in a silken cocoon resembling an open pocket with long respiratory filaments attached on the thorax. In 3-10 days, accumulation of a gas ruptures the pupa and the bubble carries the adult to the surface.

Damage. The insects are vicious biters causing server irritation. Both sexes suck blood from the head, neck and legs of cattle, horses and other domestic animals with a debilating effect. They transmit a filarial disease called *onchocerciasis* in man living in the vicinity of wooded streams in Africa, Mexico and other central American countries.

Management. The control of this insect is difficult but it can attempted by (*i*) removal of sub-merged objects to prevent oviposition, and (*ii*) destruction of the larvae by treating water with oil plus insecticide.

8. *Hippobosca maculata* Leach (Louse fly, Diptera : Hippoboscidae) (Fig 19.1E)

These flies are flattened, leathery looking more like a louse than a fly. They have a world-wide distribution living on birds and mammals as ectoparasites on whom they pass their life-cycle.

Life-history. Females are viviparous depositing 10-20 full-grown larvae on the ground; the larvae develop one at a time inside the uterus (common oviduct) whose walls provide nutritive secretion. Pupation occurs within few hours and adult emerges in 24 days.

Damage. Due to their having well developed tarsal claws, they are able to cling to their host body and become permanent ectoparasites of cattle, horse, dog, goat and sheep. Their bite is painless but irritating, without an ooze and so other flies do not gather on the wound.

Management. (*i*) Preventive measures as in the case of other blood sucking flies are helpful. (*ii*) Malathion (5%) can be applied on the back, neck and flanks of the animals every fortnightly or single spray of 0.05 per cent lindane may be carried out.

MYIASIS FLIES

Myiasis refers to an infestation of living organs or tissues of man and other mammals by maggots (larvae) of flies and disturbances resulting therefrom. This is are caused by non-sucking flies of the suborder Cylorrhapa and three subfamilies, Oestridae, Calliphoridae and Sarcophagidae. Myiasis is classified according to the region of body affected such as atrial (when the larvae invade oral, nasal, aural, ocular, sinual, vaginal and urethral cavities), cutaneous (when they live under the skin), *intestinal* (when present in stomach or itestine), and wound (when they enter artificial lesions).

BOT FLIES

1. *Gastrophilus* spp. (Horse bot fly, Diptera : Oestridae)

This genus has 3 species, *G. intestinalis* (Fig. 19.2A), *G. nasalis* and *G. haemorrhoidalis,* all attacking horses and are called horse bots. Of them, the first named is common in India and the other two in the USA and U.K. They have their site preferences for laying eggs — *G. intestinalis* laying on the inner side of the fore legs and abdomen, *G. nasalis* and *G. haemorrhoidalis* on the lower lip or jaws. The adult flies have superficial resemblance to honey bees.

Life-history. *G. intestinalis* appear during November-December, buzz around the animals (horse and mules), not for biting but for glueing their eggs called nits, 800/female on the hairs (on the inner side of the fore legs and abdomen). The animals get worried, excited or even frantic at the very sight of the flies. Eggs are licked inside the mouth and stimulated to hatch by the friction and moisture of tongue in 2 weeks time. The first instar larvae burrow into the tongue, make a linear leision up to the tongue base, moult into second instar and pass into the stomach where they attach to the wall absorb food, moult into third instar and become full-grown in 9-10 months time. Later, they pass out along with the faeces and pupate on the ground, the pupae hatching into adult flies in one month.

Damage. Horses, mules, donkeys, rarely dogs, rabbits and man (only if associated with horses) are attacked. Maggots are the injurious stage which injure tongue, stomach, and often intestine. Besides, they interfere with the glandular activity of the stomach, cause inflammations and ulcers, secrete toxins, absorb food to starve the host and, if the infestation is large, obstruct passage to the intestine. The host becomes weak, develops a rough coat and if not treated dies.

Management. (*i*) Since the flies are active during the day and in the open, horses could be stabled during the day and pastured during the night to avoid encounter with the flies. (*ii*) If larvae are detected in the faeces, 1.5 drams of carbon disulphide (or 25 ml toluene/100 kg of horse weight) in gelatin capsules could be given on empty stomach through a stomach tube so that it reaches the stomach unbroken. Dead larvae start passing out after 6 hours of treatment.

2. *Oestrus ovis* Linnaeus (Sheep bot fly, Diptera : Oestridae) (Fig. 19.2B)

These are viviparous depositing their larvae in the nostrils which after 2 or 3 weeks invade the frontal sinuses, sometimes to other parts of the head too attaching themselves by hooks to the mucosa. In another 2-3 weeks, they are full-grown and work their way back into the nostrils, drop out and pupate on the ground, emerging in 4-6 weeks later as adult flies. Heavy infestation may cause extensive mortality in sheep.

Damage. They cause profuse discharge of mucus and distress to the host.

Management. Effective treatment is possible only against the young larvae when they are still in the nostrils (or in next winter when the old larvae return to nostril and become dormant due to cold). Recommended treatments are (*i*) irrigation of nostrils with 3% lysol or spraying the nostril with 10 ml of emulsified extract of male fern, (*ii*) injection of fumigants in the nostrils (2 ml of equal parts of carbon disulphide and liquid paraffin, or same amount of tetrachloroethylene and paraffin), and (*iii*) providing salt-licks in large holes on logs of wood containing salt with the hole-margins painted with a repellent; as the sheep tries to lick, its nostrils will pick up the repellent which could be protective.

3. *Cephalopina titillator* (Clark) (Camel nasal bot fly, Diptera : Oestridae)

This fly, is present in Rajasthan. The adult fly looks somewhat like *O. ovis*, the nasal bot fly of sheep. The upper part of the head is orange and lower part is pale yellow. The thorax is reddish brown. The legs are yellowish brown and the terminal parts of tarsi are dark, the adult fly measures 8-11 mm long.

Life-history. The female fly deposits its larvae in the nostrils. The larvae bore into the nasal passages and feed for 3-11 months and then fall down on the ground to pupate in soil. The pupal stage is completed in 18-25 days. The adult fly lives for 38 days.

Damage. When the flies deposit larvae in the nostrils, the animal sneezes and snorts violently due to severe irritation. The mature larvae leave the nasopharynx and crawl down to the nostrils of the camel. The animal becomes restless, shakes its head continuously, becomes dull, stops feeding, and starts sneezing and snoring. The presence of larvae in the nasal passage of the camel sets up inflammatory changes, causing great discomfort. An offensive discharge tinged with blood comes out of the nostrils.

Management. This malady can be controlled by applying inside the nostrils 0.2 per cent suspension of trichlorphon.

4. *Hypoderma* spp. (Warble fly, Diptera : Oestridae) (Fig. 19.2C)

These are hairy yellow or black flies popularly known by the name of warble flies or heel flies. The two common species, *viz. H. bovis* (Linnaeus) and *H. lineatum* (Villers) are almost cosmopolitan in distribution. In India, they occur in drier and arid parts of Punjab, Rajasthan and U.P.

Life-history. A female fly lays during monsoon about 800 eggs in hatches on the hairs close to the hoofs of the cattle and only occassionally on the back and belly. Normally 100 eggs are laid on the animal. Even though the flies do not bite being in possession of only vestigeal mouthparts, the animals instinctively get terror-striken at the mere sight of these insects. In 3 days, the maggots hatch out, penetrate the skin and migrate through the thoracic and abdominal cavities to the under skin of back. The second to fifth instar larvae encapsulate beneath the skin of the host causing subcutaneous swelling (warbles) and perforations in the hide. The larvae moult and mature inside the warbles in 6-9 months and when about to pupate, they work their way out and fall to the ground and pupate under drier soil. The pupal period lasts for 3 weeks and the adults have a flight range of 5 km.

Damage. (*i*) In addition to causing pain and inconvenienc as an internal parasite, the holes made in the hide greatly depreciate the latter's value. In India, 50-90 per cent animals may be attacked which amounts to loss of several crores of rupees annually. Irritation, pain and annoyance lower the milk yield too. Acidentally, the flies may lay eggs on the eye lashes or eye brows and the larvae invade the interior of the eyes to cause eye myiasis.

Management. (*i*) In monsoon when the insects oviposit, the eggs could be killed by cutting hairs close to the hoofs. (*ii*) Use insecticides — (*a*) Dress the warbles with derris wash (0.5 kg powdered derris root, 113 g of soap or detergent, and 4.5 litres of water; derris could be substituted by rotenone or by a mixture of tobacco, lime and water). Applications must start before the warbles appear (say in the month of October) and carried out 4 times or more during the season. (*b*) Oral administration of a systemic organophosphorus insecticide in capsules kills the larvae before they injure the hide but does not kill them after their establishment in the warbles. (*c*) Addition of lindane at 100 ppm to cattle feed is also effective. (*d*) The water-based sprays containing 1 per cent trichlorphon or 0.05 per cent rotenone may be applied on the skin to control this pest.

Blow Flies

Insects belonging to family Calliphoridae are called blow flies. They are medium to large sized insects of bright uniform metallic (blue, green, yellowish or black) colour, oviparous depositing eggs in decaying organic matter or in cutaneous sores and abrasions causing cutaneous myiasis. Important examples of this family are *Chrysomya bezziana, Cochliomyia hominivorax, Calliphora erythrocephala* (Fig. 19.2D), *Lucilia cuprina and Phormia regina. C. hominivorax* is the screwworm of tropical America (south-western parts). It is medium-sized, metallic green or blue hairy fly which lays eggs in the wounds of domestic and wild animals, particularly cattle. The European blue bottle, *Erythrocephala* is found in hilly regions of India. It is medium to large-sized, metallic black, blue or green and essentially scavenger of animal refuge. *L. cuprina* is a serious pest of sheep in Australia, and is now reported from many parts of India. *L. serenissima* is a common bazaar fly of South India. These flies are medium-sized metallic green or blue laying eggs on meat and dead animals causing cutaneous myiasis in cattle *P. regina*, also a metallic black, blue or green fly whose larvae are the common maggots in the wool of sheep. All these flies cause cutaneous myiasis in various mammals. *Chrysomyia bezziana* is called the Indian screw-worm. It is a bluish-green fly with dark thoracic stripes and transverse abdominal bands.

Life-history. *C. bezziana* attracted to wounds in which it deposits its eggs up to 800 per female. The maggots hatch in a day and look like a screw due to their bearing small spines in each segment in a spiral fashion. They soon burrow inside the tissue, feed on it, develop rapidly to the third instar on the second or third day and sixth or seventh day, leave the host to pupate on the ground.

Damage. The larvae produce foul-smelling lesions that even erode bone. They aggravate wounds leaving gaping holes. *C. bezziana* is a common cause of human myiasis in India. Besides producing festering wounds, *C. hominivorax* can penetrate healthy tissues, even cartilage, the nasal septum can be destroyed, sinuses and even the brain infested through the middle ear. Occasionally, the larvae develop in the neglected wounds of man and other animals causing extensive tissue destruction.

Management. (*i*) Dispose of carcases properly to prevent blow flies laying their eggs. (*ii*) Where possible, remove maggots by forceps after a spray of 5 per cent chloroform water in a light vegetable oil. (*iii*) Dress wounds with pine oil which acts as a repellent.

Flesh Flies

Flies belonging to family Sacrophagidae are called flesh flies. They are medium to large sized, thick set, greyish and larviparous (viviparous) flies that are usually found in the vicinity of the latrines or near decaying animals and vegetable matter. *Sarcophaga carnaria* (Fig. 19.2E) and *S. haemorrhoidalis* are two important species of this group, which produce cutaneous and nasal myiasis in animals and have sometimes been found in the intestine following ingestion and rectum when eggs are deposited near anus in man. Management is similar to that of other myiasis flies.

LICE

Sucking Lice

Sucking lice are all apterous (wingless) insects living as blood-sucking ectoparasites of mammals (but not of birds). They are small flat-bodied insects with piercing and sucking mouthparts remaining hidden inside the head when not in use. Their thoracic segments are fused and legs are clawed.

1. *Haematopinus eurysternus* Denny (Cattle louse, Phthiraptera : Haematopinidae)

It is a wingless, grey, about 3 mm long and flat-bodied louse. Another important species are *H. quadripertusus* found in the tail, anus, vulva and eyes of cattle and *H. suis* (Fig. 19.2F) occurring on both wild and domestic pigs.

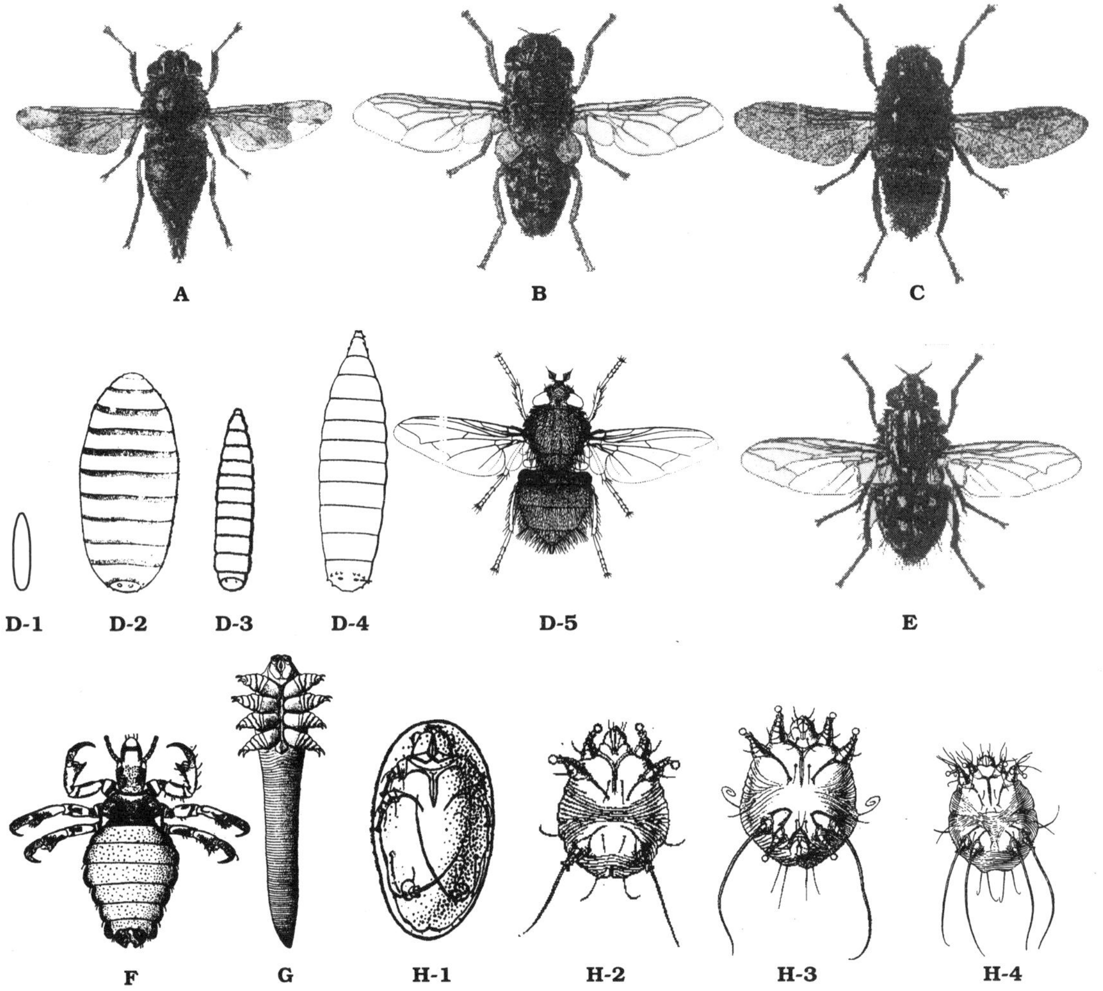

Fig. 19.2 Pests of farm animals. Myiasis flies, lice and arachnids. **A.** Horse bot fly, *Gastrophilus intestinalis*. **B.** Sheep bot fly, *Oestrus ovis*. **C.** Warble fly, *Hypoderma* spp. **D.** Common blue bottle, *Calliphora erythrocephala*; D-1. Egg, D-2. Second stage larva, D-3. Third stage larva, D-4. Pupa, D-5. Adult. **E.** Flesh fly, *Sarcophaga carnaria*. **F.** Pig louse, *Haematopinus suis*. **G.** Dog mite, *Demodex canis*. **H.** Mange mite, *Sarcoptes scabiei* ; H-1. Egg containing developing embryo, H-2. Larva, H-3. Adult male, H-4. Adult female.

Life-history. The lice are active throughout the year but breed more actively during the summer. A female lays 30-40 eggs (nits) on the basal regions of the hairs. They hatch in 15-20 days, the nymphs moult three times and mature in two weeks.

Damage. Sedentary in habit, the lice cling to the hairs, thrust their mouthparts into the skin, suck the blood and simultaneously inject saliva which causes irritation, and itching. The animal rubs itself vigorously on any hard surface. hairless patches of skin, occasionally with sores, are formed; the sores attracting more lice only to enhance the annoyance of the animal, which becomes restless, loses appetite and becomes weak with the result that the normal production of milk and meat is greatly reduced.

Management. (*i*) Application of linseed oil all over the body could kill the lice (*ii*) Use of insecticies — sprays, dips or dust containing organochlorines, malathion (5% dust or 0.05% suspension) or rotenone is effective, the last two are better since they do not accumulate in the milk and meat for long.

2. *Linognathus vituli* (Linnaeus) (Blue lice, Phthiraptera : Linognathidae)

The adults are bluish grey and so they are called blue lice. They are invariably found on the cattle in India, particularly on the stickly and emaciated ones. The hides of such animals are seriously damaged. The nature of damage and management are similar to *Haematopinus*.

BITING LICE

Biting lice resemble sucking lice in their shape and in being wingless, flattened and having reduced eyes and clawed legs. But they differ in having one of the thoracic segments (prothorax) free, biting (not sucking) mouthparts and in being ectoparasites of birds alone.

1. *Menopon gallinae* (Linnaeus) (Shaft louse, Phthiraptera : Menoponidae)

It is called shaft louse of fowl because it runs towards the body along the feather shaft when the same is being shed during moulting. Eggs are deposited on the feathers or down feathers. They hatch in 4-7 days, the nymphs moult 3 times to mature in 4 weeks. Several generations may be passed on a single host. Both nymphs and adults feed on the feathers, downs, epidermal scales and skin exudations causing abrasions (wounds), itching and annoyance. The growth of the young birds is retarded and the older birds become weak and lay fewer eggs.

2. *Menacanthus stramineus* (Nitzsch) (Chicken body louse, Phthiraptera : Monoponidae)

It is the chicken body louse of fowl and turkey. It prefers skin to feathers and may cause serious injury to adult fowls.

3. *Bevicola* spp. (Animal lice, Phthiraptera : Trichodectidae)

It has several species that are found on animals and not on birds, *e.g.B. caprae* (goat), *B. ovis* (sheep), *B. bovis* (cattle) and *B. equi* (horses and mules) Irritation caused by these pests may be severe and the infested animals often try to rid themselves of the lice by biting their skin or rubbing themselves against tree trunks, fence posts and rocks.

Management. (*i*) All biting lice could be controlled by rubbing insecticide dusts-5% malathion or carbaryl, on the body (in birds on the head, back, vent and under the wings) @ 500 g per 100 birds. (*ii*) The birds may be sprayed individually or in groups with water-based sprays of 0.5 per cent carbaryl or malathion @ 5 litres per 100 birds.

FLEAS

Like lice, fleas are also small, apterous and ectoparasitic insects but differ from them in being laterally (not dorso-ventrally) compressed and blind, and with all 3 thoracic segments free. Their mouthparts are of piercing and sucking type, and they suck blood from warm-blooded animals.

1. *Echidnophaga gallinacea* (Westwood) (Stickfast flea, Siphonaptera : Hectosyllidae)

The poultry stickfast flea is known to occur all over India. The adult is a delicate and small flea without any comb.

Life-history. The female starts ovipositing after sticking to the bird's body or wattle for a week. The eggs hatch in 6-8 days, the larvae becoming full-grown in 14-30 days when they bury into debris to pupate in a cocoon. The adult emerges in 10-20 days.

Damage. The flea attacks bare parts of the body of the fowl such as comb, wattles, around eyes and beaks, particularly of young chicks. Birds become anaemic which decreases egg production or may even lead to death.

Management. The infested birds may be dipped in 0.05 per cent malathion or carbaryl or dusted with 5 per cent malathion. The litter in the poultry house should also be dusted.

2. *Ctenocephalides canis* (Curtis) (Dog flea, Siphonaptera : Pulicidae)

It is found on the dogs and cats. These fleas are distinguished from others in having two rows of combs of heavy pigmented spines, a frontal comb on the head and a pronotal comb on each side of the pronotum of the prothorax. The spines help the flea to move through the hairs on the skin.

Life-history. A female may lay about 400 eggs in her life time which hatch into larvae in 2-10 days. The larvae feed on the blood of their host, moult twice in 24 weeks and pupate in cocoons.

Damage. Itching, irritation and annoyance are caused due to constant biting. The animals scrub their body with their nails or by rubbing against some object.

Management. Same as in case of *E. gallinacea.*

ARACHNIDS

Even though not insects, the family Acarina of the class Arachnida contains two groups of arthropods, the ticks and the mites that constitute important pests of animals (mites of plants too). Arachnids differ from insects in having their body divided only into two tagma (parts), cephalothorax (prosoma) including the head and thorax, and abdomen (opisthosoma) and also in possessing 4 pairs of appendages (instead of the 3 pairs of insects). Acarina differs from other arachnids in having its prosoma and opisthosoma fused into an undifferentiated compact body. Ticks differ from mites in being larger (macroscopic) and in having short hairs (when present), a leathery body-texture and exposed, and toothed hypostome (mouthparts). In contrast, mites are small (microscopic), with longer hairs, membranous body-texture and hidden unarmed hypostome.

TICKS

1. *Boophilus microplus* (Canestrini) (Cattle tick, Acarina : Ixodidae)

Boophilus microplus along with *Hyalomma anatolium* Koch are common cattle ticks of India. The females measure about 2.5 mm and when engorged may attain a length of 12 mm.

Life-history. A single female may lay 2-3 thousand eggs or "seed ticks" on the ground which may hatch in 2-6 weeks. The six-legged larvae attach themselves to a suitable host as it happens to pass by, feed on its blood, moult into nymphs which have 4 pairs of legs but no genital opening and finally the total life-cycle taking 3-5 weeks. *B. microplus* is a single host species while *H. anatolium* is a 3-host species, larvae on one host, nymphs on another and adults on the third. That is how the pest can live on goat, horse, donkey and camel besides cattle.

Damage. Ticks injure in 3 ways : (*i*) They cause mechanical injury — ticks normally infest softer portions of the host animals like ear lobes, udder and the base of tail. They embed their head (capitulum) deep into the skin causing inflammation, abrasion, haemorrhage, etc., which may attract other pathogens. (*ii*) They produce tick paralysis through their poisonous secretions in sheep, cattle, dog, less frequently in man. (*iii*) They transmit several diseases like tick fever, texas fever, tularemia, American spotted fever, etc.

Management. (*i*) Carefully remove ticks by hand or foreceps avoiding breakage of hypostome or capitulum. (*ii*) Dust with 2 per cent lindane or 5 per cent carbaryl or malathion or 1 per cent spray of malathion with bromocylen (0.2%) suspension. (*iii*) Apply 1 per cent cypermethrin (shampoo based) on the body of the wet animal, wait for 5-10 minutes and then wash the animal thoroughly. (*iv*) Subcutaneous injection of ivermectin (1%) is quite effective against ticks.

2. *Argas persicus* (Oken) (Fowl tick, Acarina : Argasidae)

The fowl tick is cosmopolitan in distribution attacking birds (fowl, pigeon, goose, duck, turkey, etc.)

Life-history. Up to 900 eggs in batches of 50-100 are laid in the crevices of the fowl house. Depending on weather conditions, the eggs hatch at varying periods (10-90 days). The first instar 6-legged larval stage feeds on the host's blood for 3-10 days, becomes full-grown, drops off and moult into first nymphal stage (8-legged stage). In a few days, it refixes itself on the host, becomes fully fed in a few hours, drops again to moult into second instar nymphs after 2 weeks. The second instar nymph once again engorges itself with blood for 2-3 hours, drops to the ground and after 2 weeks, moults into adult which is very hardy, capable of living without food for 3 years.

Damage. Apart from sucking blood, causing annoyance, weakness, and reduction in eggs, these ticks also transmit fowl spirochaetosis through *Spirochaeta anserina*.

Management. (*i*) The poultry houses should be cleaned throughly. The hiding places of ticks should be eliminated by removing the rubbish and closing the cracks and crevices. (*ii*) The fowls should not be allowed to roost in trees. (*iii*) The wild birds should not be allowed to nest in and around the poultry houses. (*iv*) The pest can be controlled by spraying malathion (3%) or carbaryl (2%) on walls, ceiling and floor. The spray fluid should be forced into the cracks. (*v*) The infested fowls may be dipped in 0.01 per cent solution of dichlorvos or malathion or may be given dust bath containing these pesticides.

3. *Rhipicephalus sanguineus* (Latreille) (Dog tick, Acarina : Ixodidae)

It is the commonest dog tick in India being found on most pariah dogs and also on such pedigree dogs as are not regularly treated. Its life-history is similar to that of the above mentioned ticks.

Damage. Besides blood sucking and accompanying pain and annoyance, they transmit canine piroplasmosis caused by the protozoan, *Babesia canis* (erythrocytes are destroyed due to muliplication of parasites inside them).

Management. (*i*) Apply 5 per cent derris infusion with a brush. (*ii*) Dust powders containing 2 per cent lindane, 5 per cent carbaryl or 5 per cent malathion are also effective.

MITES

1. *Demodex canis* Leydig (Dog mite, Acarina : Demodicidae) (Fig. 19.2G)

This dog mite causes a serious disease, follicular mange of dogs all over the country. The mites occur in the hair follicles and occasionally in the sebacious glands of various mammals (in dogs only in hair follicles since they lack sebacious glands).

Management. There is no satisfactory treatment though the following preparations are said to have given good results : Rotenone (1 g), alcohol 50 ml, acetone 10 ml and water 40 ml, or an ointment made up of β-naphthol 4 g, sublimed sulphur 8 g, balsam of Peru 30 ml and petroleum 30 ml. The mixture is to be applied daily or alternate days on the affected parts.

2. *Sarcoptes scabiei* Linnaeus (Mange mite, Acarina : Sarcoptidae) (Fig. 19.1H)

Popularly called mange mite (mange derived from a Latin word meaning to eat, the mite damages or eats the skin), it is an ectoparasite of horse, cattle, mule, donkey, sheep, goat and a variety of animals, *Sarcoptes scabiei* var. *hominus*, even of man.

Life-history. The mites dig galleries in the skin of the host where they undergo several generations. Mating occurs on the surface of the skin whereafter the female burrows inside the skin making galleries. Twenty to fifty eggs (in a period of 2-3 weeks @ 2-3 eggs per day) are laid in the galleries after which the female dies. The eggs hatch in a few days into 6-legged larvae which transform in 2-3 days into 8-legged nymphs. The nymphs build burrows for themselves and moult twice before becoming adults. The males are believed to stay on the surface of the skin while the females make burrows.

Damage. Preferential sites of infestation are between fingers, and toes, forearm, shoulder blades, small of back, inguinal regions and the genitalia. Intense itching, aggravated by warmth and perspiration causes scratching which helps in the spread of the parasite and produce lesions which induce secondary infections. Minute translucent vesicular swellings are possibly produced, by the irritating faecal deposits and excretions from benath the galleries.

Management. (*i*) Avoid contact with infected person and of public towels or soiled bed lines; scabies, the disease caused by these mites is highly contagious. (*ii*) Boil the clothes/ bedsheets, etc., of the patient. (*iii*) Use of ointments made up of sulphur and lanolin or cream or a mixture of equal parts of benzyl benzoate, isopropyl alcohol and soft soap or most convenient 1 per cent lindane in vanishing cream are effective.

*****

20 CHAPTER

PESTS OF PUBLIC HEALTH IMPORTANCE

Mosquitoes (Diptera : Culicidae)	1. *Aedes aegypti* (Linnaeus)
	2. *Aedes albopictus* (Skuse)
	3. *Aedes vittatus* (Bigot)
	4. *Anopheles maculipennis* Meigen
	5. *Anopheles sinensis* Wiedeman
	6. *Anopheles philippinensis* Ludlow
	7. *Culex pipiens* Linnaeus
	8. *Culex quinquefasciatus* Say
	9. *Culex vishnui* Theobold
	10. *Culex sitiens* Wiedemann
House flies (Diptera : Muscidae)	1. *Musca nebulo* Wiedemann
	2. *Musca domestica* Linnaeus
Sand flies (Diptera : Psychodidae)	1. *Phlebotomus papatasi* (Scopoli)
	2. *Phlebotomus argentipes* Annandale & Brunetti
Eye flies (Diptera : Chloropidae)	1. *Siphunculina funicola* de Meijere
	2. *Hippelates pusio* Loew

Lice (Phthiraptera : Pediculidae)	1. *Pediculus humanus corporis* Linnaeus 2. *Pediculus humanus capitis* DeGeer
Lice (Phthiraptera.: Phthridae)	1. *Pthirus pubis* (Linnaeus)
Bed bugs (Hemiptera : Cimicidae)	1. *Cimex hemipterus* (Fabricius) 2. *Cimex lectularius* Linnaeus
Fleas (Siphonaptera : Pulicidae)	1. *Xenopsylla cheopis* (Rothschild)

These insects, apart from causing annoyance and discomfort to humans, also transmit several diseases. Of the five dreadly diseases, viz. malaria, leishmaniasis, sleeping sickness, lymphatic filariasis and schistosomiasis, the first four are insect-based. Some important diseases of humans that are transmitted by insects and mites are listed in Table 20.1. The major groups of insects that are of public health importance are described in more detail.

MOSQUITOES

Culex spp., *Aedes* spp. and *Anopheles* spp. (Diptera : Culicidae)

Mosquitoes inhabit almost all parts of the world except the polar regions. They are found up to 4,200 meters attitudes in Kashmir and 1020 metres below the sea level in gold mines of South India. Their egg, larval and pupal stages are spent in water and, therefore, the presence of water in the environment is essential for their breeding and existence. They commonly breed in marshy lands, near filthy stagnant ponds, cess pools, dump cellars and standing rain or canal waters. Besides annoying humans with their painful bites, mosquitoes are also known to transmit several dreadful diseases (Table 20.1).

Classification

Mosquitoes belong to insect order Diptera, suborder Nematocera and family Culicidae. They differ from other dipterans in having (*i*) elongated piercing and sucking mouthparts, in females adapted for sucking blood, (*ii*) long antennae, plumose (feathery) in males and pilose (hairy) in females, and (*iii*) characteristic wing venation, the veins being covered with scales that vary in shape, size, structure and distribution in different species. The scaling gives an uniformally dark appearance in most culicine mosquitoes but look spotted in anopheline mosquitoes. There are 2500 species of mosquitoes which have been described in the world so far. The family Culicidae is grouped into blood-sucking and non-blood-sucking subfamilies. Our attention will center round the former since only these are important from the medical point of view. Division of Culicidae into its subfamilies with examples of the blood-sucking species is schematically shown in Fig. 20.1. Out of about the 400 known species of *Anopheles*, nearly 42 have been recorded from India of which only 10 are regarded as vectors of malaria in our country. The culicine and anopheline mosquitoes can be differentiated by the morphological features of their eggs, larva, pupa and adult (Table 20.2, Fig. 20.2).

Table 20.1 Some human diseases transmitted by insects and mites

Vector	Disease	Parasite	Transmission	Distribution
Triatoma spp.	Chagas' disease	*Trypanosoma cruzi*	Bite contamination by faeces	S. America
Pediculus humanus	Relapsing fever	*Borrelia recurrentis*	Skin contamination	Europe, Asia, Africa
	Epidemic fever	*Rickettsia prowazeki*	Bite contamination	Eurasia
	Trench fever	*Rickettsia quintana*	Bite contamination	Eurasia, Mexico
Xenopsylla cheopis	Plague	*Pasturella pestis*	Bite	Pantropical
	Murine typhus	*Rickettsia typhi*	Bite contamination	Pantropical
Anopheles spp.	Malaria	*Plasmodium* spp.	Bite	Pantropical
Aedes aegypti	Yellow fever	Virus	Bite	Africa, S. America
	Dengue	Virus	Bite	Tropics
Mosquitoes	Encephalitis	Viruses	Bite	Africa, America
Mosquitoes (*Anopheles* and *Culex)*	Filariasis (elephantiasis)	*Wuchereria bancrofti*	Bite and through skin	Pantropical
Phlebotomus spp.	Leishmaniasis (Kala-azar, etc.)	*Leishmania* spp.	Bite, etc.	Africa, Asia, S. America
Glassina spp.	Slpeeping sickness	*Trypanosoma* spp.	Bite	Africa
Simulium spp.	Onchocerciasis (river blindness)	*Onchocerca volvulus*	Invasion of bite	C. and S. America, Africa
Chrysops spp.	Loasis	*Loa loa*	Bite	Africa
Chrysops, etc.	Tularaemia	*Pasturella tularensis*	Bite	Holarctic
Cockroaches, *Musca domestica*	Dysentery, amoebic	*Entamoeba histolytica*	Food contamination	Pantropical
Musca domestica and *M. sorbens,* also *Ophyra, Atherigona,* etc.	Dysentery, bacillary	*Bacillus* spp.	Food contamination	Pantropical
	Conjunctivitis	Bacteria	Eye visits	Pantropical
	Typhoid fever	*Salmonella typhi*	Food and water contamination	Pantropical
	Cholera	*Vibrio cholerae*	Food contamination	Pantropical
	Yaws	*Treponcma pertenue*	Wound contamination	Pantropical
	Trachoma	Virus	Contamination	Pantropical
Trombicula spp.	Scrub typhus	*Rickettsia tsutsugamushi*	Bite	South East Asia
Ornithodorus spp.	African relapsing fever	*Borrelia* spp.	Bite (or contamination)	Africa
Amblifomma and *Dermiacentor* spp.	Rocky mountain spotted fever	*Rickettsia*	Bite	USA

Source **:** Hill (1997)

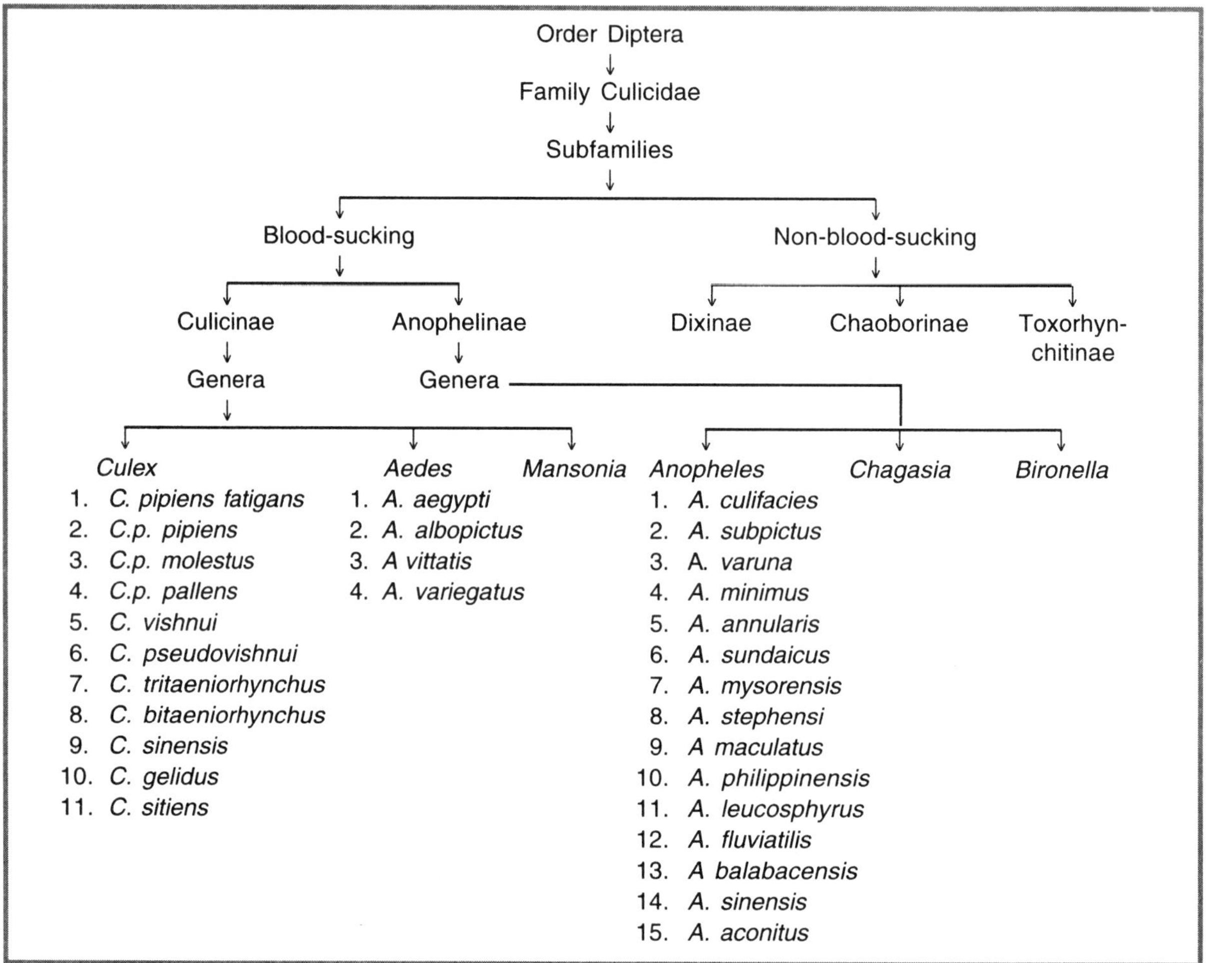

Fig. 20.1 Classification of mosquitoes belonging to family Culicidae

Life-history. In case of *Culex* mosquitoes, the eggs are laid in stagnant and somewhat dirty waters of ponds, pools and ditches The eggs are laid in rafts and the egg raft of *C. fatigans* is boat-shaped with about 200 eggs.The eggs hatch in 2-3 days. The larva breaks out of the anterior end of the egg by using a sharp projection on its head called *egg-breaker*. The larvae are called wrigglers because of their wriggling movement and they are voracious feeders feeding on algae, fungal spores and bacteria. The larval stage passes through 4 instars. The fourth and final instar is examined for determination of the species. The pupa resembles a question mark. Its tail terminates in a pair of paddles which assist the pupa to dive rapidly with jerky motions. An air vesicle situated between the future wings of the adult provides buoyancy Air from this vesicle spreads out under the pupal skin and is also swallowed which with the help of muscular action ruptures the pupal skin to allow the adult to fly out. The total life-cycle is completed in 10-15 days.

Damage. (*i*) ***Painful bites.*** Mosquitoes (females) inflict painful bites any where on the body, but the most serious bites occur in the lower extremities on account of the circulatory stasis (stagnation, slow movement). Bite-effect differs with species of mosquito and senstivity of the individual. The bite is followed by oedema (swelling), vasodilation, occasional

Table 20.2 Distinguishing features of culicine and anopheline mosquitoes

Culex	*Aedes*	*Anopheles*
	Eggs	
1. Cigar-shaped, laid in rafts, no airfloat	Elliptical, laid singly, no airfloat	Boat-shaped, laid singly, airfloat present
2. Laid in stagnant, dirty and permanent bodies of water	Laid on moist ground likely to be flooded, in domestic containers, cavities of tree with water	In flowing water, fresh or even brackish, clear or with algae
	Larva	
1. Hangs from water surface at an angle	Hangs at an angle	Lies parallel to water surface
2. Respiratory siphon long and conical	Long and conical	Absent, spiracles flush with water surface
3. Bottom feeder	Bottom feeder	Surface feeder
	Pupa	
1. Colourless with longer respiratory siphon	Colourless with longer respiratory siphon	Green with short respiratory trumpet
	Adult	
1. Resting posture horizontal to ground	Horizontal to ground	Inclined, head down at 45 degree angle
2. Body well built with stouter legs	Well built with stouter legs	Slender with delicate legs
3. Body colour uniformally grey	Blackish brown with silvery stripes on thorax and abdomen	Greyish
4. Abdomen covered with scales	Covered with scales	Few or no scales
5. Wings uniformly grey	Uniformally grey	Spotted
6. Maxillary palps longer than proboscis in male, shorter in female	Equal to proboscis in male, shorter in female	Equal to proboscis in both sexes but terminally clubbed in male and pointed in female

haemorrhage, papules (pimple-like eruption), erythema (reddening of skin) and itching. Swelling and itching may last from a few minutes to few hours to even several days. The saliva of mosquitoes contains an aenesthetic factor, an anticoagulin and atleast 4 antigenic components, each causing a positive reaction in sensitised person. The aenesthetic factor desensitises the skin so that the victim does not feel the probe of the mosquito's proboscis for some time and when he does feel the pain, the mosquito has done its job and is about to fly. Anticoagulin prevents clotting of blood and makes easy flow into the proboscis and the antigenic components cause allergic reactions. The immediate reaction to the bite is not due to histamine but due to the multiple antigens in the saliva. (*ii*) ***Vectors of diseases.*** Mosquitoes serve as cyclic or mechanical but exclusive vectors of 5 important human diseases such as (*a*) malaria, (*b*) filaria, (*c*) yellow fever, (*d*) dengue fever, (*e*) and viral encephalitis.

Management. The problem of mosquito management involves identification of the species to be controlled, its habit, topography and climate of the region. The cost of control must be

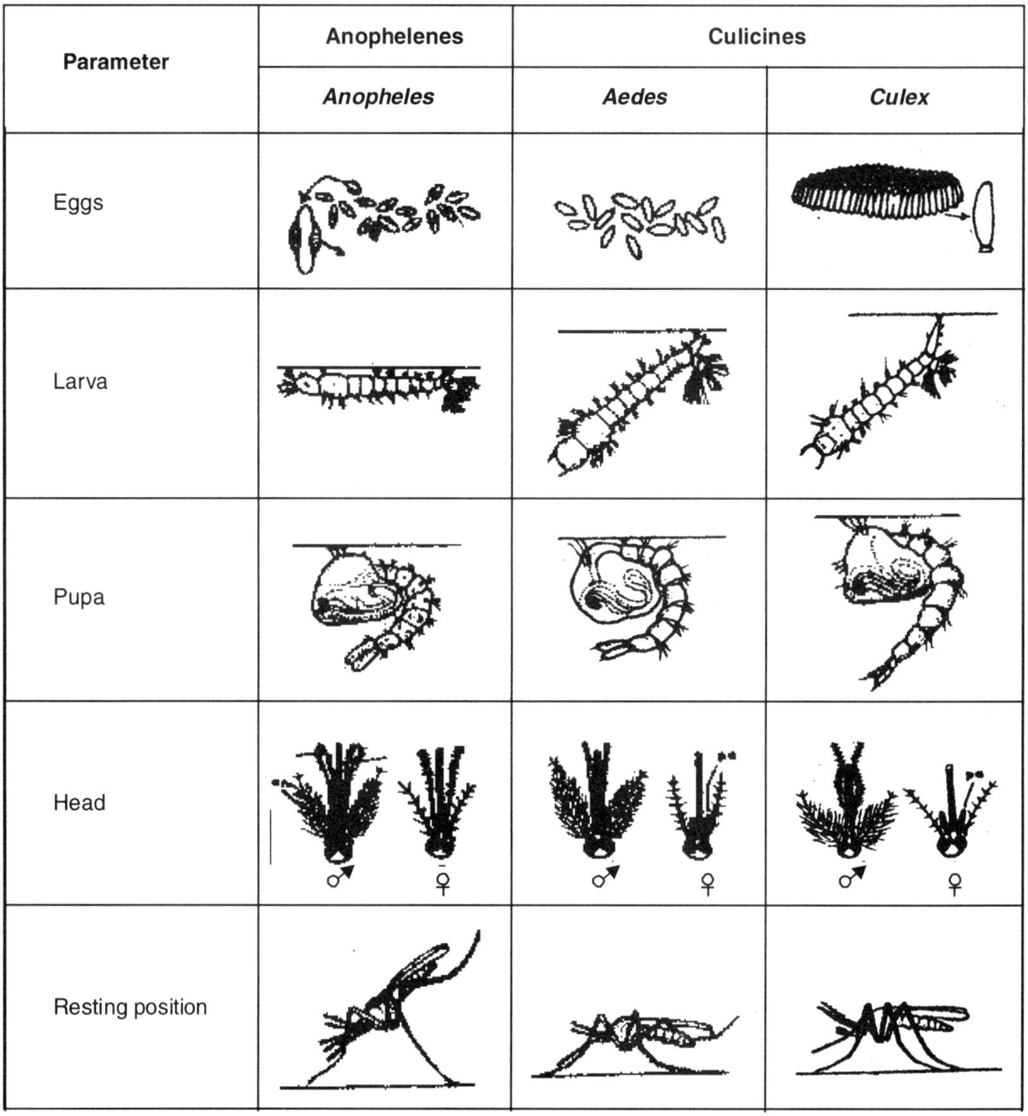

Fig. 20.2 Distinguishing features of the anopheline and culicine mosquitoes

kept commensurate with the economic status of the community. Mosquitoes may be controlled in the following ways :

(*i*) **Destruction of breeding grounds.** The only permanent method of control of most mosquitoes is to eliminate the breeding grounds entirely wherever possible. This can be achieved by (*a*) drainage of swampy areas and stagnant water, this will be applicable to mosquitoes that breed in quiet water; (*b*) changing water level in streams by intermittent flushing is useful for species that breed in flowing water; (*c*) preventing water from standing in drains, gutters and depressions; (*d*) eliminating or inverting receptacles such as tin cans, buckets, cisterns, barrels, etc. can prevent domestic species from laying their eggs; (*f*) if possible, filling up the breeding grounds, and (*f*) preventing shrubs and bushes from growing, they give shelter to mosquitoes. Of all these methods, drainage is the most difficult and expensive because it is an engineering problem. The ditches could be blasted with dynamite, the flow of a stagnant stream could be accelerated by deepening the channel and the marshes may be drained into artificially created central ponds. Drainage of rice-fields periodically results in great reduction in the number of *Anopheles* larvae.

(*ii*) **Destruction of larvae.** Mosquito larvae can be destroyed by fishes, by oiling or by toxic chemicals.

(*a*) **Fishes.** Mosquito larvae are destroyed by various minnows and the young of other fishes. In brackish breeding grounds, the killifish, *Fundulus* is effective while in fresh water breeding grounds, the viviparous top minnow, *Gambusia affinis holbrooki* is effective but less so in waters clogged by weeds and grasses or when larger predaceous fishes are present. About 50 minnows will be needed for every 9 m^2 of surface. In India, a local species *Aplocheilus panchax* has proved more economical than the pesticides. Some copepods (Crustacea) also voraciously feed on mosquito larvae.

(*b*) **Poisons.** Oiling infested water was the standard method of larval control for many years. Oil, a contact larvicide, forms a film that is toxic for the surface-inhabiting larvae. It may be sprayed or applied with a mop; oil is seldom used these days. Use of insecticides is another means of killing the larvae. Stagnant waters should be treated with fenthion or malathion (0.025%) emulsion; pyrethrum, sprayed @ 50-100 mg per 1000 litres, kills anopheline and culicine larvae. Application of fenitrothion @ 0.5-1.0g a.i. per m^2 on the surface of breeding water has given good results.

(*iii*) **Destruction of adult mosquitoes.** Destruction of adults produces the best results. Manual killing, trapping, drowning, replaying wing-vibration sound on loudspeakers, and insecticides are the methods of destroying adults. Manual killing can be done by clapping the hands over the mosquito or by hitting with fly-swatters on light coloured walls, screened windows and doors. Trapping can be done with boxes having dark coloured interiors from which mosquitoes do not readily escape. Drowning (of female) mosquitoes can be achieved by leaving a 3/4th empty bucket preferably with blackened inner surface, in the bathroom during the night. In the morning, depending on mosquito population in the house, large number of females would have accumulated in the bucket, for laying eggs. The bucket should now be covered with a sheet of cloth and the tap opened to fill the bucket under the cloth. When the bucket is full, the mosquitoes unable to fly out will drown in large numbers provided care has been taken in keeping the cloth-cover tightly in contact with the rim of the bucket. Replaying sound (wing vibration) of the female on a loudspeaker behind an electrified screen will draw a large number of males to kill them. The adults may be killed by using space sprays of certain proprietary products of pyrethrum, synthetic pyrethroids or dichlorvos. Several insecticides such as lindane (0.5 g/m^2) and propoxur, fenitrothion and malathion (2g/m^2) have also been effective. Grasses and weeds around buildings should be cut or sprayed with malathion (1%) after every week in the season when mosquitoes are very active.

(*iv*) **Protection against mosquito attack.** Persons can be protected against mosquito attack by mosquito-proofing of buildings, protective clothing and repellents.

(*a*) **Buildings.** Light airy rooms with white walls attract mosquitoes less readily than dark, damp rooms, Doors and windows should be screened preferably with 16-18 mesh per 2.5 cm^2 wire network since most species cannot penetrate such a screen. Double door screening and the outer door provided with springs could provide greater protection, particularly at highly malarial places.

(*b*) **Clothing.** In mosquito infested areas, the individual may be protected during the day with headnets, gloves, high boots and clothing, and at night by mosquito nets over the bed.

(*c*) **Repellents.** Several satisfactory mosquito repellents have been developed since the World War II. The more effective ones are oil of citronella (a constituent of the commercially available mosquito repellent cream with the trade name of Odomos), dimethyl pthalate, diethyl toluamide and Indalone (n-butyl mesityl oxide acetate). These could be applied on the exposed parts of the body.

HOUSE FLIES

***Musca nebulo* Wiedemann and *Musca domestica* Linnaeus (Diptera : Muscidae) (Fig. 20.3)**

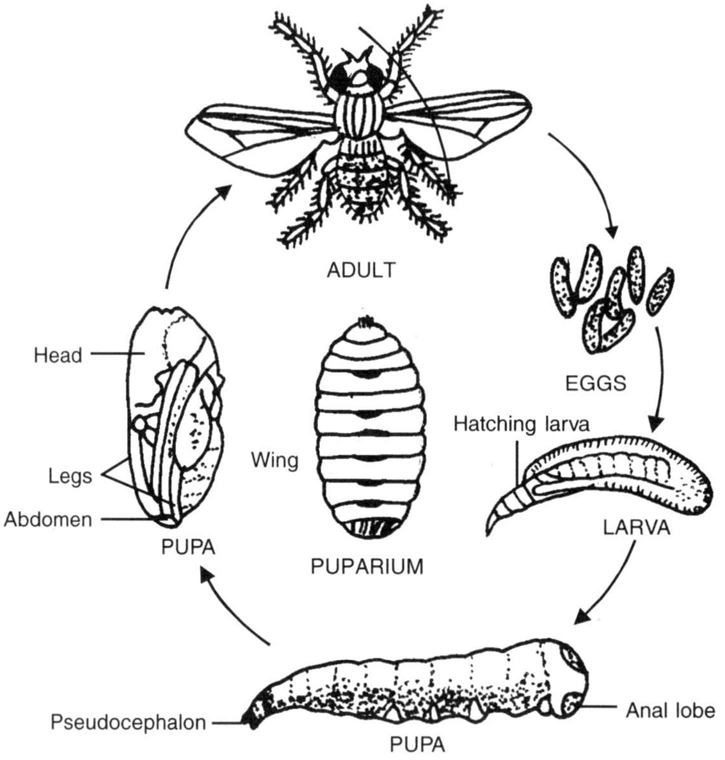

Fig. 20.3 Life-history of the house fly, *Musca nebulo*

Distribution. House flies are cosmopolitan in distribution. While *M. nebulo* is a tropical species commonly found in our houses, *M. domestica* is a temperate species found in the Himalayan regions in India, Europe and other temperate countries.

Identification. About 6-7 mm long, the insects are grey in colour with 4 whitish lines on the thorax and yellowish tinge on the ventral surface. They have a plumose appendage called arista on the terminal segment of their 3-segmented antennae and bear only one pair of wings (fore wings, so the name Diptera), the hind wings being modified into two delicate structures called halteres that function as balancing organs.

Life-history. Copulation occurs on the ground 24 hours after adult emergence and egg laying commences 6-8 days after copulation. The eggs are laid in clusters of 15-150 (about 500 eggs/female) on any decaying matter such as cow dung, horse manure, chicken manure, decomposing fruits, vegetables, seeds, human faeces, etc. Depending on weather conditions, the eggs hatch in 1-12 days and the legless (apodous), headless elongated larvae (called maggots) taper anteriorly. The first instar larva is active, crawls to the margin of the breeding material and feeds voraciously. It moults twice, the 3rd instar being the final instar. When full-grown, this larva seeks a drier place on the dung and pupates into a barrel-shaped pupa having a hard and brown coloured covering called puparium. Adult flies live for 20-30 days and there are 10-12 generations in one summer.

Damage. Flies are a source of nuisance and great annoyance, and their bites are painful. The greatest damage done by the flies is the contamination of food, resulting in the transmission of infectious diseases to human beings. No other single insect transmits as many diseases as house fly; these are typhoid dysentery (both bacillary and amoebic), cholera, yaws, tuberclosis, leprosy, trachoma, anthrax, gonorrhoea and many helminthic diseases caused by *Taenia solium*, *Hymenolepis nana*, *Enterobius vermicurlaris*, *Trichocephalus trichuris*, *Ascaris lumbricoides*, etc. and viral disease (poliomyelitis).

The house fly is a mechanical carrier of the germs of these diseases and the following features make it ideally adapted for this job : (*a*) its habit of sitting and/or feeding on all filthy material that abound in germs, (*b*) its hairy and spiny body can harbour lots of these germs, (*c*) its habit of regurgitation or vomitting before feeding enables it to transfer germs of its own gut. Truely speaking, the house fly unable to take any solid food must spit its own enzymes to predigest (liquefy) its food so that it can easily suck (sponge) it in, and (*d*) its presistent habit ensures transference of germs.

Management. The house flies can be controlled with various approaches.

1. **Prevention of breeding.** This is the best method of fly control. It can be achieved by (*i*) quick and proper disposal of manure, garbage, night soil, etc., (*ii*) keeping every premise clean and without accumulation of materials on which the flies breed, (*iii*) accumulated manures on the farms should either be kept covered with soil or polythene sheet or spread in thin layer to allow quick drying and death of eggs and larvae, and (*iv*) outdoor toilets should be dispensed with or atleast the excreta be covered with soil.
2. **Chemical treatment of breeding grounds.** Lime, crude oil, $CuSO_4$, formaldehyde or borax could be liberally sprinkled on the breeding grounds to prevent egg laying.
3. **Protection of edibles.** All edibles should be kept covered to prevent flies sitting on them; this will prevent contamination of food. In the market places, nothing should be bought or eaten that may have flies sitting on them.
4. **Destruction of adults.** (*i*) Manual killing by fly swatter, (*ii*) baiting by keeping formaline and sweetened milk in a saucer; or they can be attracted to a mixture of fermenting banana, and milk or cheese and sugar and then killed by insecticides, (*iii*) stretching

a wire smeared with boiled resin and castor; flies sitting on the wire will die, and (*iv*) Inside the houses, spraying the flies with malathion/diazinon (2%), lindane (1%) or trichlorphon (0.5%) is effective in killing them; the surfaces of windows and doors where the flies rest, may be smeared with malathion (3%) or diazinon (1.5%) emulsion with the help of a paint brush.

5. **Prevention of infection.** Patients suffering from any infectious disease should be kept in a fly-proof room.

SAND FLIES

The sand flies are small with the body and wings thickly covered with hairs. The females of Psychodinae are blood-suckers and transmit kala-azar disease caused by *Leishmania*, a flagellate, spread by *Phlebotomus argentipes*. *Pappataci* transmits the Pappataci fever prevelent in India. Verruga disease in Peru is transmitted by a species of *Phlebotomus*. The details of sand flies are discussed in chapter 19.

EYE FLIES

Siphunculina funicola de Meijere (Diptera : Chloropidae) (Fig. 20.4A)

Distribution. *Siphunculina funicola* is found throughout India, more commonly in East and South India. There are a few other species of eye flies that are found in other countries such as *Hippelates pusio H. pallipes*, etc., which occur in America.

Identification. It is a very small fly, about 2 mm long with shining black body and yellowish legs.

Life-history. The fly breeds in moist mud-contaminated environments with decomposing organic matter, near latrines, stables and surface drains. It is commonly seen to congregate in large numbers on threads or ropes hanging from roof in houses in damp warm places. The eggs are laid in batches of 5-10 and duration of the life cycle in favourable conditions is 10-21 days. It is more abundant in May and June.

Damage. The fly has the habit of hovering in front of the eyes producing buzzing sound and if allowed to enter, feeds on the secretions in the corner of the eye and thus becomes a mechanical carrier of eye infections like ophthalmia, conjunctivitis, etc. It also feeds on exudates and excretions. Conjuctivitis is believed to be transmitted by the fly.

Management. Living in good sanitary and hygienic condition is the most important precaution against this fly. Surface spray application of propuxur or etofenprox on resting places may be useful.

LICE

Prediculus humanus corporis Linnaeus (Fig. 20.4B) and *Pediculus humanus capitis* DeGeer, (Phthiraptera : Pediculidae), and *Pthirus pubis* (Linnaeus) (Phthiraptera : Pthridae) (Fig. 20.4C)

Distribution. *P. h. corporis* (body louse), *P. h. capitis* (head louse) and *Pthirus pubis* (crab louse or pubic louse) occur all over the world.

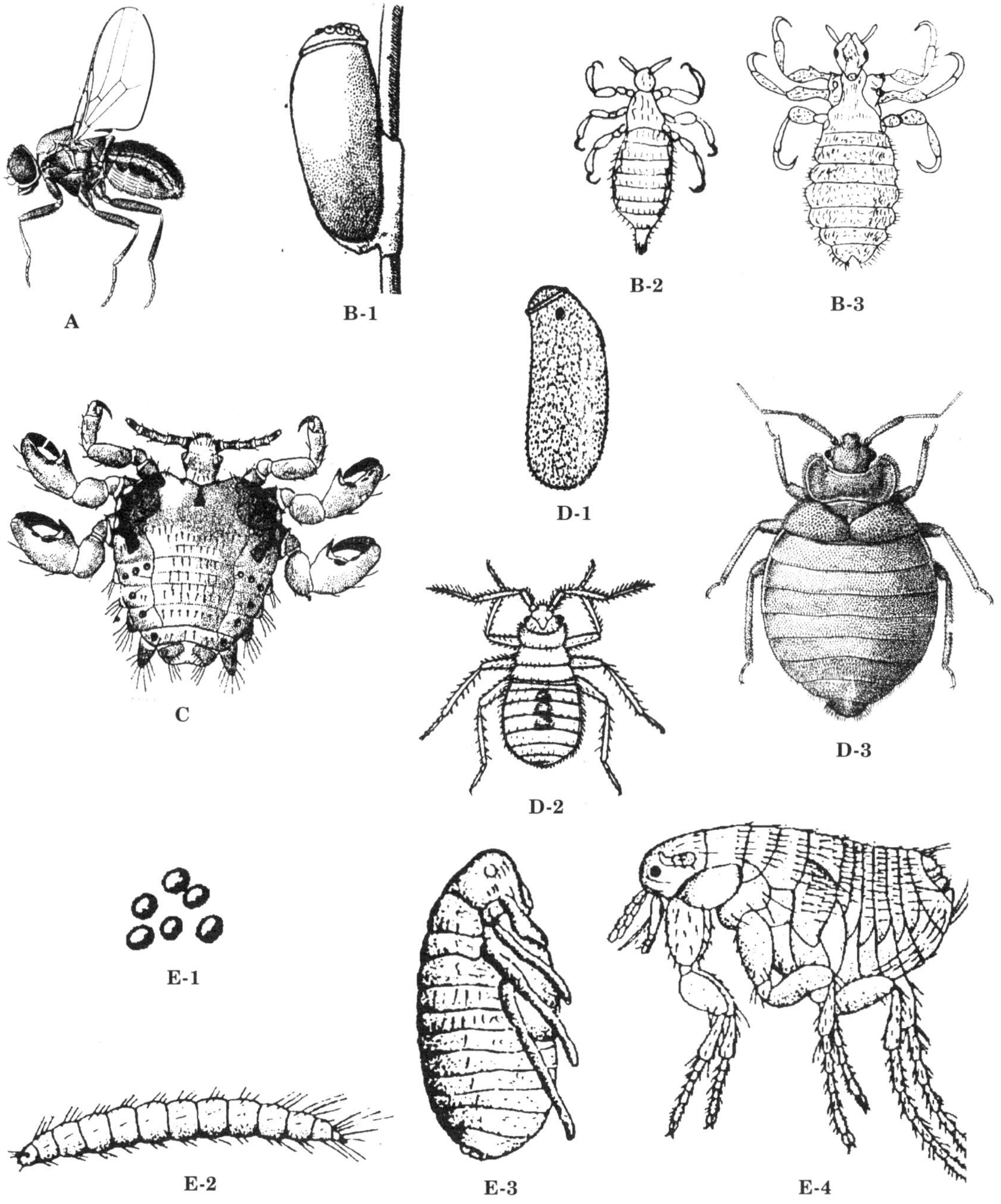

Fig. 20.4 Some public health pests. **A.** Oriental eye fly, *Siphunculina funicola.* **B.** Human louse, *Pediculus humanus corporis*; B-1. Egg attached to human hair, B-2. Nymph, B-3. Adult. **C.** Pubic louse, *Pthirus pubis*. **D.** Bed bug, *Cimex lectularius*; D-1. Egg, D-2. Newly hatached nymph, D-3. Male adult. **E.** Rat flea, *Xenopsylla cheopis*; E-1. Eggs, E-2. Larva, E-3. Pupa, E-4. Adult.

Identification. These insects are characterised by having a dorso-ventrally flattened body, lack of wings, clawed legs and piercing and sucking mouthparts. Their marks of identification are given in Table 20.4.

Table 20.3 Distinguishing features of lice parasitic to man

Sr. No.	Feature	*P. h. corporis*	*P. h. capitis*	*Pthirus pubis*
1.	Adult size (mm)			
	Male	2.0-3.0	1.0-1.5	0.8-1.0
	Female	2.0-4.0	1.8-2.0	1.0-1.2
2.	Shape	Elongate	Elongate	Oblong (turtle shaped)
3.	Colour	Greyish white	Greyish white with dark margins	Greyish white
4.	Head	Diamond-shaped	Diamond-shaped	Rectangular, neck not constricted
5.	Abdomen	Elongate, wider than thorax	Elongate, wider than thorax	Short
6.	Segments	Distinct	Distinct	Indistinct
7.	Claw size	Medium	Medium	Large, heavy
8.	Eggs deposited on	Clothing, less frequently hairs	Hairs	Hairs
9.	Egg length (mm)	0.8	0.6	0.8
10.	Principal habitat	Body	Head	Pubic and perianal regions
11.	Occurrence	Less common	Most common	Least common
12.	Transference	By contact, clothing	By contact, combs, brushes, hats	By coitus

Life-history. The female of the head house lays its eggs (nits) glued to the hairs on the head, whereas the body louse lays eggs on the seams of clothes. A female lays 8-10 eggs daily until 50-100 are laid by the head louse and 200-300 by the body louse. The incubation period is about one work. The emerging tiny slender nymphs start feeding at once and undergo 3 moultings over a period of 1-4 weeks. The adults live for about one month or more.

Damage. Both nymphs and adults bite, creating cutaneous lesions, location of the bites varying with the three species — head louse prefers to bite on the back of the head and neck, body louse at places in close contact with the clothing, and crab louse in the public region. The irritating substance injected during feeding produces roseate elevated papule accompanied by severe itching. In sever infestation (condition called pediculosis), pigmentation, discolouration, hardening and even ulceration of the skin may take place. Both body and head louse (the latter less commonly) are implicated in the transmission of various diseases like typhus, trench fever and European relapsing fever.

Management. Personal hygiene is most important for the control of all kinds of lice.

(*a*) **Body lice.** Destruction of the body lice can be achieved by thorough cleansing of the body, application of insecticides and sterilizing all clothings and bedding by boiling them.

(*b*) **Head lice.** Head lice are generally prevalent amongst school/college girls or girls and women living in groups. A powder containing malathion (2%) or lindane (1%) is useful as a delousing treatment. The application of malathion 5 per cent dust or use of lindane (0.2%) mixed with hair oil is very effective for the control of head or body louse. Kerosene containing 0.12 per cent pyrethrins or a mixture of equal parts of kerosene and olive oil has also proved satisfactory. The following morning a soap shampoo is given and the hair is combed with a fine comb to remove the nits. Treatment should be repeated in 10 days to destroy newly hatched lice and in severe infestation cutting the hair short or completely shaving them is advisable.

(*c*) **Crab lice.** The areas infested with crab lice may be treated by shaving and application of an ointment of cold cream containing 0.2 per cent lindane followed 12 hours later by washing with soap and water.

BED BUGS

Cimex hemipterus (Fabricius) and *Cimex lectularius* Linnaeus (Hemiptera.: Cimicidae (Fig. 20.4D)

Distribution. *C. hemipterus* occurs in India and other tropical countries while *C. lectularius* is found in temperate countries.

Identification. It is a small (about 13 mm long), bristly pear-shaped, wingless and dark brown insect. Before a blood meal, it is flat and active but following the meals, it becomes oval and sluggish.

Life-history. Elongate whitish eggs are laid singly at the rate of 3-4 per day in the cracks of furniture, strings of cot, loose edges of wallpaper, and on the corners of the 'durries'. The bed bug frequently returns to the same place to oviposit and may lay 75-500 eggs. The eggs hatch in 6-7 days and tiny nymphs moult 5 times during 6-8 weeks. Nymphal stages resemble each other quite closely except in increasing size and deepening colour. The wingpads appear only after the last moult. Atleast one gluttonous feed is necessary before each moult though the bug may gorge itself several times between moults. Normally an adult female lives for 2-10 months. The life-history may be completed in 15-50 weeks depending upon the weather conditions. The adult bed bugs have been observed to withstand starvation up to a year. Up to 4 generations may be produced in a single year.

Damage. Both nymphs and adults bite and suck blood during the night. In the process, they inject saliva which contains besides toxins an anticoagulin and an aenesthetic factor. The bites produce intense itching, burning and swelling.

Management. (*i*) Pouring boiling water on sites of oviposition will kill the eggs and nymphs. (*ii*) Occasionally exposing the bed sheets, durries, etc. to hot sun will also kill the eggs. (*iii*) Natural enemies of the bed bugs are the red ants, reduviid bugs and mice. (*iv*) Substitution of iron for wooden bedsteads, and liberal application of kerosene, turpentine, benzene or petroleum oils with small brushes and syringes in wooden bedsteads, furnitures, floors and walls, is helpful. (*v*) Use of 0.1 per cent malathion or 1 per cent lindane on beds, beddings, crevices, etc. would control the bed bugs.

RAT FLEA

Xenopsylla cheopis (Rothschild) (Siphonaptera : Pulicidae) (Fig. 20.4E)]

Distribution. Though named Oriental rat flea, it is cosmopolitan in its distribution.

Identification. The adult fleas are tiny, 1 mm, oblong, laterally compressed hard skinned, wingless and dark-brown insects having piercing mouth parts, concealed antennae and long jumping legs.

Life-history. About 200 minute (0.4-0.5 mm) eggs are laid in scattered clusters of 6-8 on dark and dry places in the haunts of its host, holes or even body of rat or in the dwellings of man. The eggs lie loosely on the hairs and usually slip into the ground where they incubate for 2-14 days. The three larval instars are apodous (legless), all similar except the first instar that has an egg-burster on its head, extremely active, vermiform and reaching a size of 2-6 mm. Unlike adults, they have chewing mouthparts with which they feed on the excreta or body of their rodent host (rat, mouse, squirrel). The larval stage lasts for 1-5 weeks or more. When full-grown, it pupates in a silk cocoon from which it emerges as an adult after 1-5 weeks. The duration of life-history varies with temperature — shorter (2-4 days) at higher (29-35°C) temperatures and longer (upt to 1 year) at low temperatures. On emergence, the adult must feed within 1-3 days of emergence and start ovipositing 1-4 days after the first meal. It takes 5-31 days for the bacilli taken along with the blood meal to divide into numbers large enough to be infective. This is called its incubation period. In nature, infected fleas survive not more than a few days, the uninfected ones survive much longer. In ideal laboratory conditions, the fleas can be made to live still longer.

Damage. The harm is caused by the adults alone since only they feed on blood of their hosts, rodents or man. Man is only an accidental host that the flea may or may not come across after it leaves the dead body of its main host, the rodent. Besides causing irritation, itching and lesions by their bites, fleas also transmit the germs (bacillus *Yersinia pestis*, earlier called *Pasteurella pestis*) of bubonic plague in man, endemic or murine typhus also of man, rat trypanosomiasis and tapeworms of cats and dogs.

Management. (*i*) The houses should be kept rat-free by keeping cats or by frequent poison-baiting. (*ii*) The houses should also be kept clean, well swept and ventilated, with occasional spraying of floors with lindane (1%) or malathion (0.5%). (*iii*) Dead rats should not be handled but burnt by pouring kerosene. The breeding places should be treated with propxur for controlling the fleas.

*****

INDUSTRIAL ENTOMOLOGY

PART-V

- APICULTURE
- SERICULTURE
- LAC CULTURE
- MASS PRODUCTION OF PARASITOIDS AND PREDATORS

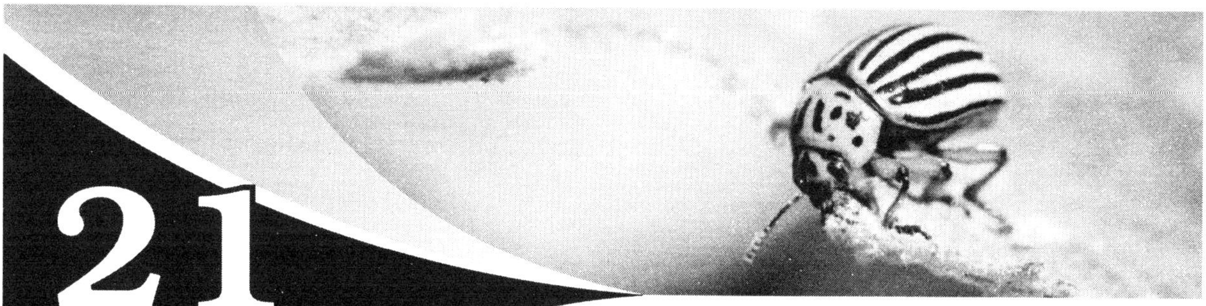

21

CHAPTER

APICULTURE

Apiculture denotes the scientific management of honey bees for commercial production of honey and other bee products. The utility of honey bees to man has been known from prehistoric times. The bees have been mentioned in the Vedas, the Ramayana, the Quran and other holy books. The carvings of honey bees, their combs and hives are found on the tombs, coffins, crowns and maces of kings and on the coins of both ancient and modern empires. Honey bees had been used as a weapon in the world war I and the mysterious property of bee venom of relieving muscular pain has also been known for a long time. Beekeeping in India has remained behind countries like the USA, Canada, Europe, Africa, Australia and New Zealand. In order to have a thorough understanding, the topic could be divided into three subheadings, i.e. honey bees, beekeeping and bee products.

HONEY BEES

Honey bees belong to the family Apidae of the order Hymenoptera. India is a unique country where all the four species of honey bees have been found foraging under natural conditions. Two of them are wild and make their nests in the open. They are *Apis dorsata* Fabricius and *Apis florea* Fabricius. The other two make their nests in the open and can be domesticated to live in hives. They are *Apis cerana* Fabricius and *Apis mellifera* Linnaeus.

(*i*) ***Apis dorsata.*** It is also called the rock bee or the giant bee. This bee is found in all parts of India from the hilly tracts (1200 m) to the plains. The bee is bigger in size to other bees, measuring about 20 mm in length. It is a very good honey gatherer. It builds a single huge comb at the face of a rock, on branches of big trees and sometimes on walls and buildings. This bee is irritable and ferocious in nature. On disturbance, it attacks human beings and domestic animals, and sometimes even death may occur. These bees are migratory in nature. In winter, they migrate to plains and come back to hills during summer. The comb is always built in open place, that's why the bees could not be domesticated up to now. The comb measures sometimes 1.5-2.0 metres across and each colony of bee is capable of storing 20 to 40 kg honey.

(*ii*) ***Apis florea.*** It is also called the little bee and is about 7 mm in length. It does not like darkness and, therefore, forms its comb in the open place, e.g. in the bushes, hedges, caves, chimneys, corners of roof, etc. It builds a single comb which is very small and only 250 g honey is obtained at a time. The honey produced by these bees is the sweetest one. This species can not tolerate cold and, therefore, is not found in hills.

(*iii*) ***Apis cerana.*** It is also called the Indian bee or Eastern honey bee and is found every where in India and its nature is quite different from rock bee, being mild in temperament and can be domesticated easily. It is about 15 mm in length. These bees like to live in dark places and, therefore, establish their comb in closed covered places such as hollowed tree trunks, burrows in the ground, hollowed places in walls, unused boxes, etc. They build several combs side by side and parallel to each other but are smaller than the rock bee. The honey and pollen are stored in the side combs while brood rearing is restricted to the central one. On an average, 3-4 kg honey is found from a comb annually. Generally, they do not migrate to leave their old combs. Two types of Indian bees, viz. plains type and hills type are found.

(*iv*) ***Apis mellifera.*** It is also called the European honey bee or the Italian honey bee and was introduced in India in 1962 by Prof. A.S. Atwal while serving at the Punjab Agricultural University at Ludhiana (India). Initially, the bee was introduced into Himachal Pradesh and Punjab, but now it has acclimatized and spread to almost all the states of India. The behavior and appearance of *A. mellifera* is similar to *A. cerana*. It makes its nest in enclosed spaces in parallel combs and is endowed with all the good qualities of a hive bee, i.e. has a prolific queen, swarms less, gentle tempered so domesticable, good honey gatherer and can guard its nests against enemies. The average honey yield of *A. mellifera* is 20-25 kg per colony, but elite beekeepers have obtained an average yield of 50 kg per colony. Prof. A.S. Atwal is called the 'Father of Modern Beekeeping' in view of the remarkable success of *A. mellifera* in India.

Organization of Bee Colony

The honey bees are social insects and live in colonies with a highly organized system of division of labour. Many combs are found in a colony in which the members of the same family used to live. A family consists of 35,000 to 70,000 members which includes a queen, 200-300 drones and workers (Fig. 21.1).

Queen. Every colony has a queen which is the mother and the only sexually developed female. All the members of colony are the products of queen, so that it is called as mother queen. She mates the drone, the male bee, in the air once or more in her life-time and lays eggs throughout her life. Her reproductive organs are well developed. A well developed queen is generally two or three times bigger than a worker, measuring 15-20 mm in length. She can be distinguished by her extended abdomen and provided with a combined sting and ovipositor. She lays 800 to 1200 eggs per day and about 15 lakh eggs are laid in her life time. A queen lives for 2 to 5 years and when it is weak or unable to lay eggs, it is replaced by one of the daughter queens.

Drone. The drone is the male bee, the main function of which is to mate with queen. It is smaller than queen and measures 15-17 mm in length. Drones are not permanent members of a colony. They are driven out of the hive before the onset of monsoon and winter. They die due to starvation and are raised only when new queens are reared. They are reared from the unfertilized eggs and do not possess structural modification, and are, therefore, incapable of collecting food or defending themselves against enemies.

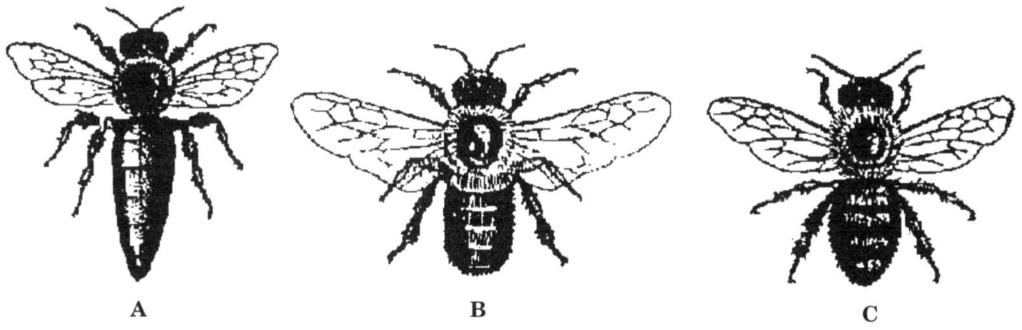

Fig. 21.1 *Apis mellifera*. **A.** Queen, **B.** Drone, **C.** Worker

Worker. Under developed females which are produced from the fertilized eggs but remain sterile due to non-availability of royal jelly are called workers. It is smaller in size than queen and has a sting on the terminal end of abdomen. The sting of the worker bee is a barbed structure which gets pulled out from her body when she stings. The bee dies as a result of pulling of the sting. On ventral side of abdomen, wax glands are found. Hind legs are modified for pollen collection. The mandibles are flattened and spoon shaped which are used for molding the wax for comb building.

They are responsible for all the work necessary for the maintenance and welfare of colony such as building of comb with wax and its maintenance; collection of honey, pollen and water for the use of the colony; to guard the colony against enemies; to take care of the queen and feeding of royal-jelly; to maintain the temperature of hive by cooling and heating the comb as per requirement and to secrete the royal jelly, prepare a 'bee bread' and to distribute these foods to grubs.

Life-history of Honey Bee

The eggs are laid by queen and when a colony wants to produce a new queen, the special cells are constructed at the lower border of the brood comb. On these cells, single egg is laid by the queen in each cell which hatches after 3 days. The newly hatched grubs are provided with royal jelly. The grub is fully developed in 5 or 6 days and then queen cell is capped where grub changes into pupa and after a week adults come out by biting the cap of queen cell. The adult which comes out earlier becomes the queen daughter and it kills the remaining pupae before their emergence.

Nuptial clight. After 2-3 days, the queen daughter takes nuptial flight accompanied by hundreds of drones during day. She overtakes her in flight. The drone which follows her gets the chance of copulation. The male dies soon after copulation and the mated queen returns to the comb. It mates only once in her life time. The seminal fluid (male sperm) is collected in a special receptacle (spermatheca) and used when required.

Oviposition. After some time, the queen daughter starts egg laying and is called as queen mother. She lays fertilized or unfertilized eggs at her will. One egg is laid in each cell. The eggs are long, oval and light brown in colour. They hatch in 3-4 days.

Grub. From the fertilized eggs, queen and workers and from the unfertilized eggs drones are born. The grubs are cylindrical and light yellow in colour. They are fed with royal jelly for 2-3 days after that they are provided honey and nectar, etc. The grub period lasts for 5-6 days.

Pupa. Full grown grub forms a cocoon and pupates inside the cell. The pupal period lasts 7-14 days depending upon the type of adult to be produced. The time required for development of different castes is given in Table 21.1.

Table 21.1 Development (days) of different castes of *Apis mellifera*

Caste	Egg	Grub	Pupa	Total
Queen	3	6.5	6.5	16
Worker	3	8.0	10.0	21
Drone	3	9.5	11.5	24

Source: Atwal (2000)

Major Activities of Honey Bees

The honey bees remain active generally throughout the year except during severe winter. Following are the main activities of honey bees:

1. Foraging. The field bees get activated in the morning and go out on foraging and collect pollen, nectar, propolis and water, carry them to the hive and make a number of trips till sunset. The bees that go out first to find out new sources of these materials are called *searcher bees* or *scout bees*. They return to the hive and communicate the message to young foraging bees by means of definite patterns of dancing. At any time bees collect most of the materials from a single or a few plant species but bees in two different colonies located side by side may visit entirely different sources, mainly due to the differences in discoveries by the scout bees. The bees collect materials from a source till they are exhausted when they may go in search of new areas. The honey bees usually forage within about 100 metres distance from the hive but they can go up to 1.5 km. They are capable of flying at a speed of 25-30 km per hour. The bees are most active in foraging within a temperature range of 25-27°C. The bees do not go out for foraging at wind speed of more than 24 km per hour.

Nectar is collected by the foragers from the flowers and is stored in the crop where it is mixed with saliva. The enzyme invertase contained in the saliva acts upon sucrose of the nectar and converts it to dextrose or levulose. The bee returns to the hive and regurgitates the contents of the stomach into comb cells which are covered by flat airtight cappings. The weight of nectar load varies from 25 to 40 mg. On a given trip, a bee visits and exploits 1-500 flowers and makes, on an average, 10-15 trips in a day. During honey flow when there is abundance of food available, bees work to their full capacity and may make upto 150 trips a day.

The pollen is collected and carried to the hive by the bees in the pollen baskets located in their hind tibiae. The bee returns to the hive and the pollen pellets are pushed down to the appropriate cells by means of spine in the middle leg. The weight of pollen load varies from 10 to 30 mg. The workers make about 6,000 trips to collect 0.5-1 g of pollen. The propolis is also carried in the pollen basket by the worker bees. As soon as the collecting bee returns to the hive, another worker unloads the propolis from the former, carries the same in its mandibles to the place requiring cementing and presses it into the crevices in the comb.

2. Combing. The comb of honey bees comprises of several hexagonal cells on both side of mid-rib. The combs are built with beeswax which is secreted by 4 pairs of wax glands located on 3-6 abdominal sterna. The wax secreted in a liquid form, collects in the intersegmental regions, hardens into thin flakes that are picked up by the legs and passed on to the spatulate mandibles for being kneaded and stuck to the top of nesting cavity and extended downwards bit by bit. Several bees hang like a sting to do the job. Usually, the cells meant for honey storage are located uppermost near the point of attachment below which are pollen cells spread in 5 cm wide band, further down are worker brood cells which are followed by the drone and queen cells. The worker cells are the smallest, drone cells larger than the worker cells and queen cells the largest. Worker and drone cells are directed sideways and queen cells vertically with open ends downwards. Cells of the size of worker and drone cells are used for storing honey and pollen. Cells containing unripe honey or developing brood are uncapped; those with fully ripe honey and fully fed grubs are capped, and pollen cells are generally not capped. Freshly built comb is generally white, but becomes dark after some time.

3. Swarming. Swarming is a method of reproduction in which a part of the colony migrates to a new site to make a new colony. During spring and summer when conditions are favourable and food is available in plenty, the bees multiply greatly with the result the comb becomes crowded and the bees begin to make preparations for swarming. At this stage, the queen daughter cells are built at the bottom and when new queen is ready to emerge out, the new queen and a large number of workers which have previously filled the cells with honey, leave the nest to start a new colony. Swarm settles in a suitable place already searched out by the workers for building new comb. In a parent colony the first queen daughter which emerges after swarming, kills the baby queen in the other cell and establishes herself as a queen mother. After that, they start their routine work of gathering nectar and pollen.

4. Absconding and migration. Complete desertion of a hive is known as absconding. This may occur due to lack of water, exhaustion of food store (either due to short supply of nectar or robbery of honey), unfavourable environment, constant pest attack (ants, wax moth, etc.) and even by excessive interference by the beekeeper in which case he is regarded as an enemy. Prior to absconding, the bees 'drink' whatever honey their nest has and then migrate leaving behind empty combs, brood and sometimes even food. Absconding can be prevented by providing water or sugar solution near the hive particularly during summer.

5. Language of bees. Honey bees have an unique and one of the best understood animal languages with which they inform each other the distance and direction of the source of food. The forager bee on return to the nest makes two kinds of dances on the surface of the comb, i.e. round dance and tail-wagging or figure of eight dance (Fig. 21.2), which the insiders perceive by contacting the forager's body with their antennae. In the round dance, which is used to indicate a short distance (less than 50 m in case of *A. mellifera*), the bee runs in circles, first in one and then in opposite direction (clock and anticlockwise), while in the tail-wagging dance which is used to indicate a longer distance (beyond 50 m in case of *A. mellifera*), the bee makes two half-circles in opposite directions with a straight run in between. During the straight run, the bee shakes its abdomen from side to side and the number of wags per unit time is related to the distance the food was located, i.e. more the wags, nearer is the food. The direction of the food is conveyed by the angle that the dancing bee makes its straight run and top of the hive which is the same as between the direction of the food and direction of the sun. Prof. Karl von Frisch was awarded the Nobel Prize in Physiology and Medicine in 1973 for discovering and interpreting the language of the honey bees in early 1920s. Later on, it was found that honey bees employ both dance and sound in their language.

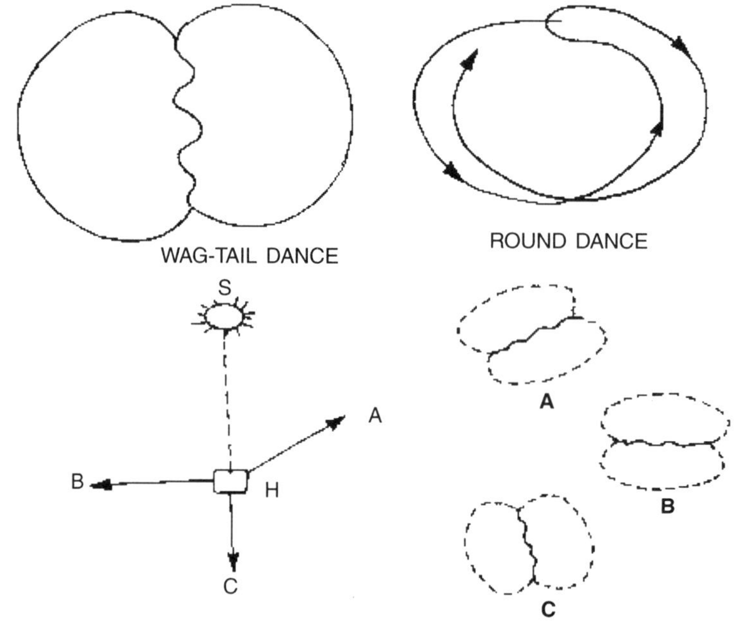

Fig. 21.2 Communication dances in honey bees according to location of the food source and direction of the sun (A, B, C = Directions, S=Sun, H=Beehive)

6. Air conditioning. Among the living creatures, honey bees are the only organisms which make their comb airconditioned. They keep their comb warm in winter and cool during summer. The brood temperature is stablized between 33 and 36°C averaging about 34.5°C. Clustering begins when the temperature inside the nest dips below 18°C and they generate heat by sitting on one another and rubbing their legs due to which the temperature of the comb rises. In summer, when the temperature rises above 33°C, the bees start fanning with their wings at the gate inside as well as outside with the result water evaporates from the honey and comb remains cool. The brood nest is usually kept at 40 per cent relative humidity.

A large number of foragers start collecting water from outside, that is received by house bees inside and carried by them to the site where most needed and evaporated. They spread minute drops of water in cells and also form thin films from regurgitated water on their tongues for evaporation. In the event of extreme hot weather they even suspend collecting concentrated nectars but prefer dilute nectars in case water is in scarcity, as the dilute nectars may be used for making thin films.

BEEKEEPING

Rearing the bees in artificial hives is known as beekeeping or apiculture. In India, the beekeeping industry started with the designing of a small hive suitable for *A. cerana* by Rev.

Father Newton in 1910. This hive named 'Newton Hive' is still popular for keeping *A. cerana*. The Father also trained a large number of beekeepers in Southern India and helped them to establish beekeeping as an economically viable proposition. Mahatama Gandhi realized the importance of beekeeping and included it in his rural development programmes. He inspired rural freedom fighters to take up beekeeping as a venture of livelihood. In earlier times, people after wrapping the blanket on the body or after smoking in night, collected honey from the comb. This was a crude method. After some times, people thought to keep the honey bees and many villagers took interest in keeping honey bees and provided various types of hives in their houses.

Thus, beekeeping can be divided into primitive and modern methods:

A. Primitive or Indigenous Methods

These methods can be divided into two categories:

(*i*) **Fixed type.** Providing a receptacle in the wall of the house with an entrance and observation holes.

(*ii*) **Movable type.** Providing a basket, empty boxes, hollowed logs, bamboo, mud pipes, earthen pots, etc. – anything that can protect bees from sun and rain.

In these indigenous methods, it was mostly left to chance whether a hive gets inhabited or not. It was not possible to have any control over the activities of bees. They could not be checked from robbing and swarming, etc. When honey was extracted, a large number of bees were killed and comb built by honey bees was destroyed. The honey obtained was not pure and contained brood juices, cocoons, pollen grains and parts of the body of the bees, with the result modern method of beekeeping was developed.

B. Modern Method or Frame Hive Method

Frame hives are fitted with movable frames on which the bees are persuaded to build their combs. They are usually composed of several boxes, one on top of the other, in which hive frames are suspended. The lower boxes (1-2) are used for holding the brood and the upper ones (1-2) are used for collection of honey, pollen and propolis (Fig. 21.3).

The artificial comb was first introduced by Revd. L.L. Langstroth in 1851 in America. In India, during 1910 Rev. Father Newton designed a small hive suitable for *A. cerana*. During 1911-17, he also trained a large number of beekeepers in Southern India. In 1928, the Royal Commission on Agriculture recommended beekeeping as a cottage industry and thereafter earnest efforts were made in Tamil Nadu (1931), Punjab (1933), Karnataka (1934), Uttar Pradesh (1938) and several other states for the adoption of this industry. All India Beekeepers Association was established in 1938-39 and subsequently it started publishing the *Indian Bee Journal.*

Bee Equipment

The following apparatus and equipments (Figs. 21.3, 21.4, 21.5) are required for bee-keeping :

1. Bee hive. Various types of bee hives are available for beekeeping. They are wooden boxes having two parts: upper ¼ comb chamber and lower ¾ brood chamber. The following two types of bee hives are more popular in India:

(*i*) Ghos box – 36 cm × 21.5 cm

(*ii*) Newton box – 20.2 cm × 14.0 cm

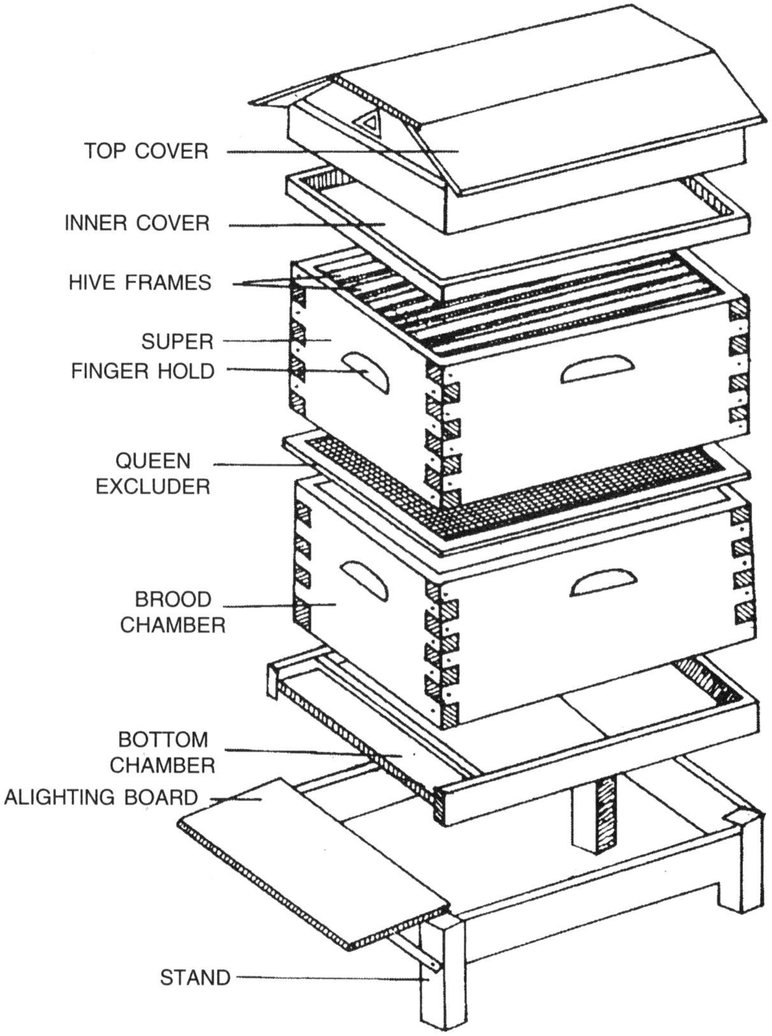

Fig. 21.3 Different parts of a Langstroth frame hive

Some other familiar boxes are as follows :

(*i*)	Langstroth box (American hive)	42.2 cm × 31.1 cm
(*ii*)	Pant, Kanje and Jeolikote No.1	42.2 cm × 12.3 cm
(*iii*)	Dadant box (Russian hive)	47 cm × 28.6 cm
(*iv*)	Thompson box	30.5 cm × 15.2 cm

A movable frame hive is composed of the following parts (Fig. 21.3).

Stand. It is a 4-legged structure, 15-20 cm high, with dimensions to support the floor board.

Floor board. The floor board is a tray with all its four sides raised by side runners and a piece 12.5 x 1.0 cm is removed from the middle of the front side runner to allow entry to the bees.

Alighting board. Sometimes, the front side runner of the floor board is replaced by a projecting piece called the alighting board. This is unnecessary, particularly if the hive is kept on a stand.

Brood chamber. It is a rectangular box without top and bottom. The number of brood boxes could be increased to 2 when the colony becomes strong.

Hive frames. These are wooden frames with their sides named as top bar, two side bars and a bottom bar. The ends of the top bar extend beyond to rest on the rabbet scooped on the long sides of the brood box and its undersurface is grooved to receive the edge of comb foundation.

Queen excluder. To obtain pure honey free from extraneous matter, it is necessary to separate the brood chamber from the supers where honey is stored. This is done with the help of a zinc or wire frame with 2.3-3.5 mm perforations to enable the workers to pass through but not the queen whose thoracic width (4.3-4.5 mm) is more than that of the perforations. The queen would be obliged to stay within the brood boxes and spare the supers of eggs and brood.

Supers. The supers are like brood boxes but shallower and are placed over the queen excluder. They are fitted with frames which are similar to those of the brood boxes except in their shorter heights. A hive could have 2-3 supers depending on its strength.

Covers. There are two covers, i.e. an inner and an outer. The inner cover is a flat board with one or two oval holes in the centre fitted with bee escapes. The escapes allow the bees to go out but do not allow them to re-enter. Such a mechanism helps to get the supers fully vacated by the bees when honey is to be extracted. The outer cover acts as a roof for the hive. It could be made of two sloping planks or could be like an inverted tray. Provision for ventilation must be made in the outer cover.

The various components of the beehive should be made from suitable timber that does not emit strong smell. Kail (*Pinus excelsa*), teak (*Tectona grandis*) and toon (*Toona ciliata*) are some of the suitable timbers.

2. Comb foundation. It is a sheet of pure beewax with the base of the workers brood cells embossed on it. It is fixed in a frame with wires and the bees construct a complete comb on it. It helps in obtaining regular strong worker brood cell comb.

3. Smoker. It is a bellow type tin container from which smoke is generated when bees are furious, which become silent due to smoke.

4. Bee gloves. These are rubber gloves and used at the time of handling the bees to protect the hands from bee stings.

5. Scraper. It is a flat iron plate with one end broad and sharpened and the other end with a wooden handle. It is used for scraping the floor of the box.

6. Hive tool. It is a flat piece of steel sharpened at one end for inserting between hive boxes to separate them and the other end bent to separate the frames. It is also used to scrape off the bee glue (propolis) and superfluous pieces of comb from various parts of the hive.

7. Division board feeder. The division board feeder is a wooden trough of the regular Langstroth frame dimension with its shoulders so made that it may hang in the hive boxes just like any other frame. A wooden strip pushed in an inclined fashion acts as a float and a perch for the bees to sit and sip sugar solution kept inside the feeder.

8. Wire embedder. It is a device to embed the comb foundation wax sheet (with hexagons embossed on it) on to the wires of the hive frame.

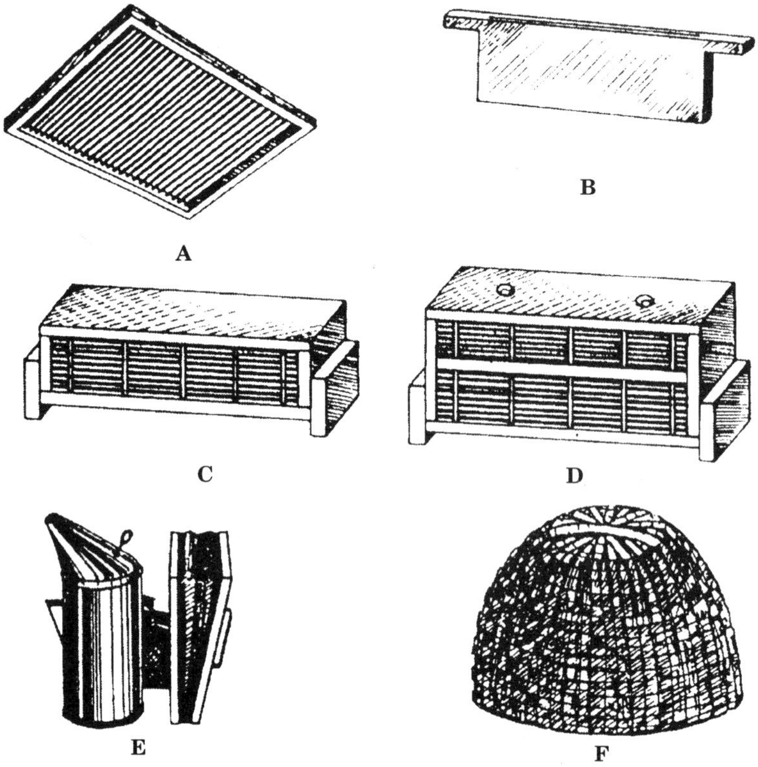

Fig. 21.4 Beekeeping equipment. **A.** Queen excluder, **B.** Feeder, **C.** Wire entrance guard, **D.** Drone trap, **E.** Smoker, **F.** Swarm catching basket

9. Comb cutter. With the comb cutter, old and worn out combs are cut and removed.

10. Bee brush. A bee brush is employed to brush off the bees from a honey comb before it is taken away for extraction.

11. Cold uncapping knife. It is a simple steel knife employed to remove the caps that seal the honey cells after filling before the combs are placed in the honey extractor.

12. Steam uncapping knife. Uncapping can be more easily done by a steam uncapping knife which has a double-walled blade that is heated by steam.

13. Uncapping basket. It is a basket in which the caps of the honey cells are collected during uncapping. A wooden T-bar rests on its mouth to support the bottom bar of the hive frame while the uncapping is carried on

14. Bee veil. It is made up of frames covered on the four sides with small mesh wire gauge and top and bottom with cloth, and used for covering the head and face to get protection from bee sting.

15. Honey extractor. The honey extractor is a drum-like device in which the uncapped frames can be rotated to create a centrifugal force that acts on the surface of the frames and drives the honey out of the cells of the combs. There are three types of honey extractors working on the same principle, i.e. tangential extractor, radial extractor and parallel radial extractor, the first being used by small beekeepers and the other two by commercial beekeepers.

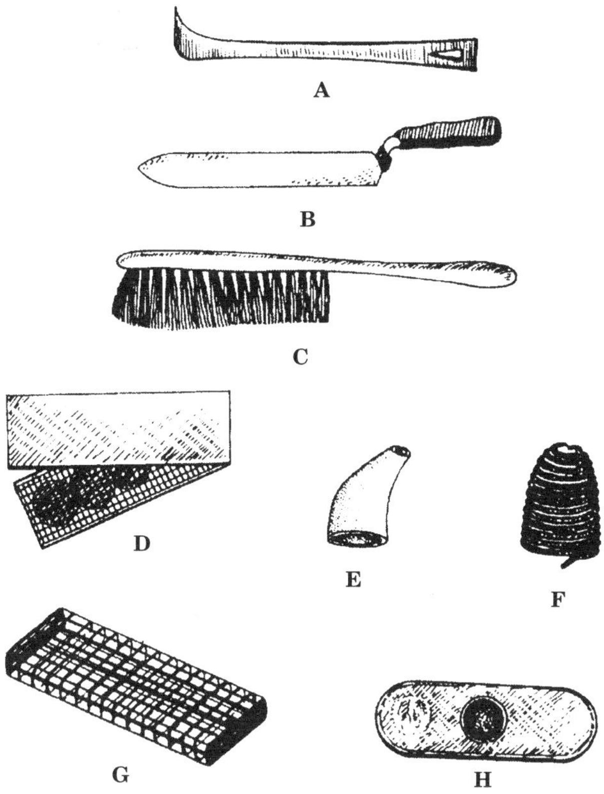

Fig. 21.5 Apiary tools. **A.** Hive tool, **B.** Uncapping knife, **C.** Bee brush, **D.** Queen cage, **E.** Conical bee-escape, **F.** Queen cell protector, **G.** Cage for queen introduction in a colony, **H.** Flat bee escape

16. Wire entrance guard. This wire gate placed in front of the hive entrance also confines the queen inside and thus helps to prevent swarming.

17. Queen cell protector. It is a cone-shaped structure made up of a piece of wire wound spirally. It fits around a queen cell, giving protection to the developing queen inside.

18. Swarm-catching basket. It is a small basket made of bamboo and is used for collecting a sitting swarm and bringing it back to the hive.

19. Drone trap. It is a rectangular box with two compartments, and on the partition in between, two wire gauge funnels are fixed with their narrow ends directed upwards. When the open end of the trap is placed against the hive entrance, the bees pass through the box and out of the distal wall of iron bars which form, in fact, the wire-screen excluder. The workers escape, whereas the drones or queen, when they reach the upper compartment, can not pass through the wire screen excluder and are thus trapped. The drone or the queen trap is used for getting rid of the drones or for confining the queen just before swarming, so as to facilitate the catching of a swarm.

20. Bee escape. It is a funnel shaped structure fitted on the inner board which allows the bees to go out of the super. The bees can not come back through the narrow end and the super frames are thus cleared of the worker bees. The removal of super frames and the extraction of honey are thereby facilitated.

21. Queen cage. It is a small cage made of wire gauge, closed at one end and open at the other. It is used when a new queen is required to be introduced into a queenless colony. A queen, with 5 or 6 workers, is confined to this cage, alongwith a little candy and the open end is closed with a piece of wood. The cage is then suspended alongside a frame in the colony. Within 24-48 hours, when the queen has acquired the odour of the colony or the workers of the colony have adopted to the queen's odour, she is accepted by the workers as the queen of the colony.

22. Dummy board. It is a wooden partition which fits perpendicular, just like an ordinary frame and serves as a movable wall. The size of the brood chamber can thus be increased or decreased according to the size of the colony.

23. Overall. An overall is made of white cloth and is useful while working in an apiary to prevent the bees from going up to the sleeves or into the garment of the beekeeper. Blue or black cloth should be avoided as the bees are attracted to these colours.

Bee Flora

Honey bees collect nectar and pollen from flowering plants. Nectar is a sweet secretion from the floral and extra-floral nectaries of flowers and is the raw material for honey. Pollen is protein-rich food for the bees. The plants that yield nectar and pollen are collectively called *bee flora, bee pasturage* or *bee forage.* The period when a good number of plants providing nectar and pollen are available to bees is called *honey flow period.* If the nectar yield is copious from a good number of plants of a particular species, it is called *major honey flow period.* When the amount of nectar to be collected is small, it is called *minor honey flow period.* The days when there is no honey flow is called the *dearth period.* As nectar and pollen are basic raw materials for beekeeping, a thorough knowledge of the bee flora of a locality is essential. Efficient beekeeping means managing honey bee colonies in such a way to obtain maximum colony population to coincide with the major honey flow in an area and to utilize the population for honey production and pollination.

In general, honey bees depend on a wide variety of plants for nectar and pollen. These include several species of wild and cultivated plants.

Field crops. Pigeonpea, lentils, clovers, lucerne, mustard, rape, linseed, sesame, gingelly, buck-wheat, Cambodia cotton, safflower, maize, millet and sunflower.

Fruit trees. Citrus, litchi, apple, peach, guava, jamun, tamarind, date palm, coconut palm, apricot, almond, plum, loquat, phalsa and cashew.

Vegetables. Cucurbits, peas, okra, beans, turnip, radish, onion, brinjal and sweet potato.

Timber trees. Tun, shisham, soapnut, *Acacia*, house chestnut, kachnar, semel, neem, weeping willow, sal, arjun, eucalyptus, privet, puna, mahua, sandal wood, fiddle wood, rain tree, wild cherry, Persian liliac and mesquite.

Ornamental flowers. Wild rose, cosmos, golden rod, hydrangea, poctulaca, poinsettia, cocal creeper, honey-suckle, cornflower, dandelion, etc.

Diseases and Enemies of Honey Bees

Honey bees like all other creatures suffer from many diseases and are attacked by several insect pests and other natural enemies.

Diseases. The honey bees are infected by various protozoans, bacteria, fungi, virus and mites which cause different diseases.

Nosema disease. This disease is caused by a protozoan, *Nosema apis,* which attacks the lining of the stomach causing dysentery. The spores of this pathogen are passed out with faeces of the infested bees and eaten up by worker bees while cleaning the combs. The disease attacks mostly in winter when the bees do not go out and quickly depletes the bee population. It is more common in temperate than in tropical countries.

The infected bees that are strong enough to make field trips for nectar and pollen often drop from fatigue on their return journey. An increasing number of bees collect in front of the hive upto some distance. The bees crawl up the blades of grass in an attempt to fly. Such disabled bees gather in depressions in the ground. The bees may also be found on the bottom or on frames, in unnatural positions with their abdomen distended with faeces. Many bees loose their body hair and become shiny. On dissection of the infected bees, the mid intestine is seen swollen and dull greyish-white in colour as it is full of spores.

Treatment lies in sterilization of brood boxes and frame hives with glacial acetic acid fumes (soaked in cotton or rag at 120 ml/hive) or ethylene oxide or 40 per cent formalin fumes only after the queen and the bees have been transferred to new foundation combs. A new drug, fumagillin, in concentrated syrup at a dose of 2 mg is highly effective in suppressing nosema disease.

Amoebic disease. It is also caused by a protozoan, *Malpighamoeba mellificae,* which infests the malpighian tubules. The bees get infected by ingesting the cysts which accumulate in the posterior end of the midgut or in the rectum. The cysts get loose from the swollen and glassy malpighian tubules, enter the intestine and are voided alongwith the faecal matter. The disease has a spring peak in April and May. In certain cases, infection is serious enough to kill the colony.

The only way to control the disease is by proper hygiene and by disinfecting the equipment. The cysts are found in faecal matter on the frames and on the bottom board, which should be scraped off and disinfected with 2 per cent carbolic acid. In the spring, the bees can be transferred to boxes that have been fumigated one week earlier with acetic acid.

American foulbrood. It is caused by a bacterium, *Bacillus larvae,* which is introduced into the hive in the form of spores in honey, on combs bearing faeces of infected bees or through the used beekeeping equipment from some previously established source of infection. The disease is most destructive brood disease and occurs worldwide. The disease is highly contagious and the bacterial spores on combs and in food, soil and larval cadavers remain viable for decades, hence there is a recurrence of the epidemic of this diseases in apiaries year after year, causing high mortality among the colonies. The disease is, however, not common in tropical countries. Young larvae, less than 53 hours of age only, are infected by spores. The infected larvae grow to almost full size but die of septicemia, sometimes in pupal stage after the cells have been sealed. The symptoms are sunken and perforated cappings of sealed brood. The cappings collapse and the dead brood is thrown out by bees showing patchiness on combs. The dead brood turns chocolate-brown and later changes into a copy (sticky) mass producing a foul smell. The diseased colony gives out a bad smell resembling a rotten fish.

The disease in case of mild infection can be treated by dusting the combs with sulphathiazole powder. Alternatively, terramycin @ of 0.25-0.40 g/ 5 litre sugar syrup should be fed to affected colonies every week for 6-7 weeks. In serious cases, the bees are shaken off the combs on a newspaper and allowed to run into an empty hive containing only foundation. Then the comb and the newspaper are burnt in a pit and the pit carefully filled to prevent any bee getting to the remains.

European foulbrood. It is caused by *Melissococcus pluton* (syn. *Streptococcus pluton* previously identified as *Bacillus alvei* and *B. pluton*) which is a nonspore forming bacterium. Young larvae within 2 days of age get infected by eating infested brood food (royal jelly) and die generally before completing development. The dead larvae turn chocolate brown but do not emit foul smell. The disease is seasonal and colonies get cured as the diseased brood is thrown out by the house bees. The treatment lies in the destruction of bees and combs by burning and burying the burnt material. Oral terramycin(as in case of American foulbrood) or ethylene oxide fumigation are effective against this disease.

Chalkbrood (Kalkbrut). It is caused by a fungus, *Ascophaera apis,* which converts larvae into chalk-white masses of mycelium. The pathogen mainly infects drone brood and less often the worker brood of the honey bee. The adults are not affected.

The fungus is spread through contaminated food, tools and combs and through the bees from infected colonies. Infection usually occurs through ingestion but may also occur through the external body surface. The larvae are most susceptible when they are 3-4 days old and those on the periphery of the brood area that are chilled and sealed become diseased readily. The ingested spores germinate particularly in the posterior end of the digestive tract of a chilled larva, and the hyphae penetrate into the tissues. The mummified larvae are white if infected by only one strain (+ or –) but when both strains occur they become dark grey or black through the formation of fruiting bodies that appear as tiny black specks on the larvae. Normally, the bees themselves are able to keep this disease under control but in the case of an outbreak, the moist combs should be destroyed and the bees transferred to a clean hive

Stonebrood (Steinbrut). It is also caused by a fungus, *Aspergillus flavus* and less frequently *A. fumigatus* and other species of *Aspergillus*. Infection takes place by germination of the spores in alimentary canal and the adults may also be attacked. The infected larvae and pupae when dead, turn into hard stone like mummies. The abdomens of dead adult bees also become mummified. The disease is rare and usually of minor importance. For prevention, the combs and equipment should be sterilized with formaldehyde fumes as in case of *Nosema.*

Sacbrood. Sacbrood may have been known as a disease of the honey bee as early as 1857 and possibly even before beekeeping by humans. The causal agent of sacbrood is a small as RNA virus which is placed in family Picornaviridae. The disease is transmitted by nurse bees when they feed royal jelly to the larvae older than two days. The diseased larva grows to a full size and outwardly appears to be healthy and is even sealed by bees from the outside. Instead of developing further into pupa, it dies and acquires a sac like appearance and its pearly white colour changes to yellow and later to dark brown. The house bees throw the dead larvae out in order to clean the cells and in this process they pick up the virus. Their own life is also shortened. Sugar feeding helps the bees and before the onset of winter the colonies are generally cleaned of the dead larvae or sick bees and the disease disappears. The virus loses its infectivity quickly within a few days outside of the living honey bee.

Thai sacbrood. It is also caused by a virus which is very similar to sacbrood virus in molecular structure but is highly virulent against *A. cerana.* Since mid-seventies, it has killed many hundred thousand *A. cerana* colonies throughout Southeast Asia. Interestingly, *A. mellifera* colonies lying in the same apiary are not affected by it and hence beekeepers are shifting to this exotic species. In the meantime, selective breeding and multiplication of resistant strains of *A. cerana* are being encouraged.

Acute bee paralysis. This disease is caused by acute bee-paralysis virus (ABPV) and affects only the adults which show signs of trembling, sprawled legs and wings. Occasionally, they also exhibit partial hairlessness and in some cases a black shiny appearance. The death rate may be high, but the disease may be mild or transient at times. Infected adult bees usually show the first symptom of acute paralysis in 2 to 4 days and then die within a day.

Chronic bee paralysis. This disease is caused by the chronic bee-paralysis virus (CBPV) and the infected adult may take many days to die in contrast to quick mortality caused by ABPV. Adult bees infected with CBPV may exhibit two distinct syndromes. In the first syndrome the adults have a bloated abdomen, which is caused by the distension of the honey sac with liquid. They do not fly, instead they crawl on the ground, exhibiting an abnormal trembling motion of the wings and bodies. Bees with the second syndrome are initially able to fly. They become almost hairless, appearing dark or almost black and shiny. Uninfected bees nibble at them and prevent their return to the colony. In a few days, they start trembling, remain flightless and die soon.

Acarine disease. The Acarine disease or Isle of Wight disease of adult honey bees is caused by a mite, *Acarapis woodi* Rennie. The mites live, feed and breed in the tracheae of the bees. They enter the spiracles on the first segment and work their way inwards into the trachea, damaging the linings while feeding on blood and depositing their faeces in the passage. It may multiply in such great numbers that the trachea are blocked, bees become sluggish and crawl around in the hives. Their wings become disjointed and they cannot fly. As more of the healthy bees get infected in a colony by the disease, it is spread in an apiary from colony to colony by the robbing bees. The disease can be very serious and may cause dwindling and ultimate death of the colony.

The other two mites which infest the honey bees are *Tropilaelaps clareae* and *Varroa jacobsoni*. *T. clareae* are active rust-red mites which live on combs and can be seen with a naked eye. They feed and breed on the brood and are seen in all developmental stages. The mites breed very fast, particularly in the monsoon period. The colony strength is reduced to a handful bees which ultimately abscond with their queen. *V. jacobsoni* are flabby rotund mites, the size of a pin head, and can be seen clinging to honey bees in the soft intersegmental membranes from where it is easy for them to feed on blood. After a good meal, mites move to the brood cells containing 5-day old larvae and later on other developmental stages. Depending upon the amount of damage caused, the adults emerge with various degrees of deformities. Owing to the fast multiplication of the mites, almost all the bees in a colony may die and many of the colonies in an apiary may be destroyed. All these three mites can be controlled by regular fumigation with menthol, chlorobenzilate or formic acid.

Smoke fumigation with chlorobenzilate (Folbex) is the most effective in killing the mites without causing damage to the bees. Two or three treatments with 350-450 mg given at 7-10 days interval give complete control. To prepare the paper strips, strong blotting paper is soaked in 5 per cent potassium nitrate solution. After drying, it is soaked in 15 per cent solution of chlorobenzilate in benzene, and is dried again. A strip (11 x 4 cm) contains the required dose. The end of the strip is ignited, kept in the hive in the evening and the entrance of the hive is shut for 20-30 minutes. Formic acid and menthol are applied on a swab of cotton at the end of a iron wire which is held in position inside the entrance. The treatment is repeated at weekly interval 3-4 times. Excessive and repeated use of one fumigant may lead to development of resistance in the mites. In India, light dusting of sulphur on top of the frames has been effectively used for the last many years against the external mites.

Enemies. Among the insect enemies of honey bees, black ants, wax moths and wasps are worrisome pests. The important animal predators include lizards and birds.

Wax moths. There are two species of wax moths causing considerable damage to honey bee colonies, viz. greater wax moth, *Galleria mellonella* and the lesser wax moth, *Achroia grisella*. The female moth lays eggs inside the hive on the covered portion of combs, in cracks and crevices in the walls, and on the bottom board of the hive. The larvae emerging from the eggs make silken tunnels in the combs under cover and they feed on beeswax. When the attack is severe, the whole comb is covered with silken tunnels. The larvae prefer darker or older combs. If this pest is not checked in time, the whole combs may be destroyed and the bees may abscond.

The prophylactic measures are more effective in keeping an apiary free from this pestilence. The combs and equipment should be kept in insect proof store rooms, boxes or even bags of thick plastic. These should be fumigated periodically with a poisonous gas to kill all stages of the wax moth. The use of paradichlorobenzene (PDB) in stored combs gives protection against this moth. Two to four table spoons of the crystals of PDB should be placed between every other super in a stack for good results.

Wasps. Several species of *Vespa*, are predacious on the bees in the plains and hills. Among these yellow banded oriental hornet, *Vespa orientalis* and the giant wasp, *V. magnifica*, are quite serious. They catch bees from blossoms or even from inside their hives, sometimes finishing off the entire colony. The wasps feed their larvae with macerated bees. The wasps are inactive in the winter, but they are very destructive in the rainy season. Being large in size, they catch bees at the entrance of the hive and forcibly take them to their own nest where they are eaten at leisure. The best method to offer protection to bees against wasps is to destroy their papery nests by burning them or by spraying an insecticide.

Ants. Several species of ants, viz. carpenter ant, *Componotus compressus*; small red household ant, *Dorylus labiatus* and other species, *Monomorium indicum* and *M. destructor*, visit bee colonies and take away honey, brood, pollen, dead bodies and other debris. The ants are more troublesome in the sub-tropical and tropical areas than in the temperate region. They are particularly bothersome to weak colonies which they can even destroy. Ants could be controlled by destroying ant nests in the vicinity of beehives by fumigating them or by the use of insecticides. In the apiaries, the hives should be placed on stands whose legs should be dipped in cups of water.

Toads, frogs and lizards. Toads and frogs are widespread in India and are seen near the hives or water holes, and cause damage to honey bees. The lizards often sit at the hive entrance and catch honey bees at ease. Some of the lizards are active at night and snap at stray honey bees which may have lost their way to the colonies.

Birds. The birds are a formidable group of bee enemies in flight. The small green bee-eater, *Merops orientalis*, is a beautiful bird of the size of a sparrow with long wings and tail with which it glides in the air with great ease, always on the look out for flying bees. Quite often it is seen near apiaries, sitting on tall grasses, telephone wires or other vantage points. As soon as it sees a flying bee, it swoops at her and catches her in the long sharp beak and then sits at a vantage point. It seems to be in no hurry and then swallows the bee in its own time. The other allied species of bee-eaters, viz. *M. apiaster* and *M. supersiliosus* have similar habits. They make their nests on the sides of mounds and hills wherever it is easy for them to dig holes for their nest. Bee eaters are also well spread in cropped areas where many species of wild bees visit flowers and become a prey to them. The honey bees with their stomachs full of nectar and legs laden with pollen, are preferred as food. The bee eaters have to be controlled effectively to make beekeeping a success in such areas. Destroying their nests and killing birds with sling shots or air guns is very rewarding in suppressing their population.

Sometimes, the bee-eaters are advantageous to apiculturists and agriculturists because of their high level of predation on hornets and locusts. Therefore, it is not always advisable to eradicate them. Efforts should be made to scare away the birds, for which two approaches have proved to be useful:

(*i*) **Plastics.** A polythene sheet is tied to a long pole and placed in the centre of the field near apiaries. As the sheet flaps and flutters in the breeze, the sound that is produced wards off the birds.

(*ii*) **Acetyl guns.** This comprises of a mechanical device wherein acetylene gas is produced by the action of water on calcium carbide and the sound scares the birds.

BEE PRODUCTS

Honey, beeswax and propolis are the major bee products which are important from commercial point of view.

Honey

Honey is a sweet viscous liquid prepared by honey bees from the nectar collected from nectar glands (nectaries) of plants and stored by them for food. The bee draws nectar by its tongue (proboscis) and carries it to the hive in its crop or honey stomach. In the hive, it is regurgitated and deposited by the hivemates into cells meant for collection of nectar and its subsequent ripening into honey. The nectar which is composed of 20-40 per cent sucrose is reduced by the enzyme invertase to glucose and fructose (Table 21.2).

Table 21.2 Chemical composition of honey

Sr. No.	Constituent	Amount (%)
1	Water	17.2
2	Fructose	38.2
3	Glucose	31.3
4	Sucrose	1.3
5	Disaccharides (maltose)	7.3
6	Higher sugars	1.5
7	Total acids (gluconic)	0.57
8	Minerals	0.17
9	Proteins and amino acids	0.04
10	Enzymes, vitamins, aroma constituents and other substance	Traces

Source: Atwal (2000)

The colour and aroma of honey depends on the species of plant from which the nectar has been collected. There is also correlation between colour and flavour, the darker honey has a stronger or more pronounced flavour and the lighter coloured honey has a delicate and more pleasant flavour for which it is preferred. If the temperature is below 24°C, glucose in the honey crystallizes and honey is said to have granulated. Some honeys granulate faster than the others. After granulation glucose settles down while fructose and water remain above increasing the danger of fermentation.

Honey is a high energy carbohydrate food. It is the best source of heat and energy giving over 5,500 calories per kg. It provides wholesome nourishment as compared to other foods. Energy value of one kg of honey is estimated to be equal to 65 eggs, 13 kg milk, 8 kg plums, 19 kg green peas, 12 kg apples and 20 kg carrots. Honey is extensively used in Ayurvedic and Unani system of medicines. It is used as a laxative, a blood purifier, a preventive agent against cold, coughs and fever and a curative for eye sores, ulcers of the tongue, throat and burns. The Indian systems of medicine belonging to both Ayurveda and Sidha schools rely on honey as a carrier which enhances the properties of drugs. Honey is the best tonic for infants and athletes. It has been acclaimed as a restorative healer and health giver since ancient times. Many religions enjoin on their followers the use of honey in various rites performed during festivals and on important occasions in the life of an individual. It is known as the food of the Gods.

Beeswax

Beeswax is secreted by the honey bees on the underside of the abdomen where there are located four pairs of wax glands. It is estimated that bees have to consume 10-15 kg of honey to produce 1 kg of beeswax. In India, the main source of beeswax is the combs of wild bees, particularly *A. dorsata*. On an average, for every 100 kg of honey produced, the corresponding wax production may range from 1 to 2 kg. Evidently, wax is costlier than honey. It has been found that 1 kg of wax can support 22 kg of honey, over 20 times its own weight.

The standard *A. mellifera* beeswax is composed of nearly 300 fractions of compounds which consist of hydrocarbons (10.5%), monoesters (35%), diesters (14%), hydroxy polyesters (8%), hydroxy monoesters (4%), free acids (8%), acid esters and polyesters (3%), triesters (3%) and unspecified (13%). Beeswax is used in more than 300 items. About 75 per cent of the beeswax produced worldwide goes into cosmetics (creams, lotions, lipsticks, eyebrow pencils, pomades, hair creams, etc.) and pharmaceutical preparations such as ointments and pill coatings. Other major use of beeswax is the manufacture of church and domestic candles. Some other uses include the production of polishes (for floor, furniture, shoe, leather, car, etc.), crayons, ink, carbon paper, lubricants, sealing wax, paints and varnishes. It is also used in telescopic lenses. It is also used as an ingredient in the composition of adhesives, chewing gums, basketball moldings and for thread and archer's bow strings. Large quantities of beeswax are also used in ammunition factories.

Propolis

It is a dark solid workable substance collected by bees from the resins and gums of plants and trees. It is used by bees as such or mixed with wax for construction and repair of their hive. It also affords protection to the colonies against unpleasant odour, bacteria and putrifying corpuses. Propolis contains 55 per cent resin and balsam, 10 per cent scented and ethereal oil, upto 30 per cent wax and 5 per cent pollen. Propolis is supposed to have antiallergic and antibacterial properties. It is effective against herpes virus and is useful for wound healing and tissue regeneration. Its extracts are a cure for many dermatological disorders. It is also known to possess antituberculosis properties.

Royal Jelly

Royal jelly is the secretion of hypopharyngeal glands of worker bees normally of 5-15 days of age. It is fed to queens throughout their larval and adult lives, and also to young worker and drone larvae. On an average, it contains moisture 66.05 per cent, proteins 12.34 per cent, fats 5.46 per cent, total reducing substances 12.49 per cent, minerals 0.82 per cent and other substances 2.84 per cent. Royal jelly is rich in vitamin B, also contains vitamin C but lacks vitamin E. It also contains a substance, 10-hydroxy decenoic acid, which exhibits antibiotic activity against many bacteria and fungi. It is believed to be a general tonic and a cure against common colds. In natural form, it is used as face cream and is applied on skin to clear blemishes and eczema. Few reports also suggest its use to increase vitality, potency and delay aging in human beings. The world production of royal jelly is about 500 tonnes.

Bee Venom

Bee venom is derived from the poison glands of honey bee workers. Bee venom is a clear liquid with sharp, bitter taste, an aromatic odour and an acid reaction. It contains histamine, apamine, tryptophan, phospholipase, hyaluronidase, lecithinase, hydrochloric acid and magnesium sulphate. It is a valuable remedy for rheumatism. It is also known to lower blood pressure and decreases cholesterol level. It also neutralizes alcohol poison.

Pollen

When bees visit flowers for nectar or pollen, they help in cross pollination. Pollen adheres to the body of the bees and carried from one flower to another and this leads to increase in yield by 30-50 per cent. The composition of pollen collected by honey bees is as follows: water 11.2 per cent, crude protein 21.6 per cent, other extracts 5.0 per cent, carbohydrates as reducing sugars 25.7 per cent, non-reducing sugars 2.7 per cent, starch 2.6 per cent, minerals 2.7 per cent and undetermined compounds 28.9 per cent. Pollen is used as a human health food and it is believed to have antibiotic and antiallergic properties.

BEE POISONING

Honey bees get poisoned when they visit flowers of poisonous plants, whose pollen and nectar are injurious, and both adults and the brood in the colony die. Some of the plants reported to be poisonous are *Aesculus californica, A. hippocastanum, A. povia, Astagalus* sp., *Crylla* sp., *Rhododendion* spp. and *Tillia* spp. Honey collected by wild bees from *R. arboreum* in Sikkim is believed to be poisonous.

The bees are susceptible to many pesticides used in agricultural crops. Based on their relative toxicity to bees, pesticides may be grouped into different categories.

(*i*) **Highly toxic.** Direct application kills all bees and treated plants remain toxic for one or two days, e.g. lindane, diazinon, phorate, quinalphos, dimethoate, monocrotophos.

(*ii*) **Moderately toxic.** Can be used around bees provided the dosages and timings are correct and also should not be applied directly over bees either in field or at the colonies, e.g. carbaryl, malathion, fenitrothion.

(*iii*) **Relatively non-toxic.** Can be safely used around bees, e.g. Bordeaux mixture, cuprous oxide, 2,4-D, methoxychlor, nicotine, pyrethrum, rotenone, sulphur, neem, endosulfan, *Bacillus thuringiensis.*

In case of pesticide application at the time of flowering of bee forage crops, any pesticide which may result in more than 10 per cent mortality of field bees should not be used during this time. If highly toxic chemicals have been used, the bees can be prevented from visiting the treated fields by closing the hive entrance. However, in case of moderately toxic chemicals it is sufficient if the hive is closed during the time of application only.

BEEKEEPING IN INDIA

The total global production of honey is about 1.31 million tonnes a year gathered by 50-60 million honey bee colonies. At present, China, USA, Turkey, Argentina and Mexico are the largest producers of honey in the world. China produces about 2.7 lakh tonnes of honey but the quality of the produce is poor. According to recent estimates there are more than 3,50,500 beekeepers in India maintaining 1.5 million colonies. The total production of honey in India is about 92000 tonnes (including wild honey), out of which more than 23,600 tonnes is exported to Germany, USA, Middle East countries and South Africa. In Punjab alone, there are about 30,000 beekeepers maintaining more than 2,50,000 *A. mellifera* colonies producing 18000 tonnes of honey annually, out of which more than 90 per cent is being exported.

A. mellifera has now spread from Punjab and Himachal Pradesh to almost all the states of India, the predominant being Bihar (1,25,000 colonies), Uttar Pradesh (80,000), Haryana (50,000), West Bengal (40,000), Jammu & Kashmir (25,000) and Kerala, Karnataka and Orissa each with 5000 colonies. There is potential to raise the number of colonies to 10-15 million in India and thus scope for future beekeeping is tremendous. The average yield can be raised from 15 to 30 kg per colony per year by using *A. mellifera* and to 60 kg by practicing migratory beekeeping.

In India, about 16 lakh people are engaged in beekeeping and allied activities. Beekeeping generally means honey production, but a beekeeper can produce many other commodities for sale and generate income. These include queen rearing, package bees, pollen and propolis collection, wax, royal jelly, bee venom and renting colonies for pollination. The honey itself can be sold in bulk or can be bottled for retail selling. Further, it can be produced as comb honey or creamed honey which are sold at a higher price. Honey can also be used in the production of alcoholic drinks. The production and marketing strategies would depend upon the type of operation or the kind of colony to be used.

The most significant feature of beekeeping industry in India is the export of honey to other countries which started at a reasonable scale in 1995-96. Under a project of Punjab Agro-Industries Cooperation, 800 tonnes of honey was exported to USA in 1996. Another 200-300 tonnes of honey was exported by other private firms to the middle-East countries. There is already a demand from Europe for litchi and other flavours from India. It is apparent now that there is a great potential of beekeeping in the country and world market is ready to purchase any amount of honey from India.

BEEKEEPING RESEARCH AND DEVELOPMENT

Commercial beekeeping in India dates back to 1911 when Rev. Father Newton devised a hive suitable for *A. cerana*. This hive, which was named after him as 'Newton hive', is still popular. The All India Beekeepers Association (AIBA) was established in 1938-39 and subsequently AIBA started publishing the Indian Bee Journal, which still has the distinction of being the only journal in the country exclusively devoted to beekeeping research and development. The Indian Council of Agricultural Research (ICAR) established a Beekeeping Research Station in Punjab in 1945 at Nagrota-Bagwan (now in Himachal Pradesh) and later at Coimbatore in Tamil Nadu in 1951. The Khadi and Village Industries Commission established Central Bee Research Institute (CBRI) at Pune in November 1962, with overall development of beekeeping as its mandate. Subsequently, training component was also added to its mandate and the institute was renamed as Central Bee Research and Training Institute (CBRTI).

On the recommendation of the National Commission on Agriculture, on All India Coordination Project on Honey Bee Research and Training was launched by ICAR in 1980, with coordinating cell at CBRTI, Pune. Later, the coordinating cell was shifted to CCS Haryana Agricultural University, Hisar. This ICAR sponsored project has now 10 centres, viz. Ludhiana (Punjab), Solan (Himachal Pradesh), New Delhi (Delhi), Pantnagar (Uttarakhand), Pusa (Bihar), Bhubaneswar (Orissa), Jorhat (Assam), Chethalli (Karnataka), Vijayari (Andhra Pradesh) and Vellayani (Kerala). Some voluntary centres, several state Agricultural Universities (SAUs), State Departments of Agriculture and National Horticulture Board are also engaged in beekeeping research and/or training. The Government of India set up a National Beekeeping Development Board (NBDB) in September 1993, which has recently been reconstituted and named as National Bee Board (NBB).

*****

22 CHAPTER

SERICULTURE

The rearing of silkworms for the production of silk is called sericulture. Silk is the secretion from the salivary glands which are found on both sides of the alimentary canal of silkworm larvae and this secretion hardens into fine threads called silk. The cocoons with which pupae are covered by the worms are utilized for silk production. Most of the lepidopteran caterpillars and some other insects spin silk, but those of only two super families, *viz.*, Bombycoidea and Noctuoidea produce silk of practical use on account of quantity and quality (Table 22.1). Silk is spun in one single reelable thread which is collected and used for manufacturing the threads and cloths, etc. The secretion is produced in a liquid form but on coming in contact with air, it solidifies into what we call silk. The silk (fibre) is composed of two proteins, fibroin and sericin. The fibroin which constitutes 75 per cent of the material is tough, elastic and insoluble making the core of the silk filament in the form of two very thin fibres called burns. The sericin which alongwith traces of wax and carotenoid pigments constitutes the rest of the material, is a gelatinous (gummy), hot-water soluble protein that holds the burns together and covers them so that the segments (loops) of the cocoon also stick together.

According to some people, India is considered the place of origin of this insect while most others consider China as its native place. Princess Lotzon of China investigated the process of making silk as early as 269 BC. China made a tremendous progress and started its export to various countries during 2000 BC. The source and method of obtaining the silk was kept secret for about 2500 years. The government made a strict rule that the person who will leak the secret to any of the foreign countries will be hanged. But still two religious bishops who went there, learnt the know-how about silkworm and collected the eggs of silkworm in hollow bamboo pieces which were carried to Kuptuntunia, from where it spread to the European and Asian countries.

Table 22.1 Moth species used for silk production

Family	Insect species	Host plant	Country
Lasiocampidae	*Gonometa postica*	*Acacia* spp.	Africa
	Trabala vishnou (Oriental Lappet Moth)	Polyphagous	South East Asia
Bombycidae	*Bombyx mori* (Silkworm; Oriental silkmoth)	Mulberry	South East Asia, etc.
	Bombyx spp.	Mulberry	India
Saturniidae	*Actias selene* (Moon moth)	Many hosts	India to China
	Antheraea assamensis (*Muga* silkworm)	Polyphagous	India
	Antheraea mylitta	*Syzygium* spp.	India
	Antheraea paphia (Tasar silkworm)	Polyphagous	South East Asia
	Antheraea pernyi (Chinese oak silkworm)	Oaks	China
	Antheraea yamamai (Japanese oak silkworm)	*Quercus* spp.	Japan
	Attacus atlas (Atlas moth)	Polyphagous	Pantropical
	Eriogyna pyretorum (Giant silkworm moth)	Camphor	South East Asia
	Naudaurelia spp. (Silkworms)	Several hosts	Africa
	Samia cynthia (Lesser Atlas moth; Wild silkmoth)	*Lantana*, etc.	India to China
	Philosamia ricini (Eri silkworm)	Castor	India, South East Asia
	Thiopaila religiosae (Deo muga silkworm)	Machilis, *Ficus*	India
Notodontidae	*Anaphe infracta* (African wild silkworm)	*Bridelia*	Uganda

Source: Hill (1997)

During ancient times, fabulous silks from China and India were carried to Europe along the famous 6000 miles 'Silk Road' which passed through Tashkent, Baghdad, Damascus and Istanbul. With the emergence of synthetic fibres, the importance of silk fibre in textile industry declined and presently it constitutes only 0.2 per cent of the fibre used in textile industry. However, it is still sought for its elegance and colours, and is rightly called the 'Queen of textiles'. China, India and South Korea are the major silk exporting countries, while exports from Japan have declined over the years.

SILKWORMS

Five silkworm species found in India are described below :

1. **Mulberry silkworm, *Bombyx mori* Linnaeus.** It is the most important silkworm and reared extensively in various part of India. Its caterpillar feeds on mulberry leaves. The cocoons are white in colour from which best quality of silk is obtained. There are several races of the mulberry silkworm which may be grouped into two categories, *viz.*, univoltine and multivoltine. The univoltine has an annual life cycle while multivoltine race passes through many generations in a year. The multivoltine race produces inferior quality of silk and is reared in West Bengal, Assam and Karnataka.

2. **Tasar silkworm, *Antheraea paphia* Linnaeus.** It is generally found in the forests of West Bengal, Assam and Uttar Pradesh and is not domesticated. The important host trees of this silkworm are sal (*Shorea robusta*), ber (*Ziziphus mauritiana*), Asan (*Terminalia tomentosa*), and Arjun (*Terminalia arjuna*). The cocoons are hard light brown to dark in colour and have to be collected from the jungle. They are reeled and if pierced are spun.
3. **Eri silkworm, *Samia cynthia ricini* Boisduval.** This silkworm was mainly found in the forests of Assam but now found in West Bengal, Bihar, U.P., Orissa and Tamil Nadu. As its scientific name indicates, it feeds on castor (*Ricinus communis*) leaves and is domesticated all over the country where castor is grown. Its cocoons which are white in colour can not be reeled and have to be spun.
4. **Muga silkworm, *Antheraea assamensis* Helfer.** This silkworm is found in Bihar, West Bengal, Orissa and Assam, and can not be domesticated. The caterpillars feed on the leaves of cinnamon and machilis plants. The cocoons are reeled and are of brilliant yellow colour from which silk of golden yellow colour is obtained.
5. **Deo muga silkworm, *Thiopaila religiosae* H.** It is found in Uttar Pradesh and Uttaranchal. The caterpillars mainly feed on the leaves of machilis and *Ficus* plant. Its thread is generally used for making the fisheries net.

I. MULBERRY SERICULTURE

Mulberry sericulture is practised by the mulberry silkworm, *Bombyx mori* Linnaeus (Lepidoptera : Bombycidae). The adult silkworm is a moth of creamy white colour measuring about 30 mm in length and a wing span of 40-50 mm. The male is smaller than female. The head is small and bears a pair of black compound eyes and bipectinate antennae. The mouth parts are vestigial, therefore, the moth does not take food and lives only for 2 to 3 days. The anterior portion of thorax is narrower than the posterior. The fore wings are provided with dirty dark coloured stripes and the body is covered with hairs. The moths copulate by keeping their mouths in opposite direction. They mate immediately after emergence during May-June.

Egg. Eggs are laid in the night in clusters on the under surface of mulberry leaves. A female lays about 300-400 eggs popularly called as silk-seeds. The eggs are small, pale white and seed like in appearance. At the time of hatching, they become black and hatch in 10-12 days during summer and 30 days during winter. In the univoltine race, the eggs do not hatch during winter but remain in hibernation, therefore, one generation is found in a year in such cases. Such type of race is found in European countries and Kashmir and Punjab in India. Contrary to this, 2-7 generations are found in multivoltine race.

Larva. The caterpillar on hatching is white to dark in colour and about 3 mm in length. There are 3 pairs of thoracic and 5 pairs of abdominal legs which are situated on the 3,4,5,6 and 10th abdominal segments. A horny appendage known as dorsal spine is found on the dorsal surface of 8th abdominal segment. Young caterpillars are reared in trays on tender mulberry leaves at 25-27°C. Each day, the feed is provided 3-4 times with small quantity of leaves. After 5th day when they become big, a net of small mesh is placed over them and the succulent leaves are put on the net. The larvae on getting the food crawl above through the meshes of the net. After about 2 hours, the net is lifted and placed on another tray. The caterpillars alongwith the unused mulberry leaves is removed. The larva moults 4-5 times after every 6-7 days and becomes mature in 30-35 days. In cold countries it takes many months to become full-grown. The full-grown caterpillar is creamy white in colour and about 7.5 cm long. The matured worms are picked up and kept in cocooning baskets. They make cocoons generally within 25 hours.

Pupa. The cocoon is 3.8 cm in length and 1.9 cm in breadth, oval in shape and white or yellow in colour. The larva pupates inside the cocoon which is made up of a single thread. It spins about 15 cm thread in an hour. The pupa inside the cocoon is reddish-brown in colour and measures 25 mm x 7 mm. The pupal period lasts for 10-15 days. At the time of emergence of adult, it secretes an alkaline fluid which pierces the cocoon and it comes out. Those cocoons which are intended for further rearing are kept separately in a cool place and moths are allowed to emerge and lay eggs.

It has been estimated that about 40-50 thousand caterpillars hatch out of 28 g of silk seed and they require about 337 to 406 kg of leaves during their development. The weight in grams of 900 m long silk filament is called a 'denier' and the size of a normal cocoon is 1.8 to 3 deniers. A single cocoon weighs 1.8 to 2 g and its shell (without the enclosed pupa), only 0.45 g. About 2500 cocoons yield 1 lb (0.45 kg) of silk.

COMPONENTS OF SERICULTURE

Sericulture is an agro-industry comprising 3 main components, *viz.* cultivation of food plants of the worms, rearing of silkworms, and reeling and spinning of silk. Since mulberry sericulture constitutes the major silk industry in India, these three components are explained here keeping this fact in view.

Cultivation of Food Plants

The cultivation of mulberry plants is called moriculture as the plant belongs to the family Moraceae. Among 20 species of mulberry, the most common are *Morus alba, M. indica, M. serrata* and *M. latifolia,* while the local *M. indica* offers certain good features (like quick growing, hardiness, remaining in flush throughout the year, etc.), its yield is rather low. Therefore, certain high yielding varieties have been developed suiting for various regions, viz. Northern and Eastern States (Punjab, J&K, U.P. and West Bengal): S-162, S-519 and S-623; and Southern States (Karnataka, Andhra Pradesh and Tamil Nadu): Kanva-2, S-30 and S-54.

The pencil-thick cuttings (22-25 cm long with 3-4 buds each) of mulberry are planted according to two systems. In the pit system, pits (45 cm wide and 45 cm deep) are dug prior to monsoon (June), filled with compost and cuttings planted after the first rainfall. The distance between the rows and plants is maintained at 95 and 45 cm, respectively. In the row system, cuttings are planted on the two margins of 60 x 30 cm ridges, keeping the distance between rows and plants at 45 and 10 cm, respectively. In each case, the plants are kept alive by pot-watering until they have taken roots and become strong. Subsequently, recommended agronomic practices are followed till good flush of leaves. The leaves are harvested for larval feeding in three ways:

(*i*) **Leaf picking method.** Individual leaves are hand picked, tender leaves for younger larvae and mature leaves for older larval instars.

(*ii*) **Branch cutting method.** The entire branch with leaves is cut and offered to third instar larvae.

(*iii*) **Top shoot harvesting method.** The tops of the shoots are clipped and given to fourth and fifth instar larvae.

Rearing of Silkworms

The room in which silkworms are reared should avoid dampness, stagnation of air, exposure to bright sunlight and strong winds. It should also ensure proper humidity, ventilation and temperature.

Rearing Equipment

The following equipment (Fig. 22.1) is required for proper rearing of the silkworms:

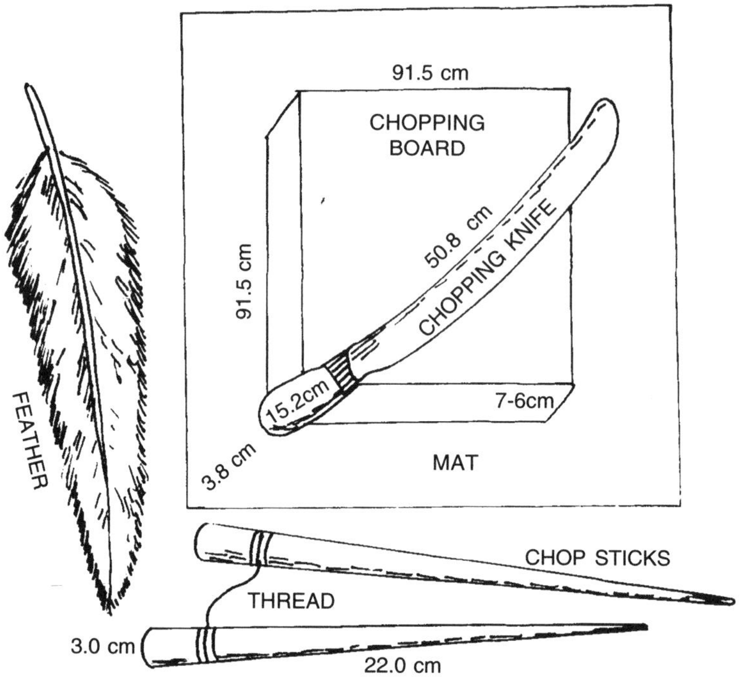

Fig. 22.1 Articles employed in handling delicate younger instars (feather and chopsticks) and for chopping mulberry leaves.

(*i*) **Rearing stands.** These are wood or bamboo stands of frames on which are placed rearing trays containing silkworms.

(*ii*) **Rearing trays.** These are trays made up of split bamboo used for rearing silkworms. These are generally circular, but sometimes box type wooden trays are employed to rear early instars.

(*iii*) **Antwells.** These are rectangular or circular enamel/concrete bowls containing water. The legs of rearing stand are kept in these bowls so that ants may not approach the caterpillars.

(*iv*) **Paraffin paper.** These are thick craft paper sheets coated with paraffin wax. These are used to cover the rearing trays to maintain humidity and prevent withering of leaves.

(*v*) **Foam rubber strips.** These are cut pieces (2.5 × 2.5 cm) of foam rubber soaked in water and kept all around silkworm rearing beds to maintain humidity. Alternatively, newspaper folded strips moistened with water could also be used.

(*vi*) **Chopsticks.** These are tapering bamboo rods required for picking up younger larvae to ensure their proper handling and avoid any injuries.

(*vii*) **Feathers.** These are usually white feathers used for brushing together freshly hatched larvae to prevent injuries.

(*viii*) **Leaf chambers.** These are chambers made up of 7.5 cm wooden strips fixed some distance apart or of some porous board. These are used for storing mulberry leaves meant for feed. The chamber with leaves is covered all over with gunny bag cloth which is kept moist during summer months and dry days.

(*ix*) **Cleaning nets.** These are nets made up of cotton or nylon of the mesh size suitable for different instars, *viz.* 2 mm^2 (I, II and III instars), 10 mm^2 (IV instar) and 20 mm^2 (V instar). These are used for changing the rearing beds so that the left over leaf-pieces and litter are filtered out without the larvae being touched by hand.

(*x*) **Chopping boards, knives and mats.** These materials are needed to chop the mulberry leaves which are offered to the larvae as food. The chopping board is made up of soft wood and placed on a mat. Two types of knives, small for chopping small pieces for younger instars and large for chopping larger pieces for older larvae, are required. The chopped leaves falling on mat are collected in an enamelled receptacle.

(*xi*) **Mountages.** These are the contrivances made up of rectangular bamboo mat tied on 4 bamboo sticks and bearing on its surface spirals of bamboo tapes. Mature worms about to spin cocoons are transferred to them and the larvae suspend themselves to the spirals and spin cocoons.

(*xii*) **Miscellaneous appliances.** These include a thermometer to record temperature of the rearing room, hygrometer to measure humidity, heater and cooler to maintain temperature and humidity, leaf-baskets to transport mulberry leaves from field to the rearing house, pads of gunny soaked in 2 per cent formalin to disinfect feet of workers entering the rearing room and wash-basin containing 2 per cent formalin to disinfect the hands of workers handling the worms.

Care of Larvae

The larvae should be reared in the room under strict hygienic conditions. The younger (I and II instars) larvae should be given tender succulent leaves with a high moisture content and old instars be given mature but soft leaves with lesser moisture. Mulberry leaves are fed to the larvae in a chopped condition. Square leaves are best when the air is dry because they prevent rapid withering. Long thin strips or oblong pieces are suitable when the season is wet. Triangular leaves take less labour and hence can be given to older instars who consume large quantities of leaves.

1. Feed bed. Feed bed is a layer of chopped leaves spread on a tray or over a large area. Finely chopped mulberry leaves are evenly scattered on the paraffin paper sheet and the I and II instar larvae are carefully brushed on to the leaves. A second sheet of paraffin paper is placed loosely over the bed and in between the two sheets and on all sides water–soaked foam rubber strips (or wet newspaper folds) are placed to maintain humidity. The older (III-V) instars can be reared by three methods:

(*i*) **Shelf rearing.** Silkworms are reared in round bamboo trays arranged one over the other in tiers on a rearing stand. Larvae are fed on chopped leaves.

(*ii*) **Floor rearing.** Fixed rearing seats or benches (5-7 x 1-1.5 m) constructed in 2-3 tiers out of wooden or bamboo strips are used for rearing silkworms. Leaves are given in a chopped state.

(*iii*) **Shoot-rearing.** The rearing seat, 1 m wide and any length long, is in single tier and larvae are offered big shoots.

2. Bed cleaning. Periodical removal of leaf leftovers and worm excreta (bed cleaning) is necessary to ensure proper growth of larvae under hygienic conditions. Four methods are adopted for bed cleaning:

(*i*) **Conventional method.** The younger worms (I-III instars) are swept together with a feather and transferred from the old to the new bed and the older worms (IV-V instars) are transferred manually.

(*ii*) **Husk method.** A thin and even layer of paddy husk is sprinkled over the bed to be changed and the chopped leaves are scattered on the husk. The worms quickly crawl through the husk to get at the feed from where they can be removed to the new tray.

(*iii*) **Net method.** A cotton or nylon net of suitable mesh size is spread over the old bed and leaves scattered on it. The larvae migrate to the net in search of fresh leaves and can be collected and transferred to a new bed.

(*iv*) **Combined husk and net method.** A thin layer of paddy husk is first sprinkled over the old bed and a net of suitable mesh is superimposed on it. Two successive feedings follow, thereafter, the net with the worms on it is transferred to another tray.

In order to avoid overcrowding of caterpillars, it is essential to increase the size of the feeding trays (area) with growth of insects, which is called spacing. For optimum results, rearing space may be doubled or trebled for I-III instars, 2-3 times more than this for IV instar and 2 times more than this for V instar. It would save time and labour if spacing is combined with bed cleaning.

3. Moulting and mounting. Moulting is a very critical event in the life of caterpillars. At each moult, leaves should be chopped to small size for pre-moult feeding. The feeding activity stops when the larvae settle down for moulting. After the last feed, it is advisable to sprinkle some lime powder which prevents early ecdysing larvae from commencing feeding and hence ensuring uniform growth.

Transferring mature fifth instar larvae to mountages is called mounting. Generally, two methods are employed for mounting:

(*i*) **Branch method.** Branches of mulberry with green leaves are kept over the rearing bed and when the worms crawl on to them, they are shaken off on a net and transferred to the mountages.

(*ii*) **Net method.** A net is spread over the bed after feeding. The non-feeding (mature) worms comeup and crawl on to the net which is then shaken on a mat and the larvae transferred to the mountages.

Care of Cocoons

The quality of the cocoons spun by the larvae depends on the environmental conditions. The optimum temperature of the room should be 24°C and the humidity 60-70 per cent. Similarly, ventilation of the room should be such that humidity is reduced but the worms are not exposed to violent dry wind or to direct sun. When the caterpillar has spun its silken cage or cocoon around itself, it casts off its skin to pupae. It is crucial to harvest the cocoons at the right time. In tropical areas (Karnataka, Andhra Pradesh, West Bengal, etc.), the proper time to harvest cocoons is 5th day after their formation, whereas in temperate areas (e.g. Kashmir), the optimum time is 7th to 8th day after cocoon formation.

Post-harvest Processing of Cocoons

With the harvesting of cocoons, begins the industrial part of silk industry. The following events are followed after harvest of the cocoons:

1. Stifling. Stifling means killing of the pupae inside the cocoons. The purpose is to prevent the emergence of moths by cutting the cocoons and rendering them unreelable. This is achieved by sunheating, putting them in boiling water or steam stifling after 10 days of cocoon formation.

2. Cocoon boiling. Immersing the cocoon in boiling water dissolves the gummy material that binds the winding segments of the thread and thus one end of the silk can easily be traced out.

3. Brushing. Brushing is done to seek the free end of the silk filament (brin) in the cocoon. It could be accomplished manually or by mechanically operated brushes.

4. Reeling. This is the process of unwinding the silk thread or brins from the cocoons, combining the required number of brins to produce silk filaments of a required thickness and gathering the same on standard reels. Three types of reeling methods are in vogue in India:

(*i*) **Country charkha.** The cooking and reeling arrangements are placed near each other, often on a common platform. The reeling arrangement comprises a wooden wheel or charkha rotated manually on its axil. The services of two persons are required in this method, i.e. one to feed the silk filaments to the thread-guide and the other to rotate the wheel.

(*ii*) **Cottage basin.** The cooking and reeling units are kept apart so that the reeling basin gets its hot supply of water through taps connected to the drum of the cooking unit. The reels which can be more than one, are also operated by hand.

(*iii*) **Filature.** It is a large factory where reeling of cocoons is carried out with the help of advanced technology. Unlike the other two methods, the number of filament ends in filature are 8-10 and heating of the cocoons is done with steam and not the boiling water. In each of the above cases, a part of the cocoon remains unreelable. These portions are spun like cotton and the silk produced by them is called spun silk.

5. Re-reeling. The raw silk is first reeled on small reels, allowed to properly dry up on them and re-reeled on large reels. Direct reeling on large reels leads to insufficient drying which causes production of hard gum spots on the thread.

6. Finishing. Finishing includes the removal of visible defects of the raw silk thread like oversize knots, loose ends, etc. The raw silk is boiled, stretched, purified by acid or by fermentation and washed repeatedly to bring out the characteristic luster of the silk. The threads are then changed into bundles or skeins, each having a diameter of 1.5 m and weight of 70 g. The skeins are made into *books* and books into bales of standard weights, which is 50 kg in India as against 60 kg at international level.

7. Testing. The raw silk is put to a number of tests to assess its size variations, winding quality, neatness, evenness, cohesion and tenacity, to meet the national and international standards.

DISEASES AND PESTS OF SILKWORM

Diseases

1. Flacherie. Flacherie is general descriptive term to describe a syndrome where the diseased larva is flaccid from dysenteric conditions and appears flabby, feeble, weak, withered and loosely hanging. This syndrome has been observed in the silkworm for many centuries and has been called by numerous names, such as la maladies des morts-blancs or morts flats, maladies de tripes, gattine, tete Claire, flacherie de Pasteur, etc. The cause of flacherie is a virus (picornavirus, a ss RNA virus) that replicates in the nuclei of mid-gut epithelial cells and a secondary invasion of a bacterium *Bacillus bombycis*. The virus is generally known as the flacherie virus (FV). Gattine is caused by a separate virus (parvovirus, a ssDNA virus) and the associated bacterium *Streptococcus bombycis*. Sudden fluctuation in temperature, bad foliage, improper incubation of eggs and overcrowding of larvae in rearing houses are main causes of occurrence and spread of disease. The FV is picked by the larvae through food. The mid-gut epithelial cells get infected. The main target are the goblet cells which degenerate after infection and are discharged into the gut lumen. The caterpillar loses appetite and ultimately dies.

2. Nucleopolyhedrosis. It is caused by another virus called the *Bombyx mori Nucleopolyhedrovirus* (BmNPV). The disease is called 'jaundice' in USA, 'giallume' in Italy, 'grasserie' in France, 'nobyo' in Japan and 'Fettsucht' in Germany. The virus enters the body orally. The infected larva loses appetite and skin becomes inelastic and shiny. Due to excessive swelling at the intersegment, the larva looks like a bomboo cane with distinct nodes.

3. Muscardine. White muscardine caused by a fungus, *Beauveria bassiana* was the first disease in animals shown to be caused by a fungus or any microorganism. Bassi de lodi demonstrated the contagious and pathogenic nature of the fungus. The fungal spores adhering to the larval body germinate under suitable conditions and penetrate the body. Larva loses appetite. The toxins produced by the fungus cause swelling and stiffening of the body and ultimately it dies.

4. Pebrine. It is another serious disease of silkworm caused by a microsporidian (protozoan), *Nosema bombycis*. The dark mottled areas or dark brown spots on the skin are signs of this disease. The disease is transmitted transovarially and also by contact and through ingestion of contaminated food. Pebrinized eggs get detached from the substratum and are visible as lumps. Moths from infected cocoons may have deformed wings, distorted antennae and poor fecundity. Two forms of the microsporidian have been reported, an acid and an amoeboid form. The acid form resembles a sporoplasm and is responsible for initial spread. The amoeboid form results in subsequent distribution of the pathogen throughout the insect.

5. Other viral diseases. A number of other viruses including the *Tipula* iridovirus (TIV), densovirus (DNV) and cytoplasmic polyhedrovirus (CPV) are known to attack silkworms and cause pathologies.

The TIV (dsDNA, non-enveloped) produces tumors that appear as white spots on the abnormally translucent integument. The virus is not very infectious even when ingested by early larval instars but the infections are generally lethal.

The DNV (ssDNA, non-enveloped) infection results in a flaccid body and pale colour of the body similar to that produced by the flacherie virus. The silkworm DNVs fall into two groups: type 1 and type 2. DNV 1 produces an acute infection with larval death at about

7 days after infection, whereas DNV 2 causes a chronic infection which may take 10-20 days till mortality and a few larvae may be able to pupate.

The CPV (Reoviridae, dsDNA, non-enveloped) has a number of strains which are distinguished by their shapes and/or intracellular locations of their inclusion bodies. The CPV infected larvae are retarded in growth and lose appetite. The infected midgut may be visible through the integument as a pale yellow or whitish area. In later stages, the polyhedra are often regurgitated and passed out with the faeces.

6. Bacterial septicemia. It may be caused by ingestion of *Bacillus thuringiensis* var. *sotto.* The infection results in loss of appetite, sluggishness, shrinkage and diarrhoea. The infection may cause a general paralysis and death within 80 minutes. It is known as the 'sotto'disease. A number of other bacteria like *Serratia marcesens, Serratia piscatorum, Streptococcus faecalis* and *Staphylococcus* sp. are also known to be associated with silkworm septicemia. The infection of *S. marcesens* which produces a characteristic red or pink larval pigment is known as the 'Rangi' disease.

Disease Management

To prevent and control silkworm diseases, great attention should be paid to the cleaning and disinfection of the silkworm's environment in the course of rearing. The following are the common methods.

Pre-rearing cleaning and disinfection. The rearing rooms, aids and the surrounding environment must be cleaned and washed before rearing begins. Silkworms and litter adhering to the room and appliances should be removed before disinfection. The disinfections may be done using physical or chemical disinfectants.

1. Physical disinfections. These include the use of sunlight, boiling and steaming to kill the pathogens.

(*i*) **Sunlight.** The bacterial effect of sunlight derives from ultraviolet rays, which denature the protein of the pathogen and kill the pathogen. Infrared rays and visible rays heat and dry the pathogen, enhancing the bacterial effect of the ultraviolet rays and accelerating the death of the pathogen.

(*ii*) **Boiling.** Small rearing tools are put into boiling water in order to kill the pathogens by making them coagulated and denatured. After the small nets, rearing chopsticks and other aids have been washed, they are put into a boiler and submerged in water. After being boiled for at least 30 minutes, they can be taken out and dried for use.

(*iii*) **Steaming.** Steaming has proved very economical and effective in disinfecting rearing tools. Proteins of the pathogens can be denatured, thus causing the pathogens to die under the conditions of steam and high pressure. A special type of steaming cabinet should be set up, and rearing tools packed in it in piles. Pour in water, close the cabinet, and raise the temperature to 100°C for half an hour, or 88°C for 40 minutes, if formalin (12.5 ml to a cubic metre of water) is added to the water.

2. Chemical disinfection. In chemical disinfection, various kinds of chemicals with varying effects are used as disinfectants. Some chemicals make the protein in the pathogen denature and precipitate. Others can hinder the metabolism of the pathogen, oxidizing the enzymes of the plasma to achieve the bacterial effects.

(*i*) **Bleaching powder.** Rearing rooms and appliances can be disinfected with bleaching powder containing 1 per cent available chlorine @ 225 cc/m^2 which exerts a strong antibiotic effect upon many pathogens, including polyhedrosis virus, flacherie virus, muscardine, aspergillus, bacterial spores and pebrine spores. A sprayer can be used to disinfect rearing rooms and appliances. Spraying should be done evenly and thoroughly. The sprayed area should be kept wet for half an hour to achieve the disinfecting effect.

(*ii*) **Formalin.** Formaldehyde present in formalin has a very strong killing effect on nuclear polyhedrosis virus, flacherie virus, muscardine, bacterial spores and pebrine spores, its effect is weaker on cytoplasmic polyhedrosis virus. Formalin containing 2 per cent formaldehyde can be used to disinfect the rearing room and appliances at a rate of 18 cc/m^2. Formalin disinfection should be conducted in airtight rooms. Before disinfection, all window and door crevices should be sealed with paper strips. After spraying, the room temperature must be raised to about 24°C for at least five hours. Sprayed rooms should be closed for 24 hours. Formalin disinfection should be completed 10 days before the rearing operation begins, otherwise the remaining odour of formaldehyde will exert an unfavorable effect on the growth of the worm. Since formalin has a strong and irritating odour, the operator must wear a gas mask or cover his mouth and nose with a wet towel while working. Disinfecting work should be done in rotation.

(*iii*) **Mixture of formalin and lime water.** Formalin solution cannot kill all cytoplasmic polyhedrosis virus. However, with the addition of fresh lime powder, its disinfecting effect can be increased remarkably. This mixture can make the cytoplasmic polyhedrosis virus lose its pathogenic ability in 20 minutes. It also has a strong killing effect on some other pathogens also. The mixture can be prepared by adding 0.5 per cent fresh lime powder to 2 per cent formalin solution. After mixing thoroughly, use the turbid fluid as the disinfectant. The mixture should be used immediately as it will lose its effect in 24 hours.

3. Disinfection and disease prevention in the rearing season. In the course of rearing silkworms, pathogens can be re-introduced to the rearing room through many channels, and disinfection should, therefore, be repeated.

(*i*) Spray the floor, corridor, entrance and exit of the rearing room and mulberry storehouse with a bleaching powder solution of 1 per cent effective chlorine at three-to-four day intervals.

(*ii*) Wash hands before entering the rearing rooms and the mulberry storehouse. Put a lime powder mat at the entrance to the rearing room.

(*iii*) After cleaning away the litter, wash hands before feeding worms.

(*iv*) Use mulberry containers and litter containers separately. These appliances should be constantly disinfected with bleaching powder.

(*v*) Throw sick worms into a lime jar. Do not throw the silkworm away randomly as it could become a source of infection.

(*vi*) Clean used nets and mats, and dry them in the sun. Do not use them again unless they are disinfected.

(*vii*) Since rearing beds are the main source for the propagation of pathogens, disinfection of the beds is essential. In production, lime powder is generally used to disinfect the worm's body and the rearing beds. Fresh lime powder has a strong disinfecting effect on many diseases. It also has an antidotal effect on chemically polluted leaves. Fresh lime powder can isolate pathogens and keep the rearing beds dry.

(*viii*) When the rearing time comes to an end, the remaining dead worms, waste matter, etc., must be cleaned away, collected and buried under the earth with some lime powder thrown on top. Rearing rooms, mounting rooms, mulberry storehouses, environments outside and inside and appliances, should be disinfected by spraying bleaching powder solution of 1 per cent available chlorine to prevent the spread of pathogens. Another disinfection is needed before a new crop begins.

4. Use of resistant strains. Silkworm strains have been selected for resistance to viral diseases like flacherie, nucleopolyhedrosis and cytoplasmic polyhedrosis. These resistant strains should be utilized for commercial production.

Pests

A number of insect and non-insect pests attack the silkworm.

1. Uzi fly. Uzi fly, *Exorista sorbillans* Wiedemann (Diptera) is the most important insect pest (endoparasite) attacking the silkworm. The flies lay their eggs on grown up larvae of silkworm and the maggots on hatching eat away the body of the caterpillar. It generally completes its life cycle in 14-17 days during summer and 26-29 days during winter. The best way of control is the prevention of fly's access to silkworm by mechanical means. Fly-proof rooms, windows and ventilators should be used in the rearing house. All crevices of the rooms should be closed to prevent maggots pupating in the soil.

Dusting of levitated china clay @ 3g/100 spinning larvae before mounting and 100g/bamboo mountage (180 x 120 cm size) before placing the dusted larvae on mountages is recommended. Dimilin (diflubenzuron 25WP) @ 1g/0.1 m^2 causes > 90 per cent sterility among flies.

2. Beetles. The adults and grubs of *Dermestes cadeverinus* (Coleoptera) and other dermestid beetles are attracted to the smell of cocoons in storage. They eat the cocoons, enclosed pupae and often the eggs (seeds) of the silkworms. The females of these beetles lay their eggs in crevices, organic matter and wooden boards. Therefore, closure of the crevices, and scruplous cleaning of the rearing room is the first requirement of prevention. Occasionally, the rooms could be fumigated with CH_3 Br (methyl bromide) and stiffled cocoons should not be stored for long.

3. Ants. The ants (Hymenoptera) attack silkworms in rearing trays. Legs of rearing stands should be dipped in antwells (filled with water + insecticide). At the time of spinning, ash or kerosene is put at the handles of the mountages to keep the ants off.

4. Lizards, birds, rats and squirrels. All these animals feed on silkworms. Mammals predate also on the pupae by biting open the cocoons. Rearing rooms should be kept free of lizards. Birds could be scared away from the vicinity and for rat and squirrel, trapping may be carried out in rearing houses.

II. NON-MULBERRY SERICULTURE

Non-mulberry sericulture is practised by Tasar silkworm, Eri silkworm and Muga silkworm.

Tasar Silkworm

The Tasar silkworm, *Antheraea paphia* Linnaeus (Lepidoptera : Saturniidae), moths are fairly large insects, female being larger and yellowish-brown in colour while males smaller and brick-red in colour, but both having prominent sye spots on their wings. Eggs are laid on tender leaves of host trees and a moth lays about 200 eggs. The egg stage lasts for 8 to 10 days. The caterpillars are stout, green with red spiracles, and the larval period is 40-50 days. The cocoons are oval and as large as hen's egg with a hard case hung from the terminal branches by a stiff attachment about 5 cm long. Pupal stage lasts for 15-30 days. The moths do not mate in captivity and so the caterpillars cannot be domesticated; as such the cocoons have to be collected from the host trees in the forest. Tasar moths are bivoltine giving two crops a year, one during August to October and the other during October to December. The silk is reelable and, therefore, the pupae have to be killed before emergence of the moth, to prevent cutting of the silk thread into pieces.

Eri Silkworm

The Eri silkworm, *Samia cynthia ricini* Boisduval (Lepidoptera : Saturniidae), moths have brown, black or green coloured wings with white crescent markings, and woolly white abdomen. The female lays about 300-500 eggs which hatch in 7-10 days. The caterpillar has a green body with a brown head and the body has small tubercles bearing short hairs. The full-grown caterpillar is about 8 cm long and the larval stage lasts for 17-25 days. The caterpillar feeds on castor leaves and it can pupate anywhere so no chandraki is required. The cocoon is not compact but loosely spun. Silk is white or brick-red in colour and not as glossy as the mulberry silk. It is not in one single strand and, therefore, not reelable, and has to be carded and spun like cotton. Since the thread is not a continuous one, the moths can be allowed to emerge from the cocoons and after emergence the cocoons are reversed to remove the pupal cases. The cocoons are then soaked in cold water for 18 hours, in warm water for 45 minutes, washed in washing soda solution, dried and spun into silk. About 28 grains of eggs will give 1600 larvae which can yield 4 kg of silk after consuming leaves from about 0.5 ha of castor crop.

Muga Silkworm

The Muga silkworm, *Antheraea assamensis* Helfer (Lepidoptera: Saturniidae), resembles Tasar silkworm. The wings and body of the female moth are copper brown to dark brown and those of the female, yellowish to brown, both pairs of wings bearing eye spots. The female moth lays 400-500 eggs on dry twigs, which hatch in 7-16 days. The larval stage lasts for 28-38 days. The duration of the pupal stage is 14 days and the moth is non-feeding and dies within 7-12 days. The Muga silkworms are polyphagous, semi-domesticated and multivoltine having 5-6 overlapping generations in a year, stifling is done by spreading the cocoons on a bamboo mat to expose them to sun to partly kill the chrysalis. The mat is then kept above an oven where hot air and smoke kill the pupae fully, Degumming is done by boiling the cocoons in alkaline solution of sodium carbonate for 10-30 minutes, after which the cocoons are reeled.

SERICULTURE IN INDIA

Sericulture is a labour-intensive industry in all its phases, namely, cultivation of silkworm food plants, silkworm rearing, silk reeling, and other post-cocoon processes such as twisting, dyeing, weaving, printing and finishing. It provides employment to approximately 60 lakh persons, most of them being small and marginal farmers, or tiny and household industry mainly in the hand reeling and hand weaving sections. Cultivation of sericulture is not very widespread being practiced regularly in contiguous districts in the three southern states of Karnataka, Andhra Pradesh and Tamil Nadu; in the North-east region; in the tribal areas of Jharkhand, Chhattisgarh, Andhra Pradesh, Orissa; and in Jammu & Kashmir and West Bengal. The cocoons and silk processing industry has traditionally existed in clusters in areas not necessarily coinciding with the sericulture areas in Karnataka, Andhra Pradesh, Tamil Nadu, West Bengal and Bihar.

India has the unique distinction of being the only country producing all the five known commercial silks, namely, mulberry, tropical tasar, oak tasar, eri and muga, of which muga with its golden yellow glitter is unique and prerogative of India. Mulberry sericulture is mainly practised in five states namely, Karnataka, Andhra Pradesh, Assam and Bodoland, West Bengal, Jharkhand and Tamil Nadu are major silk producing states in the country. North East has the unique distinction of being the only region producing four varieties of silk viz., Mulberry, Oak Tasar, Muga and Eri. Overall NE region contributes 18% of India's total silk production. India is the second largest producer of silk in the world. Among the four varieties of silk produced in 2015-16, Mulberry accounts for 71.8% (20,434 MT), Tasar 9.9% (2,818 MT), Eri 17.8% (5,054 MT) and Muga 0.6% (166 MT) of the total raw silk production of 28,472 MT. The demand for superior quality bivoltine silk is increasing in India for domestic consumption as well as value added silk products for the export market. The Ministry of Textiles Government of India and Departments of Sericulture in various states provide technical and financial assistance for enhancing the bivoltine silk production.The Indian silk goods are being exported to the traditional major markets like the USA and European countries and small markets of Asia Region. The silk goods export earnings decreased over the years due to global recession and reduction in demand for silk goods in western countries. The export earnings during 2016-17(P) were Rs.1, 871.01 crores.

SERICULTURE RESEARCH AND DEVELOPMENT

Central Silk Board, established in 1949 as statutory body under Government of India, is a national organisation for overall development of sericulture and silk industry. It is located in Bangalore. The Board has established Central Sericultural Research and Training Institutes, each at Mysore, Berhampore and Pampore; Silkworm Seed Technology Laboratory at Bangalore; Seri-biotech Research Laboratory at Bangalore ; Central Sericultural Germplasm Resources Centre at Hosur for mulberry sericulture research. National Silkworm Seed Organization is located in Bangalore. For non-mulberry sericulture research, two institutes namely, Central Tasar Research and Training Institute at Ranchi and Central Muga Eri Research and Training Institute at Ladoigarh are functioning. The post-cocoon related research is carried out at Central Silk Technological Research Institute at Banglore. As a result of research and development activities, cocoon productivity increased from 659 kg per ha in 2002 to 706 kg per ha in 2007; raw silk production increased from 75.2 kg per ha in 2002 to 86.12 kg per ha in 2007; and the renditta has improved from 8.7 in 2002 to 8.1 in 2007.

*****

23

CHAPTER

LAC CULTURE

Lac is a resinous secretion by an insect *Laccifer lacca* Kerr (Lacciferidae : Hemiptera) and the only resin of animal origin. Under natural conditions the insect is found growing on a large number of trees in India and Myanmar. Lac culture refers to the mass rearing of lac insect for lac production. Lac in India is of *puranic* antiquity. One of the earliest references to it is found in the Atharva Veda where the insect has been termed 'Laksha' and its habits and behavior have been described. Our great epic 'Mahabharta' mentions 'Lakshagriha' (house of lac) which the kauravas had got constructed to burn alive the Pandavas over 4000 years ago. The great antiquity of lac is also proved through its numerous age-old uses, e.g. for dyeing silken sarees, filling of hollow gold and silver ornaments, in wood turnery, bangle making, the use of the dye under the name of *alta* in religious ceremonies, as well as by ladies for colouring the soles of feet and palms of hand. Outside India, lac was known in Myanmar, China, Indo-China, Thailand, Sri Lanka and Madagascar. In Europe, the Greeks and Romans were familiar with the uses of lac in pigments for decorative paintings.

LAC INSECT

The lac insect, *Laccifer lacca*, is found in India, Pakistan, Sri Lanka, Myanmar, Malaysia, China and Thailand. The major lac-producing states in India include Bihar, Madhya Pradesh, West Bengal, Maharashtra, Uttar Pradesh, Orissa and Assam. In India, about 100 species of plants capable of supporting lac insect have been recorded, among which the major hosts are kusum (*Schleichera oleosa*), palas (*Butea monosperma*), ber (*Zizyphus jujuba*), khair (*Acacia catechu*), peepal (*Ficus religiosa*), ghont (*Zizyphus xylopyra*), jallari (*Shorea talura*), arhar (*Cajanus cajan*), grewia (*Grewia* spp.) and babul (*Acacia arabica*).

Life-history

Three developmental stages are found in its life cycle (Fig. 23.1), viz. egg, nymph and adult.

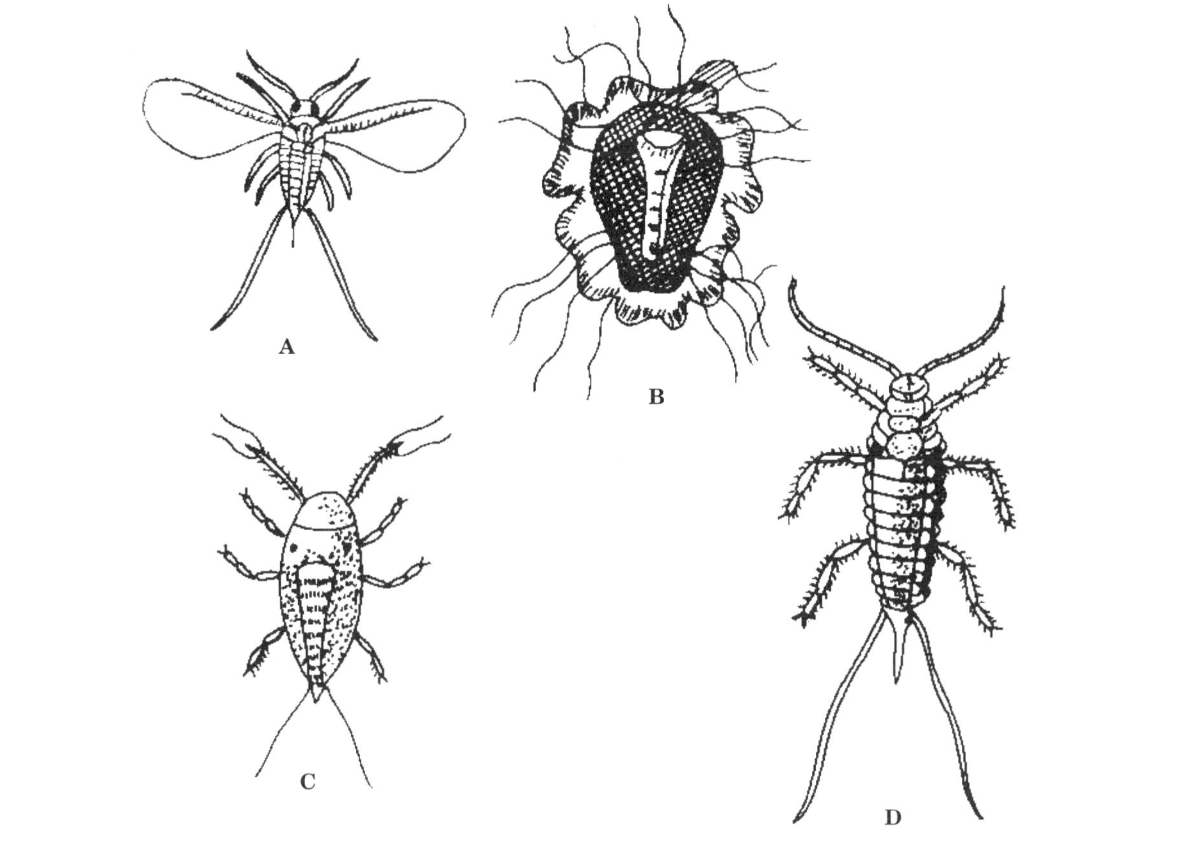

Fig. 23.1 Lac insect, *Laccifer lacca.* **A.** Winged male, **B.** Female, **C.** Nymph, **D.** Wingless male

Eggs. The eggs are laid by the female within the lac-cell. It lays about 200-500 eggs which may be fertilized or unfertilized. Both types of eggs give birth to male and female nymphs. The female lays three types of eggs: (*i*) The eggs from which both males and females hatch out in equal number. (*ii*) The eggs from which males are less than females. (*iii*) The eggs from which males are more than females. An individual egg is 0.4 mm $\times$ 0.2 mm long and pinkish in colour which changes into brown after sometimes. The female generally lays well developed eggs which hatch within a few hours. Thus, the lac insect has *ovoviviparous* mode of reproduction.

Nymphs. The newly hatched nymph (crawler) is 0.6 mm $\times$ 0.25 mm long and pinkish in colour. It possesses a pair of antennae, three pairs of legs, two compound eyes and six anal setae. The nymphs emerge in large numbers and crawl over the surface of twigs and branches of plants in search of suitable pieces for settlement. The emergence of nymphs called swarming may continue for 5 weeks or more. They mostly settle on shoots gregariously. Once settled, the nymph thrusts its proboscis into the bark of the twig and does not move from its place. After one or two days of settling, they start secreting resin from glands distributed under the cuticle all over the body, except near the mouth parts, the two breathing pores and the anus. Thus the nymphs get encased in a cell of its secretion which increases in size with the growth of the insect. They moult thrice before reaching maturity and after 1st moult the nymph loses its eyes, legs and antennae but anal setae become 10 instead of 6. The sex is readily recognized by the shape of lac cells even in the early stage of development. In the case of the male cell, the growth is more along the longitude while in the female cell it is more along the vertical axis.

The differentiation between sexes is more pronounced after the first moult. The male cell is elongated with a pair of holes at the anterior end from which thin whitish hair come out, while a female cell is somewhat globular with an irregular margin and with three holes on the top, one at the hind end and two at the anterior end. The male nymph develops the organs after second moult. Both the males and females continue to develop. From the male cells both winged and wingless males emerge after about two months. These males fertilize the females in their cells and after fertilization female develops very fast, swells up and secrets the lac at a faster rate. The size of the female as well as that of the enveloping lac cell increases rapidly and reaches a size several times that of the male lac cell. Thus, the females are the chief source of lac secretion. As the time for egg laying approaches, the posterior region of the female develops two yellow spots which is indication of egg laying. The spots enlarge and become orange-coloured. When this happens, the females have oviposited a large number of eggs in the space called *ovisac* under their tail ends. The ovisac full of eggs appears orange which indicates that the eggs would hatch in a week's time. It is at this stage that the twigs (brood lac) are cut from the trees for the purpose of inoculation to new trees. The lac insect usually passes through two generations in a year.

Adult. The adult male and female are different from each other. Female is about 3 times larger than the male.

Male. They are pinkish-red in colour and are of two types-winged and wingless. Winged male possesses only one pair of translucent membranous forewings. They are mostly found during dry season (Baisakhi and Jethawi). They survive only 3-4 days and die after copulation. The following are the main characteristics of these: (*i*) The head is large, prominent mouth parts but vestigial. (*ii*) Ocelli are 2 pairs with seven segmented antennae which have hairs on them. (*iii*) Tarsi 3 segmented. (*iv*) The abdomen is 8 segmented, broader anteriorly and narrower posteriorly. The last abdominal segment bears pointed penis.

Female. The female is pinkish in colour and about 1.5 mm in length. The ventral surface of the body is flat while dorsal surface is convex. The main characteristics are as below: (*i*) The female is deprived of eyes, legs and wings. (*ii*) Antennae are vestigial, small and 3-4 segmented. (*iii*) The mouth parts are piercing and sucking type and rostrum is two segmented. (*iv*) The female remains attached at a point and sucks the juice from the host. (*v*) Mesothorax is provided with an appendage on which spiracles open. (*vi*) The abdomen is round and on the dorsal surface, a spine is provided. The last abdominal segment is two segmented and anus is fringed.

Strains of Lac Insect

There are two distinct strains of lac insect in India called *Kusumi* and *Rangeeni*. The *Kusumi* strain is raised mainly on kusum trees or on other hosts with kusum brood and the *Rangeeni* on all other lac hosts such as palas, ber, ghont, arhar, etc. Each of the strains produces two crops in a year, thus there are four crops (Fig. 23.2).

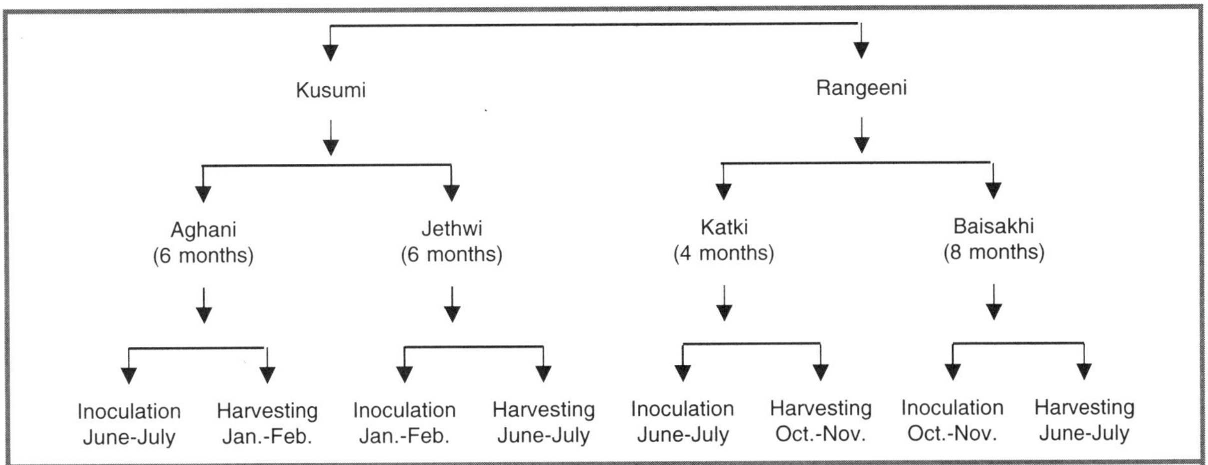

Fig. 23.2 Strains of lac insect

LAC CULTIVATION

The two methods of the lac cultivation are popular, i.e. (*i*) local cultivation, and (*ii*) modern method.

Local Cultivation

This is the crude and unscientific method of lac cultivation in which lac is collected from the trees growing in forests. Lac is left for continuous self-inoculation on the same tree and every time a partial crop is taken. This method of lac cultivation has generally failed to provide sustained supplies of brood lac for crop inoculations and optimum yield of lac because of the three reasons: (*i*) Host trees lose their capacity to throw out new succulent shoots. (*ii*) Self-inoculation leads to heavy infestation which in seasons of extreme heat results in wholesale mortality of brood. (*iii*) The trees become weak and die in course of time.

Modern Method

This method was developed by Indian Institute of Natural Resins and Gums (formerly Indian Lac Research Institute) Ranchi. The underlying principle in this method is to give the host plants rest after a harvest has been taken. Generally, a tree needs about 9-12 months for recovery of its vigour after a harvest. Such a rest without affecting lac cultivation has been made possible by adopting what has been called the *coupe system* of lac cultivation. As the term coupe means a chamber or compartment, the host trees are divided into various coupes (groups) consisting of a certain number of trees. Only a specific number of trees in a coupe are inoculated. After the harvest, these are left to rest to recover their lost vigour and the remaining resting trees are inoculated. Thus, in a coupe system alternate groups of trees are put to lac cultivation which offers two advantages : (*i*) The trees retain their vigour and capacity to produce new succulent shoots after rest. (*ii*) There is economy in money and labour to guard only the inoculated trees.

The nature of coupe differs in kusumi and rangeeni strains.

***Kusumi* strain.** Kusumi host is a slow growing tree. The trees should be divided into 4 coupes, each inoculated in a cycle of 2 years, the plants of resting coupes are pruned. As the crop is harvested in 6 months, each coupe gets a resting period of 18 months to enable the trees revitalise and produce a large number of succulent shoots.

***Rangeeni* strain.** Rangeeni strain thrives better on *palas* and *ber*. In this case, the crop is grown in 3 coupes A, B and C with a plant ratio of 3:1:3. In the two larger coupes, *baisakhi* crop is grown from October/November to June/July, in alternate years. In the smaller coupe, *katki* crop is raised every year from June/July to October/November. Under this system, the rule of full inoculation and full cropping is followed.

To get good crop, following points should be kept in mind:

1. Selection of suitable site. The site should be selected on the basis of host plants, where environmental conditions suitable for host trees should be preferred. The excessive heat and cold should be avoided and rainfall may be about 60 mm.

2. Pruning. Pruning means cutting away old, weak and diseased branches. This is an important and essential operation carried out with the object of inducing the tree to put forth maximum number of shoots suitable in condition for successful colonization by the larvae of the lac insect. Before starting lac cultivation, care should be taken that the trees have sufficient tender branches to enable the lac insect to establish itself. If it is not so, the trees should be pruned. Pruning should be done with a sharp instrument (Fig. 23.3) to give a neat cut. Pruning should always be carried out lightly and branches more than 2.5 cm in diameter should not be cut. The pruning depends upon the type of the host plant, e.g. in case of ber trees, a large number of succulent shoots are produced after pruning while palas and kusum do not ordinarily require pruning.

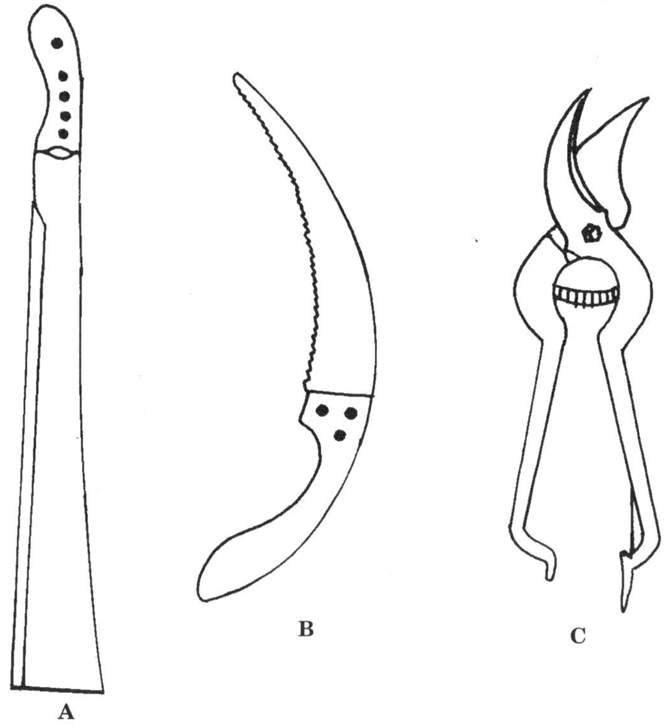

Fig. 23.3 Instruments for cutting and pruning the branches
A. Pruning knife, **B.** Pruning saw, **C.** Scateur

3. Inoculation of brood lac. Lac sticks bearing alive mother cells which produce lac larvae are known as brood lac. The brood lac sticks should be cut into convenient length of 15-30 cm and tied in succulent shoots of the host tree. The tying may be done either longitudinally or laterally. Tying of the brood lac sticks should be done securely and on upper surface of the branches. This will prevent falling of the twigs and provide full contact for quick and easy crawling of the nymphs. The correct amount of brood lac (covered 15 to 20 times of its length) should be used for inoculation. The larvae after hatching will transfer themselves into succulent shoots. The brood used for inoculation should not be left on the trees for more than 3 weeks because keeping beyond this time, there is a danger of enemies to spread. It may be advisable to use 60-80 mesh brass wire netting basket or the cheaper nylon net bags or even bamboo baskets (Fig. 23.4) to enclose the brood lac sticks for inoculation, particularly when the lac is being introduced for the first time in a new area. This helps escape of the lac nymphs and not the enemies inside. Also, enemies from outside are prevented from entering the basket due to the minuteness of the meshes.

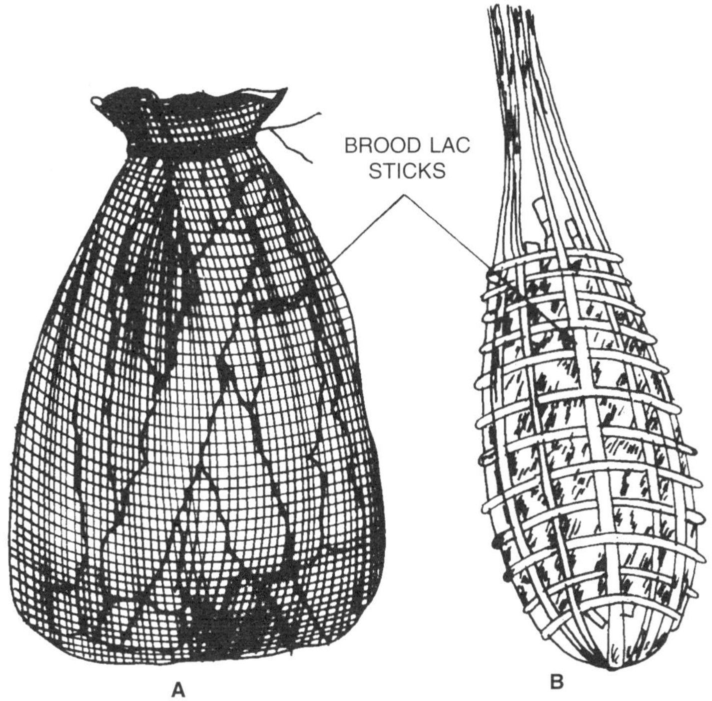

Fig. 23.4 Material for inoculation of brood lac.
A. Nylon mesh bag, **B.** Bamboo basket with brood lac

4. Lac extraction. After the escape of the nymphs from the brood lac, what has been left is the *stick lac* or *Phunki*. These sticks (Fig. 23.5) should be tied in bundles and immersed in water, preferably running water, for 3-4 days keeping them well under water by heavy stones. The stick lac should then be kept in shade for drying. Raw lac should be scraped while the sticks are still moist.

The scraped lac is crushed lightly, washed in water to remove dead insects, dry matter, etc. and dried in the open an amber coloured granular material called *seed lac*. The seed lac is then packed into 10-12 m long sausage-shaped cloth bags, held above charcoal fire and twisted when the lac starts melting. The molten lac flows out through the pores of the cloth leaving impurities called *kiri* method. The clear material or pure lac is either dropped on cold surface to solidify into round button-shaped pieces (button sac) or stretched into thin sheets called shellac.

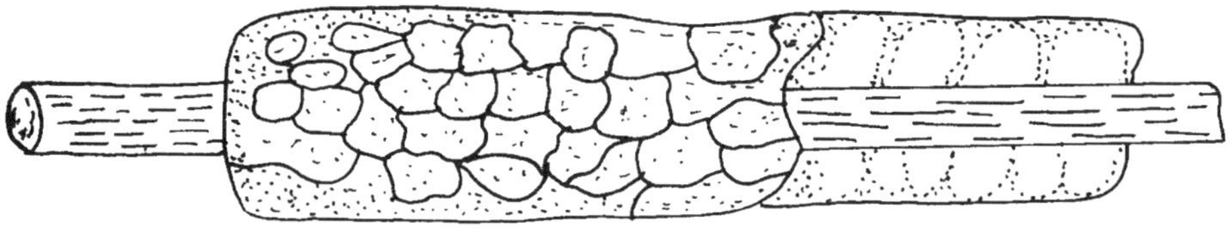

Fig. 23.5 A twig with lac

5. Preparation of shellac. The following methods are used for preparing the shellac:

Indian method. It is the oldest method in which the seed lac is put into long cloth bags of 6.5 cm width. The bag is tide with a pivot of wheel and circulated. The heat is also provided side by side. The melted lac, due to the pressure comes out which is collected and made in the form of tablets. This is an expensive method, it is estimated that to wash 1 quintal of lac requires 1 metre cloth, 1 quintal coal and 6 men in a day.

Hydraulic method. This is a machine in which the seed lac is put in a cloth on which a spray of water is provided. The bottom of the machine is heated with steam by a pipe to get the lac melted. The lac is pressed by a plunger operated by hydraulic pressure and collected. To remove the moisture, the lac is heated in another machine and then stored after cooling. This is also an expensive method and can not be used in small scale.

Solvent method. The seed lac is dissolved in spirit and separated by distillation process. The spirit may be used for further washing. The main drawback in this process is that after dissolving the second time, the spirit can not be separated by distillation hence, there is chance of fire.

Autoclave method. This process has been developed by Indian Institute of Natural Resins and Gums, Ranchi in which the seed lac is put in the bags of iron nets and heated in a special autoclave. The lac is collected on the lower surface of the autoclave. After some time it is removed from here and heated again. The melted shellac is spread in to thin sheets and dried.

Composition and Uses of Lac

Lac contains resin (75%), waxes (6%), dyes (5-6%) and albuminous material (12-13%). Lac is used for making of varnishes, paints, polishes, electrical goods, gramophone records, ornaments, toys, pottery, buttons, artificial leathers, ink, imitation fruits and vegetables, and used in aeroplanes.

Pests of Lac Insect

The insect pests attacking lac insect include parasitoids and predators. Some non-insect pests are also known to attack the lac insect.

Parasitoids. The parasitoids of lac belong to the super family Chalcidoidea which lay their eggs inside the lac cell either in or on the body of the lac insect. The grubs after hatching, feed on the lac insect and the adults come out by biting a hole in the lac cell. Five to ten per cent damage is caused by these parasitoids. The important species of parasitoids are *Coccophagous tschirchii, Tetrastichus purpureus, Marietta javensis, Eupelmus tachardiae. Tachardiaphagus tachardiae, T. somervilli, Erencyrtus dewitzi* and *Parechthrodryinus clavicornis.*

Predators. The two predators namely large white lac moth, *Eublemma amabilis* (Noctuidae) and smaller black lac moth, *Holcocera pulverea* (Gelechiidae) are more important. These moths lay their eggs on or near the lac encrusted branches. The larvae (dirty white coloured in *E. amabilis* and chocolate coloured in *H. pulverea*) on hatching bite their way inside lac encrustation to spend their whole larval life inside feeding on the lac insects as well as on the lac encrustations. Both cause a greater damage to *Katki* and *Aghani* than to *Baisakhi* and *Jethwi* lac, *E. amabilis,* however, being more destructive on the trees and *H. pulverea* on the stored lac. The three species of *Chrysopa* also attack the lac insect, the larvae of which suck the body fluid of the host. The damage caused by this predator is comparatively small unless there is a serious outbreak. The damage caused by the predatory insects is estimated to the tune of 40 per cent. The chemical control of these pests is not only uneconomical and impractical but also of doubtful value as most of these enemies spend their lives under protected condition inside lac encrustation. Simple cultural practices can help keeping the enemies in check.

Non-insect enemies. Some birds, monkeys, rats and squirrels also destroy the lac insect and lac encrustations and cause considerable loss. Rats and squirrels alone can damage upto 50 per cent of the crop. Squirrel damage during day more commonly in forest conditions and rats during night near the villages. Towards crop maturity, these pests either gnaw the mature lac encustations on the trees or brood lac sticks tied for inoculation consuming gravid females that contain plenty of eggs. The brood lac can be made to fall to the ground by these animals preventing inoculation. The only control methods available are scaring them by noise or poison-baiting. Monkeys do some damage by breaking the twigs with lac encrustations or chewing the new shoots of pruned trees.

LAC CULTURE IN INDIA

India is the major producer of lac accounting for about 70 per cent of the total world lac production. Some lac is produced in Myanmar and Thailand. Analysis of year wise lac production data in India during XI Plan (2007-2008 to 2011-2012) indicated average production by the country to the tune of 16.246 thousand tonnes. The Jharkhand state registered highest average annual production (6.306 thousand tonnes), sharing 38.82 per cent of total lac produced in the country. This is followed by Chhattisgarh (30.21%), Madhya Pradesh (13.66 %), West Bengal (6.97%), Maharashtra (4.96%), Odisha (2.27%), Uttar Pradesh (1.94 %), Assam (0.52%), Andhra Pradesh and Gujarat (0.30% each) and Meghalaya (0.06 %). In respect of state wise growth rate in lac production, the country registered negative growth rate to the tune of 8.38 per cent per annum. Amongst the major lac producing states, Jharkhand and West Bengal recorded positive growth of 12.19 and 9.94 per cent per annum respectively, during this period. Amongst the declining trend Madhya Pradesh recorded highest negative growth (-32.41 %) followed by Uttar Pradesh (-29.37%), Chhattisgarh (-26.76%), Maharashtra (-10.62%) and Odisha (-9.92%). The other minor lac producing states namely Assam, Gujarat, Meghalaya also registered declining trend during the period.

LAC RESEARCH AND DEVELOPMENT

The Indian Institute of Natural Resins and Gums (IINRG) (formerly Indian Lac Research Institute), Ranchi, is a nodal institute at national level for research and development on all aspects of lac and other natural gums and resins (excluding production) such as harvesting/ tapping, processing, product development, training, information repository, technology dissemination and national/international cooperation.

Realizing the strategic importance of lac, the then Imperial Government of India constituted the Lindsay-Harlow Committee in 1920, to look into all aspects of the country's lac trade and its development. On the suggestions of this Committee, lac merchants organized themselves into the Indian Lac Association for Research, under the aegis of which, the foundation stone of the Indian Lac Research Institute (ILRI), Ranchi, was laid on September 20,1924. Subsequently, on the recommendations of the Royal Commission on Agriculture, the Indian Lac Cess Committee (ILCC) was constituted, which took over the reigns of the ILRI on August 1, 1931. ILCC also organized and maintained the London Shellac Research Bureau, UK, and Shellac Research Bureau and Polytechnique Institute of Brooklyn, USA.

As a result of reorganization of agricultural research and education in India, the Indian Council of Agricultural Research (ICAR) took over the administrative control of the ILRI from April 1, 1966. This is one of the oldest institutes within ICAR, having completed 86 years of fruitful service to the nation. The institute mandate has been expanded in 2007 to look after other important issues related to resins and gums of Indian origin. Accordingly, ILRI has been renamed as the Indian Institute of Natural Resins and Gums (IINRG) and is known by this name since September 20, 2007.

*****

24 CHAPTER

MASS PRODUCTION OF PARASITOIDS AND PREDATORS

The natural enemies of insects including their parasitoids and predators need to be mass produced for using them to control the noxious insects acting as pests of crops and other commodities. Infact, mass production is an industrial process that requires all the logistic requirements such as substantial quantities of production materials, equipment and facilities for continuous maintenance. For mass production of parasitoids and predators, large specially designed multiroom mass rearing facilities or "biofactories" are needed along with the trained labour force with atleast one employee assigned to a particular independent rearing process. The requirements may vary depending upon the species being produced, quantity of host material, artificial diet ingredients, or growth media used.

Mass production of beneficial arthropods, is the foundation of augmentative biological control. Effective use of biological control agents to control major pests in commercial crops involves the release of tens of thousands and lakhs of individuals. Knowledge has accumulated over decades on small-scale rearing of arthropod natural enemies, but new technologies are needed to push production capabilities from thousands to millions of organisms per week. During the last more than three decades, mass production of natural enemies has seen quite a fast development; the number of available species has increased, and there had been very conspicuous developments in the area of mass production, quality control and storage.

Parasitiods can be utilised in three types of biological control i.e. conservation, classical biological control (introduction of natural enemies to a new locale), and augmentation which could be inoculative (releasing a few natural enemies at a critical time of the season) or inundative (releasing millions of natural enemies). The classical biological control, however, could not be successful in all situation; several reasons can be listed for this, such as availability of too few individuals for release, poor adaptation of the parasitoids and predators to the environmental conditions prevailing at the release location; lack of synchrony between life cycle of natural enemy and the target pest. Augmentation aims at production of sufficient numbers of bio-control agents for inoculative / inundative releases. There are many cases of successful augmentation of natural enemies round the globe. India is placed amongst top 10 countries as far as biological control practices are concerned. Innumerable attempts have been made in India to augment the populations of promising indigenous natural enemies like trichogrammatids, bethylids, chrysopids, ladybird beetles etc. Biological control through augmentation has gained maximum acceptance among sugarcane farmers of India. Use of *Trichogramma chilonis* Ishii has been effectively utilised for management of sugarcane borers. Contribution of sugarcane mills had been very significant in this venture. Subsequently, pests of other crops were targeted to achieve control with parasitoids and predators. Table 24.1 (modified after Rabindra *et al.*, 2006) contains information about parasitoids which could be utilised for the management of major insect pests of different crops:

Table 24.1: Parasitoids being used as bio-control agents against insect pests of crops

Crop/Insect-pest	Parasitoid	Dosage per ha	Frequency of application
	SUGARCANE		
Chilo spp.	*Trichogramma chilonis* (Bio SC1)	50,000	Use Tricho-cards at 10 days interval, 8 times starting on 30-day-old crop for shoot borer and 60 days for other borers or during egg laying period
Pyrilla perpusilla	*Epiricania melanoleuca*	2-3 egg masses or 5-7 cocoons in 40 selected spots	The releases are initiated before the onset of rainy season
	RICE		
Scirpophaga incertulas & *Cnaphalocrosis medinalis*	*Trichogramma japonicum* *T. chilonis*	1,00,000	30, 37 and 44 days after transplanting (DAT)
	MAIZE		
Chilo partellus	*Trichogramma chilonis*	1,00,000	Twice; first release on 10 day old crop followed by the second one 7 days after the first release
	COTTON		
Helicoverpa armigera *Earias* spp. *Pectinophora gossypiella*	*Trichogramma chilonis* (Bio C1or Bio C)	1,50,000	Weekly, 6 times starting from 40th day after planting or during the egg laying period.
	TOBACCO		
Spodoptera litura	*Telenomus remus*	1,20,000	Five times at weekly intervals
	COCONUT		
Opisina arenosella	*Goniozus nephantidis*	3,000 adults	Need based or for each generation

Crop/Insect-pest	Parasitoid	Dosage per ha	Frequency of application
		TOMATO	
Helicoverpa armigera	*Trichogramma brasiliensis* *T. pretiosum* / *T. chilonis* (Bio H1)	50,000	Weekly interval, 6 times from 25th day after transplantation or during egg laying period
		CITRUS	
Planococcus citri	*Laptomastix dactylopii*	3,000 adults	Need based; under expert supervision
		APPLE	
Eriosoma lanigerum	*Aphelinus mali*	1000 adults or mummies per infested tree	Once as soon as infestation is noticed
Quadraspidiotus perniciosus	*Encarsia perniciosi*	2000 adults per tree	Once, in Spring
Cydia pomonella	*Trichogramma embryophagum*	2000 adults per tree	Releasing at weekly intervals

Mass production

Traits of a successful parasitoid and predator include high reproductive rate, good searching ability, host specificity, be adaptable to different environmental conditions, and population needs to be synchronised with its host i.e. pest. In fact, no parasitoid has all these attributes, however those with several of the above characteristics will play an important role in the suppressing pest populations. Types of parasitoid or predator to be used depends on the target insect pest. Under certain situations nearly 40-60 per cent of insect-pest population could be reduced by releasing biocontrol agents including parasitoids-trichogrammatids, encyrtids, braconids, ichneumonids, chalcids and tachinids and predators-coccinellids beetles, lace wing bugs, predatory bugs, ants, spiders, etc. Till now, nearly 170 exotic natural enemies have been studied to explore possibility of their use against crop pests and weeds. The maximum success has been achieved with homopterous pests (> 46%).

Egg parasitoids belonging to the genus *Trichogramma and* the family Trichogrammatidae are among the most widely used biological control agents for the field insect pests. At present there are about 85 genera in the world, among which 26 have been recorded from India. Three species; a light coloured group of which *T. chilonis* is a member, a moderately pigmented group of which *T. fasciatum* is typical and a dark group of which *T. japonicum* are considered important. They parasitize insect eggs, specifically those of moths and butterflies. Entomologists since 1900s started mass rearing of *Trichogramma* realising their potential for the insect pests control.

Green lacewings of the genus *Chrysoperla* belonging to family Chrysopidae of order Neuroptera, have been well recognised and used as important predators against insect pests of vegetable, fruit, nut, fibre, and forage crops as well as ornamentals, forests, and greenhouse plantings. Now *Chrysoperla* are among the most commonly used and commercially available biological control agents in the world; their augmentative release programmes had begun since late 1940s. *Chrysoperla zastrowi sillemi* (Esben-Petersen) is the most common species of lacewings commercially available in India. *Chrysoperla* spp. larvae, sometimes called aphid lions, are carnivorous; they predominantly prey on aphids, mealybugs, thrips, spider mites, whiteflies, leafhopper nymphs and small lepidopteran larvae such as cotton bollworms; the adult primarily feed on honeydew, pollen, and nectar of flowers. Commercially sold for use in organic gardens and greenhouses, lacewings represent a lucrative industry.

Another important group of predators, the Coccinellids (ladybird beetles) belonging to family Cocinellidae and order Coleoptera, are the most important group of predators. These beetles prey upon various insect pests such as aphids, mealybugs, scales, thrips, leafhoppers, mites and insect pests of horticultural and field crops. They can be and have been employed as bioagents to regulate notorious insect pest populations. *Rodolia cardinalis* (Mulsant), *Cryptolaemus montrouzieri* Mulsant and *Curinus coeruleus* Mulsant are the coccinellids that have been successfully utilised in classical biological control programmes. Indigenous coccinellids like *Cheilomenes sexmaculata* (Fabricius), *Coccinella septempunctata* Linnaeus, *Scymnus coccivora* Ayyar, *Brumoides suturalis* (Fabricius), *Chilocorus nigrita* (Fabricius) and *Pharoscymnus horni* (Weise) stand potential for exploitation in augmentative biological control of several insect species. In India, three species, *viz., C. montrouzieri, C. coeruleus* and *R. cardinalis out of the* 22 species of coccinellids, have been introduced for controlling the sugarcane scale, *Melanaspis glomerata* (Green) which are providing substantial natural control. *B. suturalis* is an important predator of scales, mealybugs, aphids, whiteflies, eggs of pyralids and mites in sugarcane, rice, maize, sorghum, cowpea, mungbean, groundnut, mustard, brinjal and cotton ecosystems in India which can be exploited as a successful biological control agent.

Facilities for mass production

One of the most important pre-requisites for mass production of bio-agents is availability of well-lighted and ventilated low roofing rooms with windows facing north, fitted with insect proof mesh. Earlier such rooms were constructed in groves of shade trees. However, given to the modern facilities, now such rooms are constructed with insulated walls, low insulated ceiling and windows fitted with glass shutters ensuring appropriate lighting arrangements along with air-conditioning facilities to maintain the temperature at about 25-27°C and RH at 55-65%. The facilities for mass production, however, shall vary depending upon the type and number of the biocontrol agent to be produced. Other essentials include separate rooms for storage of diet ingredients, diet preparation, egg or larval implantation, insect development, adult emergence etc. General sanitation of the rooms to check entry of unwanted organisms is very important.

Rearing containers or cages of different types and sizes are required for insect rearing provisioned with the transparent material on one side or top for easy viewing. Earlier, generally wood cages were used but now these are being replaced with plastic or aluminium. Other physical facilities include tables, chairs, stools, racks etc. of varying sizes. To facilitate easy mobility, these tables or racks are provided with wheels. Other requirements include laminar flow, microscopes, air filters, furnace filters, autoclaves, hot air ovens, walk-in-incubators, ultraviolet lamps, formaldehyde gas fumigation chambers, distillation unit, refrigerators etc.

To check cannibalism, some insects need to be reared individually in plastic or glass vials. Pumpkins can be used for rearing host insects for a long time in case of multiplication of scale insect and mealy bug parasitoids and predators. Desired humidity can be maintained by keeping moist sponge or moss in the cages and spraying water over the cloth of cages. High levels of humidity is required to be maintained in rearing containers for the multiplication of bioagents of sugarcane and paddy pests. Corrugated boxes lined inside with black cloth or paper are used to rear egg parasitoids of leaf hoppers and some other which are highly photo-positive. To simulate natural rearing conditions for multiplication of natural enemies, potted plants infested with host material are kept in large sized cages or plants are grown in the field and covered with large field cages. Semi-synthetic diets have also been developed for a number of host insects to facilitate multiplication of host specific bioagents.

Production system

Continuous cultures of host insects is the most important pre-requisite for multiplication of bioagents (parasitoids and predators). To rear the host insects, natural hosts could be used as in case of aphids; there could be factitious hosts such as pumpkins to rear scale and mealy bugs while semi-synthetic diets could be used to rear lepidopterous larvae. For production of trichogrammatids and chrysopids, the most commonly used host insects are, *Corcyra cephalonica* and *Sitotroga cerealella.*Techniques have been standardised for multiplication of many bioagents.

Trichogrammatids being used in augmentative biological control in India include *Trichogramma achaeae* Nagaraja & Nagarkatti, *Trichogramma chilonis* Ishii, *Trichogramma chilotraeae* Nagaraja, *Trichogramma embryophagum* Hartig, *Trichogramma japonicum* Ashmead, and *Trichogrammatoidea bactrae* Nagaraja. The eggs of *Corcyra cephalonica* are used as host for mass production of Trichogrammatids. The 'Trichocards' containing parasitized host (*Corcyra cephalonica*) eggs safely packed in packets, indicating the date of emergence of adult parasitoids are used for shipment/field release.

Chrysoperla predators are mass multiplied on the eggs of *Corcyra cephalonica*, a laboratory host. The adults collected from the field are multiplied and after getting desired number of adults, the mass production procedure is initiated. Eggs of *Chrysoperla* sp. can be stored at 8°C for 20 days without loss of viability.

Superior strains of Trichogrammatids

To account for the poor performance of bioagents resulting from pesticide pressure, high temperature etc., genetic improvement of natural enemies has been attempted to evolve superior strains of egg parasitoid, *T. chilonis* for cotton bollworms, Bio C1 which has higher rate of increase in the North Indian conditions.; Bio C6 for peninsular Indian conditions. These strains exhibit enhanced fecundity as compared to earlier strains used. Use of Bio Sc1 against sugarcane tissue borers and Bio H1 against tomato fruit borer, provided more than 6 times higher egg parasitism. A strain of *T. chilonis* tolerant to endosulfan was developed and transferred to M/S Excell Industries Limited, Mumbai has been multiplied in a large scale and distributed to farmers under the trade name "Endogram" which was used to treat a large area of cotton and vegetable crops in 6 different states.

Mass Production Units

Augmentative biological control in India has a long history. First mass Production Unit was established at Mandya (Karnatka) in the year 1935; mass production of trichogrammatids was facilitated for control of sugarcane tissue borers. However, country's first private insectary (Biocontrol Research Laboratory) was established at Bengaluru in 1981and since then numerous companies have come up country-wide for mass production of parasitoids, predators, entomopathogens etc. National Bureau of Agricultural Insect Resources (Formerly National Bureau of Agriculturally Important Insects) has developed an infobase on bio-control producers in India showing 41 organisations/units mainly involved in production of various species of *Trichogramma* (Table 24.2); subsequently some of the units might have stopped mass production of certain bioagents while some new one would have entered the business.

Table 24.2. Organisations / units producing parasitoids

S.No.	Name and address of the Unit/Company	Parasitoid(s) produced
1	Amitul Agrochem Pvt. Ltd. Amitul House, P.O.: Railway Colony Parha Gorakhpur, Uttar Pradesh, 273012	*Trichogramma chilonis*
2	Bioved Research Society 103/42, MLN road, Allahabad, Uttar Pradesh, 211002	*T. chilonis*
3	Crop Health Bio-product Research Centre R-12/50, Rajanagar, Ghaziabad, Uttar Pradesh, 201003	*T. chilonis*
4	Biotech International Ltd VIPPS Centre, Local Shopping Centre Block-EFGH, Masjid Moth Greater Kailash-II, New Delhi, 110048	*T. achaeae, T. brasiliense,* *T. chilonis, T. japonicum*
5	Anand Biocontrol lab and Agricultural Consultancy 30 Hedgewarnagar, Dharang Erandol Jalgaon, Maharashtra, 425105	*T. chilonis; T. japonicum*
6	Excel Industries 184-87, Swami Vivekananda Road Jogeshwari West, Mumbai, Maharashtra, 400102	*T. chilonis*
7	Harit Bio-control Lab 74, Mangesh Nagar, Dehankar Layout Bhosa Road, Yavatmal – 445001, Maharashtra	*T. chilonis*
8	J.R. Biocontrol Laboratories Opp. Rest House; P.O.: Arni, Yavatmal Maharashtra-445103	*T. chilonis*
9	Mahatma Phule Krishi Vidyalaya Dept. of Entomology, College of Agriculture Pune, Maharashtra-411005	*Chelonus blackburni* *Copidosoma koehleri*
10	Nathkrupa Biocontrol laboratories 55, Sriram Nagar, Near Wireless Station Pawan Bhumi Marg, Wardha Road Nagpur, Mahashtra-440002	*Bracon hebetor*

S.No.	Name and address of the Unit/Company	Parasitoid(s) produced
11	Nominagri Bio-Pvt. Ltd. S. No. 79/2/2, Ambervet, TW Mulshi Dist. Puna, Maharashtra	*T. chilonis*
12	Wockhardt Ltd. Ready Money Terrace, 2nd Floor, 167 Dr A B Road Worli, Mumbai, Maharashtra	*T. chilonis*
13	II Floor, East Wing, New Secretariat Building Civil Lines, Nagpur, Maharashtra – 440001	*Bracon brevicornis, Bracon hebetor, Chelonus black-burni, Telenomus remus, Tetrastichus howaedi, T. Achaeae, T. Brasiliense, T. Chilonus, T. Japonicum.*
14	Basarass Biocon (India) Pvt. Ltd. 24/7, Dr Radhakrishnan Salai, Palaniappa Nagar Valasaravakham, Chennai, Tamil Nadu-600087	*T. brasiliense, T. Chilonus, T. Japonicum, T. pretiosum*
15	Bioscience laboratories 3/229-230, Gandhinagar Steel Plant P.O. Salem, Tamil Nadu – 636013	*T. chilonus*
16	Green Tech Agro Products 47-D, Parsn Residency, Rajaji Road, Ramnagar Coimbatore, Tamil Nadu – 641009	*T. brasiliense, T. Chilonus, T. Japonicum*
17	Jeypee Biotech 25 Chinnaiah School Street Virudhunag, Tamil Nadu – 626001	*T. chilonus*
18	Rajashree Sugars Theni, Tamil Nadu	*T. chilonus*
19	Shri Durga Agro Services 10/1 Kongu Nagar, Kalveerapalayam Bharathiyar University Post Coimbatore, Tamil Nadu – 641046	*T. chilonus*
20	Shrishti Bioproducts Pvt. Ltd. 48 Ramnar Koil Street, Ramnagar Coimbatore, Tamil Nadu – 641 009	*T. Chilonus, T. Japonicum*
21	Sun Agro Biosystems Pvt. Ltd. 3/340, Main Road, Madanandapuram Porur, Chennai, Tamil Nadu – 600116	*T. Chilonus*

S.No.	Name and address of the Unit/Company	Parasitoid(s) produced
22	Tamil Nadu Agricultural University Biocontrol laboratory Centre of Advanced Studies in Entomology Coimbatore, Tamil Nadu – 641 003	*T. brasiliense, T. Chilonus,* *T. Japonicum*
23	Tamil Nadu Coconut Parasite Breeding Centre Ever Bright Bus Stop A9, Kovaipudur, P.O. Coimbatore, Tamil Nadu – 641 042	*T. israeli*
24	Bio-Control Research Laboratories (BCRL) P.O.Box No. 6426, Yelahanka Post Office 36/2, Sriramanahalli, Near Rajanakunte Bangaluru, Karnataka – 560 064	*T. chilonis, T. japonicum*
25	Bio-Pest Management Pvt. Ltd. 12th Km. Opp. Takkur Aerodrome, Jakkur Post Bangaluru, Karnataka – 560 064	*T. chilonis, T. japonicum*
26	Central Coffee Research Institute Coffee Research Station, Chikamagalur Karnataka – 560 064	*Cephalonomia* *stephanoderis*
27	Indian Institute of Horticultural Research (ICAR) Hessaraghatta Lake Post Bangaluru, Karnataka – 560 089	*Trichogrammatoidea bactrae* *T. brasiliense, T. Chilonis,* *T. pretiosum*
28	Karnataka State Biocontrol laboratory V. C. Farm, Mandya, Karnataka	*T. chilonis*
29	Karnataka State Dept. of Horticulture Lal Bagh, Karnataka	*Goniozus nephantidis* *Brachymeria* sp.
30	ICAR-National Bureau of Agricultural Insect Resources, P.B.No. 2491, H. A. Farm Post Ballari Road, Hebbal, Bengaluru, Karnataka – 560 024	*Campoletis chlorideae, Chelonus blackburni, Cotesia flavipes, Cotesia plutellae, Diglyphus begini, Elasmus nephantidis, Telenomus remus, T. achaeae, T. brasiliense, T. chilonis, T. embryophagum, T. evanescens, T. japonicim, T. pretiosum, Trichogrammatoidea armigera, Tr. bectrae*
31	Central Plantation Crops Research Institute Division of Entomology & Nematology Regional Station, Krishnapuram, Kayangulam Kerala – 690 533	*Apanteles taragamae* *Brachymeria nosatoi* *Bracon brevicornis,* *T. israeli*

S.No.	Name and address of the Unit/Company	Parasitoid(s) produced
32	Andhra Pradesh State Dept. Biological Control Laboratories (i) By the side of H P Gas Godown Anantapur, Andhra Pradesh-515001 (ii) Ibrahim Patnam Krishna Dist. Andhra Pradesh-521456 (iii) Near Law College, P M Palem Vishakapatnam, Andhra Pradesh – 530041 (iv) NSCL Road, Kakinada Andhra Pradesh – 533007 (v) Mahaboobhagar Andhra Pradesh – 509001	*T. chilonis*
33	Central Tobacco Research Institute Rajahmundry, Andhra Pradesh – 533105	*Telenomus remus*
34	Kamal Herbal & Pheromone Export Pvt. Ltd. 11 Arpitha Arts, Snehapuri Colony, Macharam, Hyderabad, Andhra Pradesh – 500076	*T. chilonis*
35	Nagarjuna Agricultural Research & Development Centre 28 P & T Colony, Secunderabad Andhra Pradesh – 500009	*T. chilonis*
36	H. No. 73, 8/B, Gandhi Nagar, Jammu Jammu & Kashmir – 190008	*Chelonus blackburni* *Copidosoma koehleri*
37	16, Professors Colony, Bhanwarkua, Main Road Indore, Madhya Pradesh – 452001	*Telenoms remus*
38	Opp. Commerce College, R G Baruah Road Guwahati, Assam – 781003	*T. brasiliense, T. chilonis,* *T. japonicum*
39	Indore Biotech Inputs & Research Pvt. Ltd. 6, Sikh Mohalla Main Road Indore, Madhya Pradesh – 452 007	*T. chilonis*
40	Perunthalaivar Krishi Vigyan Kendra Biocontrol Lab Kurumbupet, Pondicherry – 605 024	*T. chilonis, T. japonicum*
41	Rajendra Foundation for Agricultural Research & Rural Development, Chittar, Bhavani (TK), Erode (Dt.)-638311	*Goniozus nephantidis* *Tetrastichus israeli,* *T. achaeae, T. brasiliense,* *T. chilonis, T. japonicum*

World scenario

Given to diversity of flora and fauna, India has contributed significantly in classical biological control at global level by providing Indian biological control agents to other countries. The success achieved in fifteen case studies has provided valuable impact. Apart from India, Many countries in the world have attempted application of biocontrol agents including parasitoids and predators to manage the insect pests. In the United States alone, more than 50 species of arthropod natural enemies are produced and marketed widely. Most of these and some additional species are used in Europe. Some of the most common predators include several phytoseiid mites, coccinellids, cecidomyiids, and chrysopids. The popular parasitic wasps used belong to the families Aphelinidae, Braconidae, Pteromalidae, and Trichogrammatidae. To control phytophagous mites, fungus gnats, and thrips, predaceous mites are used in protected situations. These are specifically useful for the control of two-spotted spider mite infesting ornamental, fruit, and vegetable crops. Lady beetles are used to control several species of scales, mealybugs, aphids, thrips, and whiteflies. The cecidomyiid, *Aphidoletes aphidimyza* (Rondani), is commonly used for biological control of aphids, like the *Chrysoperla* spp. Most extensively used aphelinid for the control of whiteflies is, *Encarsia formosa* Gahan. The braconids, *Aphidius* spp. are also released to control several species of aphids.

A large number of species of the lepidopteran egg parasitoid, *Trichogramma* spp. are mass produced since decades as the most prevalent augmentative parasitoid; these are reared on eggs of rice moth, *Corcyra cephalonica* Stainton, the angoumois grain moth, *Sitotroga cerealella* (Oliver), or Mediterranean flour moth, *Ephestia kuehniella* Zeller, that infest stored grain. Several biofactories in the former Soviet Union were known to produce millions of *Trichogramma* spp. per day. Producers of commercial natural enemies in Germany, Switzerland, and France since about 1992, have developed a number of simple, highly productive rearing systems for *Trichogramma* spp. Grains in large containers are infested with host eggs, and consequent larvae feed and subsequently moult into adults and deposit eggs. The eggs are harvested, exposed to *Trichogramma* spp. adults, and utilised to maintain the colony or glued to a substrate and released in a the field.

Challenges /Future thrust

Any biological control programme involving use of mass-produced natural enemies including parasitoids and predators has the arduous task to compete with other pest control technologies to become commercially viable and sustainable. Biological control agents need to provide effective control of the target pests at the competitive cost. One of the most challenging constraints of mass production of natural enamines is the intrinsic need of mass production of their host or prey. This doubles the cost due to production of two species where as revenue will be generated for one only. This explains that inspite of present state of mass rearing technology, only a limited number of arthropod natural enemies could be mass produced till date. Besides, the extent of mass production of parasitoids and predators is also dependent on their capacity to develop and reproduce on a diet composed of those herbivore species that have been reared on artificial diets.

The future thrust of mass production of parasitoids and predators must be aimed at ensuring availability of tens of thousands to millions of individuals for release to check pests of crops. Though, knowledge has accumulated over decades on small-scale rearing of arthropod natural enemies, but new technologies are needed to push mass production on an extensive scale. Further, new techniques need to be evolved for long-term storage and release that enhance natural enemy efficiency with a concurrent reduction in costs of biological control, making it easier and more economical.

Developing artificial diets for parasitoids and predators play a very significant role in the process of their mass production, making it more cost-effective. But this is also a fact that artificial diets do not match with the natural prey or hosts as sources of nutrition. Consequently, parasitoids and predators reared on artificial diets generally possess biological characteristics that reduce their quality as biological control agents. Development of artificial diets to address these issues is a real challenge.

Mass production of natural enemies requires substantial economic investment to develop technology and construct adequate infrastructure and hence only large organisations such as that of Government and large industry can go for such a commercial venture. Further, there is also need to focus the interaction between pests and their natural enemies in different crop ecosystems during different seasons.

*****

SELECTED BIBLIOGRAPHY

Ambrose, D.P. (2007) *The Insects : Beneficial and Harmful Aspects.* Kalyani Publishers, New Delhi.

Anonymous (2017). *Package of Practices for Crops of Punjab.* Punjab Agric. Univ., Ludhiana, India.

Atwal, A.S. (2000) *Essentials of Beekeeping and Pollination.* Kalyani Publishers, New Delhi.

Atwal, A.S. (2006) *The World of the Honey Bee.* Kalyani Publishers, New Delhi.

Atwal, A.S. and Dhaliwal, G.S. (2015) *Agricultural Pests of South Asia and Their Management.* Kalyani Publishers, New Delhi.

Awasthy, V.B. (2007) *Introduction to General and Applied Entomology.* Scientific Publishers (India), Jodhpur.

Ballal, C. R. and Yamada K. (2016). Anthocorid Predators. In: Omkar (Ed.) *Ecofriendly Pest Management for Food Security.* Academic Press. Pp. 183-216.

Barker, G.M. (ed.) (2002) *Molluscs as Crop Pests.* CAB International, Wallingford, UK.

Bhanot, J.P., Rohilla, H.R. and Kalra, V.K. (eds) (2007) *Recent Trends in Biology and Management of Polyphagous Pests of Agricultural Importance.* CCS Haryana Agricultural University, Hisar.

Chhillar, B.S., Gulati, R. and Bhatnagar, P. (2007) *Agricultural Acarology.* Daya Publishing House, New Delhi.

Chhillar, B.S., Saini, R.K. and Lal, R. (eds) (2006) *Emerging Trends in Economic Entomology.* CCS Haryana Agricultural University, Hisar.

David, B.V. (2002) *Elements of Economic Entomology.* Popular Book Depot, Chennai.

David, B.V. and Ananthakrishnan, T.N. (2004) *General and Applied Entomology.* Tata McGraw-Hill Publishing Co. Pvt. Ltd., New Delhi.

Dhaliwal, G.S. (2008) *An Outline of Entomology.* Kalyani Publishers, New Delhi.

Dhaliwal, G.S. and Arora, R. (eds) (1994) *Trends in Agricultural Insect Pest Management.* Commonwealth Publishers, New Delhi.

Dhaliwal, G.S., Jindal, V. and Mohindru, B. (2015) Crop losses due to insect pests: Global and Indian Scenario. *Indian J. Ecol.* **77** (2) : 165-168.

Dhaliwal, G.S., Singh, R. and Chhillar, B.S. (2006) *Essentials of Agricultural Entomology.* Kalyani Publishers, New Delhi.

Dhawan, A.K., Butter, N.S. and Narula, A.M. (2007). *The Cotton Whitefly, Bemisia tabaci (Gennadius).* Department of Entomology, Punjab Agricultural University, Ludhiana.

Evans, J.W. (2005) *Insect Pests and Their Control.* Asiatic Publishers, New Delhi.

Ganga, G. (2003) *Comprehensive Sericulture.* Vol. II. *Silkworm Rearing and Silk Reeling.* Oxford & IBH Publishing Co. Pvt. Ltd., New Delhi.

Gillot, C. (2005) *Entomology.* Springer, Dordrecht, The Netherlands.

Gullan, P.J. and Cranston, P.S. (2005) *The Insects : An Outline of Entomology*. Blackwell Publishing Ltd., Oxford, UK.

Hill, D.S. (2005) *Pests of Stored Foodstuffs and Their Control*. Springer (India) Pvt. Ltd., New Delhi.

Hill, D.S. (1997) *The Economic Importance of Insects*. Chapman & Hall, London.

Ignacimuthu, S. and Jayaraj, S. (eds) (2005) *Sustainable Insect Pest Management*. Narosa Publishing House, New Delhi.

Irvin, M. E. and Kampmeier, G. E. (2009) Commercial Products from Insects. In: Resh, V.H. and Carde, R. (Eds.) *Encyclopedia of Insects*. 2nd Edition. Academic Press, San Diego.

Jaiswal, A. K. and Singh, J.(2014) A review of lac production in India during XI plan. *Indian Forester* **140** (9): 907-920.

Jha, L.K. and Sen-Sarma, P.K. (eds) (2008) *Forest Entomology*. APH Publishing, New Delhi.

Khokhar, S., Saini, R.K., Ram, P. and Kumar, Y. (eds) (2010) *Recent Advances in Biointentesive Integrated Pest Management*. CCS Haryana Agricultural University, Hisar.

Maredia, K.M., Dakouo, D. and Mota-Sanchez, D. (eds) (2003) *Integrated Pest Management in the Global Arena*. CAB International, Wallingford, UK.

Mathur, Y.K. and Upadhyay, K.D. (2000) *A Text Book of Entomology*. Aman Publishing House, Meerut, India.

Misra, R.M. and Singh, M.K. (2004) *Forest Entomology in India : Important Current Problems*. Saluja Book House, Dehradun.

Mukherji, K.G. and Dubey, O.P. (eds) (2000) *IPM System in Agriculture*. Vol. 7. *Key Animal Pests*. Aditya Books Pvt. Ltd., New Delhi.

Muthukrishnan, N., Ganpathy, N., Nalini, R. and Rajendran, R. (2005) *Pest Management in Horticultural Crops*. New Madura Publishers, Madurai

Nair, K.R. (2007) *Integrated Production and Pest Management*. Gene-Tech Books, New Delhi.

Nair, M.R.G.K. (1995) *Insects and Mites of Crops in India*. Indian Council of Agricultural Research, New Delhi.

Nayar, K.K., Ananthakrishnan, T.N. and David, B.V. (2000) *General and Applied Entomology*. Tata McGraw-Hill Publishing Co. Ltd., New Delhi.

Panwar, V.P.S. (2002) *Agricultural Insect Pests of Crops and Their Control*. Kalyani Publishers, New Delhi.

Partiban, S. and David, B.V. (2007) *Management of Household Pests and Public Health Pests*. Namratha Publishers, Chennai.

Pedigo, L.P. (2002) *Entomology and Pest Management*. Prentice-Hall of India Pvt. Ltd., New Delhi.

Pradhan, S. (1983) *Agricultural Entomology and Pest Control*. Indian Council of Agricultural Research, New Delhi.

Prakash, I. and Mathur, R.P. (1987) *Management of Rodent Pests*. Indian Council of Agricultural Research, New Delhi.

Prasad, D. and Puri, S.N. (eds) (2007) *Crop Pest and Disease Management : Challenges for the Millennium*. Jyoti Publishers, New Delhi.

Pruthi, H.S. (1969) *Text Book on Agricultural Entomology*. Indian Council of Agricultural Research, New Delhi.

PSU (2002) *Mushroom Integrated Pest Management Handbook*. Pennsylvania State University, PA, USA.

Rabindra, R. J., Ballal, C. R. and Jalali S. K. (2006). Utility of parasitoids in biological control. In: *Plant protection in New Millennium*, Vol. II, pp. 197-226. (Eds. Gadewar, A V and Singh, B P). Satish Serial Publishing House, New Delhi.

Ramamurthy, V.V., Singh, V.S., Gupta, G.P. and Paul, A.V.N. (eds) (2005) *Gleanings in Entomology*. Indian Agricultural Research Institute, New Delhi.

Roy, D.N. and Brown, A.W.A. (2004) *Entomology*. Biotech Books, New Delhi.

Saha, L.R. and Dhaliwal, G.S. (2006) *Handbook of Plant Protection*. Kalyani Publishers, New Delhi.

Sarath Babu, B., Varaprasad, K.S., Anitha, K., Prasada Rao, R.D.V.J., Chakrabarty, S.K. and Chandurkar, P.S. (eds) (2002) *Resources Management in Plant Protection*. Plant Protection Association of India, Hyderabad.

Schoonhoven, L.M., van Loon, J.L.A. and Dicke, M. (2006) *Insect-Plant Biology*. Oxford University Press, New Delhi.

Sharma, V.P. and Suman, B.C. (2006) *Diseases and Pests of Mushrooms*. Agrobios (India), Jodhpur.

Singh, A., Sardana, H.R. and Sabir, N. (eds) (2004) *Validated IPM Technologies for Selected Crops*. National Centre for integrated Pest Management, New Delhi.

Singh, A., Sharma, O.P. and Garg, D.K. (eds) (2006) *Integrated Pest Management : Principles and Applications*. Vol.2. *Applications*. CBS Publishers & Distributors, New Delhi.

Singh, A., Trivedi, T.P., Sardana, H.R., Sharma, O.P. and Sabir, N. (eds) (2003) *Recent Advances in Integrated Pest Management*. National Centre for Integrated Pest Management, New Delhi.

Singh, S. P., Joshi, S. and Ballal, C. R. (2001). Innovations in mass rearing technology and techniques for mass releases, transportation and storage of natural enemies. In: *Proceedings of Symposium on Biocontrol based pest management for quality crop protection in the current millennium*, July 18-19, 2001.

Smart, J. (2003) *A Handbook for the Identification of Insects of Medical Importance*. Biotech Books, New Delhi.

Speight, M.R. and Wylie, F.R. (2001) *Insect Pests in Tropical Forestry*. CAB International, Wallingford, UK.

Sridhara, S. (ed.) (2006) *Vertebrate Pests in Agriculture : The Indian Scenario*. Scientific Publishers, Jodhpur.

Tanwar, R.K., Jeyakumar, P. and Monga, D. (2007) *Mealybugs and Their Management*. Technical Bulletin 19, National Centre for Integrated Pest Management, New Delhi.

Triplephorn, C.A. and Johnson, N.F. (2005) *Borror and Del Ong's Introduction to the Study of Insects*. Thomson Brooks/Cole, Belmont, CA, USA.

Venugopal Rao, N., Uma Maheswari, T., Prasad, R., Govardhan Naidu, V. and Savithri, P. (2003) *Integrated Insect Pest Management*. Agrobios (India), Jodhpur.

Verma, L.R., Verma, A.K. and Gautam, D.C. (eds) (2005) *Pest Management in Horticulture Crops : Principles and Practices*. Asiatech Publishers, Inc., New Delhi.

Zhang, Z.Q. (2003) *Mites of Greenhouses : Identification, Biology and Control*. CAB International, Wallingford, UK.

*****

INDEX

B

D

E

I

J

K

L

O

P

T

*****